The Definitive Guide to Java Swing

Third Edition

JOHN ZUKOWSKI

The Definitive Guide to Java Swing, Third Edition

Copyright © 2005 by John Zukowski

ISBN (pbk): 1-59059-447-9

Printed and bound in the United States of America 9 8 7 6 5 4 3 2 1

Lead Editor: Steve Anglin
Technical Reviewer: Robert Castaneda
Editorial Board: Steve Anglin, Dan Appleman, Ewan Buckingham, Gary Cornell, Tony Davis, Jason Gilmore, Jonathan Hassell, Chris Mills, Dominic Shakeshaft, Jim Sumser
Assistant Publisher: Grace Wong
Project Manager: Beth Christmas
Copy Edit Manager: Nicole LeClerc
Copy Editor: Marilyn Smith
Production Manager: Kari Brooks-Copony
Production Editor: Ellie Fountain
Compositor: Susan Glinert
Proofreaders: Linda Seifert, Liz Welch
Indexer: Michael Brinkman
Artist: Kinetic Publishing Services, LLC
Cover Designer: Kurt Krames
Manufacturing Manager: Tom Debolski

Distributed to the book trade in the United States by Springer-Verlag New York, Inc., 233 Spring Street, 6th Floor, New York, NY 10013, and outside the United States by Springer-Verlag GmbH & Co. KG, Tiergartenstr. 17, 69112 Heidelberg, Germany.

In the United States: phone 1-800-SPRINGER, fax 201-348-4505, e-mail orders@springer-ny.com, or visit http://www.springer-ny.com. Outside the United States: fax +49 6221 345229, e-mail orders@springer.de, or visit http://www.springer.de.

For information on translations, please contact Apress directly at 2560 Ninth Street, Suite 219, Berkeley, CA 94710. Phone 510-549-5930, fax 510-549-5939, e-mail info@apress.com, or visit http://www.apress.com.

The source code for this book is available to readers at http://www.apress.com in the Downloads section.

Contents at a Glance

About the Author xix

About the Technical Reviewers xxi

Acknowledgments xxiii

Introduction xxv

CHAPTER 1   Swing Overview 1

CHAPTER 2   Event Handling with the Swing Component Set 17

CHAPTER 3   The Model-View-Controller Architecture 59

CHAPTER 4   Core Swing Components 67

CHAPTER 5   Toggle Buttons 115

CHAPTER 6   Swing Menus and Toolbars 151

CHAPTER 7   Borders 211

CHAPTER 8   Root Pane Containers 235

CHAPTER 9   Pop-Ups and Choosers 267

CHAPTER 10   Layout Managers 343

CHAPTER 11   Advanced Swing Containers 377

CHAPTER 12   Bounded Range Components 419

CHAPTER 13   List Model Controls 451

CHAPTER 14   Spinner Model Controls 509

CHAPTER 15   Basic Text Components 521

CHAPTER 16   Advanced Text Capabilities 585

CHAPTER 17   Trees 623

CHAPTER 18   Tables 675

CHAPTER 19   Drag-and-Drop Support 729

CHAPTER 20   The Pluggable Look and Feel Architecture 741

CHAPTER 21   The Undo Framework 783

CHAPTER 22   Accessibility 805
APPENDIX   UI Manager Properties 813

INDEX 847

Contents

About the Author xix
About the Technical Reviewers xxi
Acknowledgments xxiii
Introduction xxv

CHAPTER 1   Swing Overview 1

Getting to Know the Swing Components 2
    AWT Component Replacements 3
    Non-AWT Upgraded Components 5
Event Handling and Layout Management 10
Undo Framework 11
SwingSet Demonstration 11
Swing Component to Chapter Mapping 12
Summary 15

CHAPTER 2   Event Handling with the Swing Component Set 17

Delegation-Based Event Handling 17
    Event Delegation Model 17
    Event Listeners As Observers 19
Multithreaded Swing Event Handling 21
    Using SwingUtilities for Mouse Button Identification 23
    Using Property Change Listeners As Observers 26
    Managing Listener Lists. 29
    Timer Class 34
Swing-Specific Event Handling 37
    Action Interface. 37
    AbstractAction Class. 38
    KeyStroke Class 41
    Using Mnemonics and Accelerators 46

Swing Focus Management 46

    Moving the Focus 48

    Examining Focus Cycles 50

    FocusTraversalPolicy Class 52

    KeyboardFocusManager Class 55

    Verifying Input During Focus Traversal 56

Summary 57

▋CHAPTER 3 **The Model-View-Controller Architecture** 59

Understanding the Flow of MVC 59

    MVC Communication 59

    UI Delegates for Swing Components 60

Sharing Data Models 61

Understanding the Predefined Data Models 63

Summary 65

▋CHAPTER 4 **Core Swing Components** 67

JComponent Class 67

    Component Pieces 69

    JComponent Properties 74

    Handling JComponent Events 80

JToolTip Class 84

    Creating a JToolTip 84

    Creating Customized JToolTip Objects 84

    Displaying Positional Tooltip Text 85

    Customizing a JToolTip Look and Feel 86

    ToolTipManager Class 86

    ToolTipManager Properties 87

JLabel Class 88

    Creating a JLabel 89

    JLabel Properties 89

    JLabel Event Handling 91

    Customizing a JLabel Look and Feel 92

Interface Icon 92

    Creating an Icon 93

    Using an Icon.. 94

    ImageIcon Class 94

    GrayFilter Class.. 97

AbstractButton Class 98
    AbstractButton Properties 98
    Handling AbstractButton Events 102
JButton Class 104
    Creating a JButton 104
    JButton Properties 105
    Handling JButton Events 106
    Customizing a JButton Look and Feel 108
JPanel Class 110
    Creating a JPanel 110
    Using a JPanel 110
    Customizing a JPanel Look and Feel 112
Summary 112

■CHAPTER 5   **Toggle Buttons** 115

ToggleButtonModel Class 115
ButtonGroup Class 116
JToggleButton Class 119
    Creating JToggleButton Components........................ 119
    JToggleButton Properties................................. 120
    Handling JToggleButton Selection Events 121
    Customizing a JToggleButton Look and Feel................ 124
JCheckBox Class 125
    Creating JCheckBox Components............................ 126
    JCheckBox Properties 127
    Handling JCheckBox Selection Events...................... 130
    Customizing a JCheckBox Look and Feel 133
JRadioButton Class 134
    Creating JRadioButton Components......................... 135
    JRadioButton Properties 136
    Grouping JRadioButton Components in a ButtonGroup 136
    Handling JRadioButton Selection Events 139
    Customizing a JRadioButton Look and Feel 147
Summary 149

■CHAPTER 6   **Swing Menus and Toolbars** 151

Working with Menus 152
    Menu Class Hierarchy 156
    JMenuBar Class 157

SingleSelectionModel Interface............................... 161

JMenuItem Class 162

JMenu Class 168

JSeparator Class... 175

JPopupMenu Class... 176

JCheckBoxMenuItem Class.................................. 184

JRadioButtonMenuItem Class............................... 189

Creating Custom MenuElement Components:
The MenuElement Interface................................. 195

Working with Pop-Ups: The Popup Class 200

Creating Pop-Up Components.............................. 200

A Complete Popup/PopupFactory Usage Example 200

Working with Toolbars: The JToolBar Class 202

Creating JToolBar Components............................. 202

Adding Components to a JToolBar 202

JToolBar Properties 203

Handling JToolBar Events 205

Customizing a JToolBar Look and Feel 205

A Complete JToolBar Usage Example 206

JToolBar.Separator Class................................. 208

Summary 208

■CHAPTER 7 **Borders** 211

Some Basics on Working with Borders 211

Exploring the Border Interface.............................. 212

Introducing BorderFactory................................. 215

Starting with AbstractBorder............................... 216

Examining the Predefined Borders 218

EmptyBorder Class....................................... 218

LineBorder Class... 219

BevelBorder Class.. 220

SoftBevelBorder Class 222

EtchedBorder Class 223

MatteBorder Class 224

CompoundBorder Class 226

TitledBorder Class.. 227

Creating Your Own Borders 232

Summary 234

■**CHAPTER 8**   **Root Pane Containers** 235

JRootPane Class 235
    Creating a JRootPane....................................... 236
    JRootPane Properties....................................... 236
    Customizing a JRootPane Look and Feel..................... 238
    RootPaneContainer Interface.............................. 239
    JLayeredPane Class.. 239
JFrame Class 242
    Creating a JFrame 243
    JFrame Properties 243
    Adding Components to a JFrame 245
    Handling JFrame Events 245
    Extending JFrame.. 246
JWindow Class 247
    Creating a JWindow 247
    JWindow Properties 248
    Handling JWindow Events 248
    Extending JWindow 248
JDialog Class 248
    Creating a JDialog 248
    JDialog Properties... 250
    Handling JDialog Events 250
    Extending JDialog... 252
JApplet Class 252
Working with a Desktop 252
    JInternalFrame Class 253
    JDesktopPane Class....................................... 262
Summary 266

■**CHAPTER 9**   **Pop-Ups and Choosers** 267

JOptionPane Class 267
    Creating a JOptionPane 268
    Displaying a JOptionPane 271
    Automatically Creating a JOptionPane in a Pop-Up Window 274
    JOptionPane Properties 280
    Customizing a JOptionPane Look and Feel 287

ProgressMonitor Class 291
     Creating a ProgressMonitor. 292
     Using a ProgressMonitor 293
     ProgressMonitor Properties. 296
     Customizing a ProgressMonitor Look and Feel. 297
ProgressMonitorInputStream Class 297
     Creating a ProgressMonitorInputStream 297
     Using a ProgressMonitorInputStream. 298
     ProgressMonitorInputStream Properties 299
JColorChooser Class 300
     Creating a JColorChooser 301
     Using JColorChooser 302
     JColorChooser Properties 307
     Customizing a JColorChooser Look and Feel 320
JFileChooser Class 322
     Creating a JFileChooser. 323
     Using JFileChooser. 323
     JFileChooser Properties. 326
     Working with File Filters 328
     Customizing a JFileChooser Look and Feel. 336
Summary 341

■CHAPTER 10   **Layout Managers** 343

Layout Manager Responsibilities 343
LayoutManager Interface 344
     Exploring the LayoutManager Interface 344
     Exploring the LayoutManager2 Interface. 345
FlowLayout Class 345
BorderLayout Class 347
GridLayout Class 349
GridBagLayout Class 350
     GridBagLayout Rows and Columns. 353
     GridBagConstraints Class 353
CardLayout Class 357
BoxLayout Class 357
     Creating a BoxLayout. 358
     Laying Out Components. 359
OverlayLayout Class 365
SizeRequirements Class 370

ScrollPaneLayout Class 370
ViewportLayout Class 371
SpringLayout Class 371
Summary 375

CHAPTER 11   Advanced Swing Containers 377

Box Class 377
    Creating a Box. 378
    Box Properties. 379
    Working with Box.Filler 380
    Creating Areas That Grow 380
    Creating Rigid Areas. 382
JSplitPane Class 383
    Creating a JSplitPane. 384
    JSplitPane Properties 385
    Listening for JSplitPane Property Changes 390
    Customizing a JSplitPane Look and Feel. 393
JTabbedPane Class 394
    Creating a JTabbedPane 395
    Adding and Removing Tabs. 397
    JTabbedPane Properties 398
    Listening for Changing Tab Selection. 399
    Customizing a JTabbedPane Look and Feel 401
JScrollPane Class 403
    Creating a JScrollPane. 404
    Changing the Viewport View 406
    Scrollable Interface. 406
    JScrollPane Properties. 407
    Customizing a JScrollPane Look and Feel. 410
JViewport Class 412
    Creating a JViewport 412
    JViewport Properties 412
    Customizing a JViewport Look and Feel 417
Summary 417

CHAPTER 12   Bounded Range Components 419

BoundedRangeModel Interface 419
DefaultBoundedRangeModel Class 420

JScrollBar Class 421

    Creating JScrollBar Components 422

    Handling Scrolling Events 423

    JScrollBar Properties 426

    Customizing a JScrollBar Look and Feel 427

JSlider Class 428

    Creating JSlider Components 428

    Handling JSlider Events 430

    JSlider Properties 431

    Customizing a JSlider Look and Feel 435

    JSlider Client Properties. 438

JProgressBar Class 439

    Creating JProgressBar Components. 439

    JProgressBar Properties 440

    Handling JProgressBar Events 445

    Customizing a JProgressBar Look and Feel 446

JTextField Class and BoundedRangeModel Interface 447

Summary 449

■CHAPTER 13   **List Model Controls** 451

ListModel Interface 451

    AbstractListModel Class. 452

    DefaultListModel Class. 453

    Listening for ListModel Events with a ListDataListener 454

    ComboBoxModel Interface. 460

    MutableComboBoxModel Interface. 460

    DefaultComboBoxModel Class 460

JList Class 463

    Creating JList Components 463

    JList Properties 464

    Scrolling JList Components. 466

    Rendering JList Elements 468

    Selecting JList Elements 473

    Displaying Multiple Columns. 479

    Customizing a JList Look and Feel. 480

    Creating a Dual List Box. 481

    Adding Element-Level Tooltips to List Items 488

JComboBox Class 490
    Creating JComboBox Components 491
    JComboBox Properties 491
    Rendering JComboBox Elements 493
    Selecting JComboBox Elements 493
    Editing JComboBox Elements 497
    Customizing a JComboBox Look and Feel 503
Sharing the Data Model for a JComboBox and JList 506
Summary 508

■CHAPTER 14 **Spinner Model Controls** 509

JSpinner Class 509
    Creating JSpinner Components 510
    JSpinner Properties 510
    Listening for JSpinner Events with a ChangeListener 511
    Customizing a JSpinner Look and Feel 512
SpinnerModel Interface 513
AbstractSpinnerModel Class 513
    SpinnerDateModel Class 514
    SpinnerListModel Class 515
    SpinnerNumberModel Class 516
    Custom Models 517
JSpinner Editors 518
    JSpinner.DefaultEditor Class 518
    JSpinner.DateEditor Class 519
    JSpinner.ListEditor Class 519
    JSpinner.NumberEditor Class 520
Summary 520

■CHAPTER 15 **Basic Text Components** 521

Overview of the Swing Text Components 521
JTextComponent Class 523
    JTextComponent Properties 523
    JTextComponent Operations 526
JTextField Class 526
    Creating a JTextField 527
    Using JLabel Mnemonics 527
    JTextField Properties 529

JTextComponent Operations with a JTextField. 530
Document Interface 537
DocumentListener and DocumentEvent Interfaces. 546
Caret and Highlighter Interfaces 547
CaretListener Interface and CaretEvent Class 550
NavigationFilter Class. 552
Keymap Interface 554
JTextComponent.KeyBinding Class 556
Handling JTextField Events 556
Customizing a JTextField Look and Feel 562
JPasswordField Class 563
Creating a JPasswordField 563
JPasswordField Properties 564
Customizing a JPasswordField Look and Feel 565
JFormattedTextField Class 566
Creating a JFormattedTextField 566
JFormattedTextField Properties 567
Customizing a JFormattedTextField Look and Feel 569
JTextArea Class 570
Creating a JTextArea 570
JTextArea Properties 571
Handling JTextArea Events 572
Customizing a JTextArea Look and Feel 572
JEditorPane Class 574
Creating a JEditorPane. 575
JEditorPane Properties. 575
Handling JEditorPane Events. 576
Customizing a JEditorPane Look and Feel. 579
JTextPane Class 580
Creating a JTextPane. 580
JTextPane Properties 580
Customizing a JTextPane Look and Feel 581
Loading a JTextPane with Content. 582
Summary 584

■CHAPTER 16   Advanced Text Capabilities 585

Using Actions with Text Components 585
Listing Actions. 586
Using Actions. 589
Finding Actions 591

Creating Styled Text 595
    StyledDocument Interface and DefaultStyledDocument Class ... 595
    AttributeSet Interface 597
    MutableAttributeSet Interface 597
    SimpleAttributeSet Class 597
    StyleConstants Class 601
    TabStop and TabSet Classes.................................. 603
    Style Interface 606
    StyleContext Class 606
The Editor Kits 607
    Loading HTML Documents...................................... 607
    Iterating Through HTML Documents............................ 608
JFormattedTextField Formats 612
    Dates and Numbers 612
    Input Masks... 618
    DefaultFormatterFactory Class 620
Summary 621

CHAPTER 17   Trees 623

Introducing Trees 623
JTree Class 624
    Creating a JTree 624
    Scrolling Trees 627
    JTree Properties 628
    Customizing a JTree Look and Feel 630
TreeCellRenderer Interface 634
    DefaultTreeCellRenderer Class 635
    DefaultTreeCellRenderer Properties 635
    Creating a Custom Renderer 637
    Working with Tree Tooltips 641
Editing Tree Nodes 643
    CellEditor Interface 644
    TreeCellEditor Interface 644
    DefaultCellEditor Class..................................... 645
    DefaultTreeCellEditor Class................................. 647
    Creating a Proper ComboBox Editor for a Tree 648
    Creating an Editor Just for Leaf Nodes...................... 648
    CellEditorListener Interface and ChangeEvent Class 650
    Creating a Better Check Box Node Editor 650

Working with the Nodes of the Tree 659
 TreeNode Interface 659
 MutableTreeNode Interface 660
 DefaultMutableTreeNode Class 661
 Traversing Trees 664
 JTree.DynamicUtilTreeNode Class 666
TreeModel Interface 667
 DefaultTreeModel Class 667
 TreeModelListener Interface and TreeModelEvent Class 668
TreeSelectionModel Interface 668
 DefaultTreeSelectionModel Class 670
 TreeSelectionListener Interface and TreeSelectionEvent Class . . . 671
 TreePath Class 671
Additional Expansion Events 672
 TreeExpansionListener Interface and
  TreeExpansionEvent Class 672
 TreeWillExpandListener Interface and
  ExpandVetoException Class 673
Summary 674

■CHAPTER 18 **Tables** 675

Introducing Tables 675
JTable Class 677
 Creating a JTable 677
 Scrolling JTable Components 678
 Manually Positioning the JTable View 679
 Removing Column Headers 680
 JTable Properties 680
 Rendering Table Cells 686
 Handling JTable Events 689
 Customizing a JTable Look and Feel 689
TableModel Interface 690
 AbstractTableModel Class 691
 DefaultTableModel Class 696
 Sorting JTable Elements 700
TableColumnModel Interface 707
 DefaultTableColumnModel Class 708
 Listening to JTable Events with a TableColumnModelListener . . . 709
 TableColumn Class 712

JTableHeader Class 715
    Creating a JTableHeader 716
    JTableHeader Properties 716
    Using Tooltips in Table Headers 716
    Customizing a JTableHeader Look and Feel 717
Editing Table Cells 718
    TableCellEditor Interface and DefaultCellEditor Class 718
    Creating a Simple Cell Editor 718
    Creating a Complex Cell Editor 722
Printing Tables 724
Summary 728

CHAPTER 19   **Drag-and-Drop Support** 729

Built-in Drag-and-Drop Support 729
TransferHandler Class 731
Drag-and-Drop Support for Images 733
Summary 740

CHAPTER 20   **The Pluggable Look and Feel Architecture** 741

LookAndFeel Class 741
    Listing the Installed Look and Feel Classes 742
    Changing the Current Look and Feel 743
    Customizing the Current Look and Feel 747
Creating a New Look and Feel 767
    Using the WindowsLookAndFeel on a Non-Windows Machine . . . 767
    Adding UI Delegates 771
Working with Metal Themes 772
    MetalTheme Class 772
    DefaultMetalTheme and OceanTheme Classes 774
Using an Auxiliary Look and Feel 776
SynthLookAndFeel Class 777
    Configuring Synth 777
    Default Synth Properties 780
    Working with Synth Images 780
Summary 781

■CHAPTER 21 **The Undo Framework** 783

  Working with the Undo Framework 783
  Using the Undo Framework with Swing Text Components 784
  The Command Design Pattern 788
  Undo Framework Components 789
    UndoableEdit Interface 789
    AbstractUndoableEdit Class 791
    CompoundEdit Class 791
    UndoManager Class 792
    UndoableEditListener Interface and UndoableEditEvent Class . . . 794
    UndoableEditSupport Class 794
    A Complete Undoable Program Example 795
  Using an Outside Object to Manage Undo States 800
    StateEditable Interface 800
    StateEdit Class 801
    A Complete StateEditable/StateEdit Example 801
  Summary 804

■CHAPTER 22 **Accessibility** 805

  Accessibility Classes 805
    Accessible Interface 806
    AccessibleContext Class 806
  Creating Accessible Components 807
  Working with the Java Access Bridge 808
  Summary 811

■APPENDIX **UI Manager Properties** 813

■INDEX 847

About the Author

JOHN ZUKOWSKI has been involved with the Java platform since it was just called Java, pushing ten years now. He currently writes a monthly column for Sun's Core Java Technologies Tech Tips (http://java.sun.com/developer/JDCTechTips/) and IBM's developerWorks (http://www-136.ibm.com/developerworks/java/). He has contributed content to numerous other sites, including jGuru (http://www.jguru.com), DevX (http://www.devx.com/, Intel (http://www.intel.com/), and JavaWorld (http://www.javaworld.com/).
He is the author of many other popular titles on Java, including *Java AWT Reference* (O'Reilly and Associates), *Mastering Java 2* (Sybex), *Borland's JBuilder: No Experience Required* (Sybex), *Learn Java with JBuilder 6* (Apress), *Java Collections* (Apress), and *Definitive Guide to Swing for Java 2* (Apress).

About the Technical Reviewers

This book was technically reviewed by Daren Klamer, David Vittor, Hido Hasimbegovic, Charlie Castaneda, and Robert Castaneda, who are all part of the CustomWare Asia Pacific team working on numerous Java and integration-based projects in Australia and the Asia Pacific region. Their web site is http://www.customware.net.

Acknowledgments

This book has been a long time coming, with various starts and stops, and getting sidetracked a few times along the way. Now that it is all done, I need to thank those who helped.

For starters, I want to thank everyone at Apress who hung in there and had patience when dealing with me throughout the project, especially project manager Beth Christmas, who I'm sure I drove nuts at times, and editor Steve Anglin, who kept nudging me along. On the production side, I'd like to thank Marilyn Smith for all the input and updates, Ellie Fountain for her hard work at ensuring little changes got done right, and, of course, my technical reviewer Rob Castaneda and the team at CustomWare for all the input on my rough work. Congrats on that marriage thing.

Some of the images used in the sample programs were made by Deb Felts, who ran a web site called the Image Addict's Attic. The site doesn't seem to be online any more, but the images are used with permission and she does retain copyright on them. Sun also maintains the Java Look and Feel Graphics Repository at `http://java.sun.com/developer/techDocs/hi/repository/`, with its own set of images to be used for Java applications.

For all the readers out there, thanks for asking me to do the update. Without your continued support, you wouldn't be holding this book in your hands.

For their continued encouragement along the way, I'd like to personally thank the following: Joe Sam Shirah, thanks for doing that long drive to visit while I was in Florida for the conference; my Aunt Mary Hamfeldt, congrats on your first grandchild; our Realtor Nancy Moore, thanks for putting up with us for so long; Miguel Muniz, thanks for all the bug reports at SavaJe; Matthew B. Doar, thanks for JDiff (`http://www.jdiff.org/`), a great little Java doclet for reporting API differences. Happy tenth birthday, Duke and Java.

I am forever grateful to my wife, Lisa, for her support, and our dog , Jaeger, for his playfulness. Thanks to Dad, too. Good luck at the casinos.

Introduction

Welcome to Learn Java 5.0 Swing in a Nutshell for Dummies in 21 Days. Since the beginning of Java time (1995), the component libraries have been actively evolving. What began as a small set of nine AWT components, plus menus and containers, has grown to a more complete and complex set of around 50 Swing components—all just to create graphical user interfaces (GUIs) for your Java client-side programs. That's where this book comes in. Its purpose is to make your life easier in creating those GUIs.

Earlier editions of this book took the approach that if the class wasn't found in the javax.swing package, it wasn't covered in the book. This third edition takes a more complete view of creating GUIs. For instance, instead of just describing the Swing layout managers, there is also material on the AWT layout managers, since you're likely to be using them.

The first edition of this book was written for a mix of the Java 1.1 and 1.2 developer. The second edition hit the 1.3 platform. This edition is wholly for the 5.0 developer. Almost all the programs will not work on a 1.4 platform, though with a little tweaking, they can be made to do so.

In this book, you'll find a tutorial-like approach to learning about the Swing libraries and related capabilities. It is not an API reference book, nor is it a primer that describes how to install the Java Development Kit (JDK), compile your programs, or run them. If you need help in those areas, consider using an integrated development environment (IDE)—such as IntelliJ IDEA, Eclipse, or Borland's JBuilder—or get one of Apress's other books, such as *Beginning Java Objects*, by Jacquie Barker.

Is this book for you? If you are new to the Java platform, you might want to start with a more introductory text first, before jumping on the Swing bandwagon. On the other hand, if you've been working with Java for a while and have decided it's time to start using the Swing component set, you'll find this book extremely useful. With this book, you won't have to drudge through the countless Swing classes for a way to accomplish that impossible task. You'll become much more productive more quickly, and you'll be able to make the most of the many reusable components and techniques available with Swing.

Book Structure

This book can be read from cover to cover, but it doesn't have to be done that way. It's true that later sections of the book assume you've absorbed knowledge from the earlier sections. However, if you want to find something on a topic covered in a later chapter, you don't need to read all the chapters that precede it first. If you come across something that's unfamiliar to you, you can always go back to the earlier chapter or search the index to locate the information you need.

The contents of this book are grouped into three logical sections:

Chapters 1 through 4 provide general knowledge that will prove to be useful as you read through the remainder of the book. In Chapter 1, you'll find an overview of the Swing component set. Chapter 2 details event handling with the Swing component set. It describes the delegation-based event model and focus management policies used by Swing. In Chapter 3, you'll learn about the Model-View-Controller (MVC) architecture. You can avoid using MVC if you wish, but to take full advantage of everything that Swing has to offer, it helps to have a good grasp of MVC concepts. In Chapter 4, you'll find the beginning coverage of the specific Swing components. All Swing components share many of the same attributes, and in Chapter 4, you'll learn the foundation for those common behaviors.

In Chapters 5 through 15, you'll discover the many aspects of the reusable Swing components. You'll find out about menus, toolbars, borders, high-level containers, pop-up dialogs, layout managers, advanced Swing containers, bounded range components, toggle components, list model components, spinners, and text components. Most of what you'll want to accomplish with the Swing libraries is discussed in these chapters.

In Chapters 16 through 22, some of the more advanced Swing topics are covered. These tend to be the areas that even the experienced developers find the most confusing. Chapter 16 goes beyond the basics of text component handling found in Chapter 15. Chapters 17 and 18 deal with the Swing tree and table components. These components allow you to display hierarchical or tabular data. In Chapter 19, you'll learn about drag-and-drop support in Swing. Chapter 20 explores how to customize the appearance of your application. Because the Swing libraries are completely Java-based, if you don't like the way something is done or how it appears, you can change it. In Chapter 21, you'll learn about the undo framework, which offers undo and redo support for your applications. Finally, in Chapter 22, you finish off with a look into the accessibility framework offered by Swing, such as support for screen readers and magnifying glasses to help those needing assistive technologies.

The Appendix contains a list of about 1,000 settable properties the user interface manager employs to configure the appearance of the Swing components for the current look and feel. The Swing components manage various defaults, such as colors and fonts applied to components, so you don't need to subclass a component in order to customize its appearance. Appendix A gathers all of the property settings listed throughout the chapters into one comprehensive list for easy reference.

Support

You can head to many places online to get technical support for Swing and answers to general Java questions. Here's a list of some of the more useful places around:

- The Java Ranch at `http://www.javaranch.com/` offers forums for just about everything in the Big Moose Saloon.

- Java Forums at `http://forums.java.sun.com/` are Sun's online forums for Java development issues.

- developerWorks at `http://www.ibm.com/developerworks/java/` is the IBM's developer community for Java with forums and tutorials.

- jGuru at `http://www.jguru.com` offers a series of FAQs and forums for finding answers.

- Marcus Green's Java Certification Exam Discussion Forum at `http://www.jchq.net/discus/` provides support for those going the certification route.

While I would love to be able to answer all reader questions, I get swamped with e-mail and real-life responsibilities. Please consider using these resources to get help.

About Java

Java is one of 13,000 islands that makes up Indonesia, whose capital is Jakarta. It is home to about 120 million people with an area about 50,000 square miles (132,000 square kilometers). While on the island, you can hear traditional music such as gamelan or angklung and enjoy Java's main export, a coffee that is considered spicy and full-bodied, with a strong, slightly acidic flavor. The island also has a dangerous volcano named Merapi, which makes up part of the Pacific "Ring of Fire." In 1891, on the island, Eugene Dubois discovered fossils from Pithecanthropus erectus, better known as Java man (homo javanensis).

For more information, see `http://encyclopedia.lockergnome.com/s/b/Java_(island)`.

CHAPTER 1

■ ■ ■

Swing Overview

According to *Encyclopedia Britannica*, Swing was a popular music in the United States, circa 1930–1945. Okay, maybe not in the Java sense. Instead, on May 23, 1995, John Gage, then director of the Science Office for Sun, introduced Java to the world. With its birth came something called the Abstract Window Toolkit, or AWT. In turn, with AWT came native widgets, and with this early native widget set came . . . trouble.

The original component set that came with the Java platform, AWT, was dependent on too many idiosyncrasies of the underlying platform. Instead of providing a mature-looking component set, Java offered the lowest common denominator version. If a feature wasn't available on all Java platforms, it wasn't available on any Java platform. And then you had to deal with all the browser/platform differences. Each Java runtime environment relied on how the component set was connected with the underlying platform-specific native widget set. If there were issues with the connection, first, they were specific to the platform (and/or browser) and second, you had to code around these problems so your programs could be write-once, run anywhere (WORA), the Java mantra of the time.

As Java technologies became more popular, users realized AWT was extremely slow and unreliable, and you couldn't really do much with the provided components. Very few of them were available, and you couldn't use them in a visual programming environment. So, new technologies were introduced, such as just-in-time (JIT) compilers to improve performance and, with Borland's help, JavaBeans for a component-based development.

With these new technologies came more and more widget sets, for the AWT component set itself was very basic. So, applet download times grew and grew, because these new widget sets weren't part of the core Java platform, and Java archive (JAR) files were introduced to improve delivery time. Eventually, each of the major browser vendors added its favorite component library to its virtual machine—AFC, IFC, and WFC, to name just a few. Yet all the libraries used different design models, and there were no true cross-browser standards.

Eventually, Sun Microsystems teamed up with Netscape Communication and other partners to create yet another library called the Java Foundation Classes, or JFC. Part of JFC is something called the Swing component set. This Swing component set is what this book is all about.

■**Note** Later technologies were introduced to help people use the Swing components within a browser and with web-based application delivery. These include the Java Plug-in (`http://java.sun.com/products/plugin/`) and Java Web Start (`http://java.sun.com/products/javawebstart/`). Alternatives to Swing, like the SWT component set with Eclipse (`http://www.eclipse.org/swt/`), have also been created. These are not discussed here.

This chapter will familiarize you with the various Swing pieces. For starters, there is the component set. Without these, there is no Swing. Next, you'll peek at the world of event handling and layout management common to both AWT and Swing components. After that, you'll take a quick look at the undo/redo framework available within the Swing architecture. Then you'll explore the SwingSet2 demonstration provided with the Java 2 Platform Standard Edition 5.0 Development Kit (JDK 5.0) so that you can see some of the capabilities. Lastly, I'll point out where in the book all these capabilities are discussed in detail.

Getting to Know the Swing Components

The book will serve as a guide to development using the Swing component set. Over the course of its pages, you'll look at every package in the `javax.swing` package hierarchy, as shown in Figure 1-1.

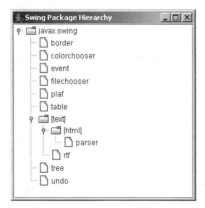

Figure 1-1. *The Swing package hierarchy*

■**Note** The `javax.swing.plaf` package contains several subpackages and related packages, some of which are located outside the `javax.swing` package hierarchy. *Plaf* stands for pluggable look and feel—a Swing concept that will be described more fully in Chapter 20.

The Swing component set is one big group of components. While the JDK 5.0 release didn't add any new Swing components to the mix, logically, you can think of them as those with duplicate components within AWT and those without.

AWT Component Replacements

The Swing component set was originally created because the basic AWT components that came with the original version of the Java libraries were insufficient for real-world, forms-based applications. All the basic components were there, but the existing set was too small and far too restrictive. For instance, you couldn't even put an image on a button. To alleviate this situation, the Swing component set offers replacements for each of the AWT components. The Swing components support all the capabilities of the original set and offer a whole lot more besides. As such, you should never need to deal with any of the basic AWT components.

Note Although the Swing components replace the AWT components, you'll still need to understand several basic AWT concepts, such as layout managers, event handling, and drawing support. In addition, you'll need to grasp the concept that all of Swing is built on top of the core AWT libraries.

The basic distinction between the Swing and equivalent AWT components is, in most cases, the Swing component class names begin with a *J* and the AWT ones don't. Swing's `JButton` is a replacement for the AWT `Button` component. One exception is the `JComboBox`, which replaces the AWT `Choice` component.

At the application programming interface (API) level, the Swing components are almost always a superset of the features the AWT components support. While they support additional capabilities, the basic AWT capabilities are there for everything but the `JList` component, whose API is completely unlike that of the AWT `List` component. Table 1-1 maps the original AWT components to their replacement Swing components.

Table 1-1. *AWT to Swing Component Mapping*

AWT Component	Nearest Swing Replacement
Button	JButton
Canvas	JPanel
Checkbox	JCheckBox
Checkbox in CheckboxGroup	JRadioButton in ButtonGroup
Choice	JComboBox
Component	JComponent
Container	JPanel
Label	JLabel
List	JList

Table 1-1. *AWT to Swing Component Mapping (Continued)*

AWT Component	Nearest Swing Replacement
Menu	JMenu
MenuBar	JMenuBar
MenuItem	JMenuItem
Panel	JPanel
PopupMenu	JPopupMenu
Scrollbar	JScrollBar
ScrollPane	JScrollPane
TextArea	JTextArea
TextField	JTextField

■**Note** For most people, the fact that the Swing components replace AWT components is irrelevant. Just treat the Swing components as an *independent* component set, and you'll be perfectly okay.

To help you understand how to use the Swing components, you'll examine each of the components in this book. For instance, Chapter 4 looks at how the JButton component works, with just a single line of text as its label, like an AWT Button, but adds capabilities, such as using image icons on buttons and working with multiple lines of text. To find out where each component is discussed in this book, see the "Swing Component to Chapter Mapping" section later in this chapter.

In addition to replacing each of the basic components, the Swing component set has a replacement for the higher-level window objects. Although the only change in most of the components' names is the beginning *J*, you'll discover in Chapter 8 how the high-level container objects are much different in the Swing world. Swing's replacement for the old FileDialog object differs even more and is discussed in Chapter 9. Table 1-2 maps the high-level window objects from the AWT component world to the Swing universe.

Table 1-2. *AWT to Swing Window Mapping*

AWT Window	Nearest Swing Replacement
Applet	JApplet
Dialog	JDialog
FileDialog	JFileChooser
Frame	JFrame
Window	JWindow

Whereas the AWT components rely on the user's operating system to provide the actual component to a Java program, Swing components are all controlled from within the Java runtime. The AWT approach is called either the *heavyweight* or the *peered* approach; most Swing components are *lightweight* or *peerless*. You'll explore the basics of this approach in Chapter 4 with the JComponent. Additional features for customizing the look and feel of components are discussed in Chapter 20.

Non-AWT Upgraded Components

In addition to offering replacements for all the basic AWT components, the Swing component set includes twice as many new components.

■**Note** If you're new to Java, just think of all of these components—both the AWT component replacements and those that were not in the AWT—as one big set of components, versus two distinct sets.

Here's a look at those components that didn't originate in the AWT world:

- JPasswordField: This specialized text field is for password entry, as shown in Figure 1-2. You cannot use cut or copy operations within the component, but you can paste text into it.

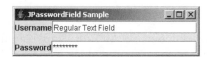

Figure 1-2. *The Swing JPasswordField*

- JEditorPane and JTextPane: These two components provide support for displaying and editing multiple-attributed content, such as an HTML and RTF viewer. Figure 1-3 shows a JEditorPane component.

Figure 1-3. *The Swing JEditorPane*

- JSpinner: This component, shown in Figure 1-4, provides selection from an ordered set of predefined values, offering arrows to scroll through the next and previous choices. The predefined values can be an array of strings, a sequential set of numbers, or a date.

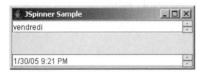

Figure 1-4. *The Swing JSpinner*

- JToggleButton: This component offers a button that stays depressed when selected. In the example shown in Figure 1-5, the North, East, and South buttons are depressed.

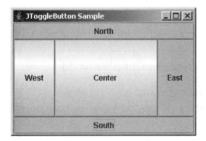

Figure 1-5. *The Swing JToggleButton*

- JSlider: This component is like the Scrollbar component of AWT (or JScrollBar in the Swing component set). However, its purpose in Swing is for user input. It offers various clues to help the user choose a value. Figure 1-6 shows an example of a JSlider component.

Figure 1-6. *The Swing JSlider*

- JProgressBar: This component allows the user to visually see the progress of an activity. Some options available include showing static text or percentage done, as shown in Figure 1-7.

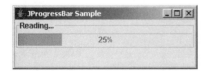

Figure 1-7. *The Swing JProgressBar*

- JFormattedTextField: This component provides for the input of formatted text, like numeric values, phone numbers, dates, or social security numbers. Figure 1-8 shows two examples of this component.

Figure 1-8. *The Swing JFormattedTextField*

- JTable: This component provides for the display of two-dimensional row and column information, such as stock quotes, as in the example shown in Figure 1-9.

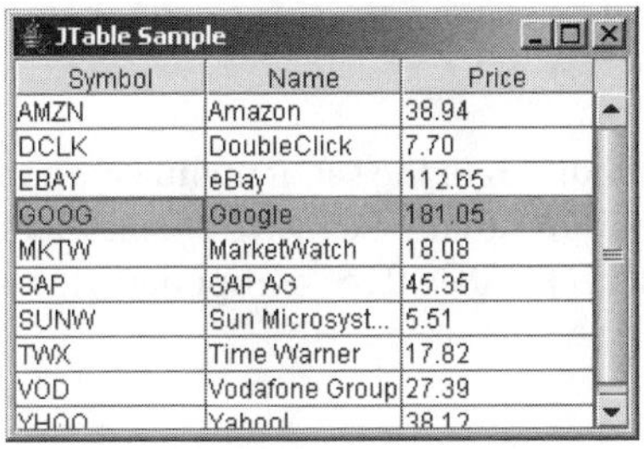

Figure 1-9. *The Swing JTable*

- JTree: This component supports the display of hierarchical data. Figure 1-10 shows an example of a JTree component.

Figure 1-10. *The Swing JTree*

- JToolTip: Through this component, all Swing components support pop-up text for offering useful tips. Figure 1-11 shows an example of a JToolTip component added to a JSlider.

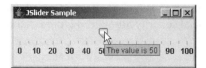

Figure 1-11. *The Swing JToolTip*

- JToolBar: This container offers a draggable toolbar to be included within any program window, as shown in Figure 1-12.

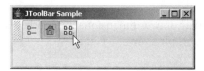

Figure 1-12. *The Swing JToolBar*

- JRadioButtonMenuItem: This component is an addition to the set of menu components. With it, you can have radio buttons on a menu for mutually exclusive choices, as shown in the example in Figure 1-13. There's also a JCheckBoxMenuItem component, for when you don't need mutually exclusive choices.

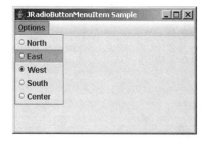

Figure 1-13. *The Swing JRadioButtonMenuItem*

- JSeparator: The menu's separator bar is now its own component and can be used outside of menus, too, as shown in Figure 1-14.

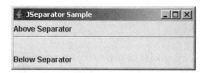

Figure 1-14. *The Swing JSeparator*

- JDesktopPane and JInternalFrame: This pair of components allows you to develop applications using the familiar Windows Multiple Document Interface (MDI). Figure 1-15 shows an example.

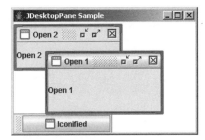

Figure 1-15. *The Swing JDesktopPane and JInternalFrame*

- JOptionPane: This component allows you to easily create pop-up windows with varied content, as shown in Figure 1-16.

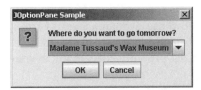

Figure 1-16. *The Swing JOptionPane*

- JColorChooser: This component is for choosing a color, with different views available to select the color, as shown in Figure 1-17.

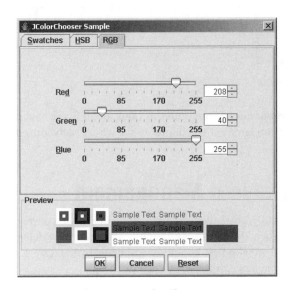

Figure 1-17. *The Swing JColorChooser*

- JSplitPane: This container allows you to place multiple components in a window. It also allows the user control over how much of each component is visible. Figure 1-18 shows an example of a JSplitPane.

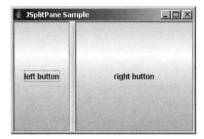

Figure 1-18. *The Swing JSplitPane*

- JTabbedPane: This component is like a container whose layout manager is CardLayout (discussed in Chapter 10), with labeled tabs automatically provided to allow the user to swap cards. This provides you with the familiar property-sheet motif, as shown in Figure 1-19.

Figure 1-19. *The Swing JTabbedPane*

You'll learn about all of these components throughout this book. Refer to the "Swing Component to Chapter Mapping" section later in this chapter to see where each component is covered.

Event Handling and Layout Management

To use the Swing components successfully, you must understand the underlying parts of the original AWT component set. For instance, the Swing components all support the delegation-based event model, which was introduced with JDK 1.1 and is supported by the AWT 1.1 component set. In addition, layout managers control screen layout.

> ■**Note** The Swing components don't support the original JDK 1.0 event model. They no longer use the `public boolean handleEvent(Event)` method and all its helper methods. If you need to convert an AWT program that uses the JDK 1.0 event model to one that uses the Swing components, you'll need to convert the program to use the delegation-based event model, in addition to changing the component set.

Although directly porting old Java AWT programs (or programmers!) to Swing programs is done most easily by continuing to use the delegation-based event model, this solution is rarely the best one. Besides supporting the delegation-based event model, the Swing components provide other, more efficient ways of dealing with events for components. In Chapter 2, you'll explore the delegation-based event model and look at the other ways of managing event handling.

In addition to the delegation-based event-handling support, the Swing components use the Model-View-Controller (MVC) design to separate their user interfaces from their underlying data models. Using the MVC architecture provides yet another way of event handling with a Swing component. While MVC might be new to most developers, the basic constructs use the delegation-based event model. MVC provides the optimal way of working with the Swing components. You'll find an overview of the MVC architecture in Chapter 3.

Besides all the support for extended event handling with the Swing classes, these classes share the need to use a layout manager for positioning components on the screen. In addition to using the layout managers that come with AWT, you can use other layout managers that come with the Swing classes. In Chapter 10, you'll learn about both the AWT and Swing layout managers.

Undo Framework

Situated within the `javax.swing` class hierarchy are the `javax.swing.undo` classes. These classes offer a framework for supporting undo and redo capabilities within Java programs. Instead of creating the basic framework yourself, the framework is provided as part of the Swing classes.

Although the undo classes don't use anything directly outside their package, the Swing text components use the undo functionality. Chapter 21 provides a detailed explanation of undo.

SwingSet Demonstration

As part of the `demo/jfc` directory with the Java 2 platform, you have available a Swing demonstration program called `SwingSet2`. This program provides a quick preview of the majority of the Swing capabilities. All the source code is included, so if you see something you like and are interested in learning how it was done, just dig through the code to find the appropriate lines.

With the Java 2 platform, you start up this demonstration from the `SwingSet2` directory with the `java -jar SwingSet2.jar` command. After starting the `SwingSet2` demonstration, you see the opening screen, as shown in Figure 1-20.

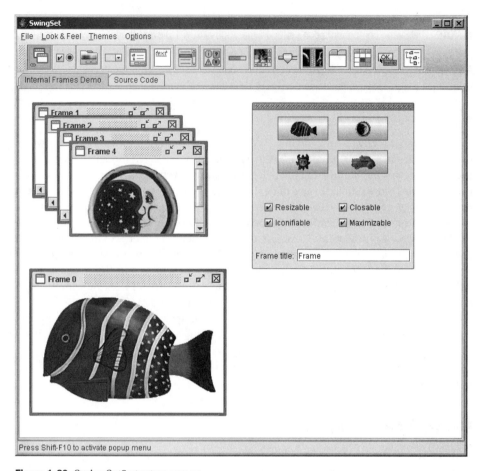

Figure 1-20. *SwingSet2 startup screen*

Choose the different buttons and tabs to see many of the features supported by the Swing components.

Swing Component to Chapter Mapping

The Swing packages contain many classes and components. To help you find where all the different components are discussed, Table 1-3 provides a handy reference (with the components listed alphabetically).

Table 1-3. *Mapping of Swing Components to Chapters in This Book*

Swing Component	Chapter
Box	11
JApplet	8
JButton	4
JCheckBox	5
JCheckBoxMenuItem	6
JColorChooser	9
JComboBox	13
JComponent	4
JDesktopPane	8
JDialog	8
JEditorPane	15
JFileChooser	9
JFormattedTextField	15
JFrame	8
JInternalFrame	8
JLabel	4
JLayeredPane	8
JList	13
JMenu	6
JMenuBar	6
JMenuItem	6
JOptionPane	9
JPanel	4
JPasswordField	15
JPopupMenu	6
JProgressBar	12
JRadioButton	5
JRadioButtonMenuItem	6

Table 1-3. *Mapping of Swing Components to Chapters in This Book (Continued)*

Swing Component	Chapter
JRootPane	8
JScrollBar	12
JScrollPane	11
JSeparator	6
JSlider	12
JSpinner	14
JSplitPane	11
JTabbedPane	11
JTable	18
JTextArea	15
JTextField	15
JTextPane	15
JToggleButton	5
JToolBar	6
JToolTip	4
JTree	17
JViewport	11
JWindow	8

In addition to information about using the different components, the following chapters feature a table for each component that lists the JavaBeans properties defined by that component. Each table notes whether a property has a setter (set*PropertyName*(*newValue*)), a getter (get*PropertyName*()), or an is*PropertyName*() method defined by the class, and whether a property is bound (you can listen for a *Property*ChangeEvent). In these property tables, inherited properties aren't listed, so even though a property for a component is listed as write-only, the parent class might still provide a getter method. As an example, Table 1-4 shows the property table for the JScrollBar component.

Table 1-4. *JScrollBar Properties*

Property Name	Data Type	Access
accessibleContext	AccessibleContext	Read-only
adjustmentListeners	AdjustmentListener[ ]	Read-only
blockIncrement	int	Read-write bound
enabled	boolean	Write-only

Table 1-4. *JScrollBar Properties (Continued)*

Property Name	Data Type	Access
maximum	int	Read-write
maximumSize	Dimension	Read-only
minimum	int	Read-write
minimumSize	Dimension	Read-only
model	BoundedRangeModel	Read-write bound
orientation	int	Read-write bound
UI	ScrollBarUI	Read-write bound
UIClassID	String	Read-only
unitIncrement	int	Read-write bound
value	int	Read-write bound
valueIsAdjusting	boolean	Read-write bound
visibleAmount	int	Read-write

Besides the property tables, you'll find information about important aspects of each component and the techniques for using them.

■**Note** This book is not intended to be an API reference, nor does it cover everything about each component. For the lesser-used aspects of a component, see the online javadoc documentation.

Summary

This chapter provided a brief overview of what will be covered in this book, such as the many essential parts of the Swing component set you need to understand in order to use Swing components. The combined set of javax.swing packages is larger than the entire first JDK, if not the first two.

In Chapter 2, you'll explore how to deal with the many aspects of event handling using the Swing components. In addition to reviewing the delegation-based event model, you'll look at different ways you can deal with events when using Swing components and get a grasp of the focus traversal policies involved with Swing.

■■■

CHAPTER 2

Event Handling with the Swing Component Set

Chapter 1 provided a brief overview of the Swing component set. In this chapter, you will start to look at the details of one aspect of using Swing components: event handling. When working with the Swing component set, the delegation-based event-handling mechanism is available, but you can also take advantage of several additional ways to respond to user-initiated actions (as well as to programmatic events). In this chapter, you'll explore all these event-handling response mechanisms. You'll also learn how Swing manages input focus and some techniques for controlling how focus is handled.

As you explore event-handling capabilities, you will start to look at some actual Swing components. In this chapter, you will be using the components in the simplest manner possible. Feel free to first read up on the components covered in later chapters of this book, and then come back to this chapter for a general discussion of event handling. The later chapters of this book also contain specific details on event handling for each component.

Delegation-Based Event Handling

Sun Microsystems introduced the delegation-based event-handling mechanism into the Java libraries with the release of JDK 1.1 and JavaBeans. Although the Java 1.0 libraries included the Observer–Observable pair of objects that followed the Observer behavioral design pattern, this wasn't an adequate long-term solution for user-interface programming. (The Java 1.0 containment event-handling mechanism was even worse.)

Event Delegation Model

The delegation-based event-handling mechanism is a specialized form of the Observer design pattern. The Observer pattern is used when an Observer wants to know when a watched object's state changes and what that state change is. In the case of the delegation-based event-handling mechanism, instead of the Observer listening for a state change, the Observer listens for events to happen.

Figure 2-1 shows the structure of the modified Observer pattern as it relates to the specific classes within the Java libraries for event handling. The generic Subject participant in the pattern manages a list (or lists) of generic Observer objects for each event that the subject can generate. The Observer objects in the list must provide a specific interface through which the Subject participant can notify them. When an event that the Observer objects are interested in happens within the Subject participant, all the registered Observer objects are notified. In the Java world, the specific interface for the Observer objects to implement must extend the java.util.EventListener interface. The specific event the Subject participant must create needs to extend the java.util.EventObject class.

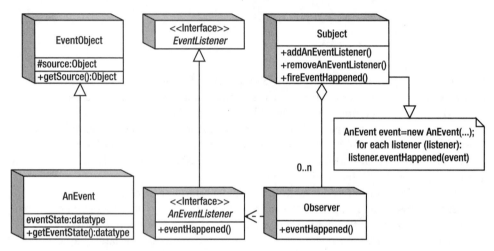

Figure 2-1. *The modified Observer pattern*

To make this a little clearer, let's take a second look at the delegation-based event-handling mechanism without all the design pattern terms. GUI components (and JavaBeans) manage lists of listeners with a pair of methods for each listener type: add*XXX*Listener() and remove*XXX*Listener(). When an event happens within the subject component, the component notifies all registered listeners of the event. Any observer class interested in such an event needs to register with the component an implementer of the appropriate interface. Then each implementation is notified when the event happens. Figure 2-2 illustrates this sequence.

■**Note** Some users like to call the event delegation model a *publish-subscribe* model, in which components publish a set of available listeners for subscription, and others can subscribe to them.

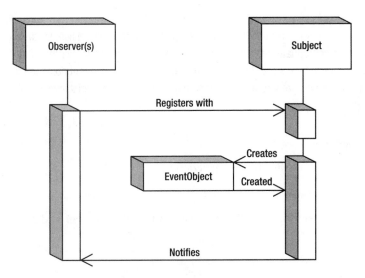

Figure 2-2. *Event delegation sequence diagram*

Event Listeners As Observers

Using event listeners to handle an event is a three-step process:

1. Define a class that implements the appropriate listener interface (this includes providing implementations for all the methods of the interface).

2. Create an instance of this listener.

3. Register this listener to the component whose events you're interested in.

Let's take a look at the three specific steps for creating a simple button that responds to selection by printing a message.

Defining the Listener

To set up event handling for a selectable button, you need to create an ActionListener, because the JButton generates ActionEvent objects when selected.

```
class AnActionListener implements ActionListener {
  public void actionPerformed(ActionEvent actionEvent) {
    System.out.println("I was selected.");
  }
}
```

Note Part of the problem of creating responsive user interfaces is figuring out which event listener to associate with a component to get the appropriate response for the event you're interested in. For the most part, this process becomes more natural with practice. Until then, you can examine the different component APIs for a pair of add/remove listener methods, or reference the appropriate component material in this book.

Creating an Instance of the Listener

Next, you simply create an instance of the listener you just defined.

```
ActionListener actionListener = new AnActionListener();
```

If you use anonymous inner classes for event listeners, you can combine steps 1 and 2:

```
ActionListener actionListener = new ActionListener() {
  public void actionPerformed(ActionEvent actionEvent) {
    System.out.println("I was selected.");
  }
};
```

Registering the Listener with a Component

Once you've created the listener, you can associate it with the appropriate component. Assuming the JButton has already been created with a reference stored in the variable button, this would merely entail calling the button's addActionListener() method:

```
button.addActionListener(actionListener);
```

If the class that you're currently defining is the class that implements the event listener interface, you don't need to create a separate instance of the listener. You just need to associate your class as the listener for the component. The following source demonstrates this:

```
public class YourClass implements ActionListener {
  ... // Other code for your class
  public void actionPerformed(ActionEvent actionEvent) {
    System.out.println("I was selected.");
  }
  // Code within some method
  JButton button = new JButton(...);
  button.addActionListener(this);
  // More code within some method
}
```

Using event handlers such as creating a listener and associating it to a component is the basic way to respond to events with the Swing components. The specifics of which listener works with which component are covered in later chapters, when each component is described. In the following sections, you'll learn about some additional ways to respond to events.

■Tip Personally, I don't like the approach of just associating a class as the event listener, because it doesn't scale well when the situation gets more complicated. For instance, as soon as you add another button onto the screen and want the same event listener to handle its selection, the `actionPerformed()` method must figure out which button triggered the event before it can respond. Although creating a separate event listener for each component adds another class to the set of deliverables, creating separate listeners is more maintainable than sharing a listener across multiple components. In addition, most integrated development environment (IDE) tools, such as Borland's JBuilder, can automatically create the listener objects as separate classes.

Multithreaded Swing Event Handling

To increase their efficiency and decrease the complexity, all Swing components were designed to *not* be thread-safe. Although this might sound scary, it simply means that all access to Swing components needs to be done from a single thread—the event-dispatch thread. If you are unsure that you're in a particular thread, you can ask the `EventQueue` class with its `public static boolean isDispatchThread()` method or the `SwingUtilities` class with its `public static boolean isEventDispatchThread()` method. The latter just acts as a proxy to the former.

■Note Earlier versions of this book showed one particular way of creating Swing programs. They were wrong. It was thought that accessing invisible (unrealized) components from outside the event-dispatch thread was okay. However, that's not true. Doing something with a Swing component can trigger a reaction within the component, and that other action would be done on the event-dispatch thread, violating the single-threaded access.

With the help of the `EventQueue` class, you create `Runnable` objects to execute on the event-dispatch thread to properly access components. If you need to execute a task on the event-dispatch thread, but you don't need any results and don't care exactly when the task finishes, you can use the `public static void invokeLater(Runnable runnable)` method of `EventQueue`. If, on the other hand, you can't continue with what you're doing until the task completes and returns a value, you can use the `public static void invokeAndWait(Runnable runnable)` method of `EventQueue`. The code to get the value is left up to *you* and is not the return value to the `invokeAndWait()` method.

■Caution The `invokeAndWait(Runnable)` method can throw an `InterruptedException` or an `InvocationTargetException`.

To demonstrate the proper way to create a Swing-based program, Listing 2-1 shows the source for a selectable button.

Listing 2-1. *Swing Application Framework*

```
import javax.swing.*;
import java.awt.*;
import java.awt.event.*;

public class ButtonSample {
  public static void main(String args[]) {
    Runnable runner = new Runnable() {
      public void run() {
        JFrame frame = new JFrame("Button Sample");
        frame.setDefaultCloseOperation(JFrame.EXIT_ON_CLOSE);
        JButton button = new JButton("Select Me");

        // Define ActionListener
        ActionListener actionListener = new ActionListener() {
          public void actionPerformed(ActionEvent actionEvent) {
            System.out.println("I was selected.");
          }
        };

        // Attach listeners
        button.addActionListener(actionListener);

        frame.add(button, BorderLayout.SOUTH);
        frame.setSize(300, 100);
        frame.setVisible(true);
      }
    };
    EventQueue.invokeLater(runner);
  }
}
```

This code produces the button shown in Figure 2-3.

Figure 2-3. *Button sample*

First, let's look at the invokeLater() method. It requires a Runnable object as its argument. You just create a Runnable object and pass it along to the invokeLater() method. Some time after the current event dispatching is done, this Runnable object will execute.

```
Runnable runnable = new Runnable() {
  public void run() {
    // Do work to be done
  }
}
EventQueue.invokeLater(runnable);
```

If you want your Swing GUI creation to be thread-safe, you should follow this pattern with all of your Swing code. If you need to access the command-line arguments, just add the `final` keyword to the argument declaration: `public static void main(final String args[])`. This may seem like overkill for a simple example like this, but it does ensure the thread safety of your program, making sure that all Swing component access is done from the event-dispatch thread. (However, calls to `repaint()`, `revalidate()`, and `invalidate()` don't need to be done from the event-dispatch thread.)

■Note In addition to the `invokeLater()` and `invokeAndWait()` methods of the `EventQueue` class, there are wrapper methods of the same name in the `SwingUtilities` class. Since the `SwingUtilities` calls just redirect the calls on to the `EventQueue` class, you should avoid the extra layer of indirection and access `EventQueue` directly. These wrapper methods were created for an early Swing version, prior to the existence of the `EventQueue` class.

One additional line from Listing 2-1 requires some extra explanation:

```
frame.setDefaultCloseOperation(JFrame.EXIT_ON_CLOSE);
```

By default, if you click the little X in the title bar of the window shown in Figure 2-3, the application does not close; instead, the frame is made invisible. Setting the default close operation to `JFrame.EXIT_ON_CLOSE`, as in Listing 2-1, causes the application to exit if the user clicks the X. You'll learn more about this behavior in Chapter 8, which explores the `JFrame` class.

Using SwingUtilities for Mouse Button Identification

The Swing component set includes a utility class called `SwingUtilities` that provides a collection of generic helper methods. You will look at this class periodically throughout this book when a particular set of methods for this class seems useful. For the button example in Listing 2-1, the methods of interest are related to determining which mouse button has been selected.

The `MouseInputListener` interface consists of seven methods: `mouseClicked(MouseEvent)`, `mouseEntered(MouseEvent)`, `mouseExited(MouseEvent)`, `mousePressed(MouseEvent)`, and `mouseReleased(MouseEvent)` from `MouseListener`; and `mouseDragged(MouseEvent)` and `mouseMoved(MouseEvent)` from `MouseMotionListener`. If you need to determine which buttons on the mouse were selected (or released) when the event happened, check the `modifiers` property of `MouseEvent` and compare it to various mask-setting constants of the `InputEvent` class.

For instance, to check if a middle mouse button is pressed for a mouse press event, you could use the following code in your mouse listener's `mousePressed()` method:

```
public void mousePressed(MouseEvent mouseEvent) {
  int modifiers = mouseEvent.getModifiers();
  if ((modifiers & InputEvent.BUTTON2_MASK) == InputEvent.BUTTON2_MASK) {
    System.out.println("Middle button pressed.");
  }
}
```

Although this works fine and dandy, the SwingUtilities class has three methods to make this process much simpler:

```
SwingUtilities.isLeftMouseButton(MouseEvent mouseEvent)
SwingUtilities.isMiddleMouseButton(MouseEvent mouseEvent)
SwingUtilities.isRightMouseButton(MouseEvent mouseEvent)
```

Now, instead of needing to manually get the modifiers and compare them against the mask, you can simply ask the SwingUtilities, as follows:

```
if (SwingUtilities.isMiddleMouseButton(mouseEvent)) {
  System.out.println("Middle button released.");
}
```

This makes your code much more readable and easier to maintain.

Listing 2-2 contains an updated ButtonSample that adds another listener to detect which mouse button was pressed.

Listing 2-2. *Button Sample with Mouse Button Detection*

```
import javax.swing.*;
import java.awt.*;
import java.awt.event.*;

public class ButtonSample {
  public static void main(String args[]) {
    Runnable runner = new Runnable() {
      public void run() {
        JFrame frame = new JFrame("Button Sample");
        frame.setDefaultCloseOperation(JFrame.EXIT_ON_CLOSE);
        JButton button = new JButton("Select Me");

        // Define ActionListener
        ActionListener actionListener = new ActionListener() {
          public void actionPerformed(ActionEvent actionEvent) {
            System.out.println("I was selected.");
          }
        };
```

```java
      // Define MouseListener
      MouseListener mouseListener = new MouseAdapter() {
        public void mousePressed(MouseEvent mouseEvent) {
          int modifiers = mouseEvent.getModifiers();
          if ((modifiers & InputEvent.BUTTON1_MASK) ==
              InputEvent.BUTTON1_MASK) {
            System.out.println("Left button pressed.");
          }
          if ((modifiers & InputEvent.BUTTON2_MASK) ==
              InputEvent.BUTTON2_MASK) {
            System.out.println("Middle button pressed.");
          }
          if ((modifiers & InputEvent.BUTTON3_MASK) ==
              InputEvent.BUTTON3_MASK) {
            System.out.println("Right button pressed.");
          }
        }
        public void mouseReleased(MouseEvent mouseEvent) {
          if (SwingUtilities.isLeftMouseButton(mouseEvent)) {
            System.out.println("Left button released.");
          }
          if (SwingUtilities.isMiddleMouseButton(mouseEvent)) {
            System.out.println("Middle button released.");
          }
          if (SwingUtilities.isRightMouseButton(mouseEvent)) {
            System.out.println("Right button released.");
          }
          System.out.println();
        }
      };

      // Attach listeners
      button.addActionListener(actionListener);
      button.addMouseListener(mouseListener);

      frame.add(button, BorderLayout.SOUTH);
      frame.setSize(300, 100);
      frame.setVisible(true);
    }
  };
  EventQueue.invokeLater(runner);
  }
}
```

Using Property Change Listeners As Observers

Besides the basic event-delegation mechanism, the JavaBeans framework introduced yet another incarnation of the Observer design pattern, this time through the property change listener. The PropertyChangeListener implementation is a truer representation of the Observer pattern. Each Observer watches for changes to an attribute of the Subject. The Observer is then notified of the new state when changed in the Subject. Figure 2-4 shows the structure of this Observer pattern as it relates to the specific classes within the JavaBeans libraries for property change handling. In this particular case, the observable Subject has a set of add/remove property change listener methods and a property (or properties) whose state is being watched.

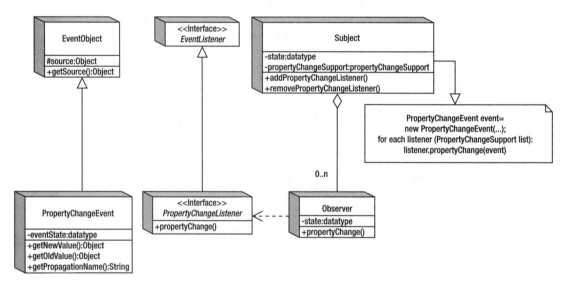

Figure 2-4. *The property change listener Observer pattern*

With a PropertyChangeListener, the registered set of listeners is managed within the PropertyChangeSupport class. When the watched property value changes, this support class notifies any registered listeners of the new and old property state values.

■**Note** Although PropertyChangeListener observers are registered at the class level, not all properties of the class might be bound. A property is bound when a change to the property causes the registered listeners to be notified. In addition, although the JavaBeans framework introduced the concept of property change listeners in JDK 1.1, none of the properties of the AWT components were bound, although this changed for the Component class in the 1.2 release. The Swing components have many of their properties bound. To find out which ones are bound, see the property tables for each Swing component that appear in later chapters of this book.

By registering `PropertyChangeListener` objects with the various components that support this type of listener, you can reduce the amount of source code you must generate after the initial listening setup. For instance, the background color of a Swing component is bound, meaning someone can register a `PropertyChangeListener` to a component to be notified when the background setting changes. When the value of the background property for that component changes, anyone listening is notified, allowing an Observer to change its background color to the new setting. Therefore, if you want all the components of your program to have the same background color, you can register them all with one component. Then, when that single component changes its background color, all the other components will be notified of the change and will modify their backgrounds to the new setting.

■**Note** Although you can use a `PropertyChangeListener` to "share" a common property setting among components, you can also map the property of a subject to a different property of the Observer.

The program in Listing 2-3 demonstrates using a `PropertyChangeListener`. It creates two buttons. When either button is selected, the background of the selected button is changed to some random color. The second button is listening for property changes within the first button. When the background color changes for the first button, the background color of the second button is changed to that new value. The first button isn't listening for property changes for the second button. Therefore, when the second button is selected, changing its background color, this change doesn't propagate back to the first button.

Listing 2-3. *Property Change Listener Sample*

```
import javax.swing.*;
import java.awt.*;
import java.awt.event.*;
import java.beans.*;
import java.util.Random;

public class BoundSample {
  public static void main(String args[]) {
    Runnable runner = new Runnable() {
      public void run() {
        JFrame frame = new JFrame("Button Sample");
        frame.setDefaultCloseOperation(JFrame.EXIT_ON_CLOSE);
        final JButton button1 = new JButton("Select Me");
        final JButton button2 = new JButton("No Select Me");
        final Random random = new Random();
```

```
      // Define ActionListener
      ActionListener actionListener = new ActionListener() {
        public void actionPerformed(ActionEvent actionEvent) {
          JButton button = (JButton)actionEvent.getSource();
          int red = random.nextInt(255);
          int green = random.nextInt(255);
          int blue = random.nextInt(255);
          button.setBackground(new Color(red, green, blue));
        }
      };

      // Define PropertyChangeListener
      PropertyChangeListener propertyChangeListener =
          new PropertyChangeListener() {
        public void propertyChange(PropertyChangeEvent propertyChangeEvent) {
          String property = propertyChangeEvent.getPropertyName();
          if ("background".equals(property)) {
            button2.setBackground((Color)propertyChangeEvent.getNewValue());
          }
        }
      };

      // Attach listeners
      button1.addActionListener(actionListener);
      button1.addPropertyChangeListener(propertyChangeListener);
      button2.addActionListener(actionListener);

      frame.add(button1, BorderLayout.NORTH);
      frame.add(button2, BorderLayout.SOUTH);
      frame.setSize(300, 100);
      frame.setVisible(true);
    }
  };
  EventQueue.invokeLater(runner);
  }
}
```

Although this example causes only a color change from button selection, imagine if the background color of the first button could be changed from a couple of hundred different places other than the one action listener! Without a property change listener, each of those places would be required to also change the background color of the second button. With the property change listener, it's only necessary to modify the background color of the primary object—the first button, in this case. The change would then automatically propagate to the other components.

The Swing library also uses the ChangeEvent/ChangeListener pair to signify state changes. Although similar to the PropertyChangeEvent/PropertyChangeListener pair, the ChangeEvent doesn't carry with it the new and old data value settings. You can think of it as a lighter-weight version of a property change listener. The ChangeEvent is useful when more than one property value changes, because ChangeEvent doesn't need to package the changes.

> **■Tip** The Swing components use the `SwingPropertyChangeSupport` class, instead of the `PropertyChangeSupport` class, to manage and notify their `PropertyChangeListener` list. The Swing version, `SwingPropertyChangeSupport`, isn't thread-safe, but it is faster and takes up less memory. Assuming it is accessed from only the event-dispatch thread, the lack of thread safety is irrelevant.

Managing Listener Lists

If you're creating your own components and want those components to fire off events, you need to maintain a list of listeners to be notified. If the listener list is for AWT events (found in `java.awt.event`), you can use the `AWTEventMulticaster` class for help with list management. Prior to the Swing libraries, if the event wasn't a predefined AWT event type, you had to manage this list of listeners yourself. With the help of the `EventListenerList` class in the `javax.swing.event` package, you no longer need to manually manage the listener list and worry about thread safety. And, if you ever need to get the list of listeners, you can ask a `Component` with `public EventListener[ ] getListeners(Class listenerType)`, or one of the type-specific methods like the `getActionListeners()` method of `JButton`. This allows you to remove listeners from an internally managed list, which helps with garbage collection.

AWTEventMulticaster Class

Whether you realize it or not, the `AWTEventMulticaster` class is used by each and every AWT component to manage event listener lists. The class implements all the AWT event listeners (`ActionListener`, `AdjustmentListener`, `ComponentListener`, `ContainerListener`, `FocusListener`, `HierarchyBoundsListener`, `HierarchyListener`, `InputMethodListener`, `ItemListener`, `KeyListener`, `MouseListener`, `MouseMotionListener`, `MouseWheelListener`, `TextListener`, `WindowFocusListener`, `WindowListener`, and `WindowStateListener`). Whenever you call a component's method to add or remove a listener, the `AWTEventMulticaster` is used for support.

If you want to create your own component and manage a list of listeners for one of these AWT event/listener pairs, you can use the `AWTEventMulticaster`. As an example, let's look at how to create a generic component that generates an `ActionEvent` object whenever a key is pressed within the component. The component uses the `public static String getKeyText (int keyCode)` method of `KeyEvent` to convert the key code to its appropriate text string and passes this string back as the action command for the `ActionEvent`. Because the component is meant to serve as the source for `ActionListener` observers, it needs a pair of add/remove methods to handle the registration of listeners. This is where the `AWTEventMulticaster` comes in, because it will manage the adding and removing of listeners from your listener list variable:

```
private ActionListener actionListenerList = null;
public void addActionListener(ActionListener actionListener) {
  actionListenerList = AWTEventMulticaster.add(
    actionListenerList, actionListener);
}
public void removeActionListener(ActionListener actionListener) {
  actionListenerList = AWTEventMulticaster.remove(
    actionListenerList, actionListener);
}
```

The remainder of the class definition describes how to handle the internal events. An internal KeyListener needs to be registered in order to send keystrokes to an ActionListener. In addition, the component must be able to get the input focus; otherwise, all keystrokes will go to other components. The complete class definition is shown in Listing 2-4. The line of source code for notification of the listener list is in boldface. That one line notifies all the registered listeners.

Listing 2-4. *Managing Listener Lists with AWTEventMulticaster*

```java
import java.awt.*;
import java.awt.event.*;
import javax.swing.*;

public class KeyTextComponent extends JComponent {
  private ActionListener actionListenerList = null;

  public KeyTextComponent() {
    setBackground(Color.CYAN);
    KeyListener internalKeyListener = new KeyAdapter() {
      public void keyPressed(KeyEvent keyEvent) {
        if (actionListenerList != null) {
          int keyCode = keyEvent.getKeyCode();
          String keyText = KeyEvent.getKeyText(keyCode);
          ActionEvent actionEvent = new ActionEvent(
            this,
            ActionEvent.ACTION_PERFORMED,
            keyText);
          actionListenerList.actionPerformed(actionEvent);
        }
      }
    };

    MouseListener internalMouseListener = new MouseAdapter() {
      public void mousePressed(MouseEvent mouseEvent) {
        requestFocusInWindow();
      }
    };

    addKeyListener(internalKeyListener);
    addMouseListener(internalMouseListener);
  }

  public void addActionListener(ActionListener actionListener) {
    actionListenerList = AWTEventMulticaster.add(
      actionListenerList, actionListener);
  }
```

```
  public void removeActionListener(ActionListener actionListener) {
    actionListenerList = AWTEventMulticaster.remove(
      actionListenerList, actionListener);
  }

  public boolean isFocusable() {
    return true;
  }
}
```

Figure 2-5 shows the component in use. The top portion of the figure is the component, and the bottom is a text field. An ActionListener is registered with the KeyTextComponent that updates the text field in order to display the text string for the key pressed.

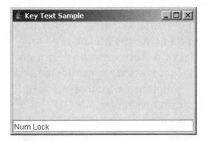

Figure 2-5. *Demonstrating the KeyTextComponent*

The source code for the example shown in Figure 2-5 follows in Listing 2-5.

Listing 2-5. *Sample Program with an AWTEventMulticaster Component*

```
import java.awt.*;
import java.awt.event.*;
import javax.swing.*;

public class KeyTextTester  {
  public static void main(String args[]) {
    Runnable runner = new Runnable() {
      public void run() {
        JFrame frame = new JFrame("Key Text Sample");
        frame.setDefaultCloseOperation(JFrame.EXIT_ON_CLOSE);
        KeyTextComponent keyTextComponent = new KeyTextComponent();
        final JTextField textField = new JTextField();

        ActionListener actionListener = new ActionListener() {
          public void actionPerformed(ActionEvent actionEvent) {
            String keyText = actionEvent.getActionCommand();
            textField.setText(keyText);
          }
        };
```

```
          keyTextComponent.addActionListener(actionListener);

          frame.add(keyTextComponent, BorderLayout.CENTER);
          frame.add(textField, BorderLayout.SOUTH);
          frame.setSize(300, 200);
          frame.setVisible(true);
        }
      };
      EventQueue.invokeLater(runner);
    }
}
```

EventListenerList Class

Although the AWTEventMulticaster class is easy to use, it doesn't work for managing lists of custom event listeners or any of the Swing event listeners found in javax.swing.event. You could create a custom extension of the class for each type of event listener list you need to manage (not practical), or you could just store the list in a data structure such as a Vector or LinkedList. Although using a Vector or LinkedList works satisfactorily, when you use this method, you need to worry about synchronization issues. If you don't program the list management properly, the listener notification may happen with the wrong set of listeners.

To help simplify this situation, the Swing component library includes a special event-listener support class, EventListenerList. One instance of the class can manage all the different types of event listeners for a component. To demonstrate the class usage, let's see how the previous example can be rewritten to use EventListenerList instead of AWTEventMulticaster. Note that in this particular example, using the AWTEventMulticaster class is actually the simpler solution. However, imagine a similar situation in which the event listener isn't one of the predefined AWT event listeners or if you need to maintain multiple listener lists.

The adding and removing of listeners is similar to the technique used with the AWTEventMulticaster in the previous example. You need to create a variable of the appropriate type—this time EventListenerList—as well as define add and remove listener methods. One key difference between the two approaches is that the initial EventListenerList is non-null, whereas the other starts off being null. A reference to an empty EventListenerList must be created to start. This removes the need for several checks for a null list variable later. The adding and removing of listeners is also slightly different. Because an EventListenerList can manage a list of listeners of any type, when you add or remove the listener, you must provide the class type for the listener being acted on.

```
EventListenerList actionListenerList = new EventListenerList();
public void addActionListener(ActionListener actionListener) {
  actionListenerList.add(ActionListener.class, actionListener);
}
public void removeActionListener(ActionListener actionListener) {
  actionListenerList.remove(ActionListener.class, actionListener);
}
```

This leaves only the notification of the listeners to be handled. No generic method exists in the class to notify all the listeners of a particular type that an event has happened, so you must create the code yourself. A call to the following code (`fireActionPerformed(actionEvent)`) will replace the one line of boldfaced source code:

`(actionListenerList.actionPerformed(actionEvent)`

from the previous example. The code gets a copy of all the listeners of a particular type from the list as an array (in a thread-safe manner). You then need to loop through the list and notify the appropriate listeners.

```
protected void fireActionPerformed(ActionEvent actionEvent) {
  EventListener listenerList[] =
    actionListenerList.getListeners(ActionListener.class);
  for (int i=0, n=listenerList.length; i<n; i++) {
    ((ActionListener)listenerList[i]).actionPerformed(actionEvent);
  }
}
```

The complete source for the new and improved class follows in Listing 2-6. When using the EventListenerList class, don't forget that the class is in the `java.swing.event` package. Other than the component class name, the testing program doesn't change.

Listing 2-6. *Managing Listener Lists with EventListenerList*

```
import java.awt.*;
import java.awt.event.*;
import javax.swing.*;
import javax.swing.event.*;
import java.util.EventListener;

public class KeyTextComponent2 extends JComponent {
  private EventListenerList actionListenerList = new EventListenerList();

  public KeyTextComponent2() {
    setBackground(Color.CYAN);
    KeyListener internalKeyListener = new KeyAdapter() {
      public void keyPressed(KeyEvent keyEvent) {
        if (actionListenerList != null) {
          int keyCode = keyEvent.getKeyCode();
          String keyText = KeyEvent.getKeyText(keyCode);
          ActionEvent actionEvent = new ActionEvent(
            this,
            ActionEvent.ACTION_PERFORMED,
            keyText);
          fireActionPerformed(actionEvent);
        }
      }
    };
```

```
  MouseListener internalMouseListener = new MouseAdapter() {
    public void mousePressed(MouseEvent mouseEvent) {
      requestFocusInWindow();
    }
  };

  addKeyListener(internalKeyListener);
  addMouseListener(internalMouseListener);
}

public void addActionListener(ActionListener actionListener) {
  actionListenerList.add(ActionListener.class, actionListener);
}
public void removeActionListener(ActionListener actionListener) {
  actionListenerList.remove(ActionListener.class, actionListener);
}

protected void fireActionPerformed(ActionEvent actionEvent) {
  EventListener listenerList[] =
    actionListenerList.getListeners(ActionListener.class);
  for (int i=0, n=listenerList.length; i<n; i++) {
    ((ActionListener)listenerList[i]).actionPerformed(actionEvent);
  }
}

public boolean isFocusable() {
  return true;
}
}
```

Timer Class

In addition to the invokeAndWait() and invokeLater() methods of EventQueue, you can use the Timer class to create actions to be executed on the event-dispatch thread. A Timer provides a way of notifying an ActionListener after a predefined number of milliseconds. The timer can repeatedly notify the listeners, or just call them once.

Creating Timer Objects

Following is the single constructor for creating a Timer that specifies the millisecond delay time between calls to the ActionListener:

```
public Timer(int delay, ActionListener actionListener);
// 1 second interval
Timer timer = new Timer(1000, anActionListener);
```

Using Timer Objects

After a Timer object has been created, you need to start() it. Once the Timer is started, the ActionListener will be notified after the given number of milliseconds. If the system is busy, the delay could be longer, but it won't be shorter.

If there comes a time when you want to stop a Timer, call its stop() method. The Timer also has a restart() method, which calls stop() and start(), restarting the delay period.

To demonstrate, Listing 2-7 defines an ActionListener that simply prints a message. You then create a Timer to call this listener every half second. After creating the timer, you need to start it.

Listing 2-7. *Swing Timer Sample*

```
import javax.swing.*;
import java.awt.*;
import java.awt.event.*;

public class TimerSample {
  public static void main(String args[]) {
    Runnable runner = new Runnable() {
      public void run() {
        ActionListener actionListener = new ActionListener() {
          public void actionPerformed(ActionEvent actionEvent) {
            System.out.println("Hello World Timer");
          }
        };
        Timer timer = new Timer(500, actionListener);
        timer.start();
      }
    };
    EventQueue.invokeLater(runner);
  }
}
```

■**Note** A Timer doesn't start up the AWT event-dispatch thread on its own.

Timer Properties

Table 2-1 lists the six properties of Timer. Four allow you to customize the behavior of the timer. running tells you if a timer has been started but not stopped, and actionListeners gets you the list of action listeners.

Table 2-1. *Timer Properties*

Property Name	Data Type	Access
actionListeners	ActionListener[ ]	Read-only
coalesce	boolean	Read-write
delay	int	Read-write
initialDelay	int	Read-write
repeats	boolean	Read-write
running	boolean	Read-only

The delay property is the same as the constructor argument. If you change the delay of a running timer, the new delay won't be used until the existing delay runs out.

The initialDelay property allows you to have another startup delay besides the periodic delay after the first execution. For instance, if you don't want to initially do a task for an hour, but then want to do it every 15 minutes thereafter, you need to change the initialDelay setting before you start the timer. By default, the initialDelay and delay properties are set to the same setting in the constructor.

The repeats property is true by default, which results in a repeating timer. When false, the timer notifies action listeners only once. You then need to restart() the timer to trigger the listener again. Nonrepeating timers are good for onetime notifications that need to happen after a triggering event.

The coalesce property allows for a busy system to throw away notifications that haven't happened yet when a new event needs to be fired to the registered ActionListener objects. By default, the coalesce value is true. This means if a timer runs every 500 milliseconds, but its system is bogged down and doesn't respond for a whole 2 seconds, the timer needs to send only one message, rather than also sending the missing ones. If the setting were false, four messages would still need to be sent.

In addition to the properties just listed, you can turn on log messages with the following line of code:

```
Timer.setLogTimers(true);
```

Log messages are good for actions that lack a visual element, allowing you to see when something happens.

■**Tip** The java.util.Timer class works in a fashion similar to the javax.swing.Timer class, except that it doesn't run the scheduled task in the event-dispatch thread. In addition, it supports executing tasks at a fixed rate, versus after a fixed delay. The latter scheme permits the repeat rate to drift between executions if the event-dispatch thread is busy.

Swing-Specific Event Handling

Keeping in mind that the Swing components are built on top of the AWT libraries, the Swing component library has several improved capabilities to make event handling much easier. The capabilities improve on several of AWT's core event-handling features, from basic action listening to focus management.

To simplify event handling, the Swing library extends the original ActionListener interface with the Action interface to store visual attributes with the event handler. This allows the creation of event handlers independent of visual components. Then, when the Action is later associated with a component, the component automatically gets information (such as a button label) directly from the event handler. This includes notification of updates for the label when the Action is modified. The AbstractAction and TextAction classes are implementations of this concept.

The Swing library also adds a KeyStroke class that allows you to more easily respond to key events. Instead of watching all key events for a specific key, you can tell a component that when a specific keystroke sequence is pressed, it must respond with a particular action. These keystroke-to-action mappings are stored in a combination of InputMap and ActionMap objects. The InputMap is specifically a ComponentInputMap when the component's window has the focus. The Swing text components can use these more readily to store the mapping of keystrokes to actions with the help of the Keymap interface. The mappings for the TextAction support are described in more detail in Chapter 16, along with the remainder of the text event-handling capabilities.

The KeyboardFocusManager and DefaultKeyboardFocusManager, along with the help of the FocusTraversalPolicy and its implementations, manage the focus subsystem. The InputVerifier helps, too, for validation of user input. These are discussed in the "Swing Focus Management" section later in this chapter.

Action Interface

The Action interface is an extension to the ActionListener interface that's very flexible for defining shared event handlers independent of the components that act as the triggering agents. The interface implements ActionListener and defines a lookup table data structure whose keys act as bound properties. Then, when an Action is associated with a component, these display properties are automatically carried over to it. The following is the interface definition:

```
public interface Action implements ActionListener {
  // Constants
  public final static String ACCELERATOR_KEY;
  public final static String ACTION_COMMAND_KEY;
  public final static String DEFAULT;
  public final static String LONG_DESCRIPTION;
  public final static String MNEMONIC_KEY;
  public final static String NAME;
  public final static String SHORT_DESCRIPTION;
  public final static String SMALL_ICON;
```

```
    // Listeners
    public void addPropertyChangeListener(PropertyChangeListener listener);
    public void removePropertyChangeListener(PropertyChangeListener listener);
    // Properties
    public boolean isEnabled();
    public void setEnabled(boolean newValue);
    // Other methods
    public Object getValue(String key);
    public void putValue(String key, Object value);
}
```

Because Action is merely an interface, the Swing libraries offer a class to implement the interface. That class is AbstractAction.

AbstractAction Class

The AbstractAction class provides a default implementation of the Action interface. This is where the bound property behavior is implemented.

Using Actions

Once you define an AbstractAction by subclassing and providing a public void actionPerformed (ActionEvent actionEvent) method, you can then pass it along to some special Swing components. JButton, JCheckBox, JRadioButton, JToggleButton, JMenuItem, JCheckBoxMenuItem, and JRadioButtonMenuItem provide constructors for creating the components from actions, whereas the Swing text components have their own built-in support for Action objects through their Keymap, InputMap, and ActionMap.

When the component with the associated Action is added to the respective Swing container, selection triggers the calling of the actionPerformed(ActionEvent actionEvent) method of the Action. The display of the component is defined by the property elements added to the internal data structure. To demonstrate, Listing 2-8 presents an Action with a "Print" label and an image icon. When this is activated, a "Hello, World" message is printed.

Listing 2-8. *Action Usage Example*

```
import java.awt.event.*;
import javax.swing.*;

public class PrintHelloAction extends AbstractAction {
  private static final Icon printIcon = new ImageIcon("Print.gif");
  PrintHelloAction() {
    super("Print", printIcon);
    putValue(Action.SHORT_DESCRIPTION, "Hello, World");
  }
  public void actionPerformed(ActionEvent actionEvent) {
    System.out.println("Hello, World");
  }
}
```

Once the Action has been defined, you can create the Action and associate it with as many other components as you want.

```
Action printAction = new PrintHelloAction();
menu.add(new JMenuItem(printAction));
toolbar.add(new JButton(printAction));
```

After the Action has been associated with the various objects, if you find that you need to modify the properties of the Action, you need to change the setting in only one place. Because the properties are all bound, they propagate to any component that uses the Action. For instance, disabling the Action (printAction.setEnabled(false)) will disable the JMenuItem and JButton created on the JMenu and JToolBar, respectively. In contrast, changing the name of the Action with printAction.putValue(Action.NAME, "Hello, World") changes the text label of the associated components.

Figure 2-6 shows what the PrintHelloAction might look like on a JToolBar and a JMenu. Selectable buttons are provided to enable or disable the Action, as well as to change its name.

Figure 2-6. *The PrintHelloAction in use*

The complete source code for this example follows in Listing 2-9. Don't worry just yet about the specifics of creating toolbars and menu bars. They'll be discussed in more detail in Chapter 6.

Listing 2-9. *PrintHelloAction Example*

```java
import java.awt.*;
import java.awt.event.*;
import javax.swing.*;

public class ActionTester {
  public static void main(String args[]) {
    Runnable runner = new Runnable() {
      public void run() {
        JFrame frame = new JFrame("Action Sample");
        frame.setDefaultCloseOperation(JFrame.EXIT_ON_CLOSE);
        final Action printAction = new PrintHelloAction();

        JMenuBar menuBar = new JMenuBar();
```

```java
      JMenu menu = new JMenu("File");
      menuBar.add(menu);
      menu.add(new JMenuItem(printAction));

      JToolBar toolbar = new JToolBar();
      toolbar.add(new JButton(printAction));

      JButton enableButton = new JButton("Enable");
      ActionListener enableActionListener = new ActionListener() {
        public void actionPerformed(ActionEvent actionEvent) {
          printAction.setEnabled(true);
        }
      };
      enableButton.addActionListener(enableActionListener);

      JButton disableButton = new JButton("Disable");
      ActionListener disableActionListener = new ActionListener() {
        public void actionPerformed(ActionEvent actionEvent) {
          printAction.setEnabled(false);
        }
      };
      disableButton.addActionListener(disableActionListener);

      JButton relabelButton = new JButton("Relabel");
      ActionListener relabelActionListener = new ActionListener() {
        public void actionPerformed(ActionEvent actionEvent) {
          printAction.putValue(Action.NAME, "Hello, World");
        }
      };
      relabelButton.addActionListener(relabelActionListener);

      JPanel buttonPanel = new JPanel();
      buttonPanel.add(enableButton);
      buttonPanel.add(disableButton);
      buttonPanel.add(relabelButton);

      frame.setJMenuBar(menuBar);

      frame.add(toolbar, BorderLayout.SOUTH);
      frame.add(buttonPanel, BorderLayout.NORTH);
      frame.setSize(300, 200);
      frame.setVisible(true);
    }
  };
  EventQueue.invokeLater(runner);
  }
}
```

AbstractAction Properties

As Table 2-2 shows, the `AbstractAction` class has three available properties.

Table 2-2. *AbstractAction Properties*

Property Name	Data Type	Access
enabled	boolean	Read-write bound
keys	Object [ ]	Read-only
propertyChangeListeners	PropertyChangeListener[ ]	Read-only

The remainder of the bound properties are placed in the lookup table with `putValue` (`String key, Object value`). Getting the current `keys` property setting allows you to find out which ones can be set en masse, instead of asking for each one individually. Table 2-3 describes the predefined set of `Action` constants that can be used as the key. You can also add your own constants, to look up later when the action happens.

Table 2-3. *AbstractAction Lookup Property Keys*

Constant	Description
NAME	Action name, used as button label
SMALL_ICON	Icon for the Action, used as button label
SHORT_DESCRIPTION	Short description of the Action; could be used as tooltip text, but not by default
LONG_DESCRIPTION	Long description of the Action; could be used for accessibility (see Chapter 22)
ACCELERATOR	KeyStroke string; can be used as the accelerator for the Action
ACTION_COMMAND_KEY	InputMap key; maps to the Action in the ActionMap of the associated JComponent
MNEMONIC_KEY	Key code; can be used as mnemonic for action
DEFAULT	Unused constant that could be used for your own property

Once a property has been placed in the lookup table, you can get it with `public Object getValue(String key)`. It works similarly to the `java.util.Hashtable` class or `java.util.Map` interface, with one distinction: if you try to put a key/value pair into the table with a `null` value, the table removes the key, if it's present.

KeyStroke Class

The `KeyStroke` class and the `inputMap` and `actionMap` properties of a specific `JComponent` provide a simple replacement for registering `KeyListener` objects to components and watching for specific keys to be pressed. The KeyStroke class allows you to define a single combination of keystrokes, such as Shift-Ctrl-P or F4. You can then activate the keystroke by registering it with a component and telling the keystroke what to do when the component recognizes it, causing the ActionListener to be notified.

Before finding out how to create keystrokes, let's look at the different conditions that can be activated and thus added to different input maps. Three conditions can activate a registered keystroke, and there are four constants in JComponent to help. The fourth is for an undefined state. The four available constants are listed in Table 2-4.

Table 2-4. *Keystroke Registration Conditions*

Constant	Description
WHEN_FOCUSED	Activates the keystroke when the actual component has the input focus
WHEN_IN_FOCUSED_WINDOW	Activates the keystroke when the window that the component is in has the input focus
WHEN_ANCESTOR_OF_FOCUSED_COMPONENT	Activates the keystroke when pressed in the component or a container of the component
UNDEFINED_CONDITION	For when no condition is defined

■**Note** In the special instance in which the keystrokes are supposed to be active only when the component is in the focused window, the InputMap is actually a ComponentInputMap.

Creating a KeyStroke

The KeyStroke class is a subclass of AWTKeyStroke and has no public constructor. You create a keystroke by using one of the following methods:

```
public static KeyStroke getKeyStroke(char keyChar)
public static KeyStroke getKeyStroke(String representation)
public static KeyStroke getKeyStroke(int keyCode, int modifiers)
public static KeyStroke getKeyStroke(int keyCode, int modifiers,
  boolean onKeyRelease)
public static KeyStroke getKeyStrokeForEvent(KeyEvent keyEvent)
```

The first version in this list, public static KeyStroke getKeyStroke(char keyChar), allows you to create a keystroke from a char variable, such as Z.

```
KeyStroke space = KeyStroke.getKeyStroke('Z');
```

■**Note** I prefer to avoid using a `char` variable to create a keystroke, because you don't know whether to specify an uppercase or lowercase letter. There is also an outdated, or deprecated, version of this method that adds a `boolean onKeyRelease` argument. This, too, should be avoided.

The `public static KeyStroke getKeyStroke(String representation)` version is the most interesting of the lot. It allows you to specify a keystroke as a text string, such as `"control F4"`. The set of modifiers to the string are `shift`, `control`, `meta`, `alt`, `button1`, `button2`, and `button3`, and multiple modifiers can be specified. The remainder of the string comes from one of the many `VK_*` constants of the `KeyEvent` class. For example, the following defines a keystroke for Ctrl-Alt-7:

```
KeyStroke controlAlt7 = KeyStroke.getKeyStroke("control alt 7");
```

The `public static KeyStroke getKeyStroke(int keyCode, int modifiers)` and `public static KeyStroke getKeyStroke(int keyCode, int modifiers, boolean onKeyRelease)` methods are the most straightforward. They allow you to directly specify the `VK_*` key constant and the `InputEvent` masks for the modifiers (or zero for no modifiers). When not specified, `onKeyRelease` is false.

```
KeyStroke enter = KeyStroke.getKeyStroke(KeyEvent.VK_ENTER, 0, true);
KeyStroke shiftF4 = KeyStroke.getKeyStroke(KeyEvent.VK_F4, InputEvent.SHIFT_MASK);
```

The last version listed, `public static KeyStroke getKeyStrokeForEvent(KeyEvent keyEvent)`, maps a specific `KeyEvent` directly to a `KeyStroke`. This is useful when you want to allow a user to supply the keystroke to activate an event. You ask the user to press a key for the event, and then register the `KeyEvent` so that the next time it happens, the event is activated.

```
KeyStroke fromKeyEvent = KeyStroke.getKeyStrokeForEvent(keyEvent);
```

Registering a KeyStroke

After you've created the keystroke, you need to register it with a component. When you register a keystroke with a component, you provide an `Action` to call when pressed (or released). Registration involves providing a mapping from keystroke to `Action`. First, you get the appropriate `InputMap` for the component based on the focus activation condition (from Table 2-4) with `getInputMap(condition)`. If no condition is provided, `WHEN_FOCUSED` is assumed. You then add a mapping from keystroke to text string in the `InputMap`:

```
component.getInputMap().put(keystroke, string)
```

If you know the action string for an existing action, you can use that; otherwise, you define the string. You then work with the `ActionMap` to map that string to an `Action`:

```
component.getActionMap.put(string, action)
```

You can share actions between components by sharing `ActionMap` instances. The example in Listing 2-10 creates four buttons, each with a different keystroke registered to it and possibly a different focus-activation condition, as listed in Table 2-4. The button label signifies the keystroke-activation conditions. The `Action` simply prints out a message and the activating button label.

Listing 2-10. *KeyStroke Listening*

```java
import javax.swing.*;
import java.awt.*;
import java.awt.event.*;

public class KeyStrokeSample {
  private static final String ACTION_KEY = "theAction";
  public static void main(String args[]) {
    Runnable runner = new Runnable() {
      public void run() {
        JFrame frame = new JFrame("KeyStroke Sample");
        frame.setDefaultCloseOperation(JFrame.EXIT_ON_CLOSE);

        JButton buttonA =
          new JButton("<html><center>FOCUSED<br>control alt 7");
        JButton buttonB =
          new JButton("<html><center>FOCUS/RELEASE<br>VK_ENTER");
        JButton buttonC =
          new JButton("<html><center>ANCESTOR<br>VK_F4+SHIFT_MASK");
        JButton buttonD =
          new JButton("<html><center>WINDOW<br>' '");

        // Define ActionListener
        Action actionListener = new AbstractAction() {
          public void actionPerformed(ActionEvent actionEvent) {
            JButton source = (JButton)actionEvent.getSource();
            System.out.println("Activated: " + source.getText());
          }
        };

        KeyStroke controlAlt7 = KeyStroke.getKeyStroke("control alt 7");
        InputMap inputMap = buttonA.getInputMap();
        inputMap.put(controlAlt7, ACTION_KEY);
        ActionMap actionMap = buttonA.getActionMap();
        actionMap.put(ACTION_KEY, actionListener);

        KeyStroke enter = KeyStroke.getKeyStroke(KeyEvent.VK_ENTER, 0, true);
        inputMap = buttonB.getInputMap();
        inputMap.put(enter, ACTION_KEY);
        buttonB.setActionMap(actionMap);
```

```
        KeyStroke shiftF4 =
          KeyStroke.getKeyStroke(KeyEvent.VK_F4, InputEvent.SHIFT_MASK);
        inputMap =
          buttonC.getInputMap(JComponent.WHEN_ANCESTOR_OF_FOCUSED_COMPONENT);
        inputMap.put(shiftF4, ACTION_KEY);
        buttonC.setActionMap(actionMap);

        KeyStroke space = KeyStroke.getKeyStroke(' ');
        inputMap = buttonD.getInputMap(JComponent.WHEN_IN_FOCUSED_WINDOW);
        inputMap.put(space, ACTION_KEY);
        buttonD.setActionMap(actionMap);

        frame.setLayout(new GridLayout(2,2));
        frame.add(buttonA);
        frame.add(buttonB);
        frame.add(buttonC);
        frame.add(buttonD);

        frame.setSize(400, 200);
        frame.setVisible(true);
      }
    };
    EventQueue.invokeLater(runner);
  }
}
```

Tip For text components, you can get the Keymap and bind an Action to a KeyStroke in one step with addActionForKeyStroke(KeyStroke, Action).

Figure 2-7 shows what the running program looks like.

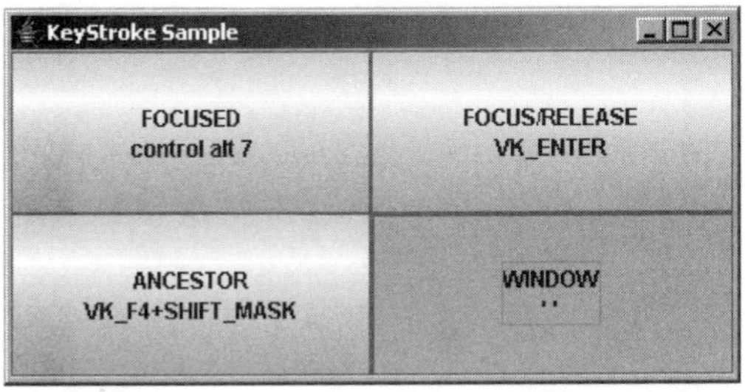

Figure 2-7. *KeyStroke listening example*

Using Mnemonics and Accelerators

The Swing libraries also use KeyStroke objects for several internal functions. Two such functions are component mnemonics and accelerators, which work as follows:

- In a component *mnemonic*, one character in a label appears underlined. When that character is pressed along with a platform-specific hotkey combination, the component is activated. For instance, pressing Alt-A in the window shown in Figure 2-8 would select the About button on a Windows XP platform.

- A menu *accelerator* activates a menu item when it is not visible. For instance, pressing Ctrl-P would select the Print menu item in the window shown in Figure 2-8 when the File menu isn't visible.

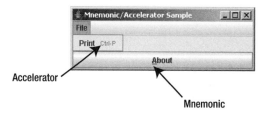

Figure 2-8. *Mnemonics and menu shortcuts*

You'll learn more about mnemonics and accelerators in Chapter 6.

Swing Focus Management

The term *focus* refers to when a component acquires the input focus. When a component has the input focus, it serves as the source for all key events, such as text input. In addition, certain components have some visual markings to indicate that they have the input focus, as shown in Figure 2-9. When certain components have the input focus, you can trigger selection with a keyboard key (usually the spacebar or Enter key), in addition to selection with a mouse. For instance, with a button, pressing the spacebar activates it.

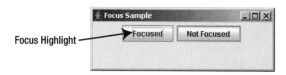

Figure 2-9. *A JButton showing it has input focus*

■**Note** The focus subsystem had a major overhaul with the 1.4 release of J2SE. All the older guts are still present, but should be avoided. The older stuff didn't work well and was very buggy. Sun's fix was to essentially throw everything away and start over, but old APIs are still present. In your quest to work with the focus subsystem, learn to use only the updated APIs, not the older ones. Classes like `javax.swing.FocusManager` and `javax.swing.DefaultFocusManager` are completely obsolete now.

An important concept in focus management is the *focus cycle*, which maps the focus traversal order for the closed set of components within a specific `Container`. The following classes are also major players in focus management:

- `FocusTraversalPolicy`: A `java.awt` class that defines the algorithm used to determine the next and previous focusable components.

- `KeyboardFocusManager`: A `java.awt` class that acts as the controller for keyboard navigation and focus changes. To request a focus change, you tell the manager to change focusable components; you don't request focus on a particular component.

You can find out when the Swing component gets the input focus by registering a `FocusListener`. The listener allows you to find out when a component gains or loses focus, which component lost focus when another component gained it, and which component got focus when another component lost focus. Additionally, a temporary focus change can happen for something like a pop-up menu. The component that lost focus will receive it again when the menu goes down.

The installed focus traversal policy describes how to move between the focusable components of a window. By default, the next component is defined by the order in which components are added to a container, as shown in Figure 2-10. For Swing applications, this focus traversal starts at the top left of the figure and goes across each row and down to the bottom right. This is the default policy, `LayoutFocusTraversalPolicy`. When all the components are in the same container, this traversal order is called a *focus cycle* and can be limited to remain within that container.

■**Note** A user can press Tab or Shift-Tab to move forward or backward through the components in a container, thus transferring the input focus.

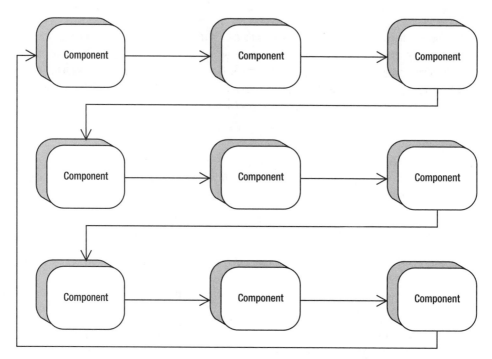

Figure 2-10. *Default focus ordering*

Moving the Focus

As an example of some basic capabilities, let's look at how to create two listeners to handle input focus: a MouseListener that moves the input focus to a component when the mouse enters its space, and an ActionListener that transfers the input focus to the next component.

The MouseListener merely needs to call requestFocusInWindow() when the mouse enters the component.

```
import java.awt.*;
import java.awt.event.*;
public class MouseEnterFocusMover extends MouseAdapter {
  public void mouseEntered(MouseEvent mouseEvent) {
    Component component = mouseEvent.getComponent();
    if (!component.hasFocus()) {
      component.requestFocusInWindow();
    }
  }
}
```

For the ActionListener, you need to call the focusNextComponent() method for the KeyboardFocusManager.

```
import java.awt.*;
import java.awt.event.*;
```

```
public class ActionFocusMover implements ActionListener {
  public void actionPerformed(ActionEvent actionEvent) {
    KeyboardFocusManager manager =
      KeyboardFocusManager.getCurrentKeyboardFocusManager();
    manager.focusNextComponent();
  }
}
```

The ActionFocusMover and MouseEnterFocusMover show two different ways of programmatically moving focus around. The ActionFocusMover uses the KeyboardFocusManager for traversal. In MouseEnterFocusMover, the call to requestFocusInWindow() says that you would like for the suggested component to get focus for the window of the application. However, getting focus can be turned off. If the component isn't focusable, either because the default setting of the focusable property is false or you called component.setFocusable(false), then the component will be skipped over and the next component after it gets focus; the component is removed from the tab focus cycle. (Think of a scrollbar that isn't in the focus cycle, but is draggable to change a setting.)

The program in Listing 2-11 uses the two event handlers for moving focus around. It creates a 3×3 grid of buttons, in which each button has an attached mouse listener and a focus listener. The even buttons are selectable but aren't focusable.

Listing 2-11. *Focus Traversal Sample*

```
import javax.swing.*;
import java.awt.*;
import java.awt.event.*;

public class FocusSample {
  public static void main(String args[]) {
    Runnable runner = new Runnable() {
      public void run() {
        JFrame frame = new JFrame("Focus Sample");
        frame.setDefaultCloseOperation(JFrame.EXIT_ON_CLOSE);

        ActionListener actionListener = new ActionFocusMover();
        MouseListener  mouseListener  = new MouseEnterFocusMover();

        frame.setLayout(new GridLayout(3,3));
        for (int i=1; i<10; i++) {
          JButton button = new JButton(Integer.toString(i));
          button.addActionListener(actionListener);
          button.addMouseListener(mouseListener);
          if ((i%2) != 0) { // odd - enabled by default
            button.setFocusable(false);
          }
          frame.add(button);
        }
```

```
        frame.setSize(300, 200);
        frame.setVisible(true);
      }
    };
    EventQueue.invokeLater(runner);
  }
}
```

Figure 2-11 shows the main window of the program.

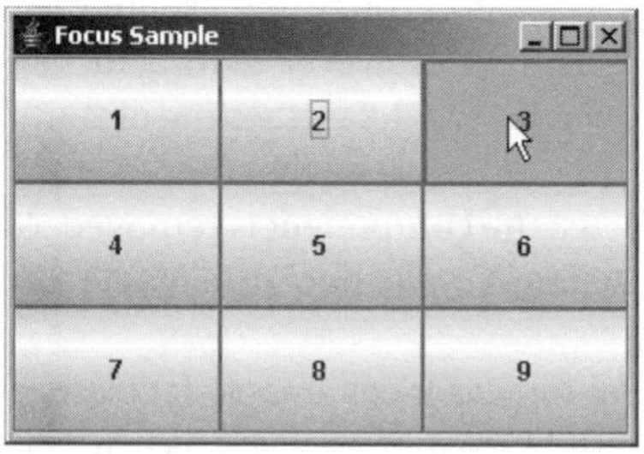

Figure 2-11. *Focus management example*

Examining Focus Cycles

One customization option available at the Swing container level is the focus cycle. Remember that the focus cycle for a container is a map of the focus traversal order for the closed set of components. You can limit the focus cycle to stay within the bounds of a container by setting the focusCycleRoot property to be true, thus restricting the focus traversal from going beyond an inner container. Then, when the Tab key is pressed within the last component of the container, the focus cycle will wrap back to the first component in the container, instead of moving the input focus to the first component outside the container. When Shift-Tab is pressed in the first component, it wraps to the last component of the container, instead of to the prior component in the outer container.

Figure 2-12 illustrates how the focus ordering would look if you placed the middle three buttons from Figure 2-10 within a container restricted in this way. In this cycle, you cannot get to the first component on the third row by pressing the Tab key to move forward. To be able to tab into the second row container, you need to set the focusTraversalPolicyProvider property to true. Otherwise, while the panel will keep the traversal policy within the second row, tabbing will never get you into the third row.

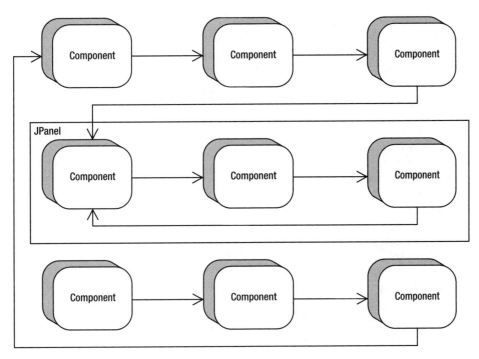

Figure 2-12. *Restrictive focus cycle*

The program in Listing 2-12 demonstrates the behavior illustrated in Figure 2-12. The on-screen program will look just like Figure 2-11; it just behaves differently.

Listing 2-12. *Restricting the Focus Cycle*

```
import javax.swing.*;
import java.awt.*;
import java.awt.event.*;

public class FocusCycleSample {
  public static void main(String args[]) {
    Runnable runner = new Runnable() {
      public void run() {
        JFrame frame = new JFrame("Focus Cycle Sample");
        frame.setDefaultCloseOperation(JFrame.EXIT_ON_CLOSE);

        frame.setLayout(new GridBagLayout());
        GridBagConstraints constraints = new GridBagConstraints();
        constraints.weightx    = 1.0;
        constraints.weighty    = 1.0;
        constraints.gridwidth  = 1;
        constraints.gridheight = 1;
        constraints.fill       = GridBagConstraints.BOTH;
```

```
      // Row One
      constraints.gridy=0;
      for (int i=0; i<3; i++) {
        JButton button = new JButton("" + i);
        constraints.gridx=i;
        frame.add(button, constraints);
      }

      // Row Two
      JPanel panel = new JPanel();
      panel.setFocusCycleRoot(true);
      panel.setFocusTraversalPolicyProvider(true);
      panel.setLayout(new GridLayout(1,3));
      for (int i=0; i<3; i++) {
        JButton button = new JButton("" + (i+3));
        panel.add(button);
      }
      constraints.gridx=0;
      constraints.gridy=1;
      constraints.gridwidth=3;
      frame.add(panel, constraints);

      // Row Three
      constraints.gridy=2;
      constraints.gridwidth=1;
      for (int i=0; i<3; i++) {
        JButton button = new JButton("" + (i+6));
        constraints.gridx=i;
        frame.add(button, constraints);
      }

      frame.setSize(300, 200);
      frame.setVisible(true);
    }
  };
  EventQueue.invokeLater(runner);
}
}
```

FocusTraversalPolicy Class

The FocusTraversalPolicy is responsible for determining the focus traversal order. It allows you to specify the next and previous components in the order. This class offers six methods for controlling traversal order:

- getComponentAfter(Container aContainer, Component aComponent)

- getComponentBefore(Container aContainer, Component aComponent)

- getDefaultComponent(Container aContainer)

- getFirstComponent(Container aContainer)

- getInitialComponent(Window window)

- getLastComponent(Container aContainer)

Swing provides five predefined traversal policies, as listed in Table 2-5. By picking the right traversal policy for your application, or rolling your own, you can determine how users will navigate around the screens.

Table 2-5. *Predefined Traversal Policies*

Policy	Description
ContainerOrderFocusTraversalPolicy	The components are traversed in the order they are added to their container. The component must be visible, displayable, enabled, and focusable to be part of the focus cycle.
DefaultFocusTraversalPolicy	The default policy for AWT programs, this extends ContainerOrderFocusTraversalPolicy to check with the component peer (the operating system) if the component hasn't explicitly set focusability. The focusability of a peer depends on the Java runtime implementation.
InternalFrameFocusTraversalPolicy	Special policy for JInternalFrame, with behavior to determine initial focusable component based on the default component of the frame.
SortingFocusTraversalPolicy	Here, you provide a Comparator to the policy constructor to define the focus cycle order.
LayoutFocusTraversalPolicy	The default policy for Swing programs, this takes into account geometric settings of components (height, width, position), and then goes top down, left to right to determine navigation order. The top-down, left-right order is determined by the current ComponentOrientation setting for your locale. For instance, Hebrew would be in right-left order instead.

To demonstrate, the program in Listing 2-13 reverses the functionality of Tab and Shift-Tab. When you run the program, it looks the same as the screen shown earlier in Figure 2-11, with the 3×3 set of buttons. However, with this version, the initial focus starts on the 9 button, and pressing Tab takes you to 8, then 7, and so on. Shift-Tab goes in the other, more normal, order.

Listing 2-13. *Reversing Focus Traversal*

```
import javax.swing.*;
import java.awt.*;
import java.awt.event.*;
import java.util.Comparator;
import java.util.Arrays;
import java.util.List;

public class NextComponentSample {
  public static void main(String args[]) {
    Runnable runner = new Runnable() {
      public void run() {
        JFrame frame = new JFrame("Reverse Sample");
        frame.setDefaultCloseOperation(JFrame.EXIT_ON_CLOSE);

        frame.setLayout(new GridLayout(3,3));
        // for (int i=1; i<10; i++) {
        for (int i=9; i>0; i--) {
          JButton button = new JButton(Integer.toString(i));
          frame.add(button, 0);
        }

        final Container contentPane = frame.getContentPane();
        Comparator<Component> comp = new Comparator<Component>() {
          public int compare(Component c1, Component c2) {
            Component comps[] = contentPane.getComponents();
            List list = Arrays.asList(comps);
            int first = list.indexOf(c1);
            int second = list.indexOf(c2);
            return second - first;
          }
        };

        FocusTraversalPolicy policy = new SortingFocusTraversalPolicy(comp);
        frame.setFocusTraversalPolicy(policy);

        frame.setSize(300, 200);
        frame.setVisible(true);
      }
    };
    EventQueue.invokeLater(runner);
  }
}
```

KeyboardFocusManager Class

The abstract KeyboardFocusManager class in the AWT library serves as the control mechanism framework for the input focus behavior of Swing components. The DefaultKeyboardFocusManager is the concrete implementation. The focus manager allows you to both programmatically discover who currently has the input focus and to change it.

The component with the current input focus is called the *focus owner*. This is accessible via the focusOwner property of KeyboardFocusManager. You can also discover the focusedWindow and activeWindow properties. The focused window is the window containing the focus owner, and the active window is either the focused window or the frame or dialog containing the focus owner.

The simple concept of moving to the previous or next component is supported in many different ways. First, you can use the shortcut API methods of Component and Container:

- Component.transferFocus()

- Component.transferFocusBackward()

- Component.transferFocusUpCycle()

- Container.transferFocusDownCycle()

The first two methods request focus to move to the next or previous component, respectively. The up and down cycle methods request that you move up out of the current focus cycle or down into the next cycle.

The following methods map directly to methods of the KeyboardFocusManager:

- focusNextComponent()

- focusPreviousComponent()

- upFocusCycle()

- downFocusCycle()

A second set of the same four methods accepts a second parameter of a Component. If the component isn't specified, these methods change the focused component based on the current focus owner. If a component is provided, the change is based on that component.

Tab and Shift-Tab are used for keyboard focus traversal because they are defined as the default focus traversal keys for most, if not all, components. To define your own traversal keys, you can replace or append to a key set via the setFocusTraversalKeys() method of Component. Different sets are available for forward, backward, and up-cycle, as specified by the FORWARD_TRAVERSAL_KEYS, BACKWARD_TRAVERSAL_KEYS, and UP_CYCLE_TRAVERSAL_KEYS constants of KeyboardFocusManager. You can set and get key sets for each. For instance, to add the F3 key as an up-cycle key for a component, use the following code:

```
Set<AWTKeyStroke> set = component.getFocusTraversalKeys(
  KeyboardFocusManager.UP_CYCLE_TRAVERSAL_KEYS);
KeyStroke stroke = KeyStroket.getKeyStroke("F3");
set.add(stroke);
component.setFocusTraversalKeys(KeyboardFocusManager.UP_CYCLE_TRAVERSAL_KEYS, set);
```

Verifying Input During Focus Traversal

Swing offers the abstract InputVerifier class for component-level verification during focus traversal with any JComponent. Just subclass InputVerifier and provide your own public boolean verify(JComponent) method to verify the contents of the component.

Listing 2-14 provides a simple numeric text field verification example, showing three text fields, of which only two have verification. Unless fields one and three are valid, you can't tab out of them.

Listing 2-14. *Numeric Input Verifier*

```
import java.awt.*;
import java.awt.event.*;
import javax.swing.*;

public class VerifierSample {
  public static void main(String args[]) {
    Runnable runner = new Runnable() {
      public void run() {
        JFrame frame = new JFrame("Verifier Sample");
        frame.setDefaultCloseOperation(JFrame.EXIT_ON_CLOSE);
        JTextField textField1 = new JTextField();
        JTextField textField2 = new JTextField();
        JTextField textField3 = new JTextField();

        InputVerifier verifier = new InputVerifier() {
          public boolean verify(JComponent comp) {
            boolean returnValue;
            JTextField textField = (JTextField)comp;
            try {
              Integer.parseInt(textField.getText());
              returnValue = true;
            } catch (NumberFormatException e) {
              returnValue = false;
            }
            return returnValue;
          }
        };

        textField1.setInputVerifier(verifier);
        textField3.setInputVerifier(verifier);

        frame.add(textField1, BorderLayout.NORTH);
        frame.add(textField2, BorderLayout.CENTER);
        frame.add(textField3, BorderLayout.SOUTH);
        frame.setSize(300, 100);
        frame.setVisible(true);
      }
```

```
    };
    EventQueue.invokeLater(runner);
  }
}
```

■**Tip** To make sure that cancel-type buttons get the input focus no matter what when using `InputVerifier`, use the `setVerifyInputWhenFocusTarget(false)` method with the component.

Summary

In this chapter, you looked at the many ways of dealing with event handling when using Swing components. Because Swing components are built *on top of* AWT components, you can use the delegation-based event-handling mechanism common with those components. You then learned about the multithreading limitations of the Swing components and how to get around them with the `invokeAndWait()` and `invokeLater()` methods of `EventQueue`. You also explored how the Swing components use the JavaBeans `PropertyChangeListener` approach for notification of bound property changes.

Besides exploring the similarities between the Swing components and AWT components, you also looked at several of the new features that the Swing library offers. You explored the `Action` interface and how it can simplify complex user-interface development by completely separating the event-handling task from the visual component. You looked at the technique for registering `KeyStroke` objects to components to simplify listening for key events. Finally, you explored Swing's focus management capabilities and how to customize the focus cycle and use the `FocusTraversalPolicy` and `KeyboardFocusManager`, as well as validating input with the `InputVerifier`.

In Chapter 3, you'll meet the Model-View-Controller (MVC) architecture of the Swing component set. You'll learn how MVC can make your user interface development efforts much easier.

■■■

CHAPTER 3

The Model-View-Controller Architecture

Chapter 2 explored how to deal with event producers and consumers with regard to Swing components. We looked at how event handling with Swing components goes beyond the event-handling capabilities of the original AWT components. In this chapter, we will take the Swing component design one step further to examine what is called the Model-View-Controller (MVC) architecture.

Understanding the Flow of MVC

First introduced in Smalltalk in the late 1980s, the MVC architecture is a special form of the Observer pattern described in Chapter 2. The *model* part of the MVC holds the state of a component and serves as the Subject. The *view* part of the MVC serves as the Observer of the Subject to display the model's state. The view creates the *controller*, which defines how the user interface reacts to user input.

MVC Communication

Figure 3-1 shows how the MVC elements communicate—in this case, with Swing's multiline text component, the JTextArea. In MVC terms, the JTextArea serves as the view part within the MVC architecture. Displayed within the component is a Document, which is the model for the JTextArea. The Document stores the state information for the JTextArea, such as the text contents. Within the JTextArea is the controller, in the form of an InputMap. It maps keyboard input to commands in an ActionMap, and those commands are mapped to TextAction objects, which can modify the Document. When the modification happens, the Document creates a DocumentEvent and sends it back to the JTextArea.

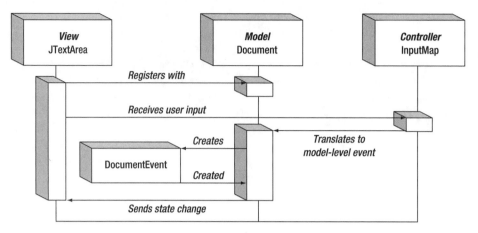

Figure 3-1. *MVC communication mechanism*

UI Delegates for Swing Components

This example demonstrates an important aspect of the MVC architecture within the Swing world. Complex interactions need to happen between the view and the controller. The Swing design combines these two elements into a *delegate* object to simplify the overall design. This results in each Swing component having a UI delegate that is in charge of rendering the current state of the component and dealing with user input events.

Sometimes, the user events result in changes to the view that don't affect the model. For instance, the cursor position is an attribute of the view. The model doesn't care about the position of the cursor, only the text contents. User input that affects the cursor position isn't passed along to the model. At other times, user input that affects the contents of the Document (for example, pressing the Backspace key) is passed along. Pressing the Backspace key results in a character being removed from the model. Because of this tight coupling, each Swing component has a UI delegate.

To demonstrate, Figure 3-2 shows the makeup of the JTextArea, with respect to the model and UI delegate. The UI delegate for the JTextArea starts with the TextUI interface, with its basic implementation in the BasicTextUI class. In turn, this is specialized with the BasicTextAreaUI for the JTextArea. The BasicTextAreaUI creates a view that is either a PlainView or a WrappedPlainView. On the model side, things are much simpler. The Document interface is implemented by the AbstractDocument class, which is further specialized by the PlainDocument.

The text components will be explained more fully in Chapters 15 and 16. As the diagram in Figure 3-2 demonstrates, much is involved in working with the text components. In most cases, you don't need to deal with the specifics to the degree shown in this figure. However, all of these classes are working behind the scenes. The UI-delegate part of the MVC architecture will be discussed further in Chapter 20, when we explore how to customize delegates.

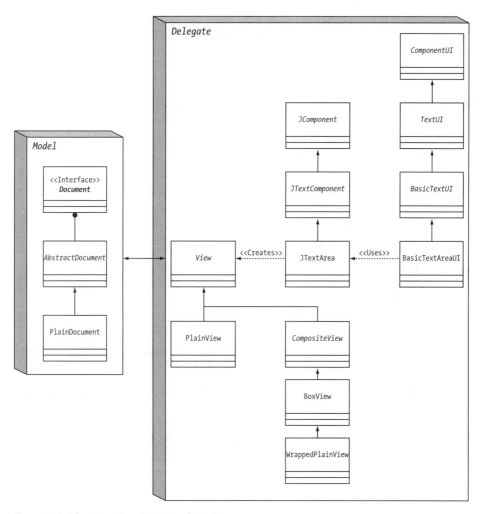

Figure 3-2. *The JTextArea MVC architecture*

Sharing Data Models

Because data models store only the state information, you can share a model across multiple components. Then each component view can be used to modify the model.

In the case of Figure 3-3, three different JTextArea components are used to modify one Document model. If a user modifies the contents of one JTextArea, the model is changed, causing the other text areas to automatically reflect the updated document state. It isn't necessary for any Document view to manually notify others sharing the model.

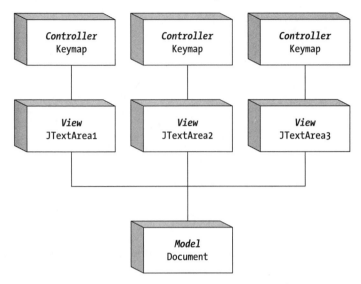

Figure 3-3. *Sharing MVC data models*

Sharing of a data model can be done in either one of two ways:

- You can create the data model apart from any component and tell each component to use the data model.

- You can create one component first, get the model from the first component, and then share it with the other components.

Listing 3-1 demonstrates how to share a data model using the latter technique.

Listing 3-1. *Sharing an MVC Model*

```
import java.awt.*;
import javax.swing.*;
import javax.swing.text.*;

public class ShareModel {
  public static void main (String args[]) {
    Runnable runner = new Runnable() {
      public void run() {
        JFrame frame = new JFrame("Sharing Sample");
        frame.setDefaultCloseOperation(JFrame.EXIT_ON_CLOSE);
        Container content = frame.getContentPane();
        JTextArea textarea1 = new JTextArea();
        Document document = textarea1.getDocument();
        JTextArea textarea2 = new JTextArea(document);
        JTextArea textarea3 = new JTextArea(document);
        content.setLayout(new BoxLayout(content, BoxLayout.Y_AXIS));
        content.add(new JScrollPane(textarea1));
```

```
      content.add(new JScrollPane(textarea2));
      content.add(new JScrollPane(textarea3));
      frame.setSize (300, 400);
      frame.setVisible (true);
     }
   };
   EventQueue.invokeLater(runner);
  }
}
```

Figure 3-4 shows how this program might look after editing the shared document. Notice that the three text areas are capable of viewing (or modifying) different areas of the document. They aren't limited to adding text only at the end, for instance. This is because each text area manages the position and cursor separately. The position and cursor are attributes of the view, not the model.

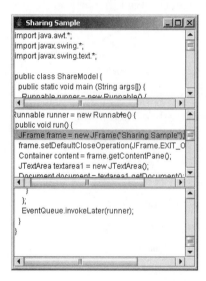

Figure 3-4. *Sharing a document between JTextArea components*

Understanding the Predefined Data Models

When working with Swing components, it's helpful to understand the data models behind each of the components because the data models store their state. Understanding the data model for each component helps you to separate the parts of the component that are visual (and thus part of the view) from those that are logical (and thus part of the data model). For example, by understanding this separation, you can see why the cursor position within a JTextArea isn't part of the data model, but rather is part of the view.

Table 3-1 provides a complete listing of the Swing components, the interface that describes the data model for each component, as well as the specific implementations. If a component isn't listed, that component inherits its data model from its parent class, most likely

AbstractButton. In addition, in some cases, multiple interfaces are used to describe a component, because the data is stored in one model and the selection of the data is in a second model. In the case of the JComboBox, the MutableComboBoxModel interface extends from ComboBoxModel. No predefined class implements the ComboBoxModel interface without also implementing the MutableComboBoxModel interface.

Table 3-1. *Swing Component Models*

Component	Data Model Interface	Implementations
AbstractButton	ButtonModel	DefaultButtonModel
JColorChooser	ColorSelectionModel	DefaultColorSelectionModel
JComboBox	ComboBoxModel	N/A
	MutableComboBoxModel	DefaultComboBoxModel
JFileChooser	ListModel	BasicDirectoryModel
JList	ListModel	AbstractListModel
		DefaultListModel
	ListSelectionModel	DefaultListSelectionModel
JMenuBar	SingleSelectionModel	DefaultSingleSelectionModel
JPopupMenu	SingleSelectionModel	DefaultSingleSelectionModel
JProgressBar	BoundedRangeModel	DefaultBoundedRangeModel
JScrollBar	BoundedRangeModel	DefaultBoundedRangeModel
JSlider	BoundedRangeModel	DefaultBoundedRangeModel
JSpinner	SpinnerModel	AbstractSpinnerModel
		SpinnerDateModel
		SpinnerListModel
		SpinnerNumberModel
JTabbedPane	SingleSelectionModel	DefaultSingleSelectionModel
JTable	TableModel	AbstractTableModel
		DefaultTableModel
	TableColumnModel	DefaultTableColumnModel
	ListSelectionModel	DefaultListSelectionModel
JTextComponent	Document	AbstractDocument
		PlainDocument
		StyledDocument
		DefaultStyleDocument
		HTMLDocument

Table 3-1. *Swing Component Models (Continued)*

Component	Data Model Interface	Implementations
JToggleButton	ButtonModel	JToggleButton
		ToggleButtonModel
JTree	TreeModel	DefaultTreeModel
	TreeSelectionModel	DefaultTreeSelectionModel
		JTree.EmptySelectionModel

When directly accessing the model of a Swing component, if you change the model, all registered views are automatically notified. This, in turn, causes the views to revalidate themselves to ensure that the components display their proper current states. This automatic propagation of state changes is one reason why MVC has become so popular. In addition, using the MVC architecture helps programs become more maintainable as they change over time and their complexity grows. No longer will you need to worry about losing state information if you change visual component libraries!

Summary

This chapter provided a quick look at how the Swing components use a modified MVC architecture. You explored what makes up this modified architecture and how one particular component, the JTextArea, maps into this architecture. In addition, the chapter discussed the sharing of data models between components and listed all the data models for the different Swing components.

In Chapter 4, you'll start to look at the individual components that make up the Swing component library. In addition, you'll explore the Swing component class hierarchy as you examine the base JComponent component from the Swing library.

■■■

CHAPTER 4

Core Swing Components

In Chapter 3, you received a quick introduction to the Model-View-Controller (MVC) pattern used by the components of the JFC/Swing project. In this chapter, you'll begin to explore how to use the key parts of the many available components.

All Swing components start with the JComponent class. Although some parts of the Swing libraries aren't rooted with the JComponent class, all the components share JComponent as the common parent class at some level of their ancestry. It's with this JComponent class that common behavior and properties are defined. In this chapter, you'll look at common functionality such as component painting, customization, tooltips, and sizing.

As far as specific JComponent descendent classes are concerned, you'll specifically look at the JLabel, JButton, and JPanel, three of the more commonly used Swing component classes. They require an understanding of the Icon interface for displaying images within components, as well as of the ImageIcon class for when using predefined images and the GrayFilter class for support. In addition, you'll look at the AbstractButton class, which serves as the parent class to the JButton. The data model shared by all AbstractButton subclasses is the ButtonModel interface; you'll explore that and the specific implementation class, the DefaultButtonModel.

JComponent Class

The JComponent class serves as the abstract root class from which all Swing components descend. The JComponent class has 42 descendent subclasses, each of which inherits much of the JComponent functionality. Figure 4-1 shows this hierarchy.

Although the JComponent class serves as the common root class for all Swing components, many classes in the libraries for the Swing project descend from classes other than JComponent. Those include all the high-level container objects such as JFrame, JApplet, and JInternalFrame; all the MVC-related classes; event-handling–related interfaces and classes; and much more. All of these will be discussed in later chapters.

Although all Swing components extend JComponent, the JComponent class extends the AWT Container class, which, in turn, extends from the AWT Component class. This means that many aspects of the JComponent are shared with both the AWT Component and Container classes.

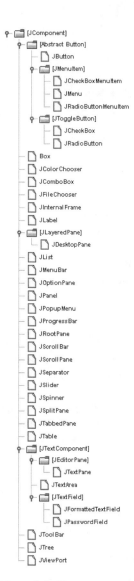

Figure 4-1. *JComponent class hierarchy diagram*

■**Note** JComponent extends from the Container class, but most of the JComponent subclasses aren't themselves containers of other components. To see if a particular Swing component is truly a container, check the BeanInfo for the class to see if the isContainer property is set to true. To get the BeanInfo for a class, ask the Introspector.

Component Pieces

The JComponent class defines many aspects of AWT components that go above and beyond the capabilities of the original AWT component set. This includes customized painting behavior and several different ways to customize display settings, such as colors, fonts, and any other client-side settings.

Painting JComponent Objects

Because the Swing JComponent class extends from the Container class, the basic AWT painting model is followed: All painting is done through the paint() method, and the repaint() method is used to trigger updates. However, many tasks are done differently. The JComponent class optimizes many aspects of painting for improved performance and extensibility. In addition, the RepaintManager class is available to customize painting behavior even further.

Note The public void update(Graphics g) method, inherited from Component, is never invoked on Swing components.

To improve painting performance and extensibility, the JComponent splits the painting operation into three tasks. The public void paint(Graphics g) method is subdivided into three separate protected method calls. In the order called, they are paintComponent(g), paintBorder(g), and paintChildren(g), with the Graphics argument passed through from the original paint() call. The component itself is first painted through paintComponent(g). If you want to customize the painting of a Swing component, you override paintComponent() instead of paint(). Unless you want to completely replace all the painting, you would call super.paintComponent() first, as shown here, to get the default paintComponent() behavior.

```
public class MyComponent extends JPanel {
  protected void paintComponent(Graphics g) {
    super.paintComponent(g);
    // Customize after calling super.paintComponent(g)
  }
  ...
}
```

Note When running a program that uses Swing components in Java 5.0, the Graphics argument passed to the paint() method and on to paintComponent() is technically a Graphics2D argument. Therefore, after casting the Graphics argument to a Graphics2D object, you could use the Java 2D capabilities of the platform, as you would when defining a drawing Stroke, Shape, or AffineTransform.

The `paintBorder()` and `paintChildren()` methods tend not to be overridden. The `paintBorder()` method draws a border around the component, a concept described more fully in Chapter 7. The `paintChildren()` method draws the components within the Swing container object, if any are present.

To optimize painting, the `JComponent` class provides three additional painting properties: `opaque`, `optimizedDrawingEnabled`, and `doubleBuffered`. These work as follows:

- **Opacity:** The `opaque` property for a `JComponent` defines whether a component is transparent. When transparent, the container of the `JComponent` must paint the background behind the component. To improve performance, you can leave the `JComponent` opaque and let the `JComponent` draw its own background, instead of relying on the container to draw the covered background.

- **Optimization:** The `optimizedDrawingEnabled` property determines whether immediate children can overlap. If children cannot overlap, the repaint time is reduced considerably. By default, optimized drawing is enabled for most Swing components, except for `JDesktopPane`, `JLayeredPane`, and `JViewport`.

- **Double buffering:** By default, all Swing components double buffer their drawing operations into a buffer shared by the complete container hierarchy; that is, all the components within a window (or subclass). This greatly improves painting performance, because when double buffering is enabled (with the `doubleBuffered` property), there is only a single screen update drawn.

■Note For synchronous painting, you can call one of the `public void paintImmediately()` methods. (Arguments are either a `Rectangle` or its parts—position and dimensions.) However, you'll rarely need to call this directly unless your program has real-time painting requirements.

The public void `revalidate()` method of `JComponent` also offers painting support. When this method is called, the high-level container of the component validates itself. This is unlike the AWT approach requiring a direct call to the `revalidate()` method of that high-level component.

The last aspect of the Swing component painting enhancements is the `RepaintManager` class.

RepaintManager Class

The `RepaintManager` class is responsible for ensuring the efficiency of repaint requests on the currently displayed Swing components, making sure the smallest "dirty" region of the screen is updated when a region becomes invalid.

Although rarely customized, `RepaintManager` is public and provides a static installation routine to use a custom manager: `public static void setCurrentManager(RepaintManager manager)`. To get the current manager, just ask with `public static void currentManager` `(JComponent)`. The argument is usually `null`, unless you've customized the manager to provide component-level support. Once you have the manager, one thing you can do is get the off-screen buffer for a component as an `Image`. Because the buffer is what is eventually shown on the screen, this effectively allows you to do a screen dump of the inside of a window (or any JComponent).

```
Component comp = ...
RepaintManager manager = RepaintManager.currentManager(null);
Image htmlImage = manager.getOffscreenBuffer(comp, comp.getWidth(),
  comp.getHeight());
// or
Image volatileImage = manager.getVolatileOffscreenBuffer(comp, comp.getWidth(),
  comp.getHeight());
```

Table 4-1 shows the two properties of RepaintManager. They allow you to disable double buffering for all drawing operations of a component (hierarchy) and to set the maximum double buffer size, which defaults to the end user's screen size.

Table 4-1. *RepaintManager Properties*

Property Name	Data Type	Access
doubleBufferingEnabled	boolean	Read-write
doubleBufferMaximumSize	Dimension	Read-write

■**Tip** To globally disable double-buffered drawing, call RepaintManager.currentManager(aComponent). setDoubleBufferingEnabled(false).

Although it's rarely done, providing your own RepaintManager subclass does allow you to customize the mechanism of painting dirty regions of the screen, or at least track when the painting is finished. Overriding any of the following four methods allows you to customize the mechanisms:

```
public synchronized void addDirtyRegion(JComponent component, int x, int y,
  int width, int height)
public Rectangle getDirtyRegion(JComponent component)
public void markCompletelyClean(JComponent component)
public void markCompletelyDirty(JComponent component)
```

UIDefaults Class

The UIDefaults class represents a lookup table containing the display settings installed for the current look and feel, such as which font to use within a JList, as well as what color or icon should be displayed within a JTree node. The use of UIDefaults will be detailed in Chapter 20 with the coverage of Java's pluggable look and feel architecture. Here, you will get a brief introduction to the UIDefaults table.

Whenever you create a component, the component automatically asks the UIManager to look in the UIDefaults table for the current settings for that component. Most color- and font-related component settings, as well as some others not related to colors and fonts, are configurable. If you don't like a particular setting, you can simply change it by updating the appropriate entry in the UIDefaults lookup table.

■**Note** All predefined resource settings in the UIDefaults table implement the UIResource interface, which allows the components to monitor which settings have been customized just by looking for those settings that don't implement the interface.

First, you need to know the name of the UIDefaults setting you want to change. You can find the setting names in Appendix A of this book, which contains a complete alphabetical listing of all known settings for the predefined look and feel types in J2SE 5.0. (These differ a little from release to release.) In addition, included with the description of each component is a table containing the UIResource-related property elements. (To find the specific component section in the book, consult the table of contents or the index.)

Once you know the name of a setting, you can store a new setting with the public static void put(Object key, Object value) method of UIManager, where key is the key string. For instance, the following code will change the default background color of newly created buttons to black and the foreground color to red:

```
UIManager.put("Button.background", Color.BLACK);
UIManager.put("Button.foreground", Color.RED);
```

Fetching UIResource Properties

If you're creating your own components, or just need to find out the current value setting, you can ask the UIManager. Although the public static Object get(Object key) method is the most generic, it requires you to cast the return value to the appropriate class type. Alternatively, you could use one of the more specific getXXX() methods, which does the casting for you, to return the appropriate type:

```
public static boolean getBoolean(Object key)
public static Border getBorder(Object key)
public static Color getColor(Object key)
public static Dimension getDimension(Object key)
public static Font getFont(Object key)
public static Icon getIcon(Object key)
public static Insets getInsets(Object key)
public static int getInt(Object key)
public static String getString(Object key)
public static ComponentUI getUI(JComponent target)
```

There is a second set of overloaded methods that accept a second argument for the Locale.

Note You can also work with the UIDefaults directly, by calling the public static UIDefaults getDefaults() method of UIManager.

Client Properties

In addition to the UIManager maintaining a table of key/value pair settings, each instance of every component can manage its own set of key/value pairs. This is useful for maintaining aspects of a component that may be specific to a particular look and feel, or for maintaining data associated with a component without requiring the definition of new classes or methods to store such data.

```
public final void putClientProperty(Object key, Object value)
public final Object getClientProperty(Object key)
```

Note Calling putClientProperty() with a value of null causes the key to be removed from the client property table.

For instance, the JTree class has a property with the Metal look and feel for configuring the line style for connecting or displaying nodes within a JTree. Because the setting is specific to one look and feel, it doesn't make sense to add something to the tree API. Instead, you set the property by calling the following on a particular tree instance:

```
tree.putClientProperty("JTree.lineStyle", "None")
```

Then, when the look and feel is the default Metal, lines will connect the nodes of the tree. If another look and feel is installed, the client property will be ignored. Figure 4-2 shows a tree with and without lines.

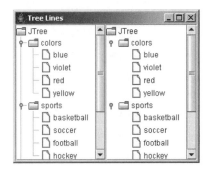

Figure 4-2. *A JTree, with and without angled lines*

■**Note** The list of client properties is probably one of the least documented aspects of Swing. Chapter 20 lists the available properties I was able to determine. Also, while Metal is the default look and feel, what you see is called Ocean. Ocean is a theme of the Metal look and feel and makes Metal look a bit flashier.

JComponent Properties

You've seen some of the pieces shared by the different JComponent subclasses. Now it's time to look at the JavaBeans properties. Table 4-2 shows the complete list of properties defined by JComponent, including those inherited through the AWT Container and Component classes.

Table 4-2. *JComponent Properties*

Property Name	Data Type	Component Access	Container Access	JComponent Access
accessibleContext	AccessibleContext	Read-only	N/A	Read-only
actionMap	ActionMap	N/A	N/A	Read-write
alignmentX	float	Read-only	Read-only	Read-write
alignmentY	float	Read-only	Read-only	Read-write
ancestorListeners	AncestorListener[ ]	N/A	N/A	Read-only
autoscrolls	boolean	N/A	N/A	Read-write
background	Color	Read-write bound	N/A	Write-only
backgroundSet	boolean	Read-only	N/A	N/A
border	Border	N/A	N/A	Read-write bound
bounds	Rectangle	Read-write	N/A	N/A
colorModel	ColorModel	Read-only	N/A	N/A
componentCount	int	N/A	Read-only	N/A
componentListeners	ComponentListener[ ]	Read-only	N/A	N/A
componentOrientation	ComponentOrientation	Read-write bound	N/A	N/A
componentPopupMenu	JPopupMenu	N/A	N/A	Read-write
components	Component[ ]	N/A	Read-only	N/A
containerListeners	ContainerListener[ ]	N/A	Read-only	N/A
cursor	Cursor	Read-write	N/A	N/A
cursorSet	boolean	Read-only	N/A	N/A
debugGraphicsOptions	int	N/A	N/A	Read-write
displayable	boolean	Read-only	N/A	N/A

Table 4-2. *JComponent Properties (Continued)*

Property Name	Data Type	Component Access	Container Access	JComponent Access
doubleBuffered	boolean	Read-only	N/A	Read-write
dropTarget	DropTarget	Read-write	N/A	N/A
enabled	boolean	Read-write	N/A	Write-only bound
focusable	boolean	Read-write bound	N/A	N/A
focusCycleRoot	boolean	N/A	Read-write bound	N/A
focusCycleRootAncestor	Container	Read-only	N/A	N/A
focusListeners	FocusListener[ ]	Read-only	N/A	N/A
focusOwner	boolean	Read-only	N/A	N/A
focusTraversalKeysEnabled	boolean	Read-write bound	N/A	N/A
focusTraversalPolicy	FocusTraversalPolicy	N/A	Read-write bound	N/A
focusTraversalPolicyProvider	boolean	N/A	Read-write bound	N/A
focusTraversalPolicySet	boolean	N/A	Read-only	N/A
font	Font	Read-write bound	Write-only	Write-only
fontSet	boolean	Read-only	N/A	N/A
foreground	Color	Read-write bound	N/A	Write-only
foregroundSet	boolean	Read-only	N/A	N/A
graphics	Graphics	Read-only	N/A	Read-only
graphicsConfiguration	GraphicsConfiguration	Read-only	N/A	N/A
height	int	Read-only	N/A	Read-only
hierarchyBoundsListeners	HierarchyBoundsListener[ ]	Read-only	N/A	N/A
hierarchyListeners	HierarchyListener[ ]	Read-only	N/A	N/A
ignoreRepaint	boolean	Read-write	N/A	N/A
inheritsPopupMenu	boolean	N/A	N/A	Read-write
inputContext	InputContext	Read-only	N/A	N/A
inputMap	InputMap	N/A	N/A	Read-only
inputMethodListeners	InputMethodListener[ ]	Read-only	N/A	N/A
inputMethodRequests	InputMethodRequests	Read-only	N/A	N/A

Table 4-2. *JComponent Properties (Continued)*

Property Name	Data Type	Component Access	Container Access	JComponent Access
inputVerifier	InputVerifier	N/A	N/A	Read-write bound
insets	Insets	N/A	Read-only	Read-only
keyListeners	KeyListener[ ]	Read-only	N/A	N/A
layout	LayoutManager	N/A	Read-write	N/A
lightweight	boolean	Read-only	N/A	N/A
locale	Locale	Read-write bound	N/A	N/A
location	Point	Read-write	N/A	N/A
locationOnScreen	Point	Read-only	N/A	N/A
maximumSize	Dimension	Read-write bound	Read-only	Read-write
maximumSizeSet	boolean	Read-only	N/A	N/A
minimumSize	Dimension	Read-write bound	Read-only	Read-write
minimumSizeSet	boolean	Read-only	N/A	N/A
mouseListeners	MouseListener[ ]	Read-only	N/A	N/A
mouseMotionListeners	MouseMotionListener[ ]	Read-only	N/A	N/A
mousePosition	Point	Read-only	N/A	N/A
mouseWheelListeners	MouseWheelListener	Read-only	N/A	N/A
name	String	Read-write bound	N/A	N/A
opaque	boolean	Read-only	N/A	Read-write bound
optimizedDrawingEnabled	boolean	N/A	N/A	Read-only
paintingTile	boolean	N/A	N/A	Read-only
parent	Container	Read-only	N/A	N/A
preferredSize	Dimension	Read-write bound	Read-only	Read-write
preferredSizeSet	boolean	Read-only	N/A	N/A
propertyChangeListeners	PropertyChangeListener[ ]	Read-only	N/A	N/A
registeredKeyStrokes	KeyStroke[ ]	N/A	N/A	Read-only
requestFocusEnabled	boolean	N/A	N/A	Read-write
rootPane	JRootPane	N/A	N/A	Read-only

Table 4-2. *JComponent Properties (Continued)*

Property Name	Data Type	Component Access	Container Access	JComponent Access
showing	boolean	Read-only	N/A	N/A
size	Dimension	Read-write	N/A	N/A
toolkit	Toolkit	Read-only	N/A	N/A
tooltipText	String	N/A	N/A	Read-write
topLevelAncestor	Container	N/A	N/A	Read-only
transferHandler	TransferHandler	N/A	N/A	Read-write bound
treeLock	Object	Read-only	N/A	N/A
uiClassID	String	N/A	N/A	Read-only
valid	boolean	Read-only	N/A	N/A
validateRoot	boolean	N/A	N/A	Read-only
verifyInputWhenFocusTarget	boolean	N/A	N/A	Read-write bound
vetoableChangeListeners	VetoableChangeListener[]	N/A	N/A	Read-only
visible	boolean	Read-write	N/A	Write-only
visibleRect	Rectangle	N/A	N/A	Read-only
width	int	Read-only	N/A	Read-only
x	int	Read-only	N/A	Read-only
y	int	Read-only	N/A	Read-only

■**Note** Additionally, there's a read-only class property defined at the Object level, the parent of the Component class.

Including the properties from the parent hierarchy, approximately 92 properties of JComponent exist. As that number indicates, the JComponent class is extremely well suited for visual development. There are roughly ten categories of JComponent properties, as described in the following sections.

Position-Oriented Properties

The x and y properties define the location of the component relative to its parent. The locationOnScreen is just another location for the component, this time relative to the screen's origin (the upper-left corner). The width and height properties define the size of the component. The visibleRect property describes the part of the component visible within the topLevelAncestor, whereas the bounds property defines the component's area, whether visible or not.

Component-Set-Oriented Properties

The components and componentCount properties enable you to find out what the children components are of the particular JComponent. For each component in the components property array, the current component would be its parent. In addition to determining a component's parent, you can find out its rootPane or topLevelAncestor.

Focus-Oriented Properties

The focusable, focusCycleRoot, focusCycleRootAncestor, focusOwner, focusTraversalKeysEnabled, focusTraversalPolicy, focusTraversalPolicyProvider, focusTraversablePolicySet, requestFocusEnabled, verifyInputWhenFocusTarget, and inputVerifier properties define the set of focus-oriented properties. These properties control the focus behavior of JComponent and were discussed in Chapter 2.

Layout-Oriented Properties

The alignmentX, alignmentY, componentOrientation, layout, maximumSize, minimumSize, preferredSize, maximumSizeSet, minimumSizeSet, and preferredSizeSet properties are used to help with layout management.

Painting Support Properties

The background and foreground properties describe the current drawing colors. The font property describes the text style to draw. The backgroundSet, foregroundSet, and fontSet properties describe if the properties are explicitly set. The insets and border properties are intermixed to describe the drawing of a border around a component. The graphics property permits real-time drawing, although the paintImmediately() method might now suffice.

To improve performance, there are the opaque (false is transparent), doubleBuffered, ignoreRepaint, and optimizedDrawingEnabled properties. The colorModel and paintingTile properties store intermediate drawing information. The graphicsConfiguration property adds support for virtual devices.

debugGraphicsOption allows you to slow down the drawing of your component if you can't figure out why it's not painted properly. The debugGraphicsOption property is set to one or more of the settings shown in Table 4-3.

Table 4-3. *DebugGraphics Settings*

DebugGraphics Settings	Description
DebugGraphics.BUFFERED_OPTION	Causes a window to pop up, displaying the drawing of the double-buffered image
DebugGraphics.FLASH_OPTION	Causes the drawing to be done more slowly, flashing between steps
DebugGraphics.LOG_OPTION	Causes a message to be printed to the screen as each step is done
DebugGraphics.NONE_OPTION	Disables all options

You can combine multiple DebugGraphics settings with the bitwise OR (|) operator, as in this example:

```
JComponent component = new ...();
component.setDebugGraphicsOptions(DebugGraphics.BUFFERED_OPTION |
  DebugGraphics.FLASH_OPTION | DebugGraphics.LOG_OPTION);
```

Internationalization Support Properties

The inputContext, inputMethodRequests, and locale properties help when creating multilingual operations.

State Support Properties

To get state information about a component, all you have to do is ask; there's much you can discover. The autoscrolls property lets you place a component within a JViewport and it automatically scrolls when dragged. The validateRoot property is used when revalidate() has been called and returns true when the current component is at the point it should stop. The remaining seven properties are self-explanatory: displayable, dropTarget, enabled, lightweight, showing, valid, and visible.

Event Support Properties

The registeredKeyStrokes, inputMap, and actionMap properties allow you to register keystroke responses with a window. All the getXXXListeners() methods allow you to get the current set of listeners for a particular listener type.

Pop-Up Support Properties

There are two types of pop-ups associated with a component: tooltips and pop-up menus. The toolTipText property is set to display pop-up support text over a component. The componentPopupMenu and inheritsPopupMenu properties are related to automatically showing pop-up menus associated with the component. The mousePosition property helps to position these.

Other Properties

The remaining properties don't seem to have any kind of logical grouping. The accessibleContext property is for support with the javax.accessibility package. The cursor property lets you change the cursor to one of the available cursors, where cursorSet is used to recognize when the property is explicitly set. The toolkit property encapsulates platform-specific behaviors for accessing system resources. The transferHandler property is there for drag-and-drop support. The name property gives you the means to recognize a particular instance of a class. The treelock property is the component tree-synchronization locking resource. The uiClassID property is new; it allows subclasses to return the appropriate class ID for their specific instance.

Handling JComponent Events

There are many different types of events that all JComponent subclasses share. Most of these come from parent classes, like Component and Container. First, you'll explore the use of PropertyChangeListener, which is inherited from Container. Then you'll look at the use of two event-handling capabilities shared by all JComponent subclasses: VetoableChangeListener and AncestorListener. Finally, you'll see the complete set of listeners inherited from Component.

Listening to Component Events with a PropertyChangeListener

The JComponent class has several component bound properties, directly and indirectly. By binding a PropertyChangeListener to the component, you can listen for particular JComponent property changes, and then respond accordingly.

```
public interface PropertyChangeListener extends EventListener {
  public void propertyChange(PropertyChangeEvent propertyChangeEvent);
}
```

To demonstrate, the PropertyChangeListener in Listing 4-1 demonstrates the behavior you might need when listening for changes to an Action type property within a JButton component. The property that changes determines which if block is executed.

Listing 4-1. *Watching for Changes to a JButton*

```
import java.beans.*;
import javax.swing.*;

public class ActionChangedListener implements PropertyChangeListener {

  private JButton button;

  public ActionChangedListener(JButton button) {
    this.button = button;
  }

  public void propertyChange(PropertyChangeEvent e) {
    String propertyName = e.getPropertyName();
    if (e.getPropertyName().equals(Action.NAME)) {
      String text = (String)e.getNewValue();
      button.setText(text);
      button.repaint();
    } else if (propertyName.equals("enabled")) {
      Boolean enabledState = (Boolean)e.getNewValue();
      button.setEnabled(enabledState.booleanValue());
      button.repaint();
```

```
    } else if (e.getPropertyName().equals(Action.SMALL_ICON)) {
      Icon icon = (Icon)e.getNewValue();
      button.setIcon(icon);
      button.invalidate();
      button.repaint();
    }
  }
}
```

■Note You can bind a PropertyChangeListener to a specific property by adding the listener with addPropertyChangeListener(String propertyName, PropertyChangeListener listener). This allows your listener to avoid having to check for the specific property that changed.

Listening to JComponent Events with a VetoableChangeListener

The VetoableChangeListener is another JavaBeans listener that Swing components use. It works with constrained properties, whereas the PropertyChangeListener works with only bound properties. A key difference between the two is that the public void vetoableChange(PropertyChangeEvent propertyChangeEvent) method can throw a PropertyVetoException if the listener doesn't like the requested change.

```
public interface VetoableChangeListener extends EventListener {
  public void vetoableChange(PropertyChangeEvent propertyChangeEvent)
    throws PropertyVetoException;
}
```

■Note Only one Swing class, JInternalFrame, has constrained properties. The listener is meant primarily for programmers to use with their own newly created components.

Listening to JComponent Events with an AncestorListener

You can use an AncestorListener to find out when a component moves, is made visible, or is made invisible. It's useful if you permit your users to customize their screens by moving components around and possibly removing components from the screens.

```
public interface  AncestorListener extends EventListener {
  public void ancestorAdded(AncestorEvent ancestorEvent);
  public void ancestorMoved(AncestorEvent ancestorEvent);
  public void ancestorRemoved(AncestorEvent ancestorEvent);
}
```

To demonstrate, Listing 4-2 associates an AncestorListener with the root pane of a JFrame. You'll see the messages Removed, Added, and Moved when the program first starts up. In addition, you'll see Moved messages when you drag the frame around.

Listing 4-2. *Listening for Ancestor Events*

```java
import java.awt.*;
import javax.swing.*;
import javax.swing.event.*;

public class AncestorSampler {
  public static void main (String args[]) {
    Runnable runner = new Runnable() {
      public void run() {
        JFrame frame = new JFrame("Ancestor Sampler");
        frame.setDefaultCloseOperation(JFrame.EXIT_ON_CLOSE);

        AncestorListener ancestorListener = new AncestorListener() {
          public void ancestorAdded(AncestorEvent ancestorEvent) {
            System.out.println ("Added");
          }
          public void ancestorMoved(AncestorEvent ancestorEvent) {
            System.out.println ("Moved");
          }
          public void ancestorRemoved(AncestorEvent ancestorEvent) {
            System.out.println ("Removed");
          }
        };
        frame.getRootPane().addAncestorListener(ancestorListener);
        frame.setSize(300, 200);
        frame.setVisible(true);
        frame.getRootPane().setVisible(false);
        frame.getRootPane().setVisible(true);
      }
    };
    EventQueue.invokeLater(runner);
  }
}
```

Listening to Inherited Events of a JComponent

In addition to the ability to listen for an instance of an AncestorEvent or PropertyChangeEvent with a JComponent, the JComponent inherits the ability to listen to many other events from its Container and Component superclasses.

Table 4-4 lists ten event listeners. You may find yourself using the JComponent listener interfaces quite a bit, but the older ones work, too. Use the ones most appropriate for the task at hand.

Table 4-4. *JComponent Inherited Event Listeners*

Class	Event Listener	Event Object
Component	ComponentListener	componentHidden(ComponentEvent)
		componentMoved(ComponentEvent)
		componentResized(ComponentEvent)
		componentShown(ComponentEvent)
Component	FocusListener	focusGained(FocusEvent)
		focusLost(FocusEvent)
Component	HierarchyBoundsListener	ancestorMoved(HierarchyEvent)
		ancestorResized(HierarchyEvent)
Component	HierarchyListener	hierarchyChanged(HierarchyEvent)
Component	InputMethodListener	caretPositionChanged(InputMethodEvent)
		inputMethodTextChanged(InputMethodEvent)
Component	KeyListener	keyPressed(KeyEvent)
		keyReleased(KeyEvent)
		keyTyped(KeyEvent)
Component	MouseListener	mouseClicked(MouseEvent)
		mouseEntered(MouseEvent)
		mouseExited(MouseEvent)
		mousePressed(MouseEvent)
		mouseReleased(MouseEvent)
Component	MouseMotionListener	mouseDragged(MouseEvent)
		mouseMoved(MouseEvent)
Component	MouseWheelListener	mouseWheelMoved(MouseWheelEvent)
Container	ContainerListener	componentAdded(ContainerEvent)
		componentRemoved(ContainerEvent)

JToolTip Class

The Swing components support the ability to display brief pop-up messages when the cursor rests over them. The class used to display pop-up messages is JToolTip.

Creating a JToolTip

Calling the `public void setToolTipText(String text)` method of JComponent automatically causes the creation of a JToolTip instance when the mouse rests over a component with the installed pop-up message. You don't normally call the JToolTip constructor directly. There's only one constructor, and it's of the no-argument variety.

Tooltip text is normally one line long. However, if the text string begins with <html> (in any case), then the contents can be any HTML 3.2 formatted text. For instance, the following line causes the pop-up message shown in Figure 4-3:

```
component.setToolTipText("<html>Tooltip<br>Message");
```

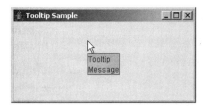

Figure 4-3. *HTML-based tooltip text*

Creating Customized JToolTip Objects

You can easily customize the display characteristics for all pop-up messages by setting UIResource elements for JToolTip, as shown in the "Customizing a JToolTip Look and Feel" section later in this chapter.

The JComponent class defines an easy way for you to customize the display characteristics of the tooltip when it's placed over a specific component. Simply subclass the component you want to customize and override its inherited `public JToolTip createToolTip()` method. The `createToolTip()` method is called when the ToolTipManager has determined that it's time to display the pop-up message.

To customize the pop-up tooltip appearance, just override the method and customize the JToolTip returned from the inherited method. For instance, the following source demonstrates the setting of a custom coloration for the tooltip for a JButton, as shown in Figure 4-4.

```
JButton b = new JButton("Hello, World") {
  public JToolTip createToolTip() {
    JToolTip tip = super.createToolTip();
    tip.setBackground(Color.YELLOW);
    tip.setForeground(Color.RED);
    return tip;
  }
};
```

Figure 4-4. *Tooltip text displayed with custom colors*

After the JToolTip has been created, you can configure the inherited JComponent properties or any of the properties specific to JToolTip, as shown in Table 4-5.

Table 4-5. *JToolTip Properties*

Property Name	Data Type	Access
accessibleContext	AccessibleContext	Read-only
component	JComponent	Read-write
tipText	String	Read-write
UI	ToolTipUI	Read-only
UIClassID	String	Read-only

Displaying Positional Tooltip Text

Swing components can even support the display of different tooltip text, depending on where the mouse pointer is located. This requires overriding the public boolean contains(int x, int y) method, which originates from the Component class.

For instance, after enhancing the customized JButton created in the previous section (Figure 4-4), the tooltip text will differ, depending on whether or not the mouse pointer is within 50 pixels from the left edge of the component.

```
JButton button = new JButton("Hello, World") {
  public JToolTip createToolTip() {
    JToolTip tip = super.createToolTip();
    tip.setBackground(Color.YELLOW);
    tip.setForeground(Color.RED);
    return tip;
  }
  public boolean contains(int x, int y) {
    if (x < 50) {
      setToolTipText("Got Green Eggs?");
    } else {
      setToolTipText("Got Ham?");
    }
    return super.contains(x, y);
  }
};
```

Customizing a JToolTip Look and Feel

Each installable Swing look and feel provides a different JToolTip appearance and a set of default UIResource value settings. Figure 4-5 shows the appearance of the JToolTip component for the preinstalled set of look and feel types: Motif, Windows, and Ocean.

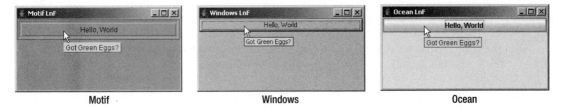

Figure 4-5. *JToolTip under different look and feel types*

The available set of UIResource-related properties for a JToolTip is shown in Table 4-6. For the JToolTip component, there are nine different properties.

Table 4-6. *JToolTip UIResource Elements*

Property String	Object Type
ToolTip.background	Color
ToolTip.backgroundInactive	Color
ToolTip.border	Border
ToolTip.borderInactive	Color
ToolTip.font	Font
ToolTip.foreground	Color
ToolTip.foregroundInactive	Color
ToolTip.hideAccelerator	Boolean
ToolTipUI	String

As noted earlier in this chapter, the JToolTip class supports the display of arbitrary HTML content. This permits the display of multiple-column and multiple-row input.

ToolTipManager Class

Although the JToolTip is something of a passive object, in the sense that the JComponent creates and shows the JToolTip on its own, there are many more configurable aspects of its usage. However, these configurable aspects are the responsibility of the class that manages tooltips, not the JToolTip itself. The class that manages tooltip usage is aptly named ToolTipManager. With the Singleton design pattern, no constructor for ToolTipManager exists. Instead, you have access to the current manager through the static sharedInstance() method of ToolTipManager.

ToolTipManager Properties

Once you have accessed the shared instance of ToolTipManager, you can customize when and if tooltip text appears. As Table 4-7 shows, there are five configurable properties.

Table 4-7. *ToolTipManager Properties*

Property Name	Data Type	Access
dismissDelay	int	Read-write
enabled	boolean	Read-write
initialDelay	int	Read-write
lightWeightPopupEnabled	boolean	Read-write
reshowDelay	int	Read-only

Initially, tooltips are enabled, but you can disable them with ToolTipManager.
sharedInstance().setEnabled(false). This allows you to always associate tooltips with components, while letting the end user enable and disable them when desired.

There are three timing-oriented properties: initialDelay, dismissDelay, and reshowDelay. They all measure time in milliseconds. The initialDelay property is the number of milliseconds the user must rest the mouse inside the component before the appropriate tooltip text appears. The dismissDelay specifies the length of time the text appears while the mouse remains motionless; if the user moves the mouse, it also causes the text to disappear. The reshowDelay determines how long a user must remain outside a component before reentry would cause the pop-up text to reappear.

The lightWeightPopupEnabled property is used to determine the pop-up window type to hold the tooltip text. If the property is true and the pop-up text fits entirely within the bounds of the top-level window, the text appears within a Swing JPanel. If this property is false and the pop-up text fits entirely within the bounds of the top-level window, the text appears within an AWT Panel. If part of the text wouldn't appear within the top-level window no matter what the property setting is, the pop-up text would appear within a Window.

Although not properties of ToolTipManager, two other methods of ToolTipManager are worth mentioning:

```
public void registerComponent(JComponent component)
public void unregisterComponent(JComponent component)
```

When you call the setToolTipText() method of JComponent, this causes the component to register itself with the ToolTipManager. There are times, however, when you need to register a component directly. This is necessary when the display of part of a component is left to another renderer. With JTree, for instance, a TreeCellRenderer displays each node of the tree. When the renderer displays the tooltip text, you "register" the JTree and tell the renderer what text to display.

```
JTree tree = new JTree(...);
ToolTipManager.sharedInstance().registerComponent(tree);
TreeCellRenderer renderer = new ATreeCellRenderer(...);
tree.setCellRenderer(renderer);
...
public class ATreeCellRenderer implements TreeCellRenderer {
...
  public Component getTreeCellRendererComponent(JTree tree, Object value,
    boolean selected, boolean expanded, boolean leaf, int row, boolean hasFocus) {
  ...
    renderer.setToolTipText("Some Tip");
    return renderer;
  }
}
```

Note If this sounds confusing, don't worry. We'll revisit the JTree in Chapter 17.

JLabel Class

The first real Swing component to examine closely is the simplest, the JLabel. The JLabel serves as the replacement component for the AWT Label but it can do *much* more. Whereas the AWT Label is limited to a single line of text, the Swing JLabel can have text, images, or both. The text can be a single line of text or HTML. In addition JLabel can support different enabled and disabled images. Figure 4-6 shows some sample JLabel components.

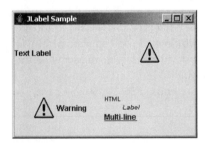

Figure 4-6. *Sample JLabel components*

Note A JLabel subclass is used as the default renderer for each of the JList, JComboBox, JTable, and JTree components.

Creating a JLabel

There are six constructors for JLabel:

```
public JLabel()
JLabel label = new JLabel();
```

```
public JLabel(Icon image)
Icon icon = new ImageIcon("dog.jpg");
JLabel label = new JLabel(icon);
```

```
public JLabel(Icon image, int horizontalAlignment)
Icon icon = new ImageIcon("dog.jpg");
JLabel label = new JLabel(icon, JLabel.RIGHT);
```

```
public JLabel(String text)
JLabel label = new JLabel("Dog");
```

```
public JLabel(String text, int horizontalAlignment)
JLabel label = new JLabel("Dog", JLabel.RIGHT);
```

```
public JLabel(String text, Icon icon, int horizontalAlignment)
Icon icon = new ImageIcon("dog.jpg");
JLabel label = new JLabel("Dog", icon, JLabel.RIGHT);
```

With the constructors for JLabel, you can customize any of three properties of the JLabel: text, icon, or horizontalAlignment. By default, the text and icon properties are empty, whereas the initial horizontalAlignment property setting depends on the constructor arguments. These settings can be any of JLabel.LEFT, JLabel.CENTER, or JLabel.RIGHT. In most cases, not specifying the horizontalAlignment setting results in a left-aligned label. However, if only the initial icon is specified, then the default alignment is centered.

JLabel Properties

Table 4-8 shows the 14 properties of JLabel. They allow you to customize the content, position, and (in a limited sense) the behavior of the JLabel.

Table 4-8. *JLabel Properties*

Property Name	Data Type	Access
accessibleContext	AccessibleContext	Read-only
disabledIcon	Icon	Read-write bound
displayedMnemonic	char	Read-write bound
displayedMnemonicIndex	int	Read-write bound
horizontalAlignment	int	Read-write bound
horizontalTextPosition	int	Read-write bound

Table 4-8. *JLabel Properties (Continued)*

Property Name	Data Type	Access
icon	Icon	Read-write bound
iconTextGap	int	Read-write bound
labelFor	Component	Read-write bound
text	String	Read-write bound
UI	LabelUI	Read-write
UIClassID	String	Read-only
verticalAlignment	int	Read-write bound
verticalTextPosition	int	Read-write bound

The content of the JLabel is the text and its associated image. Displaying an image within a JLabel will be discussed in the "Interface Icon" section later in this chapter. However, you can display different icons, depending on whether the JLabel is enabled or disabled. By default, the icon is a grayscaled version of the enabled icon, if the enabled icon comes from an Image object (ImageIcon, as described later in the chapter). If the enabled icon doesn't come from an Image, there's no icon when JLabel is disabled, unless manually specified.

The position of the contents of the JLabel is described by four different properties: horizontalAlignment, horizontalTextPosition, verticalAlignment, and verticalTextPosition. The horizontalAlignment and verticalAlignment properties describe the position of the contents of the JLabel within the container in which it's placed.

Note Alignments have an effect only if there's extra space for the layout manager to position the component. If you're using a layout manager such as FlowLayout, which sizes components to their preferred size, these settings will effectively be ignored.

The horizontal position can be any of the JLabel constants LEFT, RIGHT, or CENTER. The vertical position can be TOP, BOTTOM, or CENTER. Figure 4-7 shows various alignment settings, with the label reflecting the alignments.

The text position properties reflect where the text is positioned relative to the icon when both are present. The properties can be set to the same constants as the alignment constants. Figure 4-8 shows various text position settings, with each label reflecting the setting.

Note The constants for the different positions come from the SwingConstants interface that the JLabel class implements.

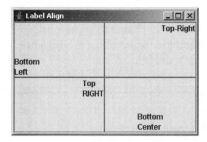

Figure 4-7. *Various JLabel alignments*

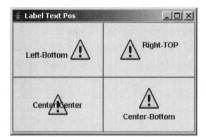

Figure 4-8. *Various JLabel text positions*

JLabel Event Handling

No event-handling capabilities are specific to the JLabel. Besides the event-handling capabilities inherited through JComponent, the closest thing there is for event handling with the JLabel is the combined usage of the displayedMnemonic, displayedMnemonicIndex, and labelFor properties.

When the displayedMnemonic and labelFor properties are set, pressing the keystroke specified by the mnemonic, along with the platform-specific hotkey (usually Alt), causes the input focus to shift to the component associated with the labelFor property. This can be helpful when a component doesn't have its own manner of displaying a mnemonic setting, such as with all the text input components. Here is an example, which results in the display shown in Figure 4-9:

```
JLabel label = new JLabel("Username");
JTextField textField = new JTextField();
label.setDisplayedMnemonic(KeyEvent.VK_U);
label.setLabelFor(textField);
```

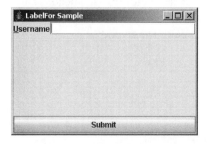

Figure 4-9. *Using a JLabel to display the mnemonic for another component*

The `displayedMnemonicIndex` property adds the ability for the mnemonic highlighted to not be the first instance of mnemonic in the label's text. The index you specify represents the position in the text, not the instance of the mnemonic. To highlight the second *e* in Username, you would specify an index of 7: `label.setDisplayedMnemonicIndex(7)`.

■**Note** The component setting of the `labelFor` property is stored as a client property of the `JLabel` with the `LABELED_BY_PROPERTY` key constant. The setting is used for accessibility purposes.

Customizing a JLabel Look and Feel

Each installable Swing look and feel provides a different `JLabel` appearance and set of default `UIResource` value settings. Although appearances differ based on the current look and feel, the differences are minimal within the preinstalled set of look and feel types. Table 4-9 shows the available set of `UIResource`-related properties for a `JLabel`. There are eight different properties for the `JLabel` component.

Table 4-9. *JLabel UIResource Elements*

Property String	Object Type
Label.actionMap	ActionMap
Label.background	Color
Label.border	Border
Label.disabledForeground	Color
Label.disabledShadow	Color
Label.font	Font
Label.foreground	Color
LabelUI	String

Interface Icon

The `Icon` interface is used to associate glyphs with various components. A *glyph* (like a symbol on a highway sign that conveys information nonverbally, such as "winding road ahead!") can be a simple drawing or a GIF image loaded from disk with the `ImageIcon` class. The interface contains two properties describing the size and a method to paint the glyph.

```
public interface Icon {
  // Properties
  public int getIconHeight();
  public int getIconWidth();
  // Other methods
  public void paintIcon(Component c, Graphics g, int x, int y);
}
```

Creating an Icon

Creating an `Icon` is as simple as implementing the interface. All you need to do is specify the size of the icon and what to draw. Listing 4-3 shows one such `Icon` implementation. The icon is a diamond-shaped glyph in which the size, color, and filled-status are all configurable.

■Tip In implementing the `paintIcon()` method of the `Icon` interface, translate the drawing coordinates of the graphics context based on the x and y position passed in, and then translate them back when the drawing is done. This greatly simplifies the different drawing operations.

Listing 4-3. *Reusable Diamond Icon Definition*

```
import javax.swing.*;
import java.awt.*;
public class DiamondIcon implements Icon {
  private Color color;
  private boolean selected;
  private int width;
  private int height;
  private Polygon poly;
  private static final int DEFAULT_WIDTH = 10;
  private static final int DEFAULT_HEIGHT = 10;

  public DiamondIcon(Color color) {
    this(color, true, DEFAULT_WIDTH, DEFAULT_HEIGHT);
  }

  public DiamondIcon(Color color, boolean selected) {
    this(color, selected, DEFAULT_WIDTH, DEFAULT_HEIGHT);
  }

  public DiamondIcon(Color color, boolean selected, int width, int height) {
    this.color = color;
    this.selected = selected;
    this.width = width;
    this.height = height;
    initPolygon();
  }

  private void initPolygon() {
    poly = new Polygon();
    int halfWidth = width/2;
    int halfHeight = height/2;
    poly.addPoint(0, halfHeight);
    poly.addPoint(halfWidth, 0);
```

```
      poly.addPoint(width, halfHeight);
      poly.addPoint(halfWidth, height);
    }

    public int getIconHeight() {
      return height;
    }

    public int getIconWidth() {
      return width;
    }

    public void paintIcon(Component c, Graphics g, int x, int y) {
      g.setColor(color);
      g.translate(x, y);
      if (selected) {
        g.fillPolygon(poly);
      } else {
        g.drawPolygon(poly);
      }
      g.translate(-x, -y);
    }
}
```

Using an Icon

Once you have your Icon implementation, using the Icon is as simple as finding a component with an appropriate property. For example, here's the icon with a JLabel:

```
Icon icon = new DiamondIcon(Color.RED, true, 25, 25);
JLabel label = new JLabel(icon);
```

Figure 4-10 shows what such a label might look like.

Figure 4-10. *Using an Icon in a JLabel*

ImageIcon Class

The ImageIcon class presents an implementation of the Icon interface for creating glyphs from AWT Image objects, whether from memory (a byte[ ]), off a disk (a file name), or over the network (a URL). Unlike with regular Image objects, the loading of an ImageIcon is immediately started when the ImageIcon is created, though it might not be fully loaded when used. In addition, unlike Image objects, ImageIcon objects are serializable so that they can be easily used by JavaBean components.

Creating an ImageIcon

There are nine constructors for an ImageIcon:

```
public ImageIcon()
Icon icon = new ImageIcon();
icon.setImage(anImage);
```

```
public ImageIcon(Image image)
Icon icon = new ImageIcon(anImage);
```

```
public ImageIcon(String filename)
Icon icon = new ImageIcon(filename);
```

```
public ImageIcon(URL location)
Icon icon = new ImageIcon(url);
```

```
public ImageIcon(byte imageData[])
Icon icon = new ImageIcon(aByteArray);
```

```
public ImageIcon(Image image, String description)
Icon icon = new ImageIcon(anImage, "Duke");
```

```
public ImageIcon(String filename, String description)
Icon icon = new ImageIcon(filename, filename);
```

```
public ImageIcon(URL location, String description)
Icon icon = new ImageIcon(url, location.getFile());
```

```
public ImageIcon(byte imageData[], String description)
Icon icon = new ImageIcon(aByteArray, "Duke");
```

The no-argument version creates an uninitialized version (empty). The remaining eight offer the ability to create an ImageIcon from an Image, byte array, file name String, or URL, with or without a description.

Using an ImageIcon

Using an ImageIcon is as simple as using an Icon: just create the ImageIcon and associate it with a component.

```
Icon icon = new ImageIcon("Warn.gif");
JLabel label3 = new JLabel("Warning", icon, JLabel.CENTER)
```

ImageIcon Properties

Table 4-10 shows the six properties of `ImageIcon`. The height and width of the `ImageIcon` are the height and width of the actual `Image` object. The `imageLoadStatus` property represents the results of the loading of the `ImageIcon` from the hidden `MediaTracker`, either `MediaTracker.ABORTED`, `MediaTracker.ERRORED`, or `MediaTracker.COMPLETE`.

Table 4-10. *ImageIcon Properties*

Property Name	Data Type	Access
description	String	Read-write
iconHeight	int	Read-only
iconWidth	int	Read-only
image	Image	Read-write
imageLoadStatus	int	Read-only
imageObserver	ImageObserver	Read-write

Sometimes, it's useful to use an `ImageIcon` to load an `Image`, and then just ask for the `Image` object from the `Icon`.

```
ImageIcon imageIcon = new ImageIcon(...);
Image image = imageIcon.getImage();
```

There is one major problem with using `ImageIcon` objects: They don't work when the image and class file using the icon are both loaded in a JAR (Java archive) file, unless you explicitly specify the full URL for the file within the JAR (`jar:http://www.example.com/directory/foo.jar!/com/example/image.gif`). You can't just specify the file name as a `String` and let the `ImageIcon` find the file. You must manually get the image data first, and then pass the data along to the `ImageIcon` constructor.

To help with loading images outside JAR files, Listing 4-4 shows an `ImageLoader` class that provides a `public static Image getImage(Class relativeClass, String filename)` method. You specify both the base class where the image file relative is found and the file name for the image file. Then you just need to pass the `Image` object returned to the constructor of `ImageIcon`.

Listing 4-4. *Image Loading Support Class*

```java
import java.awt.*;
import java.io.*;

public final class ImageLoader {

  private ImageLoader() {
  }
```

```
public static Image getImage(Class relativeClass, String filename) {
  Image returnValue = null;
  InputStream is = relativeClass.getResourceAsStream(filename);
  if (is != null) {
    BufferedInputStream bis = new BufferedInputStream(is);
    ByteArrayOutputStream baos = new ByteArrayOutputStream();
    try {
      int ch;
      while ((ch = bis.read()) != -1) {
        baos.write(ch);
      }
      returnValue = Toolkit.getDefaultToolkit().createImage(baos.toByteArray());
    } catch (IOException exception) {
      System.err.println("Error loading: " + filename);
    }
  }
  return returnValue;
}
}
```

Here's how you use the helper class:

```
Image warnImage = ImageLoader.getImage(LabelJarSample.class, "Warn.gif");
Icon warnIcon = new ImageIcon(warnImage);
JLabel label2 = new JLabel(warnIcon);
```

Tip Keep in mind that the Java platform supports GIF89A animated images.

GrayFilter Class

One additional class worth mentioning here is GrayFilter. Many of the Swing component classes rely on this class to create a disabled version of an Image to be used as an Icon. The components use the class automatically, but there might be times when you need an AWT ImageFilter that does grayscales. You can convert an Image from normal to grayed out with a call to the one useful method of the class: public static Image createDisabledImage (Image image).

```
Image normalImage = ...
Image grayImage = GrayFilter.createDisabledImage(normalImage)
```

You can now use the grayed-out image as the Icon on a component:

```
Icon warningIcon = new ImageIcon(grayImage);
JLabel warningLabel = new JLabel(warningIcon);
```

AbstractButton Class

The AbstractButton class is an important Swing class that works behind the scenes as the parent class of all the Swing button components, as shown at the top of Figure 4-1. The JButton, described in the "JButton Class" section later in this chapter, is the simplest of the subclasses. The remaining subclasses are described in later chapters.

Each of the AbstractButton subclasses uses the ButtonModel interface to store their data model. The DefaultButtonModel class is the default implementation used. In addition, you can group any set of AbstractButton objects into a ButtonGroup. Although this grouping is most natural with the JRadioButton and JRadioButtonMenuItem components, any of the AbstractButton subclasses will work.

AbstractButton Properties

Table 4-11 lists the 32 properties (with mnemonic listed twice) of AbstractButton shared by all its subclasses. They allow you to customize the appearance of all the buttons.

Table 4-11. *AbstractButton Properties*

Property Name	Data Type	Access
action	Action	Read-write bound
actionCommand	String	Read-write
actionListeners	ActionListener[ ]	Read-only
borderPainted	boolean	Read-write bound
changeListeners	ChangeListener[ ]	Read-only
contentAreaFilled	boolean	Read-write bound
disabledIcon	Icon	Read-write bound
disabledSelectedIcon	Icon	Read-write bound
displayedMnemonicIndex	int	Read-write bound
enabled	boolean	Write-only
focusPainted	boolean	Read-write bound
horizontalAlignment	int	Read-write bound
horizontalTextPosition	int	Read-write bound
icon	Icon	Read-write bound
iconTextGap	int	Read-write bound
itemListeners	ItemListener[ ]	Read-only
layout	LayoutManager	Write-only
margin	Insets	Read-write bound
mnemonic	char	Read-write bound

Table 4-11. *AbstractButton Properties (Continued)*

Property Name	Data Type	Access
mnemonic	int	Write-only
model	ButtonModel	Read-write bound
multiClickThreshhold	long	Read-write
pressedIcon	Icon	Read-write bound
rolloverEnabled	boolean	Read-write bound
rolloverIcon	Icon	Read-write bound
rolloverSelectedIcon	Icon	Read-write bound
selected	boolean	Read-write
selectedIcon	Icon	Read-write bound
selectedObjects	Object[ ]	Read-only
text	String	Read-write bound
UI	ButtonUI	Read-write
verticalAlignment	int	Read-write bound
verticalTextPosition	int	Read-write bound

■**Note** AbstractButton has a deprecated label property. You should use the equivalent text property instead.

One property worth mentioning is multiClickThreshhold. This property represents a time, in milliseconds. If a button is selected with a mouse multiple times within this time period, additional action events won't be generated. By default, the value is zero, meaning each press generates an event. To avoid accidental duplicate submissions from happening in important dialogs, set this value to some reasonable level above zero.

■**Tip** Keep in mind that all AbstractButton children can use HTML with its text property to display HTML content within the label. Just prefix the property setting with the string <html>.

ButtonModel/Class DefaultButtonModel Interface

The ButtonModel interface is used to describe the current state of the AbstractButton component. In addition, it describes the set of event listeners objects that are supported by all the different AbstractButton children. Its definition follows:

```
public interface ButtonModel extends ItemSelectable {
  // Properties
  public String getActionCommand();
  public void setActionCommand(String newValue);
  public boolean isArmed();
  public void setArmed(boolean newValue);
  public boolean isEnabled();
  public void setEnabled(boolean newValue);
  public void setGroup(ButtonGroup newValue);
  public int getMnemonic();
  public void setMnemonic(int newValue);
  public boolean isPressed();
  public void setPressed(boolean newValue);
  public boolean isRollover();
  public void setRollover(boolean newValue);
  public boolean isSelected();
  public void setSelected(boolean newValue);
  // Listeners
  public void addActionListener(ActionListener listener);
  public void removeActionListener(ActionListener listener);
  public void addChangeListener(ChangeListener listener);
  public void removeChangeListener(ChangeListener listener);
  public void addItemListener(ItemListener listener);
  public void removeItemListener(ItemListener listener);
}
```

The specific implementation of ButtonModel you'll use, unless you create your own, is the DefaultButtonModel class. The DefaultButtonModel class defines all the event registration methods for the different event listeners and manages the button state and grouping within a ButtonGroup. Its set of nine properties is shown in Table 4-12. They all come from the ButtonGroup interface, except selectedObjects, which is new to the DefaultButtonModel class, but more useful to the JToggleButton.ToggleButtonModel, which is discussed in Chapter 5.

Table 4-12. *DefaultButtonModel Properties*

Property Name	Data Type	Access
actionCommand	String	Read-write
armed	boolean	Read-write
enabled	boolean	Read-write
group	ButtonGroup	Read-write
mnemonic	int	Read-write
pressed	boolean	Read-write
rollover	boolean	Read-write
selected	boolean	Read-write
selectedObjects	Object[ ]	Read-only

Most of the time, you don't access the `ButtonModel` directly. Instead, the components that use the `ButtonModel` wrap their property calls to update the model's properties.

■**Note** The `DefaultButtonModel` also lets you get the listeners for a specific type with `public EventListener[ ] getListeners(Class listenerType)`.

Understanding AbstractButton Mnemonics

A *mnemonic* is a special keyboard accelerator that when pressed causes a particular action to happen. In the case of the `JLabel` discussed earlier in the "JLabel Class" section, pressing the displayed mnemonic causes the associated component to get the input focus. In the case of an `AbstractButton`, pressing the mnemonic for a button causes its selection.

The actual pressing of the mnemonic requires the pressing of a look-and-feel–specific hotkey (the key tends to be the Alt key). So, if the mnemonic for a button were the B key, you would need to press Alt-B to activate the button with the B-key mnemonic. When the button is activated, registered listeners will be notified of appropriate state changes. For instance, with the `JButton`, all `ActionListener` objects would be notified.

If the mnemonic key is part of the text label for the button, you'll see the character underlined. This does depend on the current look and feel and could be displayed differently. In addition, if the mnemonic isn't part of the text label, there will not be a visual indicator for selecting the particular mnemonic key, unless the look and feel shows it in the tooltip text.

Figure 4-11 shows two buttons: one with a W-key mnemonic, and the other with an H-key mnemonic. The left button has a label with *W* in its contents, so it shows the first *W* underlined. The second component doesn't benefit from this behavior on the button, but in the Ocean look and feel, identifies it only if the tooltip text is set and shown.

Figure 4-11. *AbstractButton mnemonics*

To assign a mnemonic to an abstract button, you can use either one of the `setMnemonic()` methods. One accepts a `char` argument and the other an `int`. Personally, I prefer the `int` variety, in which the value is one of the many `VK_*` constants from the `KeyEvent` class. You can also specify the mnemonic by position via the `displayedMnemonicIndex` property.

```
AbstractButton button1 = new JButton("Warning");
button1.setMnemonic(KeyEvent.VK_W);
content.add(button1);
```

Understanding AbstractButton Icons

AbstractButton has seven specific icon properties. The natural or default icon is the icon property. It is used for all cases unless a different icon is specified or there is a default behavior provided by the component. The selectedIcon property is the icon used when the button is selected. The pressedIcon is used when the button is pressed. Which of these two icons is used depends on the component, because a JButton is pressed but not selected, whereas a JCheckBox is selected but not pressed.

The disabledIcon and disabledSelectedIcon properties are used when the button has been disabled with setEnabled(false). By default, if the icon is an ImageIcon, a grayscaled version of the icon will be used.

The remaining two icon properties, rolloverIcon and rolloverSelectedIcon, allow you to display different icons when the mouse moves over the button (and rolloverEnabled is true).

Understanding Internal AbstractButton Positioning

The horizontalAlignment, horizontalTextPosition, verticalAlignment, and verticalTextPosition properties share the same settings and behavior as the JLabel class. They're listed in Table 4-13.

Table 4-13. *AbstractButton Position Constants*

Position Property	Available Settings
horizontalAlignment	LEFT, CENTER, RIGHT
horizontalTextPosition	LEFT, CENTER, RIGHT
verticalAlignment	TOP, CENTER, BOTTOM
verticalTextPosition	TOP, CENTER, BOTTOM

Handling AbstractButton Events

Although you do not create AbstractButton instances directly, you do create subclasses. All of them share a common set of event-handling capabilities. You can register PropertyChangeListener, ActionListener, ItemListener, and ChangeListener objects with abstract buttons. The PropertyChangeListener object will be discussed here, and the remaining objects listed will be discussed in later chapters, with the appropriate components.

Like the JComponent class, the AbstractButton component supports the registering of PropertyChangeListener objects to detect when bound properties of an instance of the class change. Unlike the JComponent class, the AbstractButton component provides the following set of class constants to signify the different property changes:

- BORDER_PAINTED_CHANGED_PROPERTY

- CONTENT_AREA_FILLED_CHANGED_PROPERTY

- DISABLED_ICON_CHANGED_PROPERTY

- DISABLED_SELECTED_ICON_CHANGED_PROPERTY

- FOCUS_PAINTED_CHANGED_PROPERTY

- HORIZONTAL_ALIGNMENT_CHANGED_PROPERTY

- HORIZONTAL_TEXT_POSITION_CHANGED_PROPERTY

- ICON_CHANGED_PROPERTY

- MARGIN_CHANGED_PROPERTY

- MNEMONIC_CHANGED_PROPERTY

- MODEL_CHANGED_PROPERTY

- PRESSED_ICON_CHANGED_PROPERTY

- ROLLOVER_ENABLED_CHANGED_PROPERTY

- ROLLOVER_ICON_CHANGED_PROPERTY

- ROLLOVER_SELECTED_ICON_CHANGED_PROPERTY

- SELECTED_ICON_CHANGED_PROPERTY

- TEXT_CHANGED_PROPERTY

- VERTICAL_ALIGNMENT_CHANGED_PROPERTY

- VERTICAL_TEXT_POSITION_CHANGED_PROPERTY

Therefore, instead of hard-coding specific text strings, you can create a PropertyChangeListener that uses these constants, as shown in Listing 4-5.

Listing 4-5. *Base PropertyChangeListener for AbstractButton*

```
import javax.swing.*;
import java.beans.*;

public class AbstractButtonPropertyChangeListener
    implements PropertyChangeListener {

  public void propertyChange(PropertyChangeEvent e) {
    String propertyName = e.getPropertyName();
    if (e.getPropertyName().equals(AbstractButton.TEXT_CHANGED_PROPERTY)) {
      String newText = (String) e.getNewValue();
      String oldText = (String) e.getOldValue();
      System.out.println(oldText + " changed to " + newText);
    } else if (e.getPropertyName().equals(AbstractButton.ICON_CHANGED_PROPERTY)) {
      Icon icon = (Icon) e.getNewValue();
      if (icon instanceof ImageIcon) {
        System.out.println("New icon is an image");
      }
    }
  }
}
```

JButton Class

The JButton component is the basic AbstractButton component that can be selected. It supports text, images, and HTML-based labels, as shown in Figure 4-12.

Figure 4-12. *Sample JButton components*

Creating a JButton

The JButton class has five constructors:

```
public JButton()
JButton button = new JButton();
```

```
public JButton(Icon image)
Icon icon = new ImageIcon("dog.jpg");
JButton button = new JButton(icon);
```

```
public JButton(String text)
JButton button = new JButton("Dog");
```

```
public JButton(String text, Icon icon)
Icon icon = new ImageIcon("dog.jpg");
JButton button = new JButton("Dog", icon);
```

```
public JButton(Action action)
Action action = ...;
JButton button = new JButton(action);
```

You can create a button with or without a text label or icon. The icon represents the default or selected icon property from AbstractButton.

Note Creating a JButton from an Action initializes the text label, icon, enabled status, and tooltip text. In addition, the ActionListener of the Action will be notified upon button selection.

JButton Properties

The JButton component doesn't add much to the AbstractButton. As Table 4-14 shows, of the four properties of JButton, the only new behavior added is enabling the button to be the default.

Table 4-14. *JButton Properties*

Property Name	Data Type	Access
accessibleContext	AccessibleContext	Read-only
defaultButton	boolean	Read-only
defaultCapable	boolean	Read-write bound
UIClassID	String	Read-only

The default button tends to be drawn with a different and darker border than the remaining buttons. When a button is the default, pressing the Enter key while in the top-level window causes the button to be selected. This works only as long as the component with the input focus, such as a text component or another button, doesn't consume the Enter key. Because the defaultButton property is read-only, how (you might be asking) do you set a button as the default? All top-level Swing windows contain a JRootPane, to be described in Chapter 8. You tell this JRootPane which button is the default by setting its defaultButton property. Only buttons whose defaultCapable property is true can be configured to be the default. Figure 4-13 shows the top-right button set as the default.

Figure 4-13. *Setting a default button*

Listing 4-6 demonstrates setting the default button component, as well as using a basic JButton. If the default button appearance doesn't seem that obvious in Figure 4-13, wait until the JOptionPane is described in Chapter 9, where the difference in appearance will be more obvious. Figure 4-13 uses a 2-by-2 GridLayout for the screen. The extra two arguments to the constructor represent gaps to help make the default button's appearance more obvious.

Listing 4-6. *Configuring a Default Button*

```java
import javax.swing.*;
import java.awt.*;
import java.awt.event.*;

public class DefaultButton {

  public static void main(String args[]) {
    Runnable runner = new Runnable() {
      public void run() {
        JFrame frame = new JFrame("DefaultButton");
        frame.setDefaultCloseOperation(JFrame.EXIT_ON_CLOSE);

        frame.setLayout(new GridLayout(2, 2, 10, 10));

        JButton button1 = new JButton("Text Button");
        button1.setMnemonic(KeyEvent.VK_B);
        frame.add(button1);

        Icon warnIcon = new ImageIcon("Warn.gif");
        JButton button2 = new JButton(warnIcon);
        frame.add(button2);

        JButton button3 = new JButton("Warning", warnIcon);
        frame.add(button3);

        String htmlButton = "<html><sup>HTML</sup> <sub><em>Button</em></sub><br>" +
          "<font color=\"#FF0080\"><u>Multi-line</u></font>";
        JButton button4 = new JButton(htmlButton);
        frame.add(button4);

        JRootPane rootPane = frame.getRootPane();
        rootPane.setDefaultButton(button2);

        frame.setSize(300, 200);
        frame.setVisible(true);
      }
    };
    EventQueue.invokeLater(runner);
  }
}
```

Handling JButton Events

The JButton component itself has no specific event-handling capabilities. They're all inherited from AbstractButton. Although you can listen for change events, item events, and property change events, the most helpful listener with the JButton is the ActionListener.

When the JButton component is selected, all registered ActionListener objects are notified. When the button is selected, an ActionEvent is passed to each listener. This event passes along the actionCommand property of the button to help identify which button was selected when a shared listener is used across multiple components. If the actionCommand property hasn't been explicitly set, the current text property is passed along instead. The explicit use of the actionCommand property is helpful with localization. Because the text property of the JButton is what the user sees, you as the handler of the button selection event listener cannot rely on a localized text label for determining which button was selected. So, while the text property can be localized so that a Yes button in English can say Sí in a Spanish version, if you explicitly set the actionCommand to be the "Yes" string, then no matter which language the user is running in, the actionCommand will remain "Yes" and not take on the localized text property setting.

Listing 4-7 adds the event-handling capabilities to the default button example in Listing 4-6 (see Figure 4-13). Notice that the default button behavior works properly: press Enter from any component, and button 2 (the default) will be activated.

Listing 4-7. *Watching Button Selection Events*

```java
import javax.swing.*;
import java.awt.*;
import java.awt.event.*;

public class ActionButtonSample {

  public static void main(String args[]) {
    Runnable runner = new Runnable() {
      public void run() {
        JFrame frame = new JFrame("DefaultButton");
        frame.setDefaultCloseOperation(JFrame.EXIT_ON_CLOSE);

        ActionListener actionListener = new ActionListener() {
          public void actionPerformed(ActionEvent actionEvent) {
            String command = actionEvent.getActionCommand();
            System.out.println("Selected: " + command);
          }
        };

        frame.setLayout(new GridLayout(2, 2, 10, 10));

        JButton button1 = new JButton("Text Button");
        button1.setMnemonic(KeyEvent.VK_B);
        button1.setActionCommand("First");
        button1.addActionListener(actionListener);
        frame.add(button1);
```

```
        Icon warnIcon = new ImageIcon("Warn.gif");
        JButton button2 = new JButton(warnIcon);
        button2.setActionCommand("Second");
        button2.addActionListener(actionListener);
        frame.add(button2);

        JButton button3 = new JButton("Warning", warnIcon);
        button3.setActionCommand("Third");
        button3.addActionListener(actionListener);
        frame.add(button3);

        String htmlButton = "<html><sup>HTML</sup> <sub><em>Button</em></sub><br>" +
          "<font color=\"#FF0080\"><u>Multi-line</u></font>";
        JButton button4 = new JButton(htmlButton);
        button4.setActionCommand("Fourth");
        button4.addActionListener(actionListener);
        frame.add(button4);

        JRootPane rootPane = frame.getRootPane();
        rootPane.setDefaultButton(button2);

        frame.setSize(300, 200);
        frame.setVisible(true);
      }
    };
    EventQueue.invokeLater(runner);
  }
}
```

Customizing a JButton Look and Feel

Each installable Swing look and feel provides a different JButton appearance and set of default UIResource value settings. Figure 4-14 shows the appearance of the JButton component for the preinstalled set of look and feel types: Motif, Windows, and Ocean.

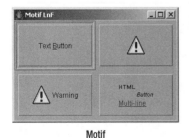

Motif

Windows

Ocean

Figure 4-14. *JButton under different look and feel types*

The available set of UIResource-related properties for a JButton is shown in Table 4-15. For the JButton component, there are 34 different properties.

Table 4-15. *JButton UIResource Elements*

Property String	Object Type
Button.actionMap	ActionMap
Button.background	Color
Button.border	Border
Button.contentAreaFilled	Boolean
Button.darkShadow	Color
Button.dashedRectGapHeight	Integer
Button.dashedRectGapWidth	Integer
Button.dashedRectGapX	Integer
Button.dashedRectGapY	Integer
Button.defaultButtonFollowsFocus	Boolean
Button.disabledForeground	Color
Button.disabledGrayRange	Integer[ ]
Button.disabledShadow	Color
Button.disabledText	Color
Button.disabledToolBarBorderBackground	Color
Button.focus	Color
Button.focusInputMap	InputMap
Button.font	Font
Button.foreground	Color
Button.gradient	List
Button.highlight	Color
Button.icon	Icon
Button.iconTextGap	Integer
Button.light	Color
Button.margin	Insets
Button.rollover	Boolean
Button.rolloverIconType	String
Button.select	Color
Button.shadow	Color
Button.showMnemonics	Boolean

Table 4-15. *JButton UIResource Elements (Continued)*

Property String	Object Type
Button.textIconGap	Integer
Button.textShiftOffset	Integer
Button.toolBarBorderBackground	Color
ButtonUI	String

JPanel Class

The last of the basic Swing components is the JPanel component. The JPanel component serves as both a general-purpose container object, replacing the AWT Panel container, and a replacement for the Canvas component, for those times when you need a drawable Swing component area.

Creating a JPanel

There are four constructors for JPanel:

```
public JPanel()
JPanel panel = new JPanel();
```

```
public JPanel(boolean isDoubleBuffered)
JPanel panel = new JPanel(false);
```

```
public JPanel(LayoutManager manager)
JPanel panel = new JPanel(new GridLayout(2,2));
```

```
public JPanel(LayoutManager manager, boolean isDoubleBuffered)
JPanel panel = new JPanel(new GridLayout(2,2), false);
```

With the constructors, you can either change the default layout manager from FlowLayout or change the default double buffering that is performed from true to false.

Using a JPanel

You can use JPanel as your general-purpose container or as a base class for a new component. For the general-purpose container, the procedure is simple: Just create the panel, set its layout manager if necessary, and add components using the add() method.

```
JPanel panel = new JPanel();
JButton okButton = new JButton("OK");
panel.add(okButton);
JButton cancelButton = new JButton("Cancel");
panel.add(cancelButton);
```

When you want to create a new component, subclass JPanel and override the public void
paintComponent(Graphics g) method. Although you can subclass JComponent directly, it seems
more appropriate to subclass JPanel. Listing 4-8 demonstrates a simple component that draws
an oval to fit the size of the component; it also includes a test driver.

Listing 4-8. *Oval Panel Component*

```
import java.awt.*;
import javax.swing.*;

public class OvalPanel extends JPanel {

  Color color;

  public OvalPanel() {
    this(Color.black);
  }
  public OvalPanel(Color color) {
    this.color = color;
  }
  public void paintComponent(Graphics g) {
    int width = getWidth();
    int height = getHeight();
    g.setColor(color);
    g.drawOval(0, 0, width, height);
  }

  public static void main(String args[]) {
    Runnable runner = new Runnable() {
      public void run() {
        JFrame frame = new JFrame("Oval Sample");
        frame.setDefaultCloseOperation(JFrame.EXIT_ON_CLOSE);

        frame.setLayout(new GridLayout(2, 2));

        Color colors[] = {Color.RED, Color.BLUE, Color.GREEN, Color.YELLOW};
        for (int i=0; i<4; i++) {
          OvalPanel panel = new OvalPanel(colors[i]);
          frame.add(panel);
        }

        frame.setSize(300, 200);
        frame.setVisible(true);
      }
    };
    EventQueue.invokeLater(runner);
  }
}
```

Figure 4-15 shows the test driver program results.

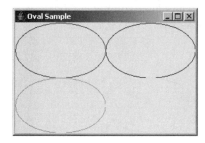

Figure 4-15. *The new OvalPanel component*

■**Note** By default, JPanel components are opaque. This differs from JComponent, whose opacity property setting by default is false. A false setting for opacity means the component is transparent.

Customizing a JPanel Look and Feel

The available set of UIResource-related properties for a JPanel is shown in Table 4-16. For the JPanel component, there are five different properties. These settings may have an effect on the components within the panel.

Table 4-16. *JPanel UIResource Elements*

Property String	Object Type
Panel.background	Color
Panel.border	Border
Panel.font	Font
Panel.foreground	Color
PanelUI	String

Summary

In this chapter, you explored the root of all Swing components: the JComponent class. From there, you looked at some of the common elements of all components, such as tooltips, as well as specific components such as JLabel. You also learned how to put glyphs (nonverbal images) on components with the help of the Icon interface and the ImageIcon class, and the GrayFilter image filter for disabled icons.

You also learned about the `AbstractButton` component, which serves as the root component for all Swing button objects. You looked at its data model interface, `ButtonModel`, and the default implementation of this interface, `DefaultButtonModel`. Next, you looked at the `JButton` class, which is the simplest of the `AbstractButton` implementations. And lastly, you looked at the `JPanel` as the basic Swing container object.

In Chapter 5, you'll start to dig into some of the more complex `AbstractButton` implementations: the toggle buttons.

CHAPTER 5

■ ■ ■

Toggle Buttons

Now that you've seen the capabilities of the relatively simple Swing components `JLabel` and `JButton`, it's time to take a look at more active components, specifically those that can be toggled. These so-called toggleable components—`JToggleButton`, `JCheckBox`, and `JRadioButton`—provide the means for your users to select from among a set of options. These options are either on or off, or enabled or disabled. When presented in a `ButtonGroup`, only one of the options in the group can be selected at a time. To deal with this selection state, the components share a common data model with `ToggleButtonModel`. Let's take a look at the data model, the components' grouping mechanism with `ButtonGroup`, and the individual components.

ToggleButtonModel Class

The `JToggleButton.ToggleButtonModel` class is a public inner class of `JToggleButton`. The class customizes the behavior of the `DefaultButtonModel` class, which, in turn, is an implementation of the `ButtonModel` interface.

The customization affects the data models of all `AbstractButton` components in the same `ButtonGroup`—a class explored next. In short, a `ButtonGroup` is a logical grouping of `AbstractButton` components. At any one time, only one of the `AbstractButton` components in the `ButtonGroup` can have the `selected` property of its data model set to `true`. The remaining ones must be `false`. This does not mean that only one selected component in the group can exist at a time. If multiple components in a `ButtonGroup` share a `ButtonModel`, multiple selected components in the group can exist. If no components share a model, at most, the user can select one component in the group. Once the user has selected that one component, the user cannot interactively deselect the selection. However, programmatically, you can deselect *all* group elements.

The definition of `JToggleButton.ToggleButtonModel` follows.

```
public class ToggleButtonModel extends DefaultButtonModel {
  // Constructors
  public ToggleButtonModel();
  // Properties
  public boolean isSelected();
  public void setPressed(boolean newValue);
  public void setSelected(boolean newvalue);
}
```

The ToggleButtonModel class defines the default data model for both the JToggleButton and its subclasses JCheckBox and JRadioButton, described in this chapter, as well as the JCheckBoxMenuItem and JRadioButtonMenuItem classes described in Chapter 6.

■**Note**   Internally, Swing's HTML viewer component uses the ToggleButtonModel for its check box and radio button input form elements.

ButtonGroup Class

Before describing the ButtonGroup class, let's demonstrate its usage. The program shown in Listing 5-1 creates objects that use the ToggleButtonModel and places them into a single group. As the program demonstrates, in addition to adding the components into the screen's container, you must add each component to the same ButtonGroup. This results in a pair of add() method calls for each component. Furthermore, the container for the button group tends to place components in a single column and to label the grouping for the user with a titled border, though neither of these treatments are required. Figure 5-1 shows the output of the program.

Listing 5-1. *Odd Collection of Button Components*

```
import javax.swing.*;
import javax.swing.border.*;
import java.awt.*;

public class AButtonGroup {
  public static void main(String args[]) {
    Runnable runner = new Runnable() {
      public void run() {
        JFrame frame = new JFrame("Button Group");
        frame.setDefaultCloseOperation(JFrame.EXIT_ON_CLOSE);
        JPanel panel = new JPanel(new GridLayout(0, 1));
        Border border =
          BorderFactory.createTitledBorder("Examples");
        panel.setBorder(border);
        ButtonGroup group = new ButtonGroup();
        AbstractButton abstract1 =
          new JToggleButton("Toggle Button");
        panel.add(abstract1);
        group.add(abstract1);
        AbstractButton abstract2 =
          new JRadioButton("Radio Button");
        panel.add(abstract2);
        group.add(abstract2);
```

```
        AbstractButton abstract3 =
          new JCheckBox("Check Box");
        panel.add(abstract3);
        group.add(abstract3);
        AbstractButton abstract4 =
          new JRadioButtonMenuItem("Radio Button Menu Item");
        panel.add(abstract4);
        group.add(abstract4);
        AbstractButton abstract5 =
          new JCheckBoxMenuItem("Check Box Menu Item");
        panel.add(abstract5);
        group.add(abstract5);
        frame.add(panel, BorderLayout.CENTER);
        frame.setSize(300, 200);
        frame.setVisible(true);
      }
    };
    EventQueue.invokeLater(runner);
  }
}
```

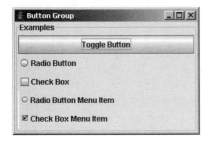

Figure 5-1. *ButtonGroup/ToggleButtonModel example*

As previously stated, the ButtonGroup class represents a logical grouping of AbstractButton components. The ButtonGroup is not a visual component; therefore, there's nothing visual on screen when a ButtonGroup is used. Any AbstractButton component can be added to the grouping with public void add(AbstractButton abstractButton). Although any AbstractButton component can belong to a ButtonGroup, only when the data model for the component is ToggleButtonModel will the grouping have any effect. The result of having a component with a data model of ToggleButtonModel in a ButtonGroup is that after the component is selected, the ButtonGroup deselects any currently selected component in the group.

■**Note** Technically speaking, the model doesn't need to be ToggleButtonModel as long as the custom model exhibits the same behavior of limiting the number of selected component models to one.

Although the add() method is typically the only ButtonGroup method you'll ever need, the following class definition shows that it's not the only method of ButtonGroup in existence:

```
public class ButtonGroup implements Serializable {
  // Constructor
  public ButtonGroup();
  // Properties
  public int getButtonCount();
  public Enumeration getElements();
  public ButtonModel getSelection();
  // Other methods
  public void add(AbstractButton aButton);
  public boolean isSelected(ButtonModel theModel) ;
  public void remove(AbstractButton aButton);
  public void setSelected(ButtonModel theModel, boolean newValue);
}
```

One interesting thing the class definition shows is that given a ButtonGroup, you cannot directly find out the selected AbstractButton. You can directly ask only which ButtonModel is selected. However, getElements() returns an Enumeration of all the AbstractButton elements in the group. You can then loop through all the buttons to find the selected one (or ones) by using code similar to the following:

```
Enumeration elements = group.getElements();
while (elements.hasMoreElements()) {
  AbstractButton button = (AbstractButton)elements.nextElement();
  if (button.isSelected()) {
    System.out.println("The winner is: " + button.getText());
    break; // Don't break if sharing models -- could show multiple buttons selected
  }
}
```

The other interesting method of ButtonGroup is setSelected(). The two arguments of the method are a ButtonModel and a boolean. If the boolean value is false, the selection request is ignored. If the ButtonModel isn't the model for a button in the ButtonGroup, then the ButtonGroup deselects the currently selected model, causing no buttons in the group to be selected. The proper usage of the method is to call the method with a model of a component in the group and a new state of true. For example, if aButton is an AbstractButton and aGroup is the ButtonGroup, then the method call would look like aGroup.setSelected(aButton.getModel(), true).

■**Note** If you add a selected button to a ButtonGroup that already has a previously selected button, the previous button retains its state and the newly added button loses its selection.

Now, let's look at the various components whose data model is the ToggleButtonModel.

JToggleButton Class

The JToggleButton is the first of the toggleable components. It's discussed first because it's the parent class of the two other components that are not menu-oriented: JCheckBox and JRadioButton. The JToggleButton is like a JButton that stays depressed when selected, instead of bouncing back to an unselected state. To deselect the selected component, you must reselect it. JToggleButton isn't a commonly used component, but you might find it useful on a toolbar, such as in Microsoft Word (for paragraph alignment, among other instances) or in a file dialog box, as shown in the upper-right corner of Figure 5-2.

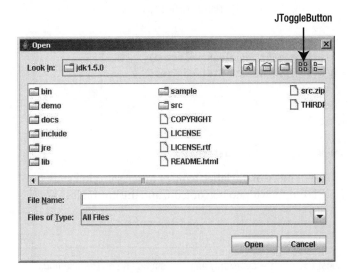

Figure 5-2. *Sample JToggleButton components from file chooser*

Defining the JToggleButton structure are two objects that customize the AbstractButton parent class: ToggleButtonModel and ToggleButtonUI. The ToggleButtonModel class represents a customized ButtonModel data model for the component, whereas ToggleButtonUI is the user interface delegate.

Now that you know about the different pieces of a JToggleButton, let's find out how to use them.

Creating JToggleButton Components

Eight constructors are available for JToggleButton:

public JToggleButton()
JToggleButton aToggleButton = new JToggleButton();

public JToggleButton(Icon icon)
JToggleButton aToggleButton = new JToggleButton(new DiamondIcon(Color.PINK))

```
public JToggleButton(Icon icon, boolean selected)
JToggleButton aToggleButton = new JToggleButton(new DiamondIcon(Color.PINK), true);

public JToggleButton(String text)
JToggleButton aToggleButton = new JToggleButton("Sicilian");

public JToggleButton(String text, boolean selected)
JToggleButton aToggleButton = new JToggleButton("Thin Crust", true);

public JToggleButton(String text, Icon icon)
JToggleButton aToggleButton = new JToggleButton("Thick Crust",
  new DiamondIcon(Color.PINK));

public JToggleButton(String text, Icon icon, boolean selected)
JToggleButton aToggleButton = new JToggleButton("Stuffed Crust",
  new DiamondIcon(Color.PINK), true);

public JToggleButton(Action action)
Action action = ...;
JToggleButton aToggleButton = new JToggleButton(action);
```

Each allows you to customize one or more of the label, icon, or initial selection state. Unless specified otherwise, the label is empty with no text or icon, and the button initially is not selected.

Note Surprisingly, Swing lacks a constructor that accepts only an initial state of a `boolean` setting. Lacking this constructor, you need to create a `JToggleButton` with the no-argument constructor variety, and then call `setSelected(boolean newValue)` directly or work with an `Action`.

JToggleButton Properties

After creating a `JToggleButton`, you can modify each of its many properties. Although there are about 100 inherited properties, Table 5-1 shows only the two introduced with `JToggleButton`. The remaining properties come from `AbstractButton`, `JComponent`, `Container`, and `Component`.

Table 5-1. *JToggleButton Properties*

Property Name	Data Type	Access
accessibleContext	AccessibleContext	Read-only
UIClassID	String	Read-only

You can change one or more of the text, icon, or selected properties set in the constructor, as well as any of the other `AbstractButton` properties described in Chapter 4. You configure the primary three properties with the appropriate getter and setter methods: get/setText(), get/setIcon(), and is/setSelected(), or setAction(action). The other properties have corresponding getter and setter methods.

The more visual configurable options of JToggleButton (and its subclasses) include the various icons for the different states of the button. Besides the standard icon, you can display a different icon when the button is selected, among other state changes. However, if you're changing icons based on the currently selected state, then JToggleButton probably isn't the most appropriate component to use. You should use one of its subclasses, JCheckBox or JRadioButton, explored later in this chapter.

■**Note** Keep in mind that the JButton component ignores the selectedIcon property.

Handling JToggleButton Selection Events

After configuring a JToggleButton, you can handle selection events in one of three ways: with an ActionListener, an ItemListener, or a ChangeListener. This is in addition to providing an Action to the constructor, which would be notified like an ActionListener.

Listening to JToggleButton Events with an ActionListener

If you're interested only in what happens when a user selects or deselects the JToggleButton, you can attach an ActionListener to the component. After the user selects the button, the component notifies any registered ActionListener objects. Unfortunately, this isn't the desired behavior, because you must then actively determine the state of the button so that you can respond appropriately for selecting or deselecting. To find out the selected state, you must get the model for the event source, and then ask for its selection state, as the following sample ActionListener source shows:

```
ActionListener actionListener = new ActionListener() {
  public void actionPerformed(ActionEvent actionEvent) {
    AbstractButton abstractButton = (AbstractButton)actionEvent.getSource();
    boolean selected = abstractButton.getModel().isSelected();
    System.out.println("Action - selected=" + selected + "\ n");
  }
};
```

Listening to JToggleButton Events with an ItemListener

The better listener to attach to a JToggleButton is the ItemListener. The ItemEvent passed to the itemStateChanged() method of ItemListener includes the current selection state of the button. This allows you to respond appropriately, without needing to search for the current button state.

To demonstrate, the following ItemListener reports the state of a selected ItemEvent-generating component:

```
ItemListener itemListener = new ItemListener() {
  public void itemStateChanged(ItemEvent itemEvent) {
    int state = itemEvent.getStateChange();
    if (state == ItemEvent.SELECTED) {
      System.out.println("Selected");
    } else {
      System.out.println("Deselected");
    }
  }
};
```

Listening to JToggleButton Events with a ChangeListener

Attaching a ChangeListener to a JToggleButton provides even more flexibility. Any attached listener will be notified of the data model changes for the button, corresponding to changes in its armed, pressed, and selected properties. Listening for notification from the three listeners—ActionListener, ItemListener, and ChangeListener—allows you to react seven different times. Figure 5-3 shows the sequencing of the ButtonModel property changes, and when the model notifies each of the listeners.

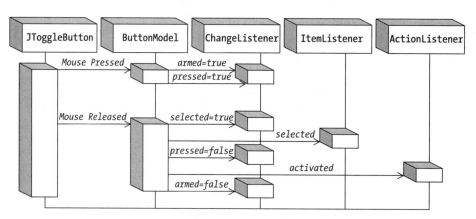

Figure 5-3. *JToggleButton notification sequencing diagram*

To demonstrate the ChangeListener notifications, the following code fragment defines a ChangeListener that reports the state changes to the three properties of the button model:

```
ChangeListener changeListener = new ChangeListener() {
  public void stateChanged(ChangeEvent changeEvent) {
    AbstractButton abstractButton = (AbstractButton)changeEvent.getSource();
    ButtonModel buttonModel = abstractButton.getModel();
    boolean armed = buttonModel.isArmed();
    boolean pressed = buttonModel.isPressed();
    boolean selected = buttonModel.isSelected();
    System.out.println("Changed: " + armed + "/" + pressed + "/" + selected);
  }
};
```

After you attach the ChangeListener to a JToggleButton and select the component by pressing and releasing the mouse over the component, the following output results:

```
Changed: true/false/false
Changed: true/true/false
Changed: true/true/true
Changed: true/false/true
Changed: false/false/true
```

With all three listeners attached to the same button, notification of registered ItemListener objects would happen after the selected property changes—in other words, between lines 3 and 4. Listing 5-2 demonstrates all three listeners attached to the same JToggleButton. With regard to the registered ActionListener objects, notification happens after releasing the button, but before the armed state changes to false, falling between lines 4 and 5.

Listing 5-2. *Listening for Toggle Selection*

```java
import javax.swing.*;
import javax.swing.event.*;
import java.awt.*;
import java.awt.event.*;

public class SelectingToggle {
  public static void main(String args[]) {
    Runnable runner = new Runnable() {
      public void run() {
        JFrame frame = new JFrame("Selecting Toggle");
        frame.setDefaultCloseOperation(JFrame.EXIT_ON_CLOSE);
        JToggleButton toggleButton = new JToggleButton("Toggle Button");
        // Define ActionListener
        ActionListener actionListener = new ActionListener() {
          public void actionPerformed(ActionEvent actionEvent) {
            AbstractButton abstractButton = (AbstractButton)actionEvent.getSource();
            boolean selected = abstractButton.getModel().isSelected();
            System.out.println("Action - selected=" + selected + "\n");
          }
        };
        // Define ChangeListener
        ChangeListener changeListener = new ChangeListener() {
          public void stateChanged(ChangeEvent changeEvent) {
            AbstractButton abstractButton = (AbstractButton)changeEvent.getSource();
            ButtonModel buttonModel = abstractButton.getModel();
            boolean armed = buttonModel.isArmed();
            boolean pressed = buttonModel.isPressed();
            boolean selected = buttonModel.isSelected();
            System.out.println("Changed: " + armed + "/" + pressed + "/" +
              selected);
          }
        };
```

```
        // Define ItemListener
        ItemListener itemListener = new ItemListener() {
          public void itemStateChanged(ItemEvent itemEvent) {
            int state = itemEvent.getStateChange();
            if (state == ItemEvent.SELECTED) {
              System.out.println("Selected");
            } else {
              System.out.println("Deselected");
            }
          }
        };
        // Attach Listeners
        toggleButton.addActionListener(actionListener);
        toggleButton.addChangeListener(changeListener);
        toggleButton.addItemListener(itemListener);
        frame.add(toggleButton, BorderLayout.NORTH);
        frame.setSize(300, 125);
        frame.setVisible(true);
      }
    };
    EventQueue.invokeLater(runner);
  }
}
```

Customizing a JToggleButton Look and Feel

Each installable Swing look and feel provides a different JToggleButton appearance and set of
default UIResource values. Figure 5-4 shows the appearance of the JToggleButton component
for the preinstalled set of look and feel types: Motif, Windows, and Ocean. As the button labels
might indicate, the first button is selected, the second has the input focus (and isn't selected),
and the third button isn't selected.

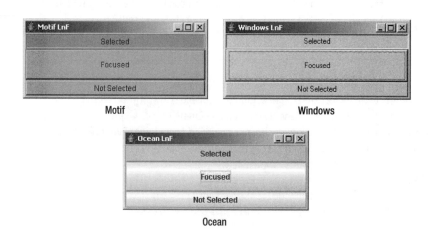

Figure 5-4. *JToggleButton under different look and feel types*

The available set of UIResource-related properties for a JToggleButton is shown in Table 5-2. The JToggleButton component has 17 different properties.

Table 5-2. *JToggleButton UIResource Elements*

Property String	Object Type
ToggleButton.background	Color
ToggleButton.border	Border
ToggleButton.darkShadow	Color
ToggleButton.disabledText	Color
ToggleButton.focus	Color
ToggleButton.focusInputMap	Object[ ]
ToggleButton.font	Font
ToggleButton.foreground	Color
ToggleButton.gradient	List
ToggleButton.highlight	Color
ToggleButton.light	Color
ToggleButton.margin	Insets
ToggleButton.select	Color
ToggleButton.shadow	Color
ToggleButton.textIconGap	Integer
ToggleButton.textShiftOffset	Integer
ToggleButtonUI	String

JCheckBox Class

The JCheckBox class represents the toggle component that, by default, displays a check box icon next to the text label for a two-state option. The check box icon uses an optional check mark to show the current state of the object, instead of keeping the button depressed, as with the JToggleButton. With the JCheckBox, the icon shows the state of the object, whereas with the JToggleButton, the icon is part of the label and isn't usually used to show state information. With the exception of the UI-related differences between JCheckBox and JToggleButton, the two components are identical. Figure 5-5 demonstrates how check box components might appear in a pizza-ordering application.

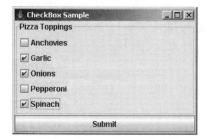

Figure 5-5. *Sample JCheckBox components*

The JCheckBox is made up of several pieces. Like JToggleButton, the JCheckBox uses a ToggleButtonModel to represent its data model. The user interface delegate is CheckBoxUI. Although the ButtonGroup is available to group together check boxes, it isn't normally appropriate. When multiple JCheckBox components are within a ButtonGroup, they behave like JRadioButton components but look like JCheckBox components. Because of this visual irregularity, you shouldn't put JCheckBox components into a ButtonGroup.

Now that you've seen the different pieces of a JCheckBox, let's find out how to use them.

Creating JCheckBox Components

Eight constructors exist for JCheckBox:

public JCheckBox()
```
JCheckBox aCheckBox = new JCheckBox();
```

public JCheckBox(Icon icon)
```
JCheckBox aCheckBox = new JCheckBox(new DiamondIcon(Color.RED, false));
aCheckBox.setSelectedIcon(new DiamondIcon(Color.PINK, true));
```

public JCheckBox(Icon icon, boolean selected)
```
JCheckBox aCheckBox = new JCheckBox(new DiamondIcon(Color.RED, false), true);
aCheckBox.setSelectedIcon(new DiamondIcon(Color.PINK, true));
```

public JCheckBox(String text)
```
JCheckBox aCheckBox = new JCheckBox("Spinach");
```

public JCheckBox(String text, boolean selected)
```
JCheckBox aCheckBox = new JCheckBox("Onions", true);
```

public JCheckBox(String text, Icon icon)
```
JCheckBox aCheckBox = new JCheckBox("Garlic", new DiamondIcon(Color.RED, false));
aCheckBox.setSelectedIcon(new DiamondIcon(Color.PINK, true));
```

```
public JCheckBox(String text, Icon icon, boolean selected)
JCheckBox aCheckBox = new JCheckBox("Anchovies", new DiamondIcon(Color.RED,
  false), true);
aCheckBox.setSelectedIcon(new DiamondIcon(Color.PINK, true));

public JCheckBox(Action action)
Action action = ...;
JCheckBox aCheckBox = new JCheckBox(action);
```

■**Note** Configuring a JCheckBox from an Action sets the label, state, and tooltip text, but not the icon.

Each allows you to customize either none or up to three properties for the label, icon, or initial selection state. Unless specified otherwise, there's no text in the label and the default selected/unselected icon for the check box appears unselected.

If you do initialize the icon in the constructor, it's the icon for the unselected state of the check box, with the same icon displayed when the check box is selected. You must also either initialize the selected icon with the setSelectedIcon(Icon newValue) method, described later, or make sure the icon is state-aware and updates itself. If you don't configure the selected icon and don't use a state-aware icon, the same icon will appear for both the selected and unselected state. Normally, an icon that doesn't change its visual appearance between selected and unselected states isn't desirable for a JCheckBox.

■**Note** A state-aware icon is one that asks the associated component for the value of the selected property.

JCheckBox Properties

After creating a JCheckBox, you can modify each of its many properties. Two properties specific to JCheckBox (shown in Table 5-3) override the behavior of its parent JToggleButton. The third borderPaintedFlat property was introduced in the 1.3 release of the JDK. All the remaining properties are inherited through parents of JToggleButton.

Table 5-3. *JCheckBox Properties*

Property Name	Data Type	Access
accessibleContext	AccessibleContext	Read-only
borderPaintedFlat	boolean	Read-write bound
UIClassID	String	Read-only

The `borderPaintedFlat` property permits a look and feel to display the border around the check icon as two-dimensional (flat) instead of three-dimensional. By default, the `borderPaintedFlat` property is `false`, meaning the border will be three-dimensional. Figure 5-6 shows what a flat border looks like, where the first, third, and fifth borders are flat, and the second and fourth are not. A look and feel may choose to ignore this property. However, it is useful for renderers for components such tables and trees, where they show only state and are not selectable. The Windows and Motif look and feel types take advantage of the property; Metal (and Ocean) does not.

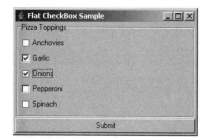

Figure 5-6. *Alternating flat JCheckBox borders for the Windows look and feel: Anchovies, Onions, and Spinach are flat; Garlic and Pepperoni are not.*

As the constructor listing demonstrated, if you choose to set an icon with a constructor, the constructor sets only one icon for the unselected state. If you want the check box icon to show the correct state visually, you must use a state-aware icon or associate a different icon for the selected state with `setSelectedIcon()`. Having two different visual state representations is what most users expect from a `JCheckBox`, so unless you have a good reason to do otherwise, it's best to follow the design convention for normal user interfaces.

The fourth button at the bottom of the screen shown in Figure 5-7 demonstrates confusing icon usage within a `JCheckBox`. The check box always appears selected. The figure displays what the screen looks like with Pizza selected, Calzone unselected, Anchovies unselected, and Stuffed Crust unselected (although the last one *appears* selected).

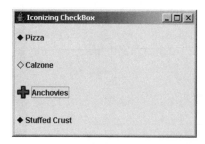

Figure 5-7. *Multiple JCheckBox components with various icons*

Listing 5-3 demonstrates three valid means of creating JCheckBox components with different icons, one using a state-aware icon. The last check box shows bad icon usage.

Listing 5-3. *Sampling JCheckBox*

```java
import javax.swing.*;
import java.awt.*;
import java.awt.event.*;

public class IconCheckBoxSample {
  private static class CheckBoxIcon implements Icon {
    private ImageIcon checkedIcon = new ImageIcon("Plus.gif");
    private ImageIcon uncheckedIcon = new ImageIcon("Minus.gif");

    public void paintIcon(Component component, Graphics g, int x, int y) {
      AbstractButton abstractButton = (AbstractButton)component;
      ButtonModel buttonModel = abstractButton.getModel();
      g.translate(x,y);
      ImageIcon imageIcon = buttonModel.isSelected() ?
        checkedIcon : uncheckedIcon;
      Image image = imageIcon.getImage();
      g.drawImage(image, 0, 0, component);
      g.translate(-x,-y);
    }
    public int getIconWidth() {
      return 20;
    }
    public int getIconHeight() {
      return 20;
    }
  }
  public static void main(String args[]) {
    Runnable runner = new Runnable() {
      public void run() {
        JFrame frame = new JFrame("Iconizing CheckBox");
        frame.setDefaultCloseOperation(JFrame.EXIT_ON_CLOSE);
        Icon checked = new DiamondIcon (Color.BLACK, true);
        Icon unchecked = new DiamondIcon (Color.BLACK, false);
        JCheckBox aCheckBox1 = new JCheckBox("Pizza", unchecked);
        aCheckBox1.setSelectedIcon(checked);
        JCheckBox aCheckBox2 = new JCheckBox("Calzone");
        aCheckBox2.setIcon(unchecked);
        aCheckBox2.setSelectedIcon(checked);
```

```
            Icon checkBoxIcon = new CheckBoxIcon();
            JCheckBox aCheckBox3 = new JCheckBox("Anchovies", checkBoxIcon);
            JCheckBox aCheckBox4 = new JCheckBox("Stuffed Crust", checked);
            frame.setLayout(new GridLayout(0,1));
            frame.add(aCheckBox1);
            frame.add(aCheckBox2);
            frame.add(aCheckBox3);
            frame.add(aCheckBox4);
            frame.setSize(300, 200);
            frame.setVisible(true);
          }
        };
        EventQueue.invokeLater(runner);
      }
    }
```

Handling JCheckBox Selection Events

As with the JToggleButton, you can handle JCheckBox events in any one of three ways: with an
ActionListener, an ItemListener, or a ChangeListener. The constructor that accepts an Action
just adds the parameter as an ActionListener.

Listening to JCheckBox Events with an ActionListener

Subscribing to ActionEvent generation with an ActionListener allows you to find out when the
user toggles the state of the JCheckBox. As with JToggleButton, the subscribed listener is told of
the selection, but not the new state. To find out the selected state, you must get the model for the
event source and ask, as the following sample ActionListener source shows. This listener
modifies the check box label to reflect the selection state.

```
ActionListener actionListener = new ActionListener() {
  public void actionPerformed(ActionEvent actionEvent) {
    AbstractButton abstractButton = (AbstractButton)actionEvent.getSource();
    boolean selected = abstractButton.getModel().isSelected();
    String newLabel = (selected ? SELECTED_LABEL : DESELECTED_LABEL);
    abstractButton.setText(newLabel);
  }
};
```

Listening to JCheckBox Events with an ItemListener

For JCheckBox, as with JToggleButton, the better listener to subscribe to is an ItemListener. The
ItemEvent passed to the itemStateChanged() method of ItemListener includes the current
state of the check box. This allows you to respond appropriately, without need to find out the
current button state.

   To demonstrate, the following ItemListener swaps the foreground and background colors
based on the state of a selected component. In this ItemListener, the foreground and background colors are swapped only when the state is selected.

```
ItemListener itemListener = new ItemListener() {
  public void itemStateChanged(ItemEvent itemEvent) {
    AbstractButton abstractButton = (AbstractButton)itemEvent.getSource();
    Color foreground = abstractButton.getForeground();
    Color background = abstractButton.getBackground();
    int state = itemEvent.getStateChange();
    if (state == ItemEvent.SELECTED) {
      abstractButton.setForeground(background);
      abstractButton.setBackground(foreground);
    }
  }
};
```

Listening to JCheckBox Events with a ChangeListener

The ChangeListener responds to the JCheckBox just as with the JToggleButton. A subscribed ChangeListener would be notified when the button is armed, pressed, selected, or released. In addition, the ChangeListener is also notified of changes to the ButtonModel, such as for the keyboard mnemonic (KeyEvent.VK_S) of the check box. Because there are no ChangeListener differences to demonstrate between a JToggleButton and a JCheckBox, you could just attach the same listener from JToggleButton to the JCheckBox, and you'll get the same selection responses.

The sample program in Listing 5-4 demonstrates all the listeners subscribed to the events of a single JCheckBox. To demonstrate that the ChangeListener is notified of changes to other button model properties, a keyboard mnemonic is associated with the component. Given that the ChangeListener is registered before the mnemonic property is changed, the ChangeListener is notified of the property change. Because the foreground and background colors and text label aren't button model properties, the ChangeListener isn't told of these changes made by the other listeners.

■**Note** If you did want to listen for changes to the foreground or background color properties, you would need to attach a PropertyChangeListener to the JCheckBox.

Listing 5-4. *Listening for JCheckBox Selection*

```
import javax.swing.*;
import javax.swing.event.*;
import java.awt.*;
import java.awt.event.*;

public class SelectingCheckBox {
  private static String DESELECTED_LABEL = "Deselected";
  private static String SELECTED_LABEL = "Selected";
```

```java
public static void main(String args[]) {
  Runnable runner = new Runnable() {
    public void run() {
      JFrame frame = new JFrame("Selecting CheckBox");
      frame.setDefaultCloseOperation(JFrame.EXIT_ON_CLOSE);
      JCheckBox checkBox = new JCheckBox(DESELECTED_LABEL);
      // Define ActionListener
      ActionListener actionListener = new ActionListener() {
        public void actionPerformed(ActionEvent actionEvent) {
          AbstractButton abstractButton =
            (AbstractButton)actionEvent.getSource();
          boolean selected = abstractButton.getModel().isSelected();
          String newLabel = (selected ? SELECTED_LABEL : DESELECTED_LABEL);
          abstractButton.setText(newLabel);
        }
      };
      // Define ChangeListener
      ChangeListener changeListener = new ChangeListener() {
        public void stateChanged(ChangeEvent changeEvent) {
          AbstractButton abstractButton =
            (AbstractButton)changeEvent.getSource();
          ButtonModel buttonModel = abstractButton.getModel();
          boolean armed = buttonModel.isArmed();
          boolean pressed = buttonModel.isPressed();
          boolean selected = buttonModel.isSelected();
          System.out.println("Changed: " + armed + "/" + pressed + "/" +
            selected);
        }
      };
      // Define ItemListener
      ItemListener itemListener = new ItemListener() {
        public void itemStateChanged(ItemEvent itemEvent) {
          AbstractButton abstractButton =
            (AbstractButton)itemEvent.getSource();
          Color foreground = abstractButton.getForeground();
          Color background = abstractButton.getBackground();
          int state = itemEvent.getStateChange();
          if (state == ItemEvent.SELECTED) {
            abstractButton.setForeground(background);
            abstractButton.setBackground(foreground);
          }
        }
      };
      // Attach Listeners
      checkBox.addActionListener(actionListener);
      checkBox.addChangeListener(changeListener);
      checkBox.addItemListener(itemListener);
```

```
        checkBox.setMnemonic(KeyEvent.VK_S);
        frame.add(checkBox, BorderLayout.NORTH);
        frame.setSize(300, 100);
        frame.setVisible(true);
      }
    };
    EventQueue.invokeLater(runner);
  }
}
```

The SelectingCheckBox class produces the screen shown in Figure 5-8, after selecting and deselecting the JCheckBox.

Figure 5-8. *SelectingCheckBox program screen*

Customizing a JCheckBox Look and Feel

Each installable Swing look and feel provides a different JCheckBox appearance and set of default UIResource values. Figure 5-9 shows the appearance of the JCheckBox component for the preinstalled set of look and feel types: Motif, Windows, and Ocean. The first, third, and fifth check boxes are selected; the third has the input focus.

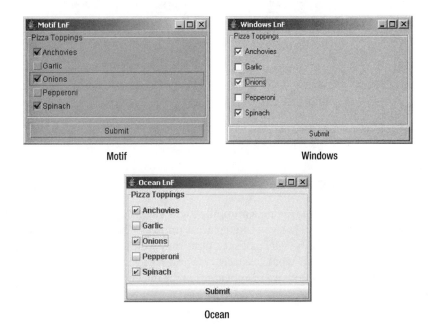

Figure 5-9. *JCheckBox under different look and feel types*

Table 5-4 shows the set of available UIResource-related properties for a JCheckBox. The JCheckBox component has 20 different properties.

Table 5-4. *JCheckBox UIResource Elements*

Property String	Object Type
CheckBox.background	Color
CheckBox.border	Border
CheckBox.darkShadow	Color
CheckBox.disabledText	Color
CheckBox.focus	Color
CheckBox.focusInputMap	Object[ ]
CheckBox.font	Font
CheckBox.foreground	Color
CheckBox.gradient	List
CheckBox.highlight	Color
CheckBox.icon	Icon
CheckBox.interiorBackground	Color
CheckBox.light	Color
CheckBox.margin	Insets
CheckBox.rollover	Boolean
Checkbox.select*	Color
CheckBox.shadow	Color
CheckBox.textIconGap	Integer
CheckBox.textShiftOffset	Integer
CheckBoxUI	String

* Lowercase b is correct.

JRadioButton Class

You use JRadioButton when you want to create a mutually exclusive group of toggleable components. Although, technically speaking, you could place a group of JCheckBox components into a ButtonGroup and only one would be selectable at a time, they wouldn't look quite right. At least with the predefined look and feel types, JRadioButton and JCheckBox components look different, as Figure 5-10 shows. This difference in appearance tells the end user to expect specific behavior from the components.

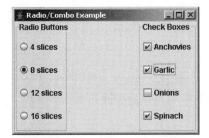

Figure 5-10. *Comparing JRadioButton to JCheckBox appearance*

The JRadioButton is made up of several pieces. Like JToggleButton and JCheckBox, the JRadioButton uses a ToggleButtonModel to represent its data model. It uses a ButtonGroup through AbstractButton to provide the mutually exclusive grouping, and the user interface delegate is the RadioButtonUI.

Let's now explore how to use the different pieces of a JRadioButton.

Creating JRadioButton Components

As with JCheckBox and JToggleButton, there are eight constructors for JRadioButton:

public JRadioButton()
```
JRadioButton aRadioButton = new JRadioButton();
```

public JRadioButton(Icon icon)
```
JRadioButton aRadioButton = new JRadioButton(new DiamondIcon(Color.CYAN, false));
aRadioButton.setSelectedIcon(new DiamondIcon(Color.BLUE, true));
```

public JRadioButton(Icon icon, boolean selected)
```
JRadioButton aRadioButton = new JRadioButton(new DiamondIcon(Color.CYAN, false),
  true);
aRadioButton.setSelectedIcon(new DiamondIcon(Color.BLUE, true));
```

public JRadioButton(String text)
```
JRadioButton aRadioButton = new JRadioButton("4 slices");
```

public JRadioButton(String text, boolean selected)
```
JRadioButton aRadioButton = new JRadioButton("8 slices", true);
```

public JRadioButton(String text, Icon icon)
```
JRadioButton aRadioButton = new JRadioButton("12 slices",
  new DiamondIcon(Color.CYAN, false));
aRadioButton.setSelectedIcon(new DiamondIcon(Color.BLUE, true));
```

public JRadioButton(String text, Icon icon, boolean selected)
```
JRadioButton aRadioButton = new JRadioButton("16 slices",
  new DiamondIcon(Color.CYAN, false), true);
aRadioButton.setSelectedIcon(new DiamondIcon(Color.BLUE, true));
```

```
public JRadioButton(Action action)
Action action = ...;
JRadioButton aRadioButton = new JRadioButton(action);
```

■**Note** As with a JCheckBox, configuring a JRadioButton from an Action sets the label, state, and tooltip text, but not the icon.

Each allows you to customize one or more of the label, icon, or initial selection state properties. Unless specified otherwise, there's no text in the label, and the default selected/unselected icon for the check box appears unselected. After creating a group of radio button components, you need to place each into a single ButtonGroup so that they work as expected, with only one button in the group selectable at a time. If you do initialize the icon in the constructor, it's the icon for the unselected state of the check box, with the same icon displayed when the check box is selected. You must also either initialize the selected icon with the setSelectedIcon(Icon newValue) method, described with JCheckBox, or make sure the icon is state-aware and updates itself.

JRadioButton Properties

JRadioButton has two properties that override the behavior of its parent JToggleButton, as listed in Table 5-5.

Table 5-5. *JRadioButton Properties*

Property Name	Data Type	Access
accessibleContext	AccessibleContext	Read-only
UIClassID	String	Read-only

Grouping JRadioButton Components in a ButtonGroup

The JRadioButton is the only JToggleButton subclass that should be placed in a ButtonGroup in order to work properly. Merely creating a bunch of radio buttons and placing them on the screen isn't enough to make them behave appropriately. In addition to adding each radio button to a container, you need to create a ButtonGroup and add each radio button to the same ButtonGroup. Once all the JRadioButton items are in a group, whenever an unselected radio button is selected, the ButtonGroup causes the currently selected radio button to be deselected.

Placing a set of JRadioButton components within a ButtonGroup on the screen is basically a four-step process:

1. Create a container for the group.

   ```
   JPanel aPanel = new JPanel(new GridLayout(0, 1));
   ```

■Note The Box class described in Chapter 11 serves as a good container for a group of JRadioButton components.

---

2. Place a border around the container, to label the grouping. This is an optional step, but you'll frequently want to add a border to label the group for the user. You can read more about borders in Chapter 7.

```
Border border = BorderFactory.createTitledBorder("Slice Count");
aPanel.setBorder(border);
```

3. Create a ButtonGroup.

```
ButtonGroup aGroup = new ButtonGroup();
```

4. For each selectable option, create a JRadioButton, add it to a container, and then add it to the group.

```
JRadioButton aRadioButton = new JRadioButton(...);
aPanel.add(aRadioButton);
aGroup.add(aRadioButton);
```

You might find the whole process, especially the fourth step, a bit tedious after a while, especially when you add another step for handling selection events. The helper class shown in Listing 5-5, with its static createRadioButtonGrouping(String elements[], String title) method, could prove useful. It takes a String array for the radio button labels as well as the border title, and then it creates a set of JRadioButton objects with a common ButtonGroup in a JPanel with a titled border.

Listing 5-5. *Initial Support Class for Working with JRadioButton*

```
import javax.swing.*;
import javax.swing.border.*;
import java.awt.*;

public class RadioButtonUtils {
  private RadioButtonUtils() {
    // Private constructor so you can't create instances
  }
  public static Container createRadioButtonGrouping (String elements[],
      String title) {
    JPanel panel = new JPanel(new GridLayout(0, 1));
// If title set, create titled border
    if (title != null) {
      Border border = BorderFactory.createTitledBorder(title);
      panel.setBorder(border);
    }
```

```
// Create group
    ButtonGroup group = new ButtonGroup();
    JRadioButton aRadioButton;
// For each String passed in:
// Create button, add to panel, and add to group
    for (int i=0, n=elements.length; i<n; i++) {
      aRadioButton = new JRadioButton(elements[i]);
      panel.add(aRadioButton);
      group.add(aRadioButton);
    }
    return panel;
  }
}
```

Now, you can create the grouping much more easily, as with the sample program in Listing 5-6.

Listing 5-6. *Sampling JRadioButton*

```
import javax.swing.*;
import java.awt.*;

public class GroupRadio {
  private static final String sliceOptions[] =
    {"4 slices", "8 slices", "12 slices", "16 slices"};
  private static final String crustOptions[] =
    {"Sicilian", "Thin Crust", "Thick Crust", "Stuffed Crust"};
  public static void main(String args[]) {
    Runnable runner = new Runnable() {
      public void run() {
        JFrame frame = new JFrame("Grouping Example");
        frame.setDefaultCloseOperation(JFrame.EXIT_ON_CLOSE);
        Container sliceContainer =
          RadioButtonUtils.createRadioButtonGrouping(
          sliceOptions, "Slice Count");
        Container crustContainer =
          RadioButtonUtils.createRadioButtonGrouping(
          crustOptions, "Crust Type");
        frame.add(sliceContainer, BorderLayout.WEST);
        frame.add(crustContainer, BorderLayout.EAST);
        frame.setSize(300, 200);
        frame.setVisible(true);
      }
    };
    EventQueue.invokeLater(runner);
  }
}
```

When you run this example, you'll see the screen shown in Figure 5-11.

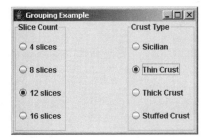

Figure 5-11. *Grouping JRadioButton components with the RadioButtonUtils helper class*

■**Note** If you're familiar with the standard AWT library, the JRadioButton/ButtonGroup combination works exactly like the Checkbox/CheckboxGroup pair.

Handling JRadioButton Selection Events

Like JToggleButton and JCheckBox, JRadioButton supports the registration of an ActionListener, an ItemListener, and a ChangeListener. And again, their usage with JRadioButton is somewhat different than with the other components.

Listening to JRadioButton Events with an ActionListener

With a JRadioButton, it's common to attach the same ActionListener to all the radio buttons in a ButtonGroup. That way, when one of the radio buttons is selected, the subscribed ActionListener will be notified. By overloading the earlier createRadioButtonGrouping() method, the method can accept an ActionListener argument and attach the listener object to each of the buttons as they're created.

```
public static Container createRadioButtonGrouping (String elements[], String title,
    ActionListener actionListener) {
  JPanel panel = new JPanel(new GridLayout(0, 1));
  // If title set, create titled border
  if (title != null) {
    Border border = BorderFactory.createTitledBorder(title);
    panel.setBorder(border);
  }
  // Create group
  ButtonGroup group = new ButtonGroup();
  JRadioButton aRadioButton;
  // For each String passed in:
  // Create button, add to panel, and add to group
```

```
  for (int i=0, n=elements.length; i<n; i++) {
    aRadioButton = new JRadioButton (elements[i]);
    panel.add(aRadioButton);
    group.add(aRadioButton);
    if (actionListener != null) {
      aRadioButton.addActionListener(actionListener);
    }
  }
  return panel;
}
```

Now if a group is created with the following source, the same ActionListener will be notified for each of the JRadioButton components created. Here, the listener prints out only the currently selected value. How you choose to respond may vary.

```
ActionListener sliceActionListener = new ActionListener() {
  public void actionPerformed(ActionEvent actionEvent) {
    AbstractButton aButton = (AbstractButton)actionEvent.getSource();
    System.out.println("Selected: " + aButton.getText());
  }
};
Container sliceContainer =
  RadioButtonUtils.createRadioButtonGrouping(sliceOptions, "Slice Count",
    sliceActionListener);
```

However, note that there are two problems with this approach. First, if a JRadioButton is already selected and then selected again, any attached ActionListener objects will still be notified once more. Although you cannot stop the double notification of subscribed ActionListener objects, with a little work, you can handle it properly. You need to retain a reference to the last selected item and check for reselection. The following modified ActionListener checks for this:

```
ActionListener crustActionListener = new ActionListener() {
  String lastSelected;
  public void actionPerformed(ActionEvent actionEvent) {
    AbstractButton aButton = (AbstractButton)actionEvent.getSource();
    String label = aButton.getText();
    String msgStart;
    if (label.equals(lastSelected)) {
      msgStart = "Reselected: ";
    } else {
      msgStart = "Selected: ";
    }
    lastSelected = label;
    System.out.println(msgStart + label);
  }
};
```

The second problem has to do with determining which JRadioButton is selected at any given time. With the overloaded RadioButtonUtils.createRadioButtonGrouping() helper methods, neither the ButtonGroup nor the individual JRadioButton components are visible outside the method. As a result, there's no direct route to find out which JRadioButton object (or objects) is selected within the ButtonGroup of the returned container. This may be necessary, for example, if there were an Order Pizza button on the screen and you wanted to find out which pizza-order options were selected after the user clicked that button.

The following helper method, public Enumeration getSelectedElements(Container container), when added to the previously created RadioButtonUtils class (Listing 5-5), will provide the necessary answer. The helper method will work only if the container passed into the method is full of AbstractButton objects. This is true for those containers created with the previously described createRadioButtonGrouping() methods, although the getSelectedElements() method can be used separately.

```
public static Enumeration<String> getSelectedElements(Container container) {
  Vector<String> selections = new Vector<String>();
  Component components[] = container.getComponents();
  for (int i=0, n=components.length; i<n; i++) {
    if (components[i] instanceof AbstractButton) {
      AbstractButton button = (AbstractButton)components[i];
      if (button.isSelected()) {
        selections.addElement(button.getText());
      }
    }
  }
  return selections.elements();
}
```

To use the getSelectedElements() method, you just need to pass the container returned from createRadioButtonGrouping() to the getSelectedElements() method to get an Enumeration of the selected items as String objects. The following example demonstrates this.

```
final Container crustContainer =
    RadioButtonUtils.createRadioButtonGrouping(crustOptions, "Crust Type");

ActionListener buttonActionListener = new ActionListener() {
  public void actionPerformed(ActionEvent actionEvent) {
    Enumeration selected = RadioButtonUtils.getSelectedElements(crustContainer);
    while (selected.hasMoreElements()) {
      System.out.println ("Selected -> " + selected.nextElement());
    }
  }
};
JButton button = new JButton ("Order Pizza");
button.addActionListener(buttonActionListener);
```

It may be necessary for getSelectedElements() to return more than one value, because if the same ButtonModel is shared by multiple buttons in the container, multiple components of the ButtonGroup will be selected. Sharing a ButtonModel between components isn't the norm. If you're sure your button model won't be shared, then you may want to provide a similar method that returns only a String.

Listening to JRadioButton Events with an ItemListener

Depending on what you're trying to do, using an ItemListener with a JRadioButton is usually not the desired event-listening approach. When an ItemListener is registered, a new JRadioButton selection notifies the listener twice: once for deselecting the old value and once for selecting the new value. For reselections (selecting the same choice again), the listener is notified only once.

To demonstrate, the following listener will detect reselections, as the ActionListener did earlier, and will report the selected (or deselected) element.

```
ItemListener itemListener = new ItemListener() {
  String lastSelected;
  public void itemStateChanged(ItemEvent itemEvent) {
    AbstractButton aButton = (AbstractButton)itemEvent.getSource();
    int state = itemEvent.getStateChange();
    String label = aButton.getText();
    String msgStart;
    if (state == ItemEvent.SELECTED) {
      if (label.equals(lastSelected)) {
        msgStart = "Reselected -> ";
      } else {
        msgStart = "Selected -> ";
      }
      lastSelected = label;
    } else {
      msgStart = "Deselected -> ";
    }
    System.out.println(msgStart + label);
  }
};
```

To work properly, some new methods will be needed for RadioButtonUtils to enable you to attach the ItemListener to each JRadioButton in the ButtonGroup. They're listed in the following section with the source for the complete example.

Listening to JRadioButton Events with a ChangeListener

The ChangeListener responds to the JRadioButton just as it does with the JToggleButton and JCheckBox. A subscribed listener is notified when the selected radio button is armed, pressed, selected, or released and for various other properties of the button model. The only difference with JRadioButton is that the ChangeListener is also notified of the state changes of the radio button being deselected. The ChangeListener from the earlier examples could be attached to the JRadioButton as well. It will just be notified more frequently.

The sample program shown in Listing 5-7 demonstrates all the listeners registered to the events of two different JRadioButton objects. In addition, a JButton reports on the selected elements of one of the radio buttons. Figure 5-12 shows the main window of the program.

Listing 5-7. *Radio Button Group Sample*

```java
import javax.swing.*;
import javax.swing.event.*;
import java.awt.*;
import java.awt.event.*;
import java.util.Enumeration;

public class GroupActionRadio {
  private static final String sliceOptions[] =
    {"4 slices", "8 slices", "12 slices", "16 slices"};
  private static final String crustOptions[] =
    {"Sicilian", "Thin Crust", "Thick Crust", "Stuffed Crust"};
  public static void main(String args[]) {
    Runnable runner = new Runnable() {
      public void run() {
        JFrame frame = new JFrame("Grouping Example");
        frame.setDefaultCloseOperation(JFrame.EXIT_ON_CLOSE);

        // Slice Parts
        ActionListener sliceActionListener = new ActionListener() {
          public void actionPerformed(ActionEvent actionEvent) {
            AbstractButton aButton = (AbstractButton)actionEvent.getSource();
            System.out.println("Selected: " + aButton.getText());
          }
        };
        Container sliceContainer =
          RadioButtonUtils.createRadioButtonGrouping(sliceOptions,
            "Slice Count", sliceActionListener);

        // Crust Parts
        ActionListener crustActionListener = new ActionListener() {
          String lastSelected;
          public void actionPerformed(ActionEvent actionEvent) {
            AbstractButton aButton = (AbstractButton)actionEvent.getSource();
            String label = aButton.getText();
            String msgStart;
            if (label.equals(lastSelected)) {
              msgStart = "Reselected: ";
            } else {
              msgStart = "Selected: ";
            }
            lastSelected = label;
            System.out.println(msgStart + label);
          }
        };
```

```java
ItemListener itemListener = new ItemListener() {
  String lastSelected;
  public void itemStateChanged(ItemEvent itemEvent) {
    AbstractButton aButton = (AbstractButton)itemEvent.getSource();
    int state = itemEvent.getStateChange();
    String label = aButton.getText();
    String msgStart;
    if (state == ItemEvent.SELECTED) {
      if (label.equals(lastSelected)) {
        msgStart = "Reselected -> ";
      } else {
        msgStart = "Selected -> ";
      }
      lastSelected = label;
    } else {
      msgStart = "Deselected -> ";
    }
    System.out.println(msgStart + label);
  }
};
ChangeListener changeListener = new ChangeListener() {
  public void stateChanged(ChangeEvent changEvent) {
    AbstractButton aButton = (AbstractButton)changEvent.getSource();
    ButtonModel aModel = aButton.getModel();
    boolean armed = aModel.isArmed();
    boolean pressed = aModel.isPressed();
    boolean selected = aModel.isSelected();
    System.out.println("Changed: " + armed + "/" + pressed + "/" +
      selected);
  }
};
final Container crustContainer =
  RadioButtonUtils.createRadioButtonGrouping(crustOptions,
    "Crust Type", crustActionListener, itemListener, changeListener);

// Button Parts
ActionListener buttonActionListener = new ActionListener() {
  public void actionPerformed(ActionEvent actionEvent) {
    Enumeration<String> selected =
      RadioButtonUtils.getSelectedElements(crustContainer);
    while (selected.hasMoreElements()) {
      System.out.println ("Selected -> " + selected.nextElement());
    }
  }
};
```

```
        JButton button = new JButton ("Order Pizza");
        button.addActionListener(buttonActionListener);

        frame.add(sliceContainer, BorderLayout.WEST);
        frame.add(crustContainer, BorderLayout.EAST);
        frame.add(button, BorderLayout.SOUTH);
        frame.setSize(300, 200);
        frame.setVisible(true);
      }
    };
    EventQueue.invokeLater(runner);
  }
}
```

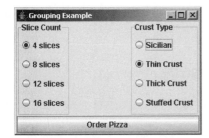

Figure 5-12. *The GroupActionRadio program sample screen*

A few more changes were made to the RadioButtonUtils class to deal with registering
ChangeListener objects to all the radio buttons in a ButtonGroup. The complete and final class
definition is shown in Listing 5-8.

Listing 5-8. *Complete Support Class for Working with JRadioButton*

```
import javax.swing.*;
import javax.swing.event.*;
import javax.swing.border.*;
import java.awt.*;
import java.awt.event.*;
import java.util.Enumeration;
import java.util.Vector;

public class RadioButtonUtils {
  private RadioButtonUtils() {
    // Private constructor so you can't create instances
  }
```

```java
public static Enumeration<String> getSelectedElements(Container container) {
  Vector<String> selections = new Vector<String>();
  Component components[] = container.getComponents();
  for (int i=0, n=components.length; i<n; i++) {
    if (components[i] instanceof AbstractButton) {
      AbstractButton button = (AbstractButton)components[i];
      if (button.isSelected()) {
        selections.addElement(button.getText());
      }
    }
  }
  return selections.elements();
}

public static Container createRadioButtonGrouping (String elements[]) {
  return createRadioButtonGrouping(elements, null, null, null, null);
}

public static Container createRadioButtonGrouping (String elements[],
    String title) {
  return createRadioButtonGrouping(elements, title, null, null, null);
}

public static Container createRadioButtonGrouping(String elements[],
    String title, ItemListener itemListener) {
  return createRadioButtonGrouping(elements, title, null, itemListener, null);
}

public static Container createRadioButtonGrouping(String elements[],
    String title, ActionListener actionListener) {
  return createRadioButtonGrouping(elements, title, actionListener, null,
    null);
}

public static Container createRadioButtonGrouping(String elements[],
    String title, ActionListener actionListener, ItemListener itemListener) {
  return createRadioButtonGrouping(elements, title, actionListener,
    itemListener, null);
}

public static Container createRadioButtonGrouping(String elements[],
    String title, ActionListener actionListener, ItemListener itemListener,
    ChangeListener changeListener) {
  JPanel panel = new JPanel(new GridLayout(0, 1));
  // If title set, create titled border
```

```
    if (title != null) {
      Border border = BorderFactory.createTitledBorder(title);
      panel.setBorder(border);
    }
    // Create group
    ButtonGroup group = new ButtonGroup();
    JRadioButton aRadioButton;
    // For each String passed in:
    // Create button, add to panel, and add to group
    for (int i=0, n=elements.length; i<n; i++) {
      aRadioButton = new JRadioButton (elements[i]);
      panel.add(aRadioButton);
      group.add(aRadioButton);
      if (actionListener != null) {
        aRadioButton.addActionListener(actionListener);
      }
      if (itemListener != null) {
        aRadioButton.addItemListener(itemListener);
      }
      if (changeListener != null) {
        aRadioButton.addChangeListener(changeListener);
      }
    }
    return panel;
  }
}
```

Note One thing not shown here but explained in Chapter 4 in the discussion of `ButtonModel` and `DefaultButtonModel` is how to get the `ButtonGroup` when given a `JRadioButton`. If you want to find the `ButtonGroup` that a `JRadioButton` is in, you need to ask the `DefaultButtonModel`: `ButtonGroup group = ((DefaultButtonModel)aJRadioButton.getModel()).getButtonGroup()`.

Customizing a JRadioButton Look and Feel

Each installable Swing look and feel provides a different `JRadioButton` appearance and set of default `UIResource` values. Figure 5-13 shows the appearance of the `JRadioButton` component for the preinstalled set of look and feel types: Motif, Windows, and Ocean. All three screens show 4 slices of Thin Crust pizza as the order. In addition, the Thick Crust option has the input focus.

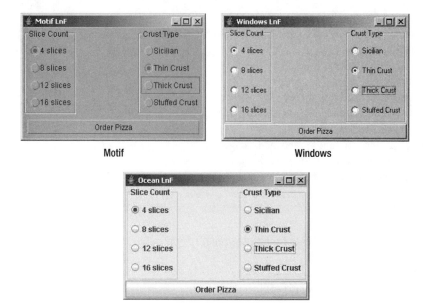

Motif

Windows

Ocean

Figure 5-13. *JRadioButton under different look and feel types*

Table 5-6 shows the set of available UIResource-related properties for a JRadioButton. The JRadioButton component has 20 different properties available.

Table 5-6. *JRadioButton UIResource Elements*

Property String	Object Type
RadioButton.background	Color
RadioButton.border	Border
RadioButton.darkShadow	Color
RadioButton.disabledText	Color
RadioButton.focus	Color
RadioButton.focusInputMap	Object[ ]
RadioButton.font	Font
RadioButton.foreground	Color
RadioButton.gradient	List
RadioButton.highlight	Color
RadioButton.icon	Icon
RadioButton.interiorBackground	Color
RadioButton.light	Color
RadioButton.margin	Insets

Table 5-6. *JRadioButton UIResource Elements (Continued)*

Property String	Object Type
RadioButton.rollover	Boolean
RadioButton.select	Color
RadioButton.shadow	Color
RadioButton.textIconGap	Integer
RadioButton.textShiftOffset	Integer
RadioButtonUI	String

Summary

This chapter described the components that can be toggled: JToggleButton, JCheckBox, and JRadioButton. You've seen how each component uses the JToggleButton.ToggleButtonModel class for its data model and how you can group the components into a ButtonGroup. In addition, you also saw how to handle selection events for each of the components.

Chapter 6 explains how to work with the various menu-oriented Swing components.

CHAPTER 6

∎∎∎

Swing Menus and Toolbars

Many of the low-level Swing components were covered in the previous two chapters of this book. This chapter will delve into Swing's menu-related components. Menus and toolbars help make your applications more user-friendly by providing visual command options. Users can avoid the somewhat archaic multiple-key command sequences that are holdovers from programs such as the early word processor WordStar and the more current emacs programmer's editor. Although Swing menus do support multiple-key command sequences, the menus (and toolbars) are designed primarily for on-screen graphical selection with a mouse, rather than the keyboard.

The menu components discussed in this chapter are used as follows:

- For each cascading menu, you create a JMenu component and add it to the JMenuBar.

- For the selections available from the JMenu, you create JMenuItem components and add them to the JMenu.

- To create submenus, you add a new JMenu to a JMenu and place JMenuItem options on the new menu.

- Then, when a JMenu is selected, the system displays its current set of components within a JPopupMenu.

In addition to the basic JMenuItem elements, this chapter covers other menu items, such as JCheckBoxMenuItem and JRadioButtonMenuItem, which you can place within a JMenu. You'll also explore the JSeparator class, which serves to divide menu items into logical groups. You'll find out how to use the JPopupMenu class for general support of pop-up menus that appear after a JMenu is selected, or in context for any component. As with abstract buttons (the AbstractButton class was introduced in Chapter 4), each menu element can have a mnemonic associated with it for keyboard selection. You'll also learn about the support for keyboard accelerators, which allow users to avoid going through all the menuing levels for selection.

Besides the individual menu-related components, in this chapter you'll look at the JMenuBar selection model and event-related classes specific to menus. The selection model interface to examine is the SingleSelectionModel interface, as well as its default implementation DefaultSingleSelectionModel. You'll explore the menu-specific listeners and events MenuListener/MenuEvent, MenuKeyListener/MenuKeyEvent, and MenuDragMouseListener/MenuDragMouseEvent. In addition, you'll examine creating other pop-up components with Popup and PopupFactory, as well as using toolbars with the JToolBar class.

Working with Menus

Let's begin with an example that demonstrates how all the menu components fit together. To start, create a frame with a menu bar, as shown in Figure 6-1.

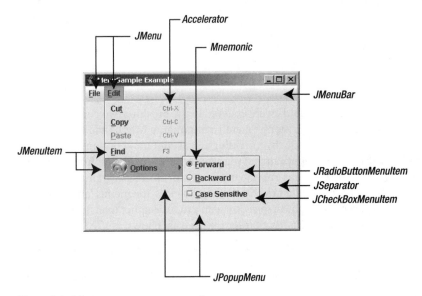

Figure 6-1. *Menu component examples*

This simple menuing example has the following features:

- On the menu bar are two ubiquitous menus: File and Edit. Under the File menu, the familiar options of New, Open, Close, and Exit will appear (although they aren't shown in Figure 6-1). Under the Edit menu are options for Cut, Copy, Paste, and Find, and a submenu of Find options. The Options submenu will contain choices for search direction— forward or backward—and a toggle for case sensitivity.

- In various places within the different menus, menu separators divide the options into logical sets.

- Each of the menu options has a mnemonic associated with it to help with keyboard navigation and selection. The mnemonic allows users to make menu selections via the keyboard, for instance, by pressing Alt-F on a Windows platform to open the File menu.

- In addition to the keyboard mnemonic, a keystroke associated with several options acts as a keyboard accelerator. Unlike the mnemonic, the accelerator can directly activate a menu option, even when the menu option isn't visible.

- The Options submenu has an icon associated with it. Although only one icon is shown in Figure 6-1, all menu components can have an icon, except for the JSeparator and JPopupMenu components.

Note that for this beginning example, none of the menu choices will do anything other than print which menu choice was selected. For example, selecting the Copy option from the Edit menu displays Selected: Copy.

Listing 6-1 shows the complete source for the class that generated the example in Figure 6-1.

Listing 6-1. *The MenuSample Class Definition*

```
import java.awt.*;
import java.awt.event.*;
import javax.swing.*;

public class MenuSample {
  static class MenuActionListener implements ActionListener {
    public void actionPerformed (ActionEvent actionEvent) {
      System.out.println ("Selected: " + actionEvent.getActionCommand());
    }
  }
  public static void main(final String args[]) {
    Runnable runner = new Runnable() {
      public void run() {
        ActionListener menuListener = new MenuActionListener();
        JFrame frame = new JFrame("MenuSample Example");
        frame.setDefaultCloseOperation(JFrame.EXIT_ON_CLOSE);
        JMenuBar menuBar = new JMenuBar();

        // File Menu, F - Mnemonic
        JMenu fileMenu = new JMenu("File");
        fileMenu.setMnemonic(KeyEvent.VK_F);
        menuBar.add(fileMenu);

        // File->New, N - Mnemonic
        JMenuItem newMenuItem = new JMenuItem("New", KeyEvent.VK_N);
        newMenuItem.addActionListener(menuListener);
        fileMenu.add(newMenuItem);

        // File->Open, O - Mnemonic
        JMenuItem openMenuItem = new JMenuItem("Open", KeyEvent.VK_O);
        openMenuItem.addActionListener(menuListener);
        fileMenu.add(openMenuItem);

        // File->Close, C - Mnemonic
        JMenuItem closeMenuItem = new JMenuItem("Close", KeyEvent.VK_C);
        closeMenuItem.addActionListener(menuListener);
        fileMenu.add(closeMenuItem);
```

```
// Separator
fileMenu.addSeparator();

// File->Save, S - Mnemonic
JMenuItem saveMenuItem = new JMenuItem("Save", KeyEvent.VK_S);
saveMenuItem.addActionListener(menuListener);
fileMenu.add(saveMenuItem);

// Separator
fileMenu.addSeparator();

// File->Exit, X - Mnemonic
JMenuItem exitMenuItem = new JMenuItem("Exit", KeyEvent.VK_X);
exitMenuItem.addActionListener(menuListener);
fileMenu.add(exitMenuItem);

// Edit Menu, E - Mnemonic
JMenu editMenu = new JMenu("Edit");
editMenu.setMnemonic(KeyEvent.VK_E);
menuBar.add(editMenu);

// Edit->Cut, T - Mnemonic, CTRL-X - Accelerator
JMenuItem cutMenuItem = new JMenuItem("Cut", KeyEvent.VK_T);
cutMenuItem.addActionListener(menuListener);
KeyStroke ctrlXKeyStroke = KeyStroke.getKeyStroke("control X");
cutMenuItem.setAccelerator(ctrlXKeyStroke);
editMenu.add(cutMenuItem);

// Edit->Copy, C - Mnemonic, CTRL-C - Accelerator
JMenuItem copyMenuItem = new JMenuItem("Copy", KeyEvent.VK_C);
copyMenuItem.addActionListener(menuListener);
KeyStroke ctrlCKeyStroke = KeyStroke.getKeyStroke("control C");
copyMenuItem.setAccelerator(ctrlCKeyStroke);
editMenu.add(copyMenuItem);

// Edit->Paste, P - Mnemonic, CTRL-V - Accelerator, Disabled
JMenuItem pasteMenuItem = new JMenuItem("Paste", KeyEvent.VK_P);
pasteMenuItem.addActionListener(menuListener);
KeyStroke ctrlVKeyStroke = KeyStroke.getKeyStroke("control V");
pasteMenuItem.setAccelerator(ctrlVKeyStroke);
pasteMenuItem.setEnabled(false);
editMenu.add(pasteMenuItem);

// Separator
editMenu.addSeparator();
```

```java
// Edit->Find, F - Mnemonic, F3 - Accelerator
JMenuItem findMenuItem = new JMenuItem("Find", KeyEvent.VK_F);
findMenuItem.addActionListener(menuListener);
KeyStroke f3KeyStroke = KeyStroke.getKeyStroke("F3");
findMenuItem.setAccelerator(f3KeyStroke);
editMenu.add(findMenuItem);

// Edit->Options Submenu, O - Mnemonic, at.gif - Icon Image File
JMenu findOptionsMenu = new JMenu("Options");
Icon atIcon = new ImageIcon ("at.gif");
findOptionsMenu.setIcon(atIcon);
findOptionsMenu.setMnemonic(KeyEvent.VK_O);

// ButtonGroup for radio buttons
ButtonGroup directionGroup = new ButtonGroup();

// Edit->Options->Forward, F - Mnemonic, in group
JRadioButtonMenuItem forwardMenuItem =
  new JRadioButtonMenuItem("Forward", true);
forwardMenuItem.addActionListener(menuListener);
forwardMenuItem.setMnemonic(KeyEvent.VK_F);
findOptionsMenu.add(forwardMenuItem);
directionGroup.add(forwardMenuItem);

// Edit->Options->Backward, B - Mnemonic, in group
JRadioButtonMenuItem backwardMenuItem =
  new JRadioButtonMenuItem("Backward");
backwardMenuItem.addActionListener(menuListener);
backwardMenuItem.setMnemonic(KeyEvent.VK_B);
findOptionsMenu.add(backwardMenuItem);
directionGroup.add(backwardMenuItem);

// Separator
findOptionsMenu.addSeparator();

// Edit->Options->Case Sensitive, C - Mnemonic
JCheckBoxMenuItem caseMenuItem =
  new JCheckBoxMenuItem("Case Sensitive");
caseMenuItem.addActionListener(menuListener);
caseMenuItem.setMnemonic(KeyEvent.VK_C);
findOptionsMenu.add(caseMenuItem);
editMenu.add(findOptionsMenu);
```

```
            frame.setJMenuBar(menuBar);
            frame.setSize(350, 250);
            frame.setVisible(true);
        }
    };
    EventQueue.invokeLater(runner);
  }
}
```

Menu Class Hierarchy

Now that you've seen an example of how to create the cascading menus for an application, you should have an idea of what's involved in using the Swing menu components. To help clarify, Figure 6-2 illustrates how all the Swing menu components are interrelated.

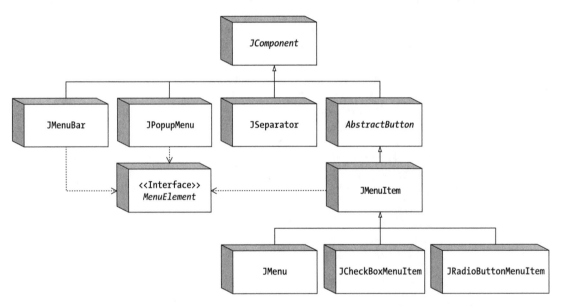

Figure 6-2. *Swing menu class hierarchy*

The most important concept illustrated in Figure 6-2 is that all the Swing menu elements, as subclasses of JComponent, are AWT components in their own right. You can place JMenuItem, JMenu, and JMenuBar components anywhere that AWT components can go, not just on a frame. In addition, because JMenuItem inherits from AbstractButton, JMenuItem and its subclasses inherit support for various icons and for HTML text labels, as described in Chapter 5.

Note Although technically possible, placing menus in locations where users wouldn't expect them to be is poor user interface design.

In addition to being part of the basic class hierarchy, each of the selectable menu components implements the MenuElement interface. The interface describes the menu behavior necessary to support keyboard and mouse navigation. The predefined menu components already implement this behavior, so you don't have to. But if you're interested in how this interface works, see the "MenuElement Interface" section later in this chapter.

Now let's take a look at the different Swing menu components.

JMenuBar Class

Swing's menu bar component is the JMenuBar. Its operation requires you to fill the menu bar with JMenu elements that have JMenuItem elements. Then you add the menu bar to a JFrame or some other user interface component requiring a menu bar. The menu bar then relies on the assistance of a SingleSelectionModel to determine which JMenu to display or post after it's selected.

Creating JMenuBar Components

JMenuBar has a single constructor of the no-argument variety: public JMenuBar(). Once you create the menu bar, you can add it to a window with the setJMenuBar() method of JApplet, JDialog, JFrame, JInternalFrame, or JRootPane. (Yes, even applets can have menu bars.)

```
JMenuBar menuBar = new JMenuBar();
// Add items to it
...
JFrame frame = new JFrame("MenuSample Example");
frame.setJMenuBar(menuBar);
```

With the system-provided look and feel types, the menu bar appears at the top of the window, below any window title (if present), with setJMenuBar(). Other look and feel types, like Aqua for the Macintosh, place the menu bar elsewhere.

You can also use the add() method of a Container to add a JMenuBar to a window. When added with the add() method, a JMenuBar is arranged by the layout manager of the Container.

After you have a JMenuBar, the remaining menu classes all work together to fill the menu bar.

Adding Menus to and Removing Menus from Menu Bars

You need to add JMenu objects to a JMenuBar. Otherwise, the only thing displayed is the border with nothing in it. There's a single method for adding menus to a JMenuBar:

```
public JMenu add(JMenu menu)
```

By default, consecutively added menus are displayed from left to right. This makes the first menu added the leftmost menu and the last menu added the rightmost menu. Menus added in between are displayed in the order in which they're added. For instance, in the sample program from Listing 6-1, the menus were added as follows:

```
JMenu fileMenu = new JMenu("File");
menuBar.add(fileMenu);
JMenu editMenu = new JMenu("Edit");
menuBar.add(editMenu);
```

■**Note** Placing a JMenuBar in the EAST or WEST area of a BorderLayout does not make the menus appear vertically, stacked one on top of another. You must customize the menu bar if you want menus to appear this way. See Figure 6-4, later in this chapter, for one implementation of a top-down menu bar.

In addition to the add() method from JMenuBar, several overloaded varieties of the add() method inherited from Container offer more control over menu positioning. Of particular interest is the add(Component component, int index) method, which allows you to specify the position in which the new JMenu is to appear. Using this second variety of add() allows you to place the File and Edit JMenu components in a JMenuBar in a different order, but with the same results:

```
menuBar.add(editMenu);
menuBar.add(fileMenu, 0);
```

If you've added a JMenu component to a JMenuBar, you can remove it with either the remove(Component component) or remove(int index) method inherited from Container:

```
bar.remove(edit);
bar.remove(0);
```

■**Tip** Adding or removing menus from a menu bar is likely to confuse users. However, sometimes it's necessary to do so—especially if you want to have an expert mode that enables a certain functionality that a nonexpert mode hides. A better approach is to disable/enable individual menu items or entire menus. If you do add or remove menus, you must then revalidate() the menu bar to display the changes.

JMenuBar Properties

Table 6-1 shows the 11 properties of JMenuBar. Half the properties are read-only, allowing you only to query the current state of the menu bar. The remaining properties allow you to alter the appearance of the menu bar by deciding whether the border of the menu bar is painted and selecting the size of the margin between menu elements. The selected property and selection model control which menu on the menu bar, if any, is currently selected. When the selected component is set to a menu on the menu bar, the menu components appear in a pop-up menu within a window.

Caution The helpMenu property, although available with a set-and-get method, is unsupported in the Swing releases through 5.0. Calling either accessor method will throw an error. With some future release of Swing, the helpMenu property will likely make a specific JMenu the designated help menu. Exactly what happens when a menu is flagged as the help menu is specific to the installed look and feel. What tends to happen is that the menu becomes the last, or rightmost, menu.

Table 6-1. *JMenuBar Properties*

Property Name	Data Type	Access
accessibleContext	AccessibleContext	Read-only
borderPainted	boolean	Read-write
component	Component	Read-only
helpMenu	JMenu	Read-write
margin	Insets	Read-write
menuCount	int	Read-only
selected	boolean/Component	Read-write
selectionModel	SingleSelectionModel	Read-write
subElements	MenuElement[ ]	Read-only
UI	MenuBarUI	Read-write
UIClassID	String	Read-only

Note The selected property of JMenuBar is nonstandard. The getter method returns a boolean to indicate if a menu component is selected on the menu bar. The setter method accepts a Component argument to select a component on the menu bar.

Customizing a JMenuBar Look and Feel

Each predefined Swing look and feel provides a different appearance and set of default UIResource values for the JMenuBar and each of the menu components. Figure 6-3 shows the appearance of all these menu components for the preinstalled set of look and feel types: Motif, Windows, and Ocean.

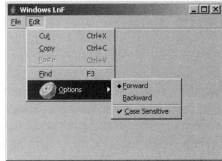

Motif   Windows

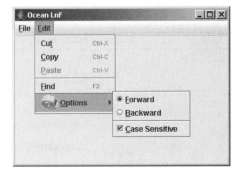

Ocean

Figure 6-3. *Menu components under different look and feel types*

In regard to the specific appearance of the JMenuBar, the available set of UIResource-related properties is shown in Table 6-2. There are 12 properties available for the JMenuBar component.

Table 6-2. *JMenuBar UIResource Elements*

Property String	Object Type
MenuBar.actionMap	ActionMap
MenuBar.background	Color
MenuBar.border	Border
MenuBar.borderColor	Color
MenuBar.darkShadow	Color
MenuBar.font	Font
MenuBar.foreground	Color
MenuBar.gradient	List
MenuBar.highlight	Color
MenuBar.shadow	Color
MenuBar.windowBindings	Object[ ]
MenuBarUI	String

If you want a vertical menu bar, instead of a horizontal one, simply change the LayoutManager of the menu bar component. A setup such as a 0 row by 1 column GridLayout does the job, as shown in the following example, because the number of rows will grow infinitely for each JMenu added:

```
import java.awt.*;
import javax.swing.*;
public class VerticalMenuBar extends JMenuBar {
  private static final LayoutManager grid = new GridLayout(0,1);
  public VerticalMenuBar() {
    setLayout(grid);
  }
}
```

Moving the menu bar shown in Figure 6-1 to the east side of a BorderLayout and making it a VerticalMenuBar instead of a JMenuBar produces the setup shown in Figure 6-4. Although the vertical menu bar may look a little unconventional here, it's more desirable to have menu items appearing stacked vertically, rather than horizontally, on the right (or left) side of a window. You may, however, want to change the MenuBar.border property to a more appropriate border.

Figure 6-4. *Using the VerticalMenuBar*

■**Note** Changing the layout manager of the JMenuBar has one negative side effect: Because top-level menus are pull-down menus, open menus on a vertical bar will obscure the menu bar. If you want to correct this pop-up placement behavior, you must extend the JMenu class and override its protected getPopupMenuOrigin() method in order to make the pop-up menu span out, rather than drop down.

SingleSelectionModel Interface

The SingleSelectionModel interface describes an index into an integer-indexed data structure where an element can be selected. The data structure behind the interface facade is most likely an array or vector in which repeatedly accessing the same position is guaranteed to return the same object. The SingleSelectionModel interface is the selection model for a JMenuBar as well as a JPopupMenu. In the case of a JMenuBar, the interface describes the currently selected JMenu that needs to be painted. In the case of a JPopupMenu, the interface describes the currently selected JMenuItem.

■**Note** SingleSelectionModel also serves as the selection model for JTabbedPane, a class described in Chapter 11.

The interface definition for SingleSelectionModel follows:

```
public interface SingleSelectionModel {
  // Listeners
  public void addChangeListener(ChangeListener listener);
  public void removeChangeListener(ChangeListener listener);
  // Properties
  public int getSelectedIndex();
  public void setSelectedIndex(int index);
  public boolean isSelected();
  // Other Methods
  public void clearSelection();
}
```

As you can see, in addition to the selection index, the interface requires maintenance of a ChangeListener list to be notified when the selection index changes.

The default Swing-provided implementation of SingleSelectionModel is the DefaultSingleSelectionModel class. For both JMenuBar and JPopupMenu, it's very unlikely that you will change their selection model from this default implementation.

The DefaultSingleSelectionModel implementation manages the list of ChangeListener objects. In addition, the model uses a value of –1 to signify that nothing is currently selected. When the selected index is –1, isSelected() returns false; otherwise, the method returns true. When the selected index changes, any registered ChangeListener objects will be notified.

JMenuItem Class

The JMenuItem component is the predefined component that a user selects on a menu bar. As a subclass of AbstractButton, JMenuItem acts as a specialized button component that behaves similarly to a JButton. Besides being a subclass of AbstractButton, the JMenuItem class shares the data model of JButton (ButtonModel interface and DefaultButtonModel implementation).

Creating JMenuItem Components

Six constructors for JMenuItem follow. They allow you to initialize the menu item's string or icon label and the mnemonic of the menu item. There's no explicit constructor permitting you to set all three options at creation time, unless you make them part of an Action.

```
public JMenuItem()
JMenuItem jMenuItem = new JMenuItem();

public JMenuItem(Icon icon)
Icon atIcon = new ImageIcon("at.gif");
JMenuItem jMenuItem = new JMenuItem(atIcon);

public JMenuItem(String text)
JMenuItem jMenuItem = new JMenuItem("Cut");

public JMenuItem(String text, Icon icon)
Icon atIcon = new ImageIcon("at.gif");
JMenuItem jMenuItem = new JMenuItem("Options", atIcon);

public JMenuItem(String text, int mnemonic)
JMenuItem jMenuItem = new JMenuItem("Cut", KeyEvent.VK_T);

public JMenuItem(Action action)
Action action = ...;
JMenuItem jMenuItem = new JMenuItem(action);
```

The mnemonic allows you to select the menu through keyboard navigation. For instance, you can simply press Alt-T on a Windows platform to select the Cut menu item if the item appears on an Edit menu that is already open. The mnemonic for a menu item usually appears underlined within the text label for the menu. However, if the letter doesn't appear within the text label or if there is no text label, the user will have no visual clue as to its setting. Letters are specified by the different key constants within the java.awt.event.KeyEvent class.

Other platforms might offer other meta-keys for selecting mnemonics. On UNIX, the meta-key is also an Alt key; on a Macintosh, it's the Command key.

Note Adding a JMenuItem with a label of "-" doesn't create a menu separator as it did with AWT's MenuItem.

JMenuItem Properties

The JMenuItem class has many properties. Roughly 100 properties are inherited through its various superclasses. The 10 properties specific to JMenuItem are shown in Table 6-3.

Table 6-3. *JMenuItem Properties*

Property Name	Data Type	Access
accelerator	KeyStroke	Read-write bound
accessibleContext	AccessibleContext	Read-only
armed	boolean	Read-write
component	Component	Read-only
enabled	boolean	Write-only bound
menuDragMouseListeners	MenuDragMouseListener[ ]	Read-only
menuKeyListeners	MenuKeyListener[ ]	Read-only
subElements	MenuElement[ ]	Read-only
UI	MenuElementUI	Write-only bound
UIClassID	String	Read-only

One truly interesting property is accelerator. As explained in Chapter 2, KeyStroke is a factory class that lets you create instances based on key and modifier combinations. For instance, the following statements, from the example in Listing 6-1 earlier in this chapter, associate Ctrl-X as the accelerator for one particular menu item:

```
KeyStroke ctrlXKeyStroke=KeyStroke.getKeyStroke("control X");
cutMenuItem.setAccelerator(ctrlXKeyStroke);
```

The read-only component and subElements properties are part of the MenuElement interface, which JMenuItem implements. The component property is the menu item renderer (the JMenuItem itself). The subElements property is empty (that is, an empty array, not null), because a JMenuItem has no children.

■**Note** Swing menus don't use AWT's MenuShortcut class.

Handling JMenuItem Events

You can handle events within a JMenuItem in at least five different ways. The component inherits the ability to allow you to listen for the firing of ChangeEvent and ActionEvent through the ChangeListener and ActionListener registration methods of AbstractButton. In addition, the JMenuItem component supports registering MenuKeyListener and MenuDragMouseListener objects when MenuKeyEvent and MenuDragMouseEvent events happen. These techniques are discussed in the following sections. A fifth way is to pass an Action to the JMenuItem constructor, which is like a specialized way of listening with an ActionListener. For more on using Action, see the discussion of using Action objects with menus, in the "JMenu Class" section a little later in this chapter.

Listening to JMenuItem Events with a ChangeListener

Normally, you wouldn't register a ChangeListener with a JMenuItem. However, demonstrating one hypothetical case helps to clarify the data model changes of the JMenuItem with respect to its ButtonModel. The changes with regard to arming, pressing, and selecting are the same as with a JButton. However, their naming might be a little confusing because the selected property of the model is never set.

A JMenuItem is *armed* when the mouse passes over the menu choice and it becomes selected. A JMenuItem is *pressed* when the user releases the mouse button over it. Immediately after being pressed, the menu item becomes unpressed and unarmed. Between the menu item being pressed and unpressed, the AbstractButton is notified of the model changes, causing any registered ActionListener objects of the menu item to be notified. The button model for a plain JMenuItem never reports being selected. If you move the mouse to another menu item without selecting, the first menu item automatically becomes unarmed. To help you better visualize the different changes, Figure 6-5 shows a sequence diagram.

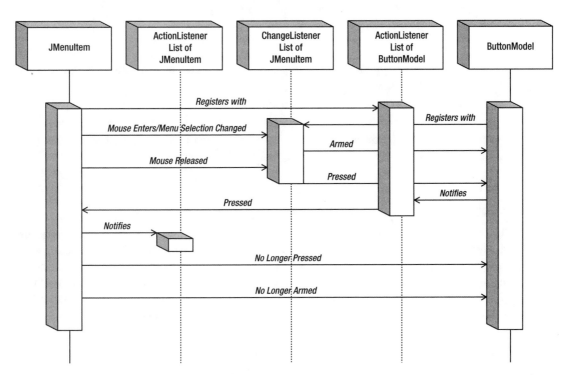

Figure 6-5. *JMenuItem selection sequence diagram*

■**Note** Subclasses of JMenuItem can have their button model selected property set, like a radio button—but the predefined JMenuItem cannot.

Listening to JMenuItem Events with an ActionListener

The better listener to attach to a JMenuItem is the ActionListener, or passing an Action to the constructor. It allows you to find out when a menu item is selected. Any registered ActionListener objects would be notified when a user releases the mouse button over a JMenuItem that is part of an open menu. Registered listeners are also notified if the user employs the keyboard (whether with arrow keys or mnemonics) or presses the menu item's keyboard accelerator to make a selection.

You must add an ActionListener to every JMenuItem for which you want an action to happen when selected. There's no automatic shortcut allowing you to register an ActionListener with a JMenu or JMenuBar and have all their contained JMenuItem objects notify a single ActionListener.

The sample program shown in Listing 6-1 associates the same ActionListener with every JMenuItem:

```
class MenuActionListener implements ActionListener {
  public void actionPerformed(ActionEvent e) {
    System.out.println("Selected: " + e.getActionCommand());
  }
}
```

However, more frequently, you would associate a different action with each item, so that each menu item can respond differently.

■**Tip** Instead of creating a custom ActionListener for the component, and adding it as a listener, you can also create a custom Action and call setAction() on the component.

Listening to JMenuItem Events with a MenuKeyListener

The MenuKeyEvent is a special kind of KeyEvent used internally by the user interface classes for a JMenu and JMenuItem, allowing the components to listen for when their keyboard mnemonic is pressed. To listen for this keyboard input, each menu component registers a MenuKeyListener to pay attention to the appropriate input. If the keyboard mnemonic is pressed, the event is consumed and not passed to any registered listeners. If the keyboard mnemonic is not pressed, any registered key listeners (instead of menu key listeners) are notified.

The MenuKeyListener interface definition follows:

```
public interface MenuKeyListener extends EventListener {
  public void menuKeyPressed(MenuKeyEvent e);
  public void menuKeyReleased(MenuKeyEvent e);
  public void menuKeyTyped(MenuKeyEvent e);
}
```

Normally, you wouldn't register objects as this type of listener yourself, although you could if you wanted to. If you do, and if a MenuKeyEvent happens (that is, a key is pressed/released), every JMenu on the JMenuBar will be notified, as will every JMenuItem (or subclass) on an open menu with a registered MenuKeyListener. That includes disabled menu items so that they can consume a pressed mnemonic. The definition of the MenuKeyEvent class follows:

```
public class MenuKeyEvent extends KeyEvent {
  public MenuKeyEvent(Component source, int id, long when, int modifiers,
    int keyCode, char keyChar, MenuElement path[], MenuSelectionManager mgr);
  public MenuSelectionManager getMenuSelectionManager();
  public MenuElement[] getPath();
}
```

It's the job of the MenuSelectionManager to determine the current selection path. The selection path is the set of menu elements from the top-level JMenu on the JMenuBar to the selected components. For the most part, the manager works behind the scenes, and you never need to worry about it.

Listening to JMenuItem Events with a MenuDragMouseListener

Like MenuKeyEvent, the MenuDragMouseEvent is a special kind of event used internally by the user interface classes for JMenu and JMenuItem. As its name implies, the MenuDragMouseEvent is a special kind of MouseEvent. By monitoring when a mouse is moved within an open menu, the user interface classes use the listener to maintain the selection path, thus determining the currently selected menu item. Its definition follows:

```
public interface MenuDragMouseListener extends EventListener {
  public void menuDragMouseDragged(MenuDragMouseEvent e);
  public void menuDragMouseEntered(MenuDragMouseEvent e);
  public void menuDragMouseExited(MenuDragMouseEvent e);
  public void menuDragMouseReleased(MenuDragMouseEvent e);
}
```

As with the MenuKeyListener, normally you don't listen for this event yourself. If you're interested in when a menu or submenu is about to be displayed, the better listener to register is the MenuListener, which can be registered with the JMenu, but not with an individual JMenuItem. You'll look at this in the next section, which describes JMenu.

The definition of the MenuDragMouseEvent class, the argument to each of the MenuDragMouseListener methods, is as follows:

```
public class MenuDragMouseEvent extends MouseEvent {
  public MenuDragMouseEvent(Component source, int id, long when, int modifiers,
    int x, int y, int clickCount, boolean popupTrigger, MenuElement path[],
    MenuSelectionManager mgr);
  public MenuSelectionManager getMenuSelectionManager();
  public MenuElement[] getPath();
}
```

Customizing a JMenuItem Look and Feel

As with the JMenuBar, the predefined look and feel types each provide a different JMenuItem appearance and set of default UIResource values. Figure 6-3 showed the appearance of the JMenuItem component for the preinstalled set: Motif, Windows, and Ocean.

The available set of UIResource-related properties for a JMenuItem are shown in Table 6-4. The JMenuItem component offers 20 different properties.

Table 6-4. *JMenuItem UIResource Elements*

Property String	Object Type
MenuItem.acceleratorDelimiter	String
MenuItem.acceleratorFont	Font
MenuItem.acceleratorForeground	Color
MenuItem.acceleratorSelectionForeground	Color
MenuItem.actionMap	ActionMap
MenuItem.arrowIcon	Icon
MenuItem.background	Color
MenuItem.border	Border
MenuItem.borderPainted	Boolean
MenuItem.checkIcon	Icon
MenuItem.commandSound	String
MenuItem.disabledForeground	Color
MenuItem.font	Font
MenuItem.foreground	Color
MenuItem.margin	Insets
MenuItem.opaque	Boolean
MenuItem.selectionBackground	Color
MenuItem.selectionForeground	Color
MenuItem.textIconGap	Integer
MenuItemUI	String

JMenu Class

The JMenu component is the basic menu item container that is placed on a JMenuBar. When a JMenu is selected, the menu displays the contained menu items within a JPopupMenu. As with JMenuItem, the data model for the JMenu is an implementation of ButtonModel, or more specifically, DefaultButtonModel.

Creating JMenu Components

Four constructors for JMenu allow you to initialize the string label of the menu if desired:

```
public JMenu()
JMenu jMenu = new JMenu();

public JMenu(String label)
JMenu jMenu = new JMenu("File");

public JMenu(String label, boolean useTearOffs)

public JMenu(Action action)
Action action = ...;
JMenu jMenu = new JMenu(action);
```

One constructor is for using a tear-off menu. However, tear-off menus aren't currently supported; therefore, the argument is ignored. The fourth constructor pulls the properties of the menu from an Action.

■**Note** Tear-off menus are menus that appear in a window and remain open after selection, instead of automatically closing.

Adding Menu Items to a JMenu

Once you have a JMenu, you need to add JMenuItem objects to it; otherwise, the menu will not display any choices. There are five methods for adding menu items defined within JMenu and one for adding a separator:

```
public JMenuItem add(JMenuItem menuItem);
public JMenuItem add(String label);
public Component add(Component component);
public Component add(Component component, int index);
public JMenuItem add(Action action);
public void addSeparator();
```

In Listing 6-1 earlier in this chapter, all the JMenuItem components were added to JMenu components with the first add() method. As a shortcut, you can pass the text label for a JMenuItem to the add() method of JMenu. This will create the menu item, set its label, and pass back the new menu item component. You can then bind a menu item event handler to this newly obtained menu item. The third add() method shows that you can place any Component on a JMenu, not solely a JMenuItem. The fourth add() lets you position the component. The last add() variety, with the Action argument, will be discussed in the next section of this chapter.

You can add separator bars with the addSeparator() method of JMenu. For instance, in Listing 6-1, the File menu was created with code similar to the following:

```
JMenu fileMenu = new JMenu("File");
JMenuItem newMenuItem = new JMenuItem("New");
fileMenu.add(newMenuItem);
JMenuItem openMenuItem = new JMenuItem("Open");
fileMenu.add(openMenuItem);
JMenuItem closeMenuItem = new JMenuItem("Close");
fileMenu.add(closeMenuItem);
fileMenu.addSeparator();
JMenuItem saveMenuItem = new JMenuItem("Save");
fileMenu.add(saveMenuItem);
fileMenu.addSeparator();
JMenuItem exitMenuItem = new JMenuItem("Exit");
fileMenu.add(exitMenuItem);
```

Notice the addSeparator() calls wrapped around the call to add the Save menu item.

In addition to adding menu items at the end of a menu, you can insert them at specific positions or insert a separator at a specific position, as follows:

```
public JMenuItem insert(JMenuItem menuItem, int pos);
public JMenuItem insert(Action a, int pos);
public void insertSeparator(int pos);
```

When a menu item is added to a JMenu, it's added to an internal JPopupMenu.

Using Action Objects with Menus

The Action interface and its associated classes are described in Chapter 2. An Action is an extension of the ActionListener interface and contains some special properties for customizing components associated with its implementations.

With the help of the AbstractAction implementation, you can easily define text labels, icons, mnemonics, tooltip text, enabled status, and an ActionListener apart from a component. Then you can create a component with an associated Action and not need to give the component a text label, icon, mnemonics, tooltip text, enabled status, or ActionListener, because those attributes would come from the Action. For a more complete description, refer to Chapter 2.

To demonstrate, Listing 6-2 creates a specific implementation of AbstractAction and adds it to a JMenu multiple times. Once the Action is added to a JMenu, selecting the JMenuItem will display a pop-up dialog box with the help of the JOptionPane class, a topic covered in Chapter 9.

Listing 6-2. *About Action Definition*

```
import java.awt.*;
import java.awt.event.*;
import javax.swing.*;
public class ShowAction extends AbstractAction {
  Component parentComponent;
  public ShowAction(Component parentComponent) {
    super("About");
    putValue(Action.MNEMONIC_KEY, new Integer(KeyEvent.VK_A));
    this.parentComponent = parentComponent;
  }
```

```
public void actionPerformed(ActionEvent actionEvent) {
    Runnable runnable = new Runnable() {
        public void run() {
            JOptionPane.showMessageDialog(
                parentComponent, "About Swing",
                "About Box V2.0", JOptionPane.INFORMATION_MESSAGE);
        }
    };
    EventQueue.invokeLater(runnable);
  }
}
```

The next source creates a ShowAction and a JMenuItem for the File and Edit menus in the sample program (Listing 6-1). Without explicitly setting the menu item properties, it will then have an "About" text label and an A mnemonic, and will perform the defined actionPerformed() method as its ActionListener. In fact, you can create the Action once, and then associate it with as many places as necessary (or other components that support adding Action objects).

```
Action showAction = new ShowAction(aComponent);
JMenuItem fileAbout = new JMenuItem(showAction);
fileMenu.add(fileAbout);
JMenuItem editAbout = new JMenuItem(showAction);
editMenu.add(editAbout);
```

One complexity-busting side effect when using AbstractAction is that it lets you disable the Action with setEnabled(false), which, in turn, will disable all components created from it.

JMenu Properties

Besides the 100-plus inherited properties of JMenu, 16 properties are available from JMenu-specific methods, as shown in Table 6-5. Several of the properties override the behavior of the inherited properties. For instance, the setter method for the accelerator property throws an error if you try to assign such a property. In other words, accelerators aren't supported within JMenu objects. The remaining properties describe the current state of the JMenu object and its contained menu components.

Table 6-5. *JMenu Properties*

Property Name	Data Type	Access
accelerator	KeyStroke	Write-only
accessibleContext	AccessibleContext	Read-only
component	Component	Read-only
delay	int	Read-write
itemCount	int	Read-only
menuComponentCount	int	Read-only
menuComponents	Component[ ]	Read-only

Table 6-5. *JMenu Properties (Continued)*

Property Name	Data Type	Access
menuListeners	MenuListener[ ]	Read-only
model	ButtonModel	Write-only bound
popupMenu	JPopupMenu	Read-only
popupMenuVisible	boolean	Read-write
selected	boolean	Read-write
subElements	MenuElement[ ]	Read-only
tearOff	boolean	Read-only
topLevelMenu	boolean	Read-only
UIClassID	String	Read-only

■**Tip** Keep in mind that many property methods are inherited and that the parent class might offer a getter method where the current class defines only a new setter method, or vice versa.

The delay property represents the value for the time that elapses between selection of a JMenu and posting of the JPopupMenu. By default, this value is zero, meaning that the submenu will appear immediately. Trying to set the value to a negative setting will throw an IllegalArgumentException.

■**Caution** Since there is no support for tear-off menus, if you try to access the tearOff property, an error will be thrown.

Selecting Menu Components

Normally, you don't need to listen for the selection of JMenu components. You listen for only selection of individual JMenuItem components. Nevertheless, you may be interested in the different ways that ChangeEvent works with a JMenu as compared with a JMenuItem. In addition, a MenuEvent can notify you whenever a menu is posted or canceled.

Listening to JMenu Events with a ChangeListener

As with a JMenuItem, you can register a ChangeListener with a JMenu if you're interested in making changes to the underlying ButtonModel. Surprisingly, the only possible state change to the ButtonModel with a JMenu is with the selected property. When selected, the JMenu displays its menu items. When not selected, the pop-up goes away.

Listening to JMenu Events with a MenuListener

The better way to listen for when a pop-up is displayed or hidden is by registering MenuListener objects with your JMenu objects. Its definition follows:

```
public interface MenuListener extends EventListener {
  public void menuCanceled(MenuEvent e);
  public void menuDeselected(MenuEvent e);
  public void menuSelected(MenuEvent e);
}
```

With a registered MenuListener, you're notified when a JMenu is selected before the pop-up menu is opened with the menu's choices. This allows you to customize its menu choices on the fly at runtime, with some potential interaction performance penalties. Besides being told when the associated pop-up menu is to be posted, you're also notified when the menu has been deselected and when the menu has been canceled. As the following MenuEvent class definition shows, the only piece of information that comes with the event is the source (the menu):

```
public class MenuEvent extends EventObject {
  public MenuEvent(Object source);
}
```

■**Tip** If you choose to customize the items on a JMenu dynamically, be sure to call revalidate(), because the component waits until you are done before updating the display.

Customizing a JMenu Look and Feel

As with the JMenuBar and JMenuItem, the predefined look and feel classes provide a different JMenu appearance and set of default UIResource values. Figure 6-3 shows the appearance of the JMenu object for the preinstalled set of look and feel types.

The available set of UIResource-related properties for a JMenu is shown in Table 6-6. For the JMenu component, there are 30 different properties.

Table 6-6. *JMenu UIResource Elements*

Property String	Object Type
menu	Color
Menu.acceleratorDelimiter	String
Menu.acceleratorFont	Font
Menu.acceleratorForeground	Color
Menu.acceleratorSelectionForeground	Color
Menu.ActionMap	ActionMap
Menu.arrowIcon	Icon
Menu.background	Color
Menu.border	Border
Menu.borderPainted	Boolean
Menu.checkIcon	Icon
Menu.delay	Integer
Menu.disabledForeground	Color
Menu.font	Font
Menu.foreground	Color
Menu.margin	Insets
Menu.menuPopupOffsetX	Integer
Menu.menuPopupOffsetY	Integer
Menu.opaque	Boolean
Menu.selectionBackground	Color
Menu.selectionForeground	Color
Menu.shortcutKeys	int[ ]
Menu.submenuPopupOffsetX	Integer
Menu.submenuPopupOffsetY	Integer
Menu.textIconGap	Integer
Menu.useMenuBarBackgroundForTopLevel	Boolean
menuPressedItemB	Color
menuPressedItemF	Color
menuText	Color
MenuUI	String

JSeparator Class

The JSeparator class is a special component that acts as a separator on a JMenu. The JPopupMenu and JToolBar classes also support separators, but each uses its own subclass of JSeparator. In addition to being placed on a menu, the JSeparator can be used anywhere you want to use a horizontal or vertical line to separate different areas of a screen.

The JSeparator is strictly a visual component; therefore, it has no data model.

Creating JSeparator Components

To create a separator for a JMenu, you don't directly create a JSeparator, although you can. Instead, you call the addSeparator() method of JMenu, and the menu will create the separator and add the separator as its next item. The fact that it's a JSeparator (which isn't a JMenuItem subclass) is hidden. There's also an insertSeparator(int index) method of JMenu that allows you to add a separator at a specific position on the menu, that isn't necessarily the next slot.

If you plan to use a JSeparator away from a menu (for example, to visually separate two panels in a layout), you should use one of the two constructors for JSeparator:

public JSeparator()
```
JSeparator jSeparator = new JSeparator();
```

public JSeparator(int orientation)
```
JSeparator jSeparator = new JSeparator(JSeparator.VERTICAL);
```

These constructors allow you to create a horizontal or vertical separator. If an orientation isn't specified, the orientation is horizontal. If you want to explicitly specify an orientation, you use either of the JSeparator constants of HORIZONTAL and VERTICAL.

JSeparator Properties

After you have a JSeparator, you add it to the screen like any other component. The initial dimensions of the component are empty (zero width and height), so if the layout manager of the screen asks the component what size it would like to be, the separator will reply that it needs no space. On the other hand, if the layout manager offers a certain amount of space, the separator will use the space if the orientation is appropriate. For instance, adding a horizontal JSeparator to the north side of a BorderLayout panel draws a separator line across the screen. However, adding a horizontal JSeparator to the east side of the same panel would result in nothing being drawn. For a vertical JSeparator, the behavior is reversed: The north side would be empty and a vertical line would appear on the east side.

The four properties of JSeparator are listed in Table 6-7.

Table 6-7. *JSeparator Properties*

Property Name	Data Type	Access
accessibleContext	AccessibleContext	Read-only
orientation	int	Read-write bound
UI	SeparatorUI	Read-write bound
UIClassID	String	Read-only

■**Caution** If the orientation property isn't set to a value equivalent to either JSeparator.HORIZONTAL or JSeparator.VERTICAL, an IllegalArgumentException is thrown.

Customizing a JSeparator Look and Feel

The appearance of the JSeparator under the preinstalled set of look and feel types is shown with the other menu components in Figure 6-3.

The available set of UIResource-related properties for a JSeparator is shown in Table 6-8. For the JSeparator component, five different properties are available.

Table 6-8. *JSeparator UIResource Elements*

Property String	Object Type
Separator.background	Color
Separator.foreground	Color
Separator.insets	Insets
Separator.thickness	Integer
SeparatorUI	String

■**Caution** Two additional properties, highlight and shadow, are present but deprecated and should not be used.

JPopupMenu Class

The JPopupMenu component is the container for pop-up menu components, displayable anywhere and used for support by JMenu. When a programmer-defined triggering event happens, you display the JPopupMenu, and the menu displays the contained menu components. Like JMenuBar, JPopupMenu uses the SingleSelectionModel to manage the currently selected element.

Creating JPopupMenu Components

There are two constructors for JPopupMenu:

public JPopupMenu()
```
JPopupMenu jPopupMenu = new JPopupMenu();
```

public JPopupMenu(String title)
```
JPopupMenu jPopupMenu = new JPopupMenu("Welcome");
```

Only one allows you to initialize the title for the menu, if desired. What happens with the title depends on the installed look and feel. The currently installed look and feel may ignore the title.

Adding Menu Items to a JPopupMenu

As with a JMenu, once you have a JPopupMenu, you need to add menu item objects to it; otherwise, the menu will be empty. There are three JPopupMenu methods for adding menu items and one for adding a separator:

```
public JMenuItem add(JMenuItem menuItem);
public JMenuItem add(String label);
public JMenuItem add(Action action);
public void addSeparator();
```

In addition, an add() method is inherited from Container for adding regular AWT components:

```
public Component add(Component component);
```

■**Note** It generally isn't wise to mix lightweight Swing components with heavyweight AWT components. However, because pop-up menus are more apt to be on top, it's less of an issue in this case.

The natural way of adding menu items is with the first add() method. You create the menu item independently of the pop-up menu, including defining its behavior, and then you attach it to the menu. With the second variety of add(), you must attach an event handler to the menu item returned from the method; otherwise, the menu choice won't respond when selected. The following source demonstrates the two approaches. Which you use depends entirely on your preference. A visual programming environment like JBuilder will use the first. Because the first approach is inherently less complex, most, if not all, programmers should also use the first approach.

```
JPopupMenu popupenu = new JPopupMenu();
ActionListener anActionListener = ...;
// The first way
JMenuItem firstItem = new JMenuItem("Hello");
firstItem.addActionListener(anActionListener);
popupMenu.add(firstItem);
// The second way
JMenuItem secondItem = popupMenu.add("World");
secondItem.addActionListener(anActionListener);
```

Using an Action to create a menu item works the same with JPopupMenu as it does with JMenu. However, according to the Javadoc for the JPopupMenu class, using the Action variety of the add() method is discouraged. Instead, pass the Action to the constructor for JMenuItem, or configure it with `setAction()`, and then add that to the `JPopupMenu`. Why the method isn't just deprecated isn't clear.

Lastly, you can add a menu separator with the `addSeparator()` method.

As well as adding menu items at the end of a menu, you can insert them at specific positions or insert a separator at a specific position:

```
public JMenuItem insert(Component component, int position);
public JMenuItem insert(Action action, int position);
```

There's no `insertSeparator()` method as there is with `JMenu`. But you can use the `add(Component component, int position)` method inherited from `Container`. If you want to remove components, use the `remove(Component component)` method specific to `JPopupMenu`.

■**Note** Accelerators on attached `JMenuItem` objects are ignored. Mnemonics might also be ignored depending on the currently installed look and feel.

Displaying the JPopupMenu

Unlike the `JMenu`, simply populating the pop-up menu isn't sufficient to use it. You need to associate the pop-up menu with an appropriate component. Prior to the 5.0 release of Swing, you needed to add event-handling code to trigger the display of the pop-up menu. Now, all you need to do is call the `setComponentPopupMenu()` method for the Swing component you wish to associate the pop-up menu with. When the platform-specific triggering event happens, the pop-up menu is automatically displayed.

■**Note** Why change the way pop-up menu display is triggered? The old code was very tightly tied to mouse events. It didn't connect well with the accessibility framework. And the same code was being added every-where to just show the pop-up menu at the x, y coordinates of the invoker.

You simply need to create an instance of `JPopupMenu` and attach it to any component you want to have display the pop-up menu, as follows:

```
JPopupMenu popupMenu = ...;
aComponent.setComponentPopupMenu(popupMenu);
```

The methods of `JComponent` that are important to pop-up menus are `getComponentPopupMenu()`, `setComponentPopupMenu()`, `getInheritsPopupMenu()`, `setInheritsPopupMenu()`, and `getPopupLocation()`. The `setInheritsPopupMenu()` method accepts a `boolean` argument. When `true`, and no component pop-up menu has been directly set for the component, the parent container will be explored for a pop-up.

JPopupMenu Properties

The 16 properties of JPopupMenu are listed in Table 6-9. Many more properties are also inherited through JComponent, Container, and Component.

Table 6-9. *JPopupMenu Properties*

Property Name	Data Type	Access
accessibleContext	AccessibleContext	Read-only
borderPainted	boolean	Read-write
component	Component	Read-only
invoker	Component	Read-only
label	String	Read-write bound
lightWeightPopupEnabled	boolean	Read-write
margin	Insets	Read-only
menuKeyListeners	MenuKeyListener[ ]	Read-only
popupMenuListeners	PopupMenuListener[ ]	Read-only
popupSize	Dimension	Write-only
selected	Component	Write-only
selectionModel	SingleSelectionModel	Read-write
subElements	MenuElement[ ]	Read-only
UI	PopupMenuUI	Read-write bound
UIClassID	String	Read-only
visible	boolean	Read-write

The most interesting property of JPopupMenu is lightWeightPopupEnabled. Normally, the JPopupMenu tries to avoid creating new heavyweight components for displaying its menu items. Instead, the pop-up menu uses a JPanel when the JPopupMenu can be displayed completely within the outermost window boundaries. Otherwise, if the menu items don't fit, the JPopupMenu uses a JWindow. If, however, you're mixing lightweight and heavyweight components on different window layers, displaying the pop-up within a JPanel might not work, because a heavyweight component displayed in the layer of the menu will appear in front of the JPanel. To correct this behavior, the pop-up menu can use a Panel for displaying the menu choices. By default, the JPopupMenu never uses a Panel.

■Note When the JPopupMenu is displayed in either a JPanel or a Panel, the outermost window relies on the layering effect of the JRootPane to ensure that the pop-up panel is displayed at the appropriate position in front of the other components. Chapter 8 describes the JRootPane class in more detail.

If you need to enable the display of a Panel, you can configure it at the individual JPopupMenu level or for your entire applet or application. At the individual pop-up level, just set the lightWeightPopupEnabled property to false. At the system level, this is done as follows:

```
// From now on, all JPopupMenus will be heavyweight
JPopupMenu.setDefaultLightWeightPopupEnabled(false);
```

The method must be called before creating the pop-up menu. JPopupMenu objects created before the change will have the original value (the default is true).

Watching for Pop-Up Menu Visibility

Like the JMenu, the JPopupMenu has a special event/listener combination to watch for when the pop-up menu is about to become visible, invisible, or canceled. The event is PopupMenuEvent, and the listener is PopupMenuListener. The event class simply references the source pop-up menu of the event.

```
public class PopupMenuEvent extends EventObject {
  public PopupMenuEvent(Object source);
}
```

When a JPopupMenu fires the event, any registered PopupMenuListener objects are notified through one of its three interface methods. This lets you customize the current menu items based on the system state or who/what the pop-up menu invoker happens to be. The PopupMenuListener interface definition follows:

```
public interface PopupMenuListener extends EventListener {
  public void popupMenuCanceled(PopupMenuEvent e);
  public void popupMenuWillBecomeInvisible(PopupMenuEvent e);
  public void popupMenuWillBecomeVisible(PopupMenuEvent e);
}
```

Customizing a JPopupMenu Look and Feel

Each installable Swing look and feel provides a different JPopupMenu appearance and set of default UIResource values. Figure 6-6 shows the appearance of the JPopupMenu component for the preinstalled set of look and feel types: Motif, Windows, and Ocean. Notice that of the predefined look and feel classes, only Motif uses the title property of the JPopupMenu.

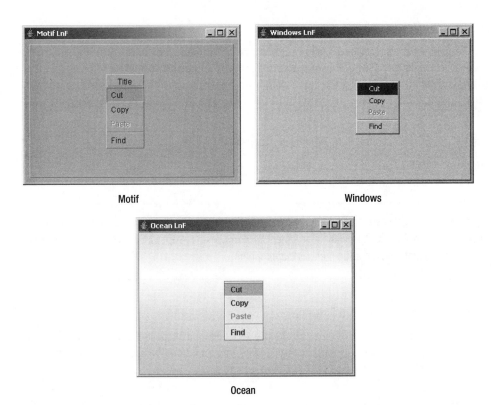

Motif

Windows

Ocean

Figure 6-6. *JPopupMenu under different look and feel types*

The available set of UIResource-related properties for a JPopupMenu is shown in Table 6-10. For the JPopupMenu component, there are five different properties.

Table 6-10. *JPopupMenu UIResource Elements*

Property String	Object Type
PopupMenu.actionMap	ActionMap
PopupMenu.background	Color
PopupMenu.border	Border
PopupMenu.consumeEventOnClose	Boolean
PopupMenu.font	Font
PopupMenu.foreground	Color
PopupMenu.popupSound	String
PopupMenu.selectedWindowInputMapBindings	Object[ ]
PopupMenu.selectedWindowInputMapBindings.RightToLeft	Object[ ]
PopupMenuSeparatorUI	String
PopupMenuUI	String

JPopupMenu.Separator Class

The JPopupMenu class maintains its own separator to permit a custom look and feel for the separator when it's on a JPopupMenu. This custom separator is an inner class to the JPopupMenu.

When you call the addSeparator() of JPopupMenu, an instance of this class is automatically created and added to the pop-up menu. In addition, you can create this separator by calling its no-argument constructor:

```
JSeparator popupSeparator = new JPopupMenu.Separator();
```

Both methods create a horizontal separator.

■**Note** If you want to change the orientation of the separator, you must call the setOrientation() method inherited from JSeparator with an argument of JPopupMenu.Separator.VERTICAL. However, having a vertical separator on a pop-up menu is inappropriate.

A Complete Pop-Up Menu Usage Example

The program in Listing 6-3 puts together all the pieces of using a JPopupMenu, including listening for selection of all the items on the menu, as well as listening for when it's displayed. The output for the program is shown in Figure 6-7, with the pop-up visible.

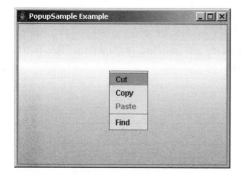

Figure 6-7. *JPopupMenu usage example output*

Listing 6-3. *PopupSample Class Definition*

```java
import java.awt.*;
import java.awt.event.*;
import javax.swing.*;
import javax.swing.event.*;

public class PopupSample {
```

```java
// Define ActionListener
static class PopupActionListener implements ActionListener {
  public void actionPerformed(ActionEvent actionEvent) {
    System.out.println("Selected: " + actionEvent.getActionCommand());
  }
}

// Define PopupMenuListener
static class MyPopupMenuListener implements PopupMenuListener {
  public void popupMenuCanceled(PopupMenuEvent popupMenuEvent) {
    System.out.println("Canceled");
  }
  public void popupMenuWillBecomeInvisible(PopupMenuEvent popupMenuEvent) {
    System.out.println("Becoming Invisible");
  }
  public void popupMenuWillBecomeVisible(PopupMenuEvent popupMenuEvent) {
    System.out.println("Becoming Visible");
  }
}

public static void main(final String args[]) {
  Runnable runner = new Runnable() {
    public void run() {
      // Create frame
      JFrame frame = new JFrame("PopupSample Example");
      frame.setDefaultCloseOperation(JFrame.EXIT_ON_CLOSE);

      ActionListener actionListener = new PopupActionListener();
      PopupMenuListener popupMenuListener = new MyPopupMenuListener();

      // Create popup menu, attach popup menu listener
      JPopupMenu popupMenu = new JPopupMenu("Title");
      popupMenu.addPopupMenuListener(popupMenuListener);

       // Cut
      JMenuItem cutMenuItem = new JMenuItem("Cut");
      cutMenuItem.addActionListener(actionListener);
      popupMenu.add(cutMenuItem);

      // Copy
      JMenuItem copyMenuItem = new JMenuItem("Copy");
      copyMenuItem.addActionListener(actionListener);
      popupMenu.add(copyMenuItem);
```

```java
        // Paste
        JMenuItem pasteMenuItem = new JMenuItem("Paste");
        pasteMenuItem.addActionListener(actionListener);
        pasteMenuItem.setEnabled(false);
        popupMenu.add(pasteMenuItem);

        // Separator
        popupMenu.addSeparator();

        // Find
        JMenuItem findMenuItem = new JMenuItem("Find");
        findMenuItem.addActionListener(actionListener);
        popupMenu.add(findMenuItem);
        JButton label = new JButton();
        frame.add(label);
        label.setComponentPopupMenu(popupMenu);

        frame.setSize(350, 250);
        frame.setVisible(true);
      }
    };
    EventQueue.invokeLater(runner);
  }
}
```

JCheckBoxMenuItem Class

Swing's `JCheckBoxMenuItem` component behaves as if you have a `JCheckBox` on a menu as a `JMenuItem`. The data model for the menu item is the `ToggleButtonModel`, described in Chapter 5. It allows the menu item to have a selected or unselected state, while showing an appropriate icon for the state. Because the data model is the `ToggleButtonModel`, when `JCheckBoxMenuItem` is placed in a `ButtonGroup`, only one component in the group is ever selected. However, this isn't the natural way to use a `JCheckBoxMenuItem` and is likely to confuse users. If you need this behavior, use `JRadioButtonMenuItem`, as described later in this chapter.

Creating JCheckBoxMenuItem Components

There are seven constructors for `JCheckBoxMenuItem`. They allow you to initialize the text label, icon, and initial state.

public JCheckBoxMenuItem()
```java
JCheckBoxMenuItem jCheckBoxMenuItem = new JCheckBoxMenuItem();
```

public JCheckBoxMenuItem(String text)
```java
JCheckBoxMenuItem jCheckBoxMenuItem = new JCheckBoxMenuItem("Boy");
```

```
public JCheckBoxMenuItem(Icon icon)
Icon boyIcon = new ImageIcon("boy-r.jpg");
JCheckBoxMenuItem jCheckBoxMenuItem = new JCheckBoxMenuItem(boyIcon);

public JCheckBoxMenuItem(String text, Icon icon)
JCheckBoxMenuItem jCheckBoxMenuItem = new JCheckBoxMenuItem("Boy", boyIcon);

public JCheckBoxMenuItem(String text, boolean state)
JCheckBoxMenuItem jCheckBoxMenuItem = new JCheckBoxMenuItem("Girl", true);

public JCheckBoxMenuItem(String text, Icon icon, boolean state)
Icon girlIcon = new ImageIcon("girl-r.jpg");
JCheckBoxMenuItem jCheckBoxMenuItem = new JCheckBoxMenuItem("Girl", girlIcon, true);

public JCheckBoxMenuItem(Action action)
Action action = ...;
JCheckBoxMenuItem jCheckBoxMenuItem = new JCheckBoxMenuItem(action);
```

Unlike the JCheckBox, the icon is part of the label and not a separate device to indicate whether something is checked. If either the text label or the icon isn't passed to the constructor, that part of the item label will be set to its default value of empty. By default, a JCheckBoxMenuItem is unselected.

■**Note** Creating a JCheckBoxMenuItem with an icon has no effect on the appearance of the check box next to the menu item. It's strictly part of the label for the JCheckBoxMenuItem.

JCheckBoxMenuItem Properties

Most of the JCheckBoxMenuItem properties are inherited from the many superclasses of JCheckBoxMenuItem. Table 6-11 lists the four properties defined by JCheckBoxMenuItem.

Table 6-11. *JCheckBoxMenuItem Properties*

Property Name	Data Type	Access
accessibleContext	AccessibleContext	Read-only
selectedObjects	Object[]	Read-only
state	boolean	Read-write
UIClassID	String	Read-only

Handling JCheckBoxMenuItem Selection Events

With a `JCheckBoxMenuItem`, you can attach many different listeners for a great variety of events:

- `MenuDragMouseListener` and `MenuKeyListener` from `JMenuItem`

- `ActionListener`, `ChangeListener`, and `ItemListener` from `AbstractButton`

- `AncestorListener` and `VetoableChangeListener` from `JComponent`

- `ContainerListener` and `PropertyChangeListener` from `Container`

- `ComponentListener`, `FocusListener`, `HierarchyBoundsListener`, `HierarchyListener`, `InputMethodListener`, `KeyListener`, `MouseListener`, `MouseMotionListener`, and `MouseWheelListener` from `Component`

Although you can listen for 18 different types of events, the most interesting are `ActionEvent` and `ItemEvent`, described next.

Listening to JCheckBoxMenuItem Events with an ActionListener

Attaching an `ActionListener` to a `JCheckBoxMenuItem` allows you to find out when the menu item is selected. The listener is told of the selection, but not of the new state. To find out the selected state, you must get the model for the event source and query the selection state, as the following sample `ActionListener` source shows. This listener modifies both the check box text and the icon label, based on the current selection state.

```
ActionListener aListener = new ActionListener() {
  public void actionPerformed(ActionEvent event) {
    Icon girlIcon = new ImageIcon("girl-r.jpg");
    Icon boyIcon = new ImageIcon("boy-r.jpg");
    AbstractButton aButton = (AbstractButton)event.getSource();
    boolean selected = aButton.getModel().isSelected();
    String newLabel;
    Icon newIcon;
    if (selected) {
      newLabel = "Girl";
      newIcon = girlIcon;
    } else {
      newLabel = "Boy";
      newIcon = boyIcon;
    }
    aButton.setText(newLabel);
    aButton.setIcon(newIcon);
  }
};
```

■**Note** Keep in mind that you can also associate an `Action` from the constructor that can do the same thing.

Listening to JCheckBoxMenuItem with an ItemListener

If you listen for JCheckBoxMenuitem selection with an ItemListener, you don't need to query the event source for the selection state—the event already carries that information. Based on this state, you respond accordingly. Re-creating the ActionListener behavior with an ItemListener requires just a few minor changes to the previously listed source, as follows:

```
ItemListener iListener = new ItemListener() {
  public void itemStateChanged(ItemEvent event) {
    Icon girlIcon = new ImageIcon("girl-r.jpg");
    Icon boyIcon = new ImageIcon("boy-r.jpg");
    AbstractButton aButton = (AbstractButton)event.getSource();
    int state = event.getStateChange();
    String newLabel;
    Icon newIcon;
    if (state == ItemEvent.SELECTED) {
      newLabel = "Girl";
      newIcon = girlIcon;
    } else {
      newLabel = "Boy";
      newIcon = boyIcon;
    }
    aButton.setText(newLabel);
    aButton.setIcon(newIcon);
  }
};
```

Customizing a JCheckBoxMenuItem Look and Feel

The appearance of the JCheckBoxMenuItem under the preinstalled set of look and feel types is shown with the other menu components in Figure 6-3.

The available set of UIResource-related properties for a JCheckBoxMenuItem is shown in Table 6-12. The JCheckBoxMenuItem component has 19 different properties.

Table 6-12. *JCheckBoxMenuItem UIResource Elements*

Property String	Object Type
CheckBoxMenuItem.acceleratorFont	Font
CheckBoxMenuItem.acceleratorForeground	Color
CheckBoxMenuItem.acceleratorSelectionForeground	Color
CheckBoxMenuItem.actionMap	ActionMap
CheckBoxMenuItem.arrowIcon	Icon
CheckBoxMenuItem.background	Color
CheckBoxMenuItem.border	Border
CheckBoxMenuItem.borderPainted	Boolean

Table 6-12. *JCheckBoxMenuItem UIResource Elements (Continued)*

Property String	Object Type
CheckBoxMenuItem.checkIcon	Icon
CheckBoxMenuItem.commandSound	String
CheckBoxMenuItem.disabledForeground	Color
CheckBoxMenuItem.font	Font
CheckBoxMenuItem.foreground	Color
CheckBoxMenuItem.gradient	List
CheckBoxMenuItem.margin	Insets
CheckBoxMenuItem.opaque	Boolean
CheckBoxMenuItem.selectionBackground	Color
CheckBoxMenuItem.selectionForeground	Color
CheckBoxMenuItemUI	String

The Icon associated with the CheckBoxMenuItem.checkIcon property key is the one displayed on the JCheckBoxMenuItem. If you don't like the default icon, you can change it with the following line of source, assuming the new icon has already been defined and created:

```
UIManager.put("CheckBoxMenuItem.checkIcon", someIcon);
```

For this new icon to display an appropriate selected image, the Icon implementation must check the state of the associated menu component within its paintIcon() method. The DiamondIcon created in Chapter 4 wouldn't work for this icon because it doesn't ask the component for its state. Instead, the state is fixed at constructor time. Listing 6-4 shows a class that represents one icon that could be used.

Listing 6-4. *State-Aware Icon Definition*

```java
import java.awt.*;
import javax.swing.*;

public class DiamondAbstractButtonStateIcon implements Icon {
  private final int width = 10;
  private final int height = 10;
  private Color color;
  private Polygon polygon;
  public DiamondAbstractButtonStateIcon(Color color) {
    this.color = color;
    initPolygon();
  }
```

```java
  private void initPolygon() {
    polygon = new Polygon();
    int halfWidth = width/2;
    int halfHeight = height/2;
    polygon.addPoint (0, halfHeight);
    polygon.addPoint (halfWidth, 0);
    polygon.addPoint (width, halfHeight);
    polygon.addPoint (halfWidth, height);
  }
  public int getIconHeight() {
    return width;
  }
  public int getIconWidth() {
    return height;
  }
  public void paintIcon(Component component, Graphics g, int x, int y) {
    boolean selected = false;
    g.setColor (color);
    g.translate (x, y);
    if (component instanceof AbstractButton) {
      AbstractButton abstractButton = (AbstractButton)component;
      selected = abstractButton.isSelected();
    }
    if (selected) {
      g.fillPolygon (polygon);
    } else {
      g.drawPolygon (polygon);
    }
    g.translate (-x, -y);
  }
}
```

Note If the `DiamondAbstractButtonStateIcon` icon were used with a component that isn't an `AbstractButton` type, the icon would always be deselected, because the selection state is a property of `AbstractButton`.

JRadioButtonMenuItem Class

The `JRadioButtonMenuItem` component has the longest name of all the Swing components. It works like a `JRadioButton`, but resides on a menu. When placed with other `JRadioButtonMenuItem` components within a `ButtonGroup`, only one component will be selected at a time. As with the `JRadioButton`, the button model for the `JRadioButtonMenuItem` is the `JToggleButton.ToggleButtonModel`.

Creating JRadioButtonMenuItem Components

The JRadioButtonMenuItem has seven constructors. They allow you to initialize the text label, icon, and initial state.

public JCheckBoxMenuItem()
```
JCheckBoxMenuItem jCheckBoxMenuItem = new JCheckBoxMenuItem();
```

public JCheckBoxMenuItem(String text)
```
JCheckBoxMenuItem jCheckBoxMenuItem = new JCheckBoxMenuItem("Boy");
```

public JCheckBoxMenuItem(Icon icon)
```
Icon boyIcon = new ImageIcon("boy-r.jpg");
JCheckBoxMenuItem jCheckBoxMenuItem = new JCheckBoxMenuItem(boyIcon);
```

public JCheckBoxMenuItem(String text, Icon icon)
```
JCheckBoxMenuItem jCheckBoxMenuItem =  new JCheckBoxMenuItem("Boy", boyIcon);
```

public JCheckBoxMenuItem(String text, boolean state)
```
JCheckBoxMenuItem jCheckBoxMenuItem = new JCheckBoxMenuItem("Girl", true);
```

public JCheckBoxMenuItem(String text, Icon icon, boolean state)
```
Icon girlIcon = new ImageIcon("girl-r.jpg");
JCheckBoxMenuItem jCheckBoxMenuItem = new JCheckBoxMenuItem("Girl", girlIcon, true);
```

public JCheckBoxMenuItem(Action action)
```
Action action = ...;
JCheckBoxMenuItem jCheckBoxMenuItem = new JCheckBoxMenuItem(action);
```

Similar to the JCheckBoxMenuItem component, the icon for the JRadioButtonMenuItem is part of the label. This is unlike the JRadioButton, in which the icon indicates whether the radio button is selected. If either the text label or icon isn't part of the constructor, that part of the item label will be empty. By default, a JRadioButtonMenuItem is unselected. If you create a JRadioButtonMenuItem that is selected and then add it to a ButtonGroup, the button group will deselect the menu item if the group already has a selected item in the group.

■**Note** After creating JRadioButtonMenuItem instances, remember to add them to a ButtonGroup, so they will work as a mutually exclusive group.

Handling JRadioButtonMenuItem Selection Events

The JRadioButtonMenuItem shares the same 18 different event/listener pairs with JCheckBoxMenuItem. To listen for selection, attaching an ActionListener is the normal approach. In addition, you might want to attach the same listener to all the JRadioButtonMenuItem objects in a ButtonGroup—after all, they're in a group for a reason. If you use the same listener, that listener can employ the current selection to perform some common operation. In other cases, such as that in Figure 6-1, selection of any JRadioButtonMenuItem option does nothing.

Only when someone selects the Find menu element would the current selection of the ButtonGroup for the set of JRadioButtonMenuItem components have any meaning.

Configuring JRadioButtonMenuItem Properties

As with JCheckBoxMenuItem, most of the JRadioButtonMenuItem properties are inherited. The two shown in Table 6-13 merely override the behavior from the superclass.

Table 6-13. *JRadioButtonMenuItem Properties*

Property Name	Data Type	Access
accessibleContext	AccessibleContext	Read-only
UIClassID	String	Read-only

Customizing a JRadioButtonMenuItem Look and Feel

The appearance of the JRadioButtonMenuItem under the preinstalled set of look and feel types is shown with the other menu components in Figure 6-3.

The available set of UIResource-related properties for a JRadioButtonMenuItem is shown in Table 6-14. For the JRadioButtonMenuItem component, there are 19 different properties.

Table 6-14. *JRadioButtonMenuItem UIResource Elements*

Property String	Object Type
RadioButtonMenuItem.acceleratorFont	Font
RadioButtonMenuItem.acceleratorForeground	Color
RadioButtonMenuItem.acceleratorSelectionForeground	Color
RadioButtonMenuItem.actionMap	ActionMap
RadioButtonMenuItem.arrowIcon	Icon
RadioButtonMenuItem.background	Color
RadioButtonMenuItem.border	Border
RadioButtonMenuItem.borderPainted	Boolean
RadioButtonMenuItem.checkIcon	Icon
RadioButtonMenuItem.commandSound	String
RadioButtonMenuItem.disabledForeground	Color
RadioButtonMenuItem.font	Font
RadioButtonMenuItem.foreground	Color
RadioButtonMenuItem.gradient	List
RadioButtonMenuItem.margin	Insets
RadioButtonMenuItem.opaque	Boolean

Table 6-14. *JRadioButtonMenuItem UIResource Elements (Continued)*

Property String	Object Type
RadioButtonMenuItem.selectionBackground	Color
RadioButtonMenuItem.selectionForeground	Color
RadioButtonMenuItemUI	String

A Complete JRadioButtonMenuItem Usage Example

To help you understand the JRadioButtonMenuItem usage, the program shown in Listing 6-5 demonstrates how to put everything together, including listening for selection of all the items on the menu, from either an ActionListener or an ItemListener. The output for the program is shown in Figure 6-8.

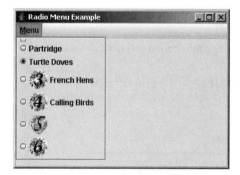

Figure 6-8. *JRadioButtonMenuItem usage example output*

Listing 6-5. *The RadioButtonSample Class Definition*

```
import javax.swing.*;
import java.awt.*;
import java.awt.event.*;

public class RadioButtonSample {
  static Icon threeIcon = new ImageIcon("3.gif");
  static Icon fourIcon = new ImageIcon("4.gif");
  static Icon fiveIcon = new ImageIcon("5.gif");
  static Icon sixIcon = new ImageIcon("6.gif");

  public static class ButtonActionListener implements ActionListener {
      public void actionPerformed (ActionEvent actionEvent) {
        AbstractButton aButton = (AbstractButton)actionEvent.getSource();
        boolean selected = aButton.getModel().isSelected();
        System.out.println (actionEvent.getActionCommand() +
          " - selected? " + selected);
      }
  }
```

```java
public static class ButtonItemListener implements ItemListener {
    public void itemStateChanged(ItemEvent itemEvent) {
        AbstractButton aButton = (AbstractButton)itemEvent.getSource();
        int state = itemEvent.getStateChange();
        String selected =
            ((state == ItemEvent.SELECTED) ? "selected" : "not selected");
        System.out.println (aButton.getText() + " - selected? " + selected);
    }
}

public static void main(String args[]) {

    Runnable runner = new Runnable() {
        public void run() {

            final ActionListener actionListener = new ButtonActionListener();
            final ItemListener itemListener = new ButtonItemListener();

            JFrame frame = new JFrame("Radio Menu Example");
            frame.setDefaultCloseOperation(JFrame.EXIT_ON_CLOSE);

            JMenuBar menuBar = new JMenuBar();
            JMenu menu = new JMenu("Menu");
            ButtonGroup buttonGroup = new ButtonGroup();
            menu.setMnemonic(KeyEvent.VK_M);

            JRadioButtonMenuItem emptyMenuItem =
                new JRadioButtonMenuItem();
            emptyMenuItem.setActionCommand("Empty");
            emptyMenuItem.addActionListener(actionListener);
            buttonGroup.add(emptyMenuItem);
            menu.add(emptyMenuItem);

            JRadioButtonMenuItem oneMenuItem =
                new JRadioButtonMenuItem("Partridge");
            oneMenuItem.addActionListener(actionListener);
            buttonGroup.add(oneMenuItem);
            menu.add(oneMenuItem);

            JRadioButtonMenuItem twoMenuItem =
                new JRadioButtonMenuItem("Turtle Doves", true);
            twoMenuItem.addActionListener(actionListener);
            buttonGroup.add(twoMenuItem);
            menu.add(twoMenuItem);
```

```
        JRadioButtonMenuItem threeMenuItem =
          new JRadioButtonMenuItem("French Hens", threeIcon);
        threeMenuItem.addItemListener(itemListener);
        buttonGroup.add(threeMenuItem);
        menu.add(threeMenuItem);

        JRadioButtonMenuItem fourMenuItem =
          new JRadioButtonMenuItem("Calling Birds", fourIcon, true);
        fourMenuItem.addActionListener(actionListener);
        buttonGroup.add(fourMenuItem);
        menu.add(fourMenuItem);

        JRadioButtonMenuItem fiveMenuItem =
          new JRadioButtonMenuItem(fiveIcon);
        fiveMenuItem.addActionListener(actionListener);
        fiveMenuItem.setActionCommand("Rings");
        buttonGroup.add(fiveMenuItem);
        menu.add(fiveMenuItem);

        JRadioButtonMenuItem sixMenuItem =
          new JRadioButtonMenuItem(sixIcon, true);
        sixMenuItem.addActionListener(actionListener);
        sixMenuItem.setActionCommand("Geese");
        buttonGroup.add(sixMenuItem);
        menu.add(sixMenuItem);

        menuBar.add(menu);
        frame.setJMenuBar(menuBar);
        frame.setSize(350, 250);
        frame.setVisible(true);
      }
    };
    EventQueue.invokeLater(runner);
  }
}
```

Note Notice that the actionCommand property is set for those menu items lacking text labels. This allows registered ActionListener objects to determine the selected object. This is only necessary when listeners are shared across components.

Creating Custom MenuElement Components: The MenuElement Interface

One thing all the selectable menu components have in common is that they implement the MenuElement interface. The JSeparator doesn't implement the interface, but that's okay because it isn't selectable. The purpose of the MenuElement interface is to allow the MenuSelectionManager to notify the different menu elements as a user moves around a program's menu structure.

As the following interface definition shows, the MenuElement interface is made up of five methods:

```
public interface MenuElement {
  public Component getComponent();
  public MenuElement[] getSubElements();
  public void menuSelectionChanged(boolean isInclude);
  public void processKeyEvent(KeyEvent event, MenuElement path[],
    MenuSelectionManager mgr);
  public void processMouseEvent(MouseEvent event, MenuElement path[],
    MenuSelectionManager mgr);
}
```

The getComponent() method returns the menu's rendering component. This is usually the menu component itself, although that isn't a requirement. The getSubElements() method returns an array of any menu elements contained within this element. If this menu element isn't the top of a submenu, the method should return a zero-length array of MenuElement objects, not null.

The menuSelectionChanged() method is called whenever the menu item is placed in or taken out of the selection path for the menu selection manager.

The two processKeyEvent() and processMouseEvent() methods are for processing a key event or mouse event that's generated over a menu. How your menu item processes events depends on what the component supports. For instance, unless you support accelerators, you probably want to respond to key events only when your menu item is in the current selection path.

Note If, for example, your new menu element was something like a JComboBoxMenuItem, where the MenuElement acted like a JComboBox, the processKeyEvent() might pass along the key character to the KeySelectionManager. See Chapter 13 for more on the KeySelectionManager.

To demonstrate the MenuElement interface, Listing 6-6 creates a new menu component called a JToggleButtonMenuItem. This component will look and act like a JToggleButton, although it can be on a menu. It's important to ensure that the menu goes away once the item is selected and that the component is displayed differently when in the current selection path.

■**Note** Although you can add any component to a menu, if the component doesn't implement the MenuElement interface, it won't act properly when a mouse moves over the component or when the component is selected.

Listing 6-6. *Toggle Button As Menu Item Class Definition*

```java
import java.awt.*;
import java.awt.event.*;
import javax.swing.*;
import javax.swing.event.*;

public class JToggleButtonMenuItem extends JToggleButton implements MenuElement {
  Color savedForeground = null;
  private static MenuElement NO_SUB_ELEMENTS[] = new MenuElement[0];
  public JToggleButtonMenuItem() {
    init();
  }
  public JToggleButtonMenuItem(String label) {
    super(label);
    init();
  }
  public JToggleButtonMenuItem(String label, Icon icon) {
    super(label, icon);
    init();
  }
  public JToggleButtonMenuItem(Action action) {
    super(action);
    init();
  }
  private void init() {
    updateUI();
    setRequestFocusEnabled(false);
    // Borrows heavily from BasicMenuUI
    MouseInputListener mouseInputListener = new MouseInputListener() {
      // If mouse released over this menu item, activate it
      public void mouseReleased(MouseEvent mouseEvent) {
        MenuSelectionManager menuSelectionManager =
          MenuSelectionManager.defaultManager();
        Point point = mouseEvent.getPoint();
        if ((point.x >= 0) &&
            (point.x < getWidth()) &&
            (point.y >= 0) &&
            (point.y < getHeight())) {
          menuSelectionManager.clearSelectedPath();
          // Component automatically handles "selection" at this point
          // doClick(0); // not necessary
```

```
      } else {
        menuSelectionManager.processMouseEvent(mouseEvent);
      }
    }
    // If mouse moves over menu item, add to selection path, so it becomes armed
    public void mouseEntered(MouseEvent mouseEvent) {
      MenuSelectionManager menuSelectionManager =
          MenuSelectionManager.defaultManager();
      menuSelectionManager.setSelectedPath(getPath());
    }
    // When mouse moves away from menu item, disarm it and select something else
    public void mouseExited(MouseEvent mouseEvent) {
      MenuSelectionManager menuSelectionManager =
        MenuSelectionManager.defaultManager();
      MenuElement path[] = menuSelectionManager.getSelectedPath();
      if (path.length > 1) {
        MenuElement newPath[] = new MenuElement[path.length-1];
        for(int i=0, c=path.length-1; i<c; i++) {
          newPath[i] = path[i];
        }
        menuSelectionManager.setSelectedPath(newPath);
      }
    }
    // Pass along drag events
    public void mouseDragged(MouseEvent mouseEvent) {
      MenuSelectionManager.defaultManager().processMouseEvent(mouseEvent);
    }
    public void mouseClicked(MouseEvent mouseEvent) {
    }
    public void mousePressed(MouseEvent mouseEvent) {
    }
    public void mouseMoved(MouseEvent mouseEvent) {
    }
  };
  addMouseListener(mouseInputListener);
  addMouseMotionListener(mouseInputListener);
}

// MenuElement methods
public Component getComponent() {
  return this;
}

public MenuElement[] getSubElements() {
  // No subelements
  return NO_SUB_ELEMENTS;
}
```

```java
public void menuSelectionChanged(boolean isIncluded) {
  ButtonModel model = getModel();
  // Only change armed state if different
  if(model.isArmed() != isIncluded) {
    model.setArmed(isIncluded);
  }

  if (isIncluded) {
    savedForeground = getForeground();
    if (!savedForeground.equals(Color.BLUE)) {
      setForeground(Color.BLUE);
    } else {
      // In case foreground blue, use something different
      setForeground(Color.RED);
    }
  } else {
    setForeground(savedForeground);
    // If null, get foreground from installed look and feel
    if (savedForeground == null) {
      updateUI();
    }
  }
}

public void processKeyEvent(KeyEvent keyEvent,
                            MenuElement path[],
                            MenuSelectionManager manager) {
  // If user presses space while menu item armed, select it
  if (getModel().isArmed()) {
    int keyChar = keyEvent.getKeyChar();
    if (keyChar == KeyEvent.VK_SPACE) {
      manager.clearSelectedPath();
      System.out.println("Selected: JToggleButtonMenuItem, by KeyEvent");
      doClick(0); // inherited from AbstractButton
    }
  }
}
public void processMouseEvent(MouseEvent mouseEvent, MenuElement path[],
    MenuSelectionManager manager) {
  // For when mouse dragged over menu and button released
  if (mouseEvent.getID() == MouseEvent.MOUSE_RELEASED) {
    manager.clearSelectedPath();
    System.out.println("Selected: JToggleButtonMenuItem, by MouseEvent");
    doClick(0); // inherited from AbstractButton
  }
}
```

```
  // Borrows heavily from BasicMenuItemUI.getPath()
  private MenuElement[] getPath() {
    MenuSelectionManager menuSelectionManager =
      MenuSelectionManager.defaultManager();
    MenuElement oldPath[] = menuSelectionManager.getSelectedPath();
    MenuElement newPath[];
    int oldPathLength = oldPath.length;
    if (oldPathLength == 0)
      return new MenuElement[0];
    Component parent = getParent();
    if (oldPath[oldPathLength-1].getComponent() == parent) {
      // Going deeper under the parent menu
      newPath = new MenuElement[oldPathLength+1];
      System.arraycopy(oldPath, 0, newPath, 0, oldPathLength);
      newPath[oldPathLength] = this;
    } else {
      // Sibling/child menu item currently selected
      int newPathPosition;
      for (newPathPosition = oldPath.length-1; newPathPosition >= 0;
          newPathPosition--) {
        if (oldPath[newPathPosition].getComponent() == parent) {
          break;
        }
      }
      newPath = new MenuElement[newPathPosition+2];
      System.arraycopy(oldPath, 0, newPath, 0, newPathPosition+1);
      newPath[newPathPosition+1] = this;
    }
    return newPath;
  }
}
```

Note The `MouseInputListener` defined in the `init()` method and the `getPath()` method borrow heavily from the system `BasicMenuUI` class. Normally, the user interface delegate deals with what happens when the mouse moves over a menu component. Because the `JToggleButton` isn't a predefined menu component, its UI class doesn't deal with it. For better modularity, these two methods should be moved into an extended `ToggleButtonUI`.

Once you've created this `JToggleButtonMenuItem` class, you can use it like any other menu item:

```
JToggleButtonMenuItem toggleItem = new JToggleButtonMenuItem("Balloon Help");
editMenu.add(toggleItem);
```

Working with Pop-Ups: The Popup Class

Not everything you want to pop up needs to be a menu. Through the `Popup` and `PopupFactory` classes, you can pop up any component over another. This is different from tooltips, which are in a read-only, unselectable label. You can pop up selectable buttons, trees, or tables.

Creating Pop-Up Components

`Popup` is a simple class with two methods—`hide()` and `show()`—with two protected constructors. Instead of creating `Popup` objects directly, you acquire them from the `PopupFactory` class.

```
PopupFactory factory = PopupFactory.getSharedInstance();
Popup popup = factory.getPopup(owner, contents, x, y);
```

The `Popup` with the `contents` component created by `PopupFactory` will thus be "above" other components within the `owner` component.

A Complete Popup/PopupFactory Usage Example

Listing 6-7 demonstrates the usage of `Popup` and `PopupFactory` to show a `JButton` above another `JButton`. Selecting the initial `JButton` will cause the second one to be created above the first, at some random location. When the second button is visible, each is selectable. Selecting the initially visible button multiple times will cause even more pop-up buttons to appear, as shown in Figure 6-9. Each pop-up button will disappear after three seconds. In this example, selecting the pop-up button just displays a message to the console.

Figure 6-9. *Popup/PopupFactory example*

Listing 6-7. *The ButtonPopupSample Class Definition*

```
import java.awt.*;
import java.awt.event.*;
import javax.swing.*;
import java.util.Random;

public class ButtonPopupSample {
```

```java
static final Random random = new Random();

// Define ActionListener
static class ButtonActionListener implements ActionListener {
  public void actionPerformed(ActionEvent actionEvent) {
    System.out.println("Selected: " + actionEvent.getActionCommand());
  }
}

// Define Show Popup ActionListener
static class ShowPopupActionListener implements ActionListener {
  private Component component;
  ShowPopupActionListener(Component component) {
    this.component = component;
  }
  public synchronized void actionPerformed(ActionEvent actionEvent) {
    JButton button = new JButton("Hello, World");
    ActionListener listener = new ButtonActionListener();
    button.addActionListener(listener);
    PopupFactory factory = PopupFactory.getSharedInstance();
    int x = random.nextInt(200);
    int y = random.nextInt(200);
    final Popup popup = factory.getPopup(component, button, x, y);
    popup.show();
    ActionListener hider = new ActionListener() {
      public void actionPerformed(ActionEvent e) {
        popup.hide();
      }
    };
    // Hide popup in 3 seconds
    Timer timer = new Timer(3000, hider);
    timer.start();
  }
}

public static void main(final String args[]) {
  Runnable runner = new Runnable() {
    public void run() {
      // Create frame
      JFrame frame = new JFrame("Button Popup Sample");
      frame.setDefaultCloseOperation(JFrame.EXIT_ON_CLOSE);

      ActionListener actionListener = new ShowPopupActionListener(frame);

      JButton start = new JButton("Pick Me for Popup");
      start.addActionListener(actionListener);
      frame.add(start);
```

```
            frame.setSize(350, 250);
            frame.setVisible(true);
        }
    };
    EventQueue.invokeLater(runner);
  }
}
```

Working with Toolbars: The JToolBar Class

Toolbars are an integral part of the main application windows in a modern user interface. Toolbars provide users with easy access to the more commonly used commands, which are usually buried within a hierarchical menuing structure. The Swing component that supports this capability is the JToolBar.

The JToolBar is a specialized Swing container for holding components. This container can then be used as a toolbar within your Java applet or application, with the potential for it to be floating or draggable, outside the main window of the program. JToolBar is a very simple component to use and understand.

Creating JToolBar Components

There are four constructors for creating JToolBar components:

```
public JToolBar()
JToolBar jToolBar = new JToolBar();
```

```
public JToolBar(int orientation)
JToolBar jToolBar = new JToolBar(JToolBar.VERTICAL);
```

```
public JToolBar(String name)
JToolBar jToolBar = new JToolBar("Window Title");
```

```
public JToolBar(String name,int orientation)
JToolBar jToolBar = new JToolBar("Window Title", ToolBar.VERTICAL);
```

By default, a toolbar is created in a horizontal direction. However, you can explicitly set the orientation by using either of the JToolBar constants of HORIZONTAL and VERTICAL.

Also by default, toolbars are floatable. Therefore, if you create the toolbar with one orientation, the user could change its orientation while dragging the toolbar around outside the window. When floating, the title will be visible on the toolbar's frame.

Adding Components to a JToolBar

Once you have a JToolBar, you need to add components to it. Any Component can be added to the toolbar. When dealing with horizontal toolbars, for aesthetic reasons, it's best if the toolbar components are all roughly the same height. For a vertical toolbar, it's best if they're roughly the same width. There's only one method defined by the JToolBar class for adding toolbar items; the remaining methods, such as add(Component), are inherited from Container. In addition, you can add a separator to a toolbar.

```
public JButton add(Action action);
public void addSeparator();
public void addSeparator(Dimension size);
```

When using the add(Action) method of JToolBar, the added Action is encapsulated within a JButton object. This is different from adding actions to JMenu or JPopupMenu components, in which JMenuItem objects are added instead. As with JMenu and JPopupMenu, adding an Action in this fashion is discouraged in the Javadoc for the class. For separators, if you don't specify the size, the installed look and feel forces a default size setting.

Note For more information about dealing with the Action interface, see Chapter 2 or the section "Using Action Objects with Menus" earlier in this chapter.

To remove components from a toolbar, use the following method:

```
public void remove(Component component)
```

JToolBar Properties

The JToolBar class defines nine properties, which are listed in Table 6-15.

Table 6-15. *JToolBar Properties*

Property Name	Data Type	Access
accessibleContext	AccessibleContext	Read-only
borderPainted	boolean	Read-write bound
floatable	boolean	Read-write bound
layout	LayoutManager	Write-only
margin	Insets	Read-write bound
orientation	int	Read-write bound
rollover	boolean	Read-write bound
UI	ToolBarUI	Read-write
UIClassID	String	Read-only

By default, the border of a JToolBar is painted. If you don't want the border painted, you can set the borderPainted property to false. Without using the borderPainted property, you would need to change the setting of the border property (inherited from the superclass JComponent).

The orientation property can be set to only one of the HORIZONTAL or VERTICAL constants of JToolBar. If another nonequivalent value is used, an IllegalArgumentException is thrown. Changing the orientation changes the layout manager of the toolbar. If you directly change the layout manager with setLayout(), changing the orientation will undo your layout change. Consequently, it's best not to manually change the layout manager of a JToolBar.

As previously mentioned, a toolbar is floatable by default. This means that a user can drag the toolbar from where you place it and move it elsewhere. To drag a toolbar, the user selects an empty part of it. The toolbar can than be left outside the original program window, floating above the main window in its own window, or dropped onto another area of the original program window. If the layout manager of the original window is BorderLayout, the droppable areas are the edges of the layout manager without any components. (You can't drop the toolbar in the center of the window.) Otherwise, the toolbar would be dropped into the last spot of the container. Figure 6-10 shows the different phases of the dragging and docking process.

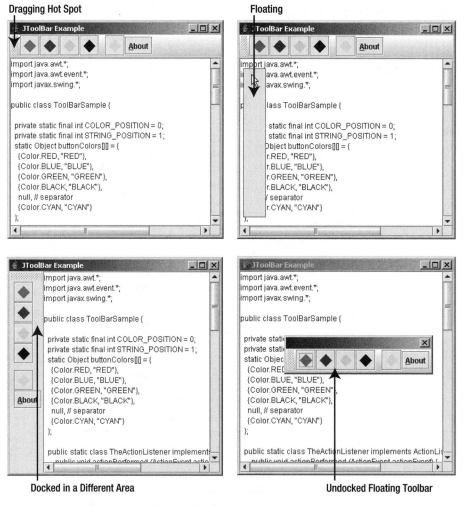

Figure 6-10. *JToolBar phases*

The rollover property defines a behavior specific to the look and feel for when the user moves the mouse over the different components within the toolbar. This behavior could involve coloration or border differences.

Handling JToolBar Events

There are no events specific to the JToolBar. You need to attach listeners to each item on the JToolBar that you want to respond to user interaction. Of course, JToolBar is a Container, so you could listen to its events.

Customizing a JToolBar Look and Feel

Each installable Swing look and feel provides its own JToolBar appearance and set of default UIResource values. Most of this appearance is controlled by the components actually within the toolbar. Figure 6-11 shows the appearance of the JToolBar component for the preinstalled set of look and feel types: Motif, Windows, and Ocean. Each toolbar has five JButton components, with a separator between the fourth and fifth.

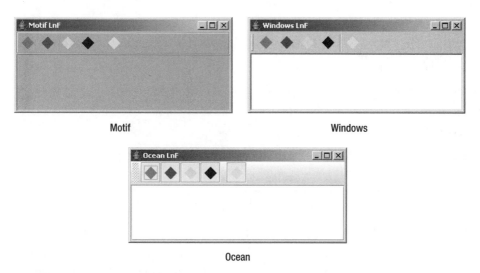

Figure 6-11. *JToolBar under different look and feel types*

The available set of UIResource-related properties for a JToolBar is shown in Table 6-16. For the JToolBar component, there are 22 different properties.

Table 6-16. *JToolBar UIResource Elements*

Property String	Object Type
ToolBar.actionMap	ActionMap
ToolBar.ancestorInputMap	InputMap
ToolBar.background	Color

Table 6-16. *JToolBar UIResource Elements (Continued)*

Property String	Object Type
ToolBar.border	Border
ToolBar.borderColor	Color
ToolBar.darkShadow	Color
ToolBar.dockingBackground	Color
ToolBar.dockingForeground	Color
ToolBar.floatingBackground	Color
ToolBar.floatingForeground	Color
ToolBar.font	Font
ToolBar.foreground	Color
ToolBar.handleIcon	Icon
ToolBar.highlight	Color
ToolBar.isRollover	Boolean
ToolBar.light	Color
ToolBar.nonrolloverBorder	Border
ToolBar.rolloverBorder	Border
ToolBar.separatorSize	Dimension
ToolBar.shadow	Color
ToolBarSeparatorUI	String
ToolBarUI	String

A Complete JToolBar Usage Example

The program in Listing 6-8 demonstrates a complete JToolBar example that results in a toolbar with a series of diamonds on the buttons. The program also reuses the ShowAction defined for the menuing example, presented in Listing 6-2 earlier in this chapter.

The rollover property is enabled to demonstrate the difference for the current look and feel. See Figure 6-12 for the output as you move your mouse over the different buttons.

Figure 6-12. *JToolBar example with isRollover enabled*

Listing 6-8. *The ToolBarSample Class Definition*

```java
import java.awt.*;
import java.awt.event.*;
import javax.swing.*;

public class ToolBarSample {

  private static final int COLOR_POSITION = 0;
  private static final int STRING_POSITION = 1;
  static Object buttonColors[][] = {
    {Color.RED, "RED"},
    {Color.BLUE, "BLUE"},
    {Color.GREEN, "GREEN"},
    {Color.BLACK, "BLACK"},
    null, // separator
    {Color.CYAN, "CYAN"}
  };

  public static class TheActionListener implements ActionListener {
      public void actionPerformed (ActionEvent actionEvent) {
        System.out.println(actionEvent.getActionCommand());
      }
  };

  public static void main(final String args[]) {

    Runnable runner = new Runnable() {
      public void run() {

        JFrame frame = new JFrame("JToolBar Example");
        frame.setDefaultCloseOperation(JFrame.EXIT_ON_CLOSE);
        ActionListener actionListener = new TheActionListener();

        JToolBar toolbar = new JToolBar();
        toolbar.setRollover(true);

        for (Object[] color: buttonColors) {
          if (color == null) {
            toolbar.addSeparator();
          } else {
            Icon icon = new DiamondIcon((Color)color[COLOR_POSITION], true, 20, 20);
            JButton button = new JButton(icon);
            button.setActionCommand((String)color[STRING_POSITION]);
            button.addActionListener(actionListener);
            toolbar.add(button);
          }
        }
```

```
        Action action = new ShowAction(frame);
        JButton button = new JButton(action);
        toolbar.add(button);

        Container contentPane = frame.getContentPane();
        contentPane.add(toolbar, BorderLayout.NORTH);
        JTextArea textArea = new JTextArea();
        JScrollPane pane = new JScrollPane(textArea);
        contentPane.add(pane, BorderLayout.CENTER);
        frame.setSize(350, 150);
        frame.setVisible(true);
      }
    };
    EventQueue.invokeLater(runner);
  }
}
```

JToolBar.Separator Class

The JToolBar class maintains its own separator to permit a custom look and feel for the separator when on a JToolBar.

This separator is automatically created when you call the addSeparator() method of JToolBar. In addition, there are two constructors for creating a JToolBar.Separator if you want to manually create the component.

public JToolBar.Separator()
```
JSeparator toolBarSeparator = new JToolBar.Separator();
```

public JToolBar.Separator(Dimension size)
```
Dimension dimension = new Dimension(10, 10);
JSeparator toolBarSeparator = new JToolBar.Separator(dimension);
```

Both constructors create a horizontal separator. You can configure the size. If you don't specify this, the look and feel decides what size to make the separator.

As with JPopupMenu.Separator, if you want to change the orientation of the separator, you must call the setOrientation() method inherited from JSeparator, this time with an argument of JToolBar.Separator.VERTICAL.

Summary

This chapter introduced the many Swing menu-related classes and their interrelationships, and Swing's toolbar class. First, you learned about the JMenuBar and its selection model, and learned how menu bars can be used within applets as well as applications.

Next, you explored the JMenuItem, which is the menu element the user selects, along with two new event/listener pairs the system uses for dealing with events, MenuKeyEvent/MenuKeyListener and MenuDragMouseEvent/MenuDragMouseListener. Then, you moved on to the JMenu component, upon which JMenuItem instances are placed, along with its new event/listener pair, MenuEvent/MenuListener, which is used to determine when a menu is about to be posted.

Next, you learned about the `JSeparator` component and how you can use it as a menu separator or as a visual display separator outside of menus.

You then explored the `JPopupMenu`, which `JMenu` uses to display its set of `JMenuItem` components. For the `JPopupMenu`, you learned about the pop-up menu's own event/listener pair, `PopupMenuEvent`/`PopupMenuListener`.

Then the selectable menu elements in `JCheckBoxMenuItem` and `JRadioButtonMenuItem` were explored with their `MenuElement` interface, and you saw how to create a custom menu component.

Menus aren't the only things that might pop up, so you explored `Popup` and `PopupFactory`. Finally, the chapter covered the `JToolBar` class, a close cousin of Swing's menu classes.

In Chapter 7, you'll look at the different classes Swing provides for customizing the border around a Swing component.

CHAPTER 7

■ ■ ■

Borders

Swing components offer the option of customizing the border area surrounding that component. With great ease, you can use any one of the eight predefined borders (including one compound border that is a combination of any of the other seven), or you can create your own individualized borders. In this chapter, you'll learn how to best use each of the existing borders and how to fashion your own.

Some Basics on Working with Borders

A border is a `JComponent` property with the standard `setBorder()` and `getBorder()` property methods. Therefore, every Swing component that is a subclass of `JComponent` can have a border. By default, a component doesn't have a custom border associated with it. (The `getBorder()` method of `JComponent` returns `null`.) Instead, the default border displayed for a component is the border appropriate for its state, based on the current look and feel. For instance, with a `JButton`, the border could appear pressed, unpressed, or disabled, with specific different borders for each look and feel (Metal, Windows, and so on).

Although the initial border property setting for every component is `null`, you can change the border of a component by calling the `setBorder(Border newValue)` method of `JComponent`. Once set, the changed value overrides the border for the current look and feel, and it draws the new border in the area of the component's insets. If at a later time, you want to reset the border back to a border that's appropriate for the state as well as the look and feel, change the border property to `null`, using `setBorder(null)`, and call `updateUI()` for the component. The `updateUI()` call notifies the look and feel to reset the border. If you don't call `updateUI()`, the component will have no border.

■Note Those Swing components that aren't subclasses of `JComponent`, such as `JApplet` and `JFrame`, lack a `setBorder()` method to change their border. If you want them to have a border, you must add a `JPanel` or other Swing component to the container, and then change the border of that component.

Examine Figure 7-1 to see a sampling of the various border configurations around a JLabel, with a text label designating the border type. How to create the different borders will be discussed in later sections of this chapter.

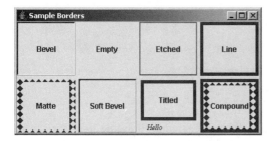

Figure 7-1. *Border examples, using a 4-by-2 GridLayout with 5-pixel horizontal and vertical gaps*

Exploring the Border Interface

The Border interface can be found in the javax.swing.border package. This interface forms the basis of all the border classes. The interface is directly implemented by the AbstractBorder class, which is the parent class of all the predefined Swing border classes: BevelBorder, CompoundBorder, EmptyBorder, EtchedBorder, LineBorder, MatteBorder, SoftBevelBorder, and TitledBorder. Of additional interest is the BorderFactory class, found in the javax.swing package. This class uses the Factory design pattern to create borders, hiding the details of the concrete implementations and caching various operations to optimize shared usages.

The Border interface shown here consists of three methods: paintBorder(), getBorderInsets(), and isBorderOpaque(). These methods are described in the following sections.

paintBorder()

The paintBorder() method is the key method of the interface. It has the following definition:

```
public void paintBorder(Component c, Graphics g, int x, int y, int
  width, int height)
```

The actual drawing of the border is done in this method. Frequently, the Border implementation will ask for the Insets dimensions first, and then draw the border in the four rectangular outer regions, as shown in Figure 7-2. If a border is opaque, the paintBorder() implementation must fill the entire insets area. If a border is opaque and doesn't fill the area, then it's a bug and needs to be corrected.

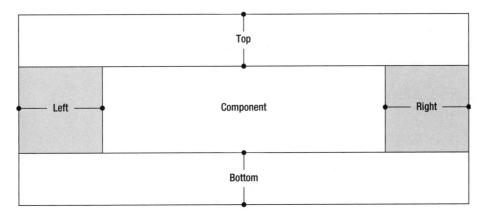

Figure 7-2. *Areas of border insets*

Listing 7-1 shows a simple paintBorder() implementation that fills in the left and right sides with a brighter color than the top and bottom.

Listing 7-1. *Filled-in Border Inset Areas*

```
public void paintBorder(Component c, Graphics g, int x, int y, int width,
    int height) {
  Insets insets = getBorderInsets(c);
  Color color = c.getForeground();
  Color brighterColor = color.brighter();

// Translate coordinate space
  g.translate(x, y);

// Top
  g.setColor(color);
  g.fillRect(0, 0, width, insets.top);

// Left
  g.setColor(brighterColor);
  g.fillRect(0, insets.top, insets.left, height-insets.top-insets.bottom);

// Bottom
  g.setColor(color);
  g.fillRect(0, height-insets.bottom, width, insets.bottom);
```

```
// Right
  g.setColor(brighterColor);
  g.fillRect(width-insets.right, insets.top, insets.right,
    height-insets.top-insets.bottom);

// Translate coordinate space back
  g.translate(-x, -y);

}
```

When creating your own borders, you'll frequently find yourself filling in the same nonoverlapping rectangular regions. The use of the `translate()` method of `Graphics` simplifies the specification of the drawing coordinates. Without translating the coordinates, you would need to offset the drawing by the origin (x, y).

■**Caution** You cannot take a shortcut by inserting `g.fillRect(x, y, width, height)`, because this would fill in the entire component area, not just the border area.

---

getBorderInsets()

The `getBorderInsets()` method returns the space necessary to draw a border around the given component c as an `Insets` object. It has the following definition:

```
public Insets getBorderInsets(Component c)
```

These inset areas, shown in Figure 7-2, define the only legal area in which a border can be drawn. The `Component` argument allows you to use some of its properties to determine the size of the insets area.

■**Caution** You can ask the component argument for font-sizing information to determine the insets' size, but if you ask about the size of the component, a `StackOverflowError` occurs because the size of the component is dependent on the size of the border insets.

---

isBorderOpaque()

Borders can be opaque or transparent. The `isBorderOpaque()` method returns `true` or `false`, to indicate which form the border is. It has the following definition:

```
public boolean isBorderOpaque()
```

When this method returns true, the border needs to be opaque, filling its entire insets area. When it returns false, any area not drawn will retain the background of the component in which the border is installed.

Introducing BorderFactory

Now that you have a basic understanding of how the Border interface works, let's take a quick look at the BorderFactory class as a means to create borders swiftly and easily. Found in the javax.swing package, the BorderFactory class offers a series of static methods for creating predefined borders. Instead of laboriously calling the specific constructors for different borders, you can create almost all the borders through this factory class. The factory class also caches the creation of some borders to avoid re-creating commonly used borders multiple times. The class definition follows.

```
public class BorderFactory {
  public static Border createBevelBorder(int type);
  public static Border createBevelBorder(int type, Color highlight,
    Color shadow);
  public static Border createBevelBorder(int type, Color highlightOuter,
    Color highlightInner, Color shadowOuter, Color shadowInner);

  public static CompoundBorder createCompoundBorder();
  public static CompoundBorder createCompoundBorder(Border outside,
    Border inside);

  public static Border createEmptyBorder();
  public static Border createEmptyBorder(int top, int left, int bottom,
    int right);

  public static Border createEtchedBorder();
  public static Border createEtchedBorder(Color highlight, Color shadow);
  public static Border createEtchedBorder(int type);
  public static Border createEtchedBorder(int type, Color highlight,
    Color shadow);

  public static Border createLineBorder(Color color);
  public static Border createLineBorder(Color color, int thickness);

  public static Border createLoweredBevelBorder();

  public static MatteBorder createMatteBorder(int top, int left, int bottom,
    int right, Color color);
  public static MatteBorder createMatteBorder(int top, int left, int bottom,
    int right, Icon icon);
```

```
    public static Border createRaisedBevelBorder();

    public static TitledBorder createTitledBorder(Border border);
    public static TitledBorder createTitledBorder(Border border, String title);
    public static TitledBorder createTitledBorder(Border border, String title,
        int justification, int position);
    public static TitledBorder createTitledBorder(Border border, String title,
        int justification, int position, Font font);
    public static TitledBorder createTitledBorder(Border border, String title,
        int justification, int position, Font font, Color color);
    public static TitledBorder createTitledBorder(String title);
}
```

I'll describe the different methods of this class during the process of describing the specific border types they create. For instance, to create a border with a red line, you can use the following statement, and then attach the border to a component.

```
Border lineBorder = BorderFactory.createLineBorder(Color.RED);
```

Note Interestingly enough, no factory method exists for creating a SoftBevelBorder.

Starting with AbstractBorder

Before looking at the individual borders available within the javax.swing.border package, one system border deserves special attention: AbstractBorder. As previously mentioned, the AbstractBorder class is the parent border of all the other predefined borders.

Tip When creating your own borders, you should create a subclass of AbstractBorder and just override the necessary methods, instead of implementing the Border interface directly yourself. There are some internal optimizations in place for subclasses.

Creating Abstract Borders

There is one constructor for AbstractBorder:

```
public AbstractBorder()
```

Because AbstractBorder is the parent class of all the other standard borders, this constructor is eventually called automatically for all of them.

■Note Borders are not meant to be used as JavaBean components. Some border classes even lack a no-argument ("no-arg" for short) constructor. Nevertheless, those border classes still call this constructor.

Examining AbstractBorder Methods

The `AbstractBorder` class provides implementations for the three methods of the `Border` interface.

```
public Insets getBorderInsets(Component c)
```

The insets of an `AbstractBorder` are zero all around. Each of the predefined subclasses overrides the `getBorderInsets()` method.

```
public boolean isBorderOpaque()
```

The default opaque property setting of an abstract border is `false`. This means that if you were to draw something like dashed lines, the component background would show through. Many predefined subclasses override the `isBorderOpaque()` method.

```
public void paintBorder(Component c, Graphics g, int x, int y,
  int width, int height)
```

The painted border for an `AbstractBorder` is empty. All subclasses should override this behavior to actually draw a border, except perhaps `EmptyBorder`.

In addition to providing default implementations of the `Border` methods, `AbstractBorder` adds two other capabilities that you can take advantage of, or just let the system use. First, there's an additional version of `getBorderInsets()` available that takes two arguments: `Component` and `Insets`:

```
public Insets getBorderInsets(Component c, Insets insets)
```

In this version of the method, instead of creating and returning a new `Insets` object, the `Insets` object passed in is first modified and then returned. Use of this method avoids the creation and later destruction of an additional `Insets` object each time the border insets is queried.

The second new method available is `getInteriorRectangle()`, which has both a static and a nonstatic version. Given the `Component`, `Border`, and four integer parameters (for x, y, width, and height), the method will return the inner `Rectangle` such that a component can paint itself only in the area within the border insets. (See the piece labeled "Component" in Figure 7-2, shown earlier in the chapter.)

■Note Currently, `getBorderInsets()` is used only once in Sun's Swing source. That place is the `MotifButtonUI` class found in the `com.sun.java.swing.plaf.motif` package.

Examining the Predefined Borders

Now that the basics have been described, let's look at the specifics of each of the predefined border classes, somewhat in order of complexity.

EmptyBorder Class

The empty border, logically enough, is a border with nothing drawn in it. You can use EmptyBorder where you might have otherwise overridden insets() or getInsets() with a regular AWT container. It allows you to reserve extra space around a component to spread your screen components out a little or to alter centering or justification somewhat. Figure 7-3 shows both an empty border and one that is not empty.

Figure 7-3. *EmptyBorder sample, with insets of 20 for top and left, 0 for right and bottom*

EmptyBorder has two constructors and two factory methods of BorderFactory:

```
public static Border createEmptyBorder()
Border emptyBorder = BorderFactory.createEmptyBorder();
```

```
public static Border createEmptyBorder(int top, int left, int bottom, int right)
Border emptyBorder = BorderFactory.createEmptyBorder(5, 10, 5, 10);
```

```
public EmptyBorder(Insets insets)
Insets insets = new Insets(5, 10, 5, 10);
Border EmptyBorder = new EmptyBorder(insets);
```

```
public EmptyBorder(int top, int left, int bottom, int right)
Border EmptyBorder = new EmptyBorder(5, 10, 5, 10);
```

Each allows you to customize the border insets in its own manner. The no-argument version creates a truly empty border with zero insets all around; otherwise, you can specify the insets as either an AWT Insets instance or as the inset pieces. The EmptyBorder is transparent by default.

Note When creating an empty border, with zeros all around, you should use the factory method to create the border, avoiding the direct constructors. This allows the factory to create one truly empty border to be shared by all. If all you want to do is hide the border, and the component is an AbstractButton subclass, just call setBorderPainted(false).

LineBorder Class

The line border is a single-color line of a user-defined thickness that surrounds a component. It can have squared-off or rounded corners. If you want to alter the thickness on different sides, you'll need to use MatteBorder, which is described in the section "Matte Border Class" later in this chapter. Figure 7-4 shows a sampling of using LineBorder, with 1- and 12-pixel line thicknesses, with and without rounded corners.

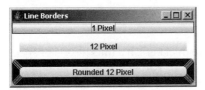

Figure 7-4. *LineBorder sample*

Creating Line Borders

The LineBorder class has three constructors, two factory methods within it, and two factory methods of BorderFactory:

public LineBorder(Color color)
```
Border lineBorder = new LineBorder (Color.RED);
```

public LineBorder(Color color, int thickness)
```
Border lineBorder = new LineBorder (Color.RED, 5);
```

public LineBorder (Color color, int thickness, boolean roundedCorners)
```
Border lineBorder = new LineBorder (Color.RED, 5, true);
```

public static Border createBlackLineBorder()
```
Border blackLine = LineBorder.createBlackLineBorder();
```

```
public static Border createGrayLineBorder()
Border grayLine = LineBorder.createGrayLineBorder();
```

```
public static Border createLineBorder(Color color)
Border lineBorder = BorderFactory.createLineBorder(Color.RED);
```

```
public static Border createLineBorder(Color color, int thickness)
Border lineBorder = BorderFactory.createLineBorder(Color.RED, 5);
```

Note The LineBorder factory methods work as follows: If you create the same border twice, the same LineBorder object will be returned. However, as with all object comparisons, you should always use the equals() method for checking object equality.

Each allows you to customize the border color and line thickness. If a thickness isn't specified, a default value of 1 is used. The two factory methods of LineBorder are for the commonly used colors of black and gray. Because the border fills in the entire insets area, the LineBorder is opaque, unless there are rounded corners. So, the opacity of the border is the opposite of the rounded-corner setting.

Configuring Line Border Properties

Table 7-1 lists the inherited borderOpaque property from AbstractBorder and the immutable properties of LineBorder.

Table 7-1. *LineBorder Properties*

Property Name	Data Type	Access
borderOpaque	boolean	Read-only
lineColor	Color	Read-only
roundedCorners	boolean	Read-only
thickness	int	Read-only

BevelBorder Class

A bevel border draws a border with a three-dimensional appearance, which can appear to be raised or lowered. When the border is raised, a shadow effect appears along the bottom and right side of the border. When lowered, the position of the shading is reversed. Figure 7-5 shows raised and lowered bevel borders with default and custom colors.

Figure 7-5. *Raised and lowered BevelBorder sample*

Drawing two different pairs of 1-pixel-wide lines around the component produces a simulated three-dimensional appearance. The border sides that aren't shaded are drawn with what is called a *highlight* color, and the other two sides are drawn with a *shadow* color. The highlight color and shadow color are each drawn in two different shades for the outer and inner edges of the bevel. As such, a drawn bevel border uses four different colors in all. Figure 7-6 shows how these four colors fit together.

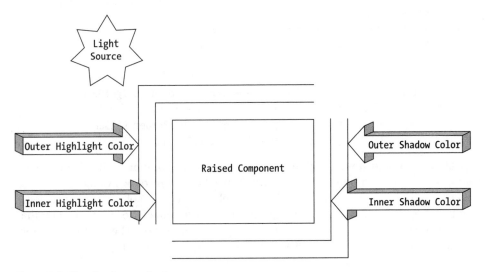

Figure 7-6. *Bevel color analysis*

There are three constructors and one factory method of BevelBorder, as well as five factory methods by which BorderFactory creates BevelBorder objects:

public BevelBorder(int bevelType)
```
Border bevelBorder = new BevelBorder(BevelBorder.RAISED);
```

public static Border createBevelBorder(int bevelType)
```
Border bevelBorder = BorderFactory.createBevelBorder(BevelBorder.RAISED);
```

public static Border createLoweredBevelBorder()
```
Border bevelBorder = BorderFactory.createLoweredBevelBorder();
```

```
public static Border createRaisedBevelBorder()
Border bevelBorder = BorderFactory.createRaisedBevelBorder();


public BevelBorder(int bevelType, Color highlight, Color shadow)
Border bevelBorder = new BevelBorder(BevelBorder.RAISED, Color.PINK, Color.RED);


public static Border createBevelBorder(int bevelType, Color highlight, Color shadow)
Border bevelBorder = BorderFactory.createBevelBorder(BevelBorder.RAISED,
  Color.PINK, Color.RED);


public BevelBorder(int bevelType, Color highlightOuter, Color highlightInner,
  Color shadowOuter, Color shadowInner)
Border bevelBorder = new BevelBorder(BevelBorder.RAISED, Color.PINK,
  Color.PINK.brighter(), Color.RED, Color.RED.darker());


public static Border createBevelBorder(int bevelType, Color highlightOuter,
  Color highlightInner, Color shadowOuter, Color shadowInner)
Border bevelBorder = BorderFactory.createBevelBorder(BevelBorder.RAISED,
  Color.PINK, Color.PINK.brighter(), Color.RED, Color.RED.darker());
```

Each allows you to customize both the bevel type and the coloration of the highlighting and shadowing within the border. The bevel type is specified by one of two values: BevelBorder.RAISED or BevelBorder.LOWERED. If highlight and shadow colors aren't specified, the appropriate colors are generated by examining the background of the component for the border. If you do specify them, remember that the highlight color should be brighter, possibly done by calling theColor.brighter(). A BevelBorder is opaque, by default.

SoftBevelBorder Class

The soft bevel border is a close cousin of the bevel border. It rounds out the corners so that their edges aren't as sharp, and it draws only one line, using the appropriate outer color for the bottom and right sides. As Figure 7-7 shows, the basic appearance of the raised and lowered SoftBevelBorder is roughly the same as that of the BevelBorder.

Figure 7-7. *Raised and lowered SoftBevelBorder sample*

SoftBevelBorder has three constructors:

public SoftBevelBorder(int bevelType)
Border softBevelBorder = new SoftBevelBorder(SoftBevelBorder.RAISED);

public SoftBevelBorder(int bevelType, Color highlight, Color shadow)
Border softBevelBorder = new SoftBevelBorder(SoftBevelBorder.RAISED, Color.RED,
  Color.PINK);

public SoftBevelBorder(int bevelType, Color highlightOuter, Color highlightInner,
  Color shadowOuter, Color shadowInner)
Border softBevelBorder = new SoftBevelBorder(SoftBevelBorder.RAISED, Color.RED,
  Color.RED.darker(), Color.PINK, Color.PINK.brighter());

Each allows you to customize both the bevel type and the coloration of the highlighting
and shadowing within the border. The bevel type is specified by one of two values:
SoftBevelBorder.RAISED or SoftBevelBorder.LOWERED. As with BevelBorder, the default coloration is derived from the background color. A soft bevel border doesn't completely fill in the
given insets area, so a SoftBevelBorder is created to be transparent (not opaque).

There are no static BorderFactory methods to create these borders.

EtchedBorder Class

An EtchedBorder is a special case of a BevelBorder, but it's not a subclass. When the outer highlight color of a BevelBorder is the same color as the inner shadow color and the outer shadow
color is the same color as the inner highlight color, you have an EtchedBorder. (See Figure 7-6
earlier in this chapter for a depiction of bevel colors.) Figure 7-8 shows what a raised and
lowered etched border might look like.

Figure 7-8. *EtchedBorder samples*

There are four constructors for EtchedBorder, as well as four factory methods of
BorderFactory for creating EtchedBorder objects:

```
public EtchedBorder()
Border etchedBorder = new EtchedBorder();


public EtchedBorder(int etchType)
Border etchedBorder = new EtchedBorder(EtchedBorder.RAISED);


public EtchedBorder(Color highlight, Color shadow)
Border etchedBorder = new EtchedBorder(Color.RED, Color.PINK);


public EtchedBorder(int etchType, Color highlight, Color shadow)
Border etchedBorder = new EtchedBorder(EtchedBorder.RAISED, Color.RED,
  Color.PINK);


public static Border createEtchedBorder()
Border etchedBorder = BorderFactory.createEtchedBorder();


public static Border createEtchedBorder(Color highlight, Color shadow)
Border etchedBorder = BorderFactory.createEtchedBorder(Color.RED, Color.PINK);


public static Border createEtchedBorder(EtchedBorder.RAISED)
Border etchedBorder = BorderFactory.createEtchedBorder(Color.RED, Color.PINK);


public static Border createEtchedBorder(int type, Color highlight, Color shadow)
Border etchedBorder = BorderFactory.createEtchedBorder(EtchedBorder.RAISED,
  Color.RED, Color.PINK);
```

Each allows you to customize both the etching type and the coloration of the highlighting and shadowing within the border. If no etching type is specified, the border is lowered. As with BevelBorder and SoftBevelBorder, you can specify the etching type through one of two constants: EtchedBorder.RAISED or EtchedBorder.LOWERED. Again, if no colors are specified, they're derived from the background color of the component passed into paintBorder(). By default, all EtchedBorder objects are created to be opaque.

MatteBorder Class

MatteBorder is one of the more versatile borders available. It comes in two varieties. The first is demonstrated in Figure 7-9 and shows a MatteBorder used like a LineBorder to fill the border with a specific color, but with a different thickness on each side (something a plain LineBorder cannot handle).

Figure 7-9. *MatteBorder color sample*

The second variety uses an Icon tiled throughout the border area. This Icon could be an ImageIcon, if created from an Image object, or it could be one you create yourself by implementing the Icon interface. Figure 7-10 demonstrates both implementations.

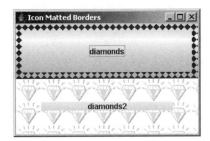

Figure 7-10. *MatteBorder icon samples*

■**Tip** When tiling an icon, the right and bottom areas may not look very attractive if the border size, component size, and icon size fail to mesh well.

There are seven constructors and two factory methods of BorderFactory for creating MatteBorder objects:

public MatteBorder(int top, int left, int bottom, int right, Color color)
```
Border matteBorder = new MatteBorder(5, 10, 5, 10, Color.GREEN);
```

public MatteBorder(int top, int left, int bottom, int right, Icon icon)
```
Icon diamondIcon = new DiamondIcon(Color.RED);
Border matteBorder = new MatteBorder(5, 10, 5, 10, diamondIcon);
```

public MatteBorder(Icon icon)
```
Icon diamondIcon = new DiamondIcon(Color.RED);
Border matteBorder = new MatteBorder(diamondIcon);
```

```
public MatteBorder(Insets insets, Color color)
Insets insets = new Insets(5, 10, 5, 10);
Border matteBorder = new MatteBorder(insets,  Color.RED);
```

```
public MatteBorder(Insets insets, Icon icon)
Insets insets = new Insets(5, 10, 5, 10);
Icon diamondIcon = new DiamondIcon(Color.RED);
Border matteBorder = new MatteBorder(insets, diamondIcon);
```

```
public static MatteBorder createMatteBorder(int top, int left, int bottom,
  int right, Color color)
Border matteBorder = BorderFactory.createMatteBorder(5, 10, 5, 10, Color.GREEN);
```

```
public static MatteBorder createMatteBorder(int top, int left, int bottom,
  int right, Icon icon)
Icon diamondIcon = new DiamondIcon(Color.RED);
Border matteBorder = BorderFactory.createMatteBorder(5, 10, 5, 10, diamondIcon);
```

Each allows you to customize what will be matted within the border area. When tiling an Icon, if you don't specify the border insets size, the actual icon dimensions will be used.

CompoundBorder Class

After EmptyBorder, the compound border is probably one of the simplest predefined borders to use. It takes two existing borders and combines them, using the Composite design pattern, into a single border. A Swing component can have only one border associated with it, therefore, the CompoundBorder allows you to combine borders *before* associating them with a component. Figure 7-11 shows two examples of CompoundBorder in action. The border on the left is a beveled, line border. The one on the right is a six-line border, with several borders combined together.

Figure 7-11. *CompoundBorder samples*

Creating Compound Borders

There are two constructors for CompoundBorder and two factory methods that BorderFactory offers for creating CompoundBorder objects (the no-argument constructor and factory methods are completely useless here, because there are no setter methods to later change the compounded borders, so no source examples are shown for them):

```
public CompoundBorder()
```

```
public static CompoundBorder createCompoundBorder()
```

```
public CompoundBorder(Border outside, Border inside)
Border compoundBorder = new CompoundBorder(lineBorder, matteBorder);
```

```
public static CompoundBorder createCompoundBorder(Border outside, Border inside)
Border compoundBorder = BorderFactory.createCompoundBorder(lineBorder,
  matteBorder);
```

■**Tip** Keep in mind that CompoundBorder is itself a Border, so you can combine multiple borders into one border many levels deep.

The opacity of a compound border depends on the opacity of the contained borders. If both contained borders are opaque, so is the compound border. Otherwise, a compound border is considered transparent.

Configuring Properties

In addition to the borderOpaque property inherited from AbstractBorder, Table 7-2 lists the two read-only properties CompoundBorder adds.

Table 7-2. *CompoundBorder Properties*

Property Name	Data Type	Access
borderOpaque	boolean	Read-only
insideBorder	Border	Read-only
outsideBorder	Border	Read-only

TitledBorder Class

Probably the most interesting border, TitledBorder can also be the most complicated to use. The titled border allows you to place a text string around a component. In addition to surrounding a single component, you can place a titled border around a group of components, like JRadioButton objects, as long as they're placed within a container such as a JPanel. The TitledBorder can be difficult to use, but there are several ways to simplify its usage. Figure 7-12 shows both a simple titled border and one that's a little more complex.

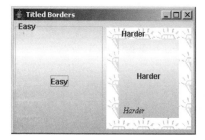

Figure 7-12. *TitledBorder samples*

Creating Titled Borders

Six constructors and six BorderFactory factory methods exist for creating TitledBorder objects. Each allows you to customize the text, position, and appearance of a title within a specified border. When unspecified, the current look and feel controls the border, title color, and title font. The default location for the title is the upper-left corner, while the default title is the empty string. A titled border is always at least partially transparent because the area beneath the title text shows through. Therefore, isBorderOpaque() reports false.

   If you look at each of the following methods, shown in pairs, this will be easier to understand. First shown is the constructor method; next shown is the equivalent BorderFactory method.

```
public TitledBorder(Border border)
Border titledBorder = new TitledBorder(lineBorder);

public static TitledBorder createTitledBorder(Border border)
Border titledBorder = BorderFactory.createTitledBorder(lineBorder);


public TitledBorder(String title)
Border titledBorder = new TitledBorder("Hello");

public static TitledBorder createTitledBorder(String title)
Border titledBorder = BorderFactory.createTitledBorder("Hello");


public TitledBorder(Border border, String title)
Border titledBorder = new TitledBorder(lineBorder, "Hello");

public static TitledBorder createTitledBorder(Border border, String title)
Border titledBorder = BorderFactory.createTitledBorder(lineBorder, "Hello");


public TitledBorder(Border border, String title, int justification, int position)
Border titledBorder = new TitledBorder(lineBorder, "Hello", TitledBorder.LEFT,
  TitledBorder.BELOW_BOTTOM);
```

```
public static TitledBorder createTitledBorder(Border border, String title,
  int justification, int position)
Border titledBorder = BorderFactory.createTitledBorder(lineBorder, "Hello",
  TitledBorder.LEFT, TitledBorder.BELOW_BOTTOM);
```

```
public TitledBorder(Border border, String title, int justification, int position,
  Font font)
Font font = new Font("Serif", Font.ITALIC, 12);
Border titledBorder = new TitledBorder(lineBorder, "Hello", TitledBorder.LEFT,
  TitledBorder.BELOW_BOTTOM, font);
```

```
public static TitledBorder createTitledBorder(Border border, String title,
  int justification, int position, Font font)
Font font = new Font("Serif", Font.ITALIC, 12);
Border titledBorder = BorderFactory.createTitledBorder(lineBorder, "Hello",
  TitledBorder.LEFT, TitledBorder.BELOW_BOTTOM, font);
```

```
public TitledBorder(Border border, String title, int justification, int position,
  Font font, Color color)
Font font = new Font("Serif", Font.ITALIC, 12);
Border titledBorder = new TitledBorder(lineBorder, "Hello", TitledBorder.LEFT,
  TitledBorder.BELOW_BOTTOM, font, Color.RED);
```

```
public static TitledBorder createTitledBorder(Border border, String title,
  int justification, int position, Font font, Color color)
Font font = new Font("Serif", Font.ITALIC, 12);
Border titledBorder = BorderFactory.createTitledBorder(lineBorder, "Hello",
  TitledBorder.LEFT, TitledBorder.BELOW_BOTTOM, font, Color.RED);
```

Configuring Properties

Unlike all the other predefined borders, titled borders have six setter methods to modify their attributes *after* border creation. As shown in Table 7-3, you can modify a titled border's underlying border, title, drawing color, font, text justification, and text position.

Table 7-3. *TitledBorder Properties*

Property Name	Data Type	Access
border	Border	Read-write
borderOpaque	boolean	Read-only
title	String	Read-write
titleColor	Color	Read-write
titleFont	Font	Read-write
titleJustification	int	Read-write
titlePosition	int	Read-write

■**Tip** To reduce screen redrawing, it's better to modify the properties of a titled border prior to placing the border around a component.

Text justification of the title string within a `TitledBorder` is specified by one of four class constants:

- `CENTER`: Place the title in the center.
- `DEFAULT_JUSTIFICATION`: Use the default setting to position the text. The value is equivalent to `LEFT`.
- `LEFT`: Place the title on the left edge.
- `RIGHT`: Place the title on the right edge.

Figure 7-13 shows the same `TitledBorder` with three different justifications.

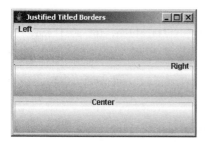

Figure 7-13. *Title justifications*

You can position title strings in any one of six different locations, as specified by one of seven class constants:

- `ABOVE_BOTTOM`: Place the title above the bottom line.
- `ABOVE_TOP`: Place the title above the top line.
- `BELOW_BOTTOM`: Place the title below the bottom line.
- `BELOW_TOP`: Place the title below the top line.
- `BOTTOM`: Place the title on the bottom line.
- `DEFAULT_POSITION`: Use the default setting to place the text. This value is equivalent to `TOP`.
- `TOP`: Place the title on the top line.

Figure 7-14 shows the six different positions available for the title on a `TitledBorder`.

Figure 7-14. *Title positioning*

Because a TitledBorder contains another Border, you can combine more than one border to place multiple titles along a single border. For example, Figure 7-15 shows a title along the top *and* bottom of the border.

Figure 7-15. *Showing multiple titles on a TitledBorder*

The program used to generate Figure 7-15 is shown in Listing 7-2.

Listing 7-2. *Multiple Titles on a TitledBorder*

```
import javax.swing.*;
import javax.swing.border.*;
import java.awt.*;

public class DoubleTitle {
  public static void main(String args[]) {
    Runnable runner = new Runnable() {
      public void run() {
        JFrame frame = new JFrame("Double Title");
        frame.setDefaultCloseOperation(JFrame.EXIT_ON_CLOSE);
        TitledBorder topBorder = BorderFactory.createTitledBorder("Top");
        topBorder.setTitlePosition(TitledBorder.TOP);
        TitledBorder doubleBorder = new TitledBorder(topBorder, "Bottom",
          TitledBorder.RIGHT, TitledBorder.BOTTOM);
        JButton doubleButton = new JButton();
        doubleButton.setBorder(doubleBorder);
        frame.add(doubleButton, BorderLayout.CENTER);
```

```
        frame.setSize(300, 100);
        frame.setVisible(true);
      }
    };
    EventQueue.invokeLater(runner);
  }
}
```

Customizing TitledBorder Look and Feel

The available set of UIResource-related properties for a TitledBorder is shown in Table 7-4. It has three different properties.

Table 7-4. *TitledBorder UIResource Elements*

Property String	Object Type
TitledBorder.font	Font
TitledBorder.titleColor	Color
TitledBorder.border	Border

Creating Your Own Borders

When you want to create your own distinctive border, you can either create a new class that implements the Border interface directly or you can extend the AbstractBorder class. As previously mentioned, extending the AbstractBorder class is the better way to go, because optimizations are built in to certain Swing classes to take advantage of some of the AbstractBorder-specific methods. For instance, if a border is an AbstractBorder, JComponent will reuse an Insets object when getting the Insets of a border. Thus, one fewer object will need to be created and destroyed each time the insets are fetched.

In addition to thinking about subclassing AbstractBorder versus implementing the Border interface yourself, you need to consider whether or not you want a static border. If you attach a border to a button, you want that button to be able to signal selection. You must examine the component passed into the paintBorder() method and react accordingly. In addition, you should also draw a disabled border to indicate when the component isn't selectable. Although setEnabled(false) disables the selection of the component, if the component has a border associated with it, the border still must be drawn, even when disabled. Figure 7-16 shows one border in action that looks at all these options for the component passed into the border's paintBorder() method.

Figure 7-16. *Active custom border examples*

The source for the custom border and the sample program is shown in Listing 7-3.

Listing 7-3. *Custom Colorized Border*

```java
import javax.swing.*;
import javax.swing.border.*;
import java.awt.*;

public class RedGreenBorder extends AbstractBorder {
  public boolean isBorderOpaque() {
    return true;
  }
  public Insets getBorderInsets(Component c) {
    return new Insets(3, 3, 3, 3);
  }
  public void paintBorder(Component c, Graphics g, int x, int y, int width,
      int height) {
    Insets insets = getBorderInsets(c);
    Color horizontalColor;
    Color verticalColor;
    if (c.isEnabled()) {
      boolean pressed = false;
      if (c instanceof AbstractButton) {
        ButtonModel model = ((AbstractButton)c).getModel();
        pressed = model.isPressed();
      }
      if (pressed) {
        horizontalColor = Color.RED;
        verticalColor = Color.GREEN;
      } else {
        horizontalColor = Color.GREEN;
        verticalColor = Color.RED;
      }
    } else {
      horizontalColor = Color.LIGHT_GRAY;
      verticalColor = Color.LIGHT_GRAY;
    }
    g.setColor(horizontalColor);

    g.translate(x, y);

    // Top
    g.fillRect(0, 0, width, insets.top);
     // Bottom
    g.fillRect(0, height-insets.bottom, width, insets.bottom);
```

```
      g.setColor(verticalColor);
      // Left
      g.fillRect(0, insets.top, insets.left, height-insets.top-insets.bottom);
       // Right
      g.fillRect(width-insets.right, insets.top, insets.right,
        height-insets.top-insets.bottom);
      g.translate(-x, -y);
    }
    public static void main(String args[]) {
      Runnable runner = new Runnable() {
        public void run() {
          JFrame frame = new JFrame("My Border");
          frame.setDefaultCloseOperation(JFrame.EXIT_ON_CLOSE);
          Border border = new RedGreenBorder();
          JButton helloButton = new JButton("Hello");
          helloButton.setBorder(border);
          JButton braveButton = new JButton("Brave New");
          braveButton.setBorder(border);
          braveButton.setEnabled(false);
          JButton worldButton = new JButton("World");
          worldButton.setBorder(border);
          frame.add(helloButton, BorderLayout.NORTH);
          frame.add(braveButton, BorderLayout.CENTER);
          frame.add(worldButton, BorderLayout.SOUTH);
          frame.setSize(300, 100);
          frame.setVisible(true);
        }
      };
      EventQueue.invokeLater(runner);
    }
}
```

■**Note** Another interesting custom border is one that displays an active component instead of a text title in
a TitledBorder. Imagine a border that has a JCheckBox or JRadioButton instead of a text string for the
title. You can also use a JLabel and pass in HTML for the text.

Summary

In this chapter, you learned about the use of the Border interface and its many predefined
implementations. You also learned how to create predefined borders using the Factory design
pattern provided by the BorderFactory class. Lastly, you saw how to define your own borders
and why subclassing AbstractBorder is beneficial.

In Chapter 8, you'll move beyond low-level components and examine the window-like
container objects available in Swing.

CHAPTER 8

■■■

Root Pane Containers

In Chapter 7, you looked at working with borders around Swing components. In this chapter, you'll explore the high-level Swing containers and discover how they differ from their AWT counterparts.

Working with top-level containers in Swing is a bit different from working with top-level AWT containers. With the AWT containers of Frame, Window, Dialog, and Applet, you added components directly to the container, and there was only one place you could add them. In the Swing world, the top-level containers of JFrame, JWindow, JDialog, and JApplet, plus the JInternalFrame container, rely on something called a JRootPane. Instead of adding components directly to the container, you add them to a part of the *root pane*. The root pane then manages them all internally.

Why was this indirect layer added? Believe it or not, it was done to simplify things. The root pane manages its components in layers so that elements such as tooltip text will always appear *above* components, and you don't need to worry about dragging some components around behind others.

The one container without an AWT counterpart, JInternalFrame, also provides some additional capabilities when placed within a desktop (within a JDesktopPane to be specific). The JInternalFrame class can be used as the basis for creating a Multiple Document Interface (MDI) application architecture within a Swing program. You can manage a series of internal frames within your program, and they'll never go beyond the bounds of your main program window.

Let's begin by exploring the new JRootPane class, which manages the internals of all the top-level containers.

JRootPane Class

The JRootPane class acts as a container delegate for the top-level Swing containers. Because the container holds only a JRootPane when you add or remove components from a top-level container, instead of directly altering the components in the container, you indirectly add or remove components from its JRootPane instance. In effect, the top-level containers are acting as proxies, with the JRootPane doing all the work.

The JRootPane container relies on its inner class RootLayout for layout management and takes up all the space of the top-level container that holds it. There are only two components within a JRootPane: a JLayeredPane and a glass pane (Component). The glass pane is in front, can be any component, and tends to be invisible. The glass pane ensures that elements such as tooltip text appear in front of any other Swing components. In the back is the JLayeredPane, which contains an optional JMenuBar on top and a content pane (Container) below it in another layer. It is within the content pane that you would normally place components in the JRootPane. Figure 8-1 should help you visualize how the RootLayout lays out the components.

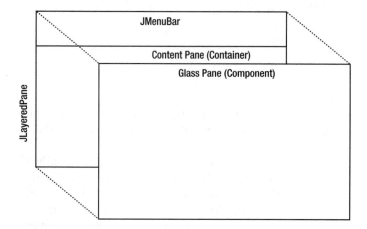

Figure 8-1. *JRootPane containment diagram*

■**Note** A JLayeredPane is just another Swing container (it's described later in this chapter). It can contain any components and has a special layering characteristic. The default JLayeredPane used within the JRootPane pane contains only a JMenuBar and a Container as its content pane. The content pane has its own layout manager, which is BorderLayout by default.

Creating a JRootPane

Although the JRootPane has a public no-argument constructor, a JRootPane isn't something you would normally create yourself. Instead, a class that implements the RootPaneContainer interface creates the JRootPane. Then, you can get the root pane from that component, through the RootPaneContainer interface, described shortly.

JRootPane Properties

As Table 8-1 shows, there are 11 properties of JRootPane. In most cases, when you get or set one of these properties for a top-level container, like JFrame, the container simply passes along the request to its JRootPane.

The glass pane for a JRootPane must not be opaque. Because the glass pane takes up the entire area in front of the JLayeredPane, an opaque glass pane would render the menu bar and content pane invisible. And, because the glass pane and content pane share the same bounds, the optimizedDrawingEnabled property returns the visibility of the glass pane as its setting.

Table 8-1. *JRootPane Properties*

Property Name	Data Type	Access
accessibleContext	AccessibleContext	Read-only
contentPane	Container	Read-write
defaultButton	JButton	Read-write bound
glassPane	Component	Read-write
jMenuBar	JMenuBar	Read-write
layeredPane	JLayeredPane	Read-write
optimizedDrawingEnabled	boolean	Read-only
UI	RootPaneUI	Read-write
UIClassID	String	Read-only
validateRoot	boolean	Read-only
windowDecorationStyle	int	Read-write bound

The windowDecorationStyle property is meant to describe the window adornments (border, title, buttons for closing window) for the window containing the JRootPane. It can be set to one of the following JRootPane class constants:

- COLOR_CHOOSER_DIALOG

- ERROR_DIALOG

- FILE_CHOOSER_DIALOG

- FRAME

- INFORMATION_DIALOG

- NONE

- PLAIN_DIALOG

- QUESTION_DIALOG

- WARNING_DIALOG

What exactly happens with the windowDecorationStyle setting depends on the current look and feel. It is just a hint. By default, this setting is NONE. If this setting is not NONE, the setUndecorated() method of JDialog or JFrame has been called with a value of true, and the getSupportsWindowDecorations() method of the current look and feel reports true, then the look and feel, rather than the window manager, will provide the window adornments. This allows you to have programs with top-level windows that look like they do not come from the platform the user is working on but from your own environment, though still providing iconify, maximize, minimize, and close buttons.

For the Metal look and feel (and Ocean theme), getSupportsWindowDecorations() reports true. The other system-provided look and feel types report false. Figure 8-2 demonstrates what a frame looks like with the window adornments provided by the Metal look and feel.

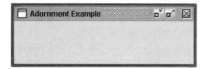

Figure 8-2. *Metal window adornments for a JFrame*

The source to produce Figure 8-2 is shown in Listing 8-1.

Listing 8-1. *Setting the Window Decoration Style*

```java
import java.awt.*;
import javax.swing.*;

public class AdornSample {

  public static void main(final String args[]) {
    Runnable runner = new Runnable() {
      public void run() {
        JFrame frame = new JFrame("Adornment Example");
        frame.setDefaultCloseOperation(JFrame.EXIT_ON_CLOSE);
        frame.setUndecorated(true);
        frame.getRootPane().setWindowDecorationStyle(JRootPane.FRAME);
        frame.setSize(300, 100);
        frame.setVisible(true);
      }
    };
    EventQueue.invokeLater(runner);
  }
}
```

Customizing a JRootPane Look and Feel

Table 8-2 shows the 12 UIResource-related properties for a JRootPane. Most of these settings have to do with the default border to use when configuring the window decoration style.

Table 8-2. *JRootPane UIResource Elements*

Property String	Object Type
RootPane.actionMap	ActionMap
RootPane.ancestorInputMap	InputMap
RootPane.colorChooserDialogBorder	Border

Table 8-2. *JRootPane UIResource Elements (Continued)*

Property String	Object Type
RootPane.defaultButtonWindowKeyBindings	Object[ ]
RootPane.errorDialogBorder	Border
RootPane.fileChooserDialogBorder	Border
RootPane.frameBorder	Border
RootPane.informationDialogBorder	Border
RootPane.plainDialogBorder	Border
RootPane.questionDialogBorder	Border
RootPane.warningDialogBorder	Border
RootPaneUI	String

RootPaneContainer Interface

The RootPaneContainer interface defines the setter/getter methods for accessing the different panes within the JRootPane, as well as accessing the JRootPane itself.

```
public interface RootPaneContainer {
  // Properties
  public Container getContentPane();
  public void setContentPane(Container contentPane);
  public Component getGlassPane();
  public void setGlassPane(Component glassPane);
  public JLayeredPane getLayeredPane();
  public void setLayeredPane(JLayeredPane layeredPane);
  public JRootPane getRootPane();
}
```

Among the predefined Swing components, the JFrame, JWindow, JDialog, JApplet, and JInternalFrame classes implement the RootPaneContainer interface. For the most part, these implementations simply pass along the request to a JRootPane implementation for the high-level container. The following source code is one such implementation for the glass pane of a RootPaneContainer implementer:

```
public Component getGlassPane() {
  return getRootPane().getGlassPane();
}
public void setGlassPane(Component glassPane) {
  getRootPane().setGlassPane(glassPane);
}
```

JLayeredPane Class

The JLayeredPane serves as the main component container of a JRootPane. The JLayeredPane manages the z-order, or layering, of components within itself. This ensures that the correct component is drawn on top of other components for tasks such as creating tooltip text, pop-up menus, and dragging for drag-and-drop. You can use the system-defined layers, or you can create your own layers.

Although initially a JLayeredPane container has no layout manager, there's nothing to stop you from setting the layout property of the container, defeating the layering aspect of the container.

Creating a JLayeredPane

As with the JRootPane, you'll almost never create an instance of the JLayeredPane class yourself. When the default JRootPane is created for one of the predefined classes that implement RootPaneContainer, the JRootPane creates a JLayeredPane for its main component area, adding an initial content pane.

Adding Components in Layers

A layer setting for each added component manages the z-order of components within a JLayeredPane. The higher the layer setting, the closer to the top the component will be drawn. You can set the layer with the layout manager constraints when you add a component to a JLayeredPane:

```
Integer layer = new Integer(20);
aLayeredPane.add(aComponent, layer);
```

You can also call the public void setLayer(Component comp, int layer) or public void setLayer(Component comp, int layer, int position) method *before* adding the component to the JLayeredPane.

```
aLayeredPane.setLayer(aComponent, 10);
aLayeredPane.add(aComponent);
```

The JLayeredPane class predefines six constants for special values. In addition, you can find out the topmost current layer with public int c and the bottom layer with public int lowestLayer(). Table 8-3 lists the six predefined layer constants.

Table 8-3. *JLayeredPane Layer Constants*

Constant	Description
FRAME_CONTENT_LAYER	Level –30,000 for holding the menu bar and content pane; not normally used by developers
DEFAULT_LAYER	Level 0 for the normal component level
PALETTE_LAYER	Level 100 for holding floating toolbars and the like
MODAL_LAYER	Level 200 for holding pop-up dialog boxes that appear on top of components on the default layer, on top of palettes, and below pop-ups
POPUP_LAYER	Level 300 for holding pop-up menus and tooltips
DRAG_LAYER	Level 400 for ensuring that dragged objects remain on top

Although you can use your own constants for layers, use them with care—because the system will use the predefined constants for *its* needs. If your constants don't fit in properly, the components may not work as you intended.

To visualize how the different layers fit in, see Figure 8-3.

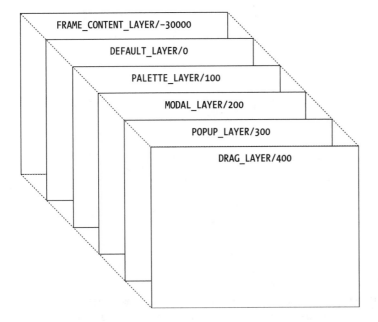

Figure 8-3. *JLayeredPane layers*

Working with Component Layers and Positions

Components in a JLayeredPane have both a layer and a position. When a single component is on a layer, it's at position 0. When multiple components are on the same layer, components added later have higher position numbers. The lower the position setting, the closer to the top the component will appear. (This is the reverse of the layering behavior.) Figure 8-4 shows the positions for four components on the same layer.

To rearrange components on a single layer, you can use either the public void moveToBack(Component component) or public void moveToFront(Component component) method. When you move a component to the front, it goes to position 0 for the layer. When you move a component to the back, it goes to the highest position number for the layer. You can also manually set the position with public void setPosition(Component component, int position). A position of –1 is automatically the bottom layer with the highest position (see Figure 8-4).

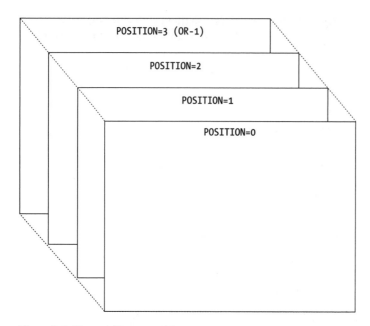

Figure 8-4. *JLayeredPane positions*

JLayeredPane Properties

Table 8-4 shows the two properties of JLayeredPane. The optimizedDrawingEnabled property determines whether components within the JLayeredPane can overlap. By default, this setting is true because in the standard usage with JRootPane the JMenuBar and content pane can't overlap. However, the JLayeredPane automatically validates the property setting to reflect the current state of the contents of the pane.

Table 8-4. *JLayeredPane Properties*

Property Name	Data Type	Access
accessibleContext	AccessibleContext	Read-only
optimizedDrawingEnabled	boolean	Read-only

JFrame Class

The JFrame class is the Swing high-level container that uses a JRootPane and implements the RootPaneContainer interface. In addition, it uses the WindowConstants interface to help manage closing operations.

Creating a JFrame

The JFrame class provides two primary constructors: one for creating a frame without a title and one for creating a frame with a title. There are two additional constructors for creating frames with a specialized GraphicsConfiguration.

public JFrame()
```
JFrame frame = new JFrame();
```

public JFrame(String title)
```
JFrame frame = new JFrame("Title Bar");
```

public JFrame(GraphicsConfiguration config)
```
GraphicsEnvironment ge = GraphicsEnvironment.getLocalGraphicsEnvironment();
GraphicsDevice gsd[] = ge.getScreenDevices();
GraphicsConfiguration gc[] = gsd[0].getConfigurations();
JFrame frame = new JFrame(gc[0]);
```

public JFrame(String title, GraphicsConfiguration config)
```
GraphicsConfiguration gc = ...;
JFrame frame = new JFrame("Title Bar", gc);
```

JFrame Properties

Table 8-5 shows the nine properties of the JFrame.

Table 8-5. *JFrame Properties*

Property Name	Data Type	Access
accessibleContext	AccessibleContext	Read-only
contentPane	Container	Read-write
defaultCloseOperation	int	Read-write
glassPane	Component	Read-write
iconImage	Image	Write-only
jMenuBar	JMenuBar	Read-write
layeredPane	JLayeredPane	Read-write
layout	LayoutManager	Write-only
rootPane	JRootPane	Read-only

Although most properties are the result of implementing the RootPaneContainer interface, two properties are special: defaultCloseOperation and layout. (You first looked at the defaultCloseOperation property in Chapter 2.) By default, a JFrame hides itself when the user closes the window. To change the setting, you can use one of the constants listed in Table 8-6 as arguments when setting the default close operation. The first comes from JFrame directly; the others are part of the WindowConstants interface.

```
aFrame.setDefaultCloseOperation(JFrame.DISPOSE_ON_CLOSE);
```

Table 8-6. *Close Operation Constants*

Constant	Description
EXIT_ON_CLOSE	Call System.exit(0).
DISPOSE_ON_CLOSE	Call dispose() on the frame.
DO_NOTHING_ON_CLOSE	Ignore the request.
HIDE_ON_CLOSE	Call setVisible(false) on the frame; this is the default.

The layout property is odd. By default, setting the layout manager of the JFrame passes the call along to the content pane. You can't change the default layout manager of the JFrame.

■Tip You can use the state property (inherited from Frame) to say whether the JFrame is currently icon-ified. When using the property, be sure to use one of the additional Frame constants of NORMAL or ICONIFIED to set its state.

There is an additional static property of JFrame: defaultLookAndFeelDecorated. This works with the windowDecorationStyle property of JRootPane. When set to true, newly created frames will be adorned with decorations from the look and feel instead of the window manager. Of course, this happens only if the current look and feel supports window decorations. Listing 8-2 shows an alternate way to generate the same screen (with the window adornments provided by the Metal look and feel) as the one shown earlier in Figure 8-2.

Listing 8-2. *Alternative Way of Setting the Window Decoration Style*

```java
import java.awt.*;
import javax.swing.*;

public class AdornSample2 {
```

```
  public static void main(final String args[]) {
    Runnable runner = new Runnable() {
      public void run() {
        JFrame.setDefaultLookAndFeelDecorated(true);
        JFrame frame = new JFrame("Adornment Example");
        frame.setDefaultCloseOperation(JFrame.EXIT_ON_CLOSE);
        frame.setSize(300, 100);
        frame.setVisible(true);
      }
    };
    EventQueue.invokeLater(runner);
  }
}
```

Adding Components to a JFrame

Because JFrame implements the RootPaneContainer interface and uses a JRootPane, you don't add components directly to the JFrame. Instead, you add them to the JRootPane contained within the JFrame. Prior to J2SE 5.0, you needed to add components like this:

```
JRootPane rootPane = aJFrame.getRootPane();
Container contentPane = rootPane.getContentPane();
contentPane.add(...);
```

This can be shortened to the following form:

```
aJFrame.getContentPane().add(...);
```

If you tried to add components directly to the JFrame, it resulted in a runtime error being thrown.

Due to many suggestions (complaints?), Sun finally decided to change the add() method into a proxy:

```
// J2SE 5.0
aJFrame.add(...);
```

With J2SE 5.0, when you add components to the JFrame, they actually are added to the content pane of the RootPaneContainer.

Handling JFrame Events

The JFrame class supports the registration of eleven different listeners:

- ComponentListener: To find out when the frame moves or is resized.

- ContainerListener: Normally not added to a JFrame because you add components to the content pane of its JRootPane.

- FocusListener: To find out when the frame gets or loses input focus.

- `HierarchyBoundsListener`: To find out when the frame moves or is resized. This works similarly to `ComponentListener`, since the frame is the top-level container of component.

- `HierarchyListener`: To find out when the frame is shown or hidden.

- `InputMethodListener`: To work with input methods for internationalization.

- `KeyListener`: Normally not added to a `JFrame`. Instead, you register a keyboard action for its content pane, like this:

```
JPanel content = (JPanel)frame.getContentPane();
KeyStroke stroke = KeyStroke.getKeyStroke(KeyEvent.VK_ESCAPE, 0);
content.registerKeyboardAction(actionListener, stroke,
  JComponent.WHEN_IN_FOCUSED_WINDOW);
```

- `MouseListener` and `MouseMotionListener`: To listen for mouse and mouse motion events.

- `PropertyChangeListener`: To listen for changes to bound properties.

- `WindowListener`: To find out when a window is iconified or deiconified or a user is trying to open or close the window.

With the help of the `defaultCloseOperation` property, you typically don't need to add a `WindowListener` to help with closing the frame or stopping the application.

Extending JFrame

If you need to extend `JFrame`, this class has two important `protected` methods:

```
protected void frameInit()
protected JRootPane createRootPane()
```

By overriding either of these methods in a subclass, you can customize the initial appearance and behavior of the frame or that of its `JRootPane`. For example, in the `ExitableJFrame` class shown in Listing 8-3, the default close operation is initialized to the `EXIT_ON_CLOSE` state. Instead of calling `setDefaultCloseOperation()` for every frame created, you can use this class instead. Because `JFrame` was subclassed, you don't need to add a call to the `frameInit()` method in either of the constructors. The parent class automatically calls the method.

Listing 8-3. *Closing Frames by Default*

```
import javax.swing.JFrame;
public class ExitableJFrame extends JFrame {
  public ExitableJFrame () {
  }
  public ExitableJFrame (String title) {
    super (title);
  }
```

```
  protected void frameInit() {
    super.frameInit();
    setDefaultCloseOperation(EXIT_ON_CLOSE);
  }
}
```

Caution If you do override the `frameInit()` method of `JFrame`, remember to call `super.frameInit()` first, to initialize the default behaviors. If you forget and don't reimplement all the default behaviors yourself, your new frame will look and act differently.

JWindow Class

The `JWindow` class is similar to the `JFrame` class. It uses a `JRootPane` for component management and implements the `RootPaneContainer` interface. Basically, it is a top-level window with no adornments.

Creating a JWindow

The `JWindow` class has five constructors:

public JWindow()
```
JWindow window = new JWindow();
```

public JWindow(Frame owner)
```
JWindow window = new JWindow(aFrame);
```

public JWindow(GraphicsConfiguration config)
```
GraphicsConfiguration gc = ...;
JWindow window = new JWindow(gc);
```

public JWindow(Window owner)
```
JWindow window = new JWindow(anotherWindow);
```

public JWindow(Window owner, GraphicsConfiguration config)
```
GraphicsConfiguration gc = ...;
JWindow window = new JWindow(anotherWindow, gc);
```

You can create a window without specifying a parent or by specifying the parent as a `Frame` or `Window`. If no parent is specified, an invisible one is used.

JWindow Properties

Table 8-7 lists the six properties of JWindow. These are similar in nature to the JFrame properties, except that JWindow has no property for a default close operation or a menu bar.

Table 8-7. *JWindow Properties*

Property Name	Data Type	Access
accessibleContext	AccessibleContext	Read-only
contentPane	Container	Read-write
glassPane	Component	Read-write
layeredPane	JLayeredPane	Read-write
layout	LayoutManager	Write-only
rootPane	JRootPane	Read-only

Handling JWindow Events

The JWindow class adds no additional event-handling capabilities beyond those of the JFrame and Window classes. See the "Handling JFrame Events" section earlier in this chapter for a list of listeners you can attach to a JWindow.

Extending JWindow

If you need to extend JWindow, the class has two protected methods of importance:

```
protected void windowInit()
protected JRootPane createRootPane()
```

JDialog Class

The JDialog class represents the standard pop-up window for displaying information related to a Frame. It acts like a JFrame, whereby its JRootPane contains a content pane and an optional JMenuBar, and it implements the RootPaneContainer and WindowConstants interfaces.

Creating a JDialog

There are 11 constructors for creating JDialog windows:

public JDialog()
```
JDialog dialog = new JDialog();
```

public JDialog(Dialog owner)
```
JDialog dialog = new JDialog(anotherDialog);
```

```
public JDialog(Dialog owner, boolean modal)
JDialog dialog = new JDialog(anotherDialog, true);

public JDialog(Dialog owner, String title)
JDialog dialog = new JDialog(anotherDialog, "Hello");

public JDialog(Dialog owner, String title, boolean modal)
JDialog dialog = new JDialog(anotherDialog, "Hello", true);

public JDialog(Dialog owner, String title, boolean modal, GraphicsConfiguration gc)
GraphicsConfiguration gc = ...;
JDialog dialog = new JDialog(anotherDialog, "Hello", true, gc);

public JDialog(Frame owner)
JDialog dialog = new JDialog(aFrame);

public JDialog(Frame owner, String windowTitle)
JDialog dialog = new JDialog(aFrame, "Hello");

public JDialog(Frame owner, boolean modal)
JDialog dialog = new JDialog(aFrame, false);

public JDialog(Frame owner, String title, boolean modal)
JDialog dialog = new JDialog(aFrame, "Hello", true);

public JDialog(Frame owner, String title, boolean modal, GraphicsConfiguration gc)
GraphicsConfiguration gc = ...;
JDialog dialog = new JDialog(aFrame, "Hello", true, gc);
```

■**Note** Instead of manually creating a JDialog and populating it, you may find yourself having JOptionPane automatically create and fill the JDialog for you. You'll explore the JOptionPane component in Chapter 9.

Each constructor allows you to customize the dialog owner, the window title, and the modality of the pop-up. When a JDialog is modal, it blocks input to the owner and the rest of the application. When a JDialog is nonmodal, it allows a user to interact with the JDialog as well as the rest of your application.

■**Caution** For modality to work properly among the different Java versions, avoid mixing heavyweight AWT components with lightweight Swing components in a JDialog.

JDialog Properties

Other than the settable icon image, the `JDialog` class has the same properties as `JFrame`. These eight properties are listed in Table 8-8.

Table 8-8. *JDialog Properties*

Property Name	Data Type	Access
accessibleContext	AccessibleContext	Read-only
contentPane	Container	Read-write
defaultCloseOperation	int	Read-write
glassPane	Component	Read-write
jMenuBar	JMenuBar	Read-write
layeredPane	JLayeredPane	Read-write
layout	LayoutManager	Write-only
rootPane	JRootPane	Read-only

The constants to use for specifying the default close operation are the `WindowConstants` shown earlier in Table 8-6 (basically all but `EXIT_ON_CLOSE`). By default, the `defaultCloseOperation` property is set to `HIDE_ON_CLOSE`, which is the desirable default behavior for a dialog pop-up.

Like `JFrame`, `JDialog` also has a static `defaultLookAndFeelDecorated` property. This controls whether or not dialogs are decorated by the look and feel, by default.

Handling JDialog Events

There are no special `JDialog` events for you to deal with; it has the same events as those for the `JFrame` class.

One thing that you may want to do with a `JDialog` is specify that pressing the Escape key cancels the dialog. The easiest way to do this is to register an Escape keystroke to a keyboard action within the `JRootPane` of the dialog, causing the `JDialog` to become hidden when Escape is pressed. Listing 8-4 demonstrates this behavior. Most of the source duplicates the constructors of `JDialog`. The `createRootPane()` method maps the Escape key to the custom `Action`.

Listing 8-4. *A JDialog That Closes When Escape Is Pressed*

```
import javax.swing.*;
import java.awt.*;
import java.awt.event.*;

public class EscapeDialog extends JDialog {
  public EscapeDialog() {
    this((Frame)null, false);
  }
```

```java
public EscapeDialog(Frame owner) {
  this(owner, false);
}
public EscapeDialog(Frame owner, boolean modal) {
  this(owner, null, modal);
}
public EscapeDialog(Frame owner, String title) {
  this(owner, title, false);
}
public EscapeDialog(Frame owner, String title, boolean modal) {
  super(owner, title, modal);
}
public EscapeDialog(Frame owner, String title, boolean modal,
    GraphicsConfiguration gc) {
  super(owner, title, modal, gc);
}
public EscapeDialog(Dialog owner) {
  this(owner, false);
}
public EscapeDialog(Dialog owner, boolean modal) {
  this(owner, null, modal);
}
public EscapeDialog(Dialog owner, String title) {
  this(owner, title, false);
}
public EscapeDialog(Dialog owner, String title, boolean modal) {
  super(owner, title, modal);
}
public EscapeDialog(Dialog owner, String title, boolean modal,
    GraphicsConfiguration gc) {
  super(owner, title, modal, gc);
}
protected JRootPane createRootPane() {
  JRootPane rootPane = new JRootPane();
  KeyStroke stroke = KeyStroke.getKeyStroke("ESCAPE");
  Action actionListener = new AbstractAction() {
    public void actionPerformed(ActionEvent actionEvent) {
      setVisible(false);
    }
  } ;
  InputMap inputMap = rootPane.getInputMap(JComponent.WHEN_IN_FOCUSED_WINDOW);
  inputMap.put(stroke, "ESCAPE");
  rootPane.getActionMap().put("ESCAPE", actionListener);

  return rootPane;
}
}
```

■Note If you use the static creation methods of JOptionPane, the JDialog windows it creates automatically have the Escape key registered to close the dialog.

Extending JDialog

If you need to extend JDialog, the class has two protected methods of importance:

```
protected void dialogInit()
protected JRootPane createRootPane()
```

The latter method is demonstrated in the previous example in Listing 8-4.

JApplet Class

The JApplet class is an extension to the AWT Applet class. For event handling to work properly within applets that use Swing components, your applets must subclass JApplet instead of Applet.

The JApplet works the same as the other high-level containers by implementing the RootPaneContainer interface. One important difference between JApplet and Applet is the default layout manager. Because you add components to the content pane of a JApplet, its default layout manager is BorderLayout. This is unlike the default layout manager of Applet, which is FlowLayout. In addition, Swing applets can also have a menu bar, or more specifically a JMenuBar, which is just another attribute of the JRootPane of the applet.

If you plan to deploy an applet that uses the Swing components, it is best to use the Java Plug-in from Sun Microsystems, because that will install the Swing libraries with the runtime.

■Tip To make sure you are running the Java Plug-in under Internet Explorer, select Internet Options from the Tools menu, and then choose the Advanced tab. Scroll down to the Java section immediately above Microsoft VM and make sure Use JRE [VERSION] for <applet> (requires restart) is selected. If [VERSION] isn't recent enough, you'll need to get a newer version from Sun at http://www.java.com.

If you need to extend the JApplet class, it has only one protected method of importance:

```
protected JRootPane createRootPane()
```

Working with a Desktop

Swing provides for the management of a set of frames within a common window or desktop. As discussed in Chapter 1, this management is commonly called MDI. The frames can be layered on top of one another or dragged around, and their appearance is specific to the current look and feel. The frames are instances of the JInternalFrame class, whereas the desktop is a specialized JLayeredPane called JDesktopPane. The management of the frames within a desktop is the responsibility of a DesktopManager, in which the default implementation that's provided is DefaultDesktopManager. The iconified form of a JInternalFrame on the desktop is represented by the `JDesktopIcon` inner class of `JInternalFrame`. There are also an `InternalFrameListener`, `InternalFrameAdapter`, and `InternalFrameEvent` for event handling.

First, let's look at the parts that make up the desktop, and then you'll see a complete example that uses all the parts.

■Note The Swing libraries provide only those tools necessary to build an application using MDI. You use these tools in whatever manner you see fit.

JInternalFrame Class

The `JInternalFrame` class is similar to the `JFrame` class. It acts as a high-level container, using the `RootPaneContainer` interface, but it isn't a top-level window. You must place internal frames within another top-level window. When dragged around, internal frames stay within the bounds of their container, which is usually a `JDesktopPane`. In addition, internal frames are lightweight and therefore offer a UI-delegate to make internal frames appear as the currently configured look and feel.

■Note As with the creation of a `JFrame`, the `JInternalFrame` is hidden when first created.

Creating a JInternalFrame

There are six constructors for `JInternalFrame`:

```
public JInternalFrame()
JInternalFrame frame = new JInternalFrame();

public JInternalFrame(String title)
JInternalFrame frame = new JInternalFrame("The Title");

public JInternalFrame(String title, boolean resizable)
JInternalFrame frame = new JInternalFrame("The Title", true);

public JInternalFrame(String title, boolean resizable, boolean closable)
JInternalFrame frame = new JInternalFrame("The Title", false, true);

public JInternalFrame(String title, boolean resizable, boolean
  closable, boolean maximizable)
JInternalFrame frame = new JInternalFrame("The Title", true, false, true);

public JInternalFrame(String title, boolean resizable, boolean
  closable, boolean maximizable, boolean iconifiable)
JInternalFrame frame = new JInternalFrame("The Title", false, true, false, true);
```

These constructors cascade in such a way that each adds a parameter to another constructor. With no arguments, the created JInternalFrame has no title and can't be resized, closed, maximized, or iconified. Internal frames can always be dragged, however.

Note In addition to your creating a JInternalFrame directly, you can rely on the JOptionPane to create an internal frame for common pop-up dialog boxes hosted by a JInternalFrame instead of being hosted by the standard JDialog.

JInternalFrame Properties

The 30 different properties for the JInternalFrame class are listed in Table 8-9. The layer property is listed twice as it has two setter methods, one for an int and another for an Integer.

Table 8-9. *JInternalFrame Properties*

Property Name	Data Type	Access
accessibleContext	AccessibleContext	Read-only
closable	boolean	Read-write bound
closed	boolean	Read-write bound constrained
contentPane	Container	Read-write bound
defaultCloseOperation	int	Read-write
desktopIcon	JInternalFrame.JDesktopIcon	Read-write bound
desktopPane	JDesktopPane	Read-only
focusCycleRoot	boolean	Read-write
focusCycleRootAncester	Container	Read-only
focusOwner	Component	Read-only
frameIcon	Icon	Read-write bound
glassPane	Component	Read-write bound
icon	boolean	Read-write bound constrained
iconifiable	boolean	Read-write
internalFrameListeners	InternalFrameListener[ ]	Read-only
jMenuBar	JMenuBar	Read-write bound
layer	int	Read-write
layer	Integer	Write-only
layeredPane	JLayeredPane	Read-write bound

Table 8-9. *JInternalFrame Properties (Continued)*

Property Name	Data Type	Access
layout	LayoutManager	Write-only
maximizable	boolean	Read-write bound
maximum	boolean	Read-write bound constrained
mostRecentFocusOwner	Component	Read-only
normalBounds	Rectangle	Read-write
resizable	boolean	Read-write bound
rootPane	JRootPane	Read-only bound
selected	boolean	Read-write bound constrained
title	String	Read-write bound
UI	InternalFrameUI	Read-write
UIClassID	String	Read-only
warningString	String	Read-only

The initial defaultCloseOperation property setting for a JInternalFrame is DISPOSE_ON_CLOSE for Java 1.3 releases and later. Earlier releases had a default setting of HIDE_ON_CLOSE. You can set this property to any of the WindowConstants settings shown earlier in Table 8-6.

The normalBounds property describes where an iconified internal frame would appear when deiconified. The focusOwner property provides the actual Component with the input focus when the specific JInternalFrame is active.

The JInternalFrame contains the only four constrained properties within the Swing classes: closed, icon, maximum, and selected. They're directly related to the four boolean constructor parameters. Each allows you to check on the current state of the property as well as change its setting. However, because the properties are constrained, whenever you try to set one, the attempt must be in a try-catch block, catching PropertyVetoException:

```
try {
  // Try to iconify internal frame
  internalFrame.setIcon(false);
} catch (PropertyVetoException propertyVetoException) {
  System.out.println("Rejected");
}
```

To help you work with some of the bound properties, the JInternalFrame class defines 11 constants, as listed in Table 8-10. They represent the string that should be returned by getPropertyName() for a PropertyChangeEvent within a PropertyChangeListener.

Table 8-10. *JInternalFrame Property Constants*

Property Name Constant	Associated Property
CONTENT_PANE_PROPERTY	contentPane
FRAME_ICON_PROPERTY	frameIcon
GLASS_PANE_PROPERTY	glassPane
IS_CLOSED_PROPERTY	closed
IS_ICON_PROPERTY	icon
IS_MAXIMUM_PROPERTY	maximum
IS_SELECTED_PROPERTY	selected
LAYERED_PANE_PROPERTY	layeredPane
MENU_BAR_PROPERTY	jMenuBar
ROOT_PANE_PROPERTY	rootPane
TITLE_PROPERTY	title

The following class example demonstrates the use of the constants within a PropertyChangeListener.

```
import java.beans.*;
import javax.swing.*;

public class InternalFramePropertyChangeHandler implements PropertyChangeListener {
  public void propertyChange(PropertyChangeEvent propertyChangeEvent) {
    String propertyName = propertyChangeEvent.getPropertyName();
    if (propertyName.equals(JInternalFrame.IS_ICON_PROPERTY)) {
      System.out.println("Icon property changed. React.");
    }
  }
}
```

Handling JInternalFrame Events

To help you use a JInternalFrame as you would use a JFrame, there's an additional event listener for responding to internal frame opening- and closing-related events. The interface is called InternalFrameListener, and its definition follows. It works similarly to the AWT WindowListener interface, but with a JInternalFrame instead of an AWT Window class.

```
public interface InternalFrameListener extends EventListener {
public void internalFrameActivated(InternalFrameEvent internalFrameEvent);
public void internalFrameClosed(InternalFrameEvent internalFrameEvent);
public void internalFrameClosing(InternalFrameEvent internalFrameEvent);
public void internalFrameDeactivated(InternalFrameEvent internalFrameEvent);
public void internalFrameDeiconified(InternalFrameEvent internalFrameEvent);
public void internalFrameIconified(InternalFrameEvent internalFrameEvent);
public void internalFrameOpened(InternalFrameEvent internalFrameEvent);
}
```

In addition, like the WindowAdapter class that has all the WindowListener methods stubbed out, there is an InternalFrameAdapter class with all the InternalFrameListener methods stubbed out. If you're not interested in all the event happenings of a JInternalFrame, you can subclass InternalFrameAdapter and override only those methods you're interested in. For instance, the listener shown in Listing 8-5 is interested in only the iconification methods. Instead of providing stubs for the other five methods of InternalFrameListener, you would need to subclass only InternalFrameAdapter and override the two relevant methods.

Listing 8-5. *Custom InternalFrameListener*

```
import javax.swing.*;
import javax.swing.event.*;

public class InternalFrameIconifyListener extends InternalFrameAdapter {
  public void internalFrameIconified(InternalFrameEvent internalFrameEvent) {
    JInternalFrame source = (JInternalFrame)internalFrameEvent.getSource();
    System.out.println ("Iconified: " + source.getTitle());
  }
  public void internalFrameDeiconified(InternalFrameEvent internalFrameEvent) {
    JInternalFrame source = (JInternalFrame)internalFrameEvent.getSource();
    System.out.println ("Deiconified: " + source.getTitle());
  }
}
```

The InternalFrameEvent class is a subclass of AWTEvent. To define the values returned by the public int getID() method of AWTEvent, the InternalFrameEvent class defines a constant for each of the specific event subtypes that can be used. In addition, two other constants designate the range of valid values. Table 8-11 lists the nine constants. You can also get the actual JInternalFrame from the event with getInternalFrame().

Table 8-11. *InternalFrameEvent Event Subtypes*

Event Subtype ID	Associated Interface Method
INTERNAL_FRAME_ACTIVATED	internalFrameActivated
INTERNAL_FRAME_CLOSED	internalFrameClosed
INTERNAL_FRAME_CLOSING	internalFrameClosing
INTERNAL_FRAME_DEACTIVATED	internalFrameDeactivated
INTERNAL_FRAME_DEICONIFIED	internalFrameDeiconified
INTERNAL_FRAME_FIRST	N/A
INTERNAL_FRAME_ICONIFIED	internalFrameIconified
INTERNAL_FRAME_LAST	N/A
INTERNAL_FRAME_OPENED	internalFrameOpened

Customizing a JInternalFrame Look and Feel

Because the JInternalFrame is a lightweight component, it has an installable look and feel. Each installable Swing look and feel provides a different JInternalFrame appearance and set of default UIResource values. Figure 8-5 shows the appearance of the JWindow container for the preinstalled set of look and feel types.

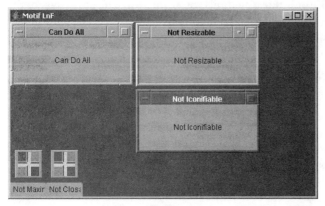

Motif

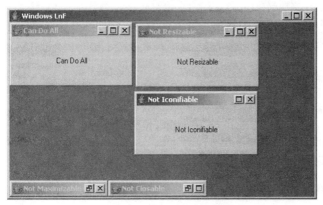

Windows

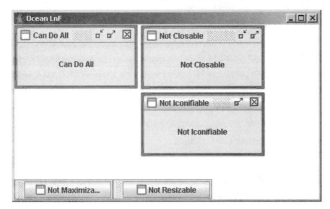

Ocean

Figure 8-5. *JInternalFrame under different look and feel types*

The available set of UIResource-related properties for a JInternalFrame is shown in Table 8-12. For the JInternalFrame component, there are 60 different properties, including those for the internal frame's title pane.

Table 8-12. *JInternalFrame UIResource Elements*

Property String	Object Type
InternalFrame.actionMap	ActionMap
InternalFrame.activeBorderColor	Color
InternalFrame.activeTitleBackground	Color
InternalFrame.activeTitleForeground	Color
InternalFrame.activeTitleGradient	List
InternalFrame.border	Border
InternalFrame.borderColor	Color
InternalFrame.borderDarkShadow	Color
InternalFrame.borderHighlight	Color
InternalFrame.borderLight	Color
InternalFrame.borderShadow	Color
InternalFrame.borderWidth	Integer
InternalFrame.closeButtonToolTip	String
InternalFrame.closeIcon	Icon
InternalFrame.closeSound	String
InternalFrame.icon	Icon
InternalFrame.iconButtonToolTip	String
InternalFrame.iconifyIcon	Icon
InternalFrame.inactiveBorderColor	Color
InternalFrame.inactiveTitleBackground	Color
InternalFrame.inactiveTitleForeground	Color
InternalFrame.inactiveTitleGradient	List
InternalFrame.layoutTitlePaneAtOrigin	Boolean
InternalFrame.maxButtonToolTip	String
InternalFrame.maximizeIcon	Icon
InternalFrame.maximizeSound	String
InternalFrame.minimizeIcon	Icon
InternalFrame.minimizeIconBackground	Color
InternalFrame.minimizeSound	String

Table 8-12. *JInternalFrame UIResource Elements (Continued)*

Property String	Object Type
InternalFrame.optionDialogBorder	Border
InternalFrame.paletteBorder	Border
InternalFrame.paletteCloseIcon	Icon
InternalFrame.paletteTitleHeight	Integer
InternalFrame.resizeIconHighlight	Color
InternalFrame.resizeIconShadow	Color
InternalFrame.restoreButtonToolTip	String
InternalFrame.restoreDownSound	String
InternalFrame.restoreUpSound	String
InternalFrame.titleButtonHeight	Integer
InternalFrame.titleButtonWidth	Integer
InternalFrame.titleFont	Font
InternalFrame.titlePaneHeight	Integer
InternalFrame.useTaskBar	Boolean
InternalFrame.windowBindings	Object[ ]
InternalFrameTitlePane.closeButtonAccessibleName	String
InternalFrameTitlePane.closeButtonText	String
InternalFrameTitlePane.closeIcon	Icon
InternalFrameTitlePane.iconifyButtonAccessibleName	String
InternalFrameTitlePane.iconifyIcon	Icon
InternalFrameTitlePane.maximizeButtonAccessibleName	String
InternalFrameTitlePane.maximizeButtonText	String
InternalFrameTitlePane.maximizeIcon	Icon
InternalFrameTitlePane.minimizeButtonText	String
InternalFrameTitlePane.minimizeIcon	Icon
InternalFrameTitlePane.moveButtonText	String
InternalFrameTitlePane.restoreButtonText	String
InternalFrameTitlePane.sizeButtonText	String
InternalFrameTitlePane.titlePaneLayout	LayoutManager
InternalFrameTitlePaneUI	String
InternalFrameUI	String

In addition to the many configurable properties in Table 8-12, with the Metal look and feel, you can designate an internal frame to be a "palette" by using a special client property, JInternalFrame.isPalette. When set to Boolean.TRUE, this internal frame will have a slightly different appearance from the others and a shorter title bar, as shown in Figure 8-6.

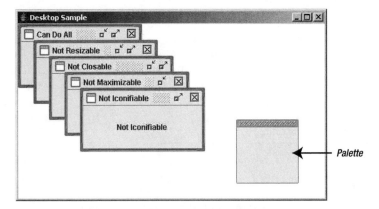

Figure 8-6. *A JInternalFrame palette with other frames*

If you also add an internal frame to the PALETTE_LAYER of the desktop, the frame will always appear on top of all the other frames (as noted in Figure 8-6):

```
JInternalFrame palette = new JInternalFrame("Palette", true, false, true, false);
palette.setBounds(150, 0, 100, 100);
palette.putClientProperty("JInternalFrame.isPalette", Boolean.TRUE);
desktop.add(palette, JDesktopPane.PALETTE_LAYER);
```

The complete source for creating the program in Figure 8-6 appears in Listing 8-6 later in this chapter.

■Note If the current look and feel is something other than Metal, the palette layer will still be honored, but its appearance won't be quite as distinctive.

Changing the JDesktopIcon

The JInternalFrame relies on an inner class, JDesktopIcon, to provide a UI delegate for the iconified view of the JInternalFrame. The class is merely a specialized JComponent for providing this capability, not a specialized Icon implementation, as the name might imply. In fact, the JDesktopIcon class comments say that the class is temporary, so you shouldn't try to customize it directly. (Of course, the class has been around for some time now.)

If you do want to customize the JDesktopIcon, you can change some of the UIResource-related properties. Table 8-13 lists the eight UIResource-related properties for the JDesktopIcon component.

Table 8-13. *JInternalFrame.DesktopIcon UIResource Elements*

Property String	Object Type
DesktopIcon.background	Color
DesktopIcon.border	Border
DesktopIcon.font	Font
DesktopIcon.foreground	Color
DesktopIcon.icon	Icon
DesktopIcon.width	Integer
DesktopIcon.windowBindings	Object[ ]
DesktopIconUI	String

JDesktopPane Class

Another class for working with groups of internal frames is the JDesktopPane class. The sole purpose of the desktop pane is to contain a set of internal frames. When internal frames are contained within a desktop pane, they delegate most of their behavior to the desktop manager of the desktop pane. You'll also learn about the DesktopManager interface in greater detail later in this chapter.

Creating a JDesktopPane

The JDesktopPane has a single no-argument constructor. Once it's created, you'd typically place the desktop in the center of a container managed by a BorderLayout. This ensures that the desktop takes up all the room in the container.

Adding Internal Frames to a JDesktopPane

The JDesktopPane doesn't implement RootPaneContainer. Instead of adding components to the different panes within a JRootPane, you add them directly to the JDesktopPane:

```
desktop.add(anInternalFrame);
```

JDesktopPane Properties

As Table 8-14 shows, there are eight properties of JDesktopPane. The JInternalFrame at index 0 of the allFrames property array is the internal frame in front of the desktop (JInternalFrame f = desktop.getAllFrames()[0]). Besides getting all the frames within the JDesktopPane, you can get only those within a specific layer: public JInternalFrame[] getAllFramesInLayer(int layer). (Remember JLayeredPane, covered earlier in this chapter in the "Working with Component Layers and Positions" section, the parent class of JDesktopPane?)

Valid dragMode property settings are the LIVE_DRAG_MODE and OUTLINE_DRAG_MODE constants of the class.

Table 8-14. *JDesktopPane Properties*

Property Name	Data Type	Access
accessibleContext	AccessibleContext	Read-only
allFrames	JInternalFrame[ ]	Read-only
desktopManager	DesktopManager	Read-write
dragMode	int	Read-write bound
opaque	boolean	Read-only
selectedFrame	JInternalFrame	Read-write
UI	DesktopPaneUI	Read-write
UIClassID	String	Read-only

■**Note** There is also a special client property (JDesktopPane.dragMode) for configuring the drawing mode when dragging an internal frame around. The client property has been replaced by the speedier versions available with the standard property.

Customizing a JDesktopPane Look and Feel

Back in Figure 8-5 you can see JInternalFrame objects within a JDesktopPane. The basic appearance of JDesktopPane is the same in each look and feel. As Table 8-15 shows, there aren't many UIResource-related properties for a JDesktopPane to configure.

Table 8-15. *JDesktopPane UIResource Elements*

Property String	Object Type
desktop	Color
Desktop.ancestorInputMap	InputMap
Desktop.background	Color
Desktop.windowBindings	Object[ ]
DesktopPane.actionMap	ActionMap
DesktopPaneUI	String

Complete Desktop Example

Now that you have the major desktop-related classes under your belt, let's look at a complete desktop example. The basic process involves creating a group of JInternalFrame objects and putting them in a single JDesktopPane. Event handling can be done for individual components on each of the internal frames, if desired, or for individual frames. In this example, simply use the InternalFrameIconifyListener class, presented earlier in Listing 8-5, to listen for internal frames being iconified and deiconified.

Figure 8-6 shows how the program looks when it first starts. One particular internal frame has been designated a palette, and the outline drag mode is enabled.

The complete source for the example is shown in Listing 8-6.

Listing 8-6. *Mixing JInternalFrames and the JDesktopPane*

```java
import javax.swing.*;
import javax.swing.event.*;
import java.awt.*;
import java.awt.event.*;

public class DesktopSample {

  public static void main(final String[] args) {
    Runnable runner = new Runnable() {
      public void run() {
        String title = (args.length==0 ? "Desktop Sample" : args[0]);
        JFrame frame = new JFrame(title);
        frame.setDefaultCloseOperation(JFrame.EXIT_ON_CLOSE);

        JDesktopPane desktop = new JDesktopPane();
        JInternalFrame internalFrames[] = {
          new JInternalFrame("Can Do All", true, true, true, true),
          new JInternalFrame("Not Resizable", false, true, true, true),
          new JInternalFrame("Not Closable", true, false, true, true),
          new JInternalFrame("Not Maximizable", true, true, false, true),
          new JInternalFrame("Not Iconifiable", true, true, true, false)
        };

        InternalFrameListener internalFrameListener =
          new InternalFrameIconifyListener();

        int pos = 0;
        for(JInternalFrame internalFrame: internalFrames) {
          // Add to desktop
          desktop.add(internalFrame);

          // Position and size
          internalFrame.setBounds(pos*25, pos*25, 200, 100);
          pos++;

          // Add listener for iconification events
          internalFrame.addInternalFrameListener(internalFrameListener);

          JLabel label = new JLabel(internalFrame.getTitle(), JLabel.CENTER);
          internalFrame.add(label, BorderLayout.CENTER);
```

```
        // Make visible
        internalFrame.setVisible(true);
      }

      JInternalFrame palette =
        new JInternalFrame("Palette", true, false, true, false);
      palette.setBounds(350, 150, 100, 100);
      palette.putClientProperty("JInternalFrame.isPalette", Boolean.TRUE);
      desktop.add(palette, JDesktopPane.PALETTE_LAYER);
      palette.setVisible(true);

      desktop.setDragMode(JDesktopPane.OUTLINE_DRAG_MODE);

      frame.add(desktop, BorderLayout.CENTER);
      frame.setSize(500, 300);
      frame.setVisible(true);
    }
  };
  EventQueue.invokeLater(runner);
  }
}
```

DesktopManager Interface

One remaining piece of the puzzle for working on a desktop is the desktop manager, which is an implementation of the DesktopManager interface, shown here:

```
public interface DesktopManager {
  public void activateFrame(JInternalFrame frame);
  public void beginDraggingFrame(JComponent frame);
  public void beginResizingFrame(JComponent frame, int direction);
  public void closeFrame(JInternalFrame frame);
  public void deactivateFrame(JInternalFrame frame);
  public void deiconifyFrame(JInternalFrame frame);
  public void dragFrame(JComponent frame, int newX, int newY);
  public void endDraggingFrame(JComponent frame);
  public void endResizingFrame(JComponent frame);
  public void iconifyFrame(JInternalFrame frame);
  public void maximizeFrame(JInternalFrame frame);
  public void minimizeFrame(JInternalFrame frame);
  public void openFrame(JInternalFrame frame);
  public void resizeFrame(JComponent frame, int newX, int newY, int newWidth,
    int newHeight);
  public void setBoundsForFrame(JComponent frame, int newX, int newY, int newWidth,
    int newHeight);
}
```

■**Note** For the `DesktopManager` methods that accept a `JComponent` argument, the arguments are usually a `JInternalFrame` or another lightweight Swing component.

When `JInternalFrame` objects are in a `JDesktopPane`, they shouldn't attempt operations such as iconifying or maximizing themselves. Instead, they should ask the desktop manager of the desktop pane in which they're installed to perform the operation:

```
getDesktopPane().getDesktopManager().iconifyFrame(anInternalFrame);
```

The `DefaultDesktopManager` class provides one such implementation of a `DesktopManager`. If the default isn't sufficient, a look and feel might provide its own `DesktopManager` implementation class, as the Windows look and feel does with the `WindowsDesktopManager`. You can also define your own manager, but this usually isn't necessary.

Summary

In this chapter, you explored the `JRootPane` class and how implementers of the `RootPaneContainer` interface rely on a `JRootPane` for internal component management. You also learned how in Swing you work with the `JRootPane` of a `JFrame`, `JDialog`, `JWindow`, `JApplet`, or `JInternalFrame` class. The root pane can then layer components with the help of a `JLayeredPane` in such a way that tooltip text and pop-up menus will always appear above their associated components.

The `JInternalFrame` can also reside within a desktop environment, in which a `JDesktopPane` and `DesktopManager` manage how and where the internal frames act and appear. You can also respond to internal frame events by associating `InternalFrameListener` implementations with a `JInternalFrame`.

In Chapter 9, you'll examine the specialized pop-up components within the Swing libraries: `JColorChooser`, `JFileChooser`, `JOptionPane`, and `ProgressMonitor`.

CHAPTER 9

■ ■ ■

Pop-Ups and Choosers

In Chapter 8, you looked at the top-level containers such as `JFrame` and `JApplet`. In addition, you explored the `JDialog` class used to create pop-up windows to display messages or get user input. Although the `JDialog` class works perfectly well, the Swing component set also offers several simpler approaches to get user input from pop-up windows, which you will explore in this chapter.

The `JOptionPane` class is useful for displaying messages, obtaining textual user input, or getting the answer to a question. The `ProgressMonitor` and `ProgressMonitorInputStream` classes enable you to monitor the progress of lengthy tasks. In addition, the `JColorChooser` and `JFileChooser` classes come equipped with feature-filled pop-up windows for getting a color choice from a user or getting a file or directory name. By using these additional classes, your user interface development tasks can be accomplished much more quickly and easily.

JOptionPane Class

`JOptionPane` is a special class for creating a panel to be placed in a pop-up window. The purpose of the panel is to display a message to a user and get a response from that user. To accomplish its task, the panel presents content in four areas (see Figure 9-1):

- **Icon:** The icon area is for the display of an `Icon` to indicate the type of message being displayed to the user. It's the responsibility of the installed look and feel to provide default icons for certain types of messages, but you can provide your own if you need to display another icon type.

- **Message:** The primary purpose of this area is to display a text message. In addition, the area can contain any optional set of objects to make the message more informational.

- **Input:** The input area allows a user to provide a response to a message. The response can be free form, in a text field, or from a pick list in a combo box or list control. For yes or no type questions, the button area should be used instead.

- **Button:** The button area is also for getting user input. Selection of a button in this area signals the end of the usage of the `JOptionPane`. Default sets of button labels are available, or you can display any number of buttons, including none, with any labels you desire.

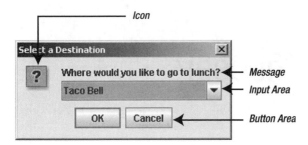

Figure 9-1. *JOptionPane parts*

All the areas are optional (although having a panel without at least a message and a button makes the option pane virtually useless).

Besides being a panel with four sections within a pop-up window, the JOptionPane is capable of automatically placing itself in a pop-up window and managing the acquisition of the user's response. It can place itself in either a JDialog or a JInternalFrame, depending on the type of GUI you're providing to the user. With the help of an Icon and set of JButton components, the JOptionPane can easily be configured to show a variety of messages and input dialogs.

■**Note** Because the JOptionPane can automatically place itself in a JDialog, you might never need to create a JDialog directly.

Creating a JOptionPane

You can either manually create a JOptionPane through one of its 7 constructors or go through one of the 25 factory methods discussed later in the chapter, in the "Automatically Creating a JOptionPane in a Pop-Up Window" section. You have the most control when manually creating the JOptionPane. However, you then must place it in a pop-up window, show the window, and finally manage getting the response.

Because of the ease of use provided by the methods that do everything automatically, you might think you would *only* use the factory methods when working with JOptionPane. However, throughout this chapter, you'll discover several other reasons why you might want to do things manually. In addition, when you use a visual-programming environment, the environment treats the JOptionPane as a JavaBean component and will ignore the factory methods.

For the seven constructors, you can have different permutations of six different arguments. The arguments allow you to configure something in one of the four different areas shown in Figure 9-1. The six arguments are the message, the message type, an option type, an icon, an array of options, and an initial option setting. The use of these arguments is shared with the factory methods.

Let's first look at the seven constructors, and then explore the different arguments. Notice that the constructor arguments are cascading and only add additional arguments to the previous constructor.

```
public JOptionPane()
JOptionPane optionPane = new JOptionPane();

public JOptionPane(Object message)
JOptionPane optionPane = new JOptionPane("Printing complete");

public JOptionPane(Object message, int messageType)
JOptionPane optionPane = new JOptionPane("Printer out of paper",
  JOptionPane.WARNING_MESSAGE);

public JOptionPane(Object message, int messageType, int optionType)
JOptionPane optionPane = new JOptionPane("Continue printing?",
  JOptionPane.QUESTION_MESSAGE, JOptionPane.YES_NO_OPTION);

public JOptionPane(Object message, int messageType, int optionType,
  Icon icon)
Icon printerIcon = new ImageIcon("printer.jpg");
JOptionPane optionPane = new JOptionPane("Continue printing?",
  JOptionPane.QUESTION_MESSAGE, JOptionPane.YES_NO_OPTION, printerIcon);

public JOptionPane(Object message, int messageType, int optionType, Icon icon,
  Object options[ ])
Icon greenIcon = new DiamondIcon(Color.GREEN);
Icon redIcon = new DiamondIcon(Color.RED);
Object optionArray[] = new Object[] { greenIcon, redIcon} ;
JOptionPane optionPane = new JOptionPane("Continue printing?",
  JOptionPane.QUESTION_MESSAGE, JOptionPane.YES_NO_OPTION, printerIcon,
  optionArray);

public JOptionPane(Object message, int messageType, int optionType, Icon icon,
  Object options[], Object initialValue)
JOptionPane optionPane = new JOptionPane("Continue printing?",
  JOptionPane.QUESTION_MESSAGE, JOptionPane.YES_NO_OPTION, printerIcon,
  optionArray, redIcon);
```

The JOptionPane Message Argument

The message argument is an Object, not a String. While you normally pass only a quoted string as this argument, with an Object argument, you can basically display anything you want in the message area. In the "Understanding the Message Property," section later in this chapter, you'll look at the more advanced uses of this argument. Briefly, though, there are four basic rules to interpret the meaning of an Object-typed message argument. For elements within the Object, recursively follow these rules:

- If the message is an array of objects (Object[ ]), make the JOptionPane place each entry onto a separate row.

- If the message is a Component, place the component in the message area.

- If the message is an Icon, place the Icon within a JLabel and display the label in the message area.

- If the message is an Object, convert it to a String with toString(), place the String in a JLabel, and display the label in the message area.

The JOptionPane Message Type and Icon Arguments

The messageType constructor argument is used to represent the type of message being displayed within the JOptionPane. If you don't provide a custom icon for the JOptionPane, the installed look and feel will use the messageType argument setting to determine which icon to display within the icon area. Five different message types are available as JOptionPane constants:

- ERROR_MESSAGE for displaying an error message

- INFORMATION_MESSAGE for displaying an informational message

- QUESTION_MESSAGE for displaying a query message

- WARNING_MESSAGE for displaying a warning message

- PLAIN_MESSAGE for displaying any other type of message

If you're using a constructor with both messageType and icon arguments and want the JOptionPane to use the default icon for the messageType, just specify null as the value for the icon argument. If the icon argument is non-null, the specified icon will be used, no matter what the message type is.

If the messageType constructor argument isn't specified, the default message type is PLAIN_MESSAGE.

The JOptionPane Option Type Argument

The optionType constructor argument is used to determine the configuration for the set of buttons in the button area. If one of the options argument described next is provided, then the optionType argument is ignored and configuration for the set of buttons is acquired from the options argument. Four different option types are available as JOptionPane constants:

- DEFAULT_OPTION for a single OK button

- OK_CANCEL_OPTION for OK and Cancel buttons

- YES_NO_CANCEL_OPTION for Yes, No, and Cancel buttons

- YES_NO_OPTION for Yes and No buttons

If the optionType constructor argument isn't specified, the default option type is DEFAULT_OPTION.

The JOptionPane Options and Initial Value Arguments

The `options` argument is an `Object` array used to construct a set of `JButton` objects for the button area of the `JOptionPane`. If this argument is `null` (or a constructor without this argument is used), the button labels will be determined by the `optionType` argument. Otherwise, the array works similarly to the message argument, but without supporting recursive arrays:

- If an `options` array element is a `Component`, place the component in the button area.

- If an `options` array element is an `Icon`, place the `Icon` within a `JButton` and place the button in the button area.

- If an `options` array element is an `Object`, convert it to a `String` with `toString()`, place the `String` in a `JButton`, and place the button in the button area.

Normally, the `options` argument will be an array of `String` objects. You may want to have an `Icon` on the `JButton`, although the resulting button won't have a label. If you want to have both an icon and a text label on the button, you can manually create a `JButton` and place it in the array. Alternatively, you can directly include any other `Component` within the array. There's one minor problem with these latter two approaches, however. It's *your* responsibility to handle responding to component selection and tell the `JOptionPane` when the user selects this component. The "Adding Components to the Button Area" section later in this chapter shows how to properly handle this behavior.

When the `options` argument is non-null, the `initialValue` argument specifies which of the buttons will be the default button when the pane is initially displayed. If it's `null`, the first component in the button area will be the default button. In either case, the first button will have the input focus, unless there is an input component in the message area, in which case, the input component will have the initial input focus.

■Tip To have no buttons on the option pane, pass an empty array as the options setting: `new Object[] { }`.

Displaying a JOptionPane

After you've created the `JOptionPane` with one of the constructors, what you have is a panel filled with components. In other words, the obtained `JOptionPane` is not yet in a pop-up window. You need to create a `JDialog`, a `JInternalFrame`, or another pop-up window, and then place the `JOptionPane` within that. In addition, if you pick this manual style of `JOptionPane` construction, you need to handle the closing of the pop-up window. You must listen for selection of a component in the button area, and then hide the pop-up window after selection.

Because there is so much to do here, the `JOptionPane` includes two helper methods to place a `JOptionPane` within either a modal `JDialog` or a `JInternalFrame` and take care of all the previously described behavior:

```
public JDialog createDialog(Component parentComponent, String title)

public JInternalFrame createInternalFrame(Component parentComponent, String title)
```

■Note When using the `createDialog()` and `createInternalFrame()` methods to create a pop-up window, selection of an automatically created button results in the closing of the created pop-up. You would then need to ask the `JOptionPane` which option the user selected with `getValue()` and, if appropriate, get the input value with `getInputValue()`.

The first argument to the methods is a component over which the pop-up window will be centered. The second argument is the title for the pop-up window. Once you create the pop-up window, whether it's a `JDialog` or `JInternalFrame`, you show it. The pop-up is then closed after one of the components in the button area is selected, at which point, your program continues. The following lines of source code show the creation of one such `JOptionPane` shown within a `JDialog`. The resulting pop-up window is shown in Figure 9-2.

```
JOptionPane optionPane = new JOptionPane("Continue printing?",
  JOptionPane.QUESTION_MESSAGE, JOptionPane.YES_NO_OPTION);
JDialog dialog = optionPane.createDialog(source, "Manual Creation");
dialog.setVisible(true);
```

Figure 9-2. *Sample JOptionPane in a JDialog*

After you create the `JOptionPane`, place it in a pop-up window, and show it, and the user has responded, you need to find out what the user selected. The selection is provided via the `public Object getValue()` method of `JOptionPane`. The value returned by `getValue()` is determined by whether an `options` array was provided to the `JOptionPane` constructor. If you provide the array, the argument selected will be returned. If you don't provide the array, an `Integer` object is returned, and its value represents the position of the button selected within the button area. In another case, `getValue()` could return `null` if nothing was selected, such as when the `JDialog` is closed by selecting the appropriate window decoration from the title bar of the pop-up window.

To make this multifaceted response easier to grasp, Listing 9-1 shows an OptionPaneUtils class that defines the method public static int getSelection(JOptionPane optionPane). Given an option pane, this method returns the position of the selected value as an int, whether or not an options array was provided. To indicate that nothing was selected, JOptionPane.CLOSED_OPTION (-1) is returned.

Listing 9-1. *JOptionPane Utility Class*

```
import javax.swing.*;

public final class OptionPaneUtils {

  private OptionPaneUtils() {
  }

  public static int getSelection(JOptionPane optionPane) {
    // Default return value, signals nothing selected
    int returnValue = JOptionPane.CLOSED_OPTION;

    // Get selected value
    Object selectedValue = optionPane.getValue();
    // If none, then nothing selected
    if (selectedValue != null) {
      Object options[] = optionPane.getOptions();
      if (options == null) {
        // Default buttons, no array specified
        if(selectedValue instanceof Integer) {
          returnValue = ((Integer)selectedValue).intValue();
        }
      } else {
        // Array of option buttons specified
        for (int i=0, n = options.length; i < n; i++) {
          if(options[i].equals(selectedValue)) {
            returnValue = i;
            break; // out of for loop
          }
        }
      }
    }
    return returnValue;
  }
}
```

With the help of this new `OptionPaneUtils.getSelection(JOptionPane)` helper method, you can now find out the option pane selection with one line of code, and then act accordingly based on the response.

```
int selection = OptionPaneUtils.getSelection(optionPane);
switch (selection) {
  case ...: ...
    break;
  case ...: ...
    break;
  default: ...
}
```

If you create a `JOptionPane` with a `null` options array, you can use the constants within the `JOptionPane` class to indicate the position of the default button labels and their return values from the `OptionPaneUtils.getSelection(JOptionPane)` method. These constants are listed in Table 9-1. Using these constants enables you to avoid hard-coding constants such as 0, 1, 2, or –1.

Table 9-1. *JOptionPane Option Position Constants*

Position	Description
CANCEL_OPTION	Used when the Cancel button is pressed
CLOSED_OPTION	Used when the pop-up window closed without the user pressing a button
NO_OPTION	Used when the No button is pressed
OK_OPTION	Used when the OK button is pressed
YES_OPTION	Used when the Yes button is pressed

Automatically Creating a JOptionPane in a Pop-Up Window

You can manually create a `JOptionPane`, place it in a `JDialog` or `JInternalFrame` (or any other container), and fetch the response. Alternatively, you could use the `JOptionPane` factory methods for creating `JOptionPane` components directly within either a `JDialog` or a `JInternalFrame`. Using the many factory methods, you can create the option pane, place it in a pop-up window, and get the response with a single line of source code.

There are 25 methods, which are first broken down into two sets: those that create the `JOptionPane` and show it within a `JDialog` and those that show the pane within a `JInternalFrame`. Methods that show the `JOptionPane` within a `JInternalFrame` are named showInternal*XXX*Dialog(), and methods that create the pane within a `JDialog` are named show*XXX*Dialog().

The second grouping of factory methods for `JOptionPane` is what fills in the *XXX* part of the method names. This represents the various message types of option panes that you can create and display. In addition, the message type defines what is returned after the user selects something in the option pane. The four different message types are as follows:

- **Message:** With a message pop-up, there's no return value. Therefore, the method is defined void show[Internal]MessageDialog(...).

- **Input:** With an input pop-up, the return value is either what the user typed in a text field (a String) or what the user picked from a list of options (an Object). Therefore, the show[Internal]InputDialog(...) methods return either a String or Object, depending on which version you use.

- **Confirm:** With the confirm pop-up, the return value signifies which, if any, button the user picked within the option pane. After a button is picked, the pop-up window is dismissed, and the returned value is one of the integer constants shown in Table 9-1. Therefore, the method here is defined as int show[Internal]ConfirmDialog(...).

- **Option:** With the option pop-up, the return value is an int, the same type as the confirm pop-up, so the methods are defined int show[Internal]OptionDialog(...). If the button labels are manually specified with a non-null argument, the integer represents the selected button position.

The information in Table 9-2 should help you understand the 25 methods and their arguments. The method names (and return types) are found on the left side of the table, and their argument lists (and data types) are on the right. The numbers that repeat across the columns for each method name indicate a specific set of arguments for that method. For instance, the showInputDialog row shows a 3 in the Parent Component column, Message column, Title column, and Message Type column. Therefore, the showInputDialog method has one version defined like this:

```
public static String showInputDialog(Component parentComponent, Object message,
  String title, int messageType)
```

Note With the exception of two of the showInputDialog() methods, the parent component argument is required for all method varieties. The message argument is the only one required for all without exception. What good is a pop-up dialog without a message?

With the way the different showXXXDialog() methods are defined, you don't need to bother with discovering the selected button yourself, or even the user input. The return value for the various methods is one of the following: nothing (void return type), an int from Table 9-1, a String, or an Object, depending on the type of dialog box shown.

Caution There is a significant difference between the JOptionPane constructors and the factory methods: The option type and message type arguments are reversed.

Table 9-2. *JOptionPane Static create and show Methods*

Method Name/Return Type	Parent Component Component	Message Object	Title String	Option Type int	Message Type int
showMessageDialog Return type: void[123]	123	123	23		23
showInternalMessageDialog Return type: void[123]	123	123	23		23
showConfirmDialog Return type: int[1234]	1234	1234	234	234	34
showInternalConfirmDialog Return type: int	1234	1234	234	234	34
showInputDialog Return type: String[12356]/Object[4]	2345	123456	34		34
showInternalInputDialog Return type: String[12]/Object[3]	123	123	23		23
showOptionDialog Return type: int[1]	1	1	1	1	1
showInternalOptionDialog Return type: int[1]	1	1	1	1	1

JOptionPane Arguments for Factory Methods

Almost all the arguments for the factory methods match the JOptionPane constructor arguments. Two lists in the "Creating a JOptionPane" section earlier in this chapter describe the acceptable values for the message type and option type arguments. In addition, the usage of the message, options, and initial value arguments are also described. The parent component and title argument are passed along to one of the createDialog() or createInternalFrame() methods, depending on the type of pop-up in which the JOptionPane is embedded.

You next need to consider the selection values argument and the initial selection value argument of the showInputDialog() method. With an input dialog box, you can ask the user for text input and allow the user to type in anything, or you can present the user with a list of predefined choices. The selection values argument to showInputDialog() determines how you provide that set of choices. The initial selection value represents the specific option to be chosen when the JOptionPane first appears. The look and feel will determine the appropriate Swing component to be used based on the number of choices presented. For small lists, a JComboBox is used. For larger lists, starting at 20 with the Motif, Metal/Ocean, and Windows look and feel types, a JList is used.

Table 9-2. *JOptionPane Static create and show Methods (Continued)*

Icon Icon	Options Object[ ]	Initial Value Object	Selection Values Object[ ]	Initial Selection Object
3				
3				
4				
4				
4			4	456
3	3	3		
1	1	1		
1	1	1		

■**Note** When the parent component argument is null, a hidden frame is used and the pop-up is centered on the screen. See the getSharedOwnerFrame() method of SwingUtilities for more details on the hidden frame. There are other focus-related usability issues that you might run into when specifying null as a parent component, if the hidden frame and dialog box are swapped to the background.

Message Pop-Ups

The showMessageDialog() and showInternalMessageDialog() methods create an INFORMATION_MESSAGE pop-up with the pop-up title "Message," unless different argument settings are specified for the message type and window title. Because the sole purpose of the message dialog box is to display a message, these dialog boxes provide only an OK button and return no value. Figure 9-3 shows sample message pop-ups created from the following lines of source:

```
JOptionPane.showMessageDialog(parent, "Printing complete");
JOptionPane.showInternalMessageDialog(desktop, "Printing complete");
```

Dialog   *Internal Frame*

Figure 9-3. *Sample JOptionPane message pop-ups*

Confirm Pop-Ups

The showConfirmDialog() and showInternalConfirmDialog() methods, by default, create a pop-up with a QUESTION_MESSAGE type and the pop-up title "Select an Option." Because confirm dialog boxes ask a question, their default option type is YES_NO_CANCEL_OPTION, giving them Yes, No, and Cancel buttons. The return value from a call to any of these methods is one of the JOptionPane class constants YES_OPTION, NO_OPTION, or CANCEL_OPTION. No prizes for guessing which constant maps to which option pane button! Figure 9-4 shows sample confirm pop-ups created from the following lines of source:

```
JOptionPane.showConfirmDialog(parent, "Continue printing?");
JOptionPane.showInternalConfirmDialog(desktop, "Continue printing?");
```

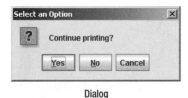
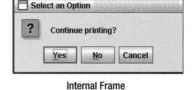

Dialog   *Internal Frame*

Figure 9-4. *Sample JOptionPane confirm pop-ups*

Input Pop-Ups

By default, the showInputDialog() and showInternalInputDialog() methods create a QUESTION_MESSAGE pop-up with an "Input" pop-up title. The option type for input dialogs is OK_CANCEL_OPTION, giving them an OK and a Cancel button, and the option type isn't changeable. The return data type for these methods is either a String or an Object. If you don't specify selection values, the pop-up prompts the user with a text field and returns the input as a String. If you do specify selection values, you get back an Object from the selection values array. Figure 9-5 shows some input pop-ups created from the following lines of source:

```
JOptionPane.showInputDialog(parent, "Enter printer name:");

// Moons of Neptune
String smallList[] = {
  "Naiad", "Thalassa", "Despina", "Galatea", "Larissa", "Proteus",
  "Triton", "Nereid"} ;
```

```
JOptionPane.showInternalInputDialog(desktop, "Pick a printer", "Input",
  JOptionPane.QUESTION_MESSAGE, null, smallList, "Triton");

// Twenty of the moons of Saturn
String bigList[] = {"Pan", "Atlas", "Prometheus", "Pandora", "Epimetheus",
  "Janus", "Mimas", "Enceladus", "Telesto", "Tethys", "Calypso", "Dione",
  "Helene", "Rhea", "Titan", "Hyperion", "Iapetus", "Phoebe", "Skadi",
  "Mundilfari"};
JOptionPane.showInputDialog(parent, "Pick a printer", "Input",
  JOptionPane.QUESTION_MESSAGE, null, bigList, "Titan");
```

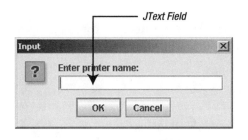

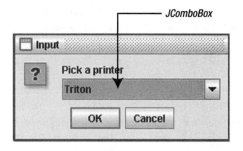

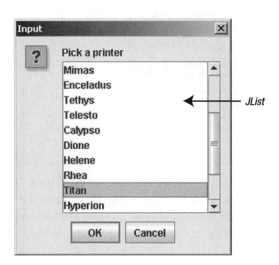

Figure 9-5. *Sample JOptionPane input pop-ups*

■**Note** It is the responsibility of the look and feel to determine the type of input component. A look and feel can use something other than a JTextField, JComboBox, or JList. It's just that all the system-provided look and feel types (from Sun) use these three components.

Option Pop-Ups

The showOptionDialog() and showInternalOptionDialog() methods provide the most flexibility because they allow you to configure all the arguments. There are no default arguments, and the return value is an int. If an options argument is not specified, the return value will be one of the constants listed in Table 9-1. Otherwise, the value returned represents the component position of the selected option from the options argument. Figure 9-6 shows a couple of input pop-ups created from the following lines of source, in which icons (instead of text) are provided on the buttons:

```
Icon greenIcon = new DiamondIcon(Color.GREEN);
Icon redIcon = new DiamondIcon(Color.RED);
Object iconArray[] = { greenIcon, redIcon} ;
JOptionPane.showOptionDialog(source, "Continue printing?", "Select an Option",
  JOptionPane.YES_NO_OPTION, JOptionPane.QUESTION_MESSAGE, null, iconArray,
  iconArray[1]);

Icon blueIcon = new DiamondIcon(Color.BLUE);
Object stringArray[] = { "Do It", "No Way"} ;
JOptionPane.showInternalOptionDialog(desktop, "Continue printing?",
  "Select an Option", JOptionPane.YES_NO_OPTION, JOptionPane.QUESTION_MESSAGE,
blueIcon, stringArray, stringArray[0]);
```

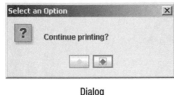
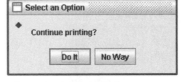

Dialog	Internal Frame

Figure 9-6. *Sample JOptionPane option pop-ups*

■**Caution** When using a factory method to show a JOptionPane within a JDialog, the dialog box is automatically modal, preventing another window from getting the input focus. When showing the JOptionPane within a JInternalFrame, the internal frame might be modal, but other windows might not be. Therefore, a user could do something within one of the other windows of the application, including an action on the JDesktopPane.

JOptionPane Properties

Table 9-3 shows the 15 properties of JOptionPane. These properties are accessible only if you don't use one of the factory methods of JOptionPane. For most of the arguments, their meaning maps directly to one of the constructor arguments.

Table 9-3. *JOptionPane Properties*

Property Name	Data Type	Access
accessibleContext	AccessibleContext	Read-only
icon	Icon	Read-write bound
initialSelectionValue	Object	Read-write bound
initialValue	Object	Read-write bound
inputValue	Object	Read-write bound
maxCharactersPerLineCount	int	Read-only
message	Object	Read-write bound
messageType	int	Read-write bound
options	Object[]	Read-write bound
optionType	int	Read-write bound
selectionValues	Object[]	Read-write bound
UI	OptionPaneUI	Read-write bound
UIClassID	String	Read-only
value	Object	Read-write bound
wantsInput	boolean	Read-write bound

The wantsInput property is automatically set to true for the input dialog boxes or when the selectionValues property is non-null. The inputValue property is the item picked from an input dialog box. The value property indicates the option selected from the button area.

Displaying Multiline Messages

The maxCharactersPerLineCount property is set to an extremely large value, Integer.MAX_VALUE, by default. For some strange reason, the Swing developers chose not to provide a setter method for this property. If you want to change the setting, you must subclass JOptionPane and override the public int getMaxCharactersPerLineCount() method. This causes a long text message to be broken up into multiple lines within an option pane. In addition, you cannot use any of the factory methods because they don't know about your subclass.

To help you create narrow JOptionPane components, you can add the source shown in Listing 9-2 to the OptionPaneUtils class definition shown earlier in Listing 9-1. The new method provides a way of specifying the desired option pane character width.

Listing 9-2. *Helper Method to Create a Narrow JOptionPane*

```
public static JOptionPane getNarrowOptionPane(int maxCharactersPerLineCount) {
  // Our inner class definition
  class NarrowOptionPane extends JOptionPane {
    int maxCharactersPerLineCount;
    NarrowOptionPane(int maxCharactersPerLineCount) {
      this.maxCharactersPerLineCount = maxCharactersPerLineCount;
    }
    public int getMaxCharactersPerLineCount() {
      return maxCharactersPerLineCount;
    }
  }
  return new NarrowOptionPane(maxCharactersPerLineCount);
}
```

Once the method and new class are defined, you can create an option pane of a specified character width, manually configure all the properties, place it in a pop-up window, show it, and then determine the user's response. The following source demonstrates using these new capabilities, with the long message trimmed a bit.

```
String msg = "this is a really long message ... this is a really long message";
JOptionPane optionPane = OptionPaneUtils.getNarrowOptionPane(72);
optionPane.setMessage(msg);
optionPane.setMessageType(JOptionPane.INFORMATION_MESSAGE);
JDialog dialog = optionPane.createDialog(source, "Width 72");
dialog.setVisible(true);
```

Figure 9-7 demonstrates what would happen if you didn't change the maxCharactersPerLineCount property. Figure 9-7 also shows the new narrow JOptionPane.

Figure 9-7. *Default JOptionPane and a narrow JOptionPane*

Although this seems like a lot of work, it's the best way to create multiline option panes, unless you want to manually parse the message into separate lines.

■Note Including the characters \ n in the message text will force the message to be displayed on multiple lines. Then it's your responsibility to count the number of characters in each message line. The message text in a JOptionPane can be formatted with HTML tags, as it can in other Swing components.

Understanding the Message Property

In all the previous examples in this chapter of using the message argument to the JOptionPane constructors and using the factory methods, the message was a single string. As described earlier in the "The JOptionPane Message Argument" section, this argument doesn't need to be a single string. For instance, if the argument were an array of strings, each string would be on a separate line. This eliminates the need to use the narrow JOptionPane, but requires you to count the characters yourself. However, because you're splitting apart the message, you can use one of the 25 factory methods. For instance, the following source creates the pop-up window shown in Figure 9-8.

```
String multiLineMsg[] = { "Hello,", "World"} ;
JOptionPane.showMessageDialog(source, multiLineMsg);
```

Figure 9-8. *Using JOptionPane with a string array*

■Caution If you manually count the characters within a long message to split it into a multiline message, the output may not be the best. For instance, when using a proportional font in which character widths vary, a line of 20 *w* characters would be much wider than a line of 20 *i* or *l* characters.

The message argument not only supports displaying an array of strings, but it also can support an array of any type of object. If an element in the array is a Component, it's placed directly into the message area. If the element is an Icon, the icon is placed within a JLabel, and the JLabel is placed into the message area. All other objects are converted to a String, placed into a JLabel, and displayed in the message area, unless the object is itself an array; in that case, these rules are applied recursively.

To demonstrate the possibilities, Figure 9-9 shows off the true capabilities of the JOptionPane. The actual content isn't meant to show anything in particular—just that you can display a lot of different stuff. The message argument is made up of the following array:

```
Object complexMsg[] = {
    "Above Message", new DiamondIcon(Color.RED), new JButton("Hello"),
    new JSlider(), new DiamondIcon(Color.BLUE), "Below Message"} ;
```

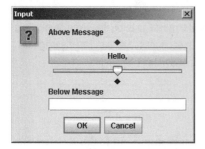

Figure 9-9. *Using JOptionPane with a complex message property*

Adding Components to the Message Area

If you were to display the pop-up in Figure 9-9, you would notice a slight problem. The option pane doesn't know about the embedded JSlider setting, unlike the way it automatically knows about input to the automatic JTextField, JComboBox, or JList components. If you want the JOptionPane (or for that matter, any input component) to get the JSlider value, you need to have your input component change the inputValue property of the JOptionPane. When this value is changed, the option pane tells the pop-up window to close because the JOptionPane has acquired its input value.

Attaching a ChangeListener to the JSlider component enables you to find out when its value has changed. Adding yet another method to the OptionPaneUtils class shown earlier in Listing 9-1 allows you to reuse this specialized JSlider with multiple JOptionPane objects more easily. The important method call is shown in boldface in Listing 9-3. A similar line would need to be added for any input component that you wanted to place within a JOptionPane. The line notifies the option pane when the user has changed the value of the input component.

Listing 9-3. *Helper Method for Creating a JSlider for Use in a JOptionPane*

```
public static JSlider getSlider(final JOptionPane optionPane) {
  JSlider slider = new JSlider();
  slider.setMajorTickSpacing (10);
  slider.setPaintTicks(true);
  slider.setPaintLabels(true);
  ChangeListener changeListener = new ChangeListener() {
    public void stateChanged(ChangeEvent changeEvent) {
      JSlider theSlider = (JSlider)changeEvent.getSource();
      if (!theSlider.getValueIsAdjusting()) {
        optionPane.setInputValue(new Integer(theSlider.getValue()));
      }
    }
  };
  slider.addChangeListener(changeListener);
  return slider;
}
```

Now that the specialized JSlider is created, you need to place it on a JOptionPane. This requires the manual creation of a JOptionPane component and, surprisingly, doesn't require the setting of the wantsInput property. The wantsInput property is set to true only when you want the JOptionPane to provide its own input component. Because you're providing one, this isn't necessary. The resulting pop-up window is shown in Figure 9-10. (The JSlider component will be more fully described in Chapter 12.)

```
JOptionPane optionPane = new JOptionPane();
JSlider slider = OptionPaneUtils.getSlider(optionPane);
optionPane.setMessage(new Object[] { "Select a value: " , slider} );
optionPane.setMessageType(JOptionPane.QUESTION_MESSAGE);
optionPane.setOptionType(JOptionPane.OK_CANCEL_OPTION);
JDialog dialog = optionPane.createDialog(source, "My Slider");
dialog.setVisible(true);
System.out.println ("Input: " + optionPane.getInputValue());
```

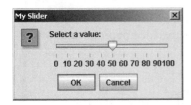

Figure 9-10. *Using JOptionPane with a JSlider*

■**Note** If the user doesn't move the slider, JOptionPane.getInputValue() correctly returns JOptionPane.UNINITIALIZED_VALUE.

Adding Components to the Button Area

In "The JOptionPane Options and Initial Value Arguments" section earlier in this chapter, you saw that if you have a Component in the array of options for the JOptionPane, you must configure the component yourself to handle selection. The same holds true for any components you add via the options property. When a component is configured to handle selection, the pop-up window that a JOptionPane is embedded in will disappear when the component is selected. The default set of buttons works this way. When installing your own components, you must notify the option pane when one of the components has been selected by setting the value property of the option pane.

　To demonstrate this mechanism, create a JButton with both an icon and a text label that can be placed in an option pane. Without defining this component yourself, the option pane supports only the display of a label or an icon on the button. When the button is selected, the button tells the option pane it was selected by setting the option pane's value property to the current text label of the button. Adding yet another method to OptionPaneUtils shown earlier in Listing 9-1 allows you to create such a button. The boldfaced line in the source shown in Listing 9-4 is the important method call to add to any other such component that you want to combine with the component array for the options property of a JOptionPane. The line would be called after selection of such a component.

Listing 9-4. *A JButton for Use on a JOptionPane*

```
public static JButton getButton(
    final JOptionPane optionPane, String text, Icon icon) {
  final JButton button = new JButton (text, icon);
  ActionListener actionListener = new ActionListener() {
    public void actionPerformed(ActionEvent actionEvent) {
      // Return current text label, instead of argument to method
      optionPane.setValue(button.getText());
    }
  };
  button.addActionListener(actionListener);
  return button;
}
```

After the specialized JButton is created, you need to place it in a JOptionPane. Unfortunately, this, too, requires the long form of the JOptionPane usage. The resulting pop-up window is shown in Figure 9-11.

```
JOptionPane optionPane = new JOptionPane();
optionPane.setMessage("I got an icon and a text label");
optionPane.setMessageType(JOptionPane.INFORMATION_MESSAGE);
Icon icon = new DiamondIcon (Color.BLUE);
JButton jButton = OptionPaneUtils.getButton(optionPane, "OK", icon);
optionPane.setOptions(new Object[] {jButton} );
JDialog dialog = optionPane.createDialog(source, "Icon/Text Button");
dialog.setVisible(true);
```

Figure 9-11. *Using JOptionPane with a JButton containing a text label and an icon*

■Tip Setting the value of the JOptionPane with setValue() will hide the option pane when a user selects the button. If you want to prevent users from closing the window without selecting a button, you can set the default close operation of the dialog containing the JOptionPane to JDialog.DO_NOTHING_ON_CLOSE. Then users won't be able to select the close icon from the window adornments. Well, they can select it; it just won't do anything.

Listening for Property Changes

The JOptionPane class defines the following 11 constants to assist with listening for bound property changes:

- ICON_PROPERTY

- INITIAL_SELECTION_VALUE_PROPERTY

- INITIAL_VALUE_PROPERTY

- INPUT_VALUE_PROPERTY

- MESSAGE_PROPERTY

- MESSAGE_TYPE_PROPERTY

- OPTION_TYPE_PROPERTY

- OPTIONS_PROPERTY

- SELECTION_VALUES_PROPERTY

- VALUE_PROPERTY

- WANTS_INPUT_PROPERTY

If you don't use the factory methods of JOptionPane, you can instead use a PropertyChangeListener to listen for changes to the bound properties. This would allow you to passively listen for changes to bound properties, instead of actively getting them after the change.

Customizing a JOptionPane Look and Feel

Each installable Swing look and feel provides a different JOptionPane appearance and set of default UIResource values. Figure 9-12 shows the appearance of the JOptionPane container for the preinstalled set of look and feel types: Motif, Windows, and Ocean.

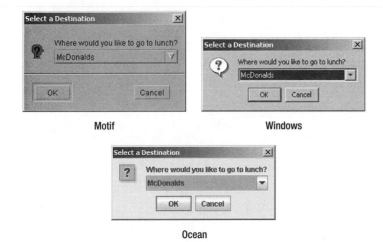

Figure 9-12. *JOptionPane under different look and feel types*

The message type of the JOptionPane helps determine the default icon to display in the icon area of the option pane. For plain messages, there are no icons. The remaining four default icons—for informational, question, warning, and error messages—are shown in Table 9-4 for the different look and feel types.

Table 9-4. *JOptionPane Icons for the Different Look and Feel Types*

Look and Feel	Informational	Question	Warning	Error
Motif				
Windows				
Metal				
Ocean				

The available set of UIResource-related properties for a JOptionPane is shown in Table 9-5. For the JOptionPane component, there are 56 different properties.

Table 9-5. *JOptionPane UIResource Elements*

Property String	Object Type
OptionPane.actionMap	ActionMap
OptionPane.background	Color
OptionPane.border	Border
OptionPane.buttonAreaBorder	Border
OptionPane.buttonClickThreshhold	Integer
OptionPane.buttonFont	Font
OptionPane.buttonOrientation	Integer
OptionPane.buttonPadding	Integer
OptionPane.cancelButtonMnemonic	String
OptionPane.cancelButtonText	String
OptionPane.cancelIcon	Icon
OptionPane.errorDialog.border.background	Color
OptionPane.errorDialog.titlePane.background	Color
OptionPane.errorDialog.titlePane.foreground	Color
OptionPane.errorDialog.titlePane.shadow	Color

Table 9-5. *JOptionPane UIResource Elements (Continued)*

Property String	Object Type
OptionPane.errorIcon	Icon
OptionPane.errorSound	String
OptionPane.font	Font
OptionPane.foreground	Color
OptionPane.informationIcon	Icon
OptionPane.informationSound	String
OptionPane.inputDialogTitle	String
OptionPane.isYesLast	Boolean
OptionPane.messageAnchor	Integer
OptionPane.messageAreaBorder	Border
OptionPane.messageFont	Font
OptionPane.messageForeground	Color
OptionPane.messageDialogTitle	String
OptionPane.minimumSize	Dimension
OptionPane.noButtonMnemonic	String
OptionPane.noButtonText	String
OptionPane.noIcon	Icon
OptionPane.okButtonMnemonic	String
OptionPane.okButtonText	String
OptionPane.okIcon	Icon
OptionPane.questionDialog.border.background	Color
OptionPane.questionDialog.titlePane.background	Color
OptionPane.questionDialog.titlePane.foreground	Color
OptionPane.questionDialog.titlePane.shadow	Color
OptionPane.questionIcon	Icon
OptionPane.questionSound	String
OptionPane.sameSizeButtons	Boolean
OptionPane.separatorPadding	Integer
OptionPane.setButtonMargin	Boolean
OptionPane.titleText	String
OptionPane.warningDialog.border.background	Color
OptionPane.warningDialog.titlePane.background	Color

Table 9-5. *JOptionPane UIResource Elements (Continued)*

Property String	Object Type
OptionPane.warningDialog.titlePane.foreground	Color
OptionPane.warningDialog.titlePane.shadow	Color
OptionPane.warningIcon	Icon
OptionPane.warningSound	String
OptionPane.windowBindings	Object[ ]
OptionPane.yesButtonMnemonic	String
OptionPane.yesButtonText	String
OptionPane.yesIcon	Icon
OptionPaneUI	String

One good use of the resources in Table 9-5 is for customizing default button labels to match the locale or language of the user. For instance, to change the four labels for the Cancel, No, OK, and Yes buttons into French, add the following code to your program. (You may be able to get the translated text from a java.util.ResourceBundle.)

```
// Set JOptionPane button labels to French
UIManager.put("OptionPane.cancelButtonText", "Annuler");
UIManager.put("OptionPane.noButtonText", "Non");
UIManager.put("OptionPane.okButtonText", "D'accord");
UIManager.put("OptionPane.yesButtonText", "Oui");
```

Now when you display the option pane, the buttons will have localized button labels. Of course, this would require translating the messages for the option pane, too. Figure 9-13 shows how a pop-up would look for the following line of source that asks if the user is 18 or older. Because the pop-up window title isn't a property, you must pass the title to every created dialog box.

```
int result = JOptionPane.showConfirmDialog(
  aFrame, "Est-ce que vous avez 18 ans ou plus?", "Choisissez une option",
  JOptionPane.YES_NO_CANCEL_OPTION);
```

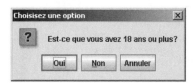

Figure 9-13. *A JOptionPane in French*

The JOptionPane component supports localized JOptionPane button labels. Out of the box, the JOptionPane displays Chinese or Japanese button labels for the standard Yes, No, Cancel, and OK buttons for the appropriate locale. For instance, the left side of Figure 9-14 shows buttons with Japanese labels for Yes, No, and Cancel, and the right side of Figure 9-14 shows buttons with Japanese labels for OK and Cancel. Obviously, you would need to change the message in the option pane, but the buttons are set for you (assuming you have the fonts to support it).

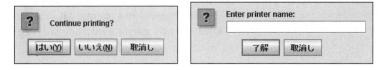

Figure 9-14. *A JOptionPane with Japanese-language buttons*

Thankfully, the 5.0 release of the JDK includes translations for the standard JOptionPane (as well as the JFileChooser and JColorChooser) labels. These are available for German (de), Spanish (es), French (fr), Italian (it), Japanese (ja), Korean (ko), English, Swedish (sv), and Chinese (Simplified/zh_CN and Traditional/zh_TW).

■Tip To start the Java runtime with a different language, just set the user.language property, as in java -Duser.language=FR ClassName. Then, whenever you create a JOptionPane, you would get the French labels for Yes, No, OK, and Cancel. The button labels would be like those shown in Figure 9-14, but without you needing to manually do the UIManager.put() calls. (Instead of *D'accord*, Sun chose to leave OK as OK.)

ProgressMonitor Class

The ProgressMonitor class is used to report on the status of a time-consuming task. The class is a special Swing class that's not a GUI component, an option pane, or a JavaBean component. Instead, you tell the ProgressMonitor when each part of the task is done. If the task is taking an extended length of time to complete, the ProgressMonitor displays a pop-up window like the one shown in Figure 9-15.

Figure 9-15. *ProgressMonitor sample*

After the `ProgressMonitor` displays the pop-up window, the user can do one of two things. The user can watch the `ProgressMonitor` display to see how much of the task has been completed; when the task is done, the `ProgressMonitor`'s display automatically disappears. Or, if the user selects the Cancel button, this tells the `ProgressMonitor` that the task needs to be canceled. To detect the cancellation, the task needs to check the `ProgressMonitor` periodically to see if the user canceled the task's operation. Otherwise, the task will continue.

The pop-up window that the `ProgressMonitor` class displays is a `JOptionPane` with a `maxCharactersPerLineCount` property setting of 60, allowing the option pane to automatically word wrap any displayed messages. The option pane is embedded within a nonmodal `JDialog` whose title is "Progress . . .". Because the `JDialog` isn't modal, a user can still interact with the main program. The `JOptionPane` for a `ProgressMonitor` will always get an informational icon within its icon area.

In addition, the message area of the option pane consists of three objects:

- At the top of the message area is a fixed message that stays the same throughout the life of the `JOptionPane`. The message can be a text string or an array of objects just like the `message` property of `JOptionPane`.

- In the middle of the message area is a note or variable message that can change as the task progresses.

- At the bottom of the message area is a progress bar (`JProgressBar` component) that fills as an increasing percentage of the task is completed.

The button area of the option pane shows a Cancel button.

Creating a ProgressMonitor

When you create a `ProgressMonitor`, there are five arguments to the single constructor:

```
public ProgressMonitor(Component parentComponent, Object message, String note,
    int minimum, int maximum)
```

The first argument represents the parent component for the `JOptionPane` for when the `ProgressMonitor` needs to appear. The parent component is the component over which the pop-up window appears, and acts like the `parentComponent` argument for the `createDialog()` method of `JOptionPane`. You then provide the static and variable message parts for the message area of the `JOptionPane`. Either of these message parts could be `null`, although `null` means that this part of the message area will never appear. Lastly, you provide `minimum` and `maximum` values as the range for the progress bar. The difference between these two values represents the expected number of operations to be performed, such as the number of files to load or the size of a file to read. Normally, the minimum setting is zero, but that isn't required. The number of completed operations determines how far the progress bar moves.

Initially, the pop-up window isn't displayed. By default, the progress monitor checks every half second (500 milliseconds) to see if the task at hand will complete in two seconds. If the task has shown some progress and it still won't complete in two seconds, then the pop-up window appears. The time to completion is configurable by changing the `millisToDecideToPopup` and `millisToPopup` properties of the `ProgressMonitor`.

The following line of source demonstrates the creation of a `ProgressMonitor` with 200 steps in the operation. A reference to the `ProgressMonitor` would need to be saved so that it can be notified as the task progresses.

```
ProgressMonitor monitor = new ProgressMonitor(
  parent, "Loading Progress", "Getting Started...", 0, 200);
```

Using a ProgressMonitor

Once you've created the `ProgressMonitor`, you need to begin the task whose progress is being monitored. As the task completes one or many steps, the `ProgressMonitor` needs to be notified of the task's progress. Notification is done with a call to the `public void setProgress(int newValue)` method, where the argument represents the progress completed thus far and the `newValue` needs to be in the `minimum...maximum` range initially specified. This progress value needs to be maintained outside the `ProgressMonitor`, because you can't ask the monitor how much progress has been made (no `public int getProgress()` method of `ProgressMonitor` exists). If the progress value were maintained in a variable named `progress`, the following two lines would update the progress value and notify the `ProgressMonitor`.

```
progress += 5;
monitor.setProgress(progress);
```

■**Note** It's possible that multiple calls to `setProgress()` may not advance the progress bar in the option pane. The changes to the `progress` setting must be enough to make the progress bar advance at least one pixel in length. For instance, if the `minimum` and `maximum` settings were zero and 2 billion, increasing the progress setting 1,000 times by 5 would have no visible effect on the progress bar, because the fractional amount would be negligible.

The `progress` setting could represent the number of files loaded thus far, or the number of bytes read in from a file. In addition to updating the count, you should update the `note` to reflect the progress. If the difference between the `minimum` and `maximum` arguments used in the `ProgressMonitor` constructor were 100, then the current progress could be viewed as a percentage of the task. Otherwise, the `progress` property merely represents the progress completed so far.

```
monitor.setNote("Loaded " + progress + " files");
```

It's the responsibility of the executing task to check whether the user pressed the Cancel button in the `ProgressMonitor` dialog box. If the task is canceled, the `ProgressMonitor` automatically closes the dialog box, but the task must actively check for the change by adding a simple check at the appropriate place or places in the source:

```
if (monitor.isCanceled()) {
// Task canceled - cleanup
  ...
}  else {
// Continue doing task
  ...
}
```

Most tasks requiring a `ProgressMonitor` will be implemented using separate threads to avoid blocking the responsiveness of the main program.

Listing 9-5 shows a program that creates a `ProgressMonitor` and allows you to either manually or automatically increase its `progress` property (see the following section for a description of this property). These tasks are handled by on-screen buttons (see Figure 9-16). Selecting the Start button creates the `ProgressMonitor`. Selecting the Manual Increase button causes the progress to increase by 5. Selecting the Automatic Increase button causes the progress to increase by 3 every 250 milliseconds (1/4 second). Pressing the Cancel button in the pop-up window during the automatic increase demonstrates what should happen when the operation is canceled; the timer stops sending updates.

Figure 9-16. *Main ProgressMonitor sample frame*

■**Note** The pop-up window won't appear until some progress is shown.

The `ProgressMonitorHandler` inner class at the start of Listing 9-5 is necessary to ensure that the `ProgressMonitor` is accessed only from the event thread. Otherwise, the access wouldn't be thread-safe in some random thread.

Listing 9-5. *Sample ProgressMonitor Usage*

```java
import javax.swing.*;
import java.awt.*;
import java.awt.event.*;

public class SampleProgress {
  static ProgressMonitor monitor;
  static int progress;
  static Timer timer;

  static class ProgressMonitorHandler implements ActionListener {
    // Called by Timer
    public void actionPerformed(ActionEvent actionEvent) {
      if (monitor == null)
        return;
```

```java
      if (monitor.isCanceled()) {
        System.out.println("Monitor canceled");
        timer.stop();
      } else {
        progress += 3;
        monitor.setProgress(progress);
        monitor.setNote("Loaded " + progress + " files");
      }
    }
  }
}

public static void main(String args[]) {

  Runnable runner = new Runnable() {
    public void run() {
      JFrame frame = new JFrame("ProgressMonitor Sample");
      frame.setDefaultCloseOperation(JFrame.EXIT_ON_CLOSE);
      frame.setLayout(new GridLayout (0, 1));

      // Define Start Button
      JButton startButton = new JButton ("Start");
      ActionListener startActionListener = new ActionListener() {
        public void actionPerformed(ActionEvent actionEvent) {
          Component parent = (Component)actionEvent.getSource();
          monitor = new ProgressMonitor(parent, "Loading Progress",
            "Getting Started...", 0, 200);
          progress = 0;
        }
      };
      startButton.addActionListener(startActionListener);
      frame.add(startButton);

      // Define Manual Increase Button
      // Pressing this button increases progress by 5
      JButton increaseButton = new JButton ("Manual Increase");
      ActionListener increaseActionListener = new ActionListener() {
        public void actionPerformed(ActionEvent actionEvent) {
          if (monitor == null)
            return;
          if (monitor.isCanceled()) {
            System.out.println("Monitor canceled");
          } else {
            progress += 5;
            monitor.setProgress(progress);
            monitor.setNote("Loaded " + progress + " files");
          }
        }
      };
```

```
      increaseButton.addActionListener(increaseActionListener);
      frame.add(increaseButton);

      // Define Automatic Increase Button
      // Start Timer to increase progress by 3 every 250 ms
      JButton autoIncreaseButton = new JButton ("Automatic Increase");
      ActionListener autoIncreaseActionListener = new ActionListener() {
        public void actionPerformed(ActionEvent actionEvent) {
          if (monitor != null) {
            if (timer == null) {
              timer = new Timer(250, new ProgressMonitorHandler());
            }
            timer.start();
          }
        }
      };
      autoIncreaseButton.addActionListener(autoIncreaseActionListener);
      frame.add(autoIncreaseButton);

      frame.setSize(300, 200);
      frame.setVisible(true);
    }
  };
  EventQueue.invokeLater(runner);
  }
}
```

ProgressMonitor Properties

Table 9-6 shows the eight properties of ProgressMonitor.

Table 9-6. *ProgressMonitor Properties*

Property Name	Data Type	Access
accessibleContext	AccessibleContext	Read-only
canceled	boolean	Read-only
maximum	int	Read-write
millisToDecideToPopup	int	Read-write
millisToPopup	int	Read-write
minimum	int	Read-write
note	String	Read-write
progress	int	Write-only

The `millisToDecideToPopup` property represents the number of milliseconds that the monitor waits before deciding if it needs to display the pop-up window. If the `progress` property hasn't changed yet, the monitor waits for another increment of this time period before checking again. When the `ProgressMonitor` checks and the `progress` property has changed, it estimates whether the task will be completed in the number of milliseconds in the `millisToPopup` property. If the `ProgressMonitor` thinks the monitored task will complete on time, the pop-up window is never displayed. Otherwise, the pop-up will display after `millisToPopup` milliseconds have passed from the time the task started.

■**Caution** Although technically possible, it isn't a good practice to move the `minimum` and `maximum` properties after the pop-up has appeared. This could result in the progress bar increasing and decreasing in an erratic manner. The same behavior happens if you move the progress setting in a nonlinear fashion.

Customizing a ProgressMonitor Look and Feel

Changing the look and feel of `ProgressMonitor` requires changing the appearance of both the `JProgressBar` and the `JLabel`, as well as the `JOptionPane` the `ProgressMonitor` uses.

The `ProgressMonitor` has one `UIResource`-related property:

- `ProgressMonitor.progressText` of type `String`

ProgressMonitorInputStream Class

The `ProgressMonitorInputStream` class represents an input stream filter that uses a `ProgressMonitor` to check the progress of the reading of an input stream. If the reading is taking too long to complete, a `ProgressMonitor` appears, and the user can select the Cancel button in the pop-up window, causing the reading to be interrupted and the input stream to throw an `InterruptedIOException`.

Creating a ProgressMonitorInputStream

Like other filtering streams, the `ProgressMonitorInputStream` is created with a reference to the stream it needs to filter. Besides a reference to this filter, the single constructor for `ProgressMonitorInputStream` requires two arguments for its `ProgressMonitor`: a parent component and a message. As seen here, the constructor takes the `ProgressMonitor` arguments first:

```
public ProgressMonitorInputStream(
  Component parentComponent, Object message, InputStream inputStream)
```

As with the `JOptionPane` and `ProgressMonitor`, the message argument is an `Object`, not a `String`, so you can display an array of components or strings on multiple lines. The following code creates one `ProgressMonitorInputStream`.

```
FileInputStream fis = new FileInputStream(filename);
ProgressMonitorInputStream pmis =
  new ProgressMonitorInputStream(parent, "Reading " + filename, fis);
```

■**Note** The `minimum...maximum` range for the `ProgressMonitorInputStream` `ProgressMonitor` is [0...*size of stream*].

Using a ProgressMonitorInputStream

As with all input streams, once you've created a `ProgressMonitorInputStream`, you need to read from it. If the input stream isn't read quickly enough, the underlying `ProgressMonitor` causes the progress pop-up window to appear. Once that window appears, a user can monitor the progress or cancel the reading by selecting the Cancel button. If the Cancel button is selected, an `InterruptedIOException` is thrown, and the `bytesTransferred` field of the exception is set to the number of bytes successfully read.

Figure 9-17 shows what one `ProgressMonitorInputStream` pop-up might look like. For a little variety, the pop-up uses two `JLabel` components in the message, instead of just one.

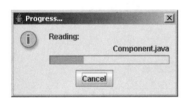

Figure 9-17. *ProgressMonitorInputStream pop-up*

Listing 9-6 shows a complete source example. The boldfaced lines are the keys to using the `ProgressMonitorInputStream`. They set up the dialog box's message and create the input stream. The program uses a file name specified from the command line, reads the file, and copies the file to standard output (the console). If the file is large enough, the progress monitor will appear. If you press the Cancel button, the reading stops and `Canceled` is printed to standard error.

Listing 9-6. *ProgressMonitorInputStream Demonstration*

```
import java.io.*;
import java.awt.*;
import javax.swing.*;

public class ProgressInputSample {
  public static final int NORMAL   = 0;
  public static final int BAD_FILE = 1;
  public static final int CANCELED = NORMAL;
  public static final int PROBLEM = 2;
```

```java
public static void main(String args[]) {
  int returnValue = NORMAL;
  if (args.length != 1) {
    System.err.println("Usage:");
    System.err.println("java ProgressInputSample filename");
  } else {
    try {
      FileInputStream fis = new FileInputStream(args[0]);
      JLabel filenameLabel = new JLabel(args[0], JLabel.RIGHT);
      Object message[] = { "Reading:", filenameLabel} ;
      ProgressMonitorInputStream pmis =
        new ProgressMonitorInputStream(null, message, fis);
      InputStreamReader isr = new InputStreamReader(pmis);
      BufferedReader br = new BufferedReader(isr);
      String line;
      while ((line = br.readLine()) != null) {
        System.out.println(line);
      }
      br.close();
    } catch (FileNotFoundException exception) {
      System.err.println("Bad File " + exception);
      returnValue = BAD_FILE;
    } catch (InterruptedIOException exception) {
      System.err.println("Canceled");
      returnValue = CANCELED;
    } catch (IOException exception) {
      System.err.println("I/O Exception " + exception);
      returnValue = PROBLEM;
    }
  }
  // AWT Thread created - must exit
  System.exit(returnValue);
}
}
```

■Note Having a `null` argument for the parent component to the `ProgressMonitorInputStream` constructor causes the pop-up window to appear centered on the screen.

ProgressMonitorInputStream Properties

Table 9-7 shows the single property of `ProgressMonitorInputStream`. The `ProgressMonitor` is created when the input stream is created. You shouldn't need to modify the `ProgressMonitor`.

However, you might want to provide a longer or shorter delay (the `millisToDecideToPopup` property of `ProgressMonitor`) before the pop-up window is displayed.

Table 9-7. *ProgressMonitorInputStream Property*

Property Name	Data Type	Access
progressMonitor	ProgressMonitor	Read-only

JColorChooser Class

You can think of a `JColorChooser` as an input-only `JOptionPane` whose input field asks you to choose a color. Like a `JOptionPane`, the `JColorChooser` is just a bunch of components in a container, not a ready-to-use pop-up window. Figure 9-18 shows how a `JColorChooser` might appear in your own application window. At the top are three selectable color chooser panels; at the bottom is a preview panel. The "I Love Swing" bit is not part of the chooser, but of the application that contains the chooser.

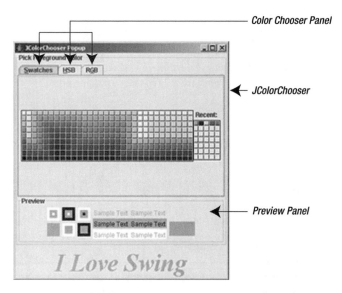

Figure 9-18. *JColorChooser sample*

In addition to appearing within your application windows, the `JColorChooser` class also provides support methods for automatically placing the group of components in a `JDialog`. Figure 9-19 shows one such automatically created pop-up.

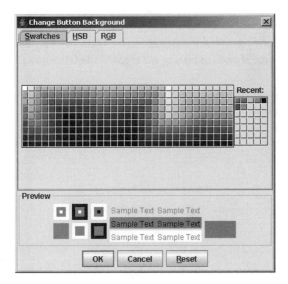

Figure 9-19. *JColorChooser pop-up sample*

In support of this behavior, the JColorChooser class requires the help of several support classes found in the javax.swing.colorchooser package. The data model for the JColorChooser is an implementation of the ColorSelectionModel interface. The javax.swing.colorchooser package provides the DefaultColorSelectionModel class as an implementation of the ColorSelectionModel interface. For the user interface, the JColorChooser class relies on the ColorChooserComponentFactory to create the default panels from which to choose a color. These panels are specific subclasses of the AbstractColorChooserPanel class, and if you don't like the default set, you can create your own.

By default, when multiple chooser panels are in a JColorChooser, each panel is shown on a tab of a JTabbedPane. However, the ColorChooserUI can deal with multiple panels in any way it desires.

Creating a JColorChooser

If you want to create a JColorChooser and place it in your own window, you use one of the following three constructors for the JColorChooser class:

public JColorChooser()
```
JColorChooser colorChooser = new JColorChooser();
```

public JColorChooser(Color initialColor)
```
JColorChooser colorChooser =
  new JColorChooser(aComponent.getBackground());
```

public JColorChooser(ColorSelectionModel model)
```
JColorChooser colorChooser = new JColorChooser(aColorSelectionModel);
```

By default, the initial color for the chooser is white. If you don't want white as the default, you can provide the initial color as a Color object or ColorSelectionModel.

Using JColorChooser

Once you've created a JColorChooser from a constructor, you can place it in any Container, just like any other Component. For instance, the source shown in Listing 9-7 created the GUI shown earlier in Figure 9-18.

Listing 9-7. *Using a JColorChooser in Your JFrame*

```java
import java.awt.*;
import javax.swing.*;
import javax.swing.event.*;
import javax.swing.colorchooser.*;

public class ColorSample {

  public static void main(String args[]) {
    Runnable runner = new Runnable() {
      public void run() {
        JFrame frame = new JFrame("JColorChooser Popup");
        frame.setDefaultCloseOperation(JFrame.EXIT_ON_CLOSE);

        final JLabel label = new JLabel("I Love Swing", JLabel.CENTER);
        label.setFont(new Font("Serif", Font.BOLD | Font.ITALIC, 48));
        frame.add(label, BorderLayout.SOUTH);

        final JColorChooser colorChooser =
          new JColorChooser(label.getBackground());
        colorChooser.setBorder(
          BorderFactory.createTitledBorder("Pick Foreground Color"));

        // More source to come
        frame.add(colorChooser, BorderLayout.CENTER);

        frame.pack();
        frame.setVisible(true);
      }
    };
    EventQueue.invokeLater(runner);
  }
}
```

Although this source code creates the GUI, selecting a different color within the JColorChooser doesn't do anything yet. Let's now look at the code that causes color changes.

Listening for Color Selection Changes

The JColorChooser uses a ColorSelectionModel as its data model. As the following interface definition shows, the data model includes a single property, selectedColor, for managing the state of the color chooser.

```
public interface ColorSelectionModel {
  // Listeners
  public void addChangeListener(ChangeListener listener);
  public void removeChangeListener(ChangeListener listener);
  // Properties
  public Color getSelectedColor();
  public void setSelectedColor(Color newValue);
}
```

When a user changes the color within the JColorChooser, the selectedColor property changes, and the JColorChooser generates a ChangeEvent to notify any registered ChangeListener objects.

Therefore, to complete the earlier ColorSample example in the previous section, and have the foreground color of the label change when the user changes the color selection within the JColorChooser, you need to register a ChangeListener with the color chooser. This involves creating a ChangeListener and adding it to the ColorSelectionModel. Placing the source code shown in Listing 9-8 where the //More source to come comment appears in the Listing 9-7 is necessary for this example to work properly.

Listing 9-8. *Activating the JColorChooser Example*

```
    ColorSelectionModel model = colorChooser.getSelectionModel();
    ChangeListener changeListener = new ChangeListener() {
      public void stateChanged(ChangeEvent changeEvent) {
        Color newForegroundColor = colorChooser.getColor();
        label.setForeground(newForegroundColor);
      }
    };
    model.addChangeListener(changeListener);
```

Once this source is added, the example is complete. Running the program brings up Figure 9-18, and selecting a new color alters the foreground of the label.

Creating and Showing a JColorChooser Pop-Up Window

Although the previous example is sufficient if you want to include a JColorChooser within your own window, more often than not, you want the JColorChooser to appear in a separate pop-up window. This window might appear as the result of selecting a button on the screen, or possibly even selecting a menu item. To support this behavior, the JColorChooser includes the following factory method:

```
public static Color showDialog(Component parentComponent,
  String title, Color initialColor)
```

When called, showDialog() creates a modal dialog box with the given parent component and title. Within the dialog box is a JColorChooser whose initial color is the one provided. As you can see in Figure 9-18 (shown earlier in the chapter), along the bottom are three buttons: OK, Cancel, and Reset. When OK is pressed, the pop-up window disappears and the showDialog() method returns the currently selected color. When Cancel is pressed, null is returned instead of the selected color or the initial color. Selection of the Reset button causes the JColorChooser to change its selected color to the initial color provided at startup.

What normally happens with the showDialog() method is that the initial color argument is some color property of an object. The returned value of the method call then becomes the new setting for the same color property. This usage pattern is shown in the following lines of code, where the changing color property is the background for a button. As with JOptionPane, the null parent-component argument causes the pop-up window to be centered on the screen instead of over any particular component.

```
Color initialBackground = button.getBackground();
Color background = JColorChooser.showDialog(
  null, "Change Button Background", initialBackground);
if (background != null) {
  button.setBackground(background);
}
```

To place this code in the context of a complete example, Listing 9-9 shows source code that offers a button that, when selected, displays a JColorChooser. The color selected within the chooser becomes the background color of the button after the OK button is selected.

Listing 9-9. *Using showDialog with the JColorChooser*

```
import java.awt.*;
import java.awt.event.*;
import javax.swing.*;

public class ColorSamplePopup {

  public static void main(String args[]) {
    Runnable runner = new Runnable() {
      public void run() {
        JFrame frame = new JFrame("JColorChooser Sample Popup");
        frame.setDefaultCloseOperation(JFrame.EXIT_ON_CLOSE);

        final JButton button = new JButton("Pick to Change Background");

        ActionListener actionListener = new ActionListener() {
          public void actionPerformed(ActionEvent actionEvent) {
            Color initialBackground = button.getBackground();
            Color background = JColorChooser.showDialog(
              null, "Change Button Background", initialBackground);
```

```
            if (background != null) {
              button.setBackground(background);
            }
          }
        }
      };
      button.addActionListener(actionListener);
      frame.add(button, BorderLayout.CENTER);

      frame.setSize(300, 100);
      frame.setVisible(true);
    }
  };
  EventQueue.invokeLater(runner);
  }
}
```

Providing Your Own OK/Cancel Event Listeners

If the showDialog() method provides too much automatic behavior, you may prefer another JColorChooser method that allows you to customize the chooser before displaying it and define what happens when the OK and Cancel buttons are selected:

```
public static JDialog createDialog(Component parentComponent, String title,
  boolean modal, JColorChooser chooserPane, ActionListener okListener,
  ActionListener cancelListener)
```

In createDialog(), the parent component and title arguments are the same as showDialog(). The modal argument allows the pop-up window to be nonmodal, unlike showDialog() in which the pop-up is always modal. When the pop-up is not modal, the user can still interact with the rest of the application. The OK and Cancel buttons in the pop-up window automatically have one associated ActionListener that hides the pop-up window after selection. It's your responsibility to add your own listeners if you need any additional response from selection.

To demonstrate proper usage of createDialog(), the program shown in Listing 9-10 duplicates the functionality of the program shown in Listing 9-9. However, instead of automatically accepting the new color, the color change is rejected if the new background is the same color as the foreground. In addition, if the user selects the Cancel button, the button background color is set to red.

Listing 9-10. *Custom Action Listeners on JColorChooser Buttons*

```
import java.awt.*;
import java.awt.event.*;
import javax.swing.*;
import javax.swing.event.*;
import javax.swing.colorchooser.*;

public class CreateColorSamplePopup {
```

```java
public static void main(String args[]) {
  Runnable runner = new Runnable() {
    public void run() {
      JFrame frame = new JFrame("JColorChooser Create Popup Sample");
      frame.setDefaultCloseOperation(JFrame.EXIT_ON_CLOSE);

      final JButton button = new JButton("Pick to Change Background");

      ActionListener actionListener = new ActionListener() {
        public void actionPerformed(ActionEvent actionEvent) {
          Color initialBackground = button.getBackground();

          final JColorChooser colorChooser =
            new JColorChooser(initialBackground);

          // For okay selection, change button background to selected color
          ActionListener okActionListener = new ActionListener() {
            public void actionPerformed(ActionEvent actionEvent) {
              Color newColor = colorChooser.getColor();
              if (newColor.equals(button.getForeground())) {
                System.out.println("Color change rejected");
              } else {
                button.setBackground(colorChooser.getColor());
              }
            }
          };

          // For cancel selection, change button background to red
          ActionListener cancelActionListener = new ActionListener() {
            public void actionPerformed(ActionEvent actionEvent) {
              button.setBackground(Color.RED);
            }
          };

          final JDialog dialog = JColorChooser.createDialog(null,
            "Change Button Background", true, colorChooser,
            okActionListener, cancelActionListener);

          // Wait for current event dispatching to complete before showing
          Runnable showDialog = new Runnable() {
            public void run() {
              dialog.setVisible(true);
            }
          };
```

```
                EventQueue.invokeLater(showDialog);
              }
            };
          button.addActionListener(actionListener);
          frame.add(button, BorderLayout.CENTER);

          frame.setSize(300, 100);
          frame.setVisible(true);
        }
      };
      EventQueue.invokeLater(runner);
    }
}
```

■Note Notice that the `actionPerformed()` method that shows the color chooser uses the `EventQueue.invokeLater()` method to show the chooser. The current event handler needs to finish before showing the chooser. Otherwise, the previous action event processing won't complete before the chooser is shown.

JColorChooser Properties

Table 9-8 lists information on the eight properties of the JColorChooser, including the three data types of the single property color.

Table 9-8. *JColorChooser Properties*

Property Name	Data Type	Access
accessibleContext	AccessibleContext	Read-only
chooserPanels	AbstractColorChooserPanel[]	Read-write bound
color	Color	Read-write
color	int rgb	Write-only
color	int red, int green, int blue	Write-only
dragEnabled	boolean	Read-write
previewPanel	JComponent	Read-write bound
selectionModel	ColorSelectionModel	Read-write bound
UI	ColorChooserUI	Read-write bound
UIClassID	String	Read-only

The `color` property is special in that it has three ways of setting itself:

- Directly from a `Color`

- From one integer representing its red-green-blue values combined into one `int` variable using the nibble allocation 0xAARRGGBB, where *A* is for alpha value (and is ignored, using 255 instead)

- From three integers, separating the red, green, and blue color components into three separate `int` variables

If you don't use `showDialog()`, you can customize the `JColorChooser` before displaying it. Besides customizing the `color` property, which is settable in the `JColorChooser` constructor, you can customize the component to be displayed in the preview area and the color chooser panels.

Changing the Preview Panel

It's the responsibility of the `ColorChooserComponentFactory` class to provide the default component for the preview area of the `JColorChooser`. For the standard look and feel types, the preview panel is in the bottom portion of the color chooser.

If you don't want a preview panel in the color chooser, you must change the `previewPanel` property to a component value that isn't `null`. When the property is set to `null`, the default preview panel for the look and feel is shown. Setting the property to an empty `JPanel` serves the purpose of not showing the preview panel.

```
colorChooser.setPreviewPanel(new JPanel());
```

Figure 9-20 shows what one such color chooser might look like without the preview panel. Because the `JPanel` has no size when nothing is in it, this effectively removes the panel.

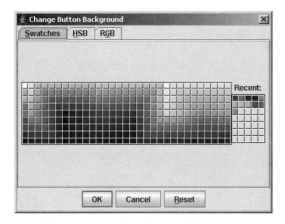

Figure 9-20. *JColorChooser without a preview panel*

If you want the preview panel present, but just don't like the default appearance, you can add your own `JComponent` to the area. Configuration entails placing your new preview panel in a title-bordered container, and having the foreground of the preview panel change when the user selects a new color.

■**Caution** A bug in the ColorChooserUI implementation class (BasicColorChooserUI) requires an extra step to properly install the preview panel. Besides calling setPreviewPanel(newPanel), you must set the panel's size and border to enable the user interface to properly configure the new preview panel. The exact steps seem to vary with which JDK release you are using. See http://bugs.sun.com/ bugdatabase/view_bug.do?bug_id=5029286 for more details. There are some other related bugs (search the Bug Parade for setPreviewPanel).

The following source demonstrates the use of a JLabel as the custom preview panel with the necessary work-around. Figure 9-21 demonstrates what the JColorChooser that uses this preview panel would look like.

```
final JLabel previewLabel = new JLabel("I Love Swing", JLabel.CENTER);
previewLabel.setFont(new Font("Serif", Font.BOLD | Font.ITALIC, 48));
previewLabel.setSize(previewLabel.getPreferredSize());
previewLabel.setBorder(BorderFactory.createEmptyBorder(0,0,1,0));
colorChooser.setPreviewPanel(previewLabel);
```

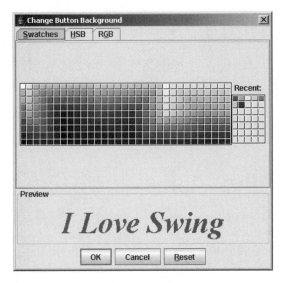

Figure 9-21. *JColorChooser with custom preview panel*

■**Note** Because the initial setting for the foreground of the preview panel is its background color, the panel will appear to be empty. This is one reason why the default preview panel shows text with contrasting background colors.

Changing the Color Chooser Panels

The various tabs in the upper part of the JColorChooser represent the AbstractColorChooserPanel implementations. Each allows the user to pick a color in a different manner. By default, the ColorChooserComponentFactory provides the JColorChooser with three panels (see Figure 9-22):

- The Swatches panel lets a user pick a color from a set of predefined color swatches, as if at a paint store.

- The HSB panel allows a user to pick a color using the Hue-Saturation-Brightness color model.

- The RGB panel is for picking colors using the Red-Green-Blue color model.

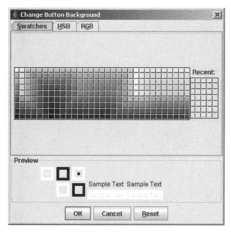

Swatches   HSB

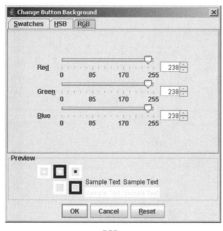

RGB

Figure 9-22. *The default JColorChooser panels*

If you don't like the default chooser panels, or you just want to add other color chooser panels that work differently, you can create your own by subclassing the AbstractColorChooserPanel class. To add a new panel to the existing set, call the following method:

```
public void addChooserPanel(AbstractColorChooserPanel panel)
```

If you later decide that you no longer want the new panel, you can remove it with this method:

```
public AbstractColorChooserPanel removeChooserPanel(AbstractColorChooserPanel panel)
```

To replace the existing set of panels, call this method:

```
setChooserPanels(AbstractColorChooserPanel panels[ ])
```

Creating a new panel entails subclassing AbstractColorChooserPanel and filling in the details of choosing a color for the new panel. The class definition, shown in the following code lines, includes five abstract methods. These five methods are what must be overridden.

```
public abstract class AbstractColorChooserPanel extends JPanel {
  public AbstractColorChooserPanel();
  protected abstract void buildChooser();
  protected Color getColorFromModel();
  public ColorSelectionModel getColorSelectionModel();
  public int getDisplayMnemonicIndex();
  public abstract String getDisplayName();
  public abstract Icon getLargeDisplayIcon();
  public int getMnemonic();
  public abstract Icon getSmallDisplayIcon();
  public void installChooserPanel(JColorChooser);
  public void paint(Graphics);
  public void uninstallChooserPanel(JColorChooser);
  public abstract void updateChooser();
}
```

To demonstrate how to work with color chooser panels, let's look at how to create a new one that displays a list of colors from the Color and SystemColor class. From this list, the user must pick one. The panel will use a JComboBox to represent the list of colors. (The details of using a JComboBox are explained in Chapter 13.) Figure 9-23 shows the finished panel. The panel is created and added with the following source:

```
SystemColorChooserPanel newChooser = new SystemColorChooserPanel();
AbstractColorChooserPanel chooserPanels[] = {newChooser};
colorChooser.setChooserPanels(chooserPanels);
```

Figure 9-23. *Replacing all panels with the new SystemColor chooser panel*

The first method to define is `public String getDisplayName()`. This method returns a text label to display on the tab when multiple chooser panels are available. If there's only one chooser panel, this name isn't shown.

```
public String getDisplayName() {
  return "SystemColor";
}
```

The return values for the two `Icon` methods do nothing with the system look and feel types. You can return `null` from them or return an `Icon` to check that nothing has been done with them. A custom `ColorChooserUI` could use the two `Icon` methods somewhere, possibly for the icon on a chooser panel tab.

```
public Icon getSmallDisplayIcon() {
  return new DiamondIcon(Color.BLUE);
}

public Icon getLargeDisplayIcon() {
  return new DiamondIcon(Color.GREEN);
}
```

The `protected void buildChooser()` method is called by the `installChooserPanel()` method of `AbstractColorChooserPanel` when the panel is added to the chooser. You use this method to add the necessary components to the container. In the sample `SystemColorChooserPanel` chooser, this involves creating the `JComboBox` and adding it to the panel. Because `AbstractColorChooserPanel` is a `JPanel` subclass, you can just add() the combo box. The combo box must be filled with options and an event handler installed for when the user selects the component. The specifics of the event handling are described after the following block of source code.

```
protected void buildChooser() {
  comboBox = new JComboBox(labels);
  comboBox.addItemListener(this);
  add(comboBox);
}
```

■**Note** In addition, if you choose to override uninstallChooserPanel (JColorChooser enclosingChooser), you need to call super.uninstallChooserPanel (JColorChooser enclosingChooser) *last*, instead of first.

When a user changes the color value in an AbstractColorChooserPanel, the panel must notify the ColorSelectionModel of the change in color. In the SystemColorChooserPanel panel, this equates to the user selecting a new choice in the JComboBox. Therefore, when the combo box value changes, find the Color that equates to the choice and tell the model about the change.

```
public void itemStateChanged(ItemEvent itemEvent) {
  int state = itemEvent.getStateChange();
  if (state == ItemEvent.SELECTED) {
    int position = findColorLabel(itemEvent.getItem());
    // Last position is bad (not selectable)
    if ((position != NOT_FOUND) && (position != labels.length-1)) {
      ColorSelectionModel selectionModel = getColorSelectionModel();
      selectionModel.setSelectedColor(colors[position]);
    }
  }
}
```

The final AbstractColorChooserPanel method to implement is public void updateChooser(). It, too, is called by installChooserPanel() at setup time. In addition, it's also called whenever the ColorSelectionModel of the JColorChooser changes. When updateChooser() is called, the chooser panel should update its display to show that the current color of the model is selected. Not all panels show which color is currently selected, so a call may do nothing. (The system-provided Swatches panel is one that doesn't display the current color.) In addition, it's possible that the current color isn't displayable on the panel. For instance, on the SystemColorChooserPanel, if the current selection isn't a SystemColor or Color constant, you can either do nothing or display something to signify a custom color. Therefore, in the updateChooser() implementation, you need to get the current color from the ColorSelectionModel and change the color for the panel. The actual setting is done in a helper method called setColor(Color newValue).

```
public void updateChooser() {
  Color color = getColorFromModel();
  setColor(color);
}
```

The setColor(Color newColor) method simply looks up the color in a lookup table using the position returned from findColorPosition(Color newColor).

```
// Change combo box to match color, if possible
private void setColor(Color newColor) {
  int position = findColorPosition(newColor);
  comboBox.setSelectedIndex(position);
}
```

The specifics of the findColorLabel(Object label) and findColorPosition(Color newColor) methods are shown in the complete source in Listing 9-11, coming up shortly.

If you don't use the showDialog() means of showing the chooser pop-up window, once the chooser panel has been defined, and you've created a chooser panel, it can be placed within a JColorChooser with addChooserPanel().

```
AbstractColorChooserPanel newChooser = new SystemColorChooserPanel();
colorChooser.addChooserPanel(newChooser);
```

After showing the JColorChooser and picking the appropriate tab, your new chooser will be available for use, as shown in Figure 9-24.

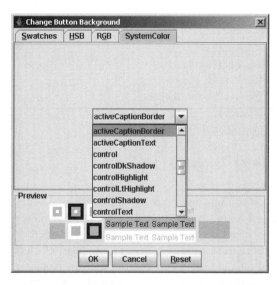

Figure 9-24. *After adding the new SystemColor chooser panel*

The complete source for the SystemColorChooserPanel is shown in Listing 9-11. The program should use the ComboBoxModel to store the labels and colors arrays of the example in one data model. However, the complexities of using the MVC capabilities of the JComboBox will be saved for Chapter 13. Feel free to change the example in order to use the appropriate data model for the JComboBox or some of the other Collections API classes available.

Listing 9-11. *Custom AbstractColorChooserPanel*

```
import javax.swing.*;
import javax.swing.colorchooser.*;
import java.awt.*;
import java.awt.event.*;

public class SystemColorChooserPanel
    extends AbstractColorChooserPanel
    implements ItemListener {
```

```java
private static int NOT_FOUND = -1;

JComboBox comboBox;
String labels[] = {
  "BLACK",
  "BLUE",
  "CYAN",
  "DARK_GRAY",
  "GRAY",
  "GREEN",
  "LIGHT_GRAY",
  "MAGENTA",
  "ORANGE",
  "PINK",
  "RED",
  "WHITE",
  "YELLOW",
  "activeCaption",
  "activeCaptionBorder",
  "activeCaptionText",
  "control",
  "controlDkShadow",
  "controlHighlight",
  "controlLtHighlight",
  "controlShadow",
  "controlText",
  "desktop",
  "inactiveCaption",
  "inactiveCaptionBorder",
  "inactiveCaptionText",
  "info",
  "infoText",
  "menu",
  "menuText",
  "scrollbar",
  "text",
  "textHighlight",
  "textHighlightText",
  "textInactiveText",
  "textText",
  "window",
  "windowBorder",
  "windowText",
  "<Custom>"};
```

```java
Color colors[] = {
  Color.BLACK,
  Color.BLUE,
  Color.CYAN,
  Color.DARK_GRAY,
  Color.GRAY,
  Color.GREEN,
  Color.LIGHT_GRAY,
  Color.MAGENTA,
  Color.ORANGE,
  Color.PINK,
  Color.RED,
  Color.WHITE,
  Color.YELLOW,
  SystemColor.activeCaption,
  SystemColor.activeCaptionBorder,
  SystemColor.activeCaptionText,
  SystemColor.control,
  SystemColor.controlDkShadow,
  SystemColor.controlHighlight,
  SystemColor.controlLtHighlight,
  SystemColor.controlShadow,
  SystemColor.controlText,
  SystemColor.desktop,
  SystemColor.inactiveCaption,
  SystemColor.inactiveCaptionBorder,
  SystemColor.inactiveCaptionText,
  SystemColor.info,
  SystemColor.infoText,
  SystemColor.menu,
  SystemColor.menuText,
  SystemColor.scrollbar,
  SystemColor.text,
  SystemColor.textHighlight,
  SystemColor.textHighlightText,
  SystemColor.textInactiveText,
  SystemColor.textText,
  SystemColor.window,
  SystemColor.windowBorder,
  SystemColor.windowText,
  null};

// Change combo box to match color, if possible
private void setColor(Color newColor) {
  int position = findColorPosition(newColor);
  comboBox.setSelectedIndex(position);
}
```

```
// Given a label, find the position of the label in the list
private int findColorLabel(Object label) {
  String stringLabel = label.toString();
  int position = NOT_FOUND;
  for (int i=0,n=labels.length; i<n; i++) {
    if (stringLabel.equals(labels[i])) {
      position=i;
      break;
    }
  }
  return position;
}

// Given a color, find the position whose color matches
// This could result in a position different from original if two are equal
// Since actual color is same, this is considered to be okay
private int findColorPosition(Color color) {
  int position = colors.length-1;
  // Cannot use equals() to compare Color and SystemColor
  int colorRGB = color.getRGB();
  for (int i=0,n=colors.length; i<n; i++) {
    if ((colors[i] != null) && (colorRGB == colors[i].getRGB())) {
      position=i;
      break;
    }
  }
  return position;
}

public void itemStateChanged(ItemEvent itemEvent) {
  int state = itemEvent.getStateChange();
  if (state == ItemEvent.SELECTED) {
    int position = findColorLabel(itemEvent.getItem());
    // last position is bad (not selectable)
    if ((position != NOT_FOUND) && (position != labels.length-1)) {
      ColorSelectionModel selectionModel = getColorSelectionModel();
      selectionModel.setSelectedColor(colors[position]);
    }
  }
}

public String getDisplayName() {
  return "SystemColor";
}
```

```
  public Icon getSmallDisplayIcon() {
    return new DiamondIcon(Color.BLUE);
  }

  public Icon getLargeDisplayIcon() {
    return new DiamondIcon(Color.GREEN);
  }

  protected void buildChooser() {
    comboBox = new JComboBox(labels);
    comboBox.addItemListener(this);
    add(comboBox);
  }

  public void updateChooser() {
    Color color = getColorFromModel();
    setColor(color);
  }
}
```

Listing 9-12 demonstrates the use of the new chooser panel. It's a slightly modified version of the CreateColorSamplePopup program shown earlier in Listing 9-10. You can uncomment the setChooserPanels() statement and comment out the addChooserPanel() call to go from adding one panel (as in Figure 9-23) to replacing all of them (as in Figure 9-24).

Listing 9-12. *Having Custom Panels in a JColorChooser*

```
import java.awt.*;
import java.awt.event.*;
import javax.swing.*;
import javax.swing.event.*;
import javax.swing.colorchooser.*;

public class CustomPanelPopup {

  public static void main(String args[]) {
    Runnable runner = new Runnable() {
      public void run() {
        JFrame frame = new JFrame("JColorChooser Custom Panel Sample");
        frame.setDefaultCloseOperation(JFrame.EXIT_ON_CLOSE);

        final JButton button = new JButton("Pick to Change Background");

        ActionListener actionListener = new ActionListener() {
          public void actionPerformed(ActionEvent actionEvent) {
            Color initialBackground = button.getBackground();
```

```
        final JColorChooser colorChooser =
          new JColorChooser(initialBackground);
        SystemColorChooserPanel newChooser =
          new SystemColorChooserPanel();
//      AbstractColorChooserPanel chooserPanels[] = {newChooser};
//      colorChooser.setChooserPanels(chooserPanels);
        colorChooser.addChooserPanel(newChooser);

        // For okay button, change button background to selected color
        ActionListener okActionListener = new ActionListener() {
          public void actionPerformed(ActionEvent actionEvent) {
            Color newColor = colorChooser.getColor();
            if (newColor.equals(button.getForeground())) {
              System.out.println("Color change rejected");
            } else {
              button.setBackground(colorChooser.getColor());
            }
          }
        };

        // For cancel button, change button background to red
        ActionListener cancelActionListener = new ActionListener() {
          public void actionPerformed(ActionEvent actionEvent) {
            button.setBackground(Color.RED);
          }
        };

        final JDialog dialog =
          JColorChooser.createDialog(
            null, "Change Button Background", true, colorChooser,
            okActionListener, cancelActionListener);

        // Wait for current event dispatching to complete before showing
        Runnable showDialog = new Runnable() {
          public void run() {
            dialog.setVisible(true);
          }
        };
        EventQueue.invokeLater(showDialog);
      }
    };
    button.addActionListener(actionListener);
    frame.add(button, BorderLayout.CENTER);
```

```
            frame.setSize(300, 100);
            frame.setVisible(true);
          }
        };
        EventQueue.invokeLater(runner);
      }
    }
```

Using the ColorChooserComponentFactory Class

One class worthy of some special attention is ColorChooserComponentFactory. Normally, this class does its work behind the scenes, and you never need to deal with it.

However, if you want to remove one of the default color choosers, you cannot use the public AbstractColorChooserPanel removeChooserPanel(AbstractColorChooserPanel panel) method of JColorChooser. Initially, the chooserPanels property of JColorChooser is null. When this property is null, the default ColorChooserUI asks the ColorChooserComponentFactory for the default panels with the public static AbstractColorChooserPanel[ ] getDefaultChooserPanels() method. So, until you modify the property, no panels will appear. If you want to remove a default panel, you must get the default array, place the panels you want to keep in a new array, and then change the chooserPanels property of the chooser to the new array. This is a little extra work, but it gets the job done.

The other method in the ColorChooserComponentFactory class is public static JComponent getPreviewPanel(), which gets the default preview panel when the previewPanel property of a JColorChooser is null. This is the reason that providing a null argument to the setPreviewPanel() method of JColorChooser doesn't remove the preview panel. For the panel to be empty, you must provide a JComponent with no size.

```
colorChooser.setPreviewPanel(new JPanel());
```

Customizing a JColorChooser Look and Feel

The JColorChooser appearance is nearly the same for all the preinstalled look and feel types. The only differences are related to how each look and feel displays the internal components, such as a JTabbedPane, JLabel, JButton, or JSlider. Changing the UIResource-related properties of those components affects the appearance of a newly created JColorChooser. In addition, the JColorChooser class has its own 39 UIResource-related properties available for customization, as listed in Table 9-9. Most of these resources are related to text labels appearing on the various default color chooser panels.

Table 9-9. *JColorChooser UIResource Elements*

Property String	Object Type
ColorChooser.background	Color
ColorChooser.cancelText	String
ColorChooser.font	Font
ColorChooser.foreground	Color

Table 9-9. *JColorChooser UIResource Elements (Continued)*

Property String	Object Type
ColorChooser.hsbBlueText	String
ColorChooser.hsbBrightnessText	String
ColorChooser.hsbDisplayedMnemonicIndex	Integer
ColorChooser.hsbGreenText	String
ColorChooser.hsbHueText	String
ColorChooser.hsbMnemonic	Integer
ColorChooser.hsbNameText	String
ColorChooser.hsbRedText	String
ColorChooser.hsbSaturationText	String
ColorChooser.okText	String
ColorChooser.panels	AbstractColorChooserPanel[ ]
ColorChooser.previewText	String
ColorChooser.resetMnemonic	Integer
ColorChooser.resetText	String
ColorChooser.rgbBlueDisplayedMnemonicIndex	Integer
ColorChooser.rgbBlueMnemonic	Integer
ColorChooser.rgbBlueText	String
ColorChooser.rgbGreenDisplayedMnemonicIndex	Integer
ColorChooser.rgbGreenMnemonic	Integer
ColorChooser.rgbGreenText	String
ColorChooser.rgbMnemonic	Integer
ColorChooser.rgbNameText	String
ColorChooser.rgbRedDisplayedMnemonicIndex	Integer
ColorChooser.rgbRedMnemonic	Integer
ColorChooser.rgbRedText	String
ColorChooser.sampleText	String
ColorChooser.showPreviewPanelText	Boolean
ColorChooser.swatchesDefaultRecentColor	Color
ColorChooser.swatchesDisplayedMnemonicIndex	Integer
ColorChooser.swatchesMnemonic	Integer
ColorChooser.swatchesNameText	String
ColorChooser.swatchesRecentSwatchSize	Dimension

Table 9-9. *JColorChooser UIResource Elements (Continued)*

Property String	Object Type
ColorChooser.swatchesRecentText	String
ColorChooser.swatchesSwatchSize	Dimension
ColorChooserUI	String

JFileChooser Class

The Swing component set also provides a chooser for the selection of file names and/or directories: the JFileChooser class. This chooser replaces the need for using the FileDialog from the
original AWT component set. Like the other Swing chooser components, JFileChooser isn't
automatically placed in a pop-up window, but it can be placed anywhere within the user interface
of your program. Figure 9-25 shows a JFileChooser with the Metal look and feel, Ocean theme,
that has been automatically placed in a modal JDialog.

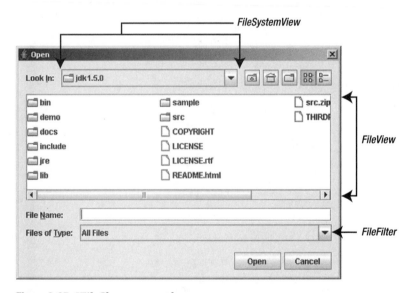

Figure 9-25. *JFileChooser sample*

In support of the JFileChooser class are a handful of classes in the javax.swing.filechooser
package. The support classes include a FileFilter class for restricting files and directories to
be listed in the FileView of the JFileChooser. The FileView controls how the directories and
files are listed within the JFileChooser. The FileSystemView is an abstract class that tries to hide
file system-related operating system specifics from the file chooser. Java 2 platform vendors
will provide operating system-specific versions so that tasks such as listing root partitions can
be done (with 100% Pure Java code).

■**Caution** Don't confuse the abstract `javax.swing.filechooser.FileFilter` class with the `java.io.FileFilter` interface. Although functionally similar, they're different. The two coexist because the `java.io.FileFilter` interface didn't exist in a Java 1.1 runtime. Because the original Swing `JFileChooser` needed to run in both Java 1.1 and Java 2 environments, the chooser needed to define a replacement. Unless otherwise specified, all `FileFilter` references in this text are to the class in the `javax.swing.filechooser` package.

Creating a JFileChooser

There are six constructors for `JFileChooser`:

```
public JFileChooser()
JFileChooser fileChooser = new JFileChooser();
```

```
public JFileChooser(File currentDirectory)
File currentDirectory = new File("."); // starting directory of program
JFileChooser fileChooser = new JFileChooser(currentDirectory);
```

```
public JFileChooser(File currentDirectory, FileSystemView fileSystemView)
FileSystemView fileSystemView = new SomeFileSystemView(...);
JFileChooser fileChooser = new JFileChooser(currentDirectory, fileSystemView);
```

```
public JFileChooser(FileSystemView fileSystemView)
JFileChooser fileChooser = new JFileChooser(fileSystemView);
```

```
public JFileChooser(String currentDirectoryPath)
String currentDirectoryPath = "."; // starting directory of program
JFileChooser fileChooser = new JFileChooser(currentDirectoryPath);
```

```
public JFileChooser(String currentDirectoryPath, FileSystemView fileSystemView)
JFileChooser fileChooser = new JFileChooser(currentDirectoryPath, fileSystemView);
```

By default, the starting directory displayed is the user's home directory (system property `user.home`). If you want to start the `JFileChooser` pointing at another directory, the directory can be specified as either a `String` or a `File` object.

You can also specify a `FileSystemView` to specify a custom representation to the operating system's top-level directory structure. When the `FileSystemView` argument is not specified, the `JFileChooser` uses a `FileSystemView` appropriate for the user's operating system.

Using JFileChooser

After creating a `JFileChooser` from a constructor, you can place it in any `Container`, because it's a `JComponent`. The `JFileChooser` object looks a little strange in an object that's not a pop-up window, but this may allow you to do a task without needing to constantly bring up a new file chooser.

Listing 9-13 demonstrates a simple window with two labels and a JFileChooser. Notice that there are no Open or Cancel buttons, but the buttons in the FileSystemView area are selectable.

Listing 9-13. *Using a JFileChooser in Your JFrame*

```
import java.io.File;
import java.awt.*;
import java.awt.event.*;
import javax.swing.*;

public class FileSamplePanel {

  public static void main(String args[]) {
    Runnable runner = new Runnable() {
      public void run() {
        JFrame frame = new JFrame("JFileChooser Popup");
        frame.setDefaultCloseOperation(JFrame.EXIT_ON_CLOSE);

        final JLabel directoryLabel = new JLabel(" ");
        directoryLabel.setFont(new Font("Serif", Font.BOLD | Font.ITALIC, 36));
        frame.add(directoryLabel, BorderLayout.NORTH);

        final JLabel filenameLabel = new JLabel(" ");
        filenameLabel.setFont(new Font("Serif", Font.BOLD | Font.ITALIC, 36));
        frame.add(filenameLabel, BorderLayout.SOUTH);

        JFileChooser fileChooser = new JFileChooser(".");
        fileChooser.setControlButtonsAreShown(false);
        frame.add(fileChooser, BorderLayout.CENTER);

        frame.pack();
        frame.setVisible(true);
      }
    };
    EventQueue.invokeLater(runner);
  }
}
```

Adding an ActionListener to a JFileChooser

The JFileChooser allows you to add ActionListener objects to listen for selection of the approval or cancel actions. Approval is double-clicking a file; cancel is pressing the Escape key. To detect which action was triggered, check the action command for the ActionEvent received by your ActionListener. Its action command setting will be either JFileChooser.APPROVE_SELECTION for file selection or JFileChooser.CANCEL_SELECTION for pressing the Escape key.

To complete the previous example in Listing 9-13, adding an ActionListener allows you to set the text for the two labels when the user selects a file. On selection, the text becomes the current directory and file name. On pressing of the Escape key, text is cleared. Listing 9-14 shows the new ActionListener.

Listing 9-14. *ActionListener for JFileChooser in Your JFrame*

```
// Create ActionListener
ActionListener actionListener = new ActionListener() {
  public void actionPerformed(ActionEvent actionEvent) {
    JFileChooser theFileChooser = (JFileChooser)actionEvent.getSource();
    String command = actionEvent.getActionCommand();
    if (command.equals(JFileChooser.APPROVE_SELECTION)) {
      File selectedFile = theFileChooser.getSelectedFile();
      directoryLabel.setText(selectedFile.getParent());
      filenameLabel.setText(selectedFile.getName());
    } else if (command.equals(JFileChooser.CANCEL_SELECTION)) {
      directoryLabel.setText(" ");
      filenameLabel.setText(" ");
    }
  }
};
fileChooser.addActionListener(actionListener);
```

With the addition of the ActionListener, the program is now complete in the sense that selection is now active. Figure 9-26 shows what this window would look like after selection of the COPYRIGHT file within the c:\jdk1.5.0 directory.

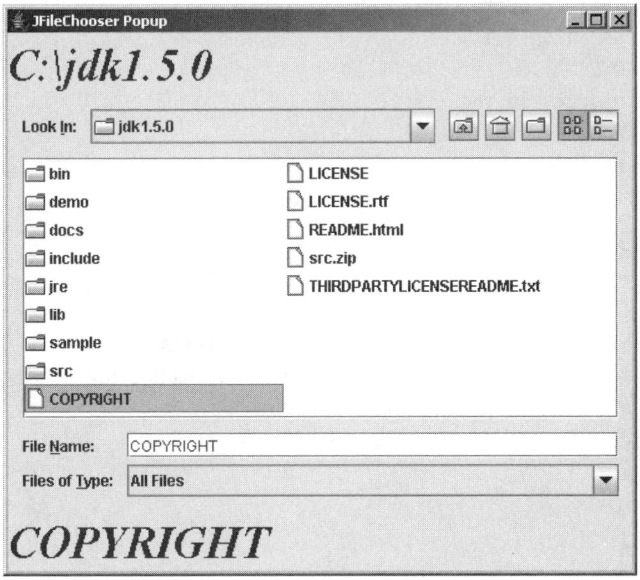

Figure 9-26. *JFileChooser within a custom window*

Showing a JFileChooser within a Pop-Up Window

Instead of placing a `JFileChooser` panel within your own window, you will more typically place it in a modal `JDialog`. There are three ways to do this, depending on the text you want to appear on the approval button:

- `public int showDialog(Component parentComponent, String approvalButtonText)`

- `public int showOpenDialog(Component parentComponent)`

- `public int showSaveDialog(Component parentComponent)`

Calling one of these methods will place the configured `JFileChooser` into a modal `JDialog` and show the dialog box centered over the parent component. Providing a `null` parent component centers the pop-up window on the screen. The call doesn't return until the user selects the approval or cancel button. After selection of one of the two buttons, the call returns a status value, depending on which button was selected. This status would be one of three `JFileChooser` constants: `APPROVE_OPTION`, `CANCEL_OPTION`, or `ERROR_OPTION`.

■**Caution** If the user clicks the approval button without selecting anything, `CANCEL_OPTION` is returned.

To perform the same task as the previous example, in which an `ActionListener` was attached to the `JFileChooser` (Listing 9-14), you can just show the dialog box and change the labels based on the return status, instead of relying on the action command, as follows:

```
JFileChooser fileChooser = new JFileChooser(".");
int status = fileChooser.showOpenDialog(null);
if (status == JFileChooser.APPROVE_OPTION) {
  File selectedFile = fileChooser.getSelectedFile();
  directoryLabel.setText(selectedFile.getParent());
  filenameLabel.setText(selectedFile.getName());
} else if (status == JFileChooser.CANCEL_OPTION) {
  directoryLabel.setText(" ");
  filenameLabel.setText(" ");
}
```

With this technique, the file chooser will be shown in another window, instead of within the window with the two labels. Notice that this version switches from checking the `String` return values of the earlier example to checking `int return values`: [if (command.equals(JFileChooser.APPROVE_SELECTION)) versus if (status == JFileChooser.APPROVE_OPTION)].

JFileChooser Properties

Once you understand the basic `JFileChooser` usage, you can customize the component's behavior and appearance by modifying its many properties. Table 9-10 shows the 26 properties of `JFileChooser`.

Table 9-10. *JFileChooser Properties*

Property Name	Data Type	Access
acceptAllFileFilter	FileFilter	Read-only
acceptAllFileFilterUsed	boolean	Read-write bound
accessibleContext	AccessibleContext	Read-only
accessory	JComponent	Read-write bound
actionListeners	ActionListener[ ]	Read-only
approveButtonMnemonic	char	Read-write bound
approveButtonText	String	Read-write bound
approveButtonToolTipText	String	Read-write bound
choosableFileFilters	FileFilter[ ]	Read-only
controlButtonsAreShown	boolean	Read-write bound
currentDirectory	File	Read-write bound
dialogTitle	String	Read-write bound
dialogType	int	Read-write bound
directorySelectionEnabled	boolean	Read-only
dragEnabled	boolean	Read-write
fileFilter	FileFilter	Read-write bound
fileHidingEnabled	boolean	Read-write bound
fileSelectionEnabled	boolean	Read-only
fileSelectionMode	int	Read-write bound
fileSystemView	FileSystemView	Read-write bound
fileView	FileView	Read-write bound
multiSelectionEnabled	boolean	Read-write bound
selectedFile	File	Read-write bound
selectedFiles	File[ ]	Read-write bound
UI	FileChooserUI	Read-only
UIClassID	String	Read-only

When the different showDialog() methods are used, the dialogType property is automatically set to one of three JOptionPane constants: OPEN_DIALOG, SAVE_DIALOG, CUSTOM_DIALOG. If you're not using showDialog(), you should set this property according to the type of dialog box you plan to work with. The controlButtonsAreShown property allows you to hide the Open, Save, and Cancel buttons.

Working with File Filters

The JFileChooser supports three ways of filtering its file and directory list. The first two involve working with the FileFilter class, and the last involves hidden files. First, let's look at the FileFilter class.

FileFilter is an abstract class that works something like FilenameFilter in AWT. However, instead of working with strings for directory and file names, it works with a File object. For every File object that is to be displayed (both files and directories), the filter decides whether the File can appear within the JFileChooser. In addition to providing an acceptance mechanism, the filter also provides a description, or name, for when the description is displayed to a user. These two capabilities are reflected in the following two methods of the class definition:

```
public abstract class FileFilter {
  public FileFilter();
  public abstract String getDescription();
  public abstract boolean accept(File file);
}
```

■**Note** Given the abstract nature of this class, it should be an interface, but it isn't.

To demonstrate a file filter, Listing 9-15 creates one that accepts an array of file extensions. If the file sent to accept() is a directory, it's automatically accepted. Otherwise, the file extension must match one of the extensions in the array provided, and the character preceding the extension must be a period. For this particular filter, the comparisons are case-insensitive.

Listing 9-15. *A Custom FileFilter for Use with a JFileChooser*

```
import javax.swing.filechooser.*;
import java.io.File; // avoid FileFilter name conflict

public class ExtensionFileFilter extends FileFilter {
  String description;
  String extensions[];

  public ExtensionFileFilter(String description, String extension) {
    this(description, new String[] { extension} );
  }
```

```
  public ExtensionFileFilter(String description, String extensions[]) {
    if (description == null) {
// Since no description, use first extension and # of extensions as description
      this.description = extensions[0]+"{ "+extensions.length+"} " ;
    } else {
      this.description = description;
    }
    // Convert array to lowercase
    // Don't alter original entries
    this.extensions = (String[])extensions.clone();
    toLower(this.extensions);
  }
  private void toLower(String array[]) {
    for (int i=0, n=array.length; i<n; i++) {
      array[i] = array[i].toLowerCase();
    }
  }

  public String getDescription() {
    return description;
  }

  // Ignore case, always accept directories
  // Character before extension must be a period
  public boolean accept(File file) {
    if (file.isDirectory()) {
      return true;
    } else {
      String path = file.getAbsolutePath().toLowerCase();
      for (int i=0, n=extensions.length; i<n; i++) {
        String extension = extensions[i];
        if ((path.endsWith(extension)  &&
            (path.charAt(path.length()-extension.length()-1)) == '.')) {
          return true;
        }
      }
    }
    return false;
  }
}
```

Using the file filter entails creating it and associating it with the JFileChooser. If you just want to make the filter selectable by the user, but not the default initial selection, call public void addChoosableFileFilter(FileFilter filter). This will keep the default accept-all-files filter selected. If, instead, you want the filter to be set when the chooser first appears, call public void setFileFilter(FileFilter filter), and the file chooser will filter the initial set of files shown.

For example, the following source will add two filters to a file chooser:

```
FileFilter jpegFilter =
  new ExtensionFileFilter(null, new String[]{ "JPG", "JPEG"} );
fileChooser.addChoosableFileFilter(jpegFilter);
FileFilter gifFilter = new ExtensionFileFilter("gif", new String[]{ "gif"} );
fileChooser.addChoosableFileFilter(gifFilter);
```

When no file filters have been associated with the JFileChooser, the filter from JFileChooser.getAcceptAllFileFilter() is used to provide a filter that accepts all files and that is also appropriate for the underlying operating system.

Figure 9-27 shows an open filter selection combo box in a Motif file chooser.

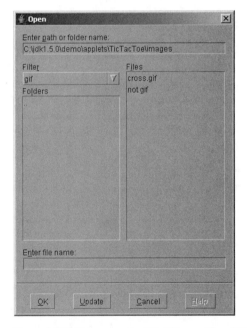

Figure 9-27. *Using custom FileFilter with a JFileChooser*

Tip Setting the `FileFilter` with `setFileFilter()` before adding filters with `add ChoosableFileFilter()` causes the accept-all-file filter to be unavailable. To put it back, call `setAcceptAllFileFilterUsed(true)`. In addition, you can reset the filter list with a call to `resetChoosableFileFilters()`.

One built-in filter isn't a `FileFilter`. It concerns hidden files, such as those that begin with a period (.) on UNIX file systems. By default, hidden files aren't shown within the `JFileChooser`. To enable the display of hidden files, you must set the `fileHidingEnabled` property to `false`:

```
aFileChooser.setFileHidingEnabled(false);
```

Tip When creating `javax.swing.filechooser.FileFilter` subclasses, you may want to have the new class also implement the `java.io.FileFilter` interface. To do this, simply add `implements java.io.FileFilter` to the class definition. This works because the method signature for the `accept()` method in the `javax.swing.filechooser` class matches the interface definition: `public boolean accept(File file)`.

Choosing Directories Instead of Files

The `JFileChooser` supports three selection modes: files only, directories only, and files and directories. The `fileSelectionMode` property setting determines the mode of the chooser. The available settings are specified by the three `JFileChooser` constants: `FILES_ONLY`, `DIRECTORIES_ONLY`, and `FILES_AND_DIRECTORIES`. Initially, the file chooser is in `JFileChooser.FILES_ONLY` mode. To change the mode, just call `public void setFileSelectionMode(int newMode)`.

In addition to the `fileSelectionMode` property, you can use the read-only `fileSelectionEnabled` and `directorySelectionEnabled` properties to determine the type of input currently supported by the file chooser.

Adding Accessory Panels

The `JFileChooser` supports the addition of an accessory component. This component can enhance the functionality of the chooser, including previewing an image or document, or playing an audio file. To respond to file selection changes, the accessory component should attach itself as a `PropertyChangeListener` to the `JFileChooser`. When the `JFileChooser.➡ SELECTED_FILE_CHANGED_PROPERTY` property changes, the accessory then changes to reflect the file selection. Figure 9-28 shows how an image previewer accessory component might appear. Configuring the accessory for a chooser is just like setting any other property.

```
fileChooser.setAccessory(new LabelAccessory(fileChooser));
```

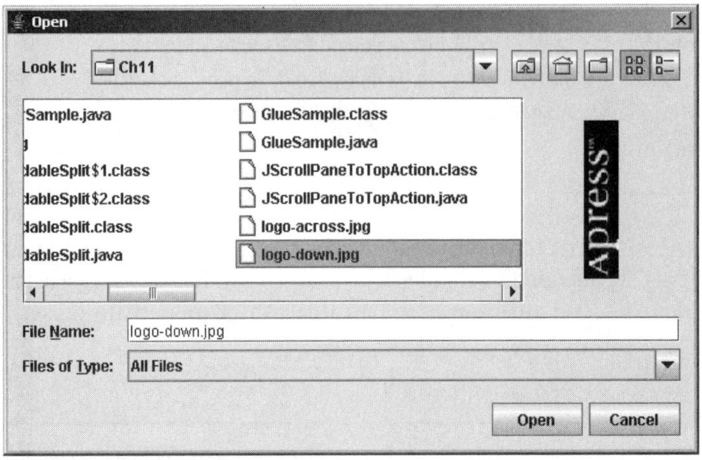

Figure 9-28. *A JFileChooser with an accessory panel*

Listing 9-16 shows source for an Image component that displays an accessory icon. The selected image file becomes the icon for a JLabel component. The component does two scaling operations to make sure the dimensions of the image are sized to fit within the accessory.

Listing 9-16. *Custom Accessory for Use with JFileChooser*

```
import javax.swing.*;
import java.beans.*;
import java.awt.*;
import java.io.*;

public class LabelAccessory extends JLabel implements PropertyChangeListener {
  private static final int PREFERRED_WIDTH = 125;
  private static final int PREFERRED_HEIGHT = 100;

  public LabelAccessory(JFileChooser chooser) {
    setVerticalAlignment(JLabel.CENTER);
    setHorizontalAlignment(JLabel.CENTER);
    chooser.addPropertyChangeListener(this);
    setPreferredSize(new Dimension(PREFERRED_WIDTH, PREFERRED_HEIGHT));
  }
  public void propertyChange(PropertyChangeEvent changeEvent) {
    String changeName = changeEvent.getPropertyName();
    if (changeName.equals(JFileChooser.SELECTED_FILE_CHANGED_PROPERTY)) {
      File file = (File)changeEvent.getNewValue();
      if (file != null) {
        ImageIcon icon = new ImageIcon(file.getPath());
        if (icon.getIconWidth() > PREFERRED_WIDTH) {
          icon = new ImageIcon(icon.getImage().getScaledInstance(
            PREFERRED_WIDTH, -1, Image.SCALE_DEFAULT));
```

```
          if (icon.getIconHeight() > PREFERRED_HEIGHT) {
            icon = new ImageIcon(icon.getImage().getScaledInstance(
            -1, PREFERRED_HEIGHT, Image.SCALE_DEFAULT));
          }
        }
      }
      setIcon(icon);
    }
  }
}
```

Using the FileSystemView Class

The FileSystemView class localizes access to platform-specific file system information. Where the JDK 1.1 version of java.io.File was fairly crippled in this respect, FileSystemView fills in to make it easier to design FileChooserUI objects. The Swing FileSystemView class provides three custom views as package-private subclasses of FileSystemView. They include support for UNIX and Windows, plus a generic handler.

Although it isn't necessary to define your own FileSystemView, the class provides some features that can be useful outside the context of a JFileChooser. To get the view specific to the user's runtime environment, call public static FileSystemView getFileSystemView(). The class definition follows.

```
public abstract class FileSystemView {
  // Constructors
  public FileSystemView();  // Properties
  // Properties
  public File getDefaultDirectory();
  public File getHomeDirectory();
  public File[] getRoots();
  // Class Methods
  public static FileSystemView getFileSystemView();
  // Other Methods
  public File createFileObject(File directory, String filename);
  public File createFileObject(String path);
  protected File createFileSystemRoot(File file);
  public abstract File createNewFolder(File containingDir) throws IOException;
  public File getChild(File parent, String filename);
  public File[] getFiles(File directory, boolean useFileHiding);
  public File getParentDirectory(File file);
  public String getSystemDisplayName(File file);
  public Icon getSystemIcon(File file);
  public String getSystemTypeDescription(File file);
  public boolean isComputerNode(File file);
  public boolean isDrive(File file);
  public boolean isFileSystem(File file);
  public boolean isFileSystemRoot(File file);
  public boolean isFloppyDrive(File file);
```

```
  public boolean isHiddenFile(File file);
  public boolean isParent(File folder, File file);
  public boolean isRoot(File file);
  public Boolean isTraversable(File file);
}
```

Note Notice that the isTraversable() method returns a Boolean, not a boolean. (I haven't a clue why the difference—perhaps somewhere an object is needed, and the primitive boolean wasn't sufficient.)

FileView Class

The final part of the JFileChooser class to examine is the FileView area where all the file names are listed. Each of the custom look and feel types has its own FileView area class. In addition, some of the predefined look and feel types, such as Motif, aren't changeable. Nevertheless, at least in the Metal and Windows file choosers, you can customize the icons for different file types or change the display name for a file.

The five methods of the FileView class allow you to change the name, icon, or description (two forms) of each File in the view. In addition, the FileView actually controls whether a directory is traversable, allowing you to program in a weak level of access control. Nontraversable directories have a different default icon, because those directories cannot be browsed for file selection.

Here's the definition of the abstract FileView class:

```
public abstract class FileView {
  public FileView();
  public String getDescription(File file);
  public Icon getIcon(File file);
  public String getName(File file);
  public String getTypeDescription(File file);
  public Boolean isTraversable(File file);
}
```

Note Like FileSystemView, the isTraversable() method returns a Boolean value, not a boolean one.

Customizing the FileView requires creating a subclass and overriding the appropriate methods. By default, all the methods return null, indicating that you don't want to define custom behavior for a specific method.

Once you've defined the file view, simply change the fileView property of your JFileChooser:

```
fileChooser.setFileView(new JavaFileView());
```

Figure 9-29 shows the changed appearance of a Metal JFileChooser after installing a custom FileView.

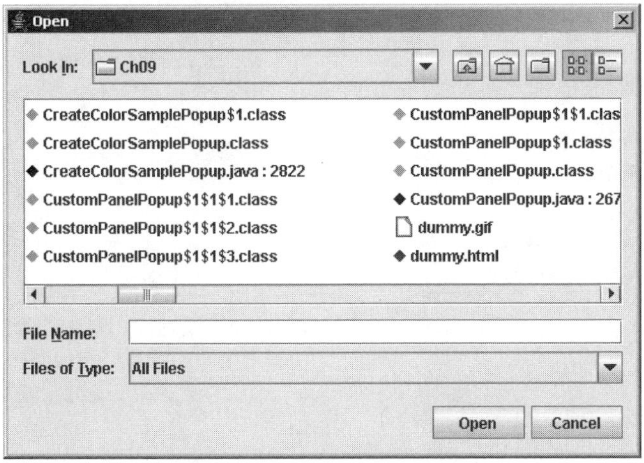

Figure 9-29. *Changing the FileView*

The JavaFileView class in Listing 9-17 provides a FileView implementation that customizes the appearance of files related to Java development—specifically, .java, .class, .jar, and .html or .htm files. (This is certainly not meant to be a comprehensive list of Java file types.) For each of these file types, a special icon instead of the default icon is displayed next to the name. In addition, for Java source files, the length of the file is displayed. (Imagine if every file attribute were being displayed!) Unfortunately, you can't modify the font or color from a FileView.

Listing 9-17. *Custom FileView for Some Java-Related File Types*

```java
import java.io.File;
import java.awt.*;
import javax.swing.*;
import javax.swing.filechooser.*;

public class JavaFileView extends FileView {
  Icon javaIcon = new DiamondIcon(Color.BLUE);
  Icon classIcon = new DiamondIcon(Color.GREEN);
  Icon htmlIcon = new DiamondIcon(Color.RED);
  Icon jarIcon = new DiamondIcon(Color.PINK);

  public String getName(File file) {
    String filename = file.getName();
    if (filename.endsWith(".java")) {
      String name = filename + " : " + file.length();
      return name;
    }
    return null;
  }
```

```java
  public String getTypeDescription(File file) {
    String typeDescription = null;
    String filename = file.getName().toLowerCase();

    if (filename.endsWith(".java")) {
      typeDescription = "Java Source";
    } else if (filename.endsWith(".class")){
      typeDescription = "Java Class File";
    } else if (filename.endsWith(".jar")){
      typeDescription = "Java Archive";
    } else if (filename.endsWith(".html") || filename.endsWith(".htm")) {
      typeDescription = "Applet Loader";
    }
    return typeDescription;
  }

  public Icon getIcon(File file) {
    if (file.isDirectory()) {
      return null;
    }
    Icon icon = null;
    String filename = file.getName().toLowerCase();
    if (filename.endsWith(".java")) {
      icon = javaIcon;
    } else if (filename.endsWith(".class")){
      icon = classIcon;
    } else if (filename.endsWith(".jar")){
      icon = jarIcon;
    } else if (filename.endsWith(".html") || filename.endsWith(".htm")) {
      icon = htmlIcon;
    }
    return icon;
  }
}
```

Customizing a JFileChooser Look and Feel

Each installable Swing look and feel provides a different JFileChooser appearance and set of default UIResource values. Figure 9-30 shows the appearance of the JFileChooser for the preinstalled set of look and feel types: Motif, Windows, and Ocean.

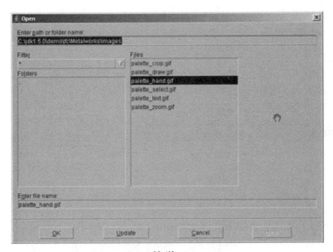

Motif

Windows

Ocean

Figure 9-30. *JFileChooser under different look and feel types*

The available set of UIResource-related properties for a JFileChooser is shown in Table 9-11. For the JFileChooser component, there are 83 different properties. Nearly all the properties relate to the button labels, mnemonics, icons, and tooltip text.

Table 9-11. *JFileChooser UIResource Elements*

Property String	Object Type
FileChooser.acceptAllFileFilterText	String
FileChooser.ancestorInputMap	InputMap
FileChooser.cancelButtonMnemonic	Integer
FileChooser.cancelButtonText	String
FileChooser.cancelButtonToolTipText	String
FileChooser.deleteFileButtonMnemonic	Integer
FileChooser.deleteFileButtonText	String
FileChooser.deleteFileButtonToolTipText	String
FileChooser.detailsViewButtonAccessibleName	String
FileChooser.detailsViewButtonToolTipText	String
FileChooser.detailsViewIcon	Icon
FileChooser.directoryDescriptionText	String
FileChooser.directoryOpenButtonMnemonic	Integer
FileChooser.directoryOpenButtonText	String
FileChooser.directoryOpenButtonToolTipText	String
FileChooser.enterFilenameLabelMnemonic	String
FileChooser.enterFilenameLabelText	String
FileChooser.fileDescriptionText	String
FileChooser.fileNameLabelMnemonic	Integer
FileChooser.fileNameLabelText	String
FileChooser.filesLabelMnemonic	Integer
FileChooser.filesLabelText	String
FileChooser.filesOfTypeLabelMnemonic	Integer
FileChooser.filesOfTypeLabelText	String
FileChooser.filterLabelMnemonic	Integer
FileChooser.filterLabelText	String
FileChooser.foldersLabelMnemonic	Integer
FileChooser.foldersLabelText	String
FileChooser.helpButtonMnemonic	Integer

Table 9-11. *JFileChooser UIResource Elements (Continued)*

Property String	Object Type
FileChooser.helpButtonText	String
FileChooser.helpButtonToolTipText	String
FileChooser.homeFolderAccessibleName	String
FileChooser.homeFolderIcon	Icon
FileChooser.homeFolderToolTipText	String
FileChooser.listFont	Font
FileChooser.listViewBackground	Color
FileChooser.listViewBorder	Border
FileChooser.listViewButtonAccessibleName	String
FileChooser.listViewButtonToolTipText	String
FileChooser.listViewIcon	Icon
FileChooser.listViewWindowsStyle	Boolean
FileChooser.lookInLabelMnemonic	Integer
FileChooser.lookInLabelText	String
FileChooser.newFolderAccessibleName	String
FileChooser.newFolderButtonMnemonic	Integer
FileChooser.newFolderButtonText	String
FileChooser.newFolderButtonToolTipText	String
FileChooser.newFolderDialogText	String
FileChooser.newFolderErrorSeparator	String
FileChooser.newFolderErrorText	String
FileChooser.newFolderIcon	Icon
FileChooser.newFolderToolTipText	String
FileChooser.openButtonMnemonic	Integer
FileChooser.openButtonText	String
FileChooser.openButtonToolTipText	String
FileChooser.openDialogTitleText	String
FileChooser.other.newFolder	String
FileChooser.other.newFolder.subsequent	String
FileChooser.win32.newFolder	String
FileChooser.win32.newFolder.subsequent	String
FileChooser.pathLabelMnemonic	Integer
FileChooser.pathLabelText	String

Table 9-11. *JFileChooser UIResource Elements (Continued)*

Property String	Object Type
FileChooser.readOnly	Boolean
FileChooser.renameFileButtonMnemonic	Integer
FileChooser.renameFileButtonText	String
FileChooser.renameFileButtonToolTipText	String
FileChooser.renameFileDialogText	String
FileChooser.renameFileErrorText	String
FileChooser.renameFileErrorTitle	String
FileChooser.saveButtonMnemonic	Integer
FileChooser.saveButtonText	String
FileChooser.saveButtonToolTipText	String
FileChooser.saveDialogTitleText	String
FileChooser.saveInLabelText	String
FileChooser.updateButtonMnemonic	Integer
FileChooser.updateButtonText	String
FileChooser.updateButtonToolTipText	String
FileChooser.upFolderAccessibleName	String
FileChooser.upFolderIcon	Icon
FileChooser.upFolderToolTipText	String
FileChooser.usesSingleFilePane	Boolean
FileChooser.useSystemExtensionHiding	Boolean
FileChooserUI	String

In addition to the more than 80 resources for JFileChooser, there are 5 additional ones as part of the FileView, which are shown in Table 9-12.

Table 9-12. *FileView UIResource Elements*

Property String	Object Type
FileView.computerIcon	Icon
FileView.directoryIcon	Icon
FileView.fileIcon	Icon
FileView.floppyDriveIcon	Icon
FileView.hardDriveIcon	Icon

Summary

In this chapter, you explored the intricacies of Swing's pop-up and chooser classes. Instead of manually creating a `JDialog` and filling it with the necessary pieces, the Swing component set includes support for many different pop-up and chooser classes. Starting with the `JOptionPane`, you learned how to create informational, question, and input pop-ups. In addition, you explored how to monitor the progress of time-consuming tasks by using the `ProgressMonitor` and `ProgressMonitorInputStream` classes.

After looking at the more general pop-up classes, you explored the specifics of Swing's color and file chooser classes: `JColorChooser` and `JFileChooser`. From each of these two classes, you can prompt the user for the requested input and customize the display in more ways than you can imagine.

Now that you have a feel for the predefined pop-ups, it is time to move on to the `LayoutManager` classes in Chapter 10. With the help of the system layout managers, you can create even better user interfaces.

CHAPTER 10

■■■

Layout Managers

In Chapter 9, you learned about the various pop-up and chooser classes available from the Swing component set. In this chapter, you'll learn about the AWT and Swing layout managers.

While this book focuses on the Swing component set, you can't use them in a vacuum. You need to understand both the AWT and Swing layout managers. In fact, you're more apt to use four of the five AWT layout managers than three of the five Swing layout managers. The AWT layout managers are FlowLayout, BorderLayout, GridLayout, CardLayout, and GridBagLayout. The Swing layouts are BoxLayout, OverlayLayout, ScrollPaneLayout, ViewportLayout, and SpringLayout. Another manager is JRootPane.RootLayout, which was described in Chapter 8.

In addition to the layout managers, you'll look at several helper classes: GridBagLayout's constraint class GridBagConstraints, the SizeRequirements class used by both the BoxLayout and OverlayLayout managers, and the SpringLayout manager's associated Spring and SpringLayout.Constraints classes.

Layout Manager Responsibilities

Every container, such as a JPanel or Container, has a layout manager. That layout manager is responsible for positioning components, regardless of the platform or screen size.

Layout managers eliminate the need to compute component placement on your own, which would be a losing proposition, since the size required for any component depends on the platform on which your program is deployed and the current look and feel. Even for a simple layout, the code required to discover component sizes and compute absolute positions could be hundreds of lines, particularly if you concern yourself with what happens when the user resizes a window. A layout manager takes care of this for you. It asks each component in the container how much space it requires, and then arranges the components on the screen as best it can, based on the component sizes on the platform in use, the available space, and the rules of the layout manager.

To find out how much space a component needs, the layout manager calls the component's getMinimumSize(), getPreferredSize(), and getMaximumSize() methods. These methods report the minimum, preferred, and maximum space that a component requires to be displayed correctly. Thus, each component must know its space requirements. The layout manager then uses the component's space requirements to resize components and arrange them on the screen. Your Java program never needs to worry about platform-dependent positioning, beyond layout manager setup.

Note that a layout manager is free to ignore some of its components; there is no requirement that a layout manager display everything. For example, a Container using a BorderLayout might include 30 or 40 components; however, the BorderLayout will display at most 5 of them (the last component placed in each of its five named areas). Likewise, a CardLayout may manage many components but displays exactly one at a time.

Besides ignoring components, a layout manager can do anything it wants with the components' minimum, preferred, and maximum size. It is free to ignore any or all of these. It makes sense that a layout manager can ignore a *preferred* size—after all, preferred means, "Give me this size if it's available." However, a layout manager can also ignore a minimum size. At times, there is no reasonable alternative because the container may not have enough room to display a component at its minimum size. How to handle this situation is left to the layout manager designer's discretion.

LayoutManager Interface

The LayoutManager interface defines the responsibilities of the manager that lays out the Component objects within a Container. As explained in the previous section, it is the duty of the layout manager to determine the position and size of each component within the Container. You will never call the methods of the LayoutManager interface directly; for the most part, layout managers do their work behind the scenes. Once you have created a LayoutManager object and told the container to use it (by calling setLayout(manager)), you're finished with it. The system calls the appropriate methods of the layout manager when necessary. Like any interface, LayoutManager specifies the methods a layout manager must implement but says nothing about how the LayoutManager does its job.

The LayoutManager interface itself is most important if you are writing a new layout manager. I'll describe this interface first because it's the foundation on which all layout managers are based. I'll also describe the LayoutManager2 interface, which is used by some layout managers.

Exploring the LayoutManager Interface

Five methods make up the LayoutManager interface:

```
public interface LayoutManager {
  public void addLayoutComponent(String name, Component comp);
  public void layoutContainer(Container parent);
  public Dimension minimumLayoutSize(Container parent);
  public Dimension preferredLayoutSize(Container parent);
  public void removeLayoutComponent(Component comp);
}
```

If you create your own class that implements LayoutManager, you must define all five. As you will see, many of the methods do not need to do anything, but you must still include a stub with the appropriate signature.

The addLayoutComponent() method is called only when you add components by calling the add(String, Component) or add(Component, Object) method, not just plain add(Component). For add(Component, Object), the Object must be of type String, or else that isn't called either.

Exploring the LayoutManager2 Interface

For layout managers that require each component to carry its layout manager constraints, the LayoutManager2 interface comes into play. The layout managers that use LayoutManager2 include BorderLayout, CardLayout, and GridBagLayout, to name a few.

LayoutManager2 has five additional methods:

```
public interface LayoutManager2 {
  public void addLayoutComponent(Component comp, Object constraints);
  public float getLayoutAlignmentX(Container target);
  public float getLayoutAlignmentY(Container target);
  public void invalidateLayout(Container target);
  public Dimension maximumLayoutSize(Container target);
}
```

The addLayoutComponent() method is called when you assign constraints to the component when adding it to the layout. In practice, this means that you added the component to the container by calling the add(Component component, Object constraints) or add(String name, Component component) methods, rather than the add(Component component) method. It is up to the layout manager to decide what, if anything, to do with the constraints. For example, GridBagLayout uses constraints to associate a GridBagConstraints object to the component added, and BorderLayout uses constraints to associate a location (like BorderLayout.CENTER) with the component.

FlowLayout Class

FlowLayout is the default layout manager for a JPanel. A FlowLayout adds components to the container in rows, working in the order defined by the getComponentOrientation() method of Component, typically left to right in the United States and western Europe. When it can't fit more components in a row, it starts a new row, similar to a word processor with word wrap enabled. When the container is resized, the components within it are repositioned based on the container's new size. Components within a FlowLayout-managed container are given their preferred size. If there is insufficient space, you do not see all the components, as illustrated in Figure 10-1.

Figure 10-1. *The default FlowLayout setup, with seven buttons and three different screen sizes. As the third example shows, if the screen is too small, the components will not be shrunk to fit all the components.*

There are three constructors for creating the FlowLayout layout manager:

```
public FlowLayout()
public FlowLayout(int alignment)
public FlowLayout(int alignment, int hgap, int vgap)
```

If an alignment is not specified, components within a FlowLayout-managed container are centered. Otherwise, the setting is controlled by one of the following constants:

- CENTER

- LEADING

- LEFT

- RIGHT

- TRAILING

For the typical left-to-right orientation, LEADING and LEFT are the same, as are TRAILING and RIGHT. For a language like Hebrew, these would be reversed. Figure 10-2 shows the effect of several different alignments.

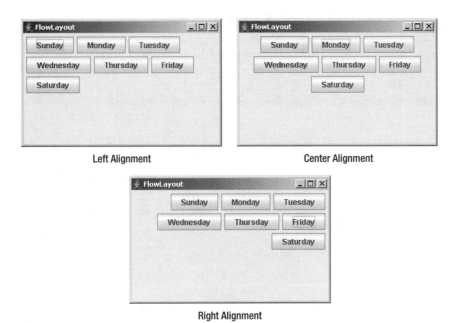

Figure 10-2. *FlowLayout with three different alignments*

You can specify the gaps, in pixels, for the spacing between components, both horizontal (hgap) and vertical (vgap). Gaps default to five pixels unless specified. It is possible to specify negative gaps if you want components to be placed on top of one another.

BorderLayout Class

BorderLayout is the default layout manager for the content pane of a JFrame, JWindow, JDialog, JInternalFrame, and JApplet. It provides for a more flexible way of positioning components along the edges of the window. Figure 10-3 shows a typical BorderLayout.

Figure 10-3. *Sample BorderLayout*

When using BorderLayout, you add components with constraints to identify in which of the five locations to place the component. If you don't specify a constraint, the component is added to the center area. Adding multiple components to the same area shows only the last component, although technically speaking, the other components are still within the container; they are just not shown.

There are two constructors for creating the BorderLayout layout manager:

```
public BorderLayout()
public BorderLayout(int hgap, int vgap)
```

Unlike FlowLayout, the default gaps for a BorderLayout are zero pixels, meaning the components are positioned right next to one another.

The constraints to use when adding a component to a BorderLayout-managed container are constants of the BorderLayout class:

- AFTER_LAST_LINE

- AFTER_LINE_ENDS

- BEFORE_FIRST_LINE

- BEFORE_LINE_BEGINS

- CENTER

- EAST

- LINE_END

- LINE_START

- NORTH

- PAGE_END

- PAGE_START

- SOUTH

- WEST

With only five regions to add a component to, you would expect only five constants. As with FlowLayout, the additional constants deal with proper positioning when the component orientation is reversed, either horizontally or vertically. For the typical left-to-right, top-to-bottom orientation, the common set of values is as follows:

- AFTER_LAST_LINE, PAGE_END, SOUTH

- AFTER_LINE_ENDS, LINE_END, EAST

- BEFORE_FIRST_LINE, PAGE_START, NORTH

- BEFORE_LINE_BEGINS, LINE_START, WEST

- CENTER

Tip Using the BEFORE and AFTER constants, as opposed to the NORTH, SOUTH, EAST, and WEST constants, is recommended, though all are supported.

You do not need specify all five areas of the container. The component in the north region takes up the entire width of the container along its top. South does the same along the bottom. The heights of north and south will be the preferred heights of the component added. The east and west areas are given the widths of the component each contains, where the height is whatever is left in the container after satisfying north's and south's height requirements. Any remaining space is given to the component in the center region.

The way to place multiple components into one of the regions of a BorderLayout-managed container is to add them to a different container first, and then add them to the BorderLayout-managed container. For instance, if you want a label and text field in the north area of a BorderLayout-managed container, place them in the west and center areas of another BorderLayout-managed container first, as shown here:

```
JPanel outerPanel = new JPanel(new BorderLayout());
JPanel topPanel = new JPanel(new BorderLayout());
JLabel label = new JLabel("Name:");
JTextField text = new JTextField();
topPanel.add(label, BorderLayout.BEFORE_LINE_BEGINS);
topPanel.add(text, BorderLayout.CENTER);
outerPanel.add(topPanel, BorderLayout.BEFORE_FIRST_LINE);
```

GridLayout Class

The GridLayout manager is ideal for laying out objects in rows and columns, where each cell in the layout has the same size. Components are added to the layout from left to right, top to bottom. A call to setLayout(new GridLayout(3, 4)) changes the layout manager of the current container to a GridLayout with three rows and four columns, as shown in Figure 10-4.

Figure 10-4. *Sample GridLayout*

There are three constructors for creating the GridLayout layout manager:

```
public GridLayout()
public GridLayout(int rows, int columns)
public GridLayout(int rows, int columns, int hgap, int vgap)
```

Typically, you would explicitly specify the overall grid size for your GridLayout-managed container. However, you can set the number of rows or columns to be zero, and the layout will grow without bounds in the direction with a zero setting.

■**Caution** If both rows and columns are specified to be zero to the GridLayout constructor, a runtime exception of IllegalArgumentException will be thrown.

The actual number of rows and columns drawn is based on the number of components within the container. The GridLayout tries to observe the number of rows requested first. If the requested number of rows is nonzero, the number of columns is determined by (*# of components* + *rows* − 1) / *rows*. If your request is for zero rows, the number of rows to use is determined by a similar formula: (*# of components* + *columns* − 1) / *columns*. Table 10-1 demonstrates this calculation. The last entry in the table is of special interest: if you request a 3×3 grid but place only four components in the layout, you actually get a 2×2 layout as a result. If you do not want to be surprised, size the GridLayout based on the actual number of objects you plan to add to the display.

Table 10-1. *GridLayout Row/Column Calculation*

Rows	Columns	# Components	Display Rows	Display Columns
0	1	10	10	1
0	2	10	5	2
1	0	10	1	10
2	0	10	2	5
2	3	10	2	5
2	3	20	2	10
3	2	10	3	4
3	3	3	3	1
3	3	4	2	2

GridBagLayout Class

GridBagLayout is the most complex and most flexible of the layout managers. Although it sounds like it should be a subclass of GridLayout, it's a different beast altogether. With GridLayout, elements are arranged in a rectangular grid, and each element in the container is sized identically (where possible). With GridBagLayout, elements can have different sizes and can occupy multiple rows or columns.

There is only the no-argument constructor for GridBagLayout:

```
public GridBagLayout()
```

The position and behavior of each element is specified by an instance of the GridBagConstraints class. By properly constraining the elements, you can specify the number of rows and columns a component occupies, which component grows when additional screen real estate is available, and various other restrictions. The actual grid size is based on the number of components within the GridBagLayout and the GridBagConstraints of those objects. For example, Figure 10-5 shows a GridBagLayout with seven components, arranged in a 3×3 grid.

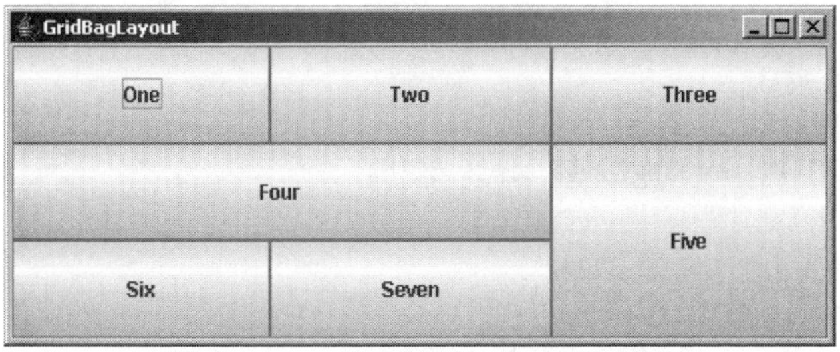

Figure 10-5. *GridBagLayout with seven components in a 3×3 grid*

■**Note** The maximum capacity of a screen using GridBagLayout is 512 rows by 512 columns. This is specified by the protected MAXGRIDSIZE constant of the layout manager.

The code used to create Figure 10-5 is shown in Listing 10-1.

Listing 10-1. *Seven-Button GridBagLayout*

```
import java.awt.*;
import java.awt.event.*;
import javax.swing.*;
import java.text.*;

public class GridBagButtons {
  private static final Insets insets = new Insets(0,0,0,0);
  public static void main(final String args[]) {
    Runnable runner = new Runnable() {
      public void run() {
        final JFrame frame = new JFrame("GridBagLayout");
        frame.setDefaultCloseOperation(JFrame.EXIT_ON_CLOSE);
        frame.setLayout(new GridBagLayout());
        JButton button;
```

```
        // Row One - Three Buttons
        button = new JButton("One");✗    ⌇
        addComponent(frame, button, 0, 0, 1, 1,
          GridBagConstraints.CENTER, GridBagConstraints.BOTH);
        button = new JButton("Two");
        addComponent(frame, button, 1, 0, 1, 1,
          GridBagConstraints.CENTER, GridBagConstraints.BOTH);
        button = new JButton("Three");
        addComponent(frame, button, 2, 0, 1, 1,
          GridBagConstraints.CENTER, GridBagConstraints.BOTH);
        // Row Two - Two Buttons
        button = new JButton("Four");
        addComponent(frame, button, 0, 1, 2, 1,
          GridBagConstraints.CENTER, GridBagConstraints.BOTH);
        button = new JButton("Five");
        addComponent(frame, button, 2, 1, 1, 2,
          GridBagConstraints.CENTER, GridBagConstraints.BOTH);
        // Row Three - Two Buttons
        button = new JButton("Six");
        addComponent(frame, button, 0, 2, 1, 1,
          GridBagConstraints.CENTER, GridBagConstraints.BOTH);
        button = new JButton("Seven");
        addComponent(frame, button, 1, 2, 1, 1,
          GridBagConstraints.CENTER, GridBagConstraints.BOTH);
        frame.setSize(500, 200);
        frame.setVisible(true);
      }
    };
    EventQueue.invokeLater(runner);
  }

  private static void addComponent(Container container, Component component,
      int gridx, int gridy, int gridwidth, int gridheight, int anchor,
      int fill) {
    GridBagConstraints gbc = new GridBagConstraints(gridx, gridy,
      gridwidth, gridheight, 1.0, 1.0, anchor, fill, insets, 0, 0);
    container.add(component, gbc);
  }
}
```

Most of the work in Listing 10-1 is done by the helper method addComponent(), which creates a set of constraints for the component to be added to the container.

GridBagLayout Rows and Columns

To help you visualize the grid of components in the GridBagLayout, Figure 10-6 indicates how the layout manager counts cells. The top-left cell in the layout has location (0, 0). There's nothing surprising about buttons one, two, three, six, and seven. Each of those occupies a 1×1 area of the layout's 3×3 grid. Button four occupies a 2×1 area; it is placed at location (0, 1), and thus occupies this cell plus the cell at (1, 1). Likewise, button five occupies a 1×2 area and takes up the cells at (2, 1) and (2, 2). The total size of the layout is determined entirely by the components that are placed in it and their constraints.

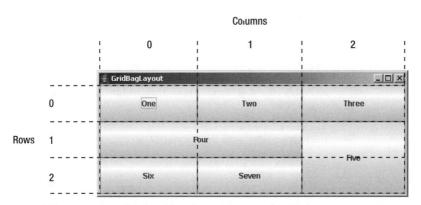

Figure 10-6. *How GridBagLayout counts rows and columns*

GridBagConstraints Class

The magic of the layout manager is strictly controlled by the different GridBagConstraints objects passed in for each component added to the container. Each specifies how to display a specific component. Unlike most other layout managers, which have a built-in idea about what to do with their display, the GridBagLayout is a blank slate. The constraints attached to the components tell the layout manager how to build its display.

Every component added to a GridBagLayout container should have a GridBagConstraints object associated with it. When an object is first added to the layout, it is given a default set of constraints (see Table 10-2). Calling container.add(Component, GridBagConstraints) or gridBagLayout.setConstraints(GridBagConstraints) applies the new set of constraints to the component.

GridBagConstraints has two constructors:

```
public GridBagConstraints()
public GridBagConstraints(int gridx, int gridy, int gridwidth, int gridheight,
   double weightx, double weighty, int anchor, int fill, Insets insets, int ipadx,
   int ipady)
```

Using the no-argument constructor for GridBagConstraints starts with all the defaults in Table 10-2. You can leave the individual settings alone and just set the individual fields. All are public, without getter methods. While you can just blindly pass in all the constraints to the GridBagConstraints constructor, it is better to describe the different fields separately.

Table 10-2. *GridBagConstraints Defaults*

Variable	Value	Description
anchor	CENTER	If the component is smaller than the space available, it will be centered within its region.
fill	NONE	The component should not resize itself if extra space is available within its region.
gridx	RELATIVE	The component associated with this constraint will be positioned relative to the last item added. If all components have gridx and gridy RELATIVE, they will be placed in a single row.
gridy	RELATIVE	The component associated with this constraint will be positioned relative to the last item added.
gridwidth	1	The component will occupy a single cell wide within the layout.
gridheight	1	The component will occupy a single cell high within the layout.
insets	0x0x0x0	No extra space is added around the edges of the component.
ipadx	0	There is no internal horizontal padding for the component.
ipady	0	There is no internal vertical padding for the component.
weightx	0	The component will not get any extra horizontal space, if available.
weighty	0	The component will not get any extra vertical space, if available.

Component Anchoring

The anchor variable specifies the direction in which the component will drift in the event it is smaller than the space available for it. CENTER is the default. The absolute values are NORTH, SOUTH, EAST, WEST, NORTHEAST, NORTHWEST, SOUTHEAST, and SOUTHWEST. The relative values are PAGE_START, PAGE_END, LINE_START, LINE_END, FIRST_LINE_START, FIRST_LINE_END, LAST_LINE_START, and LAST_LINE_END.

Component Resizing

The value of fill controls the component's resize policy. If fill is NONE (the default), the layout manager tries to give the component its preferred size. If fill is VERTICAL, it resizes in height if additional space is available. If fill is HORIZONTAL, it resizes in width. If fill is BOTH, the layout manager takes advantage of all available space in both directions. Figure 10-7 demonstrates VERTICAL, HORIZONTAL, and NONE values (generated by changing the GridBagConstraints.BOTH settings in Listing 10-1).

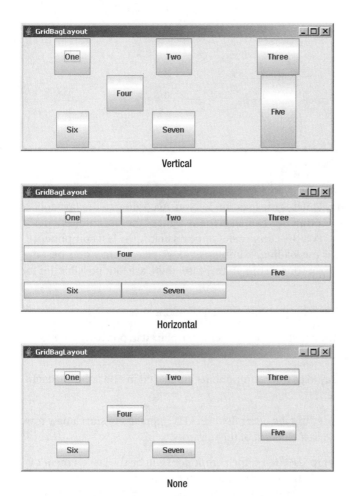

Figure 10-7. *GridBagLayout with different fill values*

Grid Positioning

The gridx and gridy variables specify the grid position where this component would be placed. (0, 0) specifies the cell at the origin of the screen. The gridwidth and gridheight variables specify the number of rows (gridwidth) and columns (gridheight) a particular component occupies. Table 10-3 shows the gridx, gridy, gridwidth, and gridheight values for the example shown earlier in Figure 10-5.

Table 10-3. *The gridx, gridy, gridwidth, and gridheight Values for Figure 10-5*

Component	gridx	gridy	gridwidth	gridheight
One	0	0	1	1
Two	1	0	1	1
Three	2	0	1	1
Four	0	1	2	1
Five	2	1	0	2
Six	0	2	1	1
Seven	1	2	1	3

It isn't necessary to set gridx and gridy to a specific location. If you set these fields to RELATIVE (the default), the system calculates the location for you. According to the Javadoc comments, if gridx is RELATIVE, the component appears to the right of the last component added to the layout. If gridy is RELATIVE, the component appears below the last component added to the layout. However, this is misleadingly simple. RELATIVE placement works best if you are adding components along a row or column. In this case, there are four possibilities for placement:

- With gridx and gridy RELATIVE, components are placed in one row.

- With gridx RELATIVE and gridy constant, components are placed in one row, each to the right of the previous component.

- With gridx constant and gridy RELATIVE, components are placed in one column, each below the previous component.

- Varying gridx or gridy while setting the other field RELATIVE appears to start a new row, placing the component as the first element of the new row.

If gridwidth or gridheight is set to REMAINDER, the component will be the last element of the row or column occupying any space that's remaining. For the components in the rightmost column of Table 10-3, for example, the gridwidth values could have been REMAINDER. Similarly, gridheight could be set to REMAINDER for the components in the bottom row.

gridwidth and gridheight may also have the value RELATIVE, which forces the component to be the next-to-last component in the row or column. Looking back to Figure 10-5, if button six had a gridwidth of RELATIVE, button seven wouldn't appear because button five is the last item in the row, and six is already next to last. If button five had a gridheight of RELATIVE, the layout manager would reserve space below it so the button could be the next-to-last item in the column.

Padding

The insets value specifies the external padding in pixels around the component (the space between the component and the edge of the cell or cells allotted to it). An Insets object can specify different padding for the top, bottom, left, or right side of the component.

ipadx and ipady specify the internal padding within the component. ipadx specifies the extra space to the right and left of the component (so the minimum width increases by 2×ipadx pixels). ipady specifies the extra space above and below the component (so the minimum height increases by 2×ipady pixels). The difference between insets (external padding) and ipadx/ipady (internal padding) can be confusing. The insets don't add space to the component itself; they are external to the component. ipadx and ipady change the component's minimum size, so they do add space to the component itself.

Weight

weightx and weighty describe how to distribute any additional space within the container. They allow you to control how components grow (or shrink) when the user resizes the container, or the container is just bigger to start.

If weightx is 0.0, the component won't get any additional space available in its row. If one or more components in a row have a positive weightx, any extra space is distributed proportionally between them. For example, if one component has a weightx value of 1.0 and the others are all 0.0, the one component will get all the additional space. If four components in a row each has a weightx value of 1.0, and the other components have weightx values of 0.0, the four components each get one quarter of the additional space. weighty behaves similarly to weightx, but in the other direction. Because weightx and weighty control the distribution of extra space in any row or column, setting either for one component may affect the position of the other components.

CardLayout Class

The CardLayout layout manager is significantly different from the other layout managers. Whereas the other layout managers attempt to display all the components within the container at once, a CardLayout displays only one component at a time. That component can be a component or container, where the latter lets you see multiple components laid out based on the layout manager of the embedded container.

Now that the JTabbedPane component (described in the next chapter) is available, CardLayout is rarely used.

BoxLayout Class

Swing's BoxLayout manager allows you to position components in either a horizontal row or a vertical column within your own container. In addition to using BoxLayout within your own container, the Box class (described in the next chapter) offers a container that uses BoxLayout as its default layout manager.

The benefit of using BoxLayout over something like FlowLayout or GridLayout is that BoxLayout works to honor each component's x and y alignment properties as well as its maximum size. And BoxLayout is much easier to use than GridBagLayout. Figure 10-8 demonstrates BoxLayout in action. Previously, you would have needed to figure out the necessary layout constraints to get GridBagLayout to behave like this.

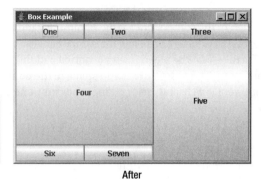

Figure 10-8. *BoxLayout example, before and after resizing*

Creating a BoxLayout

BoxLayout has a single constructor:

```
public BoxLayout(Container target, int axis)
```

The constructor takes two arguments. The first argument is the container with which this instance of the layout manager is to be associated, and the second is the layout direction. Valid directions are BoxLayout.X_AXIS for a left-to-right layout and BoxLayout.Y_AXIS for a top-to-bottom layout.

■**Caution** Trying to set the axis to something other than the equivalent value of the two constructor constants will throw an AWTError. If the layout manager is associated with a container that isn't the container passed in to the constructor, an AWTError will be thrown when the layout manager tries to lay out the other (that is, wrong) container.

Once you create a BoxLayout instance, you can associate the layout manager with a container as you would with any other layout manager.

```
JPanel panel = new JPanel();
LayoutManager layout = new BoxLayout (panel, BoxLayout.X_AXIS);
panel.setLayout(layout);
```

Unlike all the other system-provided layout managers, a BoxLayout and container are bound together in two directions, from manager to container as well as from container to manager.

■**Tip** The Box class, described in Chapter 11, lets you create a container and set its layout manager to BoxLayout all in one step.

Laying Out Components

Once you've set the layout manager of a container to BoxLayout, that's really all you do directly with the layout manager. Adding components to the container is done with either the add(Component component) or add(Component component, int index) method. Although BoxLayout implements the LayoutManager2 interface, implying the use of constraints, it currently uses none. Therefore, it isn't necessary to use add(Component component, Object constraints).

When it comes time to lay out the container, BoxLayout does its work. The BoxLayout manager tries to satisfy the minimum and maximum sizes of the components within the container, as well as their x-axis and y-axis alignments. Alignment values range from 0.0f to 1.0f. (Alignment settings are floating-point constants, not doubles, hence the need for the *f*.)

By default, all Component subclasses have an x-axis alignment of Component.CENTER_ALIGNMENT and a y-axis alignment of Component.CENTER_ALIGNMENT. However, all AbstractButton subclasses and JLabel have a default x-axis alignment of Component.LEFT_ALIGNMENT. Table 10-4 shows the constants available from Component for these component properties, settable with either setAlignmentX(float newValue) or setAlignmentY(float newValue). The different alignments work identically, except in different directions. In the case of horizontal alignments, this is similar to left-, center-, or right-justifying a paragraph.

Table 10-4. *Component Alignments*

Setting	Value
Vertical Alignment	
Component.TOP_ALIGNMENT	0.0f
Component.CENTER_ALIGNMENT	0.5f
Component.BOTTOM_ALIGNMENT	1.0f
Horizontal Alignment	
Component.LEFT_ALIGNMENT	0.0f
Component.CENTER_ALIGNMENT	0.5f
Component.RIGHT_ALIGNMENT	1.0f

Laying Out Components with the Same Alignments

The BoxLayout manager acts differently depending on the alignment of the components within the container being managed. If all the alignments are the same, those components whose maximum size is smaller than the container will be aligned based on the alignment setting. For instance, if you have a wide area with a vertical BoxLayout and small buttons within it, the horizontal alignment will serve to left-, center-, or right-justify the buttons. Figure 10-9 shows how this looks.

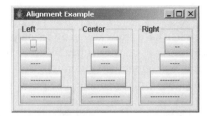

Figure 10-9. *Three y-axis BoxLayout containers, each with components having the same horizontal alignments*

The key point demonstrated here is that if all the components share the same alignment setting, the actual alignment of all the components within the managed container is the components' alignment setting.

The source used to generate Figure 10-9 is shown in Listing 10-2.

Listing 10-2. *Y-Axis Alignment*

```
import javax.swing.*;
import java.awt.*;
import java.awt.event.*;

public class YAxisAlignX {
  private static Container makeIt(String title, float alignment) {
    String labels[] = {"--", "----", "--------", "------------"};

    JPanel container = new JPanel();
    container.setBorder(BorderFactory.createTitledBorder(title));
    BoxLayout layout = new BoxLayout(container, BoxLayout.Y_AXIS);
    container.setLayout(layout);

    for (int i=0,n=labels.length; i<n; i++) {
      JButton button = new JButton(labels[i]);
      button.setAlignmentX(alignment);
      container.add(button);
    }
    return container;
  }

  public static void main(String args[]) {
    Runnable runner = new Runnable() {
      public void run() {
        JFrame frame = new JFrame("Alignment Example");
        frame.setDefaultCloseOperation(JFrame.EXIT_ON_CLOSE);

        Container panel1 = makeIt("Left", Component.LEFT_ALIGNMENT);
        Container panel2 = makeIt("Center", Component.CENTER_ALIGNMENT);
        Container panel3 = makeIt("Right", Component.RIGHT_ALIGNMENT);
```

```
        frame.setLayout(new FlowLayout());
        frame.add(panel1);
        frame.add(panel2);
        frame.add(panel3);

        frame.pack();
        frame.setVisible(true);
      }
    };
    EventQueue.invokeLater(runner);
  }
}
```

An x-axis BoxLayout works similarly when all the components have the same vertical alignments. Instead of being left-, center-, and right-justified, the components would appear at the top, center, and bottom of the container. Figure 10-10 demonstrates this appearance.

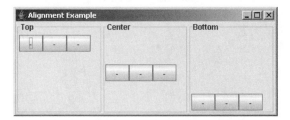

Figure 10-10. *Three x-axis BoxLayout containers that each have components with the same vertical alignments*

The source for the example shown in Figure 10-10 requires just a few changes from Listing 10-2. The complete source is provided in Listing 10-3.

Listing 10-3. *X-Axis Alignment*

```
import javax.swing.*;
import java.awt.*;
import java.awt.event.*;

public class XAxisAlignY {
  private static Container makeIt(String title, float alignment) {
    String labels[] = {"-", "-", "-"};

    JPanel container = new JPanel();
    container.setBorder(BorderFactory.createTitledBorder(title));
    BoxLayout layout = new BoxLayout(container, BoxLayout.X_AXIS);
    container.setLayout(layout);
```

```
    for (int i=0,n=labels.length; i<n; i++) {
      JButton button = new JButton(labels[i]);
      button.setAlignmentY(alignment);
      container.add(button);
    }
    return container;
  }

  public static void main(String args[]) {
    Runnable runner = new Runnable() {
      public void run() {
        JFrame frame = new JFrame("Alignment Example");
        frame.setDefaultCloseOperation(JFrame.EXIT_ON_CLOSE);

        Container panel1 = makeIt("Top",    Component.TOP_ALIGNMENT);
        Container panel2 = makeIt("Center", Component.CENTER_ALIGNMENT);
        Container panel3 = makeIt("Bottom", Component.BOTTOM_ALIGNMENT);

        frame.setLayout(new GridLayout(1, 3));
        frame.add(panel1);
        frame.add(panel2);
        frame.add(panel3);

        frame.setSize(423, 171);
        frame.setVisible(true);
      }
    };
    EventQueue.invokeLater(runner);
  }
}
```

Laying Out Components with Different Alignments

Working with small components that have the same alignment is relatively simple. However, if the components in a container managed by a BoxLayout have different alignments, things become more complex. In addition, the components won't necessarily be displayed the way you might expect. For a vertical box, the components appear as follows:

- If a component has its x alignment set to Component.LEFT_ALIGNMENT, the left edge of the component will be aligned with the center of the container.

- If a component has its x alignment set to Component.RIGHT_ALIGNMENT, the right edge of the component will be aligned with the center of the container.

- If a component has its x alignment set to Component.CENTER_ALIGNMENT, the component will be centered within the container.

- Other alignment values cause components to be placed in varying positions (depending on the value) relative to the center of the container.

To help you visualize this mixed alignment behavior, Figure 10-11 shows two BoxLayout containers. The left container has two components, one with a left alignment (the button labeled 0.0) and another with a right alignment (the button labeled 1.0). Here, you can see that the left edge of the right component is aligned to the right edge of the left component, with the common edge being the centerline of the container. The right container shows additional components placed between the 0.0 and 1.0 alignment settings. The label of each button represents its alignment setting.

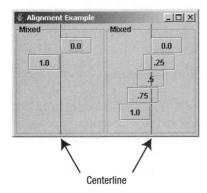

Centerline

Figure 10-11. *Two y-axis BoxLayout containers with mixed horizontal alignments*

For a horizontal box, the y alignment works the same relative to the top and bottom of the components on an x-axis, as illustrated in Figure 10-12.

Centerline

Figure 10-12. *Two x-axis BoxLayout containers with mixed vertical alignments*

Laying Out Larger Components

In the examples so far, the size of the components is always smaller than the space available. Those examples demonstrate a subtle difference between Swing and the original AWT components. The default maximum size of Swing components is the preferred size of the component. With AWT components, the default maximum size is a dimension with a width and height of Short.MAX_VALUE. If the previous examples had used AWT Button components instead of Swing JButton components, you would see surprisingly different results. You would also see different results if you manually set the maximum size property of the components to some value wider or higher than the screen for the appropriate BoxLayout. Using AWT Button components makes things a little easier to demonstrate.

Figure 10-9 showed three y-axis BoxLayout containers in which the components inside the container share the same horizontal alignment setting and the maximum size of each button is constrained. If the component's maximum size is unconstrained, or just larger than the container, you see something like Figure 10-13, in which the y-axis BoxLayout container has four Button components with the same horizontal alignment. Notice that instead of aligning to the left, center, or right, the components grow to fill all available space.

Figure 10-13. *Y-axis BoxLayout containers with the same vertical alignments and unconstrained size*

If the components had different alignments and an unconstrained maximum size, you would get yet another behavior. Any component with an alignment not at the minimum (0.0f) or maximum (1.0f) setting will grow to fill the entire space. If components with both the minimum and maximum alignment settings are present, the middle edges of those two components will align in the middle, as Figure 10-14 demonstrates.

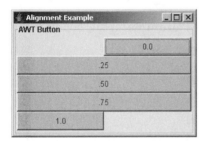

Figure 10-14. *Y-axis BoxLayout containers with different vertical alignments, unconstrained size, and both minimum/maximum alignment present*

If, however, only one component has an edge case (0.0 or 1.0) and is in a container with components having other alignments, that edge-case component will grow toward somewhere other than the middle of the container. This behavior is shown in Figure 10-15. The x-axis BoxLayout containers work similarly with different horizontal alignments.

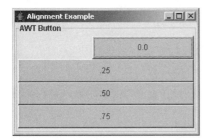

Figure 10-15. *Y-axis BoxLayout containers with different vertical alignments, unconstrained size, and only one alignment at minimum/maximum*

OverlayLayout Class

As its name implies, the OverlayLayout class is for layout management of components that lie on top of one another. When using add(Component component), the order in which you add components to a container with an OverlayLayout manager determines the component layering. If you use add(Component component, int index) instead, you can add components in any order. Although OverlayLayout implements the LayoutManager2 interface, like BoxLayout it currently doesn't use any constraints.

Determining the two-dimensional position of the components requires the layout manager to examine the x and y alignment properties of the contained components. Each component will be positioned such that its x and y alignment properties define a point shared by all the components, called the *axis point* of the layout manager. If you multiply the alignment value by the component's size in each appropriate direction, you'll get each part of the axis point for that component.

After the axis point is determined for each component, the OverlayLayout manager calculates the position of this shared point within the container. To calculate this position, the layout manager averages the different alignment properties of the components, and then multiplies each setting by the width or height of the container. This position is where the layout manager places the axis point, and the components are then positioned over this shared point.

For example, suppose you have three buttons: a 25×25 white button on top of a 50×50 gray button on top of a 100×100 black button. If the x and y alignment of each button is 0.0f, the shared axis point for the three components is their upper-left corner, and the components are all in the upper-left corner of the container. Figure 10-16 shows how this might appear.

If the x and y alignment of each button is 1.0f, the axis point for the three components is their bottom-right corner, and the components are in the bottom-right corner of the container. Figure 10-17 shows this appearance.

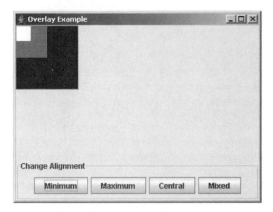

Figure 10-16. *Sample OverlayLayout with 0.0 x and y alignments*

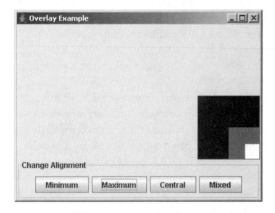

Figure 10-17. *Sample OverlayLayout with 1.0 x and y alignments*

If the x and y alignment of each button is 0.5f, the axis point for the three components is their center, and the components are in the center of the container. Figure 10-18 shows this appearance.

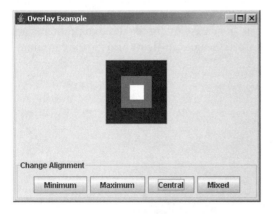

Figure 10-18. *Sample OverlayLayout with 0.5 x and y alignments*

Having all components with the same alignment is relatively easy to visualize, but what would happen if the components had different alignments? For instance, if the small button had x and y alignments of 0.0f, the medium button had alignments of 0.5f, and the large button had alignments of 1.0f, where would everything appear? Well, the first thing the layout manager calculates is the axis point. Based on the specific alignment of each button, the axis point would be the upper-left corner of the small button, the middle of the medium button, and the bottom-right corner of the large button. The position of the axis point within the container would then be the average of the alignment values multiplied by the dimensions of the container. The average of 0, 0.5, and 1 for both directions places the axis point at the center of the container. The components are then placed and layered from this position, as Figure 10-19 shows.

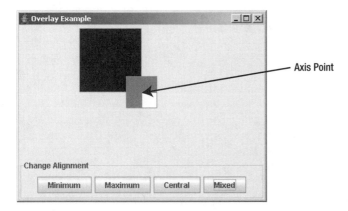

Figure 10-19. *Three buttons managed by an OverlayLayout with 0.0, 0.5, and 1.0 x and y alignments*

When you set up overlaid components, make sure that the optimizedDrawingEnabled property of the container of the components is set to false. This ensures proper repainting and event propagation.

To try out the OverlayLayout manager, use the source that follows in Listing 10-4. It provides selectable buttons to demonstrate interactively the effect of varying the alignment values. Initially, the program has everything centered.

Listing 10-4. *OverLayout Example*

```
import javax.swing.*;
import java.awt.*;
import java.awt.event.*;

public class OverlaySample {
  public static final String SET_MINIMUM = "Minimum";
  public static final String SET_MAXIMUM = "Maximum";
  public static final String SET_CENTRAL = "Central";
  public static final String SET_MIXED   = "Mixed";
```

```java
static JButton smallButton = new JButton();
static JButton mediumButton = new JButton();
static JButton largeButton = new JButton();

public static void setupButtons(String command) {
  if (SET_MINIMUM.equals(command)) {
    smallButton.setAlignmentX(0.0f);
    smallButton.setAlignmentY(0.0f);
    mediumButton.setAlignmentX(0.0f);
    mediumButton.setAlignmentY(0.0f);
    largeButton.setAlignmentX(0.0f);
    largeButton.setAlignmentY(0.0f);
  } else if (SET_MAXIMUM.equals(command)) {
    smallButton.setAlignmentX(1.0f);
    smallButton.setAlignmentY(1.0f);
    mediumButton.setAlignmentX(1.0f);
    mediumButton.setAlignmentY(1.0f);
    largeButton.setAlignmentX(1.0f);
    largeButton.setAlignmentY(1.0f);
  } else if (SET_CENTRAL.equals(command)) {
    smallButton.setAlignmentX(0.5f);
    smallButton.setAlignmentY(0.5f);
    mediumButton.setAlignmentX(0.5f);
    mediumButton.setAlignmentY(0.5f);
    largeButton.setAlignmentX(0.5f);
    largeButton.setAlignmentY(0.5f);
  } else if (SET_MIXED.equals(command)) {
    smallButton.setAlignmentX(0.0f);
    smallButton.setAlignmentY(0.0f);
    mediumButton.setAlignmentX(0.5f);
    mediumButton.setAlignmentY(0.5f);
    largeButton.setAlignmentX(1.0f);
    largeButton.setAlignmentY(1.0f);
  } else {
    throw new IllegalArgumentException("Illegal Command: " + command);
  }
  // Redraw panel
  ((JPanel)largeButton.getParent()).revalidate();
}

public static void main(String args[]) {
```

```java
final ActionListener generalActionListener = new ActionListener() {
  public void actionPerformed(ActionEvent actionEvent) {
    JComponent comp = (JComponent)actionEvent.getSource();
    System.out.println (
      actionEvent.getActionCommand() + ": " + comp.getBounds());
  }
};

final ActionListener sizingActionListener = new ActionListener() {
  public void actionPerformed(ActionEvent actionEvent) {
    setupButtons(actionEvent.getActionCommand());
  }
};

Runnable runner = new Runnable() {
  public void run() {
    JFrame frame = new JFrame("Overlay Example");
    frame.setDefaultCloseOperation(JFrame.EXIT_ON_CLOSE);

    JPanel panel = new JPanel() {
      public boolean isOptimizedDrawingEnabled() {
        return false;
      }
    };
    LayoutManager overlay = new OverlayLayout(panel);
    panel.setLayout(overlay);

    Object settings[][] = {
      {"Small", new Dimension(25, 25), Color.white},
      {"Medium", new Dimension(50, 50), Color.gray},
      {"Large", new Dimension(100, 100), Color.black}
    };
    JButton buttons[] = {smallButton, mediumButton, largeButton};

    for (int i=0, n=settings.length; i<n; i++) {
      JButton button = buttons[i];
      button.addActionListener(generalActionListener);
      button.setActionCommand((String)settings[i][0]);
      button.setMaximumSize((Dimension)settings[i][1]);
      button.setBackground((Color)settings[i][2]);
      panel.add(button);
    }
```

```
          setupButtons(SET_CENTRAL);

          JPanel actionPanel = new JPanel();
          actionPanel.setBorder(BorderFactory.createTitledBorder("Change Alignment"));
          String actionSettings[] = {SET_MINIMUM, SET_MAXIMUM, SET_CENTRAL,
            SET_MIXED};
          for (int i=0, n=actionSettings.length; i<n; i++) {
            JButton button = new JButton(actionSettings[i]);
            button.addActionListener(sizingActionListener);
            actionPanel.add(button);
          }

          frame.add(panel, BorderLayout.CENTER);
          frame.add(actionPanel, BorderLayout.SOUTH);

          frame.setSize(400, 300);
          frame.setVisible(true);
        }
      };
      EventQueue.invokeLater(runner);
    }
  }
```

SizeRequirements Class

The BoxLayout and OverlayLayout managers rely on the SizeRequirements class to determine the exact positions of the contained components. The SizeRequirements class contains various static methods to assist in the calculations necessary to position components in either an aligned or a tiled manner. The layout managers use this class to calculate their components' x coordinates and width and y coordinates and height. Each pair is calculated separately. If the associated layout manager needs both sets of attributes for positioning, the layout manager asks the SizeRequirements class separately for each.

ScrollPaneLayout Class

The JScrollPane class, a container class that will be described in Chapter 11, uses the ScrollPaneLayout manager. Trying to use the layout manager outside a JScrollPane isn't possible because the layout manager checks to see if the container object associated with the layout manager is an instance of JScrollPane. See Chapter 11 for a complete description of this layout manager (and its associated ScrollPaneConstants interface) in the context of the JScrollPane.

ViewportLayout Class

The ViewportLayout manager is used by the JViewport class, a container class (to be described in Chapter 11). The JViewport is also used within the ScrollPaneLayout/JScrollPane combination. Like ScrollPaneLayout, the ViewportLayout manager is closely tied to its component, JViewport in this case, and isn't usable outside the component, except in a subclass. In addition, the JViewport class is rarely used outside a JScrollPane. The ViewportLayout manager will be discussed in the context of its container, JViewport, in Chapter 11.

SpringLayout Class

The newest addition to the Java layout manager front is the SpringLayout manager, added with the J2SE 1.4 release. This allows you to attach "springs" to components so that they are laid out relative to other components. For instance, with SpringLayout, you can say that a button appears attached to the right border, no matter what size a user makes the screen.

The SpringLayout manager relies on SpringLayout.Constraints for the component constraints. This works similarly to the GridBagConstraints class that complements the GridBagLayout manager. Each component added to the container can have an attached SpringLayout.Constraints. Therein lies the end to the similarities between these two types of constraints.

You usually don't need to add the component with the constraints. Instead, you can add the component, and then typically attach the constraints separately. There is nothing stopping you from adding the constraints with the component, but SpringLayout.Constraints is not a simple class. It is a collection of Spring objects, each a different constraint on the component. You need to add each Spring constraint separately to SpringLayout.Constraints. You do this by setting specific constraints on an edge of the component. Using the four SpringLayout constants of EAST, WEST, NORTH, and SOUTH, you call the setContraints(String edge, Spring spring) method of SpringLayout.Constraints, where the String is one of the constants.

For instance, if you want to add a component in the top left of a container, you can set up two springs of a constant size, combine them together, and add the component to the container with the combined set, as shown here:

```
Component left = ...;
SpringLayout layout = new SpringLayout();
JPanel panel = new JPanel(layout);
Spring xPad = Spring.constant(5);
Spring yPad = Spring.constant(25);
SpringLayout.Constraints constraint = new SpringLayout.Constraints();
constraint.setConstraint(SpringLayout.WEST, xPad);
constraint.setConstraint(SpringLayout.NORTH, yPad);
frame.add(left, constraint);
```

That doesn't look too complicated, but it gets more difficult when you need to add the next component, either to the right of the first or below it. You can't just say to add the component *n* pixels over. You must actually add the padding to the edge of the earlier component. To find the edge of the earlier component, you ask the layout manager with getConstraint(), passing in the edge you want and the component, as in layout.getConstraint(SpringLayout.EAST, left), to get the location of the right edge of the first component. From that location, you can add in the necessary padding and attach it to the edge of the other component, as shown here:

```
Component right = ...;
Spring rightSideOfLeft = layout.getConstraint(SpringLayout.EAST, left);
Spring pad = Spring.constant(20);
Spring leftEdgeOfRight = Spring.sum(rightSideOfLeft, pad);
constraint = new SpringLayout.Constraints();
constraint.setConstraint(SpringLayout.WEST, leftEdgeOfRight);
constraint.setConstraint(SpringLayout.NORTH, yPad);
frame.add(right, constraint);
```

This works perfectly well, but it gets tedious as the number of components increases. To eliminate the in-between steps, you can add the components without the constraints, and then add each separately, connecting the components via the putConstraint() method of SpringLayout.

```
public void putConstraint(String e1, Component c1, int pad, String e2,
  Component c2)
public void putConstraint(String e1, Component c1, Spring s, String e2,
  Component c2)
```

Here, instead of asking for the edge and adding in the padding yourself, the putConstraint() call combines the tasks for you. To demonstrate, the following snippet adds the same component constraints to the right component as the previous one, but using putConstraint() instead of using SpringLayout.Constraints directly:

```
Component left = ...;
Component right = ...;
SpringLayout layout = new SpringLayout();
JPanel panel = new JPanel(layout);
panel.add(left);
panel.add(right);
layout.putConstraint(SpringLayout.WEST, left, 5, SpringLayout.WEST, panel);
layout.putConstraint(SpringLayout.NORTH, left, 25, SpringLayout.NORTH, panal);
layout.putConstraint(SpringLayout.NORTH, right, 25, SpringLayout.NORTH, panel);
layout.putConstraint(SpringLayout.WEST, right, 20, SpringLayout.EAST, left);
```

To help you visualize the use of SpringLayout, Sun has a tool available from https://bean-builder.dev.java.net/ called The Bean Builder. The tool is primarily intended to be used when working with JavaBean components, but it works well to see SpringLayout in action. Figure 10-20 shows what the tool looks like on startup through Java WebStart.

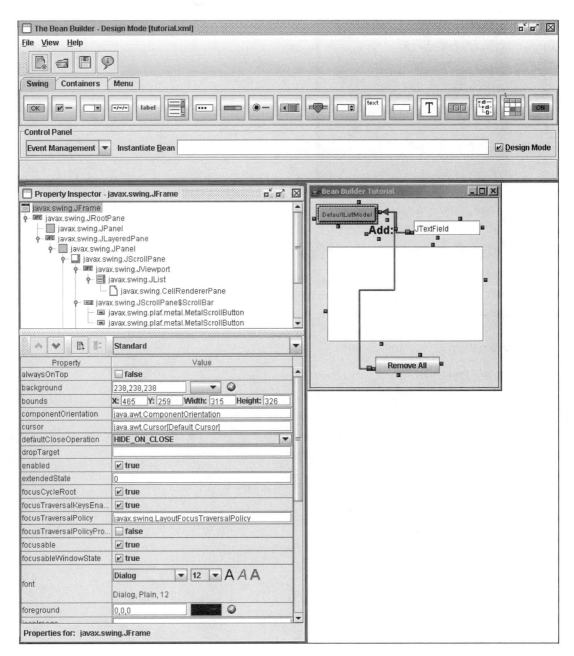

Figure 10-20. *The Bean Builder startup*

Around the edges of each component lies a set of four boxes, one each for north, south, east, and west. You can drag an arrow out of a box and connect it to any other box. Had the tool been a little more sophisticated, it would permit you to specify gap sizes for springs, too, but, as it is, the screen will look something like Figure 10-21 during screen design. Each arrow created is mapped to a specific call to the putConstraint() method.

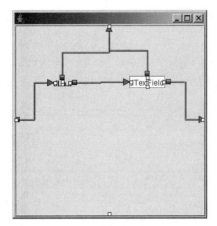

Figure 10-21. *Bean Builder and SpringLayout*

Listing 10-5 offers source similar to what would be used to generate a screen like Figure 10-21. Notice that you must use the content pane of the JFrame directly, as putConstraint() wants that container, not the frame itself.

Listing 10-5. *SpringLayout Example*

```
import java.awt.*;
import javax.swing.*;

public class SpringSample {
  public static void main(String args[]) {
    Runnable runner = new Runnable() {
      public void run() {
        JFrame frame = new JFrame("SpringLayout");
        frame.setDefaultCloseOperation(JFrame.EXIT_ON_CLOSE);
        Container contentPane = frame.getContentPane();

        SpringLayout layout = new SpringLayout();
        contentPane.setLayout(layout);

        Component left = new JLabel("Left");
        Component right = new JTextField(15);

        contentPane.add(left);
        contentPane.add(right);
```

```
        layout.putConstraint(SpringLayout.WEST,  left, 10, SpringLayout.WEST,
          contentPane);
        layout.putConstraint(SpringLayout.NORTH, left, 25, SpringLayout.NORTH,
          contentPane);
        layout.putConstraint(SpringLayout.NORTH, right, 25, SpringLayout.NORTH,
          contentPane);
        layout.putConstraint(SpringLayout.WEST, right, 20, SpringLayout.EAST, left);

        frame.setSize(300, 100);
        frame.setVisible(true);
      }
    };
    EventQueue.invokeLater(runner);
  }
}
```

Summary

This chapter introduced AWT's predefined layout managers FlowLayout, BorderLayout,
GridLayout, GridBagLayout, and CardLayout, as well as Swing's predefined layout managers
BoxLayout, OverlayLayout, ScrollPaneLayout, ViewportLayout, and SpringLayout. You saw how
the various alignment settings affect the components within a container whenever you use a
layout manager such as BoxLayout or OverlayLayout. In addition, you were introduced to the
SizeRequirements class, which is used internally by BoxLayout and OverlayLayout.

In Chapter 11, you'll look at the JScrollPane and JViewport containers, which use the
ScrollPaneLayout and ViewportLayout managers, plus several other sophisticated Swing
container classes.

CHAPTER 11

■ ■ ■

Advanced Swing Containers

Chapter 10 explored the layout managers available within AWT and Swing. In this chapter, you'll look at some of the containers that rely on these layout managers, as well as some others that work without a layout manager.

Starting with the Box class, you'll discover the best way to use the BoxLayout manager to create a single row or column of components. Next, you'll learn about the JSplitPane container, which is a bit like a specialized Box with just two components inside. The JSplitPane provides a splitter bar that acts as a divider users can drag to resize the components to suit their needs.

Then you'll explore the JTabbedPane container, which works something like a container whose layout manager is a CardLayout, except with tabs built into the container that allow you to move from card to card. You'll be able to create multiple-screen, property-sheet dialog boxes for user input with JTabbedPane.

The last two advanced Swing containers covered are the JScrollPane and JViewport. Both of these components offer the ability to display a section of a large component within a limited amount of screen real estate. The JScrollPane adds scrollbars to a display area so that you can move around a large component that sits within a small area. In fact, the JScrollPane uses the JViewport to "clip away" the part of the larger component that shouldn't be seen.

So, let's get started and look at the first container, the Box class.

Box Class

As a subclass of JComponent, the Box class is a special Java Container for creating a single row or column of components with the help of the BoxLayout manager. The Box container works like a JPanel (or Panel), but has a different default layout manager, BoxLayout. Using BoxLayout can be a little cumbersome without a Box, which simplifies working with BoxLayout. You can associate the BoxLayout manager with a container in just three steps: manually creating the container, creating the layout manager, and associating the manager with the container. When you create an instance of Box, you perform these three steps at once. In addition, you can use an inner class of Box called Box.Filler to better position components within the container.

Creating a Box

You have three ways to create a Box, offered by one constructor and two static factory methods:

```
public Box(int direction)
Box horizontalBox = new Box(BoxLayout.X_AXIS);
Box verticalBox   = new Box(BoxLayout.Y_AXIS);

public static Box createHorizontalBox()
Box horizontalBox = Box.createHorizontalBox();

public static Box createVerticalBox()
Box verticalBox   = Box.createVerticalBox();
```

■ **Note** The Box class is not designed to be used as a JavaBean component. Use of this container within an IDE can be awkward.

The less frequently used constructor requires a direction for the main axis of the layout manager. The direction is specified by either of two BoxLayout constants, X_AXIS or Y_AXIS, to create a horizontal or vertical box, respectively. Instead of manually specifying the direction, simply create a Box with the desired orientation by using one of the provided factory methods: createHorizontalBox() or createVerticalBox().

Filling a horizontal and vertical Box with a JLabel, a JTextField, and a JButton demonstrates the flexibility of BoxLayout, as shown in Figure 11-1.

Figure 11-1. *A horizontal and a vertical box*

For the horizontal container, the label and button are at their preferred widths because their maximum size is the same as their preferred size. The text field uses up the remaining space.

In the vertical container, the label and button sizes are their preferred size, too, because their maximum size is still the same as their preferred size. The text field's height fills the height that the label and button don't use, and its width is as wide as the container.

The source code for creating the screens shown in Figure 11-1 follows in Listing 11-1.

Listing 11-1. *Working with the Box*

```
import javax.swing.*;
import java.awt.*;

public class BoxSample {
  public static void main(String args[]) {
    Runnable runner = new Runnable() {
      public void run() {
        JFrame verticalFrame = new JFrame("Vertical");
        verticalFrame.setDefaultCloseOperation(JFrame.EXIT_ON_CLOSE);
        Box verticalBox = Box.createVerticalBox();
        verticalBox.add(new JLabel("Top"));
        verticalBox.add(new JTextField("Middle"));
        verticalBox.add(new JButton("Bottom"));
        verticalFrame.add(verticalBox, BorderLayout.CENTER);
        verticalFrame.setSize(150, 150);
        verticalFrame.setVisible(true);

        JFrame horizontalFrame = new JFrame("Horizontal");
        horizontalFrame.setDefaultCloseOperation(JFrame.EXIT_ON_CLOSE);
        Box horizontalBox = Box.createHorizontalBox();
        horizontalBox.add(new JLabel("Left"));
        horizontalBox.add(new JTextField("Middle"));
        horizontalBox.add(new JButton("Right"));
        horizontalFrame.add(horizontalBox, BorderLayout.CENTER);
        horizontalFrame.setSize(150, 150);
        horizontalFrame.setVisible(true);
      }
    };
    EventQueue.invokeLater(runner);
  }
}
```

Box Properties

As Table 11-1 shows, there are only two Box properties. Although the layout property inherits a setLayout(LayoutManager) method from its parent Container class, if called on a Box object, the class throws an AWTError. Once the BoxLayout manager is set during its construction, it can't be changed, nor can its direction.

Table 11-1. *Box Properties*

Property Name	Data Type	Access
accessibleContext	AccessibleContext	Read-only
layout	LayoutManager	Write-only

Working with Box.Filler

The Box class has an inner class Box.Filler to help you create invisible components for better component positioning within a container whose layout manager is BoxLayout. By directly manipulating the minimum, maximum, and preferred size of the created component, you can create components that grow to fill unused space or remain a fixed size, making screens more aesthetically pleasing to your users.

Note Technically speaking, the use of Box.Filler is not limited to containers whose layout manager is BoxLayout. You can use them anywhere you can use any other Component. The components are just invisible.

Instead of directly using the Box.Filler class, several static methods of the Box class can help you create the appropriate filler components. The factory methods allow you to categorize these components by type, instead of by minimum, maximum, or preferred size. You'll look at these methods in the next two sections.

If you're interested in the class definition, it's shown next. Like the Box class, Box.Filler isn't meant to be used as a JavaBean component.

```
public class Box.Filler extends Component implements Accessible {
  // Constructors
  public Filler(Dimension minSize, Dimension prefSize, Dimension maxSize);
  // Properties
  public AccessibleContext getAccessibleContext();
  public Dimension getMaximumSize();
  public Dimension getMinimumSize();
  public Dimension getPreferredSize();
  // Others
  protected AccessibleContext accessibleContext;
  public void changeShape(Dimension minSize, Dimension prefSize, Dimension maxSize);
}
```

Creating Areas That Grow

If a component has a dimensionless minimum and preferred size, and a maximum size bigger than the screen, the component will grow to take up unused space between components in the container along one or both axes. In the case of a Box, or more precisely, a container whose layout manager is BoxLayout, the growth occurs along the layout manager's initially chosen direction (either BoxLayout.X_AXIS or BoxLayout.Y_AXIS). For a horizontal box, the growth affects the component's width. For a vertical box, the growth is reflected in the component's height.

The name commonly given to this type of growing component is *glue*. The two flavors of glue are direction-independent glue and direction-dependent glue. The following factory methods of Box are used to create the glue components:

```
public static Component createGlue()
// Direction independent
Component glue = Box.createGlue();
aBox.add(glue);

public static Component createHorizontalGlue();
// Direction dependent: horizontal
Component horizontalGlue = Box.createHorizontalGlue();
aBox.add(horizontalGlue);

public static Component createVerticalGlue()
// Direction dependent: vertical
Component verticalGlue  = Box.createVerticalGlue();
aBox.add(verticalGlue);
```

Once you create glue, you add it to a container in the same way as any other component, by using Container.add(Component) or one of the other add() varieties. Glue allows you to align components within a container, as Figure 11-2 shows.

Figure 11-2. *Using glue in a Box*

You can add glue components to any container whose layout manager honors minimum, maximum, and preferred size properties of a component, such as BoxLayout. For instance, Figure 11-3 demonstrates what happens when you add a glue component to a JMenuBar just before adding the last JMenu. Because the layout manager for a JMenuBar is BoxLayout (actually the subclass javax.swing.plaf.basic.DefaultMenuLayout), this action pushes the last menu to the right edge of the menu bar, similar to the Motif/CDE style of help menus.

Caution I recommend that you avoid using the glue capability described here to set up help menus on menu bars. Eventually, the public void setHelpMenu(JMenu menu) of JMenuBar will be implemented and won't throw an Error. Of course, many of us are still waiting for this to happen.

Figure 11-3. *Using glue in a JMenuBar*

Creating Rigid Areas

Because a glue component grows to fill the available space, if you want to have a fixed distance between components, you need to create a rigid component, or *strut*. When doing so, you specify the strut's size. Struts can be two-dimensional, requiring you to specify the width and height of the component; or, they can be one-dimensional, requiring you to specify either the width or height.

```
public static Component createRigidArea(Dimension dimension)
// Two-dimensional
Component rigidArea = Box. createRigidArea(new Dimension(10, 10));
aBox.add(rigidArea);

public static Component createHorizontalStrut(int width)
// One-dimensional: horizontal
Component horizontalStrut = Box. createHorizontalStrut(10);
aBox.add(horizontalStrut);

public static Component createVerticalStrut(int height)
// One-dimensional: vertical
Component verticalStrut   = Box. createVerticalStrut(10);
aBox.add(verticalStrut);
```

■**Caution** Although direction-independent glue created with `createGlue()` shows no side effects if you change container direction, creating a rigid area may cause layout problems if the axis is later changed. (Imagine dragging a menu bar and dropping it along the right side from the top.) That's because the component has a dimensionless minimum size. Using `createRigidArea()` isn't recommended, unless you truly want a two-dimensional empty component.

Figure 11-4 demonstrates several struts in action. Notice that you can have varying strut distances between different components, and struts at the end of a container may have no effect. After a user resizes a screen, the strut distance between components remains fixed, as you can see in Figure 11-4.

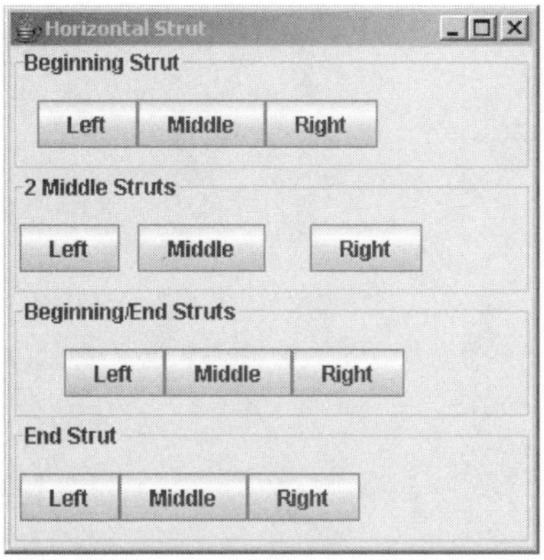

Before Resizing

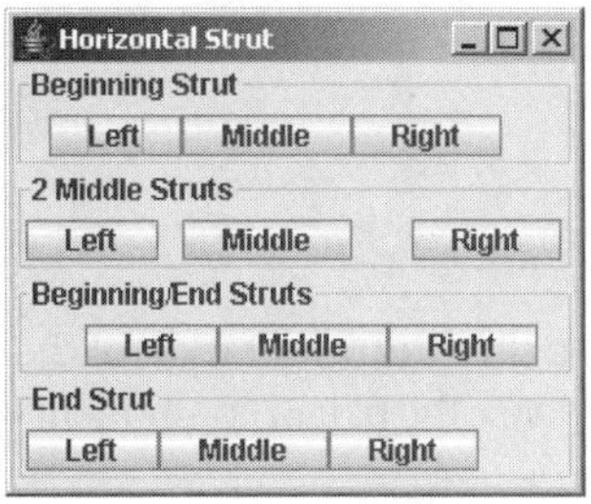

After Resizing

Figure 11-4. *Using struts in a Box*

JSplitPane Class

Similar to the Box container, the JSplitPane container allows you to display components in a single row or column. Whereas a Box can contain any number of components, a JSplitPane is meant to display two—and only two—components. The components are of variable size and separated by a movable divider. The divider is specially constructed in that the end user can grab it and drag the divider to adjust the size of the contained components. Figure 11-5 demonstrates both vertical and horizontal split panes, shown before and after moving the divider.

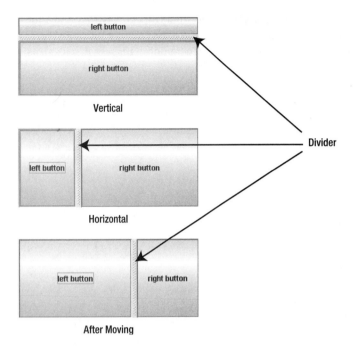

Figure 11-5. *Examples of JSplitPane containers*

Creating a JSplitPane

There are five constructors for JSplitPane. With them, you can initialize the orientation of the contained component pair, set the continuousLayout property, or initialize the pair of components for the container.

```
public JSplitPane()
JSplitPane splitPane = new JSplitPane();
```

```
public JSplitPane(int newOrientation)
JSplitPane splitPane = new JSplitPane(JSplitPane.VERTICAL_SPLIT);
```

```
public JSplitPane(int newOrientation, boolean newContinuousLayout)
JSplitPane splitPane = new JSplitPane(JSplitPane.VERTICAL_SPLIT, true);
```

```
public JSplitPane(int newOrientation, Component newLeftComponent,
  Component newRightComponent)
JComponent topComponent = new JButton("Top Button");
JComponent bottomComponent = new JButton("Bottom Button");
JSplitPane splitPane = new JSplitPane(JSplitPane.VERTICAL_SPLIT,
  topComponent, bottomComponent);
```

```
public JSplitPane(int newOrientation, boolean newContinuousLayout,
  Component newLeftComponent, Component newRightComponent)
JSplitPane splitPane = new JSplitPane(JSplitPane.VERTICAL_SPLIT, true,
  topComponent, bottomComponent);
```

Unless otherwise specified, the orientation is horizontal. Orientation can be specified by either of the JSplitPane constants VERTICAL_SPLIT or HORIZONTAL_SPLIT. The continuousLayout property setting determines how the split pane reacts when the user drags the divider. When the setting is false (the default), only the divider is redrawn when dragged. When the setting is true, the JSplitPane resizes and redraws the components on each side of the divider as the user drags the divider.

Note If the orientation is JSplitPane.VERTICAL_SPLIT, you can think of the top component as the left component and the bottom component as the right component.

If you're using the no-argument constructor, the initial set of components within the split pane is made up of buttons (two JButton components). Two other constructors explicitly set the initial two components. Surprisingly, the remaining two constructors provide no components within the container by default. To add or change the components within the JSplitPane, see the "Changing JSplitPane Components" section that's coming up shortly.

JSplitPane Properties

Table 11-2 shows the 17 properties of JSplitPane.

Table 11-2. *JSplitPane Properties*

Property Name	Data Type	Access
accessibleContext	AccessibleContext	Read-only
bottomComponent	Component	Read-write
continuousLayout	boolean	Read-write bound
dividerLocation	double	Write-only
dividerLocation	int	Read-write bound
dividerSize	int	Read-write bound
lastDividerLocation	int	Read-write bound
leftComponent	Component	Read-write
maximumDividerLocation	int	Read-only
minimumDividerLocation	int	Read-only

Table 11-2. *JSplitPane Properties (Continued)*

Property Name	Data Type	Access
oneTouchExpandable	boolean	Read-write bound
orientation	int	Read-write bound
resizeWeight	double	Read-write bound
rightComponent	Component	Read-write
topComponent	Component	Read-write
validateRoot	boolean	Read-only
UI	SplitPaneUI	Read-write bound
UIClassID	String	Read-only

Setting Orientation

Besides initializing the orientation within the constructor, you can change the JSplitPane orientation by changing the orientation property setting to either JSplitPane.VERTICAL_SPLIT or JSplitPane.HORIZONTAL_SPLIT. If you try to change the property to a nonequivalent setting, an IllegalArgumentException is thrown.

Dynamically changing the orientation at runtime is not recommended because it can confuse a user. However, if you're using a visual development tool, you can explicitly set the orientation for this property after creating the JSplitPane. When not programming visually, you would normally initialize the orientation when you create the JSplitPane.

Changing JSplitPane Components

There are four read-write properties for the different positions of a component within a JSplitPane: bottomComponent, leftComponent, rightComponent, and topComponent. In reality, these four properties represent two components internally: The left and top components are one; the right and bottom components represent the other.

You should use the properties that are appropriate for the orientation of your JSplitPane. Using the inappropriate property methods can make life difficult for the maintenance programmer. Imagine, after creating a user interface, seeing something like the following code six months later:

```
JComponent leftButton = new JButton("Left");
JComponent rightButton = new JButton("Right");
JSplitPane splitPane = new JSplitPane(JSplitPane.VERTICAL_SPLIT);
splitPane.setLeftComponent(leftButton);
splitPane.setRightComponent(rightButton);
```

If you glance at the source, you might think that the screen will contain a button to the left and one to the right based on the variable names and the set*XXX*Component() methods used. But because the instantiated JSplitPane has a vertical orientation, the interface that's created looks like Figure 11-6. The variable names are used because of the button labels, not their position.

Figure 11-6. *Adding left/right buttons to a vertical JSplitPane*

The code is more understandable if the setTopComponent() and setBottomComponent() methods are used with better variable names:

```
JComponent topButton = new JButton("Left");
JComponent bottomButton = new JButton("Right");
JSplitPane splitPane = new JSplitPane(JSplitPane.VERTICAL_SPLIT);
splitPane.setTopComponent(topButton);
splitPane.setBottomComponent(bottomButton);
```

Moving the JSplitPane Divider

Initially, the divider is shown below or to the right of the preferred size of the top or left component. At any time, you can reset the divider position to that position by calling the resetToPreferredSizes() method of JSplitPane. If you want to programmatically position the divider, you can change the dividerLocation property with setDividerLocation(newLocation). This property can be changed to an int position, representing an absolute distance from the top or left side, or it can be set to a double value between 0.0 and 1.0, representing a percentage of the JSplitPane container width.

■**Caution** Changing the property setting to a double value outside the range of 0.0 and 1.0 results in an IllegalArgumentException being thrown.

If you want to set the divider location, you must wait for the component to be realized. Essentially, that means it must be visible. While there are roundabout ways of doing this, the most direct way is to attach a HierarchyListener to the JSplitPane and watch for when the HierarchyEvent is of type SHOWING_CHANGED. This is demonstrated in the following code fragment, changing the divider location to 75%.

```
HierarchyListener hierarchyListener = new HierarchyListener() {
  public void hierarchyChanged(HierarchyEvent e) {
    long flags = e.getChangeFlags();
    if ((flags & HierarchyEvent.SHOWING_CHANGED) ==
        HierarchyEvent.SHOWING_CHANGED) {
      splitPane.setDividerLocation(.75);
    }
  }
};
splitPane.addHierarchyListener(hierarchyListener);
```

Although you can set the dividerLocation property with a double value, you can get only an int, indicating its absolute position.

■**Tip** With the system-provided look and feel classes, pressing the F8 key allows you to move the divider with the keyboard keys such as Home, End, or the arrows. F8 isn't a modifier like Shift or Alt. Instead, pressing F8 moves the focus to the divider so that it can be moved with keystrokes.

Resizing Components and Working with a One-Touch Expandable Divider

Limitations exist on the resizing of components within the JSplitPane. The JSplitPane honors the minimum size of each contained component. If grabbing and moving the divider line will cause a component to shrink to less than its minimum size, the scroll pane won't let the user drag the divider past that minimum size.

■**Note** You can always programmatically position the divider to be anywhere, even if it makes a component smaller than its minimum size. However, this isn't a good idea because the component has a minimum size for a good reason.

If the minimum dimensions of a component are too large for a JSplitPane, you need to change the component's minimum size so that the divider can use some of that component's space. For AWT components, changing the minimum size of a standard component requires subclassing. With Swing components, you can simply call the setMinimumSize() method of JComponent with a new Dimension. Nevertheless, minimum sizes are set for a reason. The component probably won't look right if you explicitly shrink its minimum size.

A better approach is available for allowing one component to take up more space than another: Set the oneTouchExpandable property of the JSplitPane to true. When this property is true, an icon is added to the divider, allowing a user to completely collapse one of the two components to give the other component the entire area. In the example in Figure 11-7, the icon is a combination up-and-down arrow.

Figure 11-7 shows how this icon might appear (as rendered by the Ocean look and feel) and illustrates what happens after selecting the up arrow on the divider to expand the lower component to its fullest size. Clicking again on the icon on the divider returns the components to their previous positions. Clicking on the divider somewhere other than on the icon will position the divider in such a way that the collapsed component is at its preferred size.

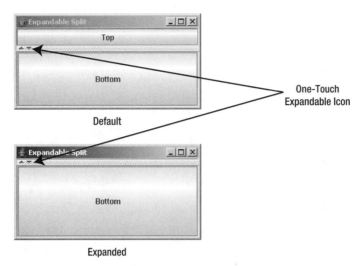

Figure 11-7. *Setting and using the oneTouchExpandable property*

Note There's no easy way to alter the one-touch expandable icon or change how the divider is rendered. Both are defined by the BasicSplitPaneDivider subclass and created in the createDefaultDivider() method of the BasicSplitPaneUI subclass for the specific look and feel. One thing you can easily change is the border around the divider, which is a custom border.

The lastDividerLocation property allows you or the system to inquire about the previous divider location. The JSplitPane uses this property when the user selects the maximizer icon to undo the minimization of one of the components in the JSplitPane.

Caution Beware of components that base their minimum size on the container size or their initial size! Placing them in a JSplitPane may require you to manually set the minimum and/or preferred size of the components. The components that most frequently cause problems when used within a JSplitPane are JTextArea and JScrollPane.

Resizing the JSplitPane

If additional space is available within the JSplitPane that is not required by the preferred size of the components it contains, this space is allocated based on the resizeWeight property setting. The initial setting of this property is 0.0, meaning the right or bottom component gets any additional space. Changing the setting to 1.0 would give all the space to the left or top component. A value of 0.5 would split the space evenly between the two components. Figure 11-8 shows the effect of these changes.

Default Resize Weight (0.0)

Resize Weight 1.0

Resize Weight 0.5

Figure 11-8. *Changing the resize weight*

Listening for JSplitPane Property Changes

The JSplitPane class defines the following constants to help with listening for bound property changes:

- CONTINUOUS_LAYOUT_PROPERTY

- DIVIDER_LOCATION_PROPERTY

- DIVIDER_SIZE_PROPERTY

- LAST_DIVIDER_LOCATION_PROPERTY

- ONE_TOUCH_EXPANDABLE_PROPERTY

- ORIENTATION_PROPERTY

- RESIZE_WEIGHT_PROPERTY

One way of listening for when the user moves the divider is to watch for changes to the lastDividerLocation property. The example in Listing 11-2 attaches a PropertyChangeListener to a JSplitPane displaying the current divider location, the current last location, and the previous last location. The component above and below the divider is the OvalPanel class (discussed in

Chapter 4), drawn to fill the dimensions of the component. This component helps to demonstrate the effect of having the continuousLayout property set to true.

Listing 11-2. *Listening for JSplitPane Property Changes*

```java
import javax.swing.*;
import java.awt.*;
import java.beans.*;

public class PropertySplit {
  public static void main(String args[]) {
    Runnable runner = new Runnable() {
      public void run() {
        JFrame frame = new JFrame("Property Split");
        frame.setDefaultCloseOperation(JFrame.EXIT_ON_CLOSE);

        // Create/configure split pane
        JSplitPane splitPane = new JSplitPane(JSplitPane.VERTICAL_SPLIT);
        splitPane.setContinuousLayout(true);
        splitPane.setOneTouchExpandable(true);

        // Create top component
        JComponent topComponent = new OvalPanel();
        splitPane.setTopComponent(topComponent);

        // Create bottom component
        JComponent bottomComponent = new OvalPanel();
        splitPane.setBottomComponent(bottomComponent);

        // Create PropertyChangeListener
        PropertyChangeListener propertyChangeListener =
            new PropertyChangeListener() {
          public void propertyChange (PropertyChangeEvent changeEvent) {
            JSplitPane sourceSplitPane = (JSplitPane)changeEvent.getSource();
            String propertyName = changeEvent.getPropertyName();
            if (propertyName.equals(
                JSplitPane.LAST_DIVIDER_LOCATION_PROPERTY)) {
              int current = sourceSplitPane.getDividerLocation();
              System.out.println ("Current: " + current);
              Integer last = (Integer)changeEvent.getNewValue();
              System.out.println ("Last: " + last);
              Integer priorLast = (Integer)changeEvent.getOldValue();
              System.out.println ("Prior last: " + priorLast);
            }
          }
        };
```

```
        // Attach listener
        splitPane.addPropertyChangeListener(propertyChangeListener);

        frame.add(splitPane, BorderLayout.CENTER);
        frame.setSize(300, 150);
        frame.setVisible(true);
      }
    };
    EventQueue.invokeLater(runner);
  }
}
```

As the following sample output demonstrates, when you run the previous program, you'll notice that the lastDividerLocation property changes to reflect the divider's being dragged. When the user stops dragging the divider, the last setting is set to the prior setting for the dividerLocation property, not to the initial last value (prior current value) when the drag started. As the divider is being dragged, the current value travels first to the last value and then to the prior last value. When the dragging stops, the final last setting (29 in this case) is set to the initial last setting to reflect the current value when the dragging started. The last three sets of output reflect the changes after pressing the one-touch expandable button.

```
Current: 11
Last: -1
Prior last: 0
Current: 12
Last: 11
Prior last: -1
Current: 12
Last: 12
Prior last: 11
Current: 12
Last: 11
Prior last: 12
Current: 15
Last: 12
Prior last: 11
Current: 15
Last: 15
Prior last: 12
Current: 15
Last: 12
Prior last: 15
Current: 112
Last: 15
Prior last: 12
Current: 112
Last: 112
```

```
Prior last: 15
Current: 112
Last: 15
Prior last: 112
```

■Note The BOTTOM, DIVIDER, LEFT, RIGHT, and TOP constants of the JSplitPane class aren't for PropertyChangeListener support. Instead, they're internal constraints used by the add(Component component, Object constraints) method.

Customizing a JSplitPane Look and Feel

Each installable Swing look and feel provides a different JSplitPane appearance and set of default UIResource values for this component. Figure 11-9 shows the appearance of the JSplitPane container for the preinstalled set of look and feel types: Motif, Windows, and Ocean.

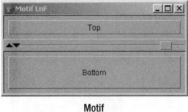

Motif

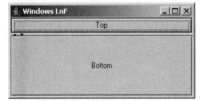

Windows

Ocean

Figure 11-9. *JSplitPane under the different look and feel types*

The available set of UIResource-related properties for a JSplitPane is shown in Table 11-3. For the JSplitPane component, there are 25 different properties, including 3 specific to the divider.

Table 11-3. *JSplitPane UIResource Elements*

Property String	Object Type
SplitPane.actionMap	ActionMap
SplitPane.activeThumb	Color
SplitPane.ancestorInputMap	InputMap
SplitPane.background	Color
SplitPane.border	Border
SplitPane.centerOneTouchButtons	Boolean
SplitPane.darkShadow	Color
SplitPane.dividerFocusColor	Color
SplitPane.dividerSize	Integer
SplitPane.foreground	Color
SplitPane.highlight	Color
SplitPane.leftButtonText	String
SplitPane.oneTouchButtonOffset	Integer
SplitPane.oneTouchButtonSize	Integer
SplitPane.oneTouchButtonsOpaque	Boolean
SplitPane.oneTouchExpandable	Boolean
SplitPane.oneTouchOffset	Integer
SplitPane.rightButtonText	String
SplitPane.shadow	Color
SplitPane.size	Integer
SplitPane.supportsOneTouchButtons	Boolean
SplitPaneDivider.border	Border
SplitPaneDivider.draggingColor	Color
SplitPaneDivider.oneTouchButtonSize	Integer
SplitPaneUI	String

JTabbedPane Class

The JTabbedPane class represents the ever-popular property sheet to support input or output from multiple panels within a single window in which only one panel is shown at a time. Using JTabbedPane is like using the CardLayout manager, except with added support for changing cards built in. While CardLayout is a LayoutManager, JTabbedPane is a full-fledged Container. In case you're not familiar with property sheets, tabbed dialog boxes, or tabbed panes (all alternate names for the same thing), Figure 11-10 shows a set of tabs from the original SwingSet demo that comes with the JDK 1.2 version of the Swing classes. (This version is more appropriate than the current one for demonstrating the features of JTabbedPane described in this section.)

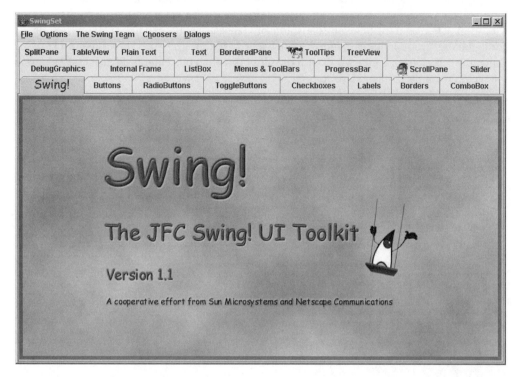

Figure 11-10. *Sample JTabbedPane screen*

To help the JTabbedPane manage which Component (tab) is selected, the model for the container is an implementation of the SingleSelectionModel interface or, more precisely, a DefaultSingleSelectionModel instance. (SingleSelectionModel and DefaultSingleSelectionModel were described with the menuing classes in Chapter 6.)

Creating a JTabbedPane

There are only three constructors for the JTabbedPane:

public JTabbedPane()
```
JTabbedPane tabbedPane = new JTabbedPane();
```

public JTabbedPane(int tabPlacement)
```
JTabbedPane tabbedPane = new JTabbedPane(JTabbedPane.RIGHT);
```

public JTabbedPane(int tabPlacement, int tabLayoutPolicy)
```
JTabbedPane tabbedPane =
  new JTabbedPane(JTabbedPane.RIGHT, JTabbedPane.SCROLL_TAB_LAYOUT);
```

The configurable options are the placement of the tabs used to change which component to display and the tab layout policy for when there are too many tabs to span one virtual row (which could be a column). By default, tabs are at the top of the container and will wrap to multiple rows when too many exist for the container width. However, you can explicitly specify a location with one of the following constants of JTabbedPane: TOP, BOTTOM, LEFT, or RIGHT or configure the layout policy with one of SCROLL_TAB_LAYOUT or WRAP_TAP_LAYOUT. Figure 11-11 shows the screen from Figure 11-10 with the other three tab placements. Figure 11-12 shows the screen with the scroll tab layout.

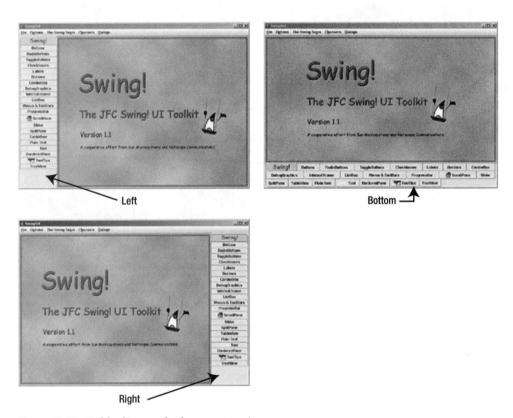

Figure 11-11. *JTabbedPane tab placement options*

■**Caution** Setting the tab placement to something other than the equivalent values for the JTabbedPane constants of TOP, BOTTOM, LEFT, or RIGHT, or the layout policy to something other than the equivalent of SCROLL_TAB_LAYOUT or WRAP_TAP_LAYOUT, will cause an IllegalArgumentException to be thrown.

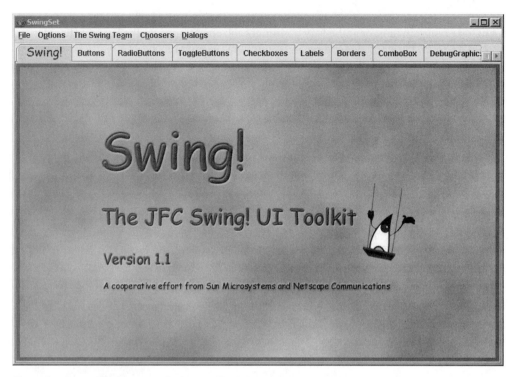

Figure 11-12. *JTabbedPane with the scroll tab layout*

Adding and Removing Tabs

Once you've created the basic JTabbedPane container, you need to add panels that make up the sheets or pages of the JTabbedPane. You can add panels in either one of two basic ways.

If you're visually creating your interface with a tool like JBuilder or Eclipse, the user interface builder will use the familiar add() methods of Container to add a Component as a panel. The panel added uses component.getName() as the default title. However, you shouldn't use the various add() methods if you're programming by hand.

The more appropriate way to add components or panels to create tabs is with any of the addTab() or insertTab() methods listed next. Any or all of the arguments other than the component and the position index of insertTab() can be null. (Passing null as the Component argument causes a NullPointerException to be thrown at runtime.) The displayed icon and tooltip settings have no default values.

- public void addTab(String title, Component component)

- public void addTab(String title, Icon icon, Component component)

- public void addTab(String title, Icon icon, Component component, String tip)

- public void insertTab(String title, Icon icon, Component component, String tip, int index)

When using `addTab()`, the tab is added to the end, which is the farthest right position for a set of top or bottom tabs, or at the very bottom for tabs positioned on the left or right side, potentially reversing sides, depending on component orientation.

After creating a panel, you can change its title, icon, mnemonic, tooltip, or component on a particular tab with one of the set*XXX*At() methods:

- `public void setTitleAt(int index, String title)`

- `public void setIconAt(int index, Icon icon)`

- `public void setMnemonicAt(int index, int mnemonic)`

- `public void setDisplayedMnemonicIndexAt(int index, int mnemonicIndex)`

- `public void setToolTipTextAt(int index, String text)`

- `public void setComponentAt(int index, Component component)`

■Tip The displayed mnemonic index refers to which time a particular character in the title should be highlighted. For instance, if you wanted the second *t* in *title* to be the highlighted mnemonic, you would set the mnemonic character to `KeyEvent.VK_T`, with `setMnemonicAt()`, and the mnemonic index to be 2, with `setDisplayedMnemonicIndexAt()`.

In addition, you can change the background or foreground of a specific tab, enable or disable a specific tab, or have a different disabled icon with additional set*XXX*At() methods:

- `public void setBackgroundAt(int index, Color background)`

- `public void setForegroundAt(int index, Color foreground)`

- `public void setEnabledAt(int index, boolean enabled)`

- `public void setDisabledIconAt(int index, Icon disabledIcon)`

To remove a tab, you can remove a specific tab with `removeTabAt(int index)`, `remove(int index)`, or `remove(Component component)`. In addition, you can remove all tabs with `removeAll()`.

JTabbedPane Properties

Table 11-4 shows the 11 properties of JTabbedPane. Because many of the setter/getter methods of JTabbedPane specify an index parameter, they aren't true properties in the literal sense.

Table 11-4. *JTabbedPane Properties*

Property Name	Data Type	Access
accessibleContext	AccessibleContext	Read-only
changeListeners	ChangeListener[ ]	Read-only
model	SingleSelectionModel	Read-write bound
selectedComponent	Component	Read-write
selectedIndex	int	Read-write
tabCount	int	Read-only
tabLayoutPolicy	int	Read-write-bound
tabPlacement	int	Read-write bound
tabRunCount	int	Read-only
UI	TabbedPaneUI	Read-write bound
UIClassID	String	Read-only

You can programmatically change the displayed tab by setting either the selectedComponent or the selectedIndex property.

The tabRunCount property represents the number of rows (for top or bottom tab placement) or columns (for right or left placement) necessary to display all the tabs.

■**Caution** Changing the LayoutManager for the JTabbedPane will throw an exception when it comes time to displaying the container. In other words, don't do it.

Listening for Changing Tab Selection

If you're interested in finding out when the selected tab changes, you need to listen for changes to the selection model. This is done by your attaching a ChangeListener to the JTabbedPane (or directly to the SingleSelectionModel). The registered ChangeListener reports when the selection model changes, as the model changes when the selected panel changes.

The program shown in Listing 11-3 demonstrates listening for changes to the selected tab and displays the title of the newly selected tab.

Listing 11-3. *Listening for Selected Tab Changes*

```java
import javax.swing.*;
import javax.swing.event.*;
import java.awt.*;
import java.awt.event.*;

public class TabSample {
  static Color colors[] = {Color.RED, Color.ORANGE, Color.YELLOW,
    Color.GREEN, Color.BLUE, Color.MAGENTA};
  static void add(JTabbedPane tabbedPane, String label, int mnemonic) {
    int count = tabbedPane.getTabCount();
    JButton button = new JButton(label);
    button.setBackground(colors[count]);
    tabbedPane.addTab(label, new DiamondIcon(colors[count]), button, label);
    tabbedPane.setMnemonicAt(count, mnemonic);
  }

  public static void main(String args[]) {
    Runnable runner = new Runnable() {
      public void run() {
        JFrame frame = new JFrame("Tabbed Pane Sample");
        frame.setDefaultCloseOperation(JFrame.EXIT_ON_CLOSE);

        JTabbedPane tabbedPane = new JTabbedPane();
        tabbedPane.setTabLayoutPolicy(JTabbedPane.SCROLL_TAB_LAYOUT);
        String titles[] = {"General", "Security", "Content", "Connection",
          "Programs", "Advanced"};
        int mnemonic[] = {KeyEvent.VK_G, KeyEvent.VK_S, KeyEvent.VK_C,
          KeyEvent.VK_O, KeyEvent.VK_P, KeyEvent.VK_A};
        for (int i=0, n=titles.length; i<n; i++) {
          add(tabbedPane, titles[i], mnemonic[i]);
        }

        ChangeListener changeListener = new ChangeListener() {
          public void stateChanged(ChangeEvent changeEvent) {
            JTabbedPane sourceTabbedPane = (JTabbedPane)changeEvent.getSource();
            int index = sourceTabbedPane.getSelectedIndex();
            System.out.println ("Tab changed to: " +
              sourceTabbedPane.getTitleAt(index));
          }
        };
        tabbedPane.addChangeListener(changeListener);
```

```
        frame.add(tabbedPane, BorderLayout.CENTER);
        frame.setSize(400, 150);
        frame.setVisible(true);
      }
    };
    EventQueue.invokeLater(runner);
  }
}
```

Customizing a JTabbedPane Look and Feel

Each installable Swing look and feel provides a different JTabbedPane appearance and set of default UIResource values for the JTabbedPane component. Figure 11-13 shows the appearance of the JTabbedPane container for the preinstalled set of look and feel types: Motif, Windows, and Ocean. Several items are specific to the look and feel: how the JTabbedPane appears when the set of available tabs is too wide for the display, how it responds when a user selects a tab in a back row, how it displays the tooltip, and how it displays the scroll tab layout.

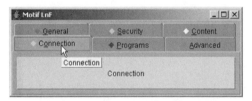

Motif

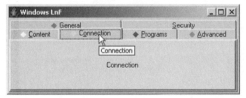

Windows

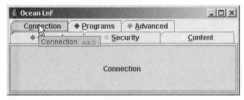

Ocean

Figure 11-13. *JTabbedPane under the different look and feel types*

The available set of UIResource-related properties for a JTabbedPane is shown in Table 11-5. For the JTabbedPane component, there are 34 different properties.

Table 11-5. *JTabbedPane UIResource Elements*

Property String	Object Type
TabbedPane.actionMap	ActionMap
TabbedPane.ancestorInputMap	InputMap
TabbedPane.background	Color
TabbedPane.borderHightlightColor	Color
TabbedPane.contentAreaColor	Color
TabbedPane.contentBorderInsets	Insets
TabbedPane.contentOpaque	Boolean
TabbedPane.darkShadow	Color
TabbedPane.focus	Color
TabbedPane.focusInputMap	InputMap
TabbedPane.font	Font
TabbedPane.foreground	Color
TabbedPane.highlight	Color
TabbedPane.light	Color
TabbedPane.opaque	Boolean
TabbedPane.selected	Color
TabbedPane.selectedForeground	Color
TabbedPane.selectedTabPadInsets	Insets
TabbedPane.selectHighlight	Color
TabbedPane.selectionFollowsFocus	Boolean
TabbedPane.shadow	Color
TabbedPane.tabAreaBackground	Color
TabbedPane.tabAreaInsets	Insets
TabbedPane.tabInsets	Insets
TabbedPane.tabRunOverlay	Integer
TabbedPane.tabsOpaque	Boolean
TabbedPane.tabsOverlapBorder	Boolean
TabbedPane.textIconGap	Integer
TabbedPane.unselectedBackground	Color

Table 11-5. *JTabbedPane UIResource Elements (Continued)*

Property String	Object Type
TabbedPane.unselectedTabBackground	Color
TabbedPane.unselectedTabForeground	Color
TabbedPane.unselectedTabHighlight	Color
TabbedPane.unselectedTabShadow	Color
TabbedPaneUI	String

JScrollPane Class

Swing's JScrollPane container provides for the display of a large component within a smaller display area, with scrolling support (if necessary) to get to the parts currently invisible. Figure 11-14 shows one such implementation, in which the large component is a JLabel with an ImageIcon on it.

Figure 11-14. *JScrollPane example*

Identifying the component to be scrolled can be done in one of two ways. Instead of adding the component to be scrolled directly to the JScrollPane container, you add the component to another component, a JViewport, already contained within the scroll pane. Alternatively, you can identify the component at construction time, by passing it into the constructor.

```
Icon icon = new ImageIcon("dog.jpg");
JLabel label = new JLabel(icon);
JScrollPane jScrollPane = new JScrollPane();
jScrollPane.setViewportView(label);
// or
JScrollPane jScrollPane2 = new JScrollPane(label);
```

Once you've added the component into the JScrollPane, users can use the scrollbars to see the parts of the large component that aren't visible within the inner area of the JScrollPane.

In addition to giving you the means to set the scrollable component for the JScrollPane, a display policy determines if and when scrollbars are shown around the JScrollPane. Swing's JScrollPane maintains separate display policies for the horizontal and vertical scrollbars.

Besides enabling you to add the JViewport and two JScrollBar components for scrolling, the JScrollPane allows you to provide two more JViewport objects for row and column headers and four Component objects to display in the scroll pane corners. The placement of all these components is managed by the ScrollPaneLayout manager, introduced in Chapter 10 and described more fully here. The actual JScrollBar components used by JScrollPane are a subclass of JScrollBar called JScrollPane.ScrollBar. They are used instead of the regular JScrollBar to properly handle scrolling the component inside the inner JViewport, when that component implements the Scrollable interface.

To help you see how all the components fit within the JScrollPane, Figure 11-15 demonstrates how the ScrollPaneLayout positions the various pieces.

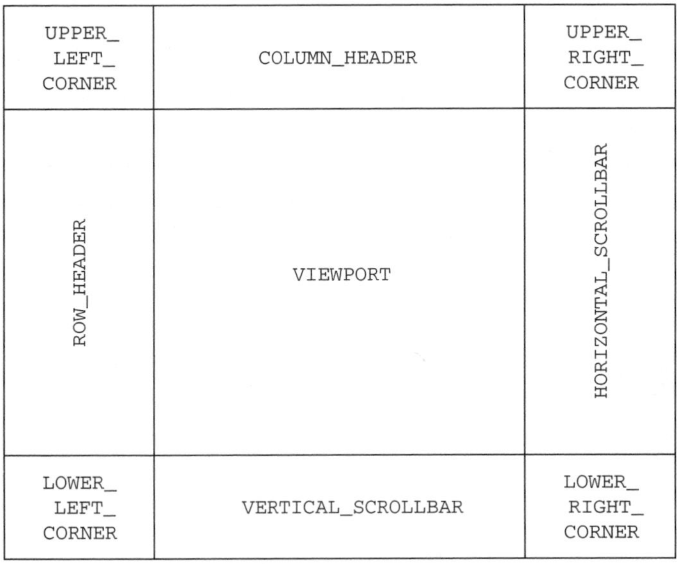

UPPER_ LEFT_ CORNER	COLUMN_HEADER	UPPER_ RIGHT_ CORNER
ROW_HEADER	VIEWPORT	HORIZONTAL_SCROLLBAR
LOWER_ LEFT_ CORNER	VERTICAL_SCROLLBAR	LOWER_ RIGHT_ CORNER

Figure 11-15. *ScrollPaneLayout regions*

■**Caution** The JScrollPane component supports scrolling only lightweight components. You should not add regular, heavyweight AWT components to the container.

Creating a JScrollPane

There are four JScrollPane constructors:

```
public JScrollPane()
JScrollPane scrollPane = new JScrollPane();
```

```
public JScrollPane(Component view)
Icon icon = new ImageIcon("largeImage.jpg");
JLabel imageLabel = new JLabel(icon);
JScrollPane scrollPane = new JScrollPane(imageLabel);
```

```
public JScrollPane(int verticalScrollBarPolicy, int horizontalScrollBarPolicy)
JScrollPane scrollPane = new
  JScrollPane(JScrollPane.VERTICAL_SCROLLBAR_ALWAYS,
  JScrollPane.HORIZONTAL_SCROLLBAR_ALWAYS);
```

```
public JScrollPane(Component view, int verticalScrollBarPolicy,
  int horizontalScrollBarPolicy)
JScrollPane scrollPane = new JScrollPane(imageLabel,
  JScrollPane.VERTICAL_SCROLLBAR_ALWAYS,
  JScrollPane.HORIZONTAL_SCROLLBAR_ALWAYS);
```

These offer the options of preinstalling a component to scroll and configuring the scrolling policies of the individual scrollbars. By default, the scrollbars are shown only when needed. Table 11-6 shows the JScrollPane constants used to explicitly set the policies for each scrollbar. Using any other nonequivalent setting results in an IllegalArgumentException being thrown.

Table 11-6. *JScrollPane Scrollbar Policies*

Policy Type	Description
VERTICAL_SCROLLBAR_AS_NEEDED	Displays designated scrollbar if viewport is too small to display its entire contents
HORIZONTAL_SCROLLBAR_AS_NEEDED	Displays designated scrollbar if viewport is too small to display its entire contents
VERTICAL_SCROLLBAR_ALWAYS	Always displays designated scrollbar
HORIZONTAL_SCROLLBAR_ALWAYS	Always displays designated scrollbar
VERTICAL_SCROLLBAR_NEVER	Never displays designated scrollbar
HORIZONTAL_SCROLLBAR_NEVER	Never displays designated scrollbar

The next section explains how to add or change the component after creating a JScrollPane.

Changing the Viewport View

If you've created a JScrollPane with an associated component to scroll, you just need to add the JScrollPane to the display, and it's ready to go. If, however, you didn't associate a component at creation time, or just want to change it later, there are two ways to associate a new component to scroll. First, you can directly change the component to scroll by setting the viewportView property:

```
scrollPane.setViewportView(dogLabel);
```

The other way of changing the component to scroll involves centering the JViewport within the JScrollPane and changing its view property:

```
scrollPane.getViewport().setView(dogLabel);
```

You'll learn more about JViewport components in the "JViewport Class" section later in this chapter.

Scrollable Interface

Unlike the AWT components such as List, which automatically provide a scrollable area when the choices are too numerous to display at once, Swing components JList, JTable, JTextComponent, and JTree don't automatically provide scrolling support. You must create the component, add it to a JScrollPane, and then add the scroll pane to the screen.

```
JList list = new JList(...);
JScrollPane scrollPane = new JScrollPane(list);
aFrame.add(scrollPane, BorderLayout.CENTER);
```

The reason that adding a component to a JScrollPane works is that each of the Swing components that might be too large for the screen (and require scrolling support) implements the Scrollable interface. With this interface implemented, when you move the scrollbars associated with the JScrollPane, the JScrollPane asks the Scrollable component within the container for its sizing information to properly position the component based on the current scrollbar positions.

The only time you need to worry about the Scrollable interface is when you're creating a new custom component that requires scrolling support. The following is the Scrollable interface definition.

```
public interface Scrollable {
  public Dimension getPreferredScrollableViewportSize();
  public boolean getScrollableTracksViewportHeight();
  public boolean getScrollableTracksViewportWidth();
  public int getScrollableBlockIncrement(Rectangle visibleRect, int orientation,
    int direction);
  public int getScrollableUnitIncrement(Rectangle visibleRect, int orientation,
    int direction);
}
```

If you create a custom `Scrollable` component and then place that component in a `JScrollPane`, it will respond appropriately when the scrollbars for the `JScrollPane` or the mouse wheel are moved.

JScrollPane Properties

Table 11-7 shows the 19 properties of `JScrollPane`.

Table 11-7. *JScrollPane Properties*

Property Name	Data Type	Access
accessibleContext	AccessibleContext	Read-only
columnHeader*	JViewport	Read-write bound
columnHeaderView	Component	Write-only
componentOrientation	ComponentOrientation	Write-only bound
horizontalScrollBar*	JScrollBar	Read-write bound
horizontalScrollBarPolicy*	int	Read-write bound
layout	LayoutManager	Write-only
rowHeader*	JViewport	Read-write bound
rowHeaderView	Component	Write-only
UI	ScrollPaneUI	Read-write bound
UIClassID	String	Read-only
validateRoot	boolean	Read-only
verticalScrollBar*	JScrollBar	Read-write bound
verticalScrollBarPolicy*	int	Read-write bound
viewport*	JViewport	Read-write bound
viewportBorder	Border	Read-write bound
viewportBorderBounds	Rectangle	Read-only
viewportView	Component	Write-only
wheelScrollingEnabled	boolean	Read-write bound

* *These properties directly map to properties of the ScrollPaneLayout manager used by the JScrollPane. Changing one of these properties for a JScrollPane causes its layout manager to change accordingly.*

■**Caution** An attempt to change the layout property of `JScrollPane` to something other than a `ScrollPaneLayout` instance or `null` will throw a `ClassCastException` at runtime, because the layout manager used by a `JScrollPane` must be a `ScrollPaneLayout`.

Working with ScrollPaneLayout

The JScrollPane relies on the ScrollPaneLayout manager for the positioning of components within the container. Whereas most layout managers are designed to lay out any type of component, all but four regions of ScrollPaneLayout accept a component of a specific type. Table 11-8 shows the type of component that can go into each of the regions shown in Figure 11-15.

Table 11-8. *ScrollPaneLayout Locations*

Location	Data Type	Description
COLUMN_HEADER	JViewport	Usually empty. If main content is a table, serves as column headers that won't scroll as vertical scrollbar is moved.
HORIZONTAL_SCROLLBAR	JScrollBar	A scrollbar for the main content region placed below that region.
LOWER_LEFT_CORNER	Component	Usually empty. For a graphic in the lower-left corner.
LOWER_RIGHT_CORNER	Component	Usually empty. For a graphic in the lower-right corner.
ROW_HEADER	JViewport	Usually empty. If main content is a table, serves as row labels that won't scroll when horizontal scrollbar is moved.
UPPER_LEFT_CORNER	Component	Usually empty. For a graphic in the upper-left corner.
UPPER_RIGHT_CORNER	Component	Usually empty. For a graphic in the upper-right corner.
VERTICAL_SCROLLBAR	JScrollBar	A scrollbar for the main content region, placed to the right of the content area.
VIEWPORT	JViewport	The main content area.

> **Note** The corners have two sets of constants. For internationalization support, you can use LOWER_LEADING_CORNER, LOWER_TRAILING_CORNER, UPPER_LEADING_CORNER, and UPPER_TRAILING_CORNER, which deal with component orientation for you. For left-to-right component orientation (United States locale), leading is left, and trailing is right.

As designed, the layout manager describes the screen layout necessary to support a main content area (VIEWPORT) that's too large for the available space. Scrollbars for navigating through the area can be placed to the right of the content area (VERTICAL_SCROLLBAR) or below it (HORIZONTAL_SCROLLBAR). Fixed headers that don't scroll can be placed above the content area (COLUMN_HEADER) or to its left (ROW_HEADER). The four corners (*_CORNER) are configurable to display any type of component, which are typically labels with images on them; however, any component can be placed there.

> **■Note** Some developers think of ScrollPaneLayout as a GridBagLayout with customized constraints (and restricted contents). Under normal circumstances, most developers won't use ScrollPaneLayout outside a JScrollPane.

Working with JScrollPane Headers and Corners

As Figure 11-15 and Table 11-8 demonstrate, many different regions exist within the JScrollPane. Normally, you work with only the central view, and let the two scrollbars do their thing. In addition, when working with the JTable component (described in Chapter 18), the table automatically places the column labels within the column header region when placed within a JScrollPane.

You can also manually add or change the column header or row header for a JScrollPane. Although you can completely replace the JViewport in these areas, it's easier to just set the columnHeaderView or rowHeaderView property to the Component for the area. This action will place the component within a JViewport for you.

To place a component in one of the corners of the JScrollPane, you need to call the setCorner(String key, Component corner) method, where key is one of the following constants from JScrollPane: LOWER_LEFT_CORNER, LOWER_RIGHT_CORNER, UPPER_LEFT_CORNER, or UPPER_RIGHT_CORNER.

Working with corners can be tricky. A corner component is displayed only if the two components at a right angle from the corner are currently shown. For instance, suppose you place a company logo within a label in the lower-right corner, and the scrollbar policy for both scrollbars is to show only when necessary. In that case, if one scrollbar were not needed, the logo in the corner wouldn't be shown. As another example, if a JScrollPane had a column header showing but didn't have a row header, any component in the upper-left corner would not be shown.

Therefore, just because you've set a corner to a component (as with scrollPane.setCorner (JScrollPane.UPPER_LEFT_CORNER, logoLabel)), don't expect it to be always or automatically shown. Moreover, as Figure 11-16 shows, the neighboring areas control the size of the corner. Don't assume a corner component can be as large as necessary. That's because its minimum, preferred, and maximum sizes are completely ignored. In Figure 11-16, the actual image used to create the corner component is larger than the space used.

Figure 11-16. *A JScrollPane with a corner component and row and column headers*

> **■Note** Changing a corner of a JScrollPane acts like a bound property where the property name is one of the corner keys shown in Table 11-8.

Resetting the Viewport Position

At times, you may want to move the contents of the inner view to the upper-left corner of the JScrollPane. This change may be needed because the view changed, or because some event happened that requires the viewport component to return to the origin of the JScrollPane. The simplest way of moving the view is to adjust the position of the scrollbar thumbs of the JScrollPane. Setting each scrollbar to its minimum value effectively moves the view of the component to the component's upper-left corner. The ActionListener shown in Listing 11-4 can be associated with a button on the screen or in the corner of the JScrollPane, causing the contents of the JScrollPane to return to their origin.

Listing 11-4. *Action to Move JScrollPane to Top*

```
import java.awt.event.*;
import javax.swing.*;

public class JScrollPaneToTopAction implements ActionListener {
  JScrollPane scrollPane;
  public JScrollPaneToTopAction(JScrollPane scrollPane) {
    if (scrollPane == null) {
      throw new IllegalArgumentException(
        "JScrollPaneToTopAction: null JScrollPane");
    }
    this.scrollPane = scrollPane;
  }
  public void actionPerformed(ActionEvent actionEvent) {
    JScrollBar verticalScrollBar   = scrollPane.getVerticalScrollBar();
    JScrollBar horizontalScrollBar = scrollPane.getHorizontalScrollBar();
    verticalScrollBar.setValue(verticalScrollBar.getMinimum());
    horizontalScrollBar.setValue(horizontalScrollBar.getMinimum());
  }
}
```

Customizing a JScrollPane Look and Feel

Each installable Swing look and feel provides a different JScrollPane appearance and set of default UIResource values for the component. Figure 11-17 shows the appearance of the JScrollPane component for the preinstalled set of look and feel types. With a JScrollPane, the primary differences between the look and feel types are related to the scrollbar's appearance and border around the viewport.

The available set of UIResource-related properties for a JScrollPane is shown in Table 11-9. For the JScrollPane component, there are ten different properties. Changing the properties related to the JScrollBar will also affect appearance when a scrollbar in a JScrollPane is visible.

Motif

Windows

Ocean

Figure 11-17. *JScrollPane under the different look and feel types*

Table 11-9. *JScrollPane UIResource Elements*

Property String	Object Type
ScrollPane.actionMap	ActionMap
ScrollPane.ancestorInputMap	InputMap
ScrollPane.ancestorInputMap.RightToLeft	InputMap
ScrollPane.background	Color
ScrollPane.border	Border
ScrollPane.font	Font
ScrollPane.foreground	Color
ScrollPane.viewportBorder	Border
ScrollPane.viewportBorderInsets	Insets
ScrollPaneUI	String

JViewport Class

The JViewport component is rarely used on its own outside a JScrollPane. It normally lives within the center of a JScrollPane and uses the ViewportLayout manager to respond to positioning requests to display a part of a large Component within a smaller space. In addition to residing in the center of a JScrollPane, JViewport is also used for the row and column headers of a JScrollPane.

Creating a JViewport

There's only one constructor for creating a JViewport: the no-argument version: public JViewport(). Once you've created the JViewport, you place a component within it by using setView(Component).

JViewport Properties

Table 11-10 shows the 13 properties of JViewport. Setting the layout manager to something other than ViewportLayout is possible but not recommended because the layout manager makes the JViewport do its work properly.

Table 11-10. *JViewport Properties*

Property Name	Data Type	Access
accessibleContext	AccessibleContext	Read-only
border	Border	Write-only
changeListeners	ChangeListener[ ]	Read-only
extentSize	Dimension	Read-write
insets	Insets	Read-only
optimizedDrawingEnabled	boolean	Read-only
scrollMode	int	Read-write
UI	ViewportUI	Read-write bound
UIClassID	String	Read-only
view	Component	Read-write
viewPosition	Point	Read-write
viewRect	Rectangle	Read-only
viewSize	Dimension	Read-write

Because of scrolling complexity and for performance reasons, the JViewport doesn't support a border. Trying to change the border to a non-null value with setBorder(Border) throws an

IllegalArgumentException. Because there can't be a border, the insets property setting is always (0, 0, 0, 0). Instead of displaying a border around the JViewport, you can display a border around the component within the view. Simply place a border around the component, or place the component inside a JPanel with a border before adding it to the JViewport. If you do place a border around the component, the border would be seen only if that part of the component is visible. If you don't want the border to scroll, you must place the JViewport within a component such as a JScrollPane that has its own border.

■**Tip** To set the background color of what appears in the JScrollPane, you need to set the background color of the viewport: aScrollPane.getViewport().setBackground(newColor).

The size of the view (viewSize property) is based on the size of the component (view property) within the JViewport. The view position (viewPosition property) is the upper-left corner of the view rectangle (viewRect property), where the rectangle's size is the extent size (extentSize property) of the viewport. If that's confusing, Figure 11-18 should help you see where all these properties lie within the JViewport.

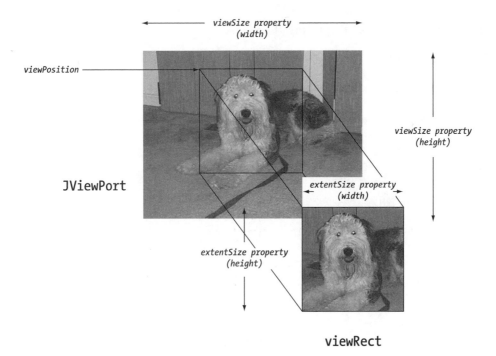

Figure 11-18. *Visualizing JViewport properties*

The scrollMode property can be set to one of the class constants shown in Table 11-11. In most cases, you can rely on the fastest and default BLIT_SCROLL_MODE mode.

Table 11-11. *JViewport Scroll Modes*

Scroll Mode	Description
BACKINGSTORE_SCROLL_MODE	A deprecated but supported mode that relies on a buffer for scrolling
BLIT_SCROLL_MODE	The default mode, which relies on Graphics.copyArea()
SIMPLE_SCROLL_MODE	Redraws entire area

To move the visible part of the view around, just change the viewPosition property. This moves the viewRect, allowing you to see a different part of the view. To demonstrate this, the program shown in Listing 11-5 attaches keyboard accelerators to the JViewport so that you can use the arrow keys to move around the view. (Normally, the JScrollPane would get these keyboard actions.) The majority of the code is necessary to set up the appropriate input/action maps. The boldfaced line of code is the one necessary to move the view.

Listing 11-5. *Keyboard Movement Control in a JViewport*

```
import javax.swing.*;
import java.awt.*;
import java.awt.event.*;

public class MoveViewSample {

  public static final int INCREASE = 0; // direction
  public static final int DECREASE = 1; // direction
  public static final int X_AXIS   = 0; // axis
  public static final int Y_AXIS   = 1; // axis
  public static final int UNIT     = 0; // type
  public static final int BLOCK    = 1; // type

  static class MoveAction extends AbstractAction {
    JViewport viewport;
    int direction;
    int axis;
    int type;
    public MoveAction(JViewport viewport, int direction, int axis, int type) {
      if (viewport == null) {
        throw new IllegalArgumentException ("null viewport not permitted");
      }
```

```
    this.viewport = viewport;
    this.direction = direction;
    this.axis = axis;
    this.type = type;
  }
  public void actionPerformed(ActionEvent actionEvent) {
    Dimension extentSize = viewport.getExtentSize();
    int horizontalMoveSize = 0;
    int verticalMoveSize = 0;
    if (axis == X_AXIS) {
      if (type == UNIT) {
        horizontalMoveSize = 1;
      } else { // type == BLOCK
        horizontalMoveSize = extentSize.width;
      }
    } else { // axis == Y_AXIS
      if (type == UNIT) {
        verticalMoveSize = 1;
      } else { // type == BLOCK
        verticalMoveSize = extentSize.height;
      }
    }
    if (direction == DECREASE) {
      horizontalMoveSize = -horizontalMoveSize;
      verticalMoveSize = -verticalMoveSize;
    }
    // Translate origin by some amount
    Point origin = viewport.getViewPosition();
    origin.x += horizontalMoveSize;
    origin.y += verticalMoveSize;
    // Set new viewing origin
    viewport.setViewPosition(origin);
  }
}

public static void main(String args[]) {
  Runnable runner = new Runnable() {
    public void run() {
      JFrame frame = new JFrame("JViewport Sample");
      frame.setDefaultCloseOperation(JFrame.EXIT_ON_CLOSE);
      Icon icon = new ImageIcon("dog.jpg");
      JLabel dogLabel = new JLabel(icon);
      JViewport viewport = new JViewport();
      viewport.setView(dogLabel);
```

```java
InputMap inputMap = viewport.getInputMap(JComponent.WHEN_IN_FOCUSED_WINDOW);
ActionMap actionMap = viewport.getActionMap();

// Up key moves view up unit
Action upKeyAction =
  new MoveAction(viewport, DECREASE, Y_AXIS, UNIT);
KeyStroke upKey = KeyStroke.getKeyStroke("UP");
inputMap.put(upKey, "up");
actionMap.put("up", upKeyAction);

// Down key moves view down unit
Action downKeyAction =
  new MoveAction(viewport, INCREASE, Y_AXIS, UNIT);
KeyStroke downKey = KeyStroke.getKeyStroke("DOWN");
inputMap.put(downKey, "down");
actionMap.put("down", downKeyAction);

// Left key moves view left unit
Action leftKeyAction =
  new MoveAction(viewport, DECREASE, X_AXIS, UNIT);
KeyStroke leftKey = KeyStroke.getKeyStroke("LEFT");
inputMap.put(leftKey, "left");
actionMap.put("left", leftKeyAction);

// Right key moves view right unit
Action rightKeyAction =
  new MoveAction(viewport, INCREASE, X_AXIS, UNIT);
KeyStroke rightKey = KeyStroke.getKeyStroke("RIGHT");
inputMap.put(rightKey, "right");
actionMap.put("right", rightKeyAction);

// PgUp key moves view up block
Action pgUpKeyAction =
  new MoveAction(viewport, DECREASE, Y_AXIS, BLOCK);
KeyStroke pgUpKey = KeyStroke.getKeyStroke("PAGE_UP");
inputMap.put(pgUpKey, "pgUp");
actionMap.put("pgUp", pgUpKeyAction);

// PgDn key moves view down block
Action pgDnKeyAction =
  new MoveAction(viewport, INCREASE, Y_AXIS, BLOCK);
KeyStroke pgDnKey = KeyStroke.getKeyStroke("PAGE_DOWN");
inputMap.put(pgDnKey, "pgDn");
actionMap.put("pgDn", pgDnKeyAction);
```

```
      // Shift-PgUp key moves view left block
      Action shiftPgUpKeyAction =
        new MoveAction(viewport, DECREASE, X_AXIS, BLOCK);
      KeyStroke shiftPgUpKey = KeyStroke.getKeyStroke("shift PAGE_UP");
      inputMap.put(shiftPgUpKey, "shiftPgUp");
      actionMap.put("shiftPgUp", shiftPgUpKeyAction);

      // Shift-PgDn key moves view right block
      Action shiftPgDnKeyAction =
        new MoveAction(viewport, INCREASE, X_AXIS, BLOCK);
      KeyStroke shiftPgDnKey = KeyStroke.getKeyStroke("shift PAGE_DOWN");
      inputMap.put(shiftPgDnKey, "shiftPgDn");
      actionMap.put("shiftPgDn", shiftPgDnKeyAction);

      frame.add(viewport, BorderLayout.CENTER);
      frame.setSize(300, 200);
      frame.setVisible(true);
    }
  };
  EventQueue.invokeLater(runner);
  }
}
```

Customizing a JViewport Look and Feel

Each installable Swing look and feel shares the same JViewport appearance with the
BasicViewportUI. There are no actual appearance differences. However, there still exists
a set of UIResource-related properties for the JViewport, as shown in Table 11-12. For the
JViewport component, there are four such properties.

Table 11-12. *JViewport UIResource Elements*

Property String	Object Type
Viewport.background	Color
Viewport.font	Font
Viewport.foreground	Color
ViewportUI	String

Summary

In this chapter, you explored several high-level Swing containers. With the Box class, you can
more easily utilize the BoxLayout manager to create a single row or column of components,
honoring the minimum, preferred, and maximum size of the components the best way possible.

With the JSplitPane component, you can create a row or column consisting of two components with a divider in between them to allow an end user to alter the components' sizes manually by moving the divider.

The JTabbedPane container displays only one component from a set of contained components at a time. The displayed component is picked by the user selecting a tab, which can contain a title with or without mnemonic, an icon, and a tooltip. This is the popular property sheet metaphor commonly seen within applications.

The JScrollPane and JViewport containers allow you to display a large component within a small area. The JScrollPane adds scrollbars to enable an end user to move the visible part around, whereas the JViewport doesn't add these scrollbars.

In Chapter 12, we'll once again examine the individual components within the Swing library, including the JProgressBar, JScrollBar, and JSlider that share the BoundedRangeModel as their data model.

■■■

CHAPTER 12

Bounded Range Components

In the previous chapter, you saw how JScrollPane provides a scrollable region for those situations when there isn't sufficient space to display an entire component on screen. Swing also offers several components that support some type of scrolling or the display of a bounded range of values. The available components are JScrollBar, JSlider, JProgressBar, and, in a more limited sense, JTextField. These components share a BoundedRangeModel as their data model. The default implementation of this data model provided with the Swing classes is the DefaultBoundedRangeModel class.

In this chapter, you'll look at the similarities and differences between these Swing components. Let's start with their shared data model, the BoundedRangeModel.

BoundedRangeModel Interface

The BoundedRangeModel interface is the Model-View-Controller (MVC) data model shared by the components described in this chapter. The interface contains four interrelated properties that are necessary to describe a range of values: minimum, maximum, value, and extent.

The minimum and maximum properties define the limits of the value of the model. The value property defines what you might think of as the current setting of the model, where the maximum setting of the value property is not necessarily the value of the maximum property of the model. Instead, the maximum setting that the value property can take is the maximum property less the extent property. To help you visualize these properties, Figure 12-1 shows these settings in relation to a JScrollBar. Any other purpose of the extent property depends on the component acting as the model's view.

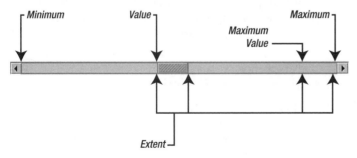

Figure 12-1. *BoundedRange properties on a JScrollBar*

The settings for the four properties must abide by the following ordering:

```
minimum <= value <= value+extent <= maximum
```

When one of the settings changes, the change may trigger changes to other settings to keep the ordering valid. For instance, changing the minimum to a setting between the current value plus extent setting and the maximum will decrease the extent and increase the value to keep the ordering valid. In addition, the original property change may result in a change to a new setting other than the requested setting. For instance, attempting to set the value below the minimum or maximum will set the value to the nearest limit of the range.

The BoundedRangeModel interface definition follows:

```
public interface BoundedRangeModel {
  // Properties
  public int  getExtent();
  public void setExtent(int newValue);
  public int  getMaximum();
  public void setMaximum(int newValue);
  public int  getMinimum();
  public void setMinimum(int newValue);
  public int  getValue();
  public void setValue(int newValue);
  public boolean getValueIsAdjusting();
  public void    setValueIsAdjusting(boolean newValue);
  // Listeners
  public void addChangeListener(ChangeListener listener);
  public void removeChangeListener(ChangeListener listener);
  // Other Methods
  public void setRangeProperties(int value, int extent, int minimum,
    int maximum, boolean adjusting);
}
```

Although the different settings available for the model are JavaBean properties, when a property setting changes, the interface uses Swing's ChangeListener approach instead of a java.beans.PropertyChangeListener.

The model's valueIsAdjusting property comes into play when the user is performing a series of rapid changes to the model, probably as a result of dragging the slider on the screen. For someone interested in knowing only when the final value is set for a model, a listener would ignore any changes until getValueIsAdjusting() returns false.

DefaultBoundedRangeModel Class

The Swing class actually implementing the BoundedRangeModel interface is DefaultBounded➥ RangeModel. This class takes care of the adjustments necessary to ensure the appropriate ordering of the different property values. It also manages a ChangeListener list to notify listeners when a model change happens.

DefaultBoundedRangeModel has two constructors:

```
public DefaultBoundedRangeModel()
```

```
public DefaultBoundedRangeModel(int value, int extent, int minimum, int maximum)
```

The no-argument version sets up the minimum, value, and extent properties of the model to have a setting of 0. The remaining maximum property gets a setting of 100.

The second constructor version takes four integer parameters, explicitly setting four properties. For both constructors, the initial value of the valueIsAdjusting property is false because the value of the model isn't yet changing beyond the initial value.

■Note Unless you're sharing a model across multiple components, it generally isn't necessary to create a BoundedRangeModel. Even if you're sharing a model across multiple components, you can create just the first component and get its BoundedRangeModel model to share.

As with practically all of the classes that manage their own listener lists, you can ask DefaultBoundedRangeModel for the listeners assigned to it. Here, you ask the model for its ChangeListener list with getListeners(ChangeListener.class). This returns an array of EventListener objects.

JScrollBar Class

The simplest of the bounded range components is the JScrollBar. The JScrollBar component is used within the JScrollPane container, described in Chapter 11, to control the scrollable region. You can also use this component within your own containers, although with the flexibility of JScrollPane this typically isn't necessary. The one point to remember about JScrollBar, however, is that it isn't used for the entry of a value, but solely for the scrolling of a region of screen real estate. For the entry of a value, you use the JSlider component discussed in the next section.

■Note The JScrollBar within a JScrollPane is actually a specialized subclass of JScrollBar that properly deals with scrollable components that implement the Scrollable interface. Although you can change the scrollbars of a JScrollPane, it's usually unnecessary—and more work than you might think.

As Figure 12-2 shows, the horizontal JScrollBar is composed of several parts. Starting from the middle and working outward, you find the scrollbar's *thumb*—also called a *knob* or *slider*. The width of the thumb is the extent property from the BoundedRangeModel. The current value of the scrollbar is at the left edge of the thumb. To the immediate left and right of the thumb are the block paging areas. Clicking to the left of the thumb will decrement the scrollbar's value, while clicking to the right increments it. The increased or decreased amount of the scrollbar's value is the scrollbar's blockIncrement property.

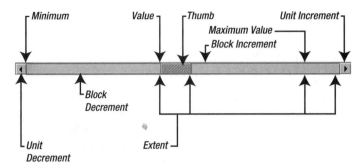

Figure 12-2. *Horizontal JScrollBar anatomy*

On the left and right edges of the scrollbar are arrow buttons. When the left arrow is pressed, the scrollbar decrements down a unit. The scrollbar's unitIncrement property specifies this unit. Typically, this value is one, though it doesn't have to be. To the immediate right of the left arrow is the minimum value of the scrollbar and the model. In addition to decreasing the value with the left arrow, clicking the right arrow causes the scrollbar to increment a unit. To the immediate left of the right arrow is the scrollbar's maximum range. The maximum value is actually a little farther to the left, where this "little farther" is specified by the model's extent property. When the thumb is next to the right arrow, this places the scrollbar value of the scrollbar at the left edge of the thumb, which is the case with all other positions, no matter where the thumb is.

A vertical JScrollBar is composed of the same parts as a horizontal JScrollBar, with the minimum and decrement parts at the top, and the value designated by the top edge of the scrollbar's thumb. The maximum and increment parts are at the bottom.

As previously mentioned, the model for the JScrollBar is the BoundedRangeModel. The delegate for the user interface is the ScrollBarUI.

Now that you've seen the different pieces of a JScrollBar, let's see how to use them.

Creating JScrollBar Components

There are three constructors for JScrollBar:

```
public JScrollBar()
JScrollBar aJScrollBar = new JScrollBar();
```

```
public JScrollBar(int orientation)
// Vertical
JScrollBar aJScrollBar = new JScrollBar(JScrollBar.VERTICAL);
// Horizontal
JScrollBar bJScrollBar = new JScrollBar(JScrollBar.HORIZONTAL);
```

```
public JScrollBar(int orientation, int value, int extent, int minimum, int maximum)
// Horizontal, initial value 500, range 0-1000, and extent of 25
JScrollBar aJScrollBar = new JScrollBar(JScrollBar.HORIZONTAL, 500, 25, 0, 1025);
```

Creating a JScrollBar with no arguments creates a vertical scrollbar with a default data model. The model has an initial value of 0, a minimum of 0, a maximum of 100, and an extent of 10. This default model offers a range of only 0 through 90. You can also explicitly set the orientation to JScrollBar.HORIZONTAL or JScrollBar.VERTICAL. If you don't like the initial model settings provided by the other two constructors, you need to explicitly set everything yourself. If the data elements aren't properly constrained, as described in the previous section about BoundedRangeModel, an IllegalArgumentException will be thrown, causing the JScrollBar construction to be aborted.

Surprisingly missing from the list of constructors is one that accepts a BoundedRangeModel argument. If you have a model instance, you can either call setModel(BoundedRangeModel newModel) after creating the scrollbar or get the individual properties from the model when creating the scrollbar, as follows:

```
JScrollBar aJScrollBar =
  new JScrollBar (JScrollBar.HORIZONTAL, aModel.getValue(), aModel.getExtent(),
    aModel.getMinimum(), aModel.getMaximum())
```

■**Tip** Starting with the 1.3 release of the J2SE platform, scrollbars do not participate in focus traversal.

Handling Scrolling Events

Once you've created your JScrollBar, it's necessary to listen for changes if you're interested in when the value changes. There are two ways of listening: the AWT 1.1 event model way and the Swing MVC way. The AWT way involves attaching an AdjustmentListener to the JScrollBar. The MVC way involves attaching a ChangeListener to the data model. Each works equally well, and both are notified if the model changes programmatically or by the user dragging the scrollbar thumb. The latter offers more flexibility and is a good choice, unless you're sharing a data model across components and need to know which component altered the model.

Listening to Scrolling Events with an AdjustmentListener

Attaching an AdjustmentListener to a JScrollBar allows you to listen for the user to change the setting of the scrollbar. The following code fragments, used for the example shown later in Figure 12-3, show how to attach an AdjustmentListener to a JScrollBar to listen for the user adjusting the value of the JScrollBar.

First, define the appropriate AdjustmentListener that simply prints out the current value of the scrollbar:

```
AdjustmentListener adjustmentListener = new AdjustmentListener() {
  public void adjustmentValueChanged (AdjustmentEvent adjustmentEvent) {
    System.out.println ("Adjusted: " + adjustmentEvent.getValue());
  }
};
```

After you've created the listener, you can create the component and attach the listener:

```
JScrollBar oneJScrollBar = new JScrollBar (JScrollBar.HORIZONTAL);
oneJScrollBar.addAdjustmentListener(adjustmentListener);
```

This manner of listening for adjustment events works perfectly well. However, you may prefer to attach a ChangeListener to the data model, as described next.

Listening to Scrolling Events with a ChangeListener

Attaching a ChangeListener to a JScrollBar data model provides more flexibility in your program designs. With an AWT AdjustmentListener, listeners are notified only when the value of the scrollbar changes. On the other hand, an attached ChangeListener is notified when there's any change in the minimum value, maximum value, current value, or extent. In addition, because the model has a valueIsAdjusting property, you can choose to ignore intermediate change events—something you can also do with an AdjustmentListener, via the property of the same name in the AdjustmentEvent.

To demonstrate, define a ChangeListener that prints out the current value of the scrollbar when the model has finished adjusting, as shown in Listing 12-1. You'll enhance this BoundedChangeListener class throughout the chapter.

Listing 12-1. *ChangeListener for BoundedRangeModel*

```
import javax.swing.*;
import javax.swing.event.*;

public class BoundedChangeListener implements ChangeListener {
  public void stateChanged(ChangeEvent changeEvent) {
    Object source = changeEvent.getSource();
    if (source instanceof BoundedRangeModel) {
      BoundedRangeModel aModel = (BoundedRangeModel)source;
      if (!aModel.getValueIsAdjusting()) {
        System.out.println ("Changed: " + aModel.getValue());
      }
    } else {
      System.out.println ("Something changed: " + source);
    }
  }
}
```

Once you create the listener, you can create the component and attach the listener. In this particular case, you need to attach the listener to the data model of the component, instead of directly to the component.

```
ChangeListener changeListener = new BoundedChangeListener();
JScrollBar anotherJScrollBar = new JScrollBar (JScrollBar.HORIZONTAL);
BoundedRangeModel model = anotherJScrollBar.getModel();
model.addChangeListener(changeListener);
```

The source for the testing program is shown in Listing 12-2.

Listing 12-2. *JScrollBar Usage Sample*

```
import javax.swing.*;
import javax.swing.event.*;
import java.awt.*;
import java.awt.event.*;

public class ScrollBarSample {
  public static void main(String args[]) {
    Runnable runner = new Runnable() {
      public void run() {
        AdjustmentListener adjustmentListener = new AdjustmentListener() {
          public void adjustmentValueChanged(AdjustmentEvent adjustmentEvent) {
            System.out.println("Adjusted: " + adjustmentEvent.getValue());
          }
        };
        JScrollBar oneJScrollBar = new JScrollBar(JScrollBar.HORIZONTAL);
        oneJScrollBar.addAdjustmentListener(adjustmentListener);

        ChangeListener changeListener = new BoundedChangeListener();
        JScrollBar anotherJScrollBar = new JScrollBar(JScrollBar.HORIZONTAL);
        BoundedRangeModel model = anotherJScrollBar.getModel();
        model.addChangeListener(changeListener);

        JFrame frame = new JFrame("ScrollBars R Us");
        frame.setDefaultCloseOperation(JFrame.EXIT_ON_CLOSE);
        frame.add(oneJScrollBar, BorderLayout.NORTH);
        frame.add(anotherJScrollBar, BorderLayout.SOUTH);
        frame.setSize(300, 200);
        frame.setVisible(true);
      }
    };
    EventQueue.invokeLater(runner);
  }
}
```

When you run this program, it shows the two horizontal scrollbars seen in Figure 12-3. The output of moving the scrollbars is sent to the console window.

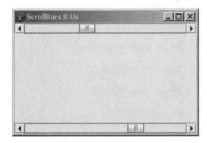

Figure 12-3. *Dual JScrollBar listening*

JScrollBar Properties

After you've created a JScrollBar, it may become necessary to modify its underlying data model. You can get the model with the public BoundedRangeModel getModel() method, and then modify the model directly. More likely, you would just call the appropriate methods of the component:

- setValue(int newValue), setExtent(int newValue), setMinimum(int newValue)

- setMaximum(int newValue)

These methods act as proxies and redirect any calls to the equivalent model method.

■**Caution** Although supported, it's not recommended that you modify a JScrollBar's orientation after displaying the component. This could seriously diminish the user's satisfaction and encourage the user to find a solution from another vendor!

In addition to the data model properties, Table 12-1 shows the 16 properties of JScrollBar.

Table 12-1. *JScrollBar Properties*

Property Name	Data Type	Access
accessibleContext	AccessibleContext	Read-only
adjustmentListeners	AdjustmentListener[ ]	Read-only
blockIncrement	int	Read-write bound
enabled	boolean	Write-only
maximum	int	Read-write
maximumSize	Dimension	Read-only
minimum	int	Read-write
minimumSize	Dimension	Read-only
model	BoundedRangeModel	Read-write bound
orientation	int	Read-write bound
UI	ScrollBarUI	Read-write bound
UIClassID	String	Read-only
unitIncrement	int	Read-write bound
value	int	Read-write bound
valueIsAdjusting	boolean	Read-write bound
visibleAmount	int	Read-write

Customizing a JScrollBar Look and Feel

Each installable Swing look and feel provides a different JScrollBar appearance and set of default UIResource values. Figure 12-4 shows the appearance of the JScrollBar component for the preinstalled set of look and feel types: Motif, Windows, and Ocean.

Figure 12-4. *JScrollBar under different look and feel types*

The available set of UIResource-related properties for a JScrollBar is shown in Table 12-2. There are 28 different properties.

Table 12-2. *JScrollBar UIResource Elements*

Property String	Object Type
scrollbar	Color
ScrollBar.actionMap	ActionMap
ScrollBar.allowsAbsolutePositioning	Boolean
ScrollBar.ancestorInputMap	InputMap
ScrollBar.ancestorInputMap.RightToLeft	InputMap
ScrollBar.background	Color
ScrollBar.border	Border
ScrollBar.darkShadow	Color
ScrollBar.focusInputMap	Object[ ]
ScrollBar.focusInputMap.RightToLeft	InputMap
ScrollBar.foreground	Color
ScrollBar.gradient	List
ScrollBar.highlight	Color
ScrollBar.maximumThumbSize	Dimension
ScrollBar.minimumThumbSize	Dimension
ScrollBar.shadow	Color
ScrollBar.squareButtons	Boolean
ScrollBar.thumb	Color
ScrollBar.thumbDarkShadow	Color
ScrollBar.thumbHeight	Integer
ScrollBar.thumbHighlight	Color

Table 12-2. *JScrollBar UIResource Elements (Continued)*

Property String	Object Type
ScrollBar.thumbShadow	Color
ScrollBar.track	Color
ScrollBar.trackForeground	Color
ScrollBar.trackHighlight	Color
ScrollBar.trackHighlightForeground	Color
ScrollBar.width	Integer
ScrollBarUI	String

JSlider Class

Although the JScrollBar component is useful for scrolling regions of the screen, it's *not* a good component for getting user input for a range of values. For that purpose, Swing offers the JSlider component. In addition to a draggable thumb like the one provided by the JScrollBar component, the JSlider component offers visible tick marks and labels to assist in showing the current setting and selecting a new one. Figure 12-5 shows several sample JSlider components.

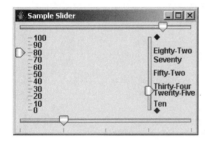

Figure 12-5. *Sample JSlider components*

The JSlider is made up of several pieces. The familiar BoundedRangeModel stores the data model for the component, and a Dictionary stores any labels for the tick marks. The user interface delegate is the SliderUI.

Now that you've seen the different pieces of a JSlider, let's find out how to use them.

Creating JSlider Components

There are six different constructors for JSlider:

```
public JSlider()
JSlider aJSlider = new JSlider();

public JSlider(int orientation)
// Vertical
JSlider aJSlider = new JSlider(JSlider.VERTICAL);
// Horizontal
JSlider bJSlider = new JSlider(JSlider.HORIZONTAL);

public JSlider(int minimum, int maximum)
// Initial value midpoint / 0
JSlider aJSlider = new JSlider(-100, 100);

public JSlider(int minimum, int maximum, int value)
JSlider aJSlider = new JSlider(-100, 100, 0);

public JSlider(int orientation, int minimum, int maximum, int value)
// Vertical, initial value 6, range 1-12 (months of year)
JSlider aJSlider = new JSlider(JSlider.VERTICAL, 6, 1, 12);

public JSlider(BoundedRangeModel model)
// Data model, initial value 3, range 1-31, and extent of 0
// JSlider direction changed to vertical prior to display on screen
DefaultBoundedRangeModel model = new DefaultBoundedRangeModel(3, 0, 1, 31);
JSlider aJSlider = new JSlider(model);
aJSlider.setOrientation(JSlider.VERTICAL);
```

Creating a JSlider with no arguments creates a horizontal slider with a default data model. The model has an initial value of 50, a minimum of 0, a maximum of 100, and an extent of 0. You can also explicitly set the orientation with JSlider.HORIZONTAL or JSlider.VERTICAL, and any of the specific model properties, with the various constructors. In addition, you can explicitly set the data model for the component.

If you're using a preconfigured BoundedRangeModel, remember to set the extent to 0 when creating the model. If the extent property is greater than 0, then the maximum setting of the value property is decreased by that amount, and the value setting will never reach the setting of the maximum property.

■**Caution** Initializing the orientation to something not equivalent to VERTICAL or HORIZONTAL throws an IllegalArgumentException. All constructors that initialize the data model could throw an IllegalArgumentException if the range and initial value fail to abide by the rules of the BoundedRangeModel described earlier in the section "BoundedRangeModel Interface."

Handling JSlider Events

You track changes to a JSlider with a ChangeListener. There's no AdjustmentListener, as there is with JScrollBar (and Scrollbar). The same BoundedChangeListener from the earlier JScrollBar example could be added to a data model of the JSlider, and you'll then be notified when the model changes.

```
ChangeListener aChangeListener = new BoundedChangeListener();
JSlider aJSlider = new JSlider ();
BoundedRangeModel model = aJSlider.getModel();
model.addChangeListener(changeListener);
```

In addition to attaching a ChangeListener to the model, you can associate the ChangeListener directly with the JSlider itself. This allows you to share the data model between views and listen independently for changes. This requires you to modify the preceding listener a bit, because the change event source will now be a JSlider instead of a BoundedRangeModel. The updated BoundedChangeListener, shown in Listing 12-3, will work for both associations, however. The changes are boldfaced in the following listing.

Listing 12-3. *ChangeListener for BoundedRangeModel and JSlider*

```
import javax.swing.*;
import javax.swing.event.*;

public class BoundedChangeListener implements ChangeListener {
  public void stateChanged(ChangeEvent changeEvent) {
    Object source = changeEvent.getSource();
    if (source instanceof BoundedRangeModel) {
      BoundedRangeModel aModel = (BoundedRangeModel)source;
      if (!aModel.getValueIsAdjusting()) {
        System.out.println ("Changed: " + aModel.getValue());
      }
    } else if (source instanceof JSlider) {
      JSlider theJSlider = (JSlider)source;
      if (!theJSlider.getValueIsAdjusting()) {
        System.out.println ("Slider changed: " + theJSlider.getValue());
      }
    } else {
      System.out.println ("Something changed: " + source);
    }
  }
}
```

The association with the slider can now be direct, instead of indirect through the model.

```
aJSlider.addChangeListener(changeListener);
```

JSlider Properties

After you've created a JSlider, you may want to modify its underlying data model. As is the case with JScrollBar, you can get the model with the public BoundedRangeModel getModel() method, and then modify the model directly. You can also directly call the methods of the component:

- setValue(int newValue), setExtent(int newValue), setMinimum(int newValue)

- setMaximum(int newValue)

As with JScrollBar, these methods act as proxies and redirect any calls to the equivalent model method.

Table 12-3 shows the 19 properties of JSlider.

Table 12-3. *JSlider Properties*

Property Name	Data Type	Access
accessibleContext	AccessibleContext	Read-only
changeListeners	ChangeListener[ ]	Read-only
extent	int	Read-write
inverted	boolean	Read-write bound
labelTable	Dictionary	Read-write bound
majorTickSpacing	int	Read-write bound
maximum	int	Read-write bound
minimum	int	Read-write bound
minorTickSpacing	int	Read-write bound
model	BoundedRangeModel	Read-write bound
orientation	int	Read-write bound
paintLabels	boolean	Read-write bound
paintTicks	boolean	Read-write bound
paintTrack	boolean	Read-write bound
snapToTicks	boolean	Read-write bound
UI	SliderUI	Read-write bound
UIClassID	String	Read-only
value	int	Read-write
valueIsAdjusting	boolean	Read-write bound

Displaying Tick Marks Within a JSlider

The JSlider component allows you to add tick marks either below a horizontal slider or to the right of a vertical slider. These tick marks allow a user to get a rough estimate of the slider's value and scale. There can be both major and minor tick marks; the major ones are simply drawn to be a little longer. Either or both can be displayed, as well as neither of them, which is the default.

■**Note** Technically, a custom look and feel could place the tick marks anywhere. However, the system-provided look and feel types place the ticks below or to the right.

To display the tick marks, you need to enable their painting with the public void setPaintTicks(boolean newValue) method. When called with a setting of true, this method enables the painting of minor and major tick marks. By default, the tick spacing for both types of tick marks is set to zero. When either is set to zero, that particular tick type isn't displayed. Because both are initially zero, you must change the value of either tick spacing to see any ticks. The public void setMajorTickSpacing(int newValue) and public void setMinorTickSpacing(int newValue) methods both support this change.

To demonstrate, Figure 12-6 shows four sliders: one with no ticks, one with aesthetically pleasing tick spacing, and two with unconventional tick spacing. It helps if the major tick spacing is a multiple of the minor tick spacing (just as a ruler shows inches, half inches, quarter inches, and so on with different tick lengths). In addition, the tick spacing shouldn't be so narrow that the ticks look like a solid block.

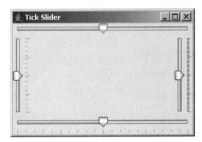

Figure 12-6. *Four JSlider controls demonstrating tick marks*

The source for the example in Figure 12-6 is shown in Listing 12-4. The top slider has no ticks. The bottom slider has the aesthetically pleasing major/minor spacing, with minor ticks at 5 units and major ones at 25 units. The left slider displays poor spacing with minor ticks at 6 and major ticks at 25. The right slider has minor ticks at each individual unit, resulting in spacing that's much too tight.

Listing 12-4. *JSlider with Tick Marks*

```java
import javax.swing.*;
import java.awt.*;

public class TickSliders {
  public static void main(String args[]) {
    Runnable runner = new Runnable() {
      public void run() {
        JFrame frame = new JFrame("Tick Slider");
        frame.setDefaultCloseOperation(JFrame.EXIT_ON_CLOSE);
        // No Ticks
        JSlider jSliderOne = new JSlider();
        // Major Tick 25 - Minor 5
        JSlider jSliderTwo = new JSlider();
        jSliderTwo.setMinorTickSpacing(5);
        jSliderTwo.setMajorTickSpacing(25);
        jSliderTwo.setPaintTicks(true);
        jSliderTwo.setSnapToTicks(true);
        // Major Tick 25 - Minor 6
        JSlider jSliderThree = new JSlider(JSlider.VERTICAL);
        jSliderThree.setMinorTickSpacing(6);
        jSliderThree.setMajorTickSpacing(25);
        jSliderThree.setPaintTicks(true);
        JSlider jSliderFour = new JSlider(JSlider.VERTICAL);
        // Major Tick 25 - Minor 1
        jSliderFour.setMinorTickSpacing(1);
        jSliderFour.setMajorTickSpacing(25);
        jSliderFour.setPaintTicks(true);

        frame.add(jSliderOne, BorderLayout.NORTH);
        frame.add(jSliderTwo, BorderLayout.SOUTH);
        frame.add(jSliderThree, BorderLayout.WEST);
        frame.add(jSliderFour, BorderLayout.EAST);
        frame.setSize(300, 200);
        frame.setVisible(true);
      }
    };
    EventQueue.invokeLater(runner);
  }
}
```

Snapping the JSlider Thumb into Position

One additional property of JSlider is related to tick marks: the snapToTicks property, set with public void setSnapToTicks(boolean newValue). When this property is true and tick marks are displayed, after you move the slider's thumb, the thumb will rest only on a tick. For instance, if a slider has a range of 0–100 with tick marks at every tenth unit, and you drop the thumb at the 33 mark, the thumb will snap to the position of the tick at 30. If tick marks aren't displayed, the property setting has no effect, including when labels are displayed without tick marks.

Labeling JSlider Positions

As Figure 12-5 (shown earlier in the chapter) demonstrates, you can label any position within the JSlider with a Component. When a position is labeled, the component will be displayed next to it. The labels are stored within a lookup table that subclasses the Dictionary class, where the key is the Integer position and the value is the Component. Any AWT Component can be the label; however, the JLabel is best suited to the role. Figure 12-7 shows how the dictionary for the right slider of Figure 12-5 might look.

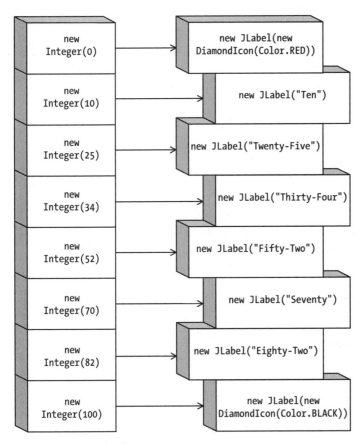

Figure 12-7. *A JSlider dictionary*

Normally, the Dictionary used to store the labels is a Hashtable. However, any class that extends the Dictionary class and that can use Integer keys will do. After you've created your dictionary of labels, you associate the dictionary with the slider with the public void setLabelTable(Dictionary newValue) method. The following source creates the label lookup table associated with Figure 12-7.

```
Hashtable<Integer, JLabel> table = new Hashtable<Integer, JLabel>();
table.put (0, new JLabel(new DiamondIcon(Color.RED)));
table.put (10, new JLabel("Ten"));
table.put (25, new JLabel("Twenty-Five"));
table.put (34, new JLabel("Thirty-Four"));
table.put (52, new JLabel("Fifty-Two"));
table.put (70, new JLabel("Seventy"));
table.put (82, new JLabel("Eighty-Two"));
table.put (100, new JLabel(new DiamondIcon(Color.BLACK)));
aJSlider.setLabelTable (table);
```

■**Note** Keep in mind that with J2SE 5.0, the compiler will auto-box an int parameter into an Integer.

Simply associating the label table with the slider won't display the labels. To enable their painting, you need to call the public void setPaintLabels(boolean newValue) method with a parameter of true. If you haven't manually created a table of labels, the system will create one with an interval of values reflecting the major tick spacing. For example, the left slider of Figure 12-5 has a slider range of 0–100 and major tick spacing of 10. When setPaintLabels(true) is called on that slider, labels are created for 0, 10, 20, and so on, all the way up to 100. The minor tick spacing is irrelevant as far as automatic generation of labels goes. And the ticks don't need to be painted for the labels to appear; the getPaintTicks() method can return false.

The automatic creation of labels is done through the public Hashtable createStandard➡ Labels(int increment) method, where the increment is the major tick spacing. You don't need to call this method directly. If you want to create the labels from other than the minimum value, you can call the overloaded public Hashtable createStandardLabels (int increment, int start) variety, and associate the hash table with the slider yourself.

Customizing a JSlider Look and Feel

Each installable Swing look and feel provides a different JSlider appearance and set of default UIResource values. Figure 12-8 shows the appearance of the JSlider component for the preinstalled set of look and feel types.

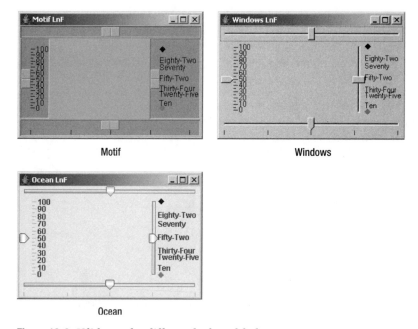

Figure 12-8. *JSlider under different look and feel types*

Two look-and-feel–related properties are part of the JSlider class definition. By default, the minimum slider value for a horizontal slider is at the left; for a vertical slider, it's at the bottom. To change the direction of a slider, call the public void setInverted(boolean newValue) method with an argument of true. In addition, the track that the slider moves along is displayed by default. You can turn it off with the public void setPaintTrack(boolean newValue) method. A value of false turns off the track display. Figure 12-9 identifies the JSlider track and points out the minimum and maximum positions of regular and inverted sliders.

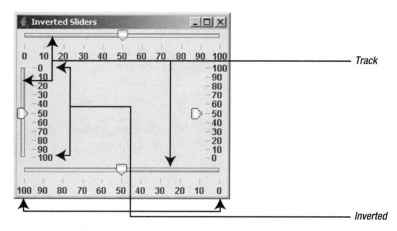

Figure 12-9. *Identifying JSlider positions and tracks*

Table 12-4 shows the 30 available UIResource-related properties for a JSlider.

Table 12-4. *JSlider UIResource Elements*

Property String	Object Type
Slider.actionMap	ActionMap
Slider.altTrackColor	Color
Slider.background	Color
Slider.border	Border
Slider.darkShadow	Color
Slider.focus	Color
Slider.focusGradient	List
Slider.focusInputMap	Object[ ]
Slider.focusInputMap.RightToLeft	InputMap
Slider.focusInsets	Insets
Slider.foreground	Color
Slider.gradient	List
Slider.highlight	Color
Slider.horizontalSize	Dimension
Slider.horizontalThumbIcon	Icon
Slider.majorTickLength	Integer
Slider.minimumHorizontalSize	Dimension
Slider.minimumVerticalSize	Dimension
Slider.paintThumbArrowShape	Boolean
Slider.paintValue	Boolean
Slider.shadow	Color
Slider.thumb	Color
Slider.thumbHeight	Integer
Slider.thumbWidth	Integer
Slider.tickColor	Color
Slider.trackBorder	Border
Slider.trackWidth	Integer
Slider.verticalSize	Dimension
Slider.verticalThumbIcon	Icon
SliderUI	String

The JSlider resources allow customization of elements that aren't accessible through JSlider or SliderUI methods. For instance, to customize the JSlider appearance of your application, you may want to alter the icon used for the draggable thumb. With just a few lines of code, you can take any icon and make it the slider's icon for every slider in your application.

```
Icon icon = new ImageIcon("logo.jpg");
UIDefaults defaults = UIManager.getDefaults();
defaults.put("Slider.horizontalThumbIcon", icon);
```

Figure 12-10 shows the results. As with all UIResource properties, this change will affect all JSlider components created after setting the property.

Figure 12-10. *A JSlider with a custom icon*

■**Note** The height and width of the icon are limited to the dimensions of the slider. Changing the icon property doesn't affect the slider size.

JSlider Client Properties

By default, with the Metal look and feel, when the track is visible, the track on which the slider moves does not change as the slider is moved over it. Nevertheless, you can enable a client property that will signal the slider to fill this track up to the point of the current value that the thumb has crossed. The name of this property is JSlider.isFilled, and a Boolean object represents the current setting. By default, this setting is Boolean.FALSE. Figure 12-11 demonstrates both a Boolean.TRUE and a Boolean.FALSE setting; the code fragment follows:

```
JSlider oneJSlider = new JSlider();
oneJSlider.putClientProperty("JSlider.isFilled", Boolean.TRUE);
JSlider anotherJSlider = new JSlider();
// Set to default setting
anotherJSlider.putClientProperty("JSlider.isFilled", Boolean.FALSE);
```

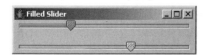

Figure 12-11. *Filled and unfilled JSlider*

This setting works only in the Metal look and feel. The Ocean theme of the Metal look and feel ignores this setting, always drawing the track filled. To get this behavior, you need to set the system property swing.metalTheme to steel, as in java -Dswing.metalTheme=steel ClassName.

JProgressBar Class

Swing's JProgressBar is different from the other BoundedRangeModel components. Its main purpose is not to get input from the user, but rather to present output. This output is in the form of a process completion percentage. As the percentage increases, a bar progresses across the component until the job is completed and the bar is filled. The movement of the bar is usually part of some multithreaded task, to avoid affecting the rest of the application.

Figure 12-12 shows several sample JProgressBar components. The top bar uses all the display defaults. The bottom bar adds a border around the component and displays the completion percentage. The right bar removes the border, and the left bar has a fixed string present instead of a completion percentage.

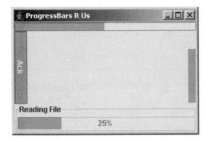

Figure 12-12. *Sample JProgressBar components*

From an object-oriented perspective, there are two primary parts to a JProgressBar: The familiar BoundedRangeModel stores the data model for the component, and the ProgressUI is the user interface delegate.

■**Note** To display a progress bar in a dialog box, use the ProgressMonitor class discussed in Chapter 9.

Creating JProgressBar Components

There are five different constructors for JProgressBar:

```
public JProgressBar()
JProgressBar aJProgressBar = new JProgressBar();
```

```
public JProgressBar(int orientation)
// Vertical
JProgressBar aJProgressBar = new JProgressBar(JProgressBar.VERTICAL);
// Horizontal
JProgressBar bJProgressBar = new JProgressBar(JProgressBar.HORIZONTAL);
```

```
public JProgressBar(int minimum, int maximum)
JProgressBar aJProgressBar = new JProgressBar(0, 500);
```

```
public JProgressBar(int orientation, int minimum, int maximum)
JProgressBar aJProgressBar = new JProgressBar(JProgressBar.VERTICAL, 0, 1000);
```

```
public JProgressBar(BoundedRangeModel model)
// Data model, initial value 0, range 0-250, and extent of 0
DefaultBoundedRangeModel model = new DefaultBoundedRangeModel(0, 0, 0, 250);
JProgressBar aJProgressBar = new JProgressBar(model);
```

Creating a JProgressBar with no arguments results in a horizontal progress bar with a default data model. The model has an initial value of 0, a minimum value of 0, a maximum value of 100, and an extent of 0. The progress bar has an extent, but it doesn't use it, even though it's part of the data model.

You can explicitly set the orientation with JProgressBar.HORIZONTAL or JProgressBar.VERTICAL, as well as any of the specific model properties, with the different constructors. In addition, you can explicitly set the data model for the component.

■**Caution** Initializing the orientation to a value not equivalent to VERTICAL or HORIZONTAL throws an IllegalArgumentException.

Creating a JProgressBar from a BoundedRangeModel is a little awkward in the sense that the progress bar virtually ignores one setting and the initial value is normally initialized to the minimum. Assuming you want the JProgressBar to start as a user might expect it to, you need to remember to set the extent to 0 and the value to the minimum when creating the model. If you increase the extent property, the maximum setting of the value property is decreased by that amount, and the value setting will never reach the setting of the maximum property.

JProgressBar Properties

After you've created a JProgressBar, you may want to modify it. Table 12-5 shows the 14 properties of JProgressBar.

Table 12-5. *JProgressBar Properties*

Property Name	Data Type	Access
accessibleContext	AccessibleContext	Read-only
borderPainted	boolean	Read-write bound
changeListeners	ChangeListener[ ]	Read-only
indeterminate	boolean	Read-write bound
maximum	int	Read-write
minimum	int	Read-write
model	BoundedRangeModel	Read-write
orientation	int	Read-write bound

Table 12-5. *JProgressBar Properties (Continued)*

Property Name	Data Type	Access
percentComplete	double	Read-only
string	String	Read-write bound
stringPainted	boolean	Read-write bound
UI	ProgressBarUI	Read-write
UIClassID	String	Read-only
value	int	Read-write

Painting JProgressBar Borders

All JComponent subclasses feature a border property by default, and the JProgressBar has a special borderPainted property to easily enable or disable the painting of the border. Calling the public void setBorderPainted(boolean newValue) method with a parameter of false turns off the painting of the progress bar's border. The right-hand progress bar in Figure 12-12 (shown earlier) has its border turned off. The source for its initialization follows:

```
JProgressBar cJProgressBar = new JProgressBar(JProgressBar.VERTICAL);
cJProgressBar.setBorderPainted(false);
```

Labeling a JProgressBar

The JProgressBar supports the display of text within the center of the component. There are three forms of this labeling:

- By default, no label exists.

- To display the percentage completed [100 × (value–minimum)/(maximum–minimum)], call the public void setStringPainted(boolean newValue) method with a parameter of true. This will result in a range from 0% to 100% displayed.

- To change the label to a fixed string, call the public void setString(String newValue) method and setStringPainted(true). On a vertical progress bar, the string is drawn rotated, so a longer string will fit better.

The left and bottom progress bars in Figure 12-12 demonstrate the fixed label and percentage label, respectively. The source code to create both progress bars follows:

```
JProgressBar bJProgressBar = new JProgressBar();
bJProgressBar.setStringPainted(true);
Border border = BorderFactory.createTitledBorder("Reading File");
bJProgressBar.setBorder(border);

JProgressBar dJProgressBar = new JProgressBar(JProgressBar.VERTICAL);
dJProgressBar.setString("Ack");
dJProgressBar.setStringPainted(true);
```

Using an Indeterminate JProgressBar

Some tasks don't have a fixed number of steps, or they do have a fixed number of steps, but you don't know what that number is until after all the steps are done. For this type of operation, the JProgressBar offers an indeterminate mode where the bar within the JProgressBar bounces back and forth from side to side, or top to bottom, depending on the direction of the progress bar. To enable this mode, just call the public void setIndeterminate(boolean newValue) method with a value of true. Figure 12-13 shows what an indeterminate progress bar looks like at different times. The length of the sliding box is one-sixth the available space and seems to not be settable.

Figure 12-13. *Sample indeterminate JProgressBar*

Stepping Along a JProgressBar

The main usage of the JProgressBar is to show progress as you step through a series of operations. Normally, you set the minimum value of the progress bar to zero and the maximum value to the number of steps to perform. Starting with a value property of zero, you increase the value to the maximum as you perform each step. All these operations imply multithreading, which is, in fact, absolutely necessary. In addition, when updating the progress bar's value, you need to remember to update it only from within the event dispatching thread (with the help of EventQueue.invokeAndWait(), if appropriate, as described in Chapter 2).

The process of having a progress bar step through its range is as follows:

1. Initialize it. This is the basic process of creating a JProgressBar with the desired orientation and range. In addition, perform any bordering and labeling here.

   ```
   JProgressBar aJProgressBar = new JProgressBar(0, 50);
   aJProgressBar.setStringPainted(true);
   ```

2. Start up the thread to perform the desired steps. Probably as the result of performing some action on the screen, you'll need to start the thread to do the work the progress bar is reporting. You need to start a new thread so that the user interface remains responsive.

   ```
   Thread stepper = new BarThread (aJProgressBar);
   stepper.start();
   ```

3. Perform the steps. Ignore updating the progress bar, and instead write the appropriate code to perform each step.

   ```
   static class BarThread extends Thread {
     private static int DELAY = 500;
     JProgressBar progressBar;
   ```

```
    public BarThread (JProgressBar bar) {
      progressBar = bar;
    }

    public void run() {
      int minimum = progressBar.getMinimum();
      int maximum = progressBar.getMaximum();
      for (int i=minimum; i<maximum; i++) {
        try {
          // Our job for each step is to just sleep
          Thread.sleep(DELAY);
        } catch (InterruptedException ignoredException) {
        } catch (InvocationTargetException ignoredException) {
          // The EventQueue.invokeAndWait() call
          // we'll add will throw this
        }
      }
    }
  }
```

4. For each step, have the thread update the progress bar in the event thread. Create the Runnable class just once outside the for loop. It isn't necessary to create one for each step.

```
Runnable runner = new Runnable() {
  public void run() {
    int value = progressBar.getValue();
    progressBar.setValue(value+1);
  }
};
```

Within the loop, tell the runner to update the progress bar. This update must be done in the event thread using the special EventQueue method invokeLater() or invokeAndWait(), because you're updating a property of the JProgressBar.

```
EventQueue.invokeAndWait (runner);
```

The complete working example is shown in Listing 12-5.

Listing 12-5. *JProgressBar Sample*

```
import javax.swing.*;
import java.awt.*;
import java.awt.event.*;
import java.lang.reflect.InvocationTargetException;

public class ProgressBarStep {
  static class BarThread extends Thread {
    private static int DELAY = 500;
    JProgressBar progressBar;
```

```java
  public BarThread(JProgressBar bar) {
    progressBar = bar;
  }

  public void run() {
    int minimum = progressBar.getMinimum();
    int maximum = progressBar.getMaximum();
    Runnable runner = new Runnable() {
      public void run() {
        int value = progressBar.getValue();
        progressBar.setValue(value+1);
      }
    };
    for (int i=minimum; i<maximum; i++) {
      try {
        EventQueue.invokeAndWait(runner);
        // Our job for each step is to just sleep
        Thread.sleep(DELAY);
      } catch (InterruptedException ignoredException) {
      } catch (InvocationTargetException ignoredException) {
      }
    }
  }
}
public static void main(String args[]) {
  Runnable runner = new Runnable() {
    public void run() {
      JFrame frame = new JFrame("Stepping Progress");
      frame.setDefaultCloseOperation(JFrame.EXIT_ON_CLOSE);
      final JProgressBar aJProgressBar = new JProgressBar(0, 50);
      aJProgressBar.setStringPainted(true);

      final JButton aJButton = new JButton("Start");

      ActionListener actionListener = new ActionListener() {
        public void actionPerformed(ActionEvent e) {
          aJButton.setEnabled(false);
          Thread stepper = new BarThread(aJProgressBar);
          stepper.start();
        }
      };
```

```
        aJButton.addActionListener(actionListener);
        frame.add(aJProgressBar, BorderLayout.NORTH);
        frame.add(aJButton, BorderLayout.SOUTH);
        frame.setSize(300, 200);
        frame.setVisible(true);
      }
    };
    EventQueue.invokeLater(runner);
  }
}
```

Figure 12-14 shows the demonstration program after selecting the button and at 22% completion.

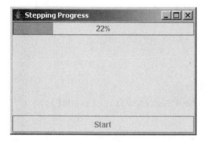

Figure 12-14. *JProgressBar in action*

By simply changing the `sleep` action in Listing 12-5 to the desired operation, this example should provide a suitable framework for reuse.

■**Note** To have the progress bar fill in the opposite direction, have the value start at the maximum and decrease it with each step. You probably don't want to display the percentage-completed string, as it will start at 100% and decrease to 0%.

Handling JProgressBar Events

Technically, the `JProgressBar` class supports notification of data model changes through a `ChangeListener`. In addition, you can attach a `ChangeListener` to its data model. Because the progress bar is meant more for visualization of output than for providing input, you typically won't use a `ChangeListener` with it. However, there may be times when this is appropriate. To reuse the `BoundedChangeListener` from Listing 12-3 earlier in this chapter, make one final change (as shown in boldface in Listing 12-6), because the source of these change events is the `JProgressBar`.

Listing 12-6. *ChangeListener for BoundedRangeModel, JSlider, and JProgressBar*

```
import javax.swing.*;
import javax.swing.event.*;

public class BoundedChangeListener implements ChangeListener {
  public void stateChanged(ChangeEvent changeEvent) {
    Object source = changeEvent.getSource();
    if (source instanceof BoundedRangeModel) {
      BoundedRangeModel aModel = (BoundedRangeModel)source;
      if (!aModel.getValueIsAdjusting()) {
        System.out.println ("Changed: " + aModel.getValue());
      }
    } else if (source instanceof JSlider) {
      JSlider theJSlider = (JSlider)source;
      if (!theJSlider.getValueIsAdjusting()) {
        System.out.println ("Slider changed: " + theJSlider.getValue());
      }
    } else if (source instanceof JProgressBar) {
      JProgressBar theJProgressBar = (JProgressBar)source;
      System.out.println ("ProgressBar changed: " + theJProgressBar.getValue());
    } else {
      System.out.println ("Something changed: " + source);
    }
  }
}
```

Customizing a JProgressBar Look and Feel

Each installable Swing look and feel provides a different JProgressBar appearance and set of default UIResource values. Figure 12-15 shows the appearance of the JProgressBar component for the preinstalled set of look and feel types.

Table 12-6 shows the set of available UIResource-related properties for a JProgressBar. It has 15 different properties.

Table 12-6. *JProgressBar UIResource Elements*

Property String	Object Type
ProgressBar.background	Color
ProgressBar.border	Border
ProgressBar.cellLength	Integer
ProgressBar.cellSpacing	Integer
ProgressBar.cycleTime	Integer
ProgressBar.font	Font
ProgressBar.foreground	Color

Table 12-6. *JProgressBar UIResource Elements (Continued)*

Property String	Object Type
ProgressBar.highlight	Color
ProgressBar.horizontalSize	Dimension
ProgressBar.repaintInterval	Integer
ProgressBar.selectionBackground	Color
ProgressBar.selectionForeground	Color
ProgressBar.shadow	Color
ProgressBar.verticalSize	Dimension
ProgressBarUI	String

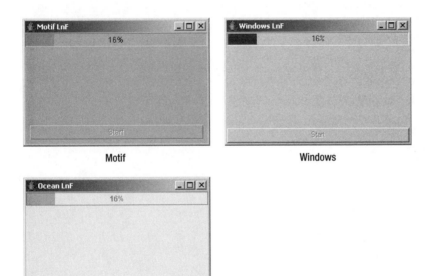

Motif   Windows

Ocean

Figure 12-15. *JProgressBar under different look and feel types*

JTextField Class and BoundedRangeModel Interface

The JTextField component is not technically a bounded-range component, but nevertheless, it uses BoundedRangeModel. Built inside the JTextField is a scrollable area used when the width of the component's contents exceeds its visible horizontal space. A BoundedRangeModel controls this scrolling area. You'll look at JTextField in more depth in Chapter 15. Here, you can see how a JScrollBar can track the scrolling area of the JTextField. Figure 12-16 shows the example in action, and Listing 12-7 shows the source.

Figure 12-16. *Tracking a JTextField width with a JScrollBar*

Listing 12-7. *JTextField with a JScrollBar for Scrolling*

```java
import javax.swing.*;
import java.awt.*;
import java.awt.event.*;
public class TextSlider extends JPanel {
  private JTextField textField;
  private JScrollBar scrollBar;
  public TextSlider() {
    setLayout(new BoxLayout(this, BoxLayout.Y_AXIS));
    textField = new JTextField();
    scrollBar = new JScrollBar(JScrollBar.HORIZONTAL);
    BoundedRangeModel brm = textField.getHorizontalVisibility();
    scrollBar.setModel(brm);
    add(textField);
    add(scrollBar);
  }
  public JTextField getTextField() {
    return textField;
  }
  public String getText() {
    return textField.getText();
  }
  public void addActionListener(ActionListener l) {
    textField.addActionListener(l);
  }
  public void removeActionListener(ActionListener l) {
    textField.removeActionListener(l);
  }
  public JScrollBar getScrollBar() {
    return scrollBar;
  }
```

```
public static void main(String args[]) {
  Runnable runner = new Runnable() {
    public void run() {
      JFrame frame = new JFrame("Text Slider");
      frame.setDefaultCloseOperation(JFrame.EXIT_ON_CLOSE);
      final TextSlider ts = new TextSlider();
      ts.addActionListener(new ActionListener() {
        public void actionPerformed(ActionEvent e) {
          System.out.println("Text: " + ts.getText());
        }
      });
      frame.add(ts, BorderLayout.NORTH);
      frame.setSize(300, 100);
      frame.setVisible(true);
    }
  };
  EventQueue.invokeLater(runner);
}
}
```

Normally, the JTextField has no associated scrollbar. In fact, most look and feel types don't offer it as an alternative. However, if this component is something you want to incorporate, you can reuse it in your own applications. Plenty of accessor methods should make reuse simpler, and you can avoid needing to access the internal pieces directly.

Summary

In this chapter, you've learned how to use Swing's JScrollBar, JSlider, and JProgressBar components. You saw how each uses the BoundedRangeModel interface to control the internal data necessary to operate the component, and how the DefaultBoundedRangeModel class offers a default implementation of this data model.

Now that you know how to use the various bounded range components, you can move on to Chapter 13, which looks at the controls that offer data selection: JList and JComboBox.

CHAPTER 13

■ ■ ■

List Model Controls

Chapter 12 explored the bounded range controls that support scrolling and the input or display of some bounded range of values. In this chapter, you'll examine two data-selection controls that present a list of choices: JList and JComboBox. The primary difference between these controls is that the JList component supports multiple selections, whereas the JComboBox does not. Also, the JComboBox lets a user provide a choice that isn't among the available options.

ListModel Interface

Figure 13-1 shows the two controls you'll be examining in this chapter.

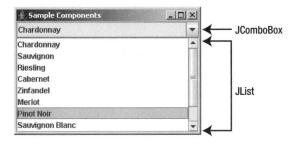

Figure 13-1. *Sample JComboBox and JList controls*

The data model shared by the two components is ListModel, which originates with the ListModel interface. The AbstractListModel class provides an implementation basis by supporting the management and notification of a set of ListDataListener objects.

In the case of a JList component, the data model implementation is the DefaultListModel class. This class adds an actual data repository, which follows the API of a Vector, for the different elements to be displayed within the JList component.

In the JComboBox component, an extension of the ListModel interface called ComboBoxModel supports the notion of a selected item within the model. The DefaultComboBoxModel class implements the ComboBoxModel interface through yet another interface, the MutableComboBoxModel, which supplies supporting methods for adding and removing elements from the model.

■**Note** The `BasicDirectoryModel` class is another `ListModel` implementation. This implementation is used by the file chooser component, `JFileChooser`, as described in Chapter 9.

The actual `ListModel` interface is rather simple. It provides for management of a `ListDataListener`, and it accesses the size of a particular element of the model.

```
public interface ListModel {
  // Properties
  public int getSize();
  // Listeners
  public void addListDataListener(ListDataListener l);
  public void removeListDataListener(ListDataListener l);
  // Other methods
  public Object getElementAt(int index);
}
```

AbstractListModel Class

The `AbstractListModel` class provides a partial implementation of the `ListModel` interface. You need to provide only the data structure and the data. The class provides for the list management of `ListDataListener` objects and the framework for notification of those listeners when the data changes. You can also get the list of listeners by using the `public ListDataListener[ ]` `getListDataListeners()` method. When you modify the data model, you must then call the appropriate method of `AbstractListModel` to notify the listening `ListDataListener` objects:

- `protected void fireIntervalAdded(Object source, int index0, int index1)`: To be called after adding a contiguous range of values to the list.

- `protected void fireIntervalRemoved(Object source, int index0, int index1)`: To be called after removing a contiguous range of values from the list.

- `protected void fireContentsChanged(Object source, int index0, int index1)`: To be called if the modified range wasn't contiguous for insertion, removal, or both.

■**Note** The ranges specified by the `fireXXX()` methods of `AbstractListModel` are closed intervals. This simply means that the indices are the endpoints of the range modified. There's no implied order for the indices; `index0`, for example, doesn't need to be less than `index1`. The only requirement is that the methods be called after the data model has changed.

If you have your data in an existing data structure, you need to convert it into a form that one of the Swing components understands or implement the `ListModel` interface yourself. As you'll see, an array or `Vector` is directly supported by `JList` and `JComboBox`. You can also wrap your data structure into an `AbstractListModel`. For instance, if your initial data structure is an

ArrayList from the Collections framework, you can convert the data structure to a ListModel with the following code:

```
final List arrayList = ...;
ListModel model = new AbstractListModel() {
  public int getSize() {
    return arrayList.size();
  }
  public Object getElementAt(int index) {
    return arrayList.get(index);
  }
}
```

The other option is to just pass the List into the Vector constructor, and then pass that Vector into the JList constructor. Effectively, you've then done the same thing.

DefaultListModel Class

The DefaultListModel class provides a data structure for you to store the data internally in the form of a Vector. You just need to add the data, because the class manages the ListDataListener list for you.

First, you create the data structure with the no-argument constructor: DefaultListModel model = new DefaultListModel(). Then you manipulate it. As shown in Table 13-1, the DefaultListModel class has only two properties.

Table 13-1. *DefaultListModel Properties*

Property Name	Data Type	Access
empty	boolean	Read-only
size	int	Read-write

The DefaultListModel class provides all its operational methods through a series of public methods. To add elements, use the following methods:

```
public void add(int index, Object element)
public void addElement(Object element)
public void insertElementAt(Object element, int index)
```

The addElement() method of DefaultListModel adds the element to the end of the data model. To change elements, use these methods:

```
public Object set(int index, Object element)
public void setElementAt(Object element, int index)
```

And to remove elements, these methods are provided:

```
public void clear()
public Object remove(int index)
public void removeAllElements()
public boolean removeElement(Object element)
public void removeElementAt(int index)
public void removeRange(int fromIndex, int toIndex)
```

The removeElement() method returns a status: true if it found the object and removed it, and false otherwise.

The DefaultListModel class is useful when you don't have your data in an existing data structure. For example, the results of a database query come back as a JDBC ResultSet. If you wish to use those results as the basis for what to display in a JList, you must store them somewhere. That somewhere can be a DefaultListModel, as demonstrated by the following:

```
ResultSet results = aJDBCStatement.executeQuery(
    "SELECT columnName FROM tableName");
DefaultListModel model = new DefaultListModel();
while (results.next()) {
  model.addElement(result.getString(1));
}
```

Listening for ListModel Events with a ListDataListener

If you're interested in finding out when the contents of the list model change, you can register a ListDataListener with the model. Three separate methods of the interface tell you when contents are added, removed, or altered. Altering the data model means adding and/or removing contents from one or more regions of the data model or changing the existing contents without adding or removing anything. The following is the interface definition:

```
public interface ListDataListener extends EventListener {
  public void contentsChanged(ListDataEvent e);
  public void intervalAdded(ListDataEvent e);
  public void intervalRemoved(ListDataEvent e);
}
```

Upon notification of the list-altering event, you're passed a ListDataEvent instance, which contains three properties, as shown in Table 13-2.

Table 13-2. *ListDataEvent Properties*

Property Name	Data Type	Access
index0	int	Read-only
index1	int	Read-only
type	int	Read-only

The indices aren't necessarily ordered, and neither are the bounds of the altered region. In the case of the list model contents changing, not everything within the region may have been altered. The area whose contents *did* change is the bounded region specified by the indices. The type property setting is one of three constants, as shown in Table 13-3, that map directly to the specific interface method called.

Table 13-3. *ListDataEvent Type Constants*

Type Constant	Method
CONTENTS_CHANGED	contentsChanged()
INTERVAL_ADDED	intervalAdded()
INTERVAL_REMOVED	intervalRemoved()

If any ListDataListener objects are attached to the data model when any one of the operational methods of the DefaultListModel class are called, each of the listeners will be notified of the data model change. To demonstrate the use of ListDataListener and the dynamic updating of the data model, the ModifyModelSample program shown in Listing 13-1 uses all the DefaultListModel class modifying methods, sending the output in the form of the event and list contents to a JTextArea.

Listing 13-1. *Modifying the Data Model*

```
import javax.swing.*;
import javax.swing.event.*;
import java.awt.*;
import java.awt.event.*;
import java.io.*;
import java.util.Enumeration;

public class ModifyModelSample {
  static String labels[] = {"Chardonnay", "Sauvignon", "Riesling", "Cabernet",
    "Zinfandel", "Merlot", "Pinot Noir", "Sauvignon Blanc", "Syrah",
    "Gewürztraminer"};

  public static void main(String args[]) {
    Runnable runner = new Runnable() {
      public void run() {
        JFrame frame = new JFrame("Modifying Model");
        frame.setDefaultCloseOperation(JFrame.EXIT_ON_CLOSE);

        // Fill model
        final DefaultListModel model = new DefaultListModel();
        for (int i=0, n=labels.length; i<n; i++) {
          model.addElement(labels[i]);
        }
```

```
        JList jlist = new JList(model);
        JScrollPane scrollPane1 = new JScrollPane(jlist);
        frame.add(scrollPane1, BorderLayout.WEST);

        final JTextArea textArea = new JTextArea();
        textArea.setEditable(false);
        JScrollPane scrollPane2 = new JScrollPane(textArea);
        frame.add(scrollPane2, BorderLayout.CENTER);

        ListDataListener listDataListener = new ListDataListener() {
          public void contentsChanged(ListDataEvent listDataEvent) {
            appendEvent(listDataEvent);
          }
          public void intervalAdded(ListDataEvent listDataEvent) {
            appendEvent(listDataEvent);
          }
          public void intervalRemoved(ListDataEvent listDataEvent) {
            appendEvent(listDataEvent);
          }
          private void appendEvent(ListDataEvent listDataEvent) {
            StringWriter sw = new StringWriter();
            PrintWriter pw = new PrintWriter(sw);
            switch (listDataEvent.getType()) {
              case ListDataEvent.CONTENTS_CHANGED:
                pw.print("Type: Contents Changed");
                break;
              case ListDataEvent.INTERVAL_ADDED:
                pw.print("Type: Interval Added");
                break;
              case ListDataEvent.INTERVAL_REMOVED:
                pw.print("Type: Interval Removed");
                break;
            }
            pw.print(", Index0: " + listDataEvent.getIndex0());
            pw.print(", Index1: " + listDataEvent.getIndex1());
            DefaultListModel theModel =
              (DefaultListModel)listDataEvent.getSource();
            pw.println(theModel);
            textArea.append(sw.toString());
          }
        };

        model.addListDataListener(listDataListener);
```

```
// Set up buttons
JPanel jp = new JPanel(new GridLayout(2, 1));
JPanel jp1 = new JPanel(new FlowLayout(FlowLayout.CENTER, 1, 1));
JPanel jp2 = new JPanel(new FlowLayout(FlowLayout.CENTER, 1, 1));
jp.add(jp1);
jp.add(jp2);
JButton jb = new JButton("add F");
jp1.add(jb);
jb.addActionListener(new ActionListener() {
  public void actionPerformed(ActionEvent actionEvent) {
    model.add(0, "First");
  }
});
jb = new JButton("addElement L");
jp1.add(jb);
jb.addActionListener(new ActionListener() {
  public void actionPerformed(ActionEvent actionEvent) {
    model.addElement("Last");
  }
});
jb = new JButton("insertElementAt M");
jp1.add(jb);
jb.addActionListener(new ActionListener() {
  public void actionPerformed(ActionEvent actionEvent) {
    int size = model.getSize();
    model.insertElementAt("Middle", size/2);
  }
});
jb = new JButton("set F");
jp1.add(jb);
jb.addActionListener(new ActionListener() {
  public void actionPerformed(ActionEvent actionEvent) {
    int size = model.getSize();
    if (size != 0)
      model.set(0, "New First");
  }
});
jb = new JButton("setElementAt L");
jp1.add(jb);
jb.addActionListener(new ActionListener() {
  public void actionPerformed(ActionEvent actionEvent) {
    int size = model.getSize();
    if (size != 0)
      model.setElementAt("New Last", size-1);
  }
});
```

```
jb = new JButton("load 10");
jp1.add(jb);
jb.addActionListener(new ActionListener() {
  public void actionPerformed(ActionEvent actionEvent) {
    for (int i=0, n=labels.length; i<n ;i++) {
      model.addElement(labels[i]);
    }
  }
});
jb. = new JButton("clear");
jp2.add(jb);
jb.addActionListener(new ActionListener() {
  public void actionPerformed(ActionEvent actionEvent) {
    model.clear();
  }
});
jb = new JButton("remove F");
jp2.add(jb);
jb.addActionListener(new ActionListener() {
  public void actionPerformed(ActionEvent actionEvent) {
    int size = model.getSize();
    if (size != 0)
      model.remove(0);
  }
});
jb = new JButton("removeAllElements");
jp2.add(jb);
jb.addActionListener(new ActionListener() {
  public void actionPerformed(ActionEvent actionEvent) {
    model.removeAllElements();
  }
});
jb = new JButton("removeElement 'Last'");
jp2.add(jb);
jb.addActionListener(new ActionListener() {
  public void actionPerformed(ActionEvent actionEvent) {
    model.removeElement("Last");
  }
});
jb = new JButton("removeElementAt M");
jp2.add(jb);
jb.addActionListener(new ActionListener() {
  public void actionPerformed(ActionEvent actionEvent) {
    int size = model.getSize();
    if (size != 0)
      model.removeElementAt(size/2);
  }
});
```

```
      jb = new JButton("removeRange FM");
      jp2.add(jb);
      jb.addActionListener(new ActionListener() {
        public void actionPerformed(ActionEvent actionEvent) {
          int size = model.getSize();
          if (size != 0)
            model.removeRange(0,size/2);
        }
      });
      frame.add(jp, BorderLayout.SOUTH);
      frame.setSize(640, 300);
      frame.setVisible(true);
    }
  };
  EventQueue.invokeLater(runner);
 }
}
```

Figure 13-2 shows the output for one such run, after several buttons were selected.

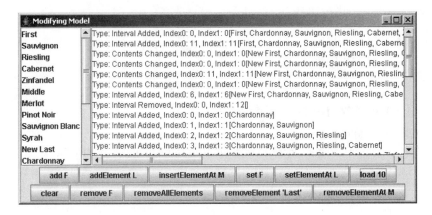

Figure 13-2. *A listing for data model changes*

■ **Note** To help you decode the button labels in Figure 13-2, an *F* means the method affects the first cell, an *M* means it affects the middle cell, and an *L* means it affects the last cell. The removeElement "Last" button will remove the first element in the data model whose content is Last.

The retrieving methods of the DefaultListModel class are quite varied in their capabilities. The class has the basic accessor methods public Object get(int index), public Object getElementAt(int index), and public Object elementAt(int index), which all do the same thing. The DefaultListModel class also has more specific methods. For instance, to work with all elements, you can obtain an instance of Enumeration using public Enumeration elements().

Or, if you want to work with all elements as an array, use either public Object[] toArray() or public void copyInto(Object anArray[]). You can also check for the existence of an element within a model with methods such as public boolean contains(Object element), public int indexOf(Object element), public int indexOf(Object element, int index), public int lastIndexOf(Object element), and public int lastIndexOf(Object element, int index).

■**Tip** Once you're finished adding elements to the data model, it's a good idea to trim its length with public void trimToSize(). This removes any extra preallocated space within the internal data structure. In addition, if you know the size of the data model in advance, you can call public void ensureCapacity(int minCapacity) to preallocate space. Both of these methods work only with DefaultListModel.

ComboBoxModel Interface

The ComboBoxModel interface extends the ListModel interface. The key reason for this extension is that the classes that implement the ComboBoxModel interface need to manage the selected item internally through a selectedItem property, as shown by the interface definition.

```
public interface ComboBoxModel extends ListModel {
  // Properties
  public Object getSelectedItem();
  public void setSelectedItem(Object anItem);
}
```

MutableComboBoxModel Interface

In addition to the ComboBoxModel interface, another data model interface, MutableComboBoxModel, extends ComboBoxModel to make methods available to modify the data model.

```
public interface MutableComboBoxModel extends ComboBoxModel {
  // Other methods
  public void addElement(Object obj);
  public void insertElementAt(Object obj, int index);
  public void removeElement(Object obj);
  public void removeElementAt(int index);
}
```

The JComboBox component uses an implementation of this interface by default.

DefaultComboBoxModel Class

The DefaultComboBoxModel class extends the AbstractListModel class to provide an appropriate data model for the JComboBox. Because of this extension, it inherits the managing of the ListDataListener list.

Like DefaultListModel, DefaultComboBoxModel adds the necessary data structure for you to collect elements to show within a component. Also, because the model is modifiable, implementing MutableComboBoxModel causes the data model to call the various file*XXX*() methods of the AbstractListModel class when the data elements within the model change.

■**Note** If you create a DefaultComboBoxModel from an array, the elements of the array are copied into an internal data structure. If you use a Vector, they're not copied; instead, the actual Vector is used internally.

To use the data model, you must first create the model with one of the three constructors:

public DefaultComboBoxModel()
```
DefaultComboBoxModel model = new DefaultComboBoxModel();
```

public DefaultComboBoxModel(Object listData[])
```
String labels[] = { "Chardonnay", "Sauvignon", "Riesling", "Cabernet", "Zinfandel",
  "Merlot", "Pinot Noir", "Sauvignon Blanc", "Syrah", "Gewürztraminer"};
DefaultComboBoxModel model = new DefaultComboBoxModel(labels);
```

public DefaultComboBoxModel(Vector listData)
```
Vector vector = aBufferedImage.getSources();
DefaultComboBoxModel model = new DefaultComboBoxModel(vector);
```

Next, you manipulate the model. Two new properties are introduced in the DefaultComboBoxModel class, as shown in Table 13-4.

Table 13-4. *DefaultComboBoxModel Properties*

Property Name	Data Type	Access
selectedItem	Object	Read-write
size	int	Read-only

The data model modification methods for the DefaultComboBoxModel are different from those for DefaultListModel. They all come from the MutableComboBoxModel interface:

```
public void addElement(Object element)
public void insertElementAt(Object element, int index)
public boolean removeElement(Object element)
public void removeElementAt(int index)
```

Due to the flexibility (and functionality) of the DefaultComboBoxModel, it's usually unnecessary to create your own ComboBoxModel implementation. Just create an instance of DefaultComboBoxModel, and then simply fill it from the appropriate data source.

■**Note** One case in which you may wish to provide your own model is when you need to support the presence of the same item within the model multiple times. With the `DefaultComboBoxModel`, if you have two items in the list whose `equals()` methods will return `true`, the model won't work properly.

If you really want to define your own model implementation, perhaps because you already have the data in your own data structure, it works best to subclass the `AbstractListModel` and implement the `ComboBoxModel` or `MutableComboBoxModel` interface methods. When subclassing the `AbstractListModel`, you merely need to provide the data structure and the access into it. Because the "selected item" part of the data model is maintained outside the primary data structure, you need a place to store that, as well. The program source in Listing 13-2 demonstrates one such implementation using an `ArrayList` as the data structure. The program includes a `main()` method to demonstrate the use of the model within a `JComboBox`.

Listing 13-2. *Using a Custom Data Model*

```
import java.awt.*;
import javax.swing.*;
import java.util.Collection;
import java.util.ArrayList;

public class ArrayListComboBoxModel
    extends AbstractListModel implements ComboBoxModel {
  private Object selectedItem;
  private ArrayList anArrayList;
  public ArrayListComboBoxModel(ArrayList arrayList) {
    anArrayList = arrayList;
  }
  public Object getSelectedItem() {
    return selectedItem;
  }
  public void setSelectedItem(Object newValue) {
    selectedItem = newValue;
  }
  public int getSize() {
    return anArrayList.size();
  }
  public Object getElementAt(int i) {
    return anArrayList.get(i);
  }

  public static void main(String args[]) {
    Runnable runner = new Runnable() {
      public void run() {
        JFrame frame = new JFrame("ArrayListComboBoxModel");
        frame.setDefaultCloseOperation(JFrame.EXIT_ON_CLOSE);
```

```
        Collection<Object> col = System.getProperties().values();
        ArrayList<Object> arrayList = new ArrayList<Object>(col);
        ArrayListComboBoxModel model = new ArrayListComboBoxModel(arrayList);

        JComboBox comboBox = new JComboBox (model);

        frame.add(comboBox, BorderLayout.NORTH);
        frame.setSize(300, 225);
        frame.setVisible(true);
      }
    };
    EventQueue.invokeLater(runner);
  }
}
```

Figure 13-3 shows the model in action using the current system properties as the source for the data model elements.

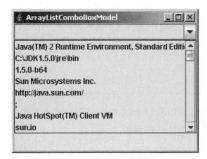

Figure 13-3. *Using an ArrayListComboBoxModel*

JList Class

The JList component is the basic Swing component for selecting one or more items from a set of choices. You present the list of choices to the user, and the user can pick one or several, depending on the selection mode of the component.

Three key elements and their implementations define the JList structure:

- A data model for holding the JList data, as defined by the ListModel interface

- A cell renderer for drawing the elements of the JList, as described by the ListCellRenderer interface

- A selection model for selecting elements of the JList, as described by the ListSelectionModel interface

Creating JList Components

The JList component has four constructors, which allow you to create a JList instance based on your initial data structure:

```
public JList()
JList jlist = new JList();

public JList(Object listData[])
String labels[] = { "Chardonnay", "Sauvignon", "Riesling", "Cabernet", "Zinfandel",
  "Merlot", "Pinot Noir", "Sauvignon Blanc", "Syrah", "Gewürztraminer"};
JList jlist = new JList(labels);

public JList(Vector listData)
Vector vector = aBufferedImage.getSources();
JList jlist = new JList(vector);

public JList(ListModel model)
ResultSet results = aJDBCStatement.executeQuery("SELECT colName FROM tableName");
DefaultListModel model = new DefaultListModel();
while (result.next())
  model.addElement(result.getString(1));
JList jlist = new JList(model);
```

If you use the no-argument constructor, you can fill in the data later. However, if you use the array or Vector constructor, you can't alter the contents without changing the whole model.

■**Note** If you want to display something other than the toString() results of each array element, see the section "Rendering JList Elements" later in this chapter for details on how to do that.

JList Properties

After creating a JList component, you can modify each of its many properties. Table 13-5 shows the 32 properties of JList.

Table 13-5. *JList Properties*

Property Name	Data Type	Access
accessibleContext	AccessibleContext	Read-only
anchorSelectionIndex	int	Read-only
cellRenderer	ListCellRenderer	Read-write bound
dragEnabled	boolean	Read-write
firstVisibleIndex	int	Read-only
fixedCellHeight	int	Read-write bound
fixedCellWidth	int	Read-write bound

Table 13-5. *JList Properties (Continued)*

Property Name	Data Type	Access
lastVisibleIndex	int	Read-only
layoutOrientation	int	Read-write bound
leadSelectionIndex	int	Read-only
listData	Vector	Write-only
listSelectionListeners	ListSelectionListener[ ]	Read-only
maxSelectionIndex	int	Read-only
minSelectionIndex	int	Read-only
model	ListModel	Read-write bound
preferredScrollableViewportSize	Dimension	Read-only
prototypeCellValue	Object	Read-write bound
scrollableTracksViewportHeight	boolean	Read-only
scrollableTracksViewportWidth	boolean	Read-only
selectedIndex	int	Read-write
selectedIndices	int[ ]	Read-write
selectedValue	Object	Read-only
selectedValues	Object[ ]	Read-only
selectionBackground	Color	Read-write bound
selectionEmpty	boolean	Read-only
selectionForeground	Color	Read-write bound
selectionMode	int	Read-write
selectionModel	ListSelectionModel	Read-write bound
UI	ListUI	Read-write
UIClassID	String	Read-only
valueIsAdjusting	boolean	Read-write
visibleRowCount	int	Read-write bound

Many of the JList properties are related to the process of selection. For instance, anchorSelectionIndex, leadSelectionIndex, maxSelectionIndex, minSelectionIndex, selectedIndex, and selectedIndices deal with the indices of the selected rows, while selectedValue and selectedValues relate to the contents of the selected elements. The anchorSelectionIndex is the most recent index0 of a ListDataEvent, whereas the leadSelectionIndex is the most recent index1.

To control the preferred number of visible rows shown, set the `visibleRowCount` property of `JList`. The default setting for this property is 8.

Scrolling JList Components

When you're working with a `JList` component, you must place the component within a `JScrollPane` if you want to allow the user to pick from all available choices. If it's not placed within a `JScrollPane` and the default number of rows displayed is smaller than the size of the data model, or if there isn't sufficient space to display the rows, the other choices aren't shown. When placed within a `JScrollPane`, the `JList` offers a vertical scrollbar to move through all the available choices.

If you don't place a `JList` in a `JScrollPane` and the number of choices exceeds the available space, only the top group of choices will be visible, as you can see in Figure 13-4.

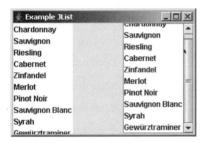

Figure 13-4. *A ten-element JList, in and out of a JScrollPane*

■**Tip** Whenever you see that a class implements the `Scrollable` interface, it should serve as a reminder to place that component within a `JScrollPane` before adding it to the application.

The `JScrollPane` relies on the dimensions provided by the `preferredScrollable`➥ `ViewportSize` property setting to determine the preferred size of the pane contents. When the data model of a `JList` is empty, a default size of 16 pixels high by 256 pixels wide per visible row is used. Otherwise, the width is determined by looping through all the cells to find the widest one, and the height is determined by the height of the first cell.

To speed the sizing of the viewport for the `JScrollPane`, you can define a prototype cell by setting the `prototypeCellValue` property. You must be sure the prototype `toString()` value is sufficiently wide and tall to accommodate all the contents of the `JList`. Then the `JScrollPane` bases the sizing of its viewport on the prototype, and it won't be necessary for the `JList` to ask each cell for its size; instead, it will ask only for the prototype.

You can also improve performance by assigning a size to the `fixedCellHeight` and `fixedCellWidth` properties. Setting these properties is another way to avoid having the `JList` ask each cell for its rendered size. Setting both properties is the fastest way to have a `JList` sized within a viewport. Of course, this is also the least flexible because it ensures that the `JList` choices aren't widened (or shortened) when the contents change. However, if you have a large number of entries in the data model, this loss of flexibility may be worthwhile to improve performance. Figure 13-5 helps you to visualize some of the sizing capabilities of a `JList`.

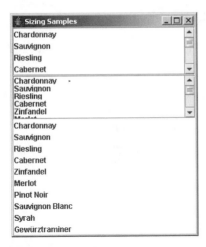

Figure 13-5. *Sizing entries within a JList*

The source used to generate the output in Figure 13-5 follows in Listing 13-3. The center list in the figure contains more than 1,000 fixed-size cells. The top list shows that you can set the number of visible rows with setVisibleRowCount(). Notice that the bottom list in the figure also uses setVisibleRowCount(). However, because the list isn't in a JScrollPane, the request to limit the number of rows is ignored.

Listing 13-3. *Sizing the List Cells*

```
import javax.swing.*;
import java.awt.*;
public class SizingSamples {
  public static void main(String args[]) {
    Runnable runner = new Runnable() {
      public void run() {
        String labels[] = {"Chardonnay", "Sauvignon", "Riesling", "Cabernet",
          "Zinfandel", "Merlot", "Pinot Noir", "Sauvignon Blanc", "Syrah",
          "Gewürztraminer"};

        JFrame frame = new JFrame("Sizing Samples");
        frame.setDefaultCloseOperation(JFrame.EXIT_ON_CLOSE);

        JList jlist1 = new JList(labels);
        jlist1.setVisibleRowCount(4);
        DefaultListModel model = new DefaultListModel();
        model.ensureCapacity(1000);
        for (int i=0;i<100;i++) {
          for (int j=0;j<10;j++) {
            model.addElement(labels[j]);
          }
        }
```

```
            JScrollPane scrollPane1 = new JScrollPane(jlist1);
            frame.add(scrollPane1, BorderLayout.NORTH);

            JList jlist2 = new JList(model);
            jlist2.setVisibleRowCount(4);
            jlist2.setFixedCellHeight(12);
            jlist2.setFixedCellWidth(200);
            JScrollPane scrollPane2 = new JScrollPane(jlist2);
            frame.add(scrollPane2, BorderLayout.CENTER);

            JList jlist3 = new JList(labels);
            jlist3.setVisibleRowCount(4);
            frame.add(jlist3, BorderLayout.SOUTH);

            frame.setSize(300, 350);
            frame.setVisible(true);
          }
        };
        EventQueue.invokeLater(runner);
    }
}
```

In addition to placing a JList within a JScrollPane, you can also find out which choices are visible or request that a specific element be made visible. The firstVisibleIndex and lastVisibleIndex properties allow you to find out which choices are currently visible within the JScrollPane. Both methods return −1 if nothing is visible; this usually happens where the data model is empty. To request that a specific element be made visible, use the public void ensureIndexIsVisible(int index) method. For instance, to programmatically move the list to the top, use the following:

```
jlist.ensureIndexIsVisible(0);
```

Rendering JList Elements

Every element within the JList is called a *cell*. Every JList has an installed cell renderer that draws every cell when the list needs to be drawn. The default renderer, DefaultListCellRenderer, is a subclass of JLabel, which means you can use either text or an icon as the graphical depiction for the cell. This tends to suit most users' needs, but sometimes the cell's appearance can benefit from some customization. And, because every JList can have at most one renderer installed, customization requires that you replace the existing renderer.

ListCellRenderer Interface and DefaultListCellRenderer Class

The JList has an installed renderer. A class that implements the ListCellRenderer interface provides this renderer.

```
public interface ListCellRenderer {
  public Component getListCellRendererComponent(JList list, Object value,
    int index, boolean isSelected, boolean cellHasFocus);
}
```

When it's time to draw each cell, the interface's sole method is called. The returned renderer provides the specific rendering for that one cell of the JList. The JList uses the rendering to draw the element, and then gets the next renderer.

A reference to the enclosing JList is provided to the getListCellRendererComponent() method so that the renderer can share display characteristics. The value of the selection contains the object in the list's data model at position index. The index is zero-based from the beginning of the data model. The last two parameters allow you to customize the cell's appearance based on the cell's state—that is, whether it's selected or has the input focus.

Listing 13-4 shows a renderer that demonstrates this technique. The sole difference for this renderer is that the cell with the input focus has a titled border. After the renderer is created, you install it by setting the cellRenderer property of the JList.

■Tip For performance reasons, it is best not to create the actual renderer in the getListCellRendererComponent() method. Either subclass Component and return this or create a class variable to hold one instance of a Component, which then may be customized and returned.

Listing 13-4. *Rendering the List Cells*

```
import java.awt.*;
import javax.swing.*;
import javax.swing.border.*;
public class FocusedTitleListCellRenderer implements ListCellRenderer {
  protected static Border noFocusBorder =
    new EmptyBorder(15, 1, 1, 1);
  protected static TitledBorder focusBorder =
    new TitledBorder(LineBorder.createGrayLineBorder(), "Focused");
  protected DefaultListCellRenderer defaultRenderer = new DefaultListCellRenderer();

  public String getTitle() {
    return focusBorder.getTitle();
  }
  public void setTitle(String newValue) {
    focusBorder.setTitle(newValue);
  }

  public Component getListCellRendererComponent(JList list, Object value,
      int index, boolean isSelected, boolean cellHasFocus) {
    JLabel renderer = (JLabel)defaultRenderer.getListCellRendererComponent(
      list, value, index, isSelected, cellHasFocus);
    renderer.setBorder(cellHasFocus ? focusBorder : noFocusBorder);
    return renderer;
  }
}
```

■**Caution** A common mistake when creating your own renderer is forgetting to make the renderer component opaque. This causes the background coloration of the renderer to be ignored and the list container's background to bleed through. With the DefaultListCellRenderer class, the renderer component is already opaque.

A sample program that uses the new renderer follows in Listing 13-5. It doesn't do anything special other than install the custom cell renderer that was just created.

Listing 13-5. *Rendering List Cells Sample*

```
import javax.swing.*;
import java.awt.*;
public class CustomBorderSample {
  public static void main(String args[]) {
    Runnable runner = new Runnable() {
      public void run() {
        String labels[] = {"Chardonnay", "Sauvignon", "Riesling", "Cabernet",
          "Zinfandel", "Merlot", "Pinot Noir", "Sauvignon Blanc", "Syrah",
          "Gewürztraminer"};
        JFrame frame = new JFrame("Custom Border");
        frame.setDefaultCloseOperation(JFrame.EXIT_ON_CLOSE);
        JList jlist = new JList(labels);
        ListCellRenderer renderer = new FocusedTitleListCellRenderer();
        jlist.setCellRenderer(renderer);
        JScrollPane sp = new JScrollPane(jlist);
        frame.add(sp, BorderLayout.CENTER);
        frame.setSize(300, 200);
        frame.setVisible(true);
      }
    };
    EventQueue.invokeLater(runner);
  }
}
```

Figure 13-6 shows the output of the sample program.

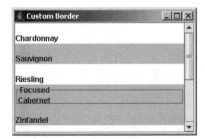

Figure 13-6. *A JList with a custom focus border cell renderer*

Creating a Complex ListCellRenderer

More often than not, custom cell renderers (like the one shown in Figure 13-6) are necessary when the data model consists of more complex data in each element—something not representable by a text string. For instance, Listing 13-6 shows the source for an example where each element of the data model consists of a font, foreground color, icon, and text string. Ensuring the proper usage of these elements within the renderer simply involves a little more work in configuring the renderer component. In this particular example, that data is stored within each element of an array in the data model. You could just as easily define a new class or use a hash table.

Listing 13-6. *Rendering Complex List Cells*

```
import java.awt.*;
import javax.swing.*;
import javax.swing.border.*;
public class ComplexCellRenderer implements ListCellRenderer {
  protected DefaultListCellRenderer defaultRenderer = new DefaultListCellRenderer();

  public Component getListCellRendererComponent(JList list, Object value, int index,
      boolean isSelected, boolean cellHasFocus) {
    Font theFont       = null;
    Color theForeground = null;
    Icon theIcon       = null;
    String theText     = null;

    JLabel renderer = (JLabel)defaultRenderer.getListCellRendererComponent(
      list, value, index, isSelected, cellHasFocus);

    if (value instanceof Object[]) {
      Object values[] = (Object[])value;
      theFont         = (Font)values[0];
      theForeground   = (Color)values[1];
      theIcon         = (Icon)values[2];
      theText         = (String)values[3];
    } else {
      theFont         = list.getFont();
      theForeground   = list.getForeground();
      theText         = "";
    }
    if (!isSelected) {
      renderer.setForeground(theForeground);
    }
    if (theIcon != null) {
      renderer.setIcon(theIcon);
    }
```

```
      renderer.setText(theText);
      renderer.setFont(theFont);
      return renderer;
   }
}
```

This renderer merely customizes the renderer component returned by the DefaultListCellRenderer. The customization is based on the data model value being passed in as an array to the value argument of the getListCellRendererComponent() method.

Listing 13-7 shows the test class. This demonstration program reuses the DiamondIcon created in Chapter 4. Most of the code is for initialization of the data model.

Listing 13-7. *Rendering Complex List Cells Sample*

```
import javax.swing.*;
import java.awt.*;
public class ComplexRenderingSample {
  public static void main(String args[]) {
    Runnable runner = new Runnable() {
      public void run() {

        Object elements[][] = {
          {new Font("Helvetica", Font.PLAIN, 20), Color.RED,
            new DiamondIcon(Color.BLUE), "Help"},
          {new Font("TimesRoman", Font.BOLD, 14), Color.BLUE,
            new DiamondIcon(Color.GREEN), "Me"},
          {new Font("Courier", Font.ITALIC, 18), Color.GREEN,
            new DiamondIcon(Color.BLACK), "I'm"},
          {new Font("Helvetica", Font.BOLD | Font.ITALIC, 12), Color.GRAY,
            new DiamondIcon(Color.MAGENTA), "Trapped"},
          {new Font("TimesRoman", Font.PLAIN, 32), Color.PINK,
            new DiamondIcon(Color.YELLOW), "Inside"},
          {new Font("Courier", Font.BOLD, 16), Color.YELLOW,
            new DiamondIcon(Color.RED), "This"},
          {new Font("Helvetica", Font.ITALIC, 8), Color.DARK_GRAY,
            new DiamondIcon(Color.PINK), "Computer"}
        };

        JFrame frame = new JFrame("Complex Renderer");
        frame.setDefaultCloseOperation(JFrame.EXIT_ON_CLOSE);

        JList jlist = new JList(elements);
        ListCellRenderer renderer = new ComplexCellRenderer();
        jlist.setCellRenderer(renderer);
        JScrollPane scrollPane = new JScrollPane(jlist);
        frame.add(scrollPane, BorderLayout.CENTER);
```

```
    // JComboBox comboBox = new JComboBox(elements);
    // comboBox.setRenderer(renderer);
    // frame.add(comboBox, BorderLayout.NORTH);

    frame.setSize(300, 200);
    frame.setVisible(true);
  }
};
EventQueue.invokeLater(runner);
  }
}
```

The output of this example is shown in Figure 13-7.

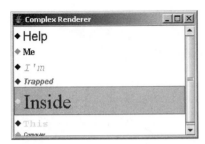

Figure 13-7. *Using a more complex list cell renderer*

■Tip When you create your own rendering components, you'll find it's best to start with the default list cell renderer. This allows you to focus on the specific details you're interested in. Otherwise, you'll need to worry about everything, such as the default selection foreground and background colors, and whether you've remembered to make the component opaque. Of course, if you want to configure everything yourself, feel free to do so.

Selecting JList Elements

By default, every JList component is in multiple-selection mode. This means that you can select multiple elements within the component. How you select multiple elements depends on the user interface you're employing. For instance, with the Ocean look and feel interface, Ctrl-select (Ctrl key and left mouse button on a right-handed mouse) acts as a selection toggle, and Shift-select acts as a means of range selection.

ListSelectionModel Interface and DefaultListSelectionModel Class

An implementation of the ListSelectionModel interface controls the selection mechanism for a JList component. The interface definition, shown here, defines constants for different selection modes and describes how to manage a list of ListSelectionListener objects. It also provides the means to describe several selection intervals.

```
public interface ListSelectionModel {
  // Constants
  public final static int MULTIPLE_INTERVAL_SELECTION;
  public final static int SINGLE_INTERVAL_SELECTION;
  public final static int SINGLE_SELECTION;
  // Properties
  public int getAnchorSelectionIndex();
  public void setAnchorSelectionIndex(int index);
  public int getLeadSelectionIndex();
  public void setLeadSelectionIndex(int index);
  public int getMaxSelectionIndex();
  public int getMinSelectionIndex();
  public boolean isSelectionEmpty();
  public int getSelectionMode();
  public void setSelectionMode(int selectionMode);
  public boolean getValueIsAdjusting();
  public void setValueIsAdjusting(boolean valueIsAdjusting);
  // Listeners
  public void addListSelectionListener(ListSelectionListener x);
  public void removeListSelectionListener(ListSelectionListener x);
  // Other methods
  public void addSelectionInterval(int index0, int index1);
  public void clearSelection();
  public void insertIndexInterval(int index, int length, boolean before);
  public boolean isSelectedIndex(int index);
  public void removeIndexInterval(int index0, int index1);
  public void removeSelectionInterval(int index0, int index1);
  public void setSelectionInterval(int index0, int index1);
}
```

Three different selection modes are available. Table 13-6 contains the name of each mode and its description.

Table 13-6. *ListSelectionModel Modes*

Mode	Description
SINGLE_SELECTION	One item at a time can be selected.
SINGLE_INTERVAL_SELECTION	One contiguous range of items can be selected.
MULTIPLE_INTERVAL_SELECTION	Any set of ranges can be selected.

Figure 13-8 shows you the results of each selection mode.

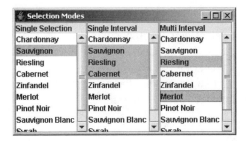

Figure 13-8. *Visual representation of selection modes*

To change the selection mode of a JList, set its selectionMode property to one of the ListSelectionModel constants shown in Table 13-6. For instance, the following would change a list to single-selection mode:

```
JList list = new JList(...);
list.setSelectionMode(ListSelectionModel.SINGLE_SELECTION);
```

The DefaultListSelectionModel class is the default implementation of the ListSelectionModel interface. You can examine any of its nine properties, shown in Table 13-7, to learn about the currently selected range.

Table 13-7. *DefaultListSelectionModel Properties*

Property Name	Data Type	Access
anchorSelectionIndex	int	Read-write
leadAnchorNotificationEnabled	boolean	Read-write
leadSelectionIndex	int	Read-write
listSelectionListeners	ListSelectionListener[ ]	Read-only
maxSelectionIndex	int	Read-only
minSelectionIndex	int	Read-only
selectionEmpty	boolean	Read-only
selectionMode	int	Read-write
valueIsAdjusting	boolean	Read-write

The selection model can show you what is currently being used in the multiple-selection mode when the selectionEmpty property is false. Simply ask each index between the minimum and maximum selection indices if it's selected with public boolean isSelectedIndex(int index). Because multiple-selection mode supports noncontiguous areas, this is the only way to find out what's selected. However, the selectedIndices property of JList provides this information without you needing to check it manually.

Listening to JList Events with a ListSelectionListener

If you want to know when elements of a JList have been selected, you need to
attach a ListSelectionListener to the JList or the ListSelectionModel. The
addListSelectionListener() and removeListenerListener() methods of the JList
only delegate to the underlying ListSelectionModel. When the set of selected elements
changes, attached listener objects are notified. The interface definition follows:

```
public interface ListSelectionListener extends EventListener {
  public void valueChanged(ListSelectionEvent e);
}
```

The ListSelectionEvent instance received by the listener describes the range of affected
elements for *this* selection event, as well as whether or not the selection is still changing, as
shown in Table 13-8. When a user is still altering selected elements, with a valueIsAdjusting
setting of true, you might want to delay performing costly operations such as drawing a high-
resolution graphics presentation.

Table 13-8. *ListSelectionEvent Properties*

Property Name	Data Type	Access
firstIndex	int	Read-only
lastIndex	int	Read-only
valueIsAdjusting	boolean	Read-only

In order to demonstrate selection with a JList, the program shown in Listing 13-8 adds a
JTextArea to a window to show the output of the selection listener. The listener prints out the
currently selected items by item position and value.

Listing 13-8. *Rendering Complex List Cells Sample*

```
import javax.swing.*;
import javax.swing.event.*;
import java.awt.*;
import java.io.*;

public class SelectingJListSample {
  public static void main(String args[]) {
    Runnable runner = new Runnable() {
      public void run() {
        String labels[] = {"Chardonnay", "Sauvignon", "Riesling", "Cabernet",
          "Zinfandel", "Merlot", "Pinot Noir", "Sauvignon Blanc", "Syrah",
          "Gewürztraminer"};
        JFrame frame = new JFrame("Selecting JList");
        frame.setDefaultCloseOperation(JFrame.EXIT_ON_CLOSE);
```

```
      JList jlist = new JList(labels);
      JScrollPane scrollPane1 = new JScrollPane(jlist);
      frame.add(scrollPane1, BorderLayout.WEST);

      final JTextArea textArea = new JTextArea();
      textArea.setEditable(false);
      JScrollPane scrollPane2 = new JScrollPane(textArea);
      frame.add(scrollPane2, BorderLayout.CENTER);

      ListSelectionListener listSelectionListener =
          new ListSelectionListener() {
        public void valueChanged(ListSelectionEvent listSelectionEvent) {
          StringWriter sw = new StringWriter();
          PrintWriter pw = new PrintWriter(sw);
          pw.print("First index: " + listSelectionEvent.getFirstIndex());
          pw.print(", Last index: " + listSelectionEvent.getLastIndex());
          boolean adjust = listSelectionEvent.getValueIsAdjusting();
          pw.println(", Adjusting? " + adjust);
          if (!adjust) {
            JList list = (JList)listSelectionEvent.getSource();
            int selections[] = list.getSelectedIndices();
            Object selectionValues[] = list.getSelectedValues();
            for (int i=0, n=selections.length; i<n; i++) {
              if (i==0) {
                pw.print("  Selections: ");
              }
              pw.print(selections[i] + "/" + selectionValues[i] + " ");
            }
            pw.println();
          }
          textArea.append(sw.toString());
        }
      };
      jlist.addListSelectionListener(listSelectionListener);

      frame.setSize(350, 200);
      frame.setVisible(true);
    }
  };
  EventQueue.invokeLater(runner);
  }
}
```

Note If you know that a JList is in single-selection mode, you can get the currently selected item with either the selectedIndex or selectedValue property.

Figure 13-9 shows the appearance of the running program.

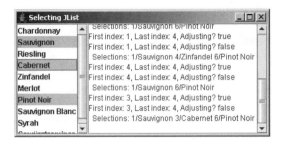

Figure 13-9. *Listening for JList selections*

The example in Listing 13-8 prints out only the currently selected items when it is not doing a rapid update (when isAdjusting reports false). Otherwise, the program merely reports the starting and ending range of selection changes, as well as the adjusting status. The example examines the selectedIndices and selectedValues properties of JList to get an ordered list of selected items. The selectedIndices and selectedValues arrays are ordered in the same way, so a particular element of the data model will show up in the same position in both lists.

There's no special selection event for double-clicking an item in the list. If you're interested in double-click events, you need to fall back to the AWT MouseEvent/MouseListener pair. Adding the following code to the program in Listing 13-8 will add appropriate text to the JTextArea for double-click events. The key method here is the public int locationToIndex(Point location) method of JList, which attempts to map screen coordinates to list elements.

```
import java.awt.event.*;
...
    MouseListener mouseListener = new MouseAdapter() {
      public void mouseClicked(MouseEvent mouseEvent) {
        JList theList = (JList)mouseEvent.getSource();
        if (mouseEvent.getClickCount() == 2) {
          int index = theList.locationToIndex(mouseEvent.getPoint());
          if (index >= 0) {
            Object o = theList.getModel().getElementAt(index);
            textArea.append("Double-clicked on: " + o.toString());
            textArea.append(System.getProperty("line.separator"));
          }
        }
      }
    };
    jlist.addMouseListener(mouseListener);
```

■**Note** The JList class also provides the public Point indexToLocation(int index) method, which produces the reverse behavior, returning a Point as the origin of the provided index.

Manually Selecting JList Events

In addition to detecting when a user selects items in a list, you can also programmatically select or deselect items. If any ListSelectionListener objects are attached to the JList, they will also be notified when the set of selected items is programmatically altered. The following methods are available:

- For a single item, public void setSelectedValue(Object element, boolean shouldScroll) selects the first item that matches the element. If the element wasn't previously selected, everything that was selected will be deselected first.

- For a range of items, public void setSelectedInterval(int index0, int index1) selects an inclusive range.

- For adding a range of selected items to the already selected set, use public void addSelectedInterval(int index0, int index1).

- You can clear all the selected items with the public void clearSelection() method.

- You can clear a range of selected items with the public void removeSelectedInterval (int index0, int index1) method.

Displaying Multiple Columns

Typically, whenever you work with a JList, you present its choices within a single column. While this is the usual manner of usage, the Swing JList control offers support for displaying its choices within multiple columns. Through the help of the setLayoutOrientation() method, you can set each JList orientation to lay out cells in columns horizontally or vertically. JList.VERTICAL is the default setting where everything appears in one column.

To lay out cells horizontally, before going to next row, use the value JList.HORIZONTAL_WRAP. For example, a list with nine elements would be displayed as shown here:

0	1	2
3	4	5
6	7	8

To lay out cells vertically, before going to next column, use the value JList.VERTICAL_WRAP. For example, a list with nine elements would be displayed as shown here:

0	3	6
1	4	7
2	5	8

Set the visibleRowCount property of JList to control the number of rows. Otherwise, the list width determines the row count for HORIZONTAL_WRAP and the list height for VERTICAL_WRAP.

Figure 13-10 shows a sample `JList` with horizontal wrap, presented as a 3×3 grid. Notice that it still supports multiple-selection mode.

Figure 13-10. *A JList with horizontal wrap*

Customizing a JList Look and Feel

Each installable Swing look and feel provides a different `JList` appearance and set of default `UIResource` value settings for the component. Figure 13-11 shows the appearance of the `JList` component for the preinstalled set of look and feel types: Motif, Windows, and Ocean.

Motif   Windows   Ocean

Figure 13-11. *JList under different look and feel types*

The available set of `UIResource`-related properties for a `JList` is shown in Table 13-9. For the `JList` component, there are 17 different properties.

Table 13-9. *JList UIResource Elements*

Property String	Object Type
List.actionMap	ActionMap
List.background	Color
List.border	Border
List.cellHeight	Integer
List.cellRenderer	ListCellRenderer
List.focusCellHighlightBorder	Border
List.focusInputMap	InputMap
List.focusInputMap.RightToLeft	InputMap
List.font	Font
List.foreground	Color

Table 13-9. *JList UIResource Elements (Continued)*

Property String	Object Type
List.lockToPositionOnScroll	Boolean
List.rendererUseListColors	Boolean
List.rendererUseUIBorder	Boolean
List.selectionBackground	Color
List.selectionForeground	Color
List.timeFactor	Long
ListUI	String

As with most of the UIResource properties, the names of most of the properties are self-explanatory. One property, List.timeFactor, requires a bit of extra descriptive text. By default, the JList comes with behavior for keyboard selection. As you type, the JList will find the entry that matches what you've typed so far. This is done with the help of the public int getNextMatch(String prefix, int startIndex, Position.Bias bias) method. The "so far" bit is controlled by the List.timeFactor setting. As long as the delay between keystrokes doesn't exceed the number of milliseconds specified by List.timeFactor (default of 1000), the new key pressed is added to the prior keys. Once the factor is exceeded, the search string is reset.

Creating a Dual List Box

The example presented in this section creates a new Swing component called a DualListBox. The primary purpose of a dual list box is to create two lists of choices: one to pick from and one that makes up your result set. This works great when the initial choice list is sizable. Trying to multi-select from a JList that contains many selections across multiple screens can be annoying, especially if you happen to deselect what you've already selected because you didn't have the Shift or Ctrl key held down. With a dual list box, the user selects items in the first list and moves them into the second. The user can easily scroll through the two lists without fear of accidentally deselecting anything. Figure 13-12 shows how the DualListBox might look in use.

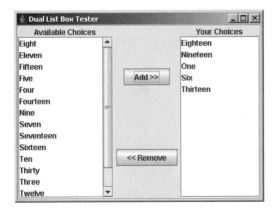

Figure 13-12. *The DualListBox in action*

To use this custom component, create it by calling the constructor, DualListBox sdual = new DualListBox(), and then fill it with data by using either setSourceElements() or addSourceElements(); each takes either a ListModel or an array argument. The add version supplements the existing choices, whereas the set version clears out the choices first. When it's time to ask the component what the user selected, you can ask for an Iterator of the chosen elements with destinationIterator(). Some properties you may want to change include the following:

- The source choices' title (Available Choices in the example)

- The destination choices' title (Your Choices in the example)

- The source or destination list cell renderer

- The source or destination visible row count

- The source or destination foreground color or background color

The complete source code for this new DualListBox component follows. Listing 13-9 contains the first class SortedListModel, which provides a sorted ListModel. Internally, this takes advantage of a TreeSet.

Listing 13-9. *Sorted List Model*

```
import javax.swing.*;
import java.util.*;

public class SortedListModel extends AbstractListModel {

  SortedSet<Object> model;

  public SortedListModel() {
    model = new TreeSet<Object>();
  }

  public int getSize() {
    return model.size();
  }

  public Object getElementAt(int index) {
    return model.toArray()[index];
  }

  public void add(Object element) {
    if (model.add(element)) {
      fireContentsChanged(this, 0, getSize());
    }
  }
```

```
  public void addAll(Object elements[]) {
    Collection<Object> c = Arrays.asList(elements);
    model.addAll(c);
    fireContentsChanged(this, 0, getSize());
  }

  public void clear() {
    model.clear();
    fireContentsChanged(this, 0, getSize());
  }

  public boolean contains(Object element) {
    return model.contains(element);
  }

  public Object firstElement() {
    return model.first();
  }

  public Iterator iterator() {
    return model.iterator();
  }

  public Object lastElement() {
    return model.last();
  }

  public boolean removeElement(Object element) {
    boolean removed = model.remove(element);
    if (removed) {
      fireContentsChanged(this, 0, getSize());
    }
    return removed;
  }
}
```

Listing 13-10 shows the DualListBox source. The included main() method demonstrates the component.

Listing 13-10. *Dual List Box Sample*

```
import java.awt.*;
import java.awt.event.*;
import javax.swing.*;
import java.util.Iterator;

public class DualListBox extends JPanel {
```

```java
  private static final Insets EMPTY_INSETS = new Insets(0,0,0,0);
  private static final String ADD_BUTTON_LABEL = "Add >>";
  private static final String REMOVE_BUTTON_LABEL = "<< Remove";
  private static final String DEFAULT_SOURCE_CHOICE_LABEL =
    "Available Choices";
  private static final String DEFAULT_DEST_CHOICE_LABEL =
    "Your Choices";
  private JLabel sourceLabel;
  private JList sourceList;
  private SortedListModel sourceListModel;
  private JList destList;
  private SortedListModel destListModel;
  private JLabel destLabel;
  private JButton addButton;
  private JButton removeButton;

  public DualListBox() {
    initScreen();
  }
  public String getSourceChoicesTitle() {
    return sourceLabel.getText();
  }
  public void setSourceChoicesTitle(String newValue) {
    sourceLabel.setText(newValue);
  }
  public String getDestinationChoicesTitle() {
    return destLabel.getText();
  }
  public void setDestinationChoicesTitle(String newValue) {
    destLabel.setText(newValue);
  }
  public void clearSourceListModel() {
    sourceListModel.clear();
  }
  public void clearDestinationListModel() {
    destListModel.clear();
  }
  public void addSourceElements(ListModel newValue) {
    fillListModel(sourceListModel, newValue);
  }
  public void setSourceElements(ListModel newValue) {
    clearSourceListModel();
    addSourceElements(newValue);
  }
  public void addDestinationElements(ListModel newValue) {
    fillListModel(destListModel, newValue);
  }
```

```java
private void fillListModel(SortedListModel model, ListModel newValues) {
  int size = newValues.getSize();
  for (int i=0; i<size; i++) {
    model.add(newValues.getElementAt(i));
  }
}
public void addSourceElements(Object newValue[]) {
  fillListModel(sourceListModel, newValue);
}
public void setSourceElements(Object newValue[]) {
  clearSourceListModel();
  addSourceElements(newValue);
}
public void addDestinationElements(Object newValue[]) {
  fillListModel(destListModel, newValue);
}
private void fillListModel(SortedListModel model, Object newValues[]) {
  model.addAll(newValues);
}
public Iterator sourceIterator() {
  return sourceListModel.iterator();
}
public Iterator destinationIterator() {
  return destListModel.iterator();
}
public void setSourceCellRenderer(ListCellRenderer newValue) {
  sourceList.setCellRenderer(newValue);
}
public ListCellRenderer getSourceCellRenderer() {
  return sourceList.getCellRenderer();
}
public void setDestinationCellRenderer(ListCellRenderer newValue) {
  destList.setCellRenderer(newValue);
}
public ListCellRenderer getDestinationCellRenderer() {
  return destList.getCellRenderer();
}
public void setVisibleRowCount(int newValue) {
  sourceList.setVisibleRowCount(newValue);
  destList.setVisibleRowCount(newValue);
}
public int getVisibleRowCount() {
  return sourceList.getVisibleRowCount();
}
```

```java
  public void setSelectionBackground(Color newValue) {
    sourceList.setSelectionBackground(newValue);
    destList.setSelectionBackground(newValue);
  }
  public Color getSelectionBackground() {
    return sourceList.getSelectionBackground();
  }
  public void setSelectionForeground(Color newValue) {
    sourceList.setSelectionForeground(newValue);
    destList.setSelectionForeground(newValue);
  }
  public Color getSelectionForeground() {
    return sourceList.getSelectionForeground();
  }
  private void clearSourceSelected() {
    Object selected[] = sourceList.getSelectedValues();
    for (int i=selected.length-1; i >= 0; --i) {
      sourceListModel.removeElement(selected[i]);
    }
    sourceList.getSelectionModel().clearSelection();
  }
  private void clearDestinationSelected() {
    Object selected[] = destList.getSelectedValues();
    for (int i=selected.length-1; i >= 0; --i) {
      destListModel.removeElement(selected[i]);
    }
    destList.getSelectionModel().clearSelection();
  }
  private void initScreen() {
    setBorder(BorderFactory.createEtchedBorder());
    setLayout(new GridBagLayout());
    sourceLabel = new JLabel(DEFAULT_SOURCE_CHOICE_LABEL);
    sourceListModel = new SortedListModel();
    sourceList = new JList(sourceListModel);
    add(sourceLabel,
      new GridBagConstraints(0, 0, 1, 1, 0, 0, GridBagConstraints.CENTER,
        GridBagConstraints.NONE, EMPTY_INSETS, 0, 0));
    add(new JScrollPane(sourceList),
      new GridBagConstraints(0, 1, 1, 5, .5, 1, GridBagConstraints.CENTER,
        GridBagConstraints.BOTH, EMPTY_INSETS, 0, 0));

    addButton = new JButton(ADD_BUTTON_LABEL);
    add(addButton,
      new GridBagConstraints(1, 2, 1, 2, 0, .25, GridBagConstraints.CENTER,
        GridBagConstraints.NONE, EMPTY_INSETS, 0, 0));
    addButton.addActionListener(new AddListener());
    removeButton = new JButton(REMOVE_BUTTON_LABEL);
```

```java
    add(removeButton,
      new GridBagConstraints(1, 4, 1, 2, 0, .25, GridBagConstraints.CENTER,
        GridBagConstraints.NONE, new Insets(0,5,0,5), 0, 0));
    removeButton.addActionListener(new RemoveListener());

    destLabel = new JLabel(DEFAULT_DEST_CHOICE_LABEL);
    destListModel = new SortedListModel();
    destList = new JList(destListModel);
    add(destLabel,
      new GridBagConstraints(2, 0, 1, 1, 0, 0, GridBagConstraints.CENTER,
        GridBagConstraints.NONE, EMPTY_INSETS, 0, 0));
    add(new JScrollPane(destList),
      new GridBagConstraints(2, 1, 1, 5, .5, 1.0, GridBagConstraints.CENTER,
        GridBagConstraints.BOTH, EMPTY_INSETS, 0, 0));
  }

  private class AddListener implements ActionListener {
    public void actionPerformed(ActionEvent e) {
      Object selected[] = sourceList.getSelectedValues();
      addDestinationElements(selected);
      clearSourceSelected();
    }
  }
  private class RemoveListener implements ActionListener {
    public void actionPerformed(ActionEvent e) {
      Object selected[] = destList.getSelectedValues();
      addSourceElements(selected);
      clearDestinationSelected();
    }
  }

  public static void main(String args[]) {
    Runnable runner = new Runnable() {
      public void run() {
        JFrame frame = new JFrame("Dual List Box Tester");
        frame.setDefaultCloseOperation(JFrame.EXIT_ON_CLOSE);
        DualListBox dual = new DualListBox();
        dual.addSourceElements(
          new String[] {"One", "Two", "Three"});
        dual.addSourceElements(
          new String[] {"Four", "Five", "Six"});
        dual.addSourceElements(
          new String[] {"Seven", "Eight", "Nine"});
        dual.addSourceElements(
          new String[] {"Ten", "Eleven", "Twelve"});
        dual.addSourceElements(
          new String[] {"Thirteen", "Fourteen", "Fifteen"});
```

```
        dual.addSourceElements(
          new String[] {"Sixteen", "Seventeen", "Eighteen"});
        dual.addSourceElements(
          new String[] {"Nineteen", "Twenty", "Thirty"});
        frame.add(dual, BorderLayout.CENTER);
        frame.setSize(400, 300);
        frame.setVisible(true);
      }
    };
    EventQueue.invokeLater(runner);
  }
}
```

Adding Element-Level Tooltips to List Items

As described in Chapter 4, all Swing components support displaying tooltip text. By calling the setToolTipText() method of a component, you can display any single text string over that component. In the case of a JList component (or for that matter, any component that contains multiple items such as a JTree or JTable), this single tooltip text string may not be sufficient. You may wish to display a different tip over each item in a component.

Displaying item-level tips takes a little more work. To display different tooltip text over each item, you must create a subclass of JList. From within this subclass, you must manually register the component with the ToolTipManager. This is normally done for you when you call setToolTipText(). But, because you won't be calling this method, you must manually notify the manager, as follows:

```
ToolTipManager.sharedInstance().registerComponent(this);
```

After you notify the ToolTipManager, the manager will then notify the component whenever the mouse moves over the component. This allows you to override the public String getToolTipText(MouseEvent mouseEvent) method to provide the appropriate tip for the item under the mouse pointer. Using some kind of Hashtable, HashMap, or Properties list allows you to map the item the mouse is over to item-specific tooltip text.

```
public String getToolTipText(MouseEvent event) {
  Point p = event.getPoint();
  int location = locationToIndex(p);
  String key = (String)model.getElementAt(location);
  String tip = tipProps.getProperty(key);
  return tip;
}
```

Figure 13-13 shows how the PropertiesList example class demonstrates various tooltips based on whichever element the mouse pointer is resting over. The complete source for the example follows in Listing 13-11.

Figure 13-13. *A JList with different element-level tooltip text*

Listing 13-11. *Custom Tooltips for List Elements*

```java
import java.awt.*;
import java.awt.event.*;
import java.util.*;
import javax.swing.*;

public class PropertiesList extends JList {

  SortedListModel model;
  Properties tipProps;

  public PropertiesList(Properties props) {
    model = new SortedListModel();
    setModel(model);
    ToolTipManager.sharedInstance().registerComponent(this);

    tipProps = props;
    addProperties(props);
  }
  private void addProperties(Properties props) {
    // Load
    Enumeration names = props.propertyNames();
    while (names.hasMoreElements()) {
      model.add(names.nextElement());
    }
  }
}
```

```
    public String getToolTipText(MouseEvent event) {
      Point p = event.getPoint();
      int location = locationToIndex(p);
      String key = (String)model.getElementAt(location);
      String tip = tipProps.getProperty(key);
      return tip;
    }
    public static void main (String args[]) {
      Runnable runner = new Runnable() {
        public void run() {
          JFrame frame = new JFrame("Custom Tip Demo");
          frame.setDefaultCloseOperation(JFrame.EXIT_ON_CLOSE);
          Properties props = System.getProperties();
          PropertiesList list = new PropertiesList(props);
          JScrollPane scrollPane = new JScrollPane(list);
          frame.add(scrollPane);
          frame.setSize(300, 300);
          frame.setVisible(true);
        }
      };
      EventQueue.invokeLater(runner);
    }
  }
}
```

JComboBox Class

The JComboBox component of the Swing component set is a multiple-part component that allows a user to choose from a predefined set of choices with the help of a pull-down list. In its basic configuration, a JComboBox acts like a JLabel to display the current user selection. Embedded within the JLabel is a pop-up menu containing choices within a JList control. When the desired choice isn't available, the JComboBox can use a JTextField to enter a new choice. The JList part is automatically embedded within a JScrollPane when desired; you don't need to manually create the JList or place it in the JScrollPane. In addition, the text field for editing is disabled by default, permitting a user to select from the set of predefined choices only. Figure 13-14 illustrates two JComboBox components: one that is not editable showing its list of choices, and another that is editable and not showing its choices.

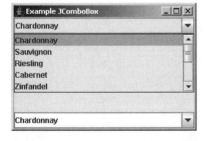

Figure 13-14. *Sample JComboBox components*

Four essential elements define the JComboBox component and its implementation:

- A data model for holding the JComboBox data, as defined by the ListModel interface

- A cell renderer for drawing the elements of the JComboBox, as described by the ListCellRenderer interface

- An editor for entering choices not part of the predefined data model, as defined by the ComboBoxEditor interface

- A keystroke manager for handling keyboard input to select elements of the JComboBox, as described by the KeySelectionManager interface

Many of the JComboBox capabilities are shared with the JList component. This isn't accidental; the two components are fairly similar. Let's now look at the JComboBox in more detail.

Creating JComboBox Components

Like the JList component, the JComboBox component has four constructors, allowing you to create one based on your initial data structure. *Unlike* the JList component, the default model used by the array and Vector constructor permits adding and removing data elements.

```
public JComboBox()
JComboBox comboBox = new JComboBox();
```

```
public JComboBox(Object listData[])
String labels[] = { "Chardonnay", "Sauvignon", "Riesling", "Cabernet", "Zinfandel",
  "Merlot", "Pinot Noir", "Sauvignon Blanc", "Syrah", "Gewürztraminer"};
JComboBox comboBox = new JComboBox(labels);
```

```
public JComboBox(Vector listData)
Vector vector = aBufferedImage.getSources();
JComboBox comboBox = new JComboBox(vector);
```

```
public JComboBox(ComboBoxModel model)
ResultSet results = aJDBCStatement.executeQuery("SELECT columnName FROM tableName");
DefaultComboBoxModel model = new DefaultComboBoxModel();
while (result.next())
  model.addElement(results.getString(1));
JComboBox comboBox = new JComboBox(model);
```

JComboBox Properties

After you create a JComboBox component, you can modify each of its many properties. Table 13-10 shows the 22 properties of JComboBox.

Table 13-10. *JComboBox Properties*

Property Name	Data Type	Access
accessibleContext	AccessibleContext	Read-only
action	Action	Read-write bound
actionCommand	String	Read-write
actionListeners	ActionListener[ ]	Read-only
editable	boolean	Read-write bound
editor	ComboBoxEditor	Read-write bound
enabled	boolean	Write-only bound
itemCount	int	Read-only
itemListeners	ItemListener[ ]	Read-only
keySelectionManager	JComboBox.KeySelectionManager	Read-write
lightWeightPopupEnabled	boolean	Read-write
maximumRowCount	int	Read-write bound
model	ComboBoxModel	Read-write bound
popupMenuListeners	PopupMenuListener[ ]	Read-only
popupVisible	boolean	Read-write
prototypeDisplayValue	Object	Read-write bound
renderer	ListCellRenderer	Read-write bound
selectedIndex	int	Read-write
selectedItem	Object	Read-write
selectedObjects	Object[ ]	Read-only
UI	ComboBoxUI	Read-write
UIClassID	String	Read-only

The significant properties of the JComboBox are concerned with the display of the pop-up list. You can control the maximum number of visible entries in the pop-up list by setting the maximumRowCount property. The lightWeightPopupEnabled property setting helps determine the type of window to use when displaying the pop-up menu of choices. If the component fits completely within the top-level window of the program, the component will be lightweight. If it doesn't fit, it will be heavyweight. If you're mixing AWT and Swing components in a program, you can force the pop-up menu of choices to be heavyweight by setting the lightWeightPopupEnabled property to true. This will force the pop-up to appear above other components. The remaining property related to the pop-up list is the popupVisible property, which allows you to programmatically display the pop-up list.

■**Note** Besides setting the `popupVisible` property, you can use the `public void hidePopup()` and `public void showPopup()` methods to toggle the pop-up list's visibility status.

Rendering JComboBox Elements

The rendering of elements within a `JComboBox` is done with a `ListCellRenderer`. This is the same renderer that is used for a `JList` component. Once you've created a renderer for either one of these two components, you can use that renderer for the other component. To reuse the `ComplexCellRenderer` from earlier in the chapter (Listing 13-6), you could add the following lines to the `ComplexRenderingSample` example (Listing 13-7) to have the two components share the same renderer.

```
JComboBox comboBox = new JComboBox(elements);
comboBox.setRenderer(renderer);
frame.add(comboBox, BorderLayout.NORTH);
```

The result of adding these lines is shown in Figure 13-15.

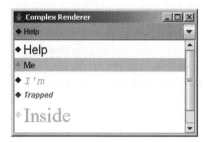

Figure 13-15. *A JComboBox with a custom renderer*

Not all renderers will work as expected with both the `JComboBox` and `JList` components. For instance, the `FocusedTitleListCellRenderer` demonstrated earlier in Figure 13-6 wouldn't show the "Focused" title border in a `JComboBox` because the choices never had the input focus. In addition, different components may have different default colors (a different unselected background color, in this case). It may be necessary to ask what color the component normally would be rendered in, and then act accordingly.

Selecting JComboBox Elements

The `JComboBox` component supports at least three different events related to selection. You can listen for keyboard input to support key selection with the help of the `JComboBox.KeySelectionManager` class. You can also listen with an `ActionListener` or an `ItemListener` to find out when the selected item of the `JComboBox` changes.

If you want to programmatically select an element, use `public void setSelectedItem(Object element)` or `public void setSelectedIndex(int index)`.

■**Tip** To programmatically deselect the current choice of a `JComboBox`, call `setSelectedIndex()` with an argument of –1.

Listening to Keyboard Events with a KeySelectionManager

The `JComboBox` has a public inner interface that's fairly important. `KeySelectionManager`, and its default implementation, manages selection from the keyboard of items within the `JComboBox`. The default manager locates the next element that corresponds to the pressed key. It has memory, so if you have entries that start with similar prefixes, users can continue typing until there is enough of a match to be unique. If you don't like this behavior, you can either turn it off or create a new key selection manager.

■**Note** The `KeySelectionManager` works only in combo boxes that are not editable.

If you want to turn off the key-selection capabilities, you can't do so by simply setting the `keySelectionManager` property to `null`. Instead, you must create an implementation of the interface with an appropriate method. The single method of the interface is `public int selectionForKey(char aKey, ComboBoxModel aModel)`. In the event the pressed key doesn't match any elements, the routine needs to return –1. Otherwise, it should return the position of the matched element. So, to ignore keyboard input, the routine should always return –1, as shown here:

```
JComboBox.KeySelectionManager manager =
  new JComboBox.KeySelectionManager() {
    public int selectionForKey(char aKey, ComboBoxModel aModel) {
      return -1;
    }
  };
aJcombo.setKeySelectionManager(manager);
```

Listening to JComboBox Events with an ActionListener

The primary means of listening for selection events is through an `ActionListener`, possibly set with `setAction(Action)`. It will tell you when an element has been selected within a `JComboBox`. Unfortunately, the listener doesn't know which element is selected.

■**Note** Setting the `ActionListener` through `setAction(Action)` also configures the tooltip text and the enabled state of the `JComboBox` based on the `Action`.

Because the ActionListener can't identify the selected element, it must ask the JComboBox that served as the source of the event. To determine the selected element from the JComboBox, use either getSelectedItem() or getSelectedIndex(). If an index of –1 is returned, then the currently selected item isn't part of the model. This seemingly impossible situation happens when the JComboBox is editable and the user has entered a value that isn't part of the original model.

■**Note** The text string comboBoxChanged is the action command for the ActionEvent sent to the ActionListener when an item within a JComboBox changes.

Listening to JComboBox Events with an ItemListener

If you use an ItemListener to find out when the selected item within a JComboBox changes, you'll also learn which item was deselected.

To demonstrate both the ActionListener and the ItemListener, the program shown in Listing 13-12 attaches both of them to the same JComboBox. The ActionListener prints its "action command," as well as the currently selected item. The ItemListener prints the affected item and the state change for it, as well as the currently selected item.

Listing 13-12. *JComboBox Selection Sample*

```
import javax.swing.*;
import javax.swing.event.*;
import java.awt.*;
import java.awt.event.*;
import java.io.*;

public class SelectingComboSample {
  static private String selectedString(ItemSelectable is) {
    Object selected[] = is.getSelectedObjects();
    return ((selected.length == 0) ? "null" : (String)selected[0]);
  }

  public static void main(String args[]) {
    Runnable runner = new Runnable() {
      public void run() {
        String labels[] = {"Chardonnay", "Sauvignon", "Riesling", "Cabernet",
          "Zinfandel", "Merlot", "Pinot Noir", "Sauvignon Blanc", "Syrah",
          "Gewürztraminer"};
        JFrame frame = new JFrame("Selecting JComboBox");
        frame.setDefaultCloseOperation(JFrame.EXIT_ON_CLOSE);

        JComboBox comboBox = new JComboBox(labels);
        frame.add(comboBox, BorderLayout.SOUTH);
```

```java
        final JTextArea textArea = new JTextArea();
        textArea.setEditable(false);
        JScrollPane sp = new JScrollPane(textArea);
        frame.add(sp, BorderLayout.CENTER);

        ItemListener itemListener = new ItemListener() {
          public void itemStateChanged(ItemEvent itemEvent) {
            StringWriter sw = new StringWriter();
            PrintWriter pw = new PrintWriter(sw);
            int state = itemEvent.getStateChange();
            String stateString =
              ((state == ItemEvent.SELECTED) ? "Selected" : "Deselected");
            pw.print("Item: " + itemEvent.getItem());
            pw.print(", State: " + stateString);
            ItemSelectable is = itemEvent.getItemSelectable();
            pw.print(", Selected: " + selectedString(is));
            pw.println();
            textArea.append(sw.toString());
          }
        };
        comboBox.addItemListener(itemListener);

        ActionListener actionListener = new ActionListener() {
          public void actionPerformed(ActionEvent actionEvent) {
            StringWriter sw = new StringWriter();
            PrintWriter pw = new PrintWriter(sw);
            pw.print("Command: " + actionEvent.getActionCommand());
            ItemSelectable is = (ItemSelectable)actionEvent.getSource();
            pw.print(", Selected: " + selectedString(is));
            pw.println();
            textArea.append(sw.toString());
          }
        };
        comboBox.addActionListener(actionListener);

        frame.setSize(400, 200);
        frame.setVisible(true);
      }
    };
    EventQueue.invokeLater(runner);
  }
}
```

Figure 13-16 shows the results after the program has been running for some time.

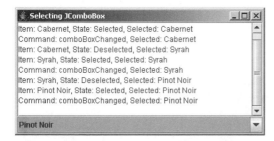

Figure 13-16. *Listening for JComboBox selections*

Listening to JComboBox Events with a ListDataListener

You can attach a ListDataListener to the data model of the JComboBox. This listener would then be notified when the selected element of the model changes. Unfortunately, the listener would also be notified of other data model changes. In other words, using a ListDataListener to find out when an element of a JComboBox is selected is *not* a recommended option.

Note Mouse movement and cursor movement events within a JComboBox don't change the selected entry; mouse release events do change the selected entry. Any registered listeners would be notified when a selected mouse button is released over an element within the JComboBox pop-up list.

Editing JComboBox Elements

You may want to use a combo box like a text field in which you list the most likely text input from the user, but also allow the user to enter something else. By enabling the editable property of the JComboBox, you've added this capability. To demonstrate, Figure 13-17 shows an editable JComboBox. The window also contains a text area that reports the current selected item and index. Even if you manually enter one of the choices within the JComboBox, getSelectedIndex() will report the proper position. Remember that if you enter a value that's not present, getSelectedIndex() returns −1.

Figure 13-17. *Using an editable JComboBox*

The source for the example in Figure 13-17 is shown in Listing 13-13.

Listing 13-13. *Editable JComboBox Sample*

```java
import java.awt.*;
import javax.swing.*;
import java.awt.event.*;
public class EditComboBox {
  public static void main(String args[]) {
    Runnable runner = new Runnable() {
      public void run() {
        String labels[] = {"Chardonnay", "Sauvignon", "Riesling", "Cabernet",
          "Zinfandel", "Merlot", "Pinot Noir", "Sauvignon Blanc", "Syrah",
          "Gewürztraminer"};
        JFrame frame = new JFrame("Editable JComboBox");
        frame.setDefaultCloseOperation(JFrame.EXIT_ON_CLOSE);

        final JComboBox comboBox = new JComboBox(labels);
        comboBox.setMaximumRowCount(5);
        comboBox.setEditable(true);
        frame.add(comboBox, BorderLayout.NORTH);

        final JTextArea textArea = new JTextArea();
        JScrollPane scrollPane = new JScrollPane(textArea);
        frame.add(scrollPane, BorderLayout.CENTER);

        ActionListener actionListener = new ActionListener() {
          public void actionPerformed(ActionEvent actionEvent) {
            textArea.append("Selected: " + comboBox.getSelectedItem());
            textArea.append(", Position: " + comboBox.getSelectedIndex());
            textArea.append(System.getProperty("line.separator"));
          }
        };
        comboBox.addActionListener(actionListener);

        frame.setSize(300, 200);
        frame.setVisible(true);
      }
    };
    EventQueue.invokeLater(runner);
  }
}
```

By default, the input field provided for editing is a JTextField. The default JTextField serves as a good editor if your data model consists of text strings. However, once your model contains a different type of object (for example, colors), you need to provide a different editor. By default, once you type in the text field (editing the results of toString() for your element), the object is treated as a String. Technically, a different editor isn't always necessary. If you can parse the contents of the text field as a string to the proper data type, then do that. But, if you want to restrict the input in any manner (for example, allow only numeric input) or provide a better input mechanism, you must provide your own editor. The interface that defines the necessary behavior is called ComboBoxEditor and its definition is shown here.

```
public interface ComboBoxEditor {
  // Properties
  public Component getEditorComponent();
  public Object getItem();
  public void setItem(Object anObject);
  // Listeners
  public void addActionListener(ActionListener l);
  public void removeActionListener(ActionListener l);
  // Other methods
  public void selectAll();
}
```

■**Note** The default editor is the BasicComboBoxEditor implementation in the javax.swing.plaf.basic package.

The add/remove listener methods are necessary for notifying any listeners when the ComboBoxEditor value has changed. It's not necessary for you to add a listener, and normally you won't do that. Nevertheless, the methods are part of the interface, so they'll need to be implemented if you want to provide your own editor.

The getEditorComponent() method returns the Component object used for the editor. You can use either an AWT or a Swing component for the editor (for example, a JColorChooser for color selection). The selectAll() method is called when the editor is first shown. It tells the editor to select everything within it. Selecting everything allows a user to merely type over the current input for the default JTextField case. Some editors may not require use of this method.

The item property methods demand the most work when you're providing a custom editor. You'll need to supply a method to map the specific pieces of the Object subclass to the components in order to present the data to be edited. You then need to get the data from the editor so that the data can be stored back in an instance of the original object.

To demonstrate, the source code in Listing 13-14 is a ComboBoxEditor for the Color class. A custom editor is necessary because there's no automatic way to parse the results of editing the default string shown for a Color. This editor will use a JColorChooser for the user to pick a new color value. The getItem() method needs to return only the current value, a Color. The setItem() method needs to convert the object passed to a Color object; the argument to setItem() is an Object. The setItem() method could be made to accept only Color arguments. However, for this example, any string that's decodable with the Color.decode() method is also supported.

Listing 13-14. *A Color Combo Box Editor*

```java
import java.awt.*;
import javax.swing.*;
import javax.swing.event.*;
import java.awt.event.*;
public class ColorComboBoxEditor implements ComboBoxEditor {
  final protected JButton editor;
  protected EventListenerList listenerList = new EventListenerList();
  public ColorComboBoxEditor(Color initialColor) {
    editor = new JButton("");
    editor.setBackground(initialColor);
    ActionListener actionListener = new ActionListener() {
      public void actionPerformed(ActionEvent e) {
        Color currentBackground = editor.getBackground();
        Color color = JColorChooser.showDialog(
          editor, "Color Chooser", currentBackground);
        if ((color != null) && (currentBackground != color)) {
          editor.setBackground(color);
          fireActionEvent(color);
        }
      }
    };
    editor.addActionListener(actionListener);
  }
  public void addActionListener(ActionListener l) {
    listenerList.add(ActionListener.class, l);
  }
  public Component getEditorComponent() {
    return editor;
  }
  public Object getItem() {
    return editor.getBackground();
  }
  public void removeActionListener(ActionListener l) {
    listenerList.remove(ActionListener.class, l);
  }
  public void selectAll() {
    // Ignore
  }
  public void setItem(Object newValue) {
    if (newValue instanceof Color) {
      Color color = (Color)newValue;
      editor.setBackground(color);
    } else {
```

```
      // Try to decode
      try {
        Color color = Color.decode(newValue.toString());
        editor.setBackground(color);
      } catch (NumberFormatException e) {
        // Ignore - value unchanged
      }
    }
  }
  protected void fireActionEvent(Color color) {
    Object listeners[] = listenerList.getListenerList();
    for (int i = listeners.length-2; i>=0; i-=2) {
      if (listeners[i] == ActionListener.class) {
        ActionEvent actionEvent =
          new ActionEvent(editor, ActionEvent.ACTION_PERFORMED, color.toString());
        ((ActionListener)listeners[i+1]).actionPerformed(actionEvent);
      }
    }
  }
}
```

To use the new editor, you need to associate it with a JComboBox. After you change the EditComboBox example shown earlier (Listing 13-13) to make the data model consist of an array of Color objects, you can then install the editor by adding the following:

```
Color color = (Color)comboBox.getSelectedItem();
ComboBoxEditor editor = new ColorComboBoxEditor(color);
comboBox.setEditor(editor);
```

A complete test program follows in Listing 13-15. It's different from the EditComboBox because below the JComboBox is a JLabel that stays in sync with the currently selected color of the JComboBox. There's also a custom cell renderer that sets the background color to the value of the cell.

Listing 13-15. *Custom JComboBox Editor Sample*

```
import java.awt.*;
import javax.swing.*;
import java.awt.event.*;
public class ColorComboBox {
  static class ColorCellRenderer implements ListCellRenderer {
    protected DefaultListCellRenderer defaultRenderer =
      new DefaultListCellRenderer();
    // Width doesn't matter as the combo box will size
    private final static Dimension preferredSize = new Dimension(0, 20);
    public Component getListCellRendererComponent(JList list, Object value,
        int index, boolean isSelected, boolean cellHasFocus) {
      JLabel renderer = (JLabel)defaultRenderer.getListCellRendererComponent(
        list, value, index, isSelected, cellHasFocus);
```

```
      if (value instanceof Color) {
        renderer.setBackground((Color)value);
      }
      renderer.setPreferredSize(preferredSize);
      return renderer;
    }
  }
  public static void main(String args[]) {
    Runnable runner = new Runnable() {
      public void run() {
        Color colors[] = {Color.BLACK, Color.BLUE, Color.CYAN, Color.DARK_GRAY,
          Color.GRAY, Color.GREEN, Color.LIGHT_GRAY, Color.MAGENTA,
          Color.ORANGE, Color.PINK, Color.RED, Color.WHITE, Color.YELLOW};
        JFrame frame = new JFrame("Color JComboBox");
        frame.setDefaultCloseOperation(JFrame.EXIT_ON_CLOSE);

        final JComboBox comboBox = new JComboBox(colors);
        comboBox.setMaximumRowCount(5);
        comboBox.setEditable(true);
        comboBox.setRenderer(new ColorCellRenderer());
        Color color = (Color)comboBox.getSelectedItem();
        ComboBoxEditor editor = new ColorComboBoxEditor(color);
        comboBox.setEditor(editor);
        frame.add(comboBox, BorderLayout.NORTH);

        final JLabel label = new JLabel();
        label.setOpaque(true);
        label.setBackground((Color)comboBox.getSelectedItem());
        frame.add(label, BorderLayout.CENTER);

        ActionListener actionListener = new ActionListener() {
          public void actionPerformed(ActionEvent actionEvent) {
            Color selectedColor = (Color)comboBox.getSelectedItem();
            label.setBackground(selectedColor);
          }
        };
        comboBox.addActionListener(actionListener);

        frame.setSize(300, 200);
        frame.setVisible(true);
      }
    };
    EventQueue.invokeLater(runner);
  }
}
```

Figure 13-18 shows the screen and a visible editor.

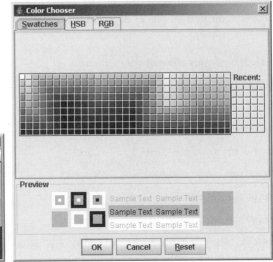

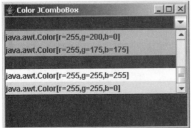

Figure 13-18. *Using a custom ComboBoxEditor*

Customizing a JComboBox Look and Feel

Each installable Swing look and feel provides a different JComboBox appearance and set of default UIResource value settings for the component. Figure 13-19 shows the appearance of the JComboBox component for the preinstalled set of look and feel types: Motif, Windows, and Ocean.

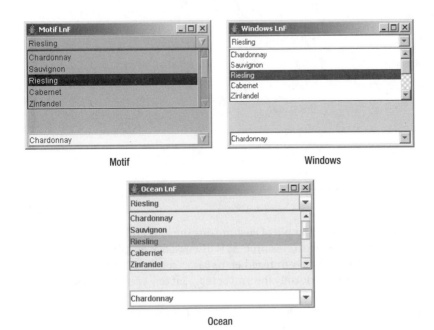

Figure 13-19. *JComboBox under different look and feel types*

The available set of UIResource-related properties for a JComboBox is shown in Table 13-11. The JComboBox component has 21 different properties.

Table 13-11. *JComboBox UIResource Elements*

Property String	Object Type
ComboBox.actionMap	ActionMap
ComboBox.ancestorInputMap	InputMap
ComboBox.background	Color
ComboBox.border	Border
ComboBox.buttonBackground	Color
ComboBox.buttonDarkShadow	Color
ComboBox.buttonHighlight	Color
ComboBox.buttonShadow	Color
ComboBox.control	Color
ComboBox.controlForeground	Color
ComboBox.disabledBackground	Color
ComboBox.disabledForeground	Color
ComboBox.font	Font
ComboBox.foreground	Color
ComboBox.rendererUseListColors	Boolean
ComboBox.selectionBackground	Color
ComboBox.selectionForeground	Color
ComboBox.showPopupOnNavigation	Boolean
ComboBox.timeFactor	Long
ComboBox.togglePopupText	String
ComboBoxUI	String

Changing the pop-up icon is one example of customizing the look and feel. To do this, you'll need to install a new user interface. (This process is discussed at length in Chapter 20.) Basically, you inherit the default functionality from either the BasicComboBoxUI or MetalComboBoxUI user interface delegate, and then override only the protected JButton createArrowButton() method.

Figure 13-20 shows the results of this change to the JComboBox user interface.

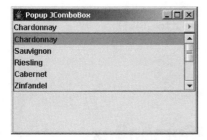

Figure 13-20. *Altering the JComboBox pop-up button*

The source for the JComboBox example shown in Figure 13-20 follows in Listing 13-16.

Listing 13-16. *Custom JComboBox Pop-up Button*

```
import java.awt.*;
import javax.swing.*;
import javax.swing.plaf.*;
import javax.swing.plaf.basic.*;
public class PopupComboSample {
  public static void main(String args[]) {
    Runnable runner = new Runnable() {
      public void run() {
        String labels[] = {"Chardonnay", "Sauvignon", "Riesling", "Cabernet",
          "Zinfandel", "Merlot", "Pinot Noir", "Sauvignon Blanc", "Syrah",
          "Gewürztraminer"};
        JFrame frame = new JFrame("Popup JComboBox");
        frame.setDefaultCloseOperation(JFrame.EXIT_ON_CLOSE);

        JComboBox comboBox = new JComboBox(labels);
        comboBox.setMaximumRowCount(5);
        comboBox.setUI((ComboBoxUI)MyComboBoxUI.createUI(comboBox));
        frame.add(comboBox, BorderLayout.NORTH);

        frame.setSize (300, 200);
        frame.setVisible (true);
      }
    };
    EventQueue.invokeLater(runner);
  }
  static class MyComboBoxUI extends BasicComboBoxUI {
    public static ComponentUI createUI(JComponent c) {
      return new MyComboBoxUI();
    }
```

```
    protected JButton createArrowButton() {
      JButton button = new BasicArrowButton(BasicArrowButton.EAST);
      return button;
    }
  }
}
```

Sharing the Data Model for a JComboBox and JList

You may have noticed several similarities between the parts that make up the JComboBox and JList. You can use the same data model and same renderer for both components. You've already seen how to share a renderer between components, in the "Rendering JComboBox Elements" section earlier in this chapter. The example presented in this section demonstrates how you could share the same data model across several components.

The example has two editable combo boxes and one JList, all sharing one data model. It also presents a button that you can click to dynamically add items to the data model. Because the data model will be associated with several components, you'll notice that each of them has additional options to choose from after selecting the button. Figure 13-21 shows what the screen might look like after adding several elements.

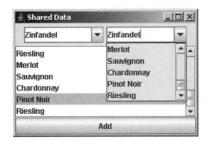

Figure 13-21. *Sharing a data model across components*

Listing 13-17 shows the source for the shared data model example.

Listing 13-17. *Shared Data Model*

```
import java.awt.*;
import java.awt.event.*;
import javax.swing.*;
public class SharedDataSample {
  public static void main(String args[]) {
    Runnable runner = new Runnable() {
      public void run() {
        final String labels[] = {"Chardonnay", "Sauvignon", "Riesling",
          "Cabernet", "Zinfandel", "Merlot", "Pinot Noir", "Sauvignon Blanc",
          "Syrah", "Gewürztraminer"};
```

```
        final DefaultComboBoxModel model = new DefaultComboBoxModel(labels);

        JFrame frame = new JFrame("Shared Data");
        frame.setDefaultCloseOperation(JFrame.EXIT_ON_CLOSE);

        JPanel panel = new JPanel();
        JComboBox comboBox1 = new JComboBox(model);
        comboBox1.setMaximumRowCount(5);
        comboBox1.setEditable(true);

        JComboBox comboBox2 = new JComboBox(model);
        comboBox2.setMaximumRowCount(5);
        comboBox2.setEditable(true);
        panel.add(comboBox1);
        panel.add(comboBox2);
        frame.add(panel, BorderLayout.NORTH);

        JList jlist = new JList(model);
        JScrollPane scrollPane = new JScrollPane(jlist);
        frame.add(scrollPane, BorderLayout.CENTER);

        JButton button = new JButton("Add");
        frame.add(button, BorderLayout.SOUTH);
        ActionListener actionListener = new ActionListener() {
          public void actionPerformed(ActionEvent actionEvent) {
            int index = (int)(Math.random()*labels.length);
            model.addElement(labels[index]);
          }
        };
        button.addActionListener(actionListener);

        frame.setSize(300, 200);
        frame.setVisible(true);
      }
    };
    EventQueue.invokeLater(runner);
  }
}
```

■**Note** When running the program shown in Listing 13-17, if you share a data model across multiple JComboBox components, there can't be a different selected element within each component. When an element is "selected" in one, it's selected in all. This seems to be a bug in the MVC design of the JComboBox. In addition, because a ListSelectionModel manages selection for the JList, changing the selected element of a JComboBox has no effect on the selected elements within a JList sharing the same model.

Summary

This chapter has demonstrated how to use Swing's `JList` and `JComboBox` components. You've seen how both components support their own data model, renderer, selection capabilities, and even a custom editor for the `JComboBox` component. Although all these capabilities are customizable, each of the components is readily usable with its default configuration.

In Chapter 14, you will start to explore the Swing text components, including `JTextField` and `JTextArea`.

■ ■ ■

CHAPTER 14

Spinner Model Controls

In the previous chapter, you learned how to work with the basic list controls: JList and JComboBox. In this chapter, you will move on to the JSpinner component, introduced with the 1.4 version of the JDK.

JSpinner Class

The JSpinner works like a cross between a JList or JComboBox component with a JFormattedTextField. In either the JList and JComboBox control, the user can select input from a predetermined set of values. The JSpinner also allows this type of selection. The other half of the component is the JFormattedTextField. How to display or enter the value isn't controlled by a list cell renderer, as in a JList; instead, you get a JFormattedTextField for entry and a couple of arrows on the side to navigate through the different values available for the text field. (The JFormattedTextField is covered in Chapters 15 and 16.)

Figure 14-1 shows what the spinner looks like for several different types of input. At the top of Figure 14-1 is a JSpinner with the days of the week in French provided to a SpinnerListModel. In the middle, you have a JSpinner for a date via the SpinnerDateModel class. On the bottom is the JSpinner usage with the SpinnerNumberModel. Each of these three work in its own mysterious way, as you'll learn later in this chapter.

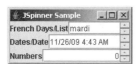

Figure 14-1. *JSpinner examples*

Many classes are involved when creating and manipulating JSpinner components, foremost the JSpinner class itself. The primary two sets of classes involved are the SpinnerModel interface, for containing the set of selectable items for the control, and, the JSpinner.DefaultEditor implementations, for catching all the selections. Thankfully, many of the other classes involved work behind the scenes, so, for example, once you provide the numeric range in a SpinnerNumberModel and associate the spinner with its model, your work is essentially done.

Creating JSpinner Components

The JSpinner class includes two constructors for initializing the component:

```
public JSpinner()
JSpinner spinner = new JSpinner();
```

```
public JSpinner(SpinnerModel model)
SpinnerModel model = new SpinnerListModel(args);
JSpinner spinner = new JSpinner(model);
```

You can start with no data model and associate it later with the tracking method of JSpinner. Alternatively, you can start up the component with a full model, in an implementation of the SpinnerModel interface, of which three concrete subclasses are available: SpinnerDateModel, SpinnerListModel, and SpinnerNumberModel, along with their abstract parent class AbstractSpinnerModel. If you don't specify a model, the SpinnerNumberModel is used. While the renderer and editor for the component is a JFormattedTextField, the editing is basically done through a series of inner classes of JSpinner: DateEditor, ListEditor, and NumberFormat, with its support class in its parent DefaultEditor.

JSpinner Properties

In addition to creating the JSpinner object, you can certainly reconfigure it, through one of the nine properties listed in Table 14-1.

Table 14-1. *JSpinner Properties*

Property Name	Data Type	Access
accessibleContext	AccessibleContext	Read-only
changeListeners	ChangeListener[ ]	Read-only
editor	JComponent	Read-write bound
model	SpinnerModel	Read-write bound
nextValue	Object	Read-only
previousValue	Object	Read-only
UI	SpinnerUI	Read-write
UIClassID	String	Read-only
value	Object	Read-write

The value property allows you to change the current setting for the component. The nextValue and previousValue properties allow you to peek at entries of the model in the different directions, without changing the selection within the application itself.

Listening for JSpinner Events with a ChangeListener

The JSpinner directly supports a single type of event listener: ChangeListener. Among other places, the listener is notified when the commitEdit() method is called for the associated component, telling you the spinner value changed. To demonstrate, Listing 14-1 attaches a custom ChangeListener to the source used to generate the program associated with Figure 14-1.

Listing 14-1. *JSpinner with ChangeListener*

```
import java.awt.*;
import javax.swing.*;
import javax.swing.event.*;
import java.text.*;
import java.util.*;

public class SpinnerSample {
  public static void main (String args[]) {
    Runnable runner = new Runnable() {
      public void run() {
        JFrame frame = new JFrame("JSpinner Sample");
        frame.setDefaultCloseOperation(JFrame.EXIT_ON_CLOSE);
        DateFormatSymbols symbols =
          new DateFormatSymbols(Locale.FRENCH);
        ChangeListener listener = new ChangeListener() {
          public void stateChanged(ChangeEvent e) {
            System.out.println("Source: " + e.getSource());
          }
        };

        String days[] = symbols.getWeekdays();
        SpinnerModel model1 = new SpinnerListModel(days);
        JSpinner spinner1 = new JSpinner(model1);
        spinner1.addChangeListener(listener);
        JLabel label1 = new JLabel("French Days/List");
        JPanel panel1 = new JPanel(new BorderLayout());
        panel1.add(label1, BorderLayout.WEST);
        panel1.add(spinner1, BorderLayout.CENTER);
        frame.add(panel1, BorderLayout.NORTH);
```

```
          SpinnerModel model2 = new SpinnerDateModel();
          JSpinner spinner2 = new JSpinner(model2);
          spinner2.addChangeListener(listener);
          JLabel label2 = new JLabel("Dates/Date");
          JPanel panel2 = new JPanel(new BorderLayout());
          panel2.add(label2, BorderLayout.WEST);
          panel2.add(spinner2, BorderLayout.CENTER);
          frame.add(panel2, BorderLayout.CENTER);

          SpinnerModel model3 = new SpinnerNumberModel();
          JSpinner spinner3 = new JSpinner(model3);
          spinner3.addChangeListener(listener);
          JLabel label3 = new JLabel("Numbers");
          JPanel panel3 = new JPanel(new BorderLayout());
          panel3.add(label3, BorderLayout.WEST);
          panel3.add(spinner3, BorderLayout.CENTER);
          frame.add(panel3, BorderLayout.SOUTH);

          frame.setSize(200, 90);
          frame.setVisible (true);
        }
      };
      EventQueue.invokeLater(runner);
    }
  }
```

Running this program demonstrates the use of this listener (of course, you'll find far more meaningful ways to use a ChangeListener).

Customizing a JSpinner Look and Feel

As with all Swing components, the JSpinner control has a different appearance under each of the system-defined look and feel types, as shown in Figure 14-2. The component primarily looks just like a text field; the difference is in the drawing of the arrows.

Figure 14-2. *JSpinner under different look and feel types*

The set of 11 UIResource properties for a JSpinner is shown in Table 14-2. These are limited to drawing the text field and the arrows.

Table 14-2. *JSpinner UIResource Elements*

Property String	Object Type
Spinner.actionMap	ActionMap
Spinner.ancestorInputMap	InputMap
Spinner.arrowButtonBorder	Border
Spinner.arrowButtonInsets	Insets
Spinner.arrowButtonSize	Dimension
Spinner.background	Color
Spinner.border	Border
Spinner.editorBorderPainted	Boolean
Spinner.font	Font
Spinner.foreground	Color
SpinnerUI	String

SpinnerModel Interface

So far, you've seen how to interact with the main JSpinner class. The SpinnerModel interface is the data model for the component. The definition of SpinnerModel follows:

```
public interface SpinnerModel {
  // Properties
  public Object getValue();
  public void setValue(Object);
  public Object getNextValue();
  public Object getPreviousValue();
  // Listeners
  public void addChangeListener(ChangeListener);
  public void removeChangeListener(ChangeListener);
}
```

The six methods of SpinnerModel map directly to those of JSpinner. The JSpinner methods just redirect the method calls to that of the model, though in the case of the listener methods, the event source is where you attach the listener.

AbstractSpinnerModel Class

The base implementation of the SpinnerModel interface is the AbstractSpinnerModel class. It provides for the management and notification of the listener list. Subclasses must implement the other four value-related methods of the interface. Three concrete implementations of the SpinnerModel interface are provided: SpinnerDateModel, SpinnerListModel, and SpinnerNumberModel.

SpinnerDateModel Class

As might be inferred from its name, the SpinnerDateModel provides for the selection of dates. This class has two constructors: one that defaults to selecting all dates and another that allows you to limit the range.

```
public SpinnerDateModel()
SpinnerModel model = new SpinnerDateModel();
JSpinner spinner = new JSpinner(model);
```

```
public SpinnerDateModel(Date value, Comparable start, Comparable end,
  int calendarField)
Calendar cal = Calendar.getInstance();
Date now = cal.getTime();
cal.add(Calendar.YEAR, -50);
Date startDate = cal.getTime();
cal.add(Calendar.YEAR, 100);
Date endDate = cal.getTime();
SpinnerModel model =
  new SpinnerDateModel(now, startDate, endDate, Calendar.YEAR);
JSpinner spinner = new JSpinner(model);
```

If you don't specify any parameters, there is no start or end point. The example shown here uses parameters to provide a 100-year range. The last field should be one of the following constants from the Calendar class:

- Calendar.AM_PM

- Calendar.DAY_OF_MONTH

- Calendar.DAY_OF_WEEK

- Calendar.DAY_OF_WEEK_IN_MONTH

- Calendar.DAY_OF_YEAR

- Calendar.ERA

- Calendar.HOUR

- Calendar.HOUR_OF_DAY

- Calendar.MILLISECOND

- Calendar.MINUTE

- Calendar.MONTH

- Calendar.SECOND

- Calendar.WEEK_OF_MONTH

- Calendar.WEEK_OF_YEAR

- Calendar.YEAR

■Note The SpinnerDateModel does not include any of the time zone-related constants of Calendar. You cannot scroll through those within a JSpinner via a SpinnerDateModel.

Table 14-3 lists the three properties from the SpinnerModel interface and four specific to the SpinnerDateModel.

Table 14-3. *SpinnerDateModel Properties*

Property Name	Data Type	Access
calendarField	int	Read-write
date	Date	Read-only
end	Comparable	Read-write
nextValue	Object	Read-only
previousValue	Object	Read-only
start	Comparable	Read-write
value	Object	Read-only

Typically, the only new property you'll use is for getting the final date, although all that does is wrap the result of getValue() in the appropriate data type. If you've provided a range of dates to the constructor, the previous or next values will be null when the current value is at an edge condition.

SpinnerListModel Class

The SpinnerListModel provides for selection from a list of entries, or at least their string representation. This class has three constructors:

```
public SpinnerListModel()
SpinnerModel model = new SpinnerListModel();
JSpinner spinner = new JSpinner(model);
```

```
public SpinnerListModel(List<?> values)
List<String> list = args;
SpinnerModel model = new SpinnerListModel(list);
JSpinner spinner = new JSpinner(model);
```

```
public SpinnerListModel(Object[] values)
SpinnerModel model = new SpinnerListModel(args);
JSpinner spinner = new JSpinner(model);
```

When no arguments are provided, the model contains a single element: the string `empty`. The `List` version retains a reference to the list. It does not copy the list. If you change the list, you change the elements in the model. The array version creates a private inner class instance of a `List` that can't be added to. For both the `List` and array versions, the initial selection will be the first element. If either is empty, an `IllegalArgumentException` will be thrown.

As shown in Table 14-4, the only property added beyond those from the interface is to get or set the list.

Table 14-4. *SpinnerListModel Properties*

Property Name	Data Type	Access
list	List<?>	Read-write
nextValue	Object	Read-only
previousValue	Object	Read-only
value	Object	Read-write

SpinnerNumberModel Class

The `SpinnerNumberModel` provides for the selection of a number from an open or closed range of values. That number can be any of the subclasses of `Number`, including `Integer` and `Double`. It has four constructors, with the first three provided just as convenience methods to the last.

```
public SpinnerNumberModel()
SpinnerModel model = new SpinnerNumberModel();
JSpinner spinner = new JSpinner(model);
```

```
public SpinnerNumberModel(double value, double minimum, double maximum,
    double stepSize)
SpinnerModel model = new SpinnerNumberModel(50, 0, 100, .25);
JSpinner spinner = new JSpinner(model);
```

```
public SpinnerNumberModel(int value, int minimum, int maximum, int stepSize)
SpinnerModel model = new SpinnerNumberModel(50, 0, 100, 1);
JSpinner spinner = new JSpinner(model);
```

```
public SpinnerNumberModel(Number value, Comparable minimum, Comparable maximum,
    Number stepSize)
Number value = new Integer(50);
Number min = new Integer(0);
Number max = new Integer(100);
Number step = new Integer(1);
SpinnerModel model = new SpinnerNumberModel(value, min, max, step);
JSpinner spinner = new JSpinner(model);
```

If the minimum or maximum value is null, the range is open-ended. For the no-argument version, the initial value is 0 and step is 1. The step size is literal, so if you set the step to .333, there will be no rounding off.

Table 14-5 shows the properties for SpinnerNumberModel. The added properties are the same as those provided by the constructor.

Table 14-5. *SpinnerNumberModel Properties*

Property Name	Data Type	Access
maximum	Comparable	Read-write
minimum	Comparable	Read-write
nextValue	Object	Read-only
number	Number	Read-only
previousValue	Object	Read-only
stepSize	Number	Read-write
value	Object	Read-write

Custom Models

Typically, the available models for the JSpinner are sufficient, so you don't need to subclass. However, that isn't always the case. For example, you might want to use a custom model that wraps the SpinnerListModel—instead of stopping at the first or last element, it wraps around to the other end. One such implementation is shown in Listing 14-2.

Listing 14-2. *RolloverSpinnerListModel Class*

```
import javax.swing.*;
import java.util.*;

public class RolloverSpinnerListModel extends SpinnerListModel {

  public RolloverSpinnerListModel(List<?> values) {
    super(values);
  }

  public RolloverSpinnerListModel(Object[] values) {
    super(values);
  }
```

```
  public Object getNextValue() {
    Object returnValue = super.getNextValue();
    if (returnValue == null) {
      returnValue = getList().get(0);
    }
    return returnValue;
  }

  public Object getPreviousValue() {
    Object returnValue = super.getPreviousValue();
    if (returnValue == null) {
      List list = getList();
      returnValue = list.get(list.size() - 1);
    }
    return returnValue;
  }
}
```

JSpinner Editors

For each of the models available for a JSpinner, a secondary support class, an inner class of JSpinner, is available. Whereas the model allows you to control what is selectable for the component, the spinner editors allow you to control how to display and edit each selectable value.

JSpinner.DefaultEditor Class

The setEditor() method of JSpinner allows you to have any JComponent as the editor for the JSpinner. While you certainly can do that, more typically, you will work with a subclass of JSpinner.DefaultEditor. It provides the basics you will need when working with simple editors based on JFormattedTextField. It contains a single constructor:

public JSpinner.DefaultEditor(JSpinner spinner)
```
JSpinner spinner = new JSpinner();
JComponent editor = JSpinner.DefaultEditor(spinner);
spinner.setEditor(editor);
```

As Table 14-6 shows, there are two properties for the editor.

Table 14-6. *JSpinner.DefaultEditor Properties*

Property Name	Data Type	Access
spinner	JSpinner	Read-only
textField	JFormattedTextField	Read-only

Without knowing which type of model you were working with, what you might do at this level is change some display characteristic of the JFormattedTextField. More typically, though, you'll change a custom aspect for the model's editor.

JSpinner.DateEditor Class

The DateEditor allows you to customize the date display (and entry) using various aspects of the SimpleDateFormat class of the java.text package. See the Javadoc for SimpleDateFormat for a complete listing of the available formatting patterns. If you don't like the default display output, you can modify it by passing in a new format to the second constructor.

```
public JSpinner.DateEditor(JSpinner spinner)
SpinnerModel model = new SpinnerDateModel();
JSpinner spinner = new JSpinner(model);
JComponent editor = JSpinner.DateEditor(spinner);
spinner.setEditor(editor);
```

```
public JSpinner.DateEditor(JSpinner spinner, String dateFormatPattern)
SpinnerModel model = new SpinnerDateModel();
JSpinner spinner = new JSpinner(model);
JComponent editor = JSpinner.DateEditor(spinner, "MMMM yyyy");
spinner.setEditor(editor);
```

By default, the format is M/d/yy h:mm a, or 12/25/04 12:34 PM for some time on Christmas in 2004 (or 1904, 1804, and so on). The latter example will show December 2004.

The editor has the two properties shown in Table 14-7.

Table 14-7. *JSpinner.DateEditor Properties*

Property Name	Data Type	Access
format	SimpleDateFormat	Read-only
model	SpinnerDateModel	Read-only

JSpinner.ListEditor Class

When working with the SpinnerListModel, the ListEditor provides no special formatting support. Instead, it offers type-ahead support. Since all entries of the model are known, the editor tries to match the characters the user has already entered with the start of one of those entries. There is only one constructor, but you should never need to access it.

```
public JSpinner.ListEditor(JSpinner spinner)
```

As shown in Table 14-8, ListEditor has only a single property.

Table 14-8. *JSpinner.ListEditor Properties*

Property Name	Data Type	Access
model	SpinnerListModel	Read-only

JSpinner.NumberEditor Class

The NumberEditor works in a manner similar to the DateEditor, allowing you to enter strings to customize the display format. Instead of working with the SimpleDateFormat, the NumberEditor is associated with the DecimalFormat class of the java.text package. Just like DateEditor, it has two constructors:

```
public JSpinner.NumberEditor(JSpinner spinner)
SpinnerModel model = new SpinnerNumberModel(50, 0, 100, .25);
JSpinner spinner = new JSpinner(model);
JComponent editor = JSpinner.NumberEditor(spinner);
spinner.setEditor(editor);
```

```
public JSpinner.NumberEditor(JSpinner spinner, String decimalFormatPattern)
SpinnerModel model = new SpinnerNumberModel(50, 0, 100, .25);
JSpinner spinner = new JSpinner(model);
JComponent editor = JSpinner.NumberEditor(spinner, "#,##0.###");
spinner.setEditor(editor);
```

The second constructor usage shows the default formatting string. It will try to use commas if the number is large enough, and it will not show decimals if the value is a whole number.

As shown in Table 14-9, this editor has two properties.

Table 14-9. *JSpinner.NumberEditor Properties*

Property Name	Data Type	Access
format	DecimalFormat	Read-only
model	SpinnerNumberModel	Read-only

Summary

In this chapter, you learned about Swing's JSpinner component. When your set of choices is limited to a fixed set or a range of values, a JSpinner allows you to select a value by spinning through the different choices. You learned how that set of choices could be provided: from a set of dates with the SpinnerDateModel and DateEditor, with the SpinnerListModel and ListEditor, or via the SpinnerNumberModel and NumberEditor.

Chapter 15 moves beyond selection from a range of values and on to where a user actually types in the whole content in the different text components.

■ ■ ■

Basic Text Components

Chapter 14 explored the dynamic input selection control offered with the JSpinner of the Swing component set. In this chapter, you will look at the basic capabilities of the Swing text components. The more advanced text component capabilities are covered in the next chapter.

The Swing component set features five text components. They all share a common parent class, JTextComponent, which defines the common behavior for all text controls.

The direct subclasses of JTextComponent are JTextField, JTextArea, and JEditorPane. JTextField is used for a single line of single-attributed text (that is, a single font and a single color). JTextField has a single subclass, JPasswordField, for when a JTextField needs to be used with an input mask for the entry of a password. JTextArea is used for multiple lines of single-attributed text input. JEditorPane is a generic editor that can support the editing of multiple-attributed input. Its subclass JTextPane is customized for input in plain-text style. In both cases, the input can be images as well as components, in addition to text.

Overview of the Swing Text Components

Like all other Swing components, text components live in an MVC world. The components shown in Figure 15-1, which is a class hierarchy diagram, are the various available UI delegates. The remaining part of the UI delegate model is the text view, which is based on the View class and discussed further in Chapter 16.

■**Note** All JTextComponent subclasses are in the javax.swing package. With the exception of the event-related pieces, the support interfaces and classes discussed in this chapter are found in the javax.swing.text package (or a subpackage). The Swing-specific, text-related event pieces are found in the javax.swing.event package, with remaining bits in java.awt.event and java.beans.

The data model for each of the components is an implementation of the Document interface, of which there are five extensions (or implementations). The single-attributed components use the PlainDocument class as their data model, while the multiple-attributed components use DefaultStyledDocument as their model. Both of these classes subclass the AbstractDocument class, which defines their common Document interface implementation. The DefaultStyledDocument class also implements the StyledDocument interface, which is an extension of Document for supporting multiple-attributed content. An additional Document implementation, HTMLDocument, is available for the `JEditorPane` when its content type is `text/html`. For restricting input into any of these documents, you can use the `DocumentFilter` class.

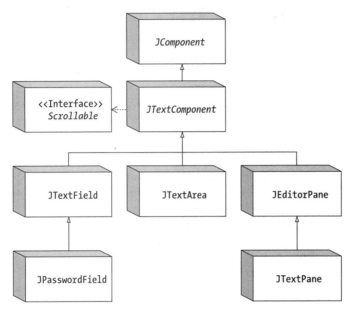

Figure 15-1. *Swing text component class hierarchy diagram*

Many other classes to be discussed in this chapter and in Chapter 16 are common among the text components. As with many of the other Swing components, you can customize the look and feel of the components without creating a new UI delegate. For the text components, the `Highlighter`, `Caret`, and `NavigationFilter` interfaces describe how text is highlighted, where text is inserted, and how to limit cursor positioning, respectively, thus allowing you to customize the text component appearance and input behavior. In addition, the `InputMap`/`ActionMap` classes define the bindings between keystrokes and text actions, letting you alter the feel of text components very easily.

Other text component model pieces are designed for event handling. You are not limited to using the `KeyListener`/`KeyEvent` or `TextEvent`/`TextListener` combination for dealing with input validation. The Swing components also can use the `DocumentEvent`/`DocumentListener` combination (as well as the `InputVerifier` described in Chapter 2). This combination provides a much more flexible manner of input validation, especially in the MVC environment of the Swing text components. Additional event handling is done through an extension of the `AbstractAction` capabilities introduced in Chapter 2. This is the `TextAction` class for tying key bindings to `Action` implementations, which is discussed in detail in Chapter 16. Many of the text framework pieces are tied together by what is called an `EditorKit`, which is also discussed in Chapter 16.

■Note Due to the many interconnections among the Swing text component classes, you'll find a number of references in this chapter to Chapter 16. Feel free to jump between this chapter and the next to read up on the full details of a particular capability.

JTextComponent Class

The JTextComponent class is the parent class for all the components used as textual views. It describes the common behavior shared by all text components. Among other things, this common behavior includes a Highlighter for selection support, a Caret for navigation throughout the content, a set of commands supported through the actions property (an array of Action implementers), a set of key bindings through a Keymap or InputMap/ActionMap combination, an implementation of the Scrollable interface so that each of the specific text components can be placed within a JScrollPane, and the text stored within the component. If that all sounds like a lot to manage, don't worry. This chapter will guide you through each of the pieces.

JTextComponent Properties

Table 15-1 shows the 27 properties of JTextComponent. These properties cover the range of capabilities you would expect from text components.

Table 15-1. *JTextComponent Properties*

Property Name	Data Type	Access
accessibleContext	AccessibleContext	Read-only
actions	Action[ ]	Read-only
caret	Caret	Read-write bound
caretColor	Color	Read-write bound
caretListeners	CaretListener[ ]	Read-only
caretPosition	int	Read-write
componentOrientation	ComponentOrientation	Write-only bound
disabledTextColor	Color	Read-write bound
document	Document	Read-write bound
dragEnabled	boolean	Read-write
editable	boolean	Read-write bound
focusAccelerator	char	Read-write bound
highlighter	Highlighter	Read-write bound
inputMethodRequests	InputMethodRequests	Read-only
keymap	Keymap	Read-write bound
margin	Insets	Read-write bound
navigationFilter	NavigationFilter	Read-write
preferredScrollableViewportSize	Dimension	Read-only
scrollableTracksViewportHeight	boolean	Read-only
scrollableTracksViewportWidth	boolean	Read-only

Table 15-1. *JTextComponent Properties (Continued)*

Property Name	Data Type	Access
selectedText	String	Read-only
selectedTextColor	Color	Read-write bound
selectionColor	Color	Read-write bound
selectionEnd	int	Read-write
selectionStart	int	Read-write
text	String	Read-write
UI	TextUI	Read-write

These properties can be grouped into eight basic categories:

- **Data model:** The document property is for the data model of all text components. The text property is used for treating this data model as a String.

- **Color:** The caretColor, disabledTextColor, selectedTextColor, and selectionColor properties, as well as the inherited foreground and background properties, specify the color for rendering the cursor, disabled text, selected text, selected text background, regular text, and regular text background.

- **Caret:** The caret, caretPosition, and navigationFilter properties are for navigating through the document.

- **Highlighter:** The highlighter, selectionStart, and selectionEnd properties are responsible for highlighting the selectedText section of the document.

- **Margin:** The margin property is for specifying how far the text contents appear from the edges of the text component.

- **Events:** The actions and keymap properties describe which capabilities the text component supports. In the case of the Action[ ] for the actions property, the capabilities are a series of ActionListener implementations that you can associate with components for event handling. For instance, instead of creating an ActionListener to perform cut, copy, and paste operations, you find the appropriate Action within the actions property and associate it with a component. The keymap property works in a similar manner, but it associates Action implementations with specific keys. For instance, it contains a key map entry for what to do when the PageUp key is pressed. The caretListeners property allows you to discover the set of CaretListener objects observing the text component. The dragEnabled setting describes if the component supports dragging text from within the component. (For information about drag-and-drop support within Swing, see Chapter 19.)

- **Scrollable interface:** The properties preferredScrollableViewportSize, scrollableTracksViewportHeight, and scrollableTracksViewportWidth are implementations of the respective Scrollable interface methods.

- **State:** The editable and focusTraversable properties describe various states of the text components. The editable property allows you to make a text component read-only. For the read-only focusTraversable property, text components are in the focus cycle (that is, they can be tabbed into) when they're enabled. The focusAccelerator is used when a neighboring JLabel has the text component set in its labelFor property, allowing you to use the visible mnemonic of the JLabel to move focus into the text component. The componentOrientation setting describes how the component's text will be drawn. Use this for languages like Hebrew where left-to-right is not necessarily the best way to draw characters. The JTextComponent inherits an opaque property from JComponent. When the opaque property is set to false, the contents of the area behind the text component bleed through, allowing you to have an image background if desired. See Figure 15-2 for how this might appear.

Listing 15-1 is the source code used to generate Figure 15-2. If you comment out the setOpaque(false) line, a background image will not be shown.

Figure 15-2. *An opaque text component with an image background*

Listing 15-1. *Drawing in the Background of a Component*

```java
import javax.swing.*;
import java.awt.*;

public class BackgroundSample {
  public static void main(String args[]) {
    Runnable runner = new Runnable() {
      public void run() {
        JFrame frame = new JFrame("Background Example");
        frame.setDefaultCloseOperation(JFrame.EXIT_ON_CLOSE);
        final ImageIcon imageIcon = new ImageIcon("draft.gif");
        JTextArea textArea = new JTextArea() {
          Image image = imageIcon.getImage();
          Image grayImage = GrayFilter.createDisabledImage(image);
          {setOpaque(false);}  // instance initializer
```

```
            public void paint (Graphics g) {
              g.drawImage(grayImage, 0, 0, this);
              super.paint(g);
            }
          };
          JScrollPane scrollPane = new JScrollPane(textArea);
          frame.add(scrollPane, BorderLayout.CENTER);
          frame.setSize(250, 250);
          frame.setVisible(true);
        }
      };
      EventQueue.invokeLater(runner);
    }
}
```

JTextComponent Operations

The JTextComponent defines the basic framework for many of the operations performed on the
text controls.

- **I/O:** The public void read(Reader in, Object description) and public void
  write(Writer out) methods (both throw IOException) allow you to read or write
  the text component contents with ease.

- **Clipboard access:** The public void cut(), public void copy(), and public void paste()
  methods provide direct access to the system clipboard.

- **Positioning:** The public void moveCaretPosition(int position) method allows you to
  position the caret. The position represents a one-dimensional location indicating the
  number of characters to precede the caret from the beginning of the text component.

- **Selection:** The public void replaceSelection(String content), public void
  selectAll(), and public void select(int selectionStart, int selectionEnd)
  methods allow you to select part of the content within the component and replace
  the content that is selected.

- **Conversion:** The public Rectangle modelToView(int position) throws
  BadLocationException and public int viewToModel(Point point) methods allow
  you (or, more likely, allow the system) to map a position within the JTextComponent to
  a physical mapping within the representation of the contents for the specific text UI
  delegate.

Now that you've had an overview of the JTextComponent class, it's time to look at its
different subclasses. First up is the JTextField, which will be used to demonstrate the operations
just listed.

JTextField Class

The JTextField component is the text component for a single line of input. The data model
for a JTextField is the PlainDocument implementation of the Document interface. The PlainDocument
model limits input to single-attributed text, meaning that it must be a single font and color.

When the Enter key is pressed within the JTextField, it automatically notifies any registered ActionListener implementations.

Creating a JTextField

There are five constructors for the JTextField component:

```
public JTextField()
JTextField textField = new JTextField();
```

```
public JTextField(String text)
JTextField textField = new JTextField("Initial Text");
```

```
public JTextField(int columnWidth)
JTextField textField = new JTextField(14);
```

```
public JTextField(String text, int columnWidth)
JTextField textField = new JTextField("Initial Text", 14);
```

```
public JTextField(Document model, String text, int columnWidth)
JTextField textField = new JTextField(aModel, null, 14);
```

By default, you get an empty text field, zero columns wide, with a default initial model. You can specify the initial text for the JTextField and how wide you want the component to be. Width is specified as the number of *m* characters in the current font that will fit within the component. There's no restriction on the number of characters that can be input. If you specify the Document data model in the constructor, you will probably want to specify a null initial-text argument. Otherwise, the current contents of the document will be replaced by the initial text for the text field.

Using JLabel Mnemonics

In the discussion of mnemonics in Chapter 4, you learned that the various button classes can have a keyboard shortcut that causes the button component to be selected. The special mnemonic character is usually underlined to indicate this visually. If the user presses the mnemonic character, along with a platform-specific mnemonic activation key, such as Alt for both Windows and UNIX, the button is activated/selected. You can provide a similar capability for a JTextField, and all other text components, with the help of a JLabel.

You can set the display mnemonic for a label, but instead of selecting the label when the mnemonic key is pressed, selection causes an associated component to get the input focus. The display mnemonic is set with the public void setDisplayedMnemonic(character) method, in which character is either an int or a char. Using the KeyEvent constants when changing the mnemonic setting simplifies initialization considerably.

The following source demonstrates how to interconnect a specific JLabel and JTextField.

```
JLabel label = new JLabel("Name: ");
label.setDisplayedMnemonic(KeyEvent.VK_N);
JTextField textField = new JTextField();
label.setLabelFor(textField);
```

In addition to calling the setDisplayedMnemonic() method, you must also call the public void setLabelFor(Component component) method of JLabel. This configures the JLabel to move input focus to the text field when the special mnemonic value is pressed.

Figure 15-3 shows what this sample program might look like. The complete source for the program follows in Listing 15-2.

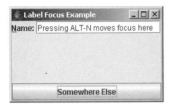

Figure 15-3. *Connecting a JLabel and a JTextField*

Listing 15-2. *Connected JLabel and JTextField*

```
import javax.swing.*;
import java.awt.*;
import java.awt.event.*;

public class LabelSample {
  public static void main(String args[]) {
    Runnable runner = new Runnable() {
      public void run() {
        JFrame frame = new JFrame("Label Focus Example");
        frame.setDefaultCloseOperation(JFrame.EXIT_ON_CLOSE);
        JPanel panel = new JPanel(new BorderLayout());
        JLabel label = new JLabel("Name: ");
        label.setDisplayedMnemonic(KeyEvent.VK_N);
        JTextField textField = new JTextField();
        label.setLabelFor(textField);
        panel.add(label, BorderLayout.WEST);
        panel.add(textField, BorderLayout.CENTER);
        frame.add(panel, BorderLayout.NORTH);
        frame.add(new JButton("Somewhere Else"), BorderLayout.SOUTH);
        frame.setSize(250, 150);
        frame.setVisible(true);
      }
    };
    EventQueue.invokeLater(runner);
  }
}
```

JTextField Properties

Table 15-2 lists the 14 properties of JTextField.

Table 15-2. *JTextField Properties*

Property Name	Data Type	Access
accessibleContext	AccessibleContext	Read-only
actionCommand	String	Write-only
action	Action	Read-write bound
actionListeners	ActionListener[ ]	Read-only
actions	Action[ ]	Read-only
columns	int	Read-write
document	Document	Write-only bound
font	Font	Write-only
horizontalAlignment	int	Read-write bound
horizontalVisibility	BoundedRangeModel	Read-only
preferredSize	Dimension	Read-only
scrollOffset	int	Read-write
UIClassID	String	Read-only
validateRoot	boolean	Read-only

There's a tight coupling between the horizontalVisibility and scrollOffset properties. The BoundedRangeModel for the horizontalVisibility property of JTextField represents the width range required for displaying the contents of the text field. If there isn't enough space to display the contents, the scrollOffset setting reflects how far off to the left the text has scrolled. As the user navigates through the text within the JTextField, the scrollOffset value is automatically updated. For example, the text field in Figure 15-4 contains the 26 letters of the alphabet plus the 10 cardinal numbers: *ABCDEFGHIJKLMNOPQRSTUVWXYZ1234567890*. Not all these characters fit in the field; therefore, the letters *A* through *J* have scrolled off to the left.

Figure 15-4. *The scrollOffset property reflects how far to the left the field's contents have scrolled; here, it is not at zero, so the beginning contents (A–J) have scrolled off to the left.*

By changing the scrollOffset setting, you can control which part of the text field is visible. To ensure that the beginning of the contents for the text field is visible, set the scrollOffset setting to zero. To make sure that the *end* of the contents is visible, you need to ask the horizontalVisibility property what the extent of the BoundedRangeModel is, to determine the width of the range, and then set the scrollOffset setting to the extent setting, as follows:

```
BoundedRangeModel model = textField.getHorizontalVisibility();
int extent = model.getExtent();
textField.setScrollOffset(extent);
```

By changing the horizontalAlignment property setting, you can right-, left-, or center-justify the contents of a JTextField. By default, the text alignment is left-justified. The public void setHorizontalAlignment(int alignment) method takes an argument of JTextField.LEFT, JTextField.CENTER, JTextField.RIGHT, JTextField.LEADING (the default), or JTextField.TRAILING to specify the contents alignment. Figure 15-5 shows how the alignment setting affects the contents.

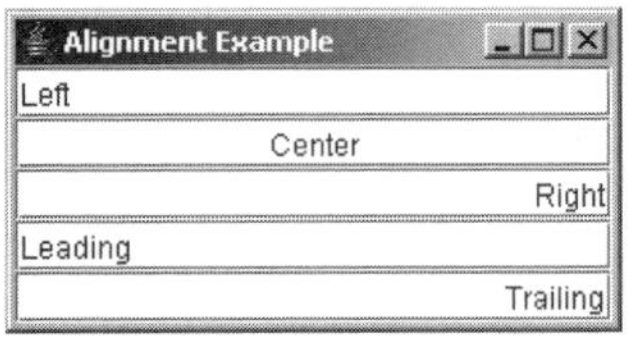

Figure 15-5. *Text field alignments*

Note You can set the document property, inherited from JTextComponent, to any implementation of the Document interface. If you use a StyledDocument with a JTextField, the UI delegate will ignore all style attributes. The StyledDocument interface is discussed in Chapter 16.

JTextComponent Operations with a JTextField

Have you ever looked for an easy way to load or save the contents of a text component? The Swing text components provide such a method. Additionally, the Swing text components have built-in support to access the system clipboard for cut, copy, and paste operations. These operations are possible with all JTextComponent subclasses. They're shown here specifically for the JTextField because they need a specific implementation to be truly demonstrated. You can perform the same tasks with the JPasswordField, JTextArea, JEditorPane, and JTextPane.

Loading and Saving Content

With the public void read(Reader in, Object description) and public void write(Writer out) methods from JTextComponent (both throw an IOException), you can easily load and save the contents from any text component. With the read() method, the description argument is added as a property of the Document data model. This allows you to retain information about where the data came from. The following example demonstrates how to read in the contents of file name and store it in textComponent. The file name is automatically retained as the description.

```
FileReader reader = null;
try {
  reader = new FileReader(filename);
  textComponent.read(reader, filename);
} catch (IOException exception) {
  System.err.println("Load oops");
} finally {
  if (reader != null) {
    try {
      reader.close();
    } catch (IOException exception) {
      System.err.println("Error closing reader");
      exception.printStackTrace();
    }
  }
}
```

If you later wanted to get the description back from the data model, which happens to be the file name in this case, you would just ask, like this:

```
Document document = textComponent.getDocument();
String filename = (String)document.getProperty(Document.StreamDescriptionProperty);
```

The properties of the Document are simply another key/value lookup table. The key in this particular case is the class constant Document.StreamDescriptionProperty. If you don't want a description stored, you pass null as the description argument to the read() method. (The Document interface will be discussed in more detail later in this chapter.)

Before you can read a file into a text component, you need to create the file to read. This could be done outside a Java program, or you could use the write() method of JTextComponent to create the file. The following demonstrates how to use the write() method to write the contents. For simplicity's sake, it doesn't deal with getting the file name from the Document, because this would not be set initially.

```
FileWriter writer = null;
try {
  writer = new FileWriter(filename);
  textComponent.write(writer);
} catch (IOException exception) {
  System.err.println("Save oops");
} finally {
  if (writer != null) {
    try {
      writer.close();
    } catch (IOException exception) {
      System.err.println("Error closing writer");
      exception.printStackTrace();
    }
  }
}
```

Figure 15-6 shows a sample program that uses the loading and saving capabilities, with these options implemented through buttons (although Load and Save options are more commonly seen under a File menu). The Clear button clears the contents of the text field.

Figure 15-6. *Loading and saving a text component*

The source in Listing 15-3 puts all the pieces together in a sample program to demonstrate loading and saving streams.

Listing 15-3. *Loading and Saving Streams with a JTextComponent*

```java
import java.awt.*;
import java.awt.event.*;
import javax.swing.*;
import javax.swing.text.*;
import java.io.*;

public class LoadSave {

  public static void main (String args[]) {
    Runnable runner = new Runnable() {
      public void run() {
        final String filename = "text.out";
        JFrame frame = new JFrame("Loading/Saving Example");
        frame.setDefaultCloseOperation(JFrame.EXIT_ON_CLOSE);

        final JTextField textField = new JTextField();
        frame.add(textField, BorderLayout.NORTH);

        JPanel panel = new JPanel();

        // Setup actions
        Action loadAction = new AbstractAction() {
          {
            putValue(Action.NAME, "Load");
          }
          public void actionPerformed(ActionEvent e) {
            doLoadCommand(textField, filename);
          }
        };
```

```java
      JButton loadButton = new JButton (loadAction);
      panel.add(loadButton);

      Action saveAction = new AbstractAction() {
        {
          putValue(Action.NAME, "Save");
        }
        public void actionPerformed(ActionEvent e) {
          doSaveCommand(textField, filename);
        }
      };
      JButton saveButton = new JButton (saveAction);
      panel.add(saveButton);

      Action clearAction = new AbstractAction() {
        {
          putValue(Action.NAME, "Clear");
        }
        public void actionPerformed(ActionEvent e) {
          textField.setText("");
        }
      };
      JButton clearButton = new JButton (clearAction);
      panel.add(clearButton);

      frame.add(panel, BorderLayout.SOUTH);

      frame.setSize(250, 150);
      frame.setVisible(true);
    }
  };
  EventQueue.invokeLater(runner);
}

public static void doSaveCommand(JTextComponent textComponent,
    String filename) {
  FileWriter writer = null;
  try {
    writer = new FileWriter(filename);
    textComponent.write(writer);
  } catch (IOException exception) {
    System.err.println("Save oops");
    exception.printStackTrace();
  } finally {
    if (writer != null) {
      try {
        writer.close();
```

```
      } catch (IOException exception) {
        System.err.println("Error closing writer");
        exception.printStackTrace();
      }
    }
  }
}

public static void doLoadCommand(JTextComponent textComponent,
    String filename) {
  FileReader reader = null;
  try {
    reader = new FileReader(filename);
    textComponent.read(reader, filename);
  } catch (IOException exception) {
    System.err.println("Load oops");
    exception.printStackTrace();
  } finally {
    if (reader != null) {
      try {
        reader.close();
      } catch (IOException exception) {
        System.err.println("Error closing reader");
        exception.printStackTrace();
      }
    }
  }
}
}
```

■Note By default, file reading and writing deals only with plain text. If the contents of a text component are styled, the styled attributes aren't saved. The `EditorKit` class can customize this loading and saving behavior. You'll explore that class in Chapter 16.

Accessing the Clipboard

To use the system clipboard for cut, copy, and paste operations, you do not need to manually concoct a `Transferable` clipboard object. Instead, you just call one of these three methods of the `JTextComponent` class: `public void cut()`, `public void copy()`, or `public void paste()`.

You could call these methods directly from `ActionListener` implementations associated with buttons or menu items, as in the following:

```
ActionListener cutListener = new ActionListener() {
  public void actionPerformed(ActionEvent actionEvent) {
    aTextComponent.cut();
  }
};
```

However, there is an easier way that doesn't require you to manually create the ActionListener implementations. This method involves finding an existing cut action by asking the text component. If you look at the set of JTextComponent properties in Table 15-1, you'll notice one property named actions, which is an array of Action objects. This property contains a predefined set of Action implementations that you can directly associate as an ActionListener with any button or menu item. Once you get the current actions for the text component, you can go through the array until you find the appropriate one. Because actions are named, you merely need to know the text string for the name. The DefaultEditorKit class has about 40 keys as public constants. Here is an example of getting the cut action:

```
Action actions[] = textField.getActions();
Action cutAction = TextUtilities.findAction(actions, DefaultEditorKit.cutAction);
```

All actions in the set for a text component are a type of TextAction, which is an extension of the AbstractAction class. The essential thing to know about a TextAction is that it acts on the last focused text component. (The TextAction class, along with the DefaultEditorKit, will be discussed more extensively in Chapter 16.) So, even though the preceding source fragment acquires the cut action from a text field, the same cut action would work for another text component on the same screen. Whichever text component had the input focus last would be the one cut when the specific cutAction is activated.

To help you visualize this behavior, Figure 15-7 shows a screen with a JTextField at the top, a JTextArea in the middle, and buttons on the bottom for the cut, copy, and paste operations (although these operations are more commonly available through an Edit menu). If you run the program, you'll notice that the cut, copy, and paste actions act on the last focused text component.

Figure 15-7. *Accessing the system clipboard from a text component*

The source code in Listing 15-4 is the complete example for finding an Action in the actions property array and using cut, copy, and paste.

Listing 15-4. *Accessing the System Clipboard*

```java
import java.awt.*;
import java.awt.event.*;
import java.util.*;
import javax.swing.*;
import javax.swing.text.*;

public class CutPasteSample {
  public static void main (String args[]) {
    Runnable runner = new Runnable() {
      public void run() {
        JFrame frame = new JFrame("Cut/Paste Example");
        frame.setDefaultCloseOperation(JFrame.EXIT_ON_CLOSE);

        JTextField textField = new JTextField();
        JTextArea textArea = new JTextArea();
        JScrollPane scrollPane = new JScrollPane(textArea);

        frame.add(textField, BorderLayout.NORTH);
        frame.add(scrollPane, BorderLayout.CENTER);

        Action actions[] = textField.getActions();

        Action cutAction =
          TextUtilities.findAction(actions, DefaultEditorKit.cutAction);
        Action copyAction =
          TextUtilities.findAction(actions, DefaultEditorKit.copyAction);
        Action pasteAction =
          TextUtilities.findAction(actions, DefaultEditorKit.pasteAction);

        JPanel panel = new JPanel();
        frame.add(panel, BorderLayout.SOUTH);

        JButton cutButton = new JButton(cutAction);
        cutButton.setText("Cut");
        panel.add(cutButton);

        JButton copyButton = new JButton(copyAction);
        copyButton.setText("Copy");
        panel.add(copyButton);

        JButton pasteButton = new JButton(pasteAction);
        pasteButton.setText("Paste");
        panel.add(pasteButton);
```

```
      frame.setSize(250, 250);
      frame.setVisible(true);
    }
  };
  EventQueue.invokeLater(runner);
 }
}
```

The example in Listing 15-4 uses the TextUtilities support class shown in Listing 15-5. There's no direct way to find out if a specific action for a specific key exists in the actions property array. Instead, you must manually search for it. The public static Action findAction(Action actions[], String key) method does the searching for you.

Listing 15-5. *TextUtilities Support Class*

```
import javax.swing.*;
import javax.swing.text.*;
import java.util.Hashtable;

public final class TextUtilities {
  private TextUtilities() {
  }

  public static Action findAction(Action actions[], String key) {
    Hashtable<Object, Action> commands = new Hashtable<Object, Action>();
    for (int i = 0; i < actions.length; i++) {
      Action action = actions[i];
      commands.put(action.getValue(Action.NAME), action);
    }
    return commands.get(key);
  }
}
```

■**Note** For security reasons, the cut() and copy() methods of the JPasswordField class do not place the current contents onto the system clipboard (the system will beep instead). You can still paste() something from the clipboard into a JPasswordField, though.

Document Interface

The Document interface defines the data model for the different text components. Implementations of the interface are meant to store both the actual content as well as any information to mark up the content (with bold, italics, or color). While all the content will be text, the way in which the text component displays the content could result in nontextual output, such as an HTML renderer.

The data model is stored apart from the text component (the view). Therefore, if you're interested in monitoring changes to the content of a text component, you must watch the Document itself, not the text component, for changes. If the changes reach the text component, it's too late—the model has already changed. To listen for changes, attach a DocumentListener to the model. However, the more likely scenario for restricting input is to provide a custom model or attach a DocumentFilter to the AbstractDocument. You can also attach an InputVerifier to the text component. However, that wouldn't be used until the input focus tried to leave the component.

■**Note** In addition to accessing the textual content through the Document interface, a framework is defined to support undo/redo capabilities. This will be explored in Chapter 21.

Now, let's look at the pieces that make up a Document. First, here's the base interface definition:

```
public interface Document {
  // Constants
  public final static String StreamDescriptionProperty;
  public final static String TitleProperty;
  // Listeners
  public void addDocumentListener(DocumentListener listener);
  public void removeDocumentListener(DocumentListener listener);
  public void addUndoableEditListener(UndoableEditListener listener);
  public void removeUndoableEditListener(UndoableEditListener listener);
  // Properties
  public Element getDefaultRootElement();
  public Position getEndPosition();
  public int getLength();
  public Element[ ] getRootElements();
  public Position getStartPosition();
  // Other methods
  public Position createPosition(int offset) throws BadLocationException;
  public Object getProperty(Object key);
  public String getText(int offset, int length) throws BadLocationException;
  public void getText(int offset, int length, Segment txt)
    throws BadLocationException;
  public void insertString(int offset, String str, AttributeSet a)
    throws BadLocationException;
  public void putProperty(Object key, Object value);
  public void remove(int offset, int len) throws BadLocationException;
  public void render(Runnable r);
}
```

The content within a Document is described by a series of elements in which each element implements the Element interface. Within each element, you can store attributes so that select content can be made bold, italic, or colorized. The elements don't store the content; they just hold the attributes. Therefore, one Document can be rendered differently from different Element sets.

The following is an example of a basic HTML document with a title and a bulleted list for content.

```
<html>

<head>
<title>Cards</title>
</head>

<body>

<h1>Suits:</h1>

<ul>
    <li>Clubs</li>
    <li>Diamonds</li>
    <li>Hearts</li>
    <li>Spades</li>
</ul>
</body>
</html>
```

Looking at the structure of the elements in this HTML document, you get a hierarchy as shown in Figure 15-8.

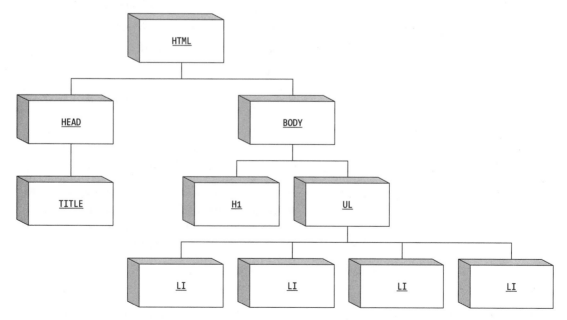

Figure 15-8. *Examining the element makeup of a document*

Although this particular document might not warrant it, multiple element hierarchies are possible. Each would store different attributes because a particular text component could have an alternative rendering of the content. Alternatively, different style sheets could be used to render the same HTML markup differently.

AbstractDocument Class

The AbstractDocument class provides the basic implementation of the Document interface. It defines the management of the listener lists, provides a read-write locking mechanism to ensure that content isn't corrupted, and enables a Dictionary for storing document properties.

Table 15-3 lists the 11 properties of the AbstractDocument class, of which 5 are defined by the Document interface itself.

Table 15-3. *AbstractDocument Properties*

Property Name	Data Type	Access
asynchronousLoadPriority*	int	Read-write
bidiRootElement*	Element	Read-only
defaultRootElement	Element	Read-only
documentFilter*	DocumentFilter	Read-write
documentListeners*	DocumentListener[ ]	Read-only
documentProperties*	Dictionary	Read-write
endPosition	Position	Read-only
length	int	Read-only
rootElements	Element[ ]	Read-only
startPosition	Position	Read-only
undoableEditListeners*	UndoableEditListener[ ]	Read-only

* These properties are specific to the AbstractDocument class. The remaining five properties are defined in the Document interface.

For the most part, you don't access any of these properties directly, except perhaps documentFilter. In the case of the documentProperties property, you get and set individual properties with the public Object getProperty(Object key) and public void putProperty(Object key, Object value) methods. For the length property, in most cases, you can simply ask for the text within a text component, and then get *its* length by using textComponent.getText().length().

The bidiRootElement property is for the bidirectional root element, which may be appropriate in certain Unicode character sets. You would normally just use the defaultRootElement. However, both are rarely accessed.

PlainDocument Class

The PlainDocument class is a specific implementation of the AbstractDocument class. It does not store any character-level attributes for the content. Instead, the elements describe where the content and each line in the content begin.

The program in Listing 15-6 walks through the Element tree for a PlainDocument, the model used for both the JTextField and the JTextArea.

Listing 15-6. *Element Walker*

```
import java.awt.*;
import java.awt.event.*;
import java.util.*;
import javax.swing.*;
import javax.swing.text.*;

public class ElementSample {
  public static void main (String args[]) {
    Runnable runner = new Runnable() {
      public void run() {
        JFrame frame = new JFrame("Element Example");
        frame.setDefaultCloseOperation(JFrame.EXIT_ON_CLOSE);

        final JTextArea textArea = new JTextArea();
        JScrollPane scrollPane = new JScrollPane(textArea);

        JButton button = new JButton("Show Elements");
        ActionListener actionListener = new ActionListener() {
          public void actionPerformed(ActionEvent actionEvent) {
            Document document = textArea.getDocument();
            ElementIterator iterator = new ElementIterator(document);
            Element element = iterator.first();
            while (element != null) {
              System.out.println(element.getStartOffset());
              element = iterator.next();
            }
          }
        };
        button.addActionListener(actionListener);

        frame.add(scrollPane, BorderLayout.CENTER);
        frame.add(button, BorderLayout.SOUTH);

        frame.setSize(250, 250);
        frame.setVisible(true);
      }
    };
    EventQueue.invokeLater(runner);
  }
}
```

Assume the contents of the JTextArea are as follows:

```
Hello, World
Welcome Home
Adios
```

The program would report Element objects starting at 0, 0, 13, and 26. The first 0 represents the start of the content; the second represents the start of the first line.

You'll learn more about Element in Chapter 16.

Filtering Document Models

In the AWT world, if you want to restrict input into a text field—such as to limit input to alphanumeric characters or to some numeric range of values—you attach a KeyListener and consume() keystrokes that you don't want to appear within the component. With the Swing text components, you could either create a new Document implementation and customize what's accepted in the Document or attach a DocumentFilter and let it filter input.

While you can certainly create a custom subclass of Document, the more object-oriented approach is to create a filter, as you don't want to change the Document; you just want to limit the input into the model. You then attach the newly created filter to the document by calling the setDocumentFilter() method of AbstractDocument. Filters work with both PlainDocument and StyledDocument subclasses.

DocumentFilter is a class, not an interface, so you must create a subclass of that to filter the text into the document of a text component. If you create a subclass of DocumentFilter, overriding these three methods allows you to customize input:

- `public void insertString(DocumentFilter.FilterBypass fb, int offset, String string, AttributeSet attributes)`: Called when a text string is inserted into the Document.

- `public void remove(DocumentFilter.FilterBypass fb, int offset, int length)`: Called when something is deleted.

- `public void replace(DocumentFilter.FilterBypass fb, int offset, int length, String text, AttributeSet attrs)`: Called when something is inserted into the currently selected text.

To restrict input, just override each method and check to see if the new content would be valid. If the content would not be valid, reject it.

For example, to create a DocumentFilter subclass to limit to a numeric range, you need to override the behavior of insertString(), remove(), and replace(). Because you're ensuring that the input is numeric and within a valid range, you must validate the proposed input to see if it's acceptable. If it is acceptable, then you can modify the document model by calling the insertString(), remove(), or replace() method of the DocumentFilter.FilterBypass argument of each original method call. When the input is unacceptable, you throw a BadLocationException. Seeing this exception thrown ensures the input method framework understands the user input was invalid. This will typically trigger the system to beep. Listing 15-7 shows a custom document filter for limiting an integer range.

Listing 15-7. *Custom Document Filter*

```java
import javax.swing.text.*;
import java.awt.Toolkit;

public class IntegerRangeDocumentFilter extends DocumentFilter {

  int minimum, maximum;
  int currentValue = 0;

  public IntegerRangeDocumentFilter(int minimum, int maximum) {
    this.minimum = minimum;
    this.maximum = maximum;
  }

  public void insertString(DocumentFilter.FilterBypass fb, int offset,
      String string, AttributeSet attr) throws BadLocationException {

    if (string == null) {
      return;
    } else {
      String newValue;
      Document doc = fb.getDocument();
      int length = doc.getLength();
      if (length == 0) {
        newValue = string;
      } else {
        String currentContent = doc.getText(0, length);
        StringBuffer currentBuffer = new StringBuffer(currentContent);
        currentBuffer.insert(offset, string);
        newValue = currentBuffer.toString();
      }
      currentValue = checkInput(newValue, offset);
      fb.insertString(offset, string, attr);
    }
  }

  public void remove(DocumentFilter.FilterBypass fb, int offset, int length)
      throws BadLocationException {

    Document doc = fb.getDocument();
    int currentLength = doc.getLength();
    String currentContent = doc.getText(0, currentLength);
    String before = currentContent.substring(0, offset);
    String after = currentContent.substring(length+offset, currentLength);
    String newValue = before + after;
    currentValue = checkInput(newValue, offset);
    fb.remove(offset, length);
  }
```

```
public void replace(DocumentFilter.FilterBypass fb, int offset, int length,
    String text, AttributeSet attrs) throws BadLocationException {

  Document doc = fb.getDocument();
  int currentLength = doc.getLength();
  String currentContent = doc.getText(0, currentLength);
  String before = currentContent.substring(0, offset);
  String after = currentContent.substring(length+offset, currentLength);
  String newValue = before + (text == null ? "" : text) + after;
  currentValue = checkInput(newValue, offset);
  fb.replace(offset, length, text, attrs);
}

private int checkInput(String proposedValue, int offset)
    throws BadLocationException {
  int newValue = 0;
  if (proposedValue.length() > 0) {
    try {
      newValue = Integer.parseInt(proposedValue);
    } catch (NumberFormatException e) {
      throw new BadLocationException(proposedValue, offset);
    }
  }
  if ((minimum <= newValue) && (newValue <= maximum)) {
    return newValue;
  } else {
    throw new BadLocationException(proposedValue, offset);
  }
}
}
```

Figure 15-9 shows the numeric range filter in use.

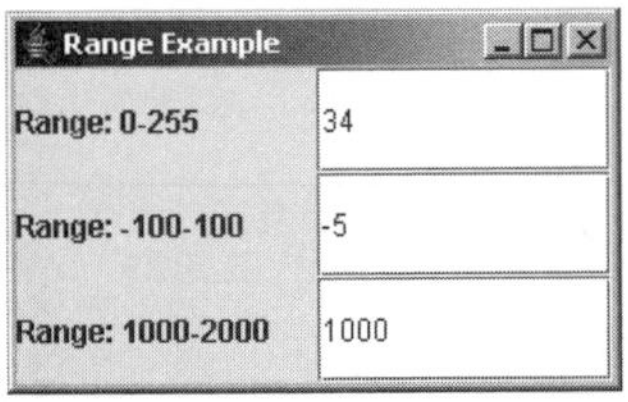

Figure 15-9. *Using a Document that restricts input to a range of values*

The sample program using the new IntegerRangeDocumentFilter follows in Listing 15-8.

Listing 15-8. *Program Using a Custom Document Filter*

```java
import javax.swing.*;
import javax.swing.text.*;
import java.awt.*;
import java.awt.event.*;

public class RangeSample {
  public static void main(String args[]) {
    Runnable runner = new Runnable() {
      public void run() {
        JFrame frame = new JFrame("Range Example");
        frame.setDefaultCloseOperation(JFrame.EXIT_ON_CLOSE);
        frame.setLayout(new GridLayout(3, 2));

        frame.add(new JLabel("Range: 0-255"));
        JTextField textFieldOne = new JTextField();
        Document textDocOne = textFieldOne.getDocument();
        DocumentFilter filterOne = new IntegerRangeDocumentFilter(0, 255);
        ((AbstractDocument)textDocOne).setDocumentFilter(filterOne);
        frame.add(textFieldOne);

        frame.add(new JLabel("Range: -100-100"));
        JTextField textFieldTwo = new JTextField();
        Document textDocTwo = textFieldTwo.getDocument();
        DocumentFilter filterTwo = new IntegerRangeDocumentFilter(-100, 100);
        ((AbstractDocument)textDocTwo).setDocumentFilter(filterTwo);
        frame.add(textFieldTwo);

        frame.add(new JLabel("Range: 1000-2000"));
        JTextField textFieldThree = new JTextField();
        Document textDocThree = textFieldThree.getDocument();
        DocumentFilter filterThree = new IntegerRangeDocumentFilter(1000, 2000);
        ((AbstractDocument)textDocThree).setDocumentFilter(filterThree);
        frame.add(textFieldThree);

        frame.setSize(250, 150);
        frame.setVisible(true);
      }
    };
    EventQueue.invokeLater(runner);
  }
}
```

If you try out this program, you'll notice a couple of interesting issues. The first text field, with a range of 0 to 255, works fine. You can enter and delete characters at will, as long as the content is within the range.

In the second text field, the valid range is –100 to +100. Although you can enter any of the 201 numbers into the text field, if you want a negative number, you need to enter something like 3, left arrow, and minus sign (-). Because the text field validates input with each key, the - by itself isn't valid. You would need to either specifically accept a - as valid input in the checkInput() method of the custom DocumentFilter or force users to enter negative numbers in an awkward manner.

The third text field presents an even more troublesome situation. The valid range of input is 1000–2000. As you press each key to enter a number, such as 1500, it's rejected. You can't build up the input to 1500 because, by themselves, 1, 5, and 0 are not valid input. Instead, to enter a number into this text field, you must enter it somewhere *else*, place it into the system clipboard, and then use Ctrl-V to paste it into the text field as the field's final value. You can't use Backspace to correct a mistake, because no three-digit numbers are valid.

While the IntegerRangeDocumentFilter class shown in Listing 15-7 presents a workable DocumentFilter for any integer range, it works best with ranges of positive numbers that begin at zero. If you don't mind seeing the temporarily invalid input in the fields, it may be better to just attach an InputVerifier to deal with validation when leaving the text field.

DocumentListener and DocumentEvent Interfaces

If you're interested in finding out when the content of a text component changes, you can attach an implementation of the DocumentListener interface to the Document model of the component.

```
public interface DocumentListener implements EventListener {
  public void changedUpdate(DocumentEvent documentEvent);
  public void insertUpdate(DocumentEvent documentEvent);
  public void removeUpdate(DocumentEvent documentEvent);
}
```

From the three interface methods, you can find out if the contents were added to (insertUpdate()), removed (removeUpdate()), or stylistically changed (changedUpdate()). Notice that the latter is an attribute change versus a content change.

The interface method will receive an instance of DocumentEvent, from which you can find out where the change occurred, as well as the type of change, as follows:

```
public interface DocumentEvent {
  public Document getDocument();
  public int getLength();
  public int getOffset();
  public DocumentEvent.EventType getType();
  public DocumentEvent.ElementChange getChange(Element element);
}
```

The offset property of the event is where the change started. The length property of the event tells the length of the change that happened. The type of the event can be derived from whichever one of the three DocumentListener methods were called. In addition, the DocumentEvent.EventType class has three constants—CHANGE, INSERT, and REMOVE—so you can find out which event type happened directly from the type property.

The getChange() method of DocumentEvent requires an Element to return a DocumentEvent.ElementChange. You normally use the default root element from the Document, as in the following example.

```
Document documentSource = documentEvent.getDocument();
Element rootElement = documentSource.getDefaultRootElement();
DocumentEvent.ElementChange change = documentEvent.getChange(rootElement);
```

Once you have your DocumentEvent.ElementChange instance, you can find out the added and removed elements, if you need that level of information.

```
public interface DocumentEvent.ElementChange {
  public Element[ ] getChildrenAdded();
  public Element[ ] getChildrenRemoved();
  public Element getElement();
  public int getIndex();
}
```

Caret and Highlighter Interfaces

Now that you understand the data model aspect of a text component, you can look at some aspects of its selection rendering through the Caret and Highlighter interfaces. Remember that these are properties of the text component, not the data model.

The Caret interface describes what's usually referred to as the *cursor*: the location in the document where you can insert text. The Highlighter interface provides the basis for how to paint selected text. These two interfaces, their related interfaces, and their implementations are rarely altered. The text components simply use their default implementations with the DefaultCaret and DefaultHighlighter classes.

Although you probably won't alter the caret and highlighter behavior for a text component, you should know that there are many interrelated classes working together. For the Highlighter interface, the predefined implementation is called DefaultHighlighter, which extends another implementation called LayeredHighlighter. The Highlighter also manages a collection of Highlighter.Highlight objects to designate highlighted sections.

The DefaultHighlighter creates a DefaultHighlighter.HighlightPainter to paint the highlighted section(s) of text. The HighlightPainter is an implementation of the Highlighter.HighlightPainter interface and extends the LayeredHighlighter.LayerPainter class. Each section to paint is described by a Highlighter.Highlight, where the Highlighter manages the set. The actual HighlightPainter is created by the DefaultCaret implementation.

The Highlighter interface describes how to paint selected text within a text component. If you don't like the color, you can simply change the TextField.selectionBackground UI property setting to a different color.

```
public interface Highlighter {
  // Properties
  public Highlighter.Highlight[ ] getHighlights();
  // Other methods
  public Object addHighlight(int p0, int p1, Highlighter.HighlightPainter p)
    throws BadLocationException;
```

```
   public void changeHighlight(Object tag, int p0, int p1)
     throws BadLocationException;
   public void deinstall(JTextComponent component);
   public void install(JTextComponent component)
   public void paint(Graphics g);
   public void removeAllHighlights();
   public void removeHighlight(Object tag);
}
```

The Caret interface describes the current cursor, as well as several selection attributes. Of the Highlighter and Caret interfaces, the latter is the one that you would actually use, although it isn't necessary to subclass it.

```
public interface Caret {
  // Properties
  public int getBlinkRate();
  public void setBlinkRate(int newValue);
  public int getDot();
  public void setDot(int newValue);
  public Point getMagicCaretPosition();
  public void setMagicCaretPosition(Point newValue);
  public int getMark();
  public boolean isSelectionVisible();
  public void setSelectionVisible(boolean newValue);
  public boolean isVisible();
  public void setVisible(boolean newValue);
  // Listeners
  public void addChangeListener(ChangeListener l);
  public void removeChangeListener(ChangeListener l);
  // Other methods
  public void deinstall(JTextComponent c);
  public void install(JTextComponent c);
  public void moveDot(int dot);
  public void paint(Graphics g);
}
```

Table 15-4 lists the six attributes of Caret.

Table 15-4. *Caret Properties*

Property Name	Data Type	Access
blinkRate	int	Read-write
dot	int	Read-write
magicCaretPosition	Point	Read-write
mark	int	Read-only
selectionVisible	boolean	Read-write
visible	boolean	Read-write

The blinkRate is the millisecond delay between the flashes of the caret. The dot property is the current position within the text component of the cursor. To move the cursor to another position so that some text will be highlighted, add a call to the moveDot(int newPosition) method. This sets the mark property to the old dot position and sets the new dot setting to the new position.

The magicCaretPosition property deals with moving up and down lines of different lengths. For example, suppose the following three lines of text were on your screen:

```
Friz Freleng
Mel Blanc
What's up Doc?
```

Now suppose that the current cursor position is between the *n* and *g* on the first line. If you pressed the down arrow twice, you would want the cursor to stay at the same horizontal position, instead of moving to the end of the shorter second line. It's the magicCursorPosition property that retains this information, so that the cursor ends up being between the *D* and the *o* in the third line. Without the magic position retained, the cursor would fall in between the *p* and the word space of the last line.

One useful instance of using the caret is to find the current screen location in response to a keystroke. That way, you can pop up a menu at the current cursor position. This would be similar to the Code Insights option in JBuilder or IntelliSense in Visual Studio, in which the tool helps you complete method calls by popping up a menu of methods. Given the current dot location in the model, map it to the position in the view with the public Rectangle modelToView(int position) method of JTextComponent (which can throw a BadLocationException). Then use the Rectangle returned as the location to pop up the menu, as shown in Figure 15-10.

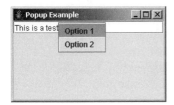

Figure 15-10. *Using the Caret to determine a pop-up location*

The program in Listing 15-9 will show a JPopupMenu at the location where the period (.) key is pressed in the text field.

Listing 15-9. *Mapping Caret Location to Pop-Up Position*

```
import javax.swing.*;
import javax.swing.text.*;
import javax.swing.plaf.*;
import java.awt.*;
import java.awt.event.*;
```

```
public class PopupSample {
  public static void main(String args[]) {
    Runnable runner = new Runnable() {
      public void run() {
        JFrame frame = new JFrame("Popup Example");
        frame.setDefaultCloseOperation(JFrame.EXIT_ON_CLOSE);

        final JPopupMenu popup = new JPopupMenu();
        JMenuItem menuItem1 = new JMenuItem("Option 1");
        popup.add(menuItem1);

        JMenuItem menuItem2 = new JMenuItem("Option 2");
        popup.add(menuItem2);

        final JTextField textField = new JTextField();
        frame.add(textField, BorderLayout.NORTH);

        ActionListener actionListener = new ActionListener() {
          public void actionPerformed(ActionEvent actionEvent) {
            try {
              int dotPosition = textField.getCaretPosition();
              Rectangle popupLocation = textField.modelToView(dotPosition);
              popup.show(textField, popupLocation.x, popupLocation.y);
            } catch (BadLocationException badLocationException) {
              System.err.println("Oops");
            }
          }
        };
        KeyStroke keystroke =
          KeyStroke.getKeyStroke(KeyEvent.VK_PERIOD, 0, false);
        textField.registerKeyboardAction(actionListener, keystroke,
          JComponent.WHEN_FOCUSED);

        frame.setSize(250, 150);
        frame.setVisible(true);
      }
    };
    EventQueue.invokeLater(runner);
  }
}
```

CaretListener Interface and CaretEvent Class

You can listen for cursor movements in two ways: associate a ChangeListener with the Caret or associate a CaretListener with the JTextComponent. Working directly with the JTextComponent is the easier approach, though both will function equally well.

In the case of the CaretListener, there's a single method defined by the interface:

```
public interface CaretListener implements EventListener {
  public void caretUpdate (CaretEvent caretEvent);
}
```

When the listener is notified, a CaretEvent is sent, which reports on the new dot and mark locations.

```
public abstract class CaretEvent extends EventObject {
  public CaretEvent(Object source);
  public abstract int getDot();
  public abstract int getMark();
}
```

To demonstrate, Figure 15-11 shows a program with a CaretListener attached to the inner JTextArea. When the CaretEvent happens, the current dot value is sent to the top text field and the current mark setting is sent to the button. In the example, the cursor dot is at the beginning of the second line, with the mark at the end.

Figure 15-11. *CaretListener sample*

Listing 15-10 shows the source associated with the example in Figure 15-11.

Listing 15-10. *Listening for Caret Changes*

```
import javax.swing.*;
import javax.swing.event.*;
import java.awt.*;

public class CaretSample {
  public static void main(String args[]) {
    Runnable runner = new Runnable() {
      public void run() {
        JFrame frame = new JFrame("Caret Example");
        frame.setDefaultCloseOperation(JFrame.EXIT_ON_CLOSE);

        JTextArea textArea = new JTextArea();
        JScrollPane scrollPane = new JScrollPane(textArea);
        frame.add(scrollPane, BorderLayout.CENTER);
```

```
        final JTextField dot = new JTextField();
        dot.setEditable(false);
        JPanel dotPanel = new JPanel(new BorderLayout());
        dotPanel.add(new JLabel("Dot: "), BorderLayout.WEST);
        dotPanel.add(dot, BorderLayout.CENTER);
        frame.add(dotPanel, BorderLayout.NORTH);

        final JTextField mark = new JTextField();
        mark.setEditable(false);
        JPanel markPanel = new JPanel(new BorderLayout());
        markPanel.add(new JLabel("Mark: "), BorderLayout.WEST);
        markPanel.add(mark, BorderLayout.CENTER);
        frame.add(markPanel, BorderLayout.SOUTH);

        CaretListener listener = new CaretListener() {
          public void caretUpdate(CaretEvent caretEvent) {
            dot.setText(Integer.toString(caretEvent.getDot()));
            mark.setText(Integer.toString(caretEvent.getMark()));
          }
        };

        textArea.addCaretListener(listener);

        frame.setSize(250, 150);
        frame.setVisible(true);
      }
    };
    EventQueue.invokeLater(runner);
  }
}
```

NavigationFilter Class

Similar to the way you can limit input to the text component's document by associating
a DocumentFilter with a Document, you can limit where the caret can go by associating a
NavigationFilter with a JTextComponent. The class has three methods:

```
public void setDot(NavigationFilter.FilterBypass fb, int dot, Position.Bias bias)

public void moveDot(NavigationFilter.FilterBypass fb, int dot, Position.Bias bias)

public int getNextVisualPositionFrom(JTextComponent text, int pos,
  Position.Bias bias, int direction, Position.Bias[] biasRet)
```

To limit movement, you would typically override the first two, leaving the default implementation of the latter. For instance, Listing 15-11 shows a program that has a reserved area
(say, the title of a report) at the beginning of the JTextArea. If you try to set or move the caret
(dot) to the reserved area, the filter rejects the change and moves the caret to after the area.

Listing 15-11. *Restricting Caret Movement*

```java
import javax.swing.*;
import javax.swing.text.*;
import javax.swing.event.*;
import java.awt.*;

public class NavigationSample {
  private static final String START_STRING = "Start\n";
  private static final int START_STRING_LENGTH = START_STRING.length();

  public static void main(String args[]) {
    Runnable runner = new Runnable() {
      public void run() {
        JFrame frame = new JFrame("Navigation Example");
        frame.setDefaultCloseOperation(JFrame.EXIT_ON_CLOSE);

        JTextArea textArea = new JTextArea(START_STRING);
        textArea.setCaretPosition(START_STRING_LENGTH);
        JScrollPane scrollPane = new JScrollPane(textArea);
        frame.add(scrollPane, BorderLayout.CENTER);

        NavigationFilter filter = new NavigationFilter() {
          public void setDot(NavigationFilter.FilterBypass fb, int dot,
              Position.Bias bias) {
            if (dot < START_STRING_LENGTH) {
              fb.setDot(START_STRING_LENGTH, bias);
            } else {
              fb.setDot(dot, bias);
            }
          }
          public void moveDot(NavigationFilter.FilterBypass fb, int dot,
              Position.Bias bias) {
            if (dot < START_STRING_LENGTH) {
              fb.setDot(START_STRING_LENGTH, bias);
            } else {
              fb.setDot(dot, bias);
            }
          }
        };

        textArea.setNavigationFilter(filter);

        frame.setSize(250, 150);
        frame.setVisible(true);
      }
    };
    EventQueue.invokeLater(runner);
  }
}
```

Figure 15-12 shows the screen after typing some information into the text component.

Figure 15-12. *NavigationFilter sample*

Keymap Interface

In "MVC-speak," the keymap property of the text component is the Controller part. It maps KeyStroke objects to individual actions through the Keymap interface. (The KeyStroke class was discussed in Chapter 2.) When you register the KeyStroke to the JTextComponent with registerKeyboardAction(), as in the PopupSample program shown in Listing 15-9 earlier in this chapter, the text component stores this mapping from KeyStroke to Action in a Keymap. For instance, the Backspace key is mapped to delete the previous character. If you want to add another binding, you just register another keystroke.

■**Note** In reality, the Keymap is just a front to the ActionMap/InputMap pair. The JTextComponent relies on some internal workings to indirectly use the ActionMap/InputMap classes.

You can also add actions for keystrokes directly to the Keymap. This allows you to share a key map across multiple text components, as long as they all share the same extended behavior.

```
public interface Keymap {
  // Properties
  public Action[ ] getBoundActions();
  public KeyStroke[ ] getBoundKeyStrokes();
  public Action getDefaultAction();
  public void setDefaultAction(Action action);
  public String getName();
  public Keymap getResolveParent();
  public void setResolveParent(Keymap parent);
  // Other methods
  public void addActionForKeyStroke(KeyStroke keystroke, Action action);
  public Action getAction(KeyStroke keystroke);
  public KeyStroke[ ] getKeyStrokesForAction(Action action);
  public boolean isLocallyDefined(KeyStroke keystroke);
  public void removeBindings();
  public void removeKeyStrokeBinding(KeyStroke keystroke);
}
```

For some applications, you may also want to *remove* keystrokes from the key map. For instance, the JTextField has an entry in the key map for the Enter key so that any registered ActionListener objects are notified. If the JTextField is on a screen where a button has been designated as the default, pressing Enter won't select the default button, as desired. Getting rid of the default behavior is a simple process of requesting the removal of the single KeyStroke from the Keymap, as shown here:

```
Keymap keymap = textField.getKeymap();
KeyStroke keystroke = KeyStroke.getKeyStroke(KeyEvent.VK_ENTER, 0, false);
keymap.removeKeyStrokeBinding(keystroke);
```

Then, when you press Enter in the text field, the default button is activated, as shown in Figure 15-13.

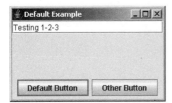

Figure 15-13. *Using the default button after removing the Enter binding from the Keymap*

The program source for the example in Figure 15-13 is shown in Listing 15-12.

Listing 15-12. *Working with the Default Button*

```java
import javax.swing.*;
import javax.swing.text.*;
import java.awt.*;
import java.awt.event.*;

public class DefaultSample {
  public static void main(String args[]) {
    Runnable runner = new Runnable() {
      public void run() {
        JFrame frame = new JFrame("Default Example");
        frame.setDefaultCloseOperation(JFrame.EXIT_ON_CLOSE);

        JTextField textField = new JTextField();
        frame.add(textField, BorderLayout.NORTH);

        ActionListener actionListener = new ActionListener() {
          public void actionPerformed(ActionEvent actionEvent) {
            System.out.println(actionEvent.getActionCommand() + " selected");
          }
        };
```

```
        JPanel panel = new JPanel();
        JButton defaultButton = new JButton("Default Button");
        defaultButton.addActionListener(actionListener);
        panel.add(defaultButton);

        JButton otherButton = new JButton("Other Button");
        otherButton.addActionListener(actionListener);
        panel.add(otherButton);

        frame.add(panel, BorderLayout.SOUTH);

        Keymap keymap = textField.getKeymap();
        KeyStroke keystroke =
          KeyStroke.getKeyStroke(KeyEvent.VK_ENTER, 0, false);
        keymap.removeKeyStrokeBinding(keystroke);

        frame.getRootPane().setDefaultButton(defaultButton);

        frame.setSize(250, 150);
        frame.setVisible(true);
      }
    };
    EventQueue.invokeLater(runner);
  }
}
```

JTextComponent.KeyBinding Class

The JTextComponent class stores the specific key bindings with the help of the JTextComponent.KeyBinding class. The current look and feel defines the default set of the key bindings for text components, such as the familiar Ctrl-X for cut, Ctrl-C for copy, and Ctrl-V for paste on a Microsoft Windows platform.

Handling JTextField Events

Dealing with events in Swing text components is completely different from dealing with events in AWT text components. Although you can still attach an ActionListener to listen for when the user presses the Enter key in the text field, attaching a KeyListener or a TextListener is no longer useful.

To validate input, it is better to attach an InputVerifier than a FocusListener. However, input validation tends to be best left to the Document to accomplish or implemented when a user submits a form.

Listening to JTextField Events with an ActionListener

The JTextField will notify any registered ActionListener objects when the user presses Enter from within the text field. The component sends an ActionEvent to the ActionListener objects.

Part of this ActionEvent is an action command. By default, the action command of the event is the current contents of the component. With the Swing JTextField, you can also set this action command to be something different from the content. The JTextField has an actionCommand property. When it is set to null (the default setting), the action command for the ActionEvent takes the contents of the component. However, if you set the actionCommand property for the JTextField, then that actionCommand setting is part of the ActionEvent.

The following code demonstrates this difference. There are two text fields. When Enter is pressed in the first text field, causing the registered ActionListener to be notified, "Yo" is printed out. When Enter is pressed in the second text field, the contents are printed out.

```
JTextField nameTextField = new JTextField();
JTextField cityTextField = new JTextField();
ActionListener actionListener = new ActionListener() {
  public void actionPerformed(ActionEvent actionEvent) {
    System.out.println("Command: " + actionEvent.getActionCommand());
  }
};
nameTextField.setActionCommand("Yo");
nameTextField.addActionListener(actionListener);
cityTextField.addActionListener(actionListener);
```

Listening to JTextField Events with an KeyListener

With the Swing text components, you normally don't listen for key events with a KeyListener—at least not to validate input. Running the following example demonstrates that you can still find out when a key has been pressed or released, not just when it has been typed.

```
KeyListener keyListener = new KeyListener() {
  public void keyPressed(KeyEvent keyEvent) {
    printIt("Pressed", keyEvent);
  }
  public void keyReleased(KeyEvent keyEvent) {
    printIt("Released", keyEvent);
  }
  public void keyTyped(KeyEvent keyEvent) {
    printIt("Typed", keyEvent);
  }
  private void printIt(String title, KeyEvent keyEvent) {
    int keyCode = keyEvent.getKeyCode();
    String keyText = KeyEvent.getKeyText(keyCode);
    System.out.println(title + " : " + keyText);
  }
};
nameTextField.addKeyListener(keyListener);
cityTextField.addKeyListener(keyListener);
```

Listening to JTextField Events with an InputVerifier

Implementing the InputVerifier interface allows you to do field-level validation of a JTextField. Before focus moves out of a text component, the verifier runs. If the input isn't valid, the verifier rejects the change and keeps input focus within the given component.

In the following example, if you try to move the input focus beyond the text field, you'll find that you can't, unless the contents of the text field are empty or the contents consist of the string "Exit".

```
InputVerifier verifier = new InputVerifier() {
  public boolean verify(JComponent input) {
    final JTextComponent source = (JTextComponent)input;
    String text = source.getText();
    if ((text.length() != 0) && !(text.equals("Exit"))) {
      Runnable runnable = new Runnable() {
        public void run() {
          JOptionPane.showMessageDialog (source, "Can't leave.",
            "Error Dialog", JOptionPane.ERROR_MESSAGE);
        }
      };
      EventQueue.invokeLater(runnable);
      return false;
    } else {
      return true;
    }
  }
};
nameTextField.setInputVerifier(verifier);
cityTextField.setInputVerifier(verifier);
```

Listening to JTextField Events with a DocumentListener

To find out when the contents of the text component changed, you need to associate a listener with the data model. In this case, the data model is Document and the listener is a DocumentListener. The following example just tells you when and how the model changed. Remember that changedUpdate() is for attribute changes. Do not use a DocumentListener for input validation.

```
DocumentListener documentListener = new DocumentListener() {
  public void changedUpdate(DocumentEvent documentEvent) {
    printIt(documentEvent);
  }
  public void insertUpdate(DocumentEvent documentEvent) {
    printIt(documentEvent);
  }
  public void removeUpdate(DocumentEvent documentEvent) {
    printIt(documentEvent);
  }
  private void printIt(DocumentEvent documentEvent) {
    DocumentEvent.EventType type = documentEvent.getType();
```

```
    String typeString = null;
    if (type.equals(DocumentEvent.EventType.CHANGE)) {
      typeString = "Change";
    } else if (type.equals(DocumentEvent.EventType.INSERT)) {
      typeString = "Insert";
    } else if (type.equals(DocumentEvent.EventType.REMOVE)) {
      typeString = "Remove";
    }
    System.out.print("Type  :   " + typeString + " / ");
    Document source = documentEvent.getDocument();
    int length = source.getLength();
    try {
      System.out.println("Contents: " + source.getText(0, length));
    } catch (BadLocationException badLocationException) {
      System.out.println("Contents: Unknown");
    }
  }
};
nameTextField.getDocument().addDocumentListener(documentListener);
cityTextField.getDocument().addDocumentListener(documentListener);
```

Putting It All Together

Now that you've seen the usage of the listeners separately, let's put them all together within one example. Figure 15-14 shows the end result of this endeavor. Keep in mind that the magic word to tab out of a component is "Exit."

Figure 15-14. *JTextField event demonstration*

The source behind the program in Figure 15-14 is shown in Listing 15-13.

Listing 15-13. *Text Event Handling*

```java
import javax.swing.*;
import javax.swing.text.*;
import javax.swing.event.*;
import java.awt.*;
import java.awt.event.*;

public class JTextFieldSample {
  public static void main(String args[]) {
    Runnable runner = new Runnable() {
```

```java
public void run() {
  JFrame frame = new JFrame("TextField Listener Example");
  frame.setDefaultCloseOperation(JFrame.EXIT_ON_CLOSE);

  JPanel namePanel = new JPanel(new BorderLayout());
  JLabel nameLabel = new JLabel("Name: ");
  nameLabel.setDisplayedMnemonic(KeyEvent.VK_N);
  JTextField nameTextField = new JTextField();
  nameLabel.setLabelFor(nameTextField);
  namePanel.add(nameLabel, BorderLayout.WEST);
  namePanel.add(nameTextField, BorderLayout.CENTER);
  frame.add(namePanel, BorderLayout.NORTH);

  JPanel cityPanel = new JPanel(new BorderLayout());
  JLabel cityLabel = new JLabel("City: ");
  cityLabel.setDisplayedMnemonic(KeyEvent.VK_C);
  JTextField cityTextField = new JTextField();
  cityLabel.setLabelFor(cityTextField);
  cityPanel.add(cityLabel, BorderLayout.WEST);
  cityPanel.add(cityTextField, BorderLayout.CENTER);
  frame.add(cityPanel, BorderLayout.SOUTH);

  ActionListener actionListener = new ActionListener() {
    public void actionPerformed(ActionEvent actionEvent) {
      System.out.println("Command: " + actionEvent.getActionCommand());
    }
  };
  nameTextField.setActionCommand("Yo");
  nameTextField.addActionListener(actionListener);
  cityTextField.addActionListener(actionListener);

  KeyListener keyListener = new KeyListener() {
    public void keyPressed(KeyEvent keyEvent) {
      printIt("Pressed", keyEvent);
    }
    public void keyReleased(KeyEvent keyEvent) {
      printIt("Released", keyEvent);
    }
    public void keyTyped(KeyEvent keyEvent) {
      printIt("Typed", keyEvent);
    }
    private void printIt(String title, KeyEvent keyEvent) {
      int keyCode = keyEvent.getKeyCode();
      String keyText = KeyEvent.getKeyText(keyCode);
      System.out.println(title + " : " + keyText + " / " +
        keyEvent.getKeyChar());
    }
  };
```

```
nameTextField.addKeyListener(keyListener);
cityTextField.addKeyListener(keyListener);

InputVerifier verifier = new InputVerifier() {
  public boolean verify(JComponent input) {
    final JTextComponent source = (JTextComponent)input;
    String text = source.getText();
    if ((text.length() != 0) && !(text.equals("Exit"))) {
      JOptionPane.showMessageDialog (source, "Can't leave.",
        "Error Dialog", JOptionPane.ERROR_MESSAGE);
      return false;
    } else {
      return true;
    }
  }
};
nameTextField.setInputVerifier(verifier);
cityTextField.setInputVerifier(verifier);

DocumentListener documentListener = new DocumentListener() {
  public void changedUpdate(DocumentEvent documentEvent) {
    printIt(documentEvent);
  }
  public void insertUpdate(DocumentEvent documentEvent) {
    printIt(documentEvent);
  }
  public void removeUpdate(DocumentEvent documentEvent) {
    printIt(documentEvent);
  }
  private void printIt(DocumentEvent documentEvent) {
    DocumentEvent.EventType type = documentEvent.getType();
    String typeString = null;
    if (type.equals(DocumentEvent.EventType.CHANGE)) {
      typeString = "Change";
    } else if (type.equals(DocumentEvent.EventType.INSERT)) {
      typeString = "Insert";
    } else if (type.equals(DocumentEvent.EventType.REMOVE)) {
      typeString = "Remove";
    }
    System.out.print("Type  :    " + typeString + " / ");
    Document source = documentEvent.getDocument();
    int length = source.getLength();
```

```
          try {
            System.out.println("Contents: " + source.getText(0, length));
          } catch (BadLocationException badLocationException) {
            System.out.println("Contents: Unknown");
          }
        }
      }
    };
    nameTextField.getDocument().addDocumentListener(documentListener);
    cityTextField.getDocument().addDocumentListener(documentListener);

    frame.setSize(250, 100);
    frame.setVisible(true);
    }
  };
  EventQueue.invokeLater(runner);
  }
}
```

Customizing a JTextField Look and Feel

Each installable Swing look and feel provides a different JTextField appearance and set of default UIResource values. The available set of 25 UIResource-related properties for a JTextField is shown in Table 15-5.

Table 15-5. *JTextField UIResource Elements*

Property String	Object Type
text	Color
textHighlight	Color
textHighlightText	Color
textInactiveText	Color
TextField.actionMap	ActionMap
TextField.background	Color
TextField.border	Border
TextField.caretAspectRatio	Number
TextField.caretBlinkRate	Integer
TextField.caretForeground	Color
TextField.darkShadow	Color
TextField.disabledBackground	Color
TextField.focusInputMap	InputMap
TextField.font	Font

Table 15-5. *JTextField UIResource Elements (Continued)*

Property String	Object Type
TextField.foreground	Color
TextField.highlight	Color
TextField.inactiveBackground	Color
TextField.inactiveForeground	Color
TextField.keyBindings	KeyBinding[ ]
TextField.light	Color
TextField.margin	Insets
TextField.selectionBackground	Color
TextField.selectionForeground	Color
TextField.shadow	Color
TextFieldUI	String

Figure 15-15 shows the appearance of the JTextField component for the preinstalled set of look and feel types: Motif, Windows, and Ocean.

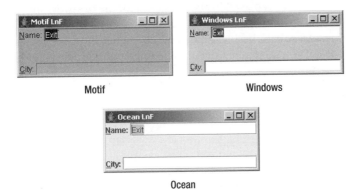

Motif   Windows

Ocean

Figure 15-15. *JTextField under different look and feel types*

JPasswordField Class

The JPasswordField component is designed for input of passwords. Instead of echoing what the user types, a special input mask is displayed. It works like a JTextField with an input mask of *. You can't unset the mask, nor can you cut or copy the contents of the password component. The intention is to enhance security.

Creating a JPasswordField

The JPasswordField class has the same five constructors as the JTextField:

```
public JPasswordField()
JPasswordField passwordField = new JPasswordField();

public JPasswordField(String text)
JPasswordField passwordField = new JPasswordField("Initial Password");

public JPasswordField(int columnWidth)
JPasswordField passwordField = new JPasswordField(14);

public JPasswordField(String text, int columnWidth)
JPasswordField passwordField = new JPasswordField("Initial Password", 14);

public JPasswordField(Document model, String text, int columnWidth)
JPasswordField passwordField = new JPasswordField(aModel, "Initial Password", 14);
```

With the no-argument constructor, you get an empty input field zero columns wide, a default initial Document model, and an echo character of *. Although you can specify the initial text in the constructor, you're usually prompting a user for a password to verify the user's identity, not to see if the user can submit a form. Therefore, a JPasswordField tends to be empty at startup. As with the JTextField, you can also specify the initial width, assuming that the layout manager of the container in which the JPasswordField is placed will honor this request.

You can also specify the Document data model for the password field in a constructor. When specifying the Document data model, you should specify a null initial-text argument; otherwise, the current contents of the document will be replaced by the initial text for the password field. In addition, you should *not* try to use a custom Document with a JPasswordField. Because the component doesn't display any visual feedback besides how many characters have been entered, it can be confusing to a user if you tried to restrict input to only numeric data.

JPasswordField Properties

Table 15-6 shows the four properties of JPasswordField.

Table 15-6. *JPasswordField Properties*

Property Name	Data Type	Access
accessibleContext	AccessibleContext	Read-only
echoChar	char	Read-write
password	char[ ]	Read-only
UIClassID	String	Read-only

Setting the echoChar property allows you to use a mask character other than the default asterisk (*) character. If the echoChar property is set to the character \ u0000 (0), the public boolean echoCharIsSet() method returns false. In all other cases, the method returns true.

■**Caution** The JPasswordField also has a deprecated read-only text property, which you should avoid using. You should use the password property instead, because it returns a char[] that can be cleared immediately after usage. A String must wait for the garbage collector to dispose of it.

Customizing a JPasswordField Look and Feel

The JPasswordField is a subclass of a JTextField. It has the same appearance under all the predefined look and feel types as the JTextField (see Figure 15-15). The one difference is that the current echoChar property setting masks the content. This is shown in Figure 15-16. The top text component is a JTextField; the bottom one is a JPasswordField.

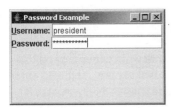

Figure 15-16. *JPasswordField sample in Ocean theme*

The set of 17 UIResource-related properties for a JPasswordField is shown in Table 15-7.

Table 15-7. *JPasswordField UIResource Elements*

Property String	Object Type
PasswordField.actionMap	ActionMap
PasswordField.background	Color
PasswordField.border	Border
PasswordField.caretAspectRatio	Number
PasswordField.caretBlinkRate	Integer
PasswordField.caretForeground	Color
PasswordField.disabledBackground	Color
PasswordField.focusInputMap	InputMap
PasswordField.font	Font
PasswordField.foreground	Color
PasswordField.inactiveBackground	Color
PasswordField.inactiveForeground	Color
PasswordField.keyBindings	KeyBinding[ ]

Table 15-7. *JPasswordField UIResource Elements (Continued)*

Property String	Object Type
PasswordField.margin	Insets
PasswordField.selectionBackground	Color
PasswordField.selectionForeground	Color
PasswordFieldUI	String

JFormattedTextField Class

The JFormattedTextField provides support for the input of formatted text. When the component is created, you define a mask for the input. That mask can be in the form of one of four styles: a java.text.Format object, an AbstractFormatter, an AbstractFormatterFactory, or an actual value of a different type (such as 3.141592).

The system provides several abstract formatters for you to work with, depending on the type of data you want a user to input. For instance, the NumberFormatter is available to enter numbers, and the DateFormatter is available for entering dates. There is also a MaskFormatter for describing input with edit strings, like "XXX-XX-XXX" for a United States social security number. If you want different display and edit formats, you can use the AbstractFormatterFactory. You'll learn more about formatters and formatter factories in Chapter 16.

Creating a JFormattedTextField

There are six constructors for the JFormattedTextField class:

public JFormattedTextField()
```
JFormattedTextField formattedField = new JFormattedTextField();
```

public JFormattedTextField(Format format)
```
DateFormat format = new SimpleDateFormat("yyyy--MMMM--dd");
JFormattedTextField formattedField = new JFormattedTextField(format);
```

public JFormattedTextField(JFormattedTextField.AbstractFormatter formatter)
```
DateFormat displayFormat = new SimpleDateFormat("yyyy--MMMM--dd");
DateFormatter displayFormatter = new DateFormatter(displayFormat);
JFormattedTextField formattedField = new JFormattedTextField(displayFormatter);
```

public JFormattedTextField(JFormattedTextField.AbstractFormatterFactory factory)
```
DateFormat displayFormat = new SimpleDateFormat("yyyy--MMMM--dd");
DateFormatter displayFormatter = new DateFormatter(displayFormat);
DateFormat editFormat = new SimpleDateFormat("MM/dd/yy");
DateFormatter editFormatter = new DateFormatter(editFormat);
DefaultFormatterFactory factory = new DefaultFormatterFactory(
  displayFormatter, displayFormatter, editFormatter);
JFormattedTextField formattedField = new JFormattedTextField(factory);
```

```
public JFormattedTextField(JFormattedTextField.AbstractFormatterFactory factory,
  Object currentValue)
DateFormat displayFormat = new SimpleDateFormat("yyyy--MMMM--dd");
DateFormatter displayFormatter = new DateFormatter(displayFormat);
DateFormat editFormat = new SimpleDateFormat("MM/dd/yy");
DateFormatter editFormatter = new DateFormatter(editFormat);
DefaultFormatterFactory factory = new DefaultFormatterFactory(
  displayFormatter, displayFormatter, editFormatter);
JFormattedTextField formattedField = new JFormattedTextField(factory, new Date());

public JFormattedTextField(Object value)
JFormattedTextField formattedField = new JFormattedTextField(new Date());
```

The no-argument version requires you to configure it later. The other constructors allow you to configure what and how input will be accepted into the component.

JFormattedTextField Properties

Table 15-8 shows the eight properties of JFormattedTextField. Instead of getting the contents of the JFormattedTextField as a String via the text property, as you would with a JTextField, you get it as an Object via the value property. Thus, if your formatter were for a Date object, the value you get back could be cast to type java.util.Date.

Table 15-8. *JFormattedTextField Properties*

Property Name	Data Type	Access
actions	Action[ ]	Read-only
document	Document	Write-only
editValid	boolean	Read-only
focusLostBehavior	int	Read-write
formatter	JFormattedTextField.AbstractFormatter	Read-only
formatterFactory	JFormattedTextField.AbstractFormatterFactory	Read-write bound
UIClassID	String	Read-only
value	Object	Read-write bound

Listing 15-14 demonstrates the user of JFormattedTextField with custom formatters and factories. Notice that when you edit the bottom text field, the display format and edit format are different.

Listing 15-14. *JFormattedTextField Example*

```java
import javax.swing.*;
import javax.swing.text.*;
import javax.swing.event.*;
import java.awt.*;
import java.awt.event.*;
import java.util.*;
import java.text.*;

public class FormattedSample {
  public static void main(final String args[]) {
    Runnable runner = new Runnable() {
      public void run() {
        JFrame frame = new JFrame("Formatted Example");
        frame.setDefaultCloseOperation(JFrame.EXIT_ON_CLOSE);

        JPanel datePanel = new JPanel(new BorderLayout());
        JLabel dateLabel = new JLabel("Date: ");
        dateLabel.setDisplayedMnemonic(KeyEvent.VK_D);
        DateFormat format = new SimpleDateFormat("yyyy--MMMM--dd");
        JFormattedTextField dateTextField = new JFormattedTextField(format);
        dateLabel.setLabelFor(dateTextField);
        datePanel.add(dateLabel, BorderLayout.WEST);
        datePanel.add(dateTextField, BorderLayout.CENTER);
        frame.add(datePanel, BorderLayout.NORTH);

        JPanel date2Panel = new JPanel(new BorderLayout());
        JLabel date2Label = new JLabel("Date 2: ");
        date2Label.setDisplayedMnemonic(KeyEvent.VK_A);
        DateFormat displayFormat = new SimpleDateFormat("yyyy--MMMM--dd");
        DateFormatter displayFormatter = new DateFormatter(displayFormat);
        DateFormat editFormat = new SimpleDateFormat("MM/dd/yy");
        DateFormatter editFormatter = new DateFormatter(editFormat);
        DefaultFormatterFactory factory = new DefaultFormatterFactory(
          displayFormatter, displayFormatter, editFormatter);
        JFormattedTextField date2TextField = new JFormattedTextField(factory,
          new Date());
        date2Label.setLabelFor(date2TextField);
        date2Panel.add(date2Label, BorderLayout.WEST);
        date2Panel.add(date2TextField, BorderLayout.CENTER);
        frame.add(date2Panel, BorderLayout.SOUTH);

        ActionListener actionListener = new ActionListener() {
          public void actionPerformed(ActionEvent actionEvent) {
            JFormattedTextField source =
              (JFormattedTextField)actionEvent.getSource();
            Object value = source.getValue();
```

```
        System.out.println("Class: " + value.getClass());
        System.out.println("Value: " + value);
      }
    };
    dateTextField.addActionListener(actionListener);
    date2TextField.addActionListener(actionListener);

    frame.setSize(250, 100);
    frame.setVisible(true);
    }
  };
  EventQueue.invokeLater(runner);
  }
}
```

Customizing a JFormattedTextField Look and Feel

Like the JPasswordField, JFormattedTextField is a subclass of a JTextField. It, too, has the
same appearance as the JTextField under all the predefined look and feel types (see Figure 15-15).
To customize its display, you can change any of the set of 16 UIResource-related properties for
a JFormattedTextField, as shown in Table 15-9.

Table 15-9. *JFormattedTextField UIResource Elements*

Property String	Object Type
FormattedTextField.actionMap	ActionMap
FormattedTextField.background	Color
FormattedTextField.border	Border
FormattedTextField.caretAspectRatio	Number
FormattedTextField.caretBlinkRate	Integer
FormattedTextField.caretForeground	Color
FormattedTextField.focusInputMap	InputMap
FormattedTextField.font	Font
FormattedTextField.foreground	Color
FormattedTextField.inactiveBackground	Color
FormattedTextField.inactiveForeground	Color
FormattedTextField.keyBindings	KeyBinding[ ]
FormattedTextField.margin	Insets
FormattedTextField.selectionBackground	Color
FormattedTextField.selectionForeground	Color
FormattedTextFieldUI	String

JTextArea Class

The JTextArea component is the text component for multiple-line input. Similar to the JTextField, the data model for a JTextArea is the PlainDocument implementation of the Document interface. Therefore, the JTextArea is limited to single-attributed text. As with other Swing components that may require scrolling, the JTextArea doesn't support scrolling itself. You need to place each JTextArea within a JScrollPane to allow a user to properly scroll through the contents of a JTextArea.

Creating a JTextArea

There are six constructors for creating a JTextArea:

public JTextArea()
```
JTextArea textArea = new JTextArea();
```

public JTextArea(Document document)
```
Document document = new PlainDocument();
JTextArea textArea = new JTextArea(document);
```

public JTextArea(String text)
```
JTextArea textArea = new JTextArea("...");
```

public JTextArea(int rows, int columns)
```
JTextArea textArea = new JTextArea(10, 40);
```

public JTextArea(String text, int rows, int columns)
```
JTextArea textArea = new JTextArea("...", 10, 40);
```

public JTextArea(Document document, String text, int rows, int columns)
```
JTextArea textArea = new JTextArea(document, null, 10, 40);
```

Unless otherwise specified, the text area is able to hold zero rows and columns of content. Although this might sound like a serious limitation, you're just telling the text area to let the current LayoutManager worry about the size of your text area. The contents of the JTextArea are initially empty unless specified from either the starting text string or the Document model.

■**Note** Other initial settings for a JTextArea include having a tab stop every eight positions and turning off word wrap. For more on tab stops, see the TabStop and TabSet class descriptions in Chapter 16.

After creating a JTextArea, remember to place the JTextArea into a JScrollPane. Then if there isn't sufficient space on the screen, the JScrollPane will manage the scrolling for you.

```
JTextArea textArea = new JTextArea();
JScrollPane scrollPane = new JScrollPane(textArea);
content.add(scrollPane);
```

Figure 15-17 shows how a JTextArea looks within a JScrollPane and outside a JScrollPane. In the JTextArea not in the JScrollPane, you can't see the text that falls below the bottom screen border. By design, moving the cursor into that area doesn't cause the content at the top to move up.

Figure 15-17. *A JTextArea without a JScrollPane and one within a JScrollPane*

JTextArea Properties

Table 15-10 shows the 12 properties of JTextArea.

Table 15-10. *JTextArea Properties*

Property Name	Data Type	Access
accessibleContext	AccessibleContext	Read-only
columns	int	Read-write
font	Font	Write-only
lineCount	int	Read-only
lineWrap	boolean	Read-write bound
preferredScrollableViewportSize	Dimension	Read-only
preferredSize	Dimension	Read-only
rows	int	Read-write
scrollableTracksViewportWidth	boolean	Read-only
tabSize	int	Read-write bound
UIClassID	String	Read-only
wrapStyleWord	boolean	Read-write bound

The rows and columns properties come directly from the constructor arguments. The preferredScrollableViewportSize and scrollableTracksViewportWidth properties come from implementing the Scrollable interface for scrolling support. The font and preferredSize properties merely customize the behavior inherited from JTextComponent.

That leaves the more interesting properties of lineCount, tabSize, and lineWrap with wrapStyleWord to examine. The lineCount property allows you to find out how many lines are in the text area. This is useful for sizing purposes. The tabSize property allows you to control the tab position interval within the text area. By default, this value is 8.

The lineWrap and wrapStyleWord properties work together. By default, the wrapping of long lines is disabled. If you enable line wrapping (by setting the lineWrap property to true), the point at which long lines wrap depends on the wrapStyleWord property setting. Initially, this property is false, which means that if the lineWrap property is true, line wrapping happens at character boundaries. If both lineWrap and wrapStyleWord are true, then each word from a line that doesn't fit is wrapped to another line, as it is in a word processor. So, to get the word wrap capabilities that most people want, you should set both properties to true for your JTextArea:

```
JTextArea textArea = new JTextArea("...");
textArea.setLineWrap(true);
textArea.setWrapStyleWord(true);
JScrollPane scrollPane = new JScrollPane(textArea);
```

Note The Ctrl-Tab and Shift-Ctrl-Tab key combinations allow users to change focus from within JTextArea components without needing to subclass the component.

Handling JTextArea Events

No events are specific to a JTextArea. You can use one of the inherited listeners from JTextComponent (or one of its parents) or attach an InputVerifier.

At times, you'll just have a JTextArea on the screen and get its contents after the user presses a button. Other times, there's a bit more planning involved, where you might monitor input as it is entered, and possibly convert something like :-) to a smiley face: ☺.

Customizing a JTextArea Look and Feel

Each installable Swing look and feel provides a different JTextArea appearance and set of default UIResource values. Figure 15-18 shows the appearance of the JTextArea component for the preinstalled set of look and feel types. Notice that the primary difference in the appearance of each is the scrollbar from the JScrollPane, which is not a part of the actual JTextArea.

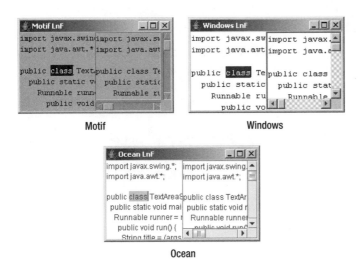

Figure 15-18. *JTextArea under different look and feel types*

The available set of 15 UIResource-related properties for a JTextArea is listed in Table 15-11.

Table 15-11. *JTextArea UIResource Elements*

Property String	Object Type
TextArea.actionMap	ActionMap
TextArea.background	Color
TextArea.border	Border
TextArea.caretAspectRatio	Number
TextArea.caretBlinkRate	Integer
TextArea.caretForeground	Color
TextArea.focusInputMap	InputMap
TextArea.font	Font
TextArea.foreground	Color
TextArea.inactiveForeground	Color
TextArea.keyBindings	KeyBinding[ ]
TextArea.margin	Insets
TextArea.selectionBackground	Color
TextArea.selectionForeground	Color
TextAreaUI	String

JEditorPane Class

The JEditorPane class provides the ability to display and edit multiple-attributed text. While the JTextField and JTextArea support only single-color, single-font content, the JEditorPane allows you to tag your content with various styles (such as bold, italics, 14-point Helvetica, right-justified paragraphs) or with the appearance of an HTML viewer, as shown in Figure 15-19.

Figure 15-19. *Sample JEditorPane as an HTML viewer*

> ■**Note** The HTML support for JEditorPane is only at the HTML 3.2 level with some extensions, whereas HTML 4.0x is the current version as of this writing. Cascading Style Sheets (CSS) are partially supported.

The JEditorPane supports the display and editing of multiple-attributed text through the help of an EditorKit specific to the text-markup mechanism. Predefined kits exist to support raw text, HTML documents, and Rich Text Format (RTF) documents. Because the content is multiple-attributed, the PlainDocument model is no longer sufficient. Instead, Swing provides a StyledDocument in the form of the DefaultStyledDocument class for maintaining the document model. The remaining part of the mix is the new HyperlinkListener/HyperlinkEvent event-handling pair for monitoring hyperlink operations within the document.

Creating a JEditorPane

The JEditorPane has four constructors:

```
public JEditorPane()
JEditorPane editorPane = new JEditorPane();
```

```
public JEditorPane(String type, String text)
String content = "<H1>Got Java?</H1>";
String type = "text/html";
JEditorPane editorPane = new JEditorPane(type, content);
```

```
public JEditorPane(String urlString) throws IOException
JEditorPane editorPane = new JEditorPane("http://www.apress.com");
```

```
public JEditorPane(URL url) throws IOException
URL url = new URL("http://www.apress.com");
JEditorPane editorPane = new JEditorPane(url);
```

The no-argument constructor creates an empty JEditorPane. If you want to initialize the contents, you can directly specify the text and its MIME type. Or, you can specify the URL for where to get the contents. The URL can be specified as either a String or a URL object. When you specify the contents as a URL, the JEditorPane determines the MIME type from the response.

JEditorPane Properties

Table 15-12 shows the 11 properties of JEditorPane. Most of the properties just customize the behavior of the parent classes.

Table 15-12. *JEditorPane Properties*

Property Name	Data Type	Access
accessibleContext	AccessibleContext	Read-only
contentType	String	Read-write
editorKit	EditorKit	Read-write bound
hyperlinkListeners	HyperlinkListener[ ]	Read-only
page	URL	Read-write bound
page	String	Write-only bound
preferredSize	Dimension	Read-only
scrollableTracksViewportHeight	boolean	Read-only
scrollableTracksViewportWidth	boolean	Read-only
text	String	Read-write
UIClassID	String	Read-only

■**Note** The page property is nonstandard in the sense it has two setter methods, but only one getter.

Four interesting properties of JEditorPane are the editorKit, contentType, page, and text. The editorKit property is configured based on the type of content in the editor pane. It is covered in more detail in Chapter 16, with its DefaultEditorKit, StyledEditorKit, and HTMLEditorKit implementations. The contentType property represents the MIME type of the content inside the document. This property tends to be automatically set when you set up the content in the constructor (or elsewhere). In the event the editor kit is unable to determine the MIME type, you can manually set it. The three MIME types with built-in support are text/html, text/plain, and text/rtf, as reported by the getContentType() method of the predefined editor kits.

The page property allows you to change the displayed contents to reflect the contents of a specific URL so that you can use the contents in some manner not programmed into the environment. The text property allows you to find out what the textual content is based on the current Document model.

Handling JEditorPane Events

Because JEditorPane is just another text area component with some special display characteristics, it supports the same set of listeners for event handling as does the JTextArea component. In addition, the JEditorPane provides a special listener-event combination to deal with hyperlinks within a document.

The HyperlinkListener interface defines one method, public void hyperlinkUpdate (HyperlinkEvent hyperlinkEvent), which works with a HyperlinkEvent to respond to—not surprisingly—a hyperlink event. The event includes a HyperlinkEvent.EventType that reports on the type of event and allows you to react differently, either by following the link when selected or possibly changing the cursor when moving the mouse over (or off) the hyperlink (although this happens by default).

Here is the HyperlinkListener definition:

```
public interface HyperlinkListener implements EventListener {
  public void hyperlinkUpdate(HyperlinkEvent hyperlinkEvent);
}
```

And, here is the HyperlinkEvent definition:

```
public class HyperlinkEvent extends EventObject {
  // Constructors
  public HyperlinkEvent(Object source, HyperlinkEvent.EventType type, URL url);
  public HyperlinkEvent(Object source, HyperlinkEvent.EventType type, URL url,
    String description);
  public HyperlinkEvent(Object source, HyperlinkEvent.EventType type, URL url,
    String description, Element sourceElement)
  // Properties
  public String getDescription();
```

```
  public HyperlinkEvent.EventType getEventType();
  public Element getSourceElement();
  public URL getURL();
}
```

The hyperlink event types will be one of three constants within the HyperlinkEvent.EventType class:

- ACTIVATED: Usually involving a mouse click over the appropriate content

- ENTERED: Moving the mouse over the hyperlink content

- EXITED: Moving the mouse out of the hyperlink content

Therefore, if you want to create a HyperlinkListener that displays the URL in a status bar while over a hyperlink and follows the hyperlink when activated, you can create your own miniature HTML help viewer. The HyperlinkListener implementation in Listing 15-15 will do the trick for you. There are println statements present in the listener to display the URL when the mouse is over the URL and when the URL is activated.

Listing 15-15. *HyperlinkListener Example*

```java
import java.awt.*;
import javax.swing.*;
import javax.swing.text.*;
import javax.swing.event.*;
import java.io.*;
import java.net.*;

public class ActivatedHyperlinkListener implements HyperlinkListener {

  Frame frame;
  JEditorPane editorPane;

  public ActivatedHyperlinkListener(Frame frame, JEditorPane editorPane) {
    this.frame = frame;
    this.editorPane = editorPane;
  }

  public void hyperlinkUpdate(HyperlinkEvent hyperlinkEvent) {
    HyperlinkEvent.EventType type = hyperlinkEvent.getEventType();
    final URL url = hyperlinkEvent.getURL();
    if (type == HyperlinkEvent.EventType.ENTERED) {
      System.out.println("URL:  " + url );
    } else if (type == HyperlinkEvent.EventType.ACTIVATED) {
      System.out.println("Activated");
      Runnable runner = new Runnable() {
        public void run() {
```

```
                    // Retain reference to original
                    Document doc = editorPane.getDocument();
                    try {
                      editorPane.setPage(url);
                    }  catch (IOException ioException) {
                      JOptionPane.showMessageDialog(frame, "Error following link",
                        "Invalid link", JOptionPane.ERROR_MESSAGE);
                      editorPane.setDocument(doc);
                    }
                  }
                }
              };
              EventQueue.invokeLater(runner);
          }
        }
      }
```

■**Tip** Don't forget to make the JEditorPane read-only with a call to setEditable(false). Otherwise, the viewer acts as an editor.

Listing 15-16 is a complete example using our new ActivatedHyperlinkListener class. The frame it creates looks like the page shown earlier in Figure 15-19, although in the figure, the About link has been followed.

Listing 15-16. *JEditorPane Example*

```java
import javax.swing.*;
import javax.swing.event.*;
import java.awt.*;
import java.io.*;

public class EditorPaneSample {
  public static void main(String args[]) {
    Runnable runner = new Runnable() {
      public void run() {
        JFrame frame = new JFrame("EditorPane Example");
        frame.setDefaultCloseOperation(JFrame.EXIT_ON_CLOSE);

        try {
          JEditorPane editorPane = new JEditorPane("http://www.google.com");
          editorPane.setEditable(false);

          HyperlinkListener hyperlinkListener =
            new ActivatedHyperlinkListener(frame, editorPane);
          editorPane.addHyperlinkListener(hyperlinkListener);
```

```
            JScrollPane scrollPane = new JScrollPane(editorPane);
            frame.add(scrollPane);
          } catch (IOException e) {
            System.err.println("Unable to load: " + e);
          }

          frame.setSize(640, 480);
          frame.setVisible(true);
        }
      };
    EventQueue.invokeLater(runner);
  }
}
```

Customizing a JEditorPane Look and Feel

The appearance of the JEditorPane is similar to that of a JTextArea (see Figure 15-18). Although the supported contents differ, the look-and-feel–related attributes usually aren't different.

The available set of 15 UIResource-related properties for a JEditorPane is shown in Table 15-13. Their names are similar to those of the JTextArea settings.

Table 15-13. *JEditorPane UIResource Elements*

Property String	Object Type
EditorPane.actionMap	ActionMap
EditorPane.background	Color
EditorPane.border	Border
EditorPane.caretAspectRatio	Number
EditorPane.caretBlinkRate	Integer
EditorPane.caretForeground	Color
EditorPane.focusInputMap	InputMap
EditorPane.font	Font
EditorPane.foreground	Color
EditorPane.inactiveForeground	Color
EditorPane.keyBindings	KeyBinding[ ]
EditorPane.margin	Insets
EditorPane.selectionBackground	Color
EditorPane.selectionForeground	Color
EditorPaneUI	String

JTextPane Class

The JTextPane is a specialized form of the JEditorPane designed especially for the editing (and display) of styled text. It differs from the JEditorPane only in its manner of providing the content to display because the text isn't tagged with the styles as it would be in an HTML or RTF document.

The JTextPane relies on three interfaces for the setting of text attributes: AttributeSet for a basic collection of attributes, MutableAttributeSet for a changeable collection of attributes, and Style for a set of attributes to be associated with a part of a StyledDocument.

This section will introduce JTextPane. See Chapter 16 for additional information about configuring styles for different parts of the styled content within a JTextPane.

Creating a JTextPane

There are only two constructors for JTextPane:

public JTextPane()
```
JTextPane textPane = new JTextPane();
JScrollPane scrollPane = new JScrollPane(textPane);
```

public JTextPane(StyledDocument document)
```
StyledDocument document = new DefaultStyledDocument();
JTextPane textPane = new JTextPane(document);
JScrollPane scrollPane = new JScrollPane(textPane);
```

The no-argument constructor initially has zero contents. The second constructor allows you to create the Document first, and then use it in the JTextPane.

■**Tip** Remember to place your JTextPane within a JScrollPane if the contents will be larger than the available screen space.

JTextPane Properties

Table 15-14 shows the eight properties of JTextPane. You'll look at these in greater detail in Chapter 16.

Table 15-14. *JTextPane Properties*

Property Name	Data Type	Access
characterAttributes	AttributeSet	Read-only
document	Document	Write-only bound
editorKit	EditorKit	Write-only bound

Table 15-14. *JTextPane Properties (Continued)*

Property Name	Data Type	Access
inputAttributes	MutableAttributeSet	Read-only
logicalStyle	Style	Read-write
paragraphAttributes	AttributeSet	Read-only
styledDocument	StyledDocument	Read-write*
UIClassID	String	Read-only

* Changing the styledDocument property triggers a bound property notification on the document property.

Customizing a JTextPane Look and Feel

The JTextPane is a subclass of a JEditorPane. It has the same appearance under all the predefined look and feel types as the JTextArea (see Figure 15-18). Although the contents might differ, the look and feel is the same.

The available set of UIResource-related properties for a JTextPane is shown in Table 15-15. For the JTextPane component, there are 15 different properties. Their names are similar to the JTextArea settings.

Table 15-15. *JTextPane UIResource Elements*

Property String	Object Type
TextPane.actionMap	ActionMap
TextPane.background	Color
TextPane.border	Border
TextPane.caretAspectRatio	Number
TextPane.caretBlinkRate	Integer
TextPane.caretForeground	Color
TextPane.focusInputMap	InputMap
TextPane.font	Font
TextPane.foreground	Color
TextPane.inactiveForeground	Color
TextPane.keyBindings	KeyBinding[ ]
TextPane.margin	Insets
TextPane.selectionBackground	Color
TextPane.selectionForeground	Color
TextPaneUI	String

Loading a JTextPane with Content

Listing 15-17 provides an example that loads the content for a StyledDocument for a JTextPane. This is just to give you an idea of the possibilities. The details of using Style, SimpleAttributeSet, and StyleConstants will be discussed in Chapter 16.

Listing 15-17. *JTextPane Example*

```java
import javax.swing.*;
import javax.swing.text.*;
import javax.swing.event.*;
import java.awt.*;

public class TextPaneSample {
  private static String message =
    "In the beginning, there was COBOL, then there was FORTRAN, " +
    "then there was BASIC, ... and now there is Java.\n";

  public static void main(String args[]) {
    Runnable runner = new Runnable() {
      public void run() {
        JFrame frame = new JFrame("TextPane Example");
        frame.setDefaultCloseOperation(JFrame.EXIT_ON_CLOSE);

        StyleContext context = new StyleContext();
        StyledDocument document = new DefaultStyledDocument(context);

        Style style = context.getStyle(StyleContext.DEFAULT_STYLE);
        StyleConstants.setAlignment(style, StyleConstants.ALIGN_RIGHT);
        StyleConstants.setFontSize(style, 14);
        StyleConstants.setSpaceAbove(style, 4);
        StyleConstants.setSpaceBelow(style, 4);

        // Insert content
        try {
          document.insertString(document.getLength(), message, style);
        } catch (BadLocationException badLocationException) {
          System.err.println("Oops");
        }

        SimpleAttributeSet attributes = new SimpleAttributeSet();
        StyleConstants.setBold(attributes, true);
        StyleConstants.setItalic(attributes, true);

        // Insert content
        try {
          document.insertString(document.getLength(), "Hello Java", attributes);
```

```
      } catch (BadLocationException badLocationException) {
        System.err.println("Oops");
      }

      // Third style for icon/component
      Style labelStyle = context.getStyle(StyleContext.DEFAULT_STYLE);

      Icon icon = new ImageIcon("Computer.gif");
      JLabel label = new JLabel(icon);
      StyleConstants.setComponent(labelStyle, label);

      // Insert content
      try {
        document.insertString(document.getLength(), "Ignored", labelStyle);
      } catch (BadLocationException badLocationException) {
        System.err.println("Oops");
      }

      JTextPane textPane = new JTextPane(document);
      textPane.setEditable(false);
      JScrollPane scrollPane = new JScrollPane(textPane);
      frame.add(scrollPane, BorderLayout.CENTER);

      frame.setSize(300, 150);
      frame.setVisible(true);
    }
  };
  EventQueue.invokeLater(runner);
  }
}
```

The key line of the source code is the call to insertString() and its style argument:

```
document.insertString(document.getLength(), message, style);
```

Figure 15-20 shows how a JTextPane might look like with a few paragraphs of content. Notice that the content is not restricted to just text; it can have images as well.

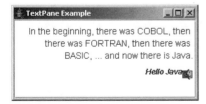

Figure 15-20. *Sample JTextPane*

Summary

In this chapter, you began to explore the details of the Swing text components. You initially looked at the root text component, JTextComponent, and the many operations it defines for all other text components. You then explored the specific text components of JTextField, JPasswordField, JFormattedTextField, JTextArea, JEditorPane, and JTextPane.

You also explored the various pieces that make up the different components. You delved into the data model for the text components, based on the Document interface, for the AbstractDocument and PlainDocument classes. You also looked at creating a custom document filter via DocumentFilter for restricting input to a text component. In addition, you explored the Caret and Highlighter interfaces for displaying the cursor and highlighted text, the NavigationFilter for limiting movement within the text component, as well as the Keymap to make the text component act as the controller. As the controller, the Keymap converts a user's keystrokes into specific actions that affect the model for the text component.

You also looked at how events are handled within the Swing text components. In addition to the basic AWT event handling classes, Swing adds some new ones designed for listening for cursor movement with the CaretListener and document content changes with the DocumentListener. The JEditorPane also provides another event handler with the HyperlinkListener. And there is the general Swing support for input verification through InputVerifier.

In Chapter 16, you'll further explore the Swing text components. This chapter touched on the basic features of all the components, while the next chapter goes into all the gory details of working with the TextAction, formatting input for a JFormattedTextField, and configuring Style objects to work with a StyledDocument. You'll also look into shuffling through the tags of your HTMLDocument.

CHAPTER 16

■ ■ ■

Advanced Text Capabilities

In Chapter 15, you were introduced to the myriad capabilities of the Swing text components. In this chapter, you'll continue on the same path by looking at some advanced capabilities that will prove useful in special situations.

The Swing text components ship with many prefabricated features. For instance, as you saw in Chapter 15, although text components have methods such as cut(), copy(), and paste() to work with the system clipboard, you really don't need to use them. This is because the Swing text components come with their own predefined set of Action objects, which you'll explore in this chapter. To use Action objects, just attach them to a component, such as a button or menu item, and then simply select the component that triggers the Action. For text components, the Action object is an instance of TextAction, which has a nice additional feature of knowing which text component last had the input focus.

In this chapter, you'll also look at how to create stylized text for display in a JTextPane. If you want to display multicolored text documents or different font styles, the JTextPane component provides a series of interfaces and classes to describe the attributes attached to the document. The AttributeSet interface gives you these on a read-only basis, and the MutableAttributeSet interface extends AttributeSet in order to set attributes. You'll see how the SimpleAttributeSet class implements both of these interfaces by offering a Hashtable to store the text attributes, and how the StyleConstants class helps to configure the many text attributes you can apply. And, you'll learn how to work with tab stops within your text documents, including how to define leader characters and how text is aligned.

Next, you'll get a glimpse of the different editor kits that Swing provides, focusing on the inner workings of the HTMLDocument. When the JEditorPane displays HTML, the HTMLEditorKit controls how to load and display the HTML content into an HTMLDocument. You'll see how the parser loads the content and how to iterate through the different tags in the document.

Lastly, you'll learn how to take advantage of the formatted input options and validation available with the JFormattedTextField component. You'll see how to provide for formatted dates and numbers, as well as masked input like telephone and social security numbers.

Using Actions with Text Components

The TextAction class is a special case of the Action interface that was defined with the other Swing event-handling capabilities in Chapter 2 and briefly reviewed in Chapter 15. The purpose of the TextAction class is to provide concrete Action implementations that can work with text components. These implementations are smart enough to know which text component most recently had the input focus and therefore should be the subject of the action.

For every text component, you need a way to associate keystrokes with specific actions. This is done via the Keymap interface, which maps a KeyStroke to a TextAction, so that separate KeyListener objects don't need to be associated with the text component for each keystroke in order to listen for it. Key maps can be shared across multiple components and/or customized for a particular look and feel. The JTextComponent also has getKeymap() and setKeymap() methods that allow you to read or customize the key map.

■**Note** Although the Swing text components use TextAction, KeyStroke, and Keymap, they still support the ability to attach a KeyListener. Using a KeyListener, however, usually isn't appropriate, especially when you want to restrict input to match certain criteria. The better approach for restricting input is to come up with a custom DocumentFilter, as demonstrated in Chapter 15, or use an InputVerifier. In addition, the actual Keymap implementation is just a wrapper to the InputMap/ActionMap combination used for keyboard-action mapping in the nontextual Swing components.

The text components come with many predefined TextAction implementations. Through a default key map, the text components know about these predefined actions, so they know how to insert and remove content, as well as how to track the positions of both the cursor and caret. If the text component supports stylized content, as JTextPane does, there are additional default actions to support this content. All these implementations derive from the JFC/Swing technology editor kits. As discussed in the "The Editor Kits" section later in this chapter, an editor kit provides a logical grouping of the various ways to edit a specific type of text component.

Listing Actions

To find out which actions a JTextComponent supports, you merely ask by using the public Action[ ] getActions() method. This will return an array of Action objects, usually of type TextAction, that can be used like any other Action, such as for creating buttons on a JToolBar.

Figure 16-1 shows a program that will list the actions for the different predefined components. Pick a component from the JRadioButton group, and its list of text actions will be displayed in the text area. For each action, the program shows the action name and class name.

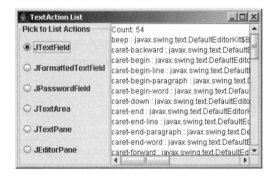

Figure 16-1. *TextAction list demonstration*

The same set of 53 actions is available for all text components. JTextField, JFormattedTextField, and JPasswordField have one extra action, called notify-field-accept, used for detecting when the Enter key is pressed while in the text component. The JFormattedTextField has a second extra action, reset-field-edit, for when the contents don't validate against the provided format mask. JTextPane adds its own set of about 20 more actions for dealing with multiple-attributed text.

Listing 16-1 shows the source used to generate Figure 16-1. The RadioButtonUtils class was created in Chapter 5.

Listing 16-1. *Listing Text Component Actions*

```java
import javax.swing.*;
import javax.swing.text.*;
import java.awt.*;
import java.awt.event.*;
import java.io.*;
import java.util.*;

public class ListActions {
  public static void main(String args[]) {
    Runnable runner = new Runnable() {
      public void run() {
        JFrame frame = new JFrame("TextAction List");
        frame.setDefaultCloseOperation(JFrame.EXIT_ON_CLOSE);

        String components[] = {
          "JTextField", "JFormattedTextField", "JPasswordField",
          "JTextArea", "JTextPane", "JEditorPane"};

        final JTextArea textArea = new JTextArea();
        textArea.setEditable(false);
        JScrollPane scrollPane = new JScrollPane(textArea);
        frame.add(scrollPane, BorderLayout.CENTER);

        ActionListener actionListener = new ActionListener() {
          public void actionPerformed(ActionEvent actionEvent) {
            // Determine which component selected
            String command = actionEvent.getActionCommand();
            JTextComponent component = null;
            if (command.equals("JTextField")) {
              component = new JTextField();
            } else if (command.equals("JFormattedTextField")) {
              component = new JFormattedTextField();
            } else if (command.equals("JPasswordField")) {
              component = new JPasswordField();
```

```java
      } else if (command.equals("JTextArea")) {
        component = new JTextArea();
      } else if (command.equals("JTextPane")) {
        component = new JTextPane();
      } else {
        component = new JEditorPane();
      }

      // Process action list
      Action actions[] = component.getActions();
      // Define comparator to sort actions
      Comparator<Action> comparator = new Comparator<Action>() {
        public int compare(Action a1, Action a2) {
          String firstName = (String)a1.getValue(Action.NAME);
          String secondName = (String)a2.getValue(Action.NAME);
          return firstName.compareTo(secondName);
        }
      };
      Arrays.sort(actions, comparator);
      StringWriter sw = new StringWriter();
      PrintWriter pw = new PrintWriter(sw, true);
      int count = actions.length;
      pw.println("Count: " + count);
      for (int i=0; i<count; i++) {
        pw.print  (actions[i].getValue(Action.NAME));
        pw.print  (" : ");
        pw.println(actions[i].getClass().getName());
      }
      pw.close();
      textArea.setText(sw.toString());
      textArea.setCaretPosition(0);
    }
  };

  final Container componentsContainer =
    RadioButtonUtils.createRadioButtonGrouping(components,
      "Pick to List Actions", actionListener);

  frame.add(componentsContainer, BorderLayout.WEST);
  frame.setSize(400, 250);
  frame.setVisible(true);
 }
};
EventQueue.invokeLater(runner);
 }
}
```

Using Actions

So far, you've seen that there are many predefined TextAction implementations available for the various text components, but you haven't used any of them. By making a few minor changes to Listing 16-1, you can enhance the program in order to activate it. The modified program is shown in Listing 16-2. With this version, when one of the radio buttons is selected, that type of text component will be displayed where the text list of Action objects appears in Figure 16-1. In addition, the different Action objects are added to a new JMenuBar placed at the top of the display window.

Note In the program shown in Listing 16-2, after all the menu buttons are activated, you're stuck with a text label that might not be exactly what you want. However, you can easily change this with the public void setText(String label) method of JMenuItem. If you do this, remember that you need to know what's in the menu item to change the label to something meaningful.

Listing 16-2. *Enabling Text Component Actions*

```
import javax.swing.*;
import javax.swing.text.*;
import java.awt.*;
import java.awt.event.*;
import java.io.*;
import java.util.*;

public class ActionsMenuBar {
  public static void main(String args[]) {
    Runnable runner = new Runnable() {
      public void run() {
        final JFrame frame = new JFrame("TextAction Usage");
        frame.setDefaultCloseOperation(JFrame.EXIT_ON_CLOSE);
        final JScrollPane scrollPane = new JScrollPane();
        frame.add(scrollPane, BorderLayout.CENTER);

        final JMenuBar menuBar = new JMenuBar();
        frame.setJMenuBar(menuBar);

        ActionListener actionListener = new ActionListener() {
          JTextComponent component;
          public void actionPerformed(ActionEvent actionEvent) {
            // Determine which component selected
            String command = actionEvent.getActionCommand();
            if (command.equals("JTextField")) {
              component = new JTextField();
```

```java
          } else if (command.equals("JFormattedTextField")) {
            component = new JFormattedTextField();
          } else if (command.equals("JPasswordField")) {
            component = new JPasswordField();
          } else if (command.equals("JTextArea")) {
            component = new JTextArea();
          } else if (command.equals("JTextPane")) {
            component = new JTextPane();
          } else {
            component = new JEditorPane();
          }
          scrollPane.setViewportView(component);
          // Process action list
          Action actions[] = component.getActions();
          menuBar.removeAll();
          menuBar.revalidate();
          JMenu menu = null;
          for (int i=0, n=actions.length; i<n; i++) {
            if ((i % 10) == 0) {
              menu = new JMenu("From " + i);
              menuBar.add(menu);
            }
            menu.add(actions[i]);
          }
          menuBar.revalidate();
        }
      };

      String components[] = {
        "JTextField", "JFormattedTextField", "JPasswordField",
        "JTextArea", "JTextPane", "JEditorPane"};
      final Container componentsContainer =
        RadioButtonUtils.createRadioButtonGrouping(components,
          "Pick to List Actions", actionListener);
      frame.add(componentsContainer, BorderLayout.WEST);

      frame.setSize(400, 300);
      frame.setVisible(true);
    }
  };
  EventQueue.invokeLater(runner);
  }
}
```

Figure 16-2 shows some of the available operations for a JTextArea. When you select the different menu options, the JTextComponent is appropriately affected.

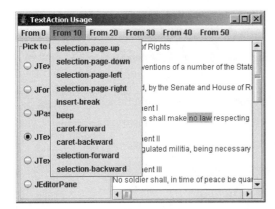

Figure 16-2. *TextAction list usage demonstration*

This technique is useful because it shows that you can readily discover the supported operations of a text component and provide access to that behavior without knowing precisely what the actual behavior is. This is just one demonstration of the many ways you can use TextAction objects.

Finding Actions

Although listing and using Action objects related to a text component is a fairly malleable process, unless you know what you're looking for, it isn't very useful. Thankfully, the DefaultEditorKit has 46 class constants that match many of the shared 46 (out of 53) Action objects of all the text components. The class constants' names more or less reflect their functionality. The JTextField adds an additional constant for the Action shared with JFormattedTextField and JPasswordField. Unfortunately, the names associated with the extra actions available to the JTextPane aren't class constants of any text component and are just used internally within the StyledEditorKit, where you will find the additional Action implementations defined.

■**Note** One additional Action exists primarily for debugging purposes. Its Action name is dump-model, and it lacks a class constant to go with it. When initiated, the method literally dumps out the Document model Element structure for the text component.

Table 16-1 lists the 47 constants available to help you locate the predefined Action you're seeking.

Table 16-1. *TextAction Name Constants*

DefaultEditorKit.backwardAction	DefaultEditorKit.previousWordAction
DefaultEditorKit.beepAction	DefaultEditorKit.readOnlyAction
DefaultEditorKit.beginAction	DefaultEditorKit.selectAllAction
DefaultEditorKit.beginLineAction	DefaultEditorKit.selectionBackwardAction
DefaultEditorKit.beginParagraphAction	DefaultEditorKit.selectionBeginAction
DefaultEditorKit.beginWordAction	DefaultEditorKit.selectionBeginLineAction
DefaultEditorKit.copyAction	DefaultEditorKit.selectionBeginParagraphAction
DefaultEditorKit.cutAction	DefaultEditorKit.selectionBeginWordAction
DefaultEditorKit.defaultKeyTypedAction	DefaultEditorKit.selectionDownAction
DefaultEditorKit.deleteNextCharAction	DefaultEditorKit.selectionEndAction
DefaultEditorKit.deletePrevCharAction	DefaultEditorKit.selectionEndLineAction
DefaultEditorKit.downAction	DefaultEditorKit.selectionEndParagraphAction
DefaultEditorKit.endAction	DefaultEditorKit.selectionEndWordAction
DefaultEditorKit.endLineAction	DefaultEditorKit.selectionForwardAction
DefaultEditorKit.endParagraphAction	DefaultEditorKit.selectionNextWordAction
DefaultEditorKit.endWordAction	DefaultEditorKit.selectionPreviousWordAction
DefaultEditorKit.forwardAction	DefaultEditorKit.selectionUpAction
DefaultEditorKit.insertBreakAction	DefaultEditorKit.selectLineAction
DefaultEditorKit.insertContentAction	DefaultEditorKit.selectParagraphAction
DefaultEditorKit.insertTabAction	DefaultEditorKit.selectWordAction
DefaultEditorKit.nextWordAction	DefaultEditorKit.upAction
DefaultEditorKit.pageDownAction	DefaultEditorKit.writableAction
DefaultEditorKit.pageUpAction	JTextField.notifyAction
DefaultEditorKit.pasteAction	

With such a huge list of constants, what on earth do you *do* with them? Well, first you find the constant for the predefined TextAction you want to use (or learn the necessary text string if no constant is provided). This is relatively easy because the names are fairly self-explanatory.

To demonstrate, Listing 16-3 contains a program that shows how to work with these constants. The program has two text areas to show that TextAction objects really know to work with the last text component that had the input focus. One set of menu items includes two options that are used to switch the text area from read-only to writable. This action is done using the DefaultEditorKit.readOnlyAction and DefaultEditorKit.writableAction names. The other set of menu items includes options for cut, copy, and paste support, whose constants are DefaultEditorKit.cutAction, DefaultEditorKit.copyAction, and DefaultEditorKit.pasteAction. Because the constants are String values, you need to look up the actual Action object to use.

The lookup process requires getting the ActionMap for the component with getActionMap(), and then searching for the key with the get() method of ActionMap, as in this example:

```
Action readAction = component.getActionMap().get(DefaultEditorKit.readOnlyAction);
```

Listing 16-3. *Using Text Component Actions*

```java
import javax.swing.*;
import javax.swing.text.*;
import java.awt.*;
import java.awt.event.*;
import java.io.*;
import java.util.*;

public class UseActions {
  public static void main(String args[]) {
    Runnable runner = new Runnable() {
      public void run() {
        JFrame frame = new JFrame("Use TextAction");
        frame.setDefaultCloseOperation(JFrame.EXIT_ON_CLOSE);
        Dimension empty = new Dimension(0,0);

        final JTextArea leftArea = new JTextArea();
        JScrollPane leftScrollPane = new JScrollPane(leftArea);
        leftScrollPane.setPreferredSize(empty);

        final JTextArea rightArea = new JTextArea();
        JScrollPane rightScrollPane = new JScrollPane(rightArea);
        rightScrollPane.setPreferredSize(empty);

        JSplitPane splitPane = new JSplitPane(JSplitPane.HORIZONTAL_SPLIT,
          leftScrollPane, rightScrollPane);

        JMenuBar menuBar = new JMenuBar();
        frame.setJMenuBar(menuBar);
        JMenu menu = new JMenu("Options");
        menuBar.add(menu);
        JMenuItem menuItem;

        Action readAction =
          leftArea.getActionMap().get(DefaultEditorKit.readOnlyAction);
        menuItem = menu.add(readAction);
        menuItem.setText("Make read-only");
        Action writeAction  =
          leftArea.getActionMap().get(DefaultEditorKit.writableAction);
        menuItem = menu.add(writeAction);
        menuItem.setText("Make writable");
```

```
        menu.addSeparator();

        Action cutAction =
          leftArea.getActionMap().get(DefaultEditorKit.cutAction);
        menuItem = menu.add(cutAction);
        menuItem.setText("Cut");
        Action copyAction =
          leftArea.getActionMap().get(DefaultEditorKit.copyAction);
        menuItem = menu.add(copyAction);
        menuItem.setText("Copy");
        Action pasteAction =
          leftArea.getActionMap().get(DefaultEditorKit.pasteAction);
        menuItem = menu.add(pasteAction);
        menuItem.setText("Paste");

        frame.add(splitPane, BorderLayout.CENTER);
        frame.setSize(400, 250);
        frame.setVisible(true);
        splitPane.setDividerLocation(.5);
      }
    };
    EventQueue.invokeLater(runner);
  }
}
```

Figure 16-3 shows the program at work. Notice that for each JMenuItem created, the text label changes to give it a more user-friendly setting.

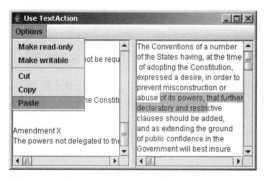

Figure 16-3. *Specific TextAction usage demonstration*

By asking for specific TextAction instances, you don't need to constantly recode repetitive operations. In fact, if you constantly find yourself repeating the same operations over and over with a text component, it's probably time for you to create your own TextAction objects.

Creating Styled Text

In Chapter 15, you looked at displaying plain text and HTML. With the Swing text components—or at least the JTextPane—you can also display stylized text, in which different blocks of text can have multiple attributes. These attributes might include boldface, italics, a different font or color at the character level, or justification at the paragraph level, just as with any of the modern word processors.

To support these capabilities, Swing supplies many different interfaces and classes, all of which start with the specialized Document interface extension of StyledDocument. The Document interface was introduced in Chapter 15, focusing on the PlainDocument implementation class. The StyledDocument interface, or more precisely, the DefaultStyledDocument implementation, manages a series of styles and attribute sets for the contents of a Document.

The various styles used by a StyledDocument are described initially by the AttributeSet interface, which is a set of key/value pairs of read-only attributes. The key for an attribute might be "current font," in which the setting would be the font to use. To actually change the font, you need to move on to the MutableAttributeSet interface, which supplies the ability to add and remove attributes. For instance, if you had an AttributeSet for "bold," you could use MutableAttributeSet to also add italics, underlining, or colorization (or all three) to the set.

For a simple implementation of AttributeSet, there is the StyleContext.SmallAttributeSet class, which uses an array to manage the set of attributes. For an implementation of the MutableAttributeSet interface, there is the SimpleAttributeSet class, which uses a Hashtable to manage the attributes. More complex attribute sets move on to the Style interface, which adds a name to the set of attributes as defined by a MutableAttributeSet. The actual Style implementation class is the StyleContext.NamedStyle class. Besides adding a name, the Style interface adds the ability to have a ChangeListener monitor a set of attributes for changes.

The class that manages the set of Style objects for a StyledDocument is the StyleContext class. An implementation of the AbstractDocument.AttributeContext interface, StyleContext uses the StyleConstants class, which defines various attributes for commonly used styles. When working with HTML documents, the StyleContext is actually a StyleSheet, which may help you in understanding the whole arrangement. Keep in mind that all of the classes and interfaces discussed here (except StyleSheet) are required just to set up the Document data model for a particular JTextPane.

StyledDocument Interface and DefaultStyledDocument Class

The StyledDocument interface extends the Document interface by adding the ability to store styles for the content of the document. These styles can describe the character or paragraph attributes, such as color, orientation, or font.

```
public interface StyledDocument extends Document {
  public Style addStyle(String nm, Style parent);
  public Color getBackground(AttributeSet attribute);
  public Element getCharacterElement(int position);
  public Font getFont(AttributeSet attribute);
  public Color getForeground(AttributeSet attribute);
```

```
  public Style getLogicalStyle(int position);
  public Element getParagraphElement(int position);
  public Style getStyle(String name);
  public void removeStyle(String name);
  public void setCharacterAttributes(int offset, int length, AttributeSet s,
    boolean replace);
  public void setLogicalStyle(int position, Style style);
  public void setParagraphAttributes(int offset, int length, AttributeSet s,
    boolean replace);
}
```

The DefaultStyledDocument class is the implementation of the StyledDocument interface provided with the Swing components. It serves as the data model for the JTextPane component.

Creating a DefaultStyledDocument

You can create a DefaultStyledDocument in any one of the three ways listed here:

public DefaultStyledDocument()
```
DefaultStyledDocument document = new DefaultStyledDocument();
```

public DefaultStyledDocument(StyleContext styles)
```
StyleContext context = new StyleContext();
DefaultStyledDocument document = new DefaultStyledDocument(context);
```

public DefaultStyledDocument(AbstractDocument.Content content, StyleContext styles)
```
AbstractDocument.Content content = new StringContent();
DefaultStyledDocument document = new DefaultStyledDocument(content, context);
```

You can share the StyleContext between multiple documents or use the default context. In addition, you can predefine the content using one of the AbstractDocument.Content implementations, either GapContent or StringContent. It is the responsibility of one of these Content implementations to store the actual Document content.

DefaultStyledDocument Properties

Besides having a default root element to describe the contents of the document, the DefaultStyledDocument makes available the style names as an Enumeration. These are the only two properties defined at the DefaultStyledDocument level, as shown in Table 16-2. There are other properties you can get for a DefaultStyledDocument; however, they require the position or AttributeSet from which to get them.

Table 16-2. *DefaultStyledDocument Properties*

Property Name	Data Type	Access
defaultRootElement	Element	Read-only
styleNames	Enumeration	Read-only

AttributeSet Interface

The AttributeSet interface describes a read-only set of key/value attributes, allowing you access to the descriptive content of a series of attributes. If the set of attributes lacks a specific key defined for it, the AttributeSet supports the ability to look elsewhere by traveling up a chain to a resolving parent for the parent's definition of the attribute. This allows the AttributeSet to define a core set of attributes and lets developers (or possibly even users) modify only the set of attributes they want to change. Unless you want someone to change the defaults globally, you shouldn't provide direct access to the resolving parent. That way, you never lose any of the original settings.

```
public interface AttributeSet {
  // Constants
  public final static Object NameAttribute;
  public final static Object ResolveAttribute;
  // Properties
  public int getAttributeCount();
  public Enumeration getAttributeNames();
  public AttributeSet getResolveParent();
  // Other methods
  public boolean containsAttribute(Object name, Object value);
  public boolean containsAttributes(AttributeSet attributes);
  public AttributeSet copyAttributes();
  public Object getAttribute(Object key);
  public boolean isDefined(Object attrName);
  public boolean isEqual(AttributeSet attr);
}
```

MutableAttributeSet Interface

The MutableAttributeSet interface describes how you would go about adding to or removing from the set of attributes, as well as how to set the resolving parent.

```
public interface MutableAttributeSet extends AttributeSet {
  public void addAttribute(Object name, Object value);
  public void addAttributes(AttributeSet attributes);
  public void removeAttribute(Object name);
  public void removeAttributes(AttributeSet attributes);
  public void removeAttributes(Enumeration names);
  public void setResolveParent(AttributeSet parent);
}
```

SimpleAttributeSet Class

The SimpleAttributeSet class is the first implementation of the AttributeSet interface. When you begin using it, you'll finally be able to see just how to create the multiple-attributed text for display in the JTextPane. The SimpleAttributeSet class is a specific implementation of AttributeSet that relies on a standard Hashtable for managing the key/attribute pairs.

Creating a SimpleAttributeSet

SimpleAttributeSet has two constructors:

public SimpleAttributeSet()
SimpleAttributeSet attributeSet1 = new SimpleAttributeSet();

public SimpleAttributeSet(AttributeSet source)
SimpleAttributeSet attributeSet2 = new SimpleAttributeSet(attributeSet1);

You would typically create an empty SimpleAttributeSet, and then set its attributes, as in the first constructor listed. Or, you can instead provide the initial settings for the set of attributes in the constructor. Note that this is *not* the resolving parent—it's just an initialized data structure.

SimpleAttributeSet Properties

Table 16-3 displays the four properties of SimpleAttributeSet. They provide access to the set of attributes, let you know whether any attributes exist, and identify the resolving parent (if any).

Table 16-3. *SimpleAttributeSet Properties*

Property Name	Data Type	Access
attributeCount	int	Read-only
attributeNames	Enumeration	Read-only
empty	boolean	Read-only
resolveParent	AttributeSet	Read-write

Using a SimpleAttributeSet

To create an appropriate AttributeSet to use with a SimpleAttributeSet, you need to discover the keys for the attributes you want to alter. You'll see some helper methods shortly in the StyleConstants class covered in the next section. All the keys are hidden away in four public inner classes of StyleConstants: CharacterConstants, ColorConstants, FontConstants, and ParagraphConstants, as shown in Table 16-4.

Table 16-4. *Key Constants for Storing AttributeSet Values*

AttributeSet Key Constants	Value Type	Default Setting
CharacterConstants.Background	Color	Color.BLACK
ColorConstants.Background	Color	Color.BLACK
CharacterConstants.BidiLevel	Integer	0
CharacterConstants.Bold	Boolean	false
FontConstants.Bold	Boolean	false

Table 16-4. *Key Constants for Storing AttributeSet Values*

AttributeSet Key Constants	Value Type	Default Setting
CharacterConstants.ComponentAttribute	Component	null
CharacterConstants.Family	String	"Monospaced"
FontConstants.Family	String	"Monospaced"
CharacterConstants.Foreground	Color	Color.BLACK
ColorConstants.Foreground	Color	Color.BLACK
CharacterConstants.IconAttribute	Icon	null
CharacterConstants.Italic	Boolean	false
FontConstants.Italic	Boolean	false
CharacterConstants.Size	Integer	12
FontConstants.Size	Integer	12
CharacterConstants.StrikeThrough	Boolean	false
CharacterConstants.Subscript	Boolean	false
CharacterConstants.Superscript	Boolean	false
CharacterConstants.Underline	Boolean	false
ParagraphConstants.Alignment	Integer	ALIGN_LEFT
ParagraphConstants.FirstLineIndent	Float	0
ParagraphConstants.LeftIndent	Float	0
ParagraphConstants.LineSpacing	Float	0
ParagraphConstants.Orientation	unknown	unknown
ParagraphConstants.RightIndent	Float	0
ParagraphConstants.SpaceAbove	Float	0
ParagraphConstants.SpaceBelow	Float	0
ParagraphConstants.TabSet	TabSet	null

For example, to populate the StyledDocument for a JTextPane, after creating the DefaultStyledDocument, you add content to it by calling the public void insertString(int offset, String contents, AttributeSet attributes) method, which happens to throw a BadLocationException. You can then change the attribute set and add more attributes. So, if you wanted to create content that was both bold *and* italic, you would add two attributes to a SimpleAttributeSet and insert the content into the document:

```
SimpleAttributeSet attributes = new SimpleAttributeSet();
attributes.addAttribute(StyleConstants.CharacterConstants.Bold, Boolean.TRUE);
attributes.addAttribute(StyleConstants.CharacterConstants.Italic, Boolean.TRUE);
```

```
// Insert content
try {
  document.insertString(document.getLength(), "Hello, Java", attributes);
} catch (BadLocationException badLocationException) {
  System.err.println("Oops");
}
```

Figure 16-4 shows how a JTextPane would appear with the words "Hello, Java" and a second insertion displayed.

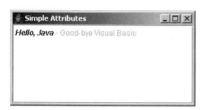

Figure 16-4. *SimpleAttributeSet usage demonstration*

The source for the program shown in Figure 16-4 is presented in Listing 16-4.

Listing 16-4. *Using a SimpleAttributeSet*

```
import javax.swing.*;
import javax.swing.text.*;
import javax.swing.event.*;
import java.awt.*;

public class SimpleAttributeSample {
  public static void main(String args[]) {
    Runnable runner = new Runnable() {
      public void run() {
        JFrame frame = new JFrame("Simple Attributes");
        frame.setDefaultCloseOperation(JFrame.EXIT_ON_CLOSE);

        StyledDocument document = new DefaultStyledDocument();

        SimpleAttributeSet attributes = new SimpleAttributeSet();
        attributes.addAttribute(StyleConstants.CharacterConstants.Bold,
          Boolean.TRUE);
        attributes.addAttribute(StyleConstants.CharacterConstants.Italic,
          Boolean.TRUE);
```

```
      // Insert content
      try {
        document.insertString(document.getLength(), "Hello, Java",
          attributes);
      } catch (BadLocationException badLocationException) {
        System.err.println("Bad insert");
      }

      attributes = new SimpleAttributeSet();
      attributes.addAttribute(StyleConstants.CharacterConstants.Bold,
        Boolean.FALSE);
      attributes.addAttribute(StyleConstants.CharacterConstants.Italic,
        Boolean.FALSE);
      attributes.addAttribute(StyleConstants.CharacterConstants.Foreground,
        Color.LIGHT_GRAY);

      // Insert content
      try {
        document.insertString(document.getLength(),
          " - Good-bye Visual Basic", attributes);
      } catch (BadLocationException badLocationException) {
        System.err.println("Bad insert");
      }

    JTextPane textPane = new JTextPane(document);
      textPane.setEditable(false);
      JScrollPane scrollPane = new JScrollPane(textPane);
      frame.add(scrollPane, BorderLayout.CENTER);

      frame.setSize(300, 150);
      frame.setVisible(true);
    }
  };
  EventQueue.invokeLater(runner);
  }
}
```

In summary, to specify the style of the content, simply set up the attribute set, insert the content, and then repeat the steps for each bit of content you want to add.

StyleConstants Class

The StyleConstants class is chock-full of helper methods to simplify setting attribute sets. And you don't need to burrow into the constants of the inner classes of StyleConstants, because the class makes them available through class constants at the StyleConstants level.

```
public static final Object Alignment;
public static final Object Background;
public static final Object BidiLevel;
public static final Object Bold;
public static final Object ComponentAttribute;
public static final String ComponentElementName;
public static final Object ComposedTextAttribute;
public static final Object Family;
public static final Object FirstLineIndent;
public static final Object FontFamily;
public static final Object FontSize;
public static final Object Foreground;
public static final Object IconAttribute;
public static final String IconElementName;
public static final Object Italic;
public static final Object LeftIndent;
public static final Object LineSpacing;
public static final Object ModelAttribute;
public static final Object NameAttribute;
public static final Object Orientation;
public static final Object ResolveAttribute;
public static final Object RightIndent;
public static final Object Size;
public static final Object SpaceAbove;
public static final Object SpaceBelow;
public static final Object StrikeThrough;
public static final Object Subscript;
public static final Object Superscript;
public static final Object TabSet;
public static final Object Underline;
```

Several static methods allow you to modify a MutableAttributeSet using more logical method names, without requiring you to know the more obscure AttributeSet name. Use the StyleConstants variables of ALIGN_CENTER, ALIGN_JUSTIFIED, ALIGN_LEFT, and ALIGN_RIGHT for the int argument to setAlignment(). The remaining settings are self-explanatory.

```
public static void setAlignment(MutableAttributeSet a, int align);
public static void setBackground(MutableAttributeSet a, Color fg);
public static void setBidiLevel(MutableAttributeSet a, int o);
public static void setBold(MutableAttributeSet a, boolean b);
public static void setComponent(MutableAttributeSet a, Component c);
public static void setFirstLineIndent(MutableAttributeSet a, float i);
public static void setFontFamily(MutableAttributeSet a, String fam);
public static void setFontSize(MutableAttributeSet a, int s);
public static void setForeground(MutableAttributeSet a, Color fg);
public static void setIcon(MutableAttributeSet a, Icon c);
public static void setItalic(MutableAttributeSet a, boolean b);
public static void setLeftIndent(MutableAttributeSet a, float i);
```

```
public static void setLineSpacing(MutableAttributeSet a, float i);
public static void setRightIndent(MutableAttributeSet a, float i);
public static void setSpaceAbove(MutableAttributeSet a, float i);
public static void setSpaceBelow(MutableAttributeSet a, float i);
public static void setStrikeThrough(MutableAttributeSet a, boolean b);
public static void setSubscript(MutableAttributeSet a, boolean b);
public static void setSuperscript(MutableAttributeSet a, boolean b);
public static void setTabSet(MutableAttributeSet a, TabSet tabs);
public static void setUnderline(MutableAttributeSet a, boolean b);
```

For instance, instead of calling the following to make the SimpleAttributeSet both bold and italic:

```
attributes.addAttribute(StyleConstants.CharacterConstants.Bold, Boolean.TRUE)
attributes.addAttribute(StyleConstants.CharacterConstants.Italic, Boolean.TRUE)
```

you could use the following:

```
StyleConstants.setBold(attributes, true);
StyleConstants.setItalic(attributes, true);
```

As you can see, the latter form is much more readable and easier to maintain!

■Tip Besides methods to change AttributeSet objects, the StyleConstants class provides many other methods that let you check the status of an AttributeSet to see if a setting is currently enabled or disabled.

TabStop and TabSet Classes

One of the key constants for storing AttributeSet values is the ParagraphConstants.TabSet attribute. The TabSet class represents a collection of TabStop objects, each defining a tab position, alignment, and leader. If you wanted to define your own tab stops for a JTextPane, you could create a set of TabStop objects, one for each tab stop, create the TabSet, and then associate the TabSet with a MutableAttributeSet.

Creating a TabStop

The TabStop class isn't a JavaBean component in the typical sense; it does not have a no-argument constructor. Instead, you must specify the position, in pixels, at which to place the tab stop. It has two constructors:

```
public TabStop(float position)
TabStop stop = new TabStop(40);
```

```
public TabStop(float position, int align, int leader)
TabStop stop = new TabStop(40, TabStop.ALIGN_DECIMAL, TabStop.LEAD_DOTS);
```

■**Note** Although theoretically it can be specified, the leader argument to the TabStop constructor is currently ignored by the predefined text components.

TabStop Properties

Table 16-5 displays the three properties of TabStop, each initialized by the constructor.

Table 16-5. *TabStop Properties*

Property Name	Data Type	Access
alignment	int	Read-only
leader	int	Read-only
position	int	Read-only

Four alignment settings are specified by the five constants listed in Table 16-6. Figure 16-5 shows how the different settings are displayed.

Table 16-6. *TabStop Alignment Settings*

Alignment	Description
ALIGN_BAR	Starts at tab position
ALIGN_LEFT	Starts at tab position
ALIGN_CENTER	Centers over tab position
ALIGN_DECIMAL	Places decimal point at tab position
ALIGN_RIGHT	Ends at tab position

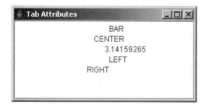

Figure 16-5. *TabStop alignment*

■**Note** Although the ALIGN_BAR and ALIGN_LEFT are technically different constants, their alignment setting currently yields the same result. They are defined per the Rich Text Format (RTF) specification.

Using TabStop Objects

Once you have a TabStop object, or a group of them, you pass the object to the TabSet constructor in an array of TabStop objects like this:

```
TabSet tabset = new TabSet(new TabStop[] {tabstop})
```

As an example, Listing 16-5 shows the source for the TabStop alignment program shown in Figure 16-5.

Listing 16-5. *Using Tabs*

```java
import javax.swing.*;
import javax.swing.text.*;
import javax.swing.event.*;
import java.awt.*;

public class TabSample {
  public static void main(String args[]) {
    Runnable runner = new Runnable() {
      public void run() {
        JFrame frame = new JFrame("Tab Attributes");
        frame.setDefaultCloseOperation(JFrame.EXIT_ON_CLOSE);

        StyledDocument document = new DefaultStyledDocument();

        int positions[] = {TabStop.ALIGN_BAR, TabStop.ALIGN_CENTER,
          TabStop.ALIGN_DECIMAL, TabStop.ALIGN_LEFT, TabStop.ALIGN_RIGHT};
        String strings[] = {"\tBAR\n", "\tCENTER\n", "\t3.14159265\n",
          "\tLEFT\n", "\tRIGHT\n"};

        SimpleAttributeSet attributes = new SimpleAttributeSet();

        for (int i=0, n=positions.length; i<n; i++) {
          TabStop tabstop = new TabStop(150, positions[i], TabStop.LEAD_DOTS);
          try {
            int position = document.getLength();
            document.insertString(position, strings[i], null);
            TabSet tabset = new TabSet(new TabStop[] {tabstop});
            StyleConstants.setTabSet(attributes, tabset);
            document.setParagraphAttributes(position, 1, attributes, false);
          } catch (BadLocationException badLocationException) {
            System.err.println("Bad Location");
          }
        }
```

```
            JTextPane textPane = new JTextPane(document);
            textPane.setEditable(false);
            JScrollPane scrollPane = new JScrollPane(textPane);
            frame.add(scrollPane, BorderLayout.CENTER);

            frame.setSize(300, 150);
            frame.setVisible(true);
          }
        };
        EventQueue.invokeLater(runner);
      }
}
```

In addition to specifying a position and alignment, you can specify which character you want to appear as a leader in the white space created by the tab character. By default, nothing exists there; therefore, the constant is LEAD_NONE. The other TabStop values create a line of periods (dots), equal signs, hyphens, thick lines, or underlines: LEAD_DOTS, LEAD_EQUALS, LEAD_HYPHENS, LEAD_THICKLINE, or LEAD_UNDERLINE. Unfortunately, this option is available but unsupported. While a nonstandard Swing component *might* support this capability, the standard ones currently do not support the different leader settings.

Style Interface

The Style interface is one more of the enhanced ways to specify an AttributeSet. It adds a name to the MutableAttributeSet and the ability to attach a ChangeListener to a Style in order to monitor changes to the attribute settings. For instance, you can configure a bold-italic style as shown here:

```
String BOLD_ITALIC = "BoldItalic";
Style style = (Style)document.getStyle(StyleContext.DEFAULT_STYLE);
StyleConstants.setBold(style, true);
StyleConstants.setItalic(style, true);
document.addStyle(BOLD_ITALIC, null);
```

Later, you can attach the style to some text:

```
style = document.getStyle(BOLD_ITALIC);
document.insertString(document.getLength(), "Hello, Java", style);
```

StyleContext Class

The StyleContext class manages the styles for a styled document. With the help of the StyleContext.NamedStyle class, you can just let the JTextPane to do its own thing, because the StyleContext knows when something needs to be done. For HTML documents, the StyleContext is more specifically a StyleSheet.

The Editor Kits

You briefly saw some of the default EditorKit capabilities of TextAction objects earlier in this chapter, in the "Using Actions with Text Components" section. The EditorKit class serves as the mastermind for pulling together all the different aspects of the text components. It creates documents, manages actions, and creates the visual representation of the document or View. In addition, an EditorKit knows how to read or write the document to a stream. Each document type requires its own EditorKit, so different ones are provided with the JFC/Project Swing components for both HTML and RTF text, as well as plain and styled text.

The actual display of the Document contents is done through the EditorKit with the help of a ViewFactory. For each Element of the Document, the ViewFactory determines which View is created for that element and rendered by the text component delegate. For each different type of element, there is a different View subclass.

Loading HTML Documents

In Chapter 15, you saw how the read() and write() methods of the JTextComponent allow you to read in and write out content for a text component. While the LoadSave example from Listing 15-3 in Chapter 15 demonstrated this process for the JTextField, it works with all the text components, as you would expect. The only requirement for making sure the loading and saving is done for the proper document type is to change the editor kit for the document.

To demonstrate, here's how you could load an HTML file as a StyledDocument into a JEditorPane:

```
JEditorPane editorPane = new JEditorPane();
editorPane.setEditorKit(new HTMLEditorKit());
reader = new FileReader(filename);
editorPane.read(reader, filename);
```

It is that easy. The content type of the component is set to be text/html and loads in the content from filename to be displayed as HTML content. One thing worth noting is that the loading is done asynchronously.

If you need to load the content in synchronously, so that you can wait until everything is loaded, such as for parsing purposes, the process is a bit more involved. You need to work with the HTML parser (HTMLEditorKit.Parser class in javax.swing.text.html package), the parser delegator (ParserDelegator in the javax.swing.text.html.parser package), and the parser callback (HTMLEditorKit.ParserCallback) that you get from the HTMLDocument (as an HTMLDocument.HTMLReader). It sounds more complicated than it really is. To demonstrate, the following code loads a file synchronously into the JEditorPane.

```
reader = new FileReader(filename);
// First create empty empty HTMLDocument to read into
HTMLEditorKit htmlKit = new HTMLEditorKit();
HTMLDocument htmlDoc = (HTMLDocument)htmlKit.createDefaultDocument();
// Next create the parser
HTMLEditorKit.Parser parser = new ParserDelegator();
// Then get HTMLReader (parser callback) from document
HTMLEditorKit.ParserCallback callback = htmlDoc.getReader(0);
```

```
// Finally load the reader into it
// The final true argument says to ignore the character set
parser.parse(reader, callback, true);
// Examine contents
```

Iterating Through HTML Documents

After you have the HTML document loaded, in addition to just displaying the content inside a JEditorPane, you may find it necessary to parse through the content yourself to pull out various pieces. The HTMLDocument supports at least two manners of iteration through the content via the HTMLDocument.Iterator and ElementIterator classes.

HTMLDocument.Iterator Class

To use the HTMLDocument.Iterator, you ask an HTMLDocument to give you the iterator for a specific HTML.Tag. Then, for each instance of the tag in the document, you can look at the attributes of the tag.

The HTML.Tag class includes 76 class constants for all the standard HTML tags (which the HTMLEditorKit understands), such as HTML.Tag.H1 for the <H1> tag. These constants are listed in Table 16-7.

Table 16-7. *HTML Tag Constants*

A	DIR	IMG	SCRIPT
ADDRESS	DIV	IMPLIED	SELECT
APPLET	DL	INPUT	SMALL
AREA	DT	ISINDEX	SPAN
B	EM	KBD	STRIKE
BASE	FONT	LI	STRONG
BASEFONT	FORM	LINK	STYLE
BIG	FRAME	MAP	SUB
BLOCKQUOTE	FRAMESET	MENU	SUP
BODY	H1	META	TABLE
BR	H2	NOFRAMES	TD
CAPTION	H3	OBJECT	TEXTAREA
CENTER	H4	OL	TH
CITE	H5	OPTION	TITLE
CODE	H6	P	TR
COMMENT	HEAD	PARAM	TT
CONTENT	HR	PRE	U
DD	HTML	S	UL
DFN	I	SAMP	VAR

■Note Only those HTML tag constants that have been previously flagged as a block tag—where the isBlock() method for the tag returns true—will work with the HTMLDocument.Iterator. For instance, STRONG is not a block tag, while H1 is.

After you have the specific iterator to work with, you can look at the specific attributes and content of each instance of the tag through the help of the class properties shown in Table 16-8.

Table 16-8. *HTMLDocument.Iterator Properties*

Property Name	Data Type	Access
attributes	AttributeSet	Read-only
endOffset	int	Read-only
startOffset	int	Read-only
tag	HTML.Tag	Read-only
valid	boolean	Read-only

The other piece of the iteration process is the next() method, which lets you get the next instance of the tag in the document. The basic structure of using this iterator is as follows:

```
// Get the iterator
HTMLDocument.Iterator iterator = htmlDoc.getIterator(HTML.Tag.A);

// For each valid one
while (iterator.isValid()) {

// Process element

// Get the next one
 iterator.next();
}
```

This can also be expressed in a basic for loop construct:

```
for (HTMLDocument.Iterator iterator = htmlDoc.getIterator(HTML.Tag.A);
        iterator.isValid();
        iterator.next()) {
  // Process element
}
```

Listing 16-6 demonstrates the use of HTMLDocument.Iterator. This program prompts you for a URL from the command line, loads the file synchronously, looks for all the <A> tags, and then displays all the anchors listed as HREF attributes. Think of this as a simple "spidering" application in which you can build up a database of URL links between documents. The start and end offsets are also used to get the linking text. Just pass in the URL of the location you want to scan to run the program.

Listing 16-6. *Iterating Across HTML Documents for Links*

```java
import java.io.*;
import java.net.*;
import javax.swing.*;
import javax.swing.text.*;
import javax.swing.text.html.*;
import javax.swing.text.html.parser.*;
public class DocumentIteratorExample {

  public static void main(String args[]) throws Exception {

    if (args.length != 1) {
      System.err.println("Usage: java DocumentIteratorExample input-URL");
    }

    // Load HTML file synchronously
    URL url = new URL(args[0]);
    URLConnection connection = url.openConnection();
    InputStream is = connection.getInputStream();
    InputStreamReader isr = new InputStreamReader(is);
    BufferedReader br = new BufferedReader(isr);

    HTMLEditorKit htmlKit = new HTMLEditorKit();
    HTMLDocument htmlDoc = (HTMLDocument)htmlKit.createDefaultDocument();
    HTMLEditorKit.Parser parser = new ParserDelegator();
    HTMLEditorKit.ParserCallback callback = htmlDoc.getReader(0);
    parser.parse(br, callback, true);

    // Parse
    for (HTMLDocument.Iterator iterator = htmlDoc.getIterator(HTML.Tag.A);
         iterator.isValid();
         iterator.next()) {

      AttributeSet attributes = iterator.getAttributes();
      String srcString = (String)attributes.getAttribute(HTML.Attribute.HREF);
      System.out.print(srcString);
      int startOffset = iterator.getStartOffset();
      int endOffset = iterator.getEndOffset();
      int length = endOffset - startOffset;
      String text = htmlDoc.getText(startOffset, length);
      System.out.println(" - " + text);
    }
    System.exit(0);
  }
}
```

ElementIterator Class

Another way of examining the contents of an HTMLDocument is through the ElementIterator (which is not specific to HTML documents). When working with an ElementIterator, you basically see all the Element objects of the document and ask each one what it is. If the object is something you are interested in working with, you can get a closer look.

To get the iterator for a document, just ask like this:

```
ElementIterator iterator = new ElementIterator(htmlDoc);
```

The ElementIterator is not meant to be a simple sequential iterator. It is bidirectional with next() and previous() methods and supports going back to the beginning with first(). Although next() and previous() return the next or previous element to work with, you can also get the element at the current position by using current(). Here is the basic looping method through a document:

```
Element element;
ElementIterator iterator = new ElementIterator(htmlDoc);
while ((element = iterator.next()) != null) {
 // Process element
}
```

How do you find out which element you have in case you want to ignore it if it isn't interesting? You need to get its name and type from its attribute set.

```
AttributeSet attributes = element.getAttributes();
Object name = attributes.getAttribute(StyleConstants.NameAttribute);
if (name instanceof HTML.Tag) {
```

Now you can look for specific tag types, such as HTML.Tag.H1, HTML.Tag.H2, and so on. The actual content for the tag would be in a child element of the element. To demonstrate, the following shows how to search for H1, H2, and H3 tags in a document, while displaying the appropriate titles associated with the tags.

```
if ((name instanceof HTML.Tag) && ((name == HTML.Tag.H1) ||
    (name == HTML.Tag.H2) || (name == HTML.Tag.H3))) {
  // Build up content text as it may be within multiple elements
  StringBuffer text = new StringBuffer();
  int count = element.getElementCount();
  for (int i=0; i<count; i++) {
    Element child = element.getElement(i);
    AttributeSet childAttributes = child.getAttributes();
    if (childAttributes.getAttribute(StyleConstants.NameAttribute) ==
        HTML.Tag.CONTENT) {
      int startOffset = child.getStartOffset();
      int endOffset = child.getEndOffset();
      int length = endOffset - startOffset;
      text.append(htmlDoc.getText(startOffset, length));
    }
  }
}
```

To try this out, you'll need to actually find a web page that uses H1, H2, or H3 tags. This isn't easy these days. Alternatively, you can just switch the H1, H2, and H3 to different tags that you know you will find.

JFormattedTextField Formats

In Chapter 15, you got a little taste of the JFormattedTextField component. Now, you'll get the rest of the meal. A JFormattedTextField is used for accepting formatted input from a user. This sounds simple, but is actually quite important and involved. Without a JFormattedTextField, getting formatted input isn't as easy as it sounds. Throwing in localization requirements makes life really interesting.

Not only does the JFormattedTextField component support entering input in a formatted fashion, but it also allows the user to use the keyboard to increment and decrement the input value; for example, to scroll through the available months in a date.

For a JFormattedTextField, the validation magic is controlled by the focusLostBehavior property. This can be set to one of four values:

- COMMIT_OR_REVERT: This is the default. When the component loses focus, the component automatically calls the commitEdit() method internally. This will parse the component's contents and throw a ParseException on error, reverting the contents to the most recent valid value.

- COMMIT: This setting is similar to COMMIT_OR_REVERT, but it leaves the invalid contents within the field, allowing the user to modify the setting.

- REVERT: This setting always reverts the value.

- PERSIST: This setting essentially does nothing. When the focusLostBehavior property is set to PERSIST, you should manually call commitEdit() yourself to see if the contents are valid before using the contents.

Dates and Numbers

For starters, let's see how to use the JFormattedTextField to accept input that should be internationalized. This includes all forms of dates, times, and numbers—basically, anything whose format can be acquired from a DateFormat or NumberFormat object.

If you provide a Date object or Number subclass to the JFormattedTextField constructor, the component passes the input String to the constructor of that object type to do the input validation. Instead, you should work with the InternationalFormatter class in the java.swing.text package by passing a DateFormat or NumberFormat into the constructor. This allows you to specify long versus short form for dates and times, as well as currency, percentage, floats, and integers for numbers.

Date and Time Formats

To demonstrate date and time formatting, the example in Listing 16-7 accepts various date and time input. From top to bottom, the inputs are short date format for default locale, full date format for United States English, medium date format for Italian, day of week in French, and short time format for the default locale.

Listing 16-7. *Formatted Date and Time Input*

```java
import javax.swing.*;
import javax.swing.text.*;
import javax.swing.event.*;
import java.awt.*;
import java.text.*;
import java.util.*;

public class DateInputSample {
  public static void main(String args[]) {
    Runnable runner = new Runnable() {
      public void run() {
        JFrame frame = new JFrame("Date/Time Input");
        frame.setDefaultCloseOperation(JFrame.EXIT_ON_CLOSE);

        JLabel label;
        JFormattedTextField input;
        JPanel panel;

        BoxLayout layout =
          new BoxLayout(frame.getContentPane(), BoxLayout.Y_AXIS);
        frame.setLayout(layout);

        Format shortDate =
          DateFormat.getDateInstance(DateFormat.SHORT);
        label = new JLabel("Short date:");
        input = new JFormattedTextField(shortDate);
        input.setValue(new Date());
        input.setColumns(20);
        panel = new JPanel(new FlowLayout(FlowLayout.RIGHT));
        panel.add(label);
        panel.add(input);
        frame.add(panel);

        Format fullUSDate =
          DateFormat.getDateInstance(DateFormat.FULL, Locale.US);
        label = new JLabel("Full US date:");
        input = new JFormattedTextField(fullUSDate);
        input.setValue(new Date());
        input.setColumns(20);
        panel = new JPanel(new FlowLayout(FlowLayout.RIGHT));
        panel.add(label);
        panel.add(input);
        frame.add(panel);
```

```
        Format mediumItalian =
            DateFormat.getDateInstance(DateFormat.MEDIUM, Locale.ITALIAN);
        label = new JLabel("Medium Italian date:");
        input = new JFormattedTextField(mediumItalian);
        input.setValue(new Date());
        input.setColumns(20);
        panel = new JPanel(new FlowLayout(FlowLayout.RIGHT));
        panel.add(label);
        panel.add(input);
        frame.add(panel);

        Format dayOfWeek = new SimpleDateFormat("E", Locale.FRENCH);
        label = new JLabel("French day of week:");
        input = new JFormattedTextField(dayOfWeek);
        input.setValue(new Date());
        input.setColumns(20);
        panel = new JPanel(new FlowLayout(FlowLayout.RIGHT));
        panel.add(label);
        panel.add(input);
        frame.add(panel);

        Format shortTime = DateFormat.getTimeInstance(DateFormat.SHORT);
        label = new JLabel("Short time:");
        input = new JFormattedTextField(shortTime);
        input.setValue(new Date());
        input.setColumns(20);
        panel = new JPanel(new FlowLayout(FlowLayout.RIGHT));
        panel.add(label);
        panel.add(input);
        frame.add(panel);

        frame.pack();
        frame.setVisible(true);
      }
    };
    EventQueue.invokeLater(runner);
  }
}
```

Figure 16-6 shows an example of running the program. To start the program in a different locale, you can set the user.language and user.country settings from the command line with a command similar to the following:

```
java -Duser.language=fr -Duser.country=FR DateInputSample
```

However, this will alter the valid input only for those formats without a specific locale set.

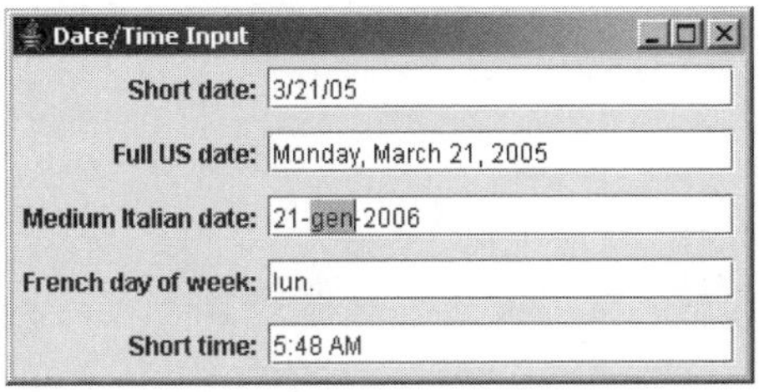

Figure 16-6. *Formatted JFormattedTextField date and time input*

Number Formats

Numbers work similarly to dates, just with the `java.text.NumberFormat` class, instead of the `DateFormat` class. The localization that can be done here is with `getCurrencyInstance()`, `getInstance()`, `getIntegerInstance()`, `getNumberInstance()`, and `getPercentInstance()`.

The `NumberFormat` class will deal with the placement of the necessary commas, periods, percent signs, and so on. While inputting the numbers, extra characters like commas for thousands aren't required. The component will add them after they are input where appropriate, as shown in the example in Figure 16-7. Notice the positions of decimal points and commas and how they differ from locale to locale.

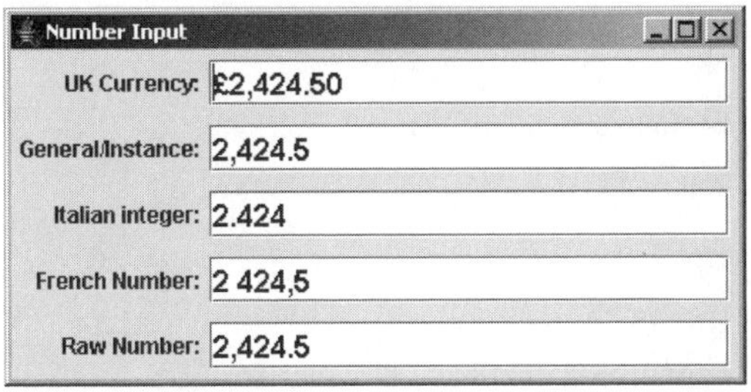

Figure 16-7. *Formatted JFormattedTextField numeric input*

Listing 16-8 shows the program that generated Figure 16-7. Each input field starts with a value of 2424.50. In the case of the integer version, the input value is rounded. When setting the contents of a `JFormattedTextField`, use the `setValue()` method, not the `setText()` method. This will ensure that the text contents are validated.

Listing 16-8. *Formatted Numeric Input*

```
import javax.swing.*;
import javax.swing.text.*;
import javax.swing.event.*;
import java.awt.*;
import java.text.*;
import java.util.*;
```

```java
public class NumberInputSample {
  public static void main(String args[]) {
    Runnable runner = new Runnable() {
      public void run() {
        JFrame frame = new JFrame("Number Input");
        frame.setDefaultCloseOperation(JFrame.EXIT_ON_CLOSE);
        Font font = new Font("SansSerif", Font.BOLD, 16);

        JLabel label;
        JFormattedTextField input;
        JPanel panel;

        BoxLayout layout =
          new BoxLayout(frame.getContentPane(), BoxLayout.Y_AXIS);
        frame.setLayout(layout);

        Format currency =
          NumberFormat.getCurrencyInstance(Locale.UK);
        label = new JLabel("UK Currency:");
        input = new JFormattedTextField(currency);
        input.setValue(2424.50);
        input.setColumns(20);
        input.setFont(font);
        panel = new JPanel(new FlowLayout(FlowLayout.RIGHT));
        panel.add(label);
        panel.add(input);
        frame.add(panel);

        Format general = NumberFormat.getInstance();
        label = new JLabel("General/Instance:");
        input = new JFormattedTextField(general);
        input.setValue(2424.50);
        input.setColumns(20);
        input.setFont(font);
        panel = new JPanel(new FlowLayout(FlowLayout.RIGHT));
        panel.add(label);
        panel.add(input);
        frame.add(panel);

        Format integer = NumberFormat.getIntegerInstance(Locale.ITALIAN);
        label = new JLabel("Italian integer:");
        input = new JFormattedTextField(integer);
        input.setValue(2424.50);
        input.setColumns(20);
        input.setFont(font);
```

```
        panel = new JPanel(new FlowLayout(FlowLayout.RIGHT));
        panel.add(label);
        panel.add(input);
        frame.add(panel);

        Format number = NumberFormat.getNumberInstance(Locale.FRENCH);
        label = new JLabel("French Number:");
        input = new JFormattedTextField(number);
        input.setValue(2424.50);
        input.setColumns(20);
        input.setFont(font);
        panel = new JPanel(new FlowLayout(FlowLayout.RIGHT));
        panel.add(label);
        panel.add(input);
        frame.add(panel);

        label = new JLabel("Raw Number:");
        input = new JFormattedTextField(2424.50);
        input.setColumns(20);
        input.setFont(font);
        panel = new JPanel(new FlowLayout(FlowLayout.RIGHT));
        panel.add(label);
        panel.add(input);
        frame.add(panel);
        frame.pack();
        frame.setVisible(true);
      }
    };
    EventQueue.invokeLater(runner);
  }
}
```

The last of the five JFormattedTextField examples in Figure 16-7 initializes the component with a double. The value 2424.50 is auto-boxed into a Double object. There's nothing wrong with passing an object to the constructor. However, you might notice some irregularities while entering values into the field. A value seems to always start with one decimal point, even though more input digits are accepted. Instead of using a Format object to go from text to Object and back, the Double constructor that accepts a String is used.

When you pass in a java.text.Format object to the JFormattedTextField constructor, this internally is mapped to either a DateFormatter or NumberFormatter object. Both of these are subclasses of the InternationalFormatter class. The inner class named JFormattedTextField. AbstractFormatterFactory manages the use of the formatter objects within JFormattedTextField. The factory will install() the formatter as the user enters the JFormattedTextField and uninstall() it on departure, ensuring the formatter is active in only one text field at a time. These install() and uninstall() methods are inherited by the formatter classes from the JFormattedTextField.AbstractFormatter superclass of all formatters.

Input Masks

Beyond numbers and dates, the JFormattedTextField supports user input following a pattern or mask. For instance, if an input field is a United States social security number (SSN), it has a typical pattern of number, number, number, dash, number, number, dash, number, number, number, number. With the help of the MaskFormatter class, you can specify the mask using the characters listed in Table 16-9.

Table 16-9. *Special Characters for Masks*

Character	Description
#	Matches numeric character (Character.isDigit())
H	Matches hexadecimal number (0–9, a–f, and A–F)
A	Matches alphanumeric character (Character.is LetterOrDigit())
?	Matches alphabetic character (Character.isLetter())
U	Matches uppercase letter; maps lowercase to uppercase
L	Matches lowercase letter; maps uppercase to lowercase
*	Wildcard, matches any character
'	Escape character to have literal strings/separators in input field

For example, this formatter creates an SSN mask:

```
new MaskFormatter("###'-##'-####")
```

The apostrophes in the mask mean the character after each is treated literally—in this case, as a dash. You have the option of passing this formatter to the JFormattedTextField constructor or configuring the text field with the setMask() method.

To demonstrate, Listing 16-9 includes two JFormattedTextField components: one to accept SSNs and the other United States phone numbers.

Listing 16-9. *Formatted Masked Input*

```
import javax.swing.*;
import javax.swing.text.*;
import javax.swing.event.*;
import java.awt.*;
import java.text.*;
import java.util.*;

public class MaskInputSample {
  public static void main(String args[]) {
    Runnable runner = new Runnable() {
      public void run() {
        JFrame frame = new JFrame("Mask Input");
        frame.setDefaultCloseOperation(JFrame.EXIT_ON_CLOSE);
```

```
        JLabel label;
        JFormattedTextField input;
        JPanel panel;
        MaskFormatter formatter;

        BoxLayout layout =
          new BoxLayout(frame.getContentPane(), BoxLayout.Y_AXIS);
        frame.setLayout(layout);

        try {
          label = new JLabel("SSN");
          formatter = new MaskFormatter("###'-##'-####");
          input = new JFormattedTextField(formatter);
          input.setValue("123-45-6789");
          input.setColumns(20);
          panel = new JPanel(new FlowLayout(FlowLayout.RIGHT));
          panel.add(label);
          panel.add(input);
          frame.add(panel);
        } catch (ParseException e) {
          System.err.println("Unable to add SSN");
        }

        try {
          label = new JLabel("US Phone");
          formatter = new MaskFormatter("'(###')' ###'-####");
          input = new JFormattedTextField(formatter);
          input.setColumns(20);
          panel = new JPanel(new FlowLayout(FlowLayout.RIGHT));
          panel.add(label);
          panel.add(input);
          frame.add(panel);
        } catch (ParseException e) {
          System.err.println("Unable to add Phone");
        }

        frame.pack();
        frame.setVisible(true);
      }
    };
    EventQueue.invokeLater(runner);
  }
}
```

Figure 16-8 shows the output of the program. In this example, the SSN field starts with an initial value, while the phone number field does not.

Figure 16-8. *Formatted masked input in JFormattedTextFields*

The MaskFormatter does provide some customization options. By default, the formatter is in overwrite mode, so as you type, the entered digits will replace each number and space in the input field. Set the overwriteMode property to false to disable this. Typically, this isn't necessary, though for entering in long dates, it can be helpful.

If you wish to have a different character as the placeholder character, before a position is filled in the mask, set the placeholderCharacter property of the MaskFormatter. To demonstrate, add the following line to the phone number formatter in Listing 16-9:

```
formatter.setPlaceholder('*');
```

You'll see the results in the bottom text field shown in Figure 16-9.

Figure 16-9. *Formatted masked input with a placeholder*

Another useful MaskFormatter property is validCharacters, for restricting which alphanumeric characters are valid for an input field.

DefaultFormatterFactory Class

The DefaultFormatterFactory class found in the javax.swing.text package offers a way to have different formatters for displaying values, editing values, and a special case of a null value. It offers five constructors, starting with no parameters and then adding an additional AbstractFormatter parameter for each constructor.

```
public DefaultFormatterFactory()
DefaultFormatterFactory factory = new DefaultFormatterFactory()

public DefaultFormatterFactory(JFormattedTextField.AbstractFormatter defaultFormat)
DateFormat defaultFormat = new SimpleDateFormat("yyyy--MMMM--dd");
DateFormatter defaultFormatter = new DateFormatter(displayFormat);
DefaultFormatterFactory factory = new DefaultFormatterFactory(defaultFormatter);

public DefaultFormatterFactory(JFormattedTextField.AbstractFormatter defaultFormat,
    JFormattedTextField.AbstractFormatter displayFormat)
DateFormat displayFormat = new SimpleDateFormat("yyyy--MMMM--dd");
DateFormatter displayFormatter = new DateFormatter(displayFormat);
DefaultFormatterFactory factory = new DefaultFormatterFactory(displayFormatter,
    displayFormatter);
```

```
public DefaultFormatterFactory(JFormattedTextField.AbstractFormatter defaultFormat,
  JFormattedTextField.AbstractFormatter displayFormat,
  JFormattedTextField.AbstractFormatter editFormat)
DateFormat displayFormat = new SimpleDateFormat("yyyy--MMMM--dd");
DateFormatter displayFormatter = new DateFormatter(displayFormat);
DateFormat editFormat = new SimpleDateFormat("MM/dd/yy");
DateFormatter editFormatter = new DateFormatter(editFormat);
DefaultFormatterFactory factory = new DefaultFormatterFactory(
  displayFormatter, displayFormatter, editFormatter);

public DefaultFormatterFactory(JFormattedTextField.AbstractFormatter defaultFormat,
  JFormattedTextField.AbstractFormatter displayFormat,
  JFormattedTextField.AbstractFormatter editFormat,
  JFormattedTextField.AbstractFormatter nullFormat)
DateFormat displayFormat = new SimpleDateFormat("yyyy--MMMM--dd");
DateFormatter displayFormatter = new DateFormatter(displayFormat);
DateFormat editFormat = new SimpleDateFormat("MM/dd/yy");
DateFormatter editFormatter = new DateFormatter(editFormat);
DateFormat nullFormat = new SimpleDateFormat("'null'");
DateFormatter nullFormatter = new DateFormatter(nullFormat);
DefaultFormatterFactory factory = new DefaultFormatterFactory(
  displayFormatter, displayFormatter, editFormatter, nullFormatter);
```

There isn't much magic in the use of DefaultFormatterFactory. Just create one and pass it along to the JFormattedTextField constructor. Then the state of the text field will determine which formatter is used to show the current value. Typically, the display formatter is repeated for the default settings. If any of the formatters is null or unset, the default formatter will be used instead.

Summary

In this chapter, you saw several of the more advanced aspects of working with the JFC/Project Swing text components. You looked into how to use the predefined TextAction objects to create working user interfaces without defining any of your own event-handling capabilities. In addition, you explored the JTextPane and how to create multiple-attributed text within a JTextPane through the AttributeSet, MutableAttributeSet, SimpleAttributeSet, and StyleConstants. You also saw how to create tab stops within a Document and glanced at the EditorKit facilities of Swing, exploring the details of the HTMLEditorKit specifically. Finally, you learned more about accepting formatted input with the JFormattedTextField.

For additional information about the Swing text package, be sure to stop by The Swing Connection at http://java.sun.com/products/jfc/tsc/articles/text/overview/.

In Chapter 17, you'll explore the Swing component for displaying hierarchical data: the JTree.

CHAPTER 17

■ ■ ■

Trees

In Chapter 16, you looked at how to work with the text document capabilities within the Swing component set. In this chapter, you'll learn how to work with Swing's tree class, the JTree component.

Introducing Trees

The JTree component is the visual component for displaying hierarchical data elements, also known as *nodes*. Using this tree metaphor, imagine the tree is flipped upside down. The node at the top of the tree is called the *root*. Extending from the root node of the tree are branches to other nodes. If a node does not have any branches coming out of it, that node is called a *leaf node*. See Figure 17-1 for a simple JTree.

Figure 17-1. *Sample JTree*

Many interconnected classes are used in the composition of the JTree. First, the JTree implements the Scrollable interface, so that you can place the tree within a JScrollPane for scroll management. The display of each node within the tree is controlled by implementations of the TreeCellRenderer interface; by default, the implementation is the DefaultTreeCellRenderer class. Nodes of a tree are editable with implementations of TreeCellEditor. Two editor implementations are available: one offering a text field with DefaultTreeCellEditor and one offering a check box or combo box with DefaultCellEditor, which extends from the generic AbstractCellEditor. If these classes don't provide what you need, you can place custom editors within an EditorContainer.

> ■**Note** The DefaultCellEditor class can also be used as a cell editor with the JTable component. The JTable component is described in Chapter 18.

By default, the actual nodes of the JTree are implementations of the TreeNode interface or its subinterface MutableTreeNode. The DefaultMutableTreeNode class is one such implementation that's commonly used, with the JTree.DynamicUtilTreeNode inner class helping to create the tree nodes. The many tree nodes make up the TreeModel for the JTree, stored by default into an instance of the DefaultTreeModel class.

Tree selection is managed by a TreeSelectionModel implementation, with a default implementation of DefaultTreeSelectionModel available. The JTree.EmptySelectionModel is also available if you do not want the nodes of the tree to be selectable. The path of nodes from the root of the tree to the selected node is maintained within a TreePath, with the help of a RowMapper implementation to map rows to paths.

> ■**Note** The tree-specific classes are found in the javax.swing.tree package. The event-related classes are in the javax.swing.event package.

JTree Class

The JTree class forms the basis for visually displaying a set of hierarchical data elements.

Creating a JTree

There are seven different ways to create a JTree, with five different ways to specify the nodes:

```
public JTree()
JTree tree = new JTree();
```

```
public JTree(Hashtable value)
JTree tree = new JTree(System.getProperties());
```

```
public JTree(Object value[])
public static void main (String args[]) {
  JTree tree = new JTree(args);
  ...
}
```

```
public JTree(Vector value)
Vector vector = new Vector();
vector.add("One");
vector.add("Two");
JTree tree = new JTree(vector);
```

```
public JTree(TreeModel value)
JTree tree = new JTree(aTreeModel);
```

```
public JTree(TreeNode value)
JTree tree = new JTree(aTreeNode);
```

```
public JTree(TreeNode value, boolean asksAllowsChildren)
JTree tree = new JTree(aTreeNode, true);
```

The first of the constructors is the no-argument variety. Surprisingly, it has a default data model with some nodes in it (see Figure 17-1). Normally, you would change the data model of the default tree after creation with setModel(TreeModel newModel).

The next three constructors seem to belong together. Creation of a JTree from a Hashtable made up of key/value pairs uses the set of keys for the nodes and values for the children, whereas creation from an array or Vector uses the elements as the nodes. This may seem to imply that the tree is only one level deep, but actually the tree can be infinitely deep if the key or element itself is in a Hashtable, an array, or a Vector.

The remaining three constructors use the custom data structures of JTree, which will be explained later in this chapter. By default, only those nodes that have children are leaf nodes. However, trees can be constructed with partial nodes that won't get children until later. The last of these three constructors causes a method to be called when you try to open a parent node, instead of the parent node just looking for child nodes.

■**Tip** If the value for a key in a Hashtable is another Hashtable, array, or Vector, you can create a multi-level tree by using the top-level Hashtable as the constructor argument.

As I mentioned, using a Hashtable, an array, or a Vector as the argument in the constructor tree does, in fact, allow you to create multilevel trees. There are two minor problems with this, however: the root node isn't visible, and it automatically has a data element of root. The text label for any other nodes of type Hashtable, array, or Vector is the result of toString(). The default text is not desirable in any of these three instances. You get either the results of the toString() method of the Object class for an array or a label that includes a list of all the elements in the Hashtable or Vector. In the case of an Object array, the output would look something like [Ljava.lang.Object;@fa8d8993. This is certainly not something you want to show a user.

Although you cannot override toString()(because there is no array class to subclass), you can subclass Hashtable or Vector to provide a different toString() behavior. Offering a name to the constructor of this new class allows you to provide a text label to use in the tree when the Hashtable or Vector is not the root node. The class shown in Listing 17-1 defines this behavior for a Vector subclass. In addition to the constructor providing a name, the class also adds a constructor that initializes the Vector to the contents of an array.

Listing 17-1. *Named Vector*

```java
import java.util.Vector;
public class NamedVector<E> extends Vector<E> {
  String name;
  NamedVector(String name) {
    this.name = name;
  }
  NamedVector(String name, E elements[]) {
    this.name = name;
    for (int i=0, n=elements.length; i<n; i++) {
      add(elements[i]);
    }
  }
  public String toString() {
    return "[" + name + "]";
  }
}
```

Figure 17-2 shows an example of the NamedVector class in action.

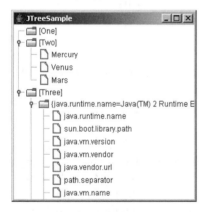

Figure 17-2. *Sample JTree with the Vector subclass node*

Listing 17-2 shows the source used to generate the example in Figure 17-2.

Listing 17-2. *Named Vector Usage*

```java
import javax.swing.*;
import javax.swing.tree.*;
import java.awt.*;
import java.util.*;

public class TreeArraySample {
  public static void main(final String args[]) {
    Runnable runner = new Runnable() {
```

```
    public void run() {
      JFrame frame = new JFrame("JTreeSample");
      frame.setDefaultCloseOperation(JFrame.EXIT_ON_CLOSE);

      Vector<String> oneVector = new NamedVector<String>("One", args);
      Vector<String> twoVector = new NamedVector<String>("Two",
        new String[]{"Mercury", "Venus", "Mars"});
      Vector<Object> threeVector = new NamedVector<Object>("Three");
      threeVector.add(System.getProperties());
      threeVector.add(twoVector);
      Object rootNodes[] = {oneVector, twoVector, threeVector};
      Vector<Object> rootVector = new NamedVector<Object>("Root", rootNodes);
      JTree tree = new JTree(rootVector);
      frame.add(tree, BorderLayout.CENTER);
      frame.setSize(300, 300);
      frame.setVisible(true);
    }
  };
  EventQueue.invokeLater(runner);
  }
}
```

Scrolling Trees

If you created and ran the program in Listing 17-2, you would notice one small problem. When all the parent nodes are open, the tree is too big for the initial screen size. Not only that, but you also can't see the nodes at the bottom of the tree. To fix this situation, it's necessary to place instances of the JTree class within a JScrollPane so that the scroll pane can manage the scrolling aspects of the tree. Similar to the JTextArea class described in Chapter 15, the JTree class implements the Scrollable interface for scrolling support.

Replacing the two boldfaced lines in the example in Listing 17-2 with the following three lines will place the tree within a scroll pane. This will cause the tree to appear in a scrollable region when the tree is too large for the available display space.

```
// Change from
JTree tree = new JTree(rootVector);
frame.add(tree, BorderLayout.CENTER);
// To
JTree tree = new JTree(rootVector);
JScrollPane scrollPane = new JScrollPane(tree);
frame.add(scrollPane, BorderLayout.CENTER);
```

In addition to using a JScrollPane for scrolling, you can manually scroll the visible content in the scrolling region. Use the public void scrollPathToVisible(TreePath path) and public void scrollRowToVisible(int row) methods to move a particular tree path or row into some part of the visible area. The *row* of a node indicates the number of nodes above the current node to the top of the tree. This differs from the *level* of the tree, which is the number of ancestors (or parent nodes) a node has. Figure 17-3 should help you visualize this difference. In the window on the left, the soccer node is at level 2 and row 8. When the colors node is closed, as in the window on the right, the soccer node remains on level 2 but moves to row 4, because the blue, violet, red, and yellow rows are no longer visible.

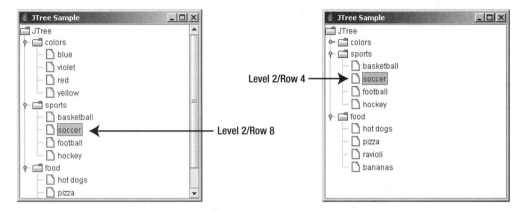

Figure 17-3. *Rows versus levels of a tree*

JTree Properties

Table 17-1 lists the 40 specific properties of JTree. You will explore many of these as you look at the different classes that make up JTree.

Table 17-1. *JTree Properties*

Property Name	Data Type	Access
accessibleContext	AccessibleContext	Read-only
anchorSelectionPath	TreePath	Read-write bound
cellEditor	TreeCellEditor	Read-write bound
cellRenderer	TreeCellRenderer	Read-write bound
dragEnabled	boolean	Read-write
editable	boolean	Read-write bound
editing	boolean	Read-only
editingPath	TreePath	Read-only
expandsSelectedPath	boolean	Read-write bound
fixedRowHeight	boolean	Read-only
invokesStopCellEditing	boolean	Read-write bound
largeModel	boolean	Read-write bound
lastSelectedPathComponent	Object	Read-only
leadSelectionPath	TreePath	Read-write bound

Table 17-1. *JTree Properties (Continued)*

Property Name	Data Type	Access
leadSelectionRow	int	Read-only
maxSelectionRow	int	Read-only
minSelectionRow	int	Read-only
model	TreeModel	Read-write bound
preferredScrollableViewportSize	Dimension	Read-only
rootVisible	boolean	Read-write bound
rowCount	int	Read-only
rowHeight	int	Read-write bound
scrollableTracksViewportHeight	boolean	Read-only
scrollableTracksViewportWidth	boolean	Read-only
scrollsOnExpand	boolean	Read-write bound
selectionCount	int	Read-only
selectionEmpty	boolean	Read-only
selectionModel	TreeSelectionModel	Read-write bound
selectionPath	TreePath	Read-write
selectionPaths	TreePath[ ]	Read-write
selectionRow	int	Write-only
selectionRows	int[ ]	Read-write
showsRootHandles	boolean	Read-write bound
toggleClickCount	int	Read-write bound
treeExpansionListeners	TreeExpansionListener[ ]	Read-only
treeSelectionListeners	TreeSelectionListener[ ]	Read-only
treeWillExpandListeners	TreeWillExpandListener[ ]	Read-only
UI	TreeUI	Read-write
UIClassID	String	Read-only
visibleRowCount	int	Read-write bound

Some JTree properties are closely interrelated. For instance, when the rowHeight property is positive, it means that the node at each row is displayed with a fixed height, no matter what size the nodes within the tree should be. When the rowHeight property is negative, the cellRenderer property determines the rowHeight. So, the value of rowHeight determines the setting of the fixedRowHeight property. Changing the value of rowHeight to a value such as 12 pixels results in the fixedRowHeight property having a setting of true.

The largeModel property setting is a suggestion to the TreeUI to help it display the tree. Initially, this setting is false because a tree has many data elements and you don't want the user interface component to cache excessive information (such as node renderer sizes) about the tree. For smaller models, caching information about a tree doesn't require as much memory.

The current setting of lastSelectedPathComponent property is the contents of the last selected node. At any time, you can ask a tree what is selected. If nothing is selected, this property's value will be null. Because trees support multiple selections, the lastSelectedPathComponent property doesn't necessarily return *all* selected nodes. You can also modify the selection path with the anchorSelectionPath and leadSelectionPath properties.

The three selection row properties—leadSelectionRow, minSelectionRow, and maxSelectionRow—are interesting in that the row values can change based on another parent node's opening or closing. When a single node in the tree is selected, all three properties have the same setting. You can get an array of all selected row indices with the selectionRows property. However, there is no way to map a row number to a node in the tree. Instead, use the selectionPaths property, which provides an array of TreePath elements. As you'll soon see, each TreePath includes the selected node and all nodes on the path from the root node to the selected node.

There are three visibility-related settings of a tree. You can adjust the preferred number of rows to display for the tree by setting the visibleRowCount property. By default, the setting is 20. This setting is valid only when a particular tree is within a JScrollPane or some other component that uses the Scrollable interface. The second visibility-related setting has to do with whether the root node is visible. When the tree is created from a Hashtable, array, or Vector constructor, the root isn't visible. Otherwise, it will be visible initially. Changing the rootVisible property allows you to alter this setting. The other visibility-related setting has to do with the icon next to the root node. By default, there is no icon at the root level to show the open or closed state of the root of the tree. All nonroot nodes always have this type of icon. To show the root icon, set the showsRootHandles property to true.

Three additional selection-oriented properties are also available. The toggleClickCount property allows you to control how many clicks over a parent node will trigger selection or expansion of the node. The default setting is 2. The scrollsOnExpand property causes the tree to scroll when a node is expanded such that as many descendants as possible will be visible. By default, this is true. The third property, expandsSelectedPath, is true by default, causing the selected path for a node to be expanded when programmatically selected. If, however, you don't wish to expand the tree upon programmatic selection, you can set this to false and leave the path hidden.

Customizing a JTree Look and Feel

Each installable Swing look and feel provides a different JTree appearance and set of default UIResource values. Figure 17-4 shows the appearance of the JTree container for the preinstalled set of look and feel types: Motif, Windows, and Ocean.

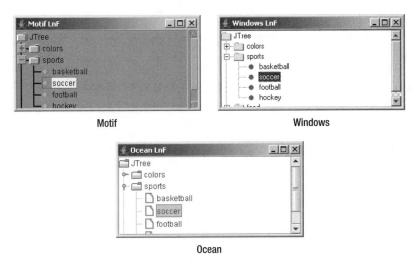

Figure 17-4. *JTree under different look and feel types*

The available set of UIResource-related properties for a JTree is shown in Table 17-2. For the JTree component, there are 43 different properties.

Table 17-2. *JTree UIResource Elements*

Property String	Object Type
Tree.actionMap	ActionMap
Tree.ancestorInputMap	InputMap
Tree.background	Color
Tree.changeSelectionWithFocus	Boolean
Tree.closedIcon	Icon
Tree.collapsedIcon	Icon
Tree.drawDashedFocusIndicator	Boolean
Tree.drawHorizontalLines	Boolean
Tree.drawsFocusBorderAroundIcon	Boolean
Tree.drawVerticalLines	Boolean
Tree.editorBorder	Border
Tree.editorBorderSelectionColor	Color
Tree.expandedIcon	Icon
Tree.expanderSize	Integer

Table 17-2. *JTree UIResource Elements (Continued)*

Property String	Object Type
Tree.focusInputMap	InputMap
Tree.focusInputMap.RightToLeft	InputMap
Tree.font	Font
Tree.foreground	Color
Tree.hash	Color
Tree.iconBackground	Color
Tree.iconForeground	Color
Tree.iconHighlight	Color
Tree.iconShadow	Color
Tree.leafIcon	Icon
Tree.leftChildIndent	Integer
Tree.line	Color
Tree.lineTypeDashed	Boolean
Tree.openIcon	Icon
Tree.padding	Integer
Tree.paintLines	Boolean
Tree.rendererUseTreeColors	Boolean
Tree.rightChildIndent	Integer
Tree.rowHeight	Integer
Tree.scrollsHorizontallyAndVertically	Boolean
Tree.scrollsOnExpand	Boolean
Tree.selectionBackground	Color
Tree.selectionBorderColor	Color
Tree.selectionForeground	Color
Tree.showsRootHandles	Boolean
Tree.textBackground	Color
Tree.textForeground	Color
Tree.timeFactor	Integer
TreeUI	String

Of the many different JTree resources, five are for the various icons displayed within the JTree. To see how the five icons are positioned, examine Figure 17-5. If you just want to change the icons (and possibly the colors) of a tree, all you need to do is change the icon properties with lines such as the following:

```
UIManager.put("Tree.openIcon", new DiamondIcon(Color.RED, false));
```

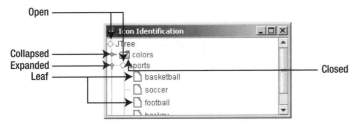

Figure 17-5. *JTree icons*

The purpose of the Tree.hash color property may not be immediately obvious. This color is for the lines drawn to connect nodes. With the Metal look and feel, and Ocean theme, by default, angled lines connect the nodes. To enable the drawing of these lines, you must set the JTree.lineStyle client property. This property isn't a UIResource property, but rather a client property set with the public final void putClientProperty(Object key, Object value) method of JComponent. The JTree.lineStyle property has the following valid settings:

- None, for not drawing lines to connect nodes

- Angled, the default setting for Ocean, for drawing lines in the Tree.hash color to connect the nodes

- Horizontal, for drawing horizontal lines between first-level nodes in the Tree.line color

---

Note The JTree.lineStyle client property is used only by the Metal look and feel. If the current look and feel isn't Metal or one of its themes like Ocean, the property setting will be ignored if set (unless a custom look and feel takes advantage of the setting). The other system-provided look and feel classes don't use this setting.

With client properties, you first must create the tree and then set the property. This client property is specific to tree components, and it is not set for all trees. Therefore, creating a tree with no lines entails using the following lines of code:

```
JTree tree = new JTree();
tree.putClientProperty("JTree.lineStyle", "None");
```

Figure 17-6 shows the results.

Figure 17-6. *A JTree with no connection lines*

The following lines produce horizontal lines between level-one nodes:

```
UIManager.put("Tree.line", Color.GREEN);
JTree tree = new JTree();
tree.putClientProperty("JTree.lineStyle", "Horizontal");
```

Figure 17-7 shows how the horizontal lines appear.

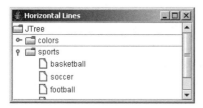

Figure 17-7. *A JTree with horizontal level lines*

TreeCellRenderer Interface

Each of the nodes within the JTree has an installed cell *renderer*. It's the responsibility of the renderer to draw the node and clearly display its state. The default renderer is basically a JLabel, which allows you to have both text and an icon within the node. However, any component can serve as the node renderer. The default renderer displays an icon that represents the state of the node.

■**Note** The tree cell renderer is just that—a renderer. If the renderer were, say, a JButton, it wouldn't be selectable but would nevertheless be drawn to look just like a JButton.

The configuration of each node renderer is defined by the TreeCellRenderer interface. Any class implementing this interface can serve as a renderer for your JTree.

```
public interface TreeCellRenderer {
  public Component getTreeCellRendererComponent(JTree tree, Object value,
    boolean selected, boolean expanded, boolean leaf, int row, boolean hasFocus);
}
```

When it's time to draw a tree node, that tree asks its registered TreeCellRenderer how to display that specific node. The node itself is passed in as the value argument so that the renderer has access to its current state to determine how to render this state. To change the installed renderer, use public void setCellRenderer(TreeCellRenderer renderer).

DefaultTreeCellRenderer Class

The DefaultTreeCellRenderer class serves as the default tree cell renderer. This class is a JLabel subclass, so it can support capabilities such as displaying tooltip text or pop-up menus specific to a node. It has only a no-argument constructor.

When used by a JTree, the DefaultTreeCellRenderer uses the various default icons (as shown earlier in Figure 17-5) to display the current state of the node and a text representation of the data for the node. The text representation is acquired by calling the toString() method for each node of the tree.

DefaultTreeCellRenderer Properties

Table 17-3 shows the 14 properties added (or altered) with DefaultTreeCellRenderer. Because the default renderer happens to be a JLabel, you also acquire many additional properties from it.

Table 17-3. *DefaultTreeCellRenderer Properties*

Property Name	Data Type	Access
background	Color	Write-only
backgroundNonSelectionColor	Color	Read-write
backgroundSelectionColor	Color	Read-write
borderSelectionColor	Color	Read-write
closedIcon	Icon	Read-write
defaultClosedIcon	Icon	Read-only
defaultLeafIcon	Icon	Read-only
defaultOpenIcon	Icon	Read-only
font	Font	Read-write
leafIcon	Icon	Read-write
openIcon	Icon	Read-write
preferredSize	Dimension	Read-only
textNonSelectionColor	Color	Read-write
textSelectionColor	Color	Read-write

If you don't like working with the UIManager or just want to change the icons, font, or colors for a single tree, you don't need to create a custom tree cell renderer. Instead, you can ask the tree for its renderer and customize it to display the icons, font, or colors you want. Figure 17-8 shows a JTree with an altered renderer. Instead of creating a new renderer, the existing default renderer was customized with the following source:

```
JTree tree = new JTree();
DefaultTreeCellRenderer renderer = (DefaultTreeCellRenderer)tree.getCellRenderer();
// Swap background colors
Color backgroundSelection = renderer.getBackgroundSelectionColor();
renderer.setBackgroundSelectionColor(renderer.getBackgroundNonSelectionColor());
renderer.setBackgroundNonSelectionColor(backgroundSelection);
// Swap text colors
Color textSelection = renderer.getTextSelectionColor();
renderer.setTextSelectionColor(renderer.getTextNonSelectionColor());
renderer.setTextNonSelectionColor(textSelection);
```

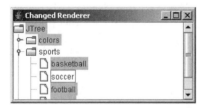

Figure 17-8. *A JTree with an altered default renderer*

Remember that TreeUI caches renderer size information. If a change to the renderer changes the renderer size, this cache isn't updated. To get around the problem, it's necessary to signal to the tree that the cache is invalid. One such signal is to change the rowHeight property. As long as the current rowHeight property setting isn't positive, the TreeUI must ask the renderer for its height. Therefore, decreasing the value by 1 has a side effect of invalidating the cached renderer size information, causing the tree to be displayed with the proper initial sizes for all the renderers. Adding the following source to the previous example demonstrates this.

```
renderer.setFont(new Font("Dialog", Font.BOLD | Font.ITALIC, 32));
int rowHeight = tree.getRowHeight();
if (rowHeight <= 0) {
  tree.setRowHeight(rowHeight - 1);
}
```

The window on the left in Figure 17-9 shows the effect this addition has on Figure 17-8. If you didn't change the rowHeight property to invalidate the display cache, you would get the effect shown in the right window instead.

With size-change notification   Without size-change notification

Figure 17-9. *You must properly modify the size of a tree renderer.*

Creating a Custom Renderer

If the nodes of your JTree consist of information that is too complex to display within the text of a single JLabel, you can create your own renderer. As an example, consider a tree in which the nodes describe books by their title, author, and price, as shown in Figure 17-10. In this case, the renderer can be a container in which a separate component displays each part.

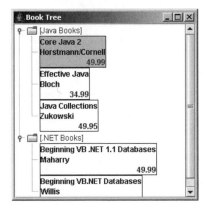

Figure 17-10. *A JTree with a custom renderer*

To describe each book in this example, you need to define a class for storing the necessary information, as shown in Listing 17-3.

Listing 17-3. *Book Class Definition*

```
public class Book {
  String title;
  String authors;
  float price;
  public Book(String title, String authors, float price) {
    this.title = title;
    this.authors = authors;
    this.price = price;
  }
```

```java
  public String getTitle() {
    return title;
  }
  public String getAuthors() {
    return authors;
  }
  public float getPrice() {
    return price;
  }
}
```

To render a book as a node in the tree, you need to create a TreeCellRenderer implementation. Because the books are leaf nodes, the custom renderer will use a DefaultTreeCellRenderer to render all the other nodes. The key part of the renderer is the getTreeCellRendererComponent(). In the event that the node data received by this method is of type Book, it stores the appropriate information in the different labels and returns a JPanel as the renderer, with labels for each of the book titles, authors, and prices. Otherwise, the getTreeCellRendererComponent() method returns the default renderer.

Listing 17-4 contains the source for this custom renderer. Notice that it uses the same selection colors as the remaining nodes of the tree so that the book nodes don't appear out of place.

Listing 17-4. *Book Cell Renderer*

```java
import javax.swing.*;
import javax.swing.tree.*;
import java.awt.*;

public class BookCellRenderer implements TreeCellRenderer {
  JLabel titleLabel;
  JLabel authorsLabel;
  JLabel priceLabel;
  JPanel renderer;
  DefaultTreeCellRenderer defaultRenderer = new DefaultTreeCellRenderer();
  Color backgroundSelectionColor;
  Color backgroundNonSelectionColor;
  public BookCellRenderer() {
    renderer = new JPanel(new GridLayout(0, 1));
    titleLabel = new JLabel(" ");
    titleLabel.setForeground(Color.BLUE);
    renderer.add(titleLabel);
    authorsLabel = new JLabel(" ");
    authorsLabel.setForeground(Color.BLUE);
    renderer.add(authorsLabel);
    priceLabel = new JLabel(" ");
    priceLabel.setHorizontalAlignment(JLabel.RIGHT);
```

```
      priceLabel.setForeground(Color.RED);
      renderer.add(priceLabel);
      renderer.setBorder(BorderFactory.createLineBorder(Color.BLACK));
      backgroundSelectionColor = defaultRenderer.getBackgroundSelectionColor();
      backgroundNonSelectionColor = defaultRenderer.getBackgroundNonSelectionColor();
    }
    public Component getTreeCellRendererComponent(JTree tree, Object value,
        boolean selected, boolean expanded, boolean leaf, int row, boolean hasFocus) {
      Component returnValue = null;
      if ((value != null) && (value instanceof DefaultMutableTreeNode)) {
        Object userObject = ((DefaultMutableTreeNode)value).getUserObject();
        if (userObject instanceof Book) {
          Book book = (Book)userObject;
          titleLabel.setText(book.getTitle());
          authorsLabel.setText(book.getAuthors());
          priceLabel.setText("" + book.getPrice());
          if (selected) {
            renderer.setBackground(backgroundSelectionColor);
          } else {
            renderer.setBackground(backgroundNonSelectionColor);
          }
          renderer.setEnabled(tree.isEnabled());
          returnValue = renderer;
        }
      }
      if (returnValue == null) {
        returnValue = defaultRenderer.getTreeCellRendererComponent(tree, value,
            selected, expanded, leaf, row, hasFocus);
      }
      return returnValue;
    }
}
```

▉Tip The JLabel components are created with an initial text label consisting of a space. Having a nonempty label gives each component some dimensions. The TreeUI caches node sizes to improve performance. Having an initial size for the labels ensures that the cache is initialized properly.

The last remaining part is the test program, shown in Listing 17-5. The majority of it just creates arrays of Book objects. It reuses the NamedVector class from Listing 17-1 to help create the tree branches. The code lines necessary for changing the tree cell renderer are boldfaced. Running the program demonstrates the custom renderer, as shown earlier in Figure 17-10.

Listing 17-5. *Using the Custom Book Cell Renderer*

```java
import javax.swing.*;
import javax.swing.tree.*;
import java.awt.*;
import java.util.*;

public class BookTree {
  public static void main(String args[]) {
    Runnable runner = new Runnable() {
      public void run() {
        JFrame frame = new JFrame("Book Tree");
        frame.setDefaultCloseOperation(JFrame.EXIT_ON_CLOSE);
        Book javaBooks[] = {
          new Book("Core Java 2", "Horstmann/Cornell", 49.99f),
          new Book("Effective Java", "Bloch", 34.99f),
          new Book("Java Collections", "Zukowski", 49.95f)
        };
        Book netBooks[] = {
          new Book("Beginning VB .NET 1.1 Databases", "Maharry", 49.99f),
          new Book("Beginning VB.NET Databases", "Willis", 39.99f)
        };
        Vector<Book> javaVector = new NamedVector<Book>("Java Books", javaBooks);
        Vector<Book> netVector = new NamedVector<Book>(".NET Books", netBooks);
        Object rootNodes[] = {javaVector, netVector};
        Vector<Object> rootVector = new NamedVector<Object>("Root", rootNodes);
        JTree tree = new JTree(rootVector);
        TreeCellRenderer renderer = new BookCellRenderer();
        tree.setCellRenderer(renderer);
        JScrollPane scrollPane = new JScrollPane(tree);
        frame.add(scrollPane, BorderLayout.CENTER);
        frame.setSize(300, 300);
        frame.setVisible(true);
      }
    };
    EventQueue.invokeLater(runner);
  }
}
```

■Note Don't worry about the details of `DefaultMutableTreeNode` just yet. Unless otherwise directed, all the nodes of every tree are a `DefaultMutableTreeNode`. Each array element placed in a `Vector` in Listing 17-5 defines the data for that specific node. This data is then stored in the `userObject` property of its `DefaultMutableTreeNode`.

Working with Tree Tooltips

If you want a tree to display tooltips for the nodes, you must register the component with the ToolTipManager. If you don't register the component, the renderer will never get the opportunity to display tooltips. The renderer displays the tip, not the tree, so setting tooltip text for the tree is ignored. The following line shows how you to register a specific tree with the ToolTipManager.

```
ToolTipManager.sharedInstance().registerComponent(aTree);
```

Once you've notified the ToolTipManager that you want the tree to display tooltip text, you must tell the renderer what text to display. Although you can directly set the text with the following lines, this results in a constant setting for all nodes.

```
DefaultTreeCellRenderer renderer = (DefaultTreeCellRenderer)aTree.getCellRenderer();
renderer.setToolTipText("Constant Tool Tip Text");
```

Instead of providing a constant setting, one alternative is to provide the renderer with a table of tooltip strings so that the renderer can determine at runtime the string to display as the tooltip text. The renderer in Listing 17-6 is one such example that relies on a java.util.Dictionary implementation (like a Hashtable) to store a mapping from nodes to tooltip text. If a tip exists for a specific node, the renderer associates the tip with it.

Listing 17-6. *Tooltip Cell Renderer*

```
import javax.swing.*;
import javax.swing.tree.*;
import java.awt.*;
import java.util.*;

public class ToolTipTreeCellRenderer implements TreeCellRenderer {
  DefaultTreeCellRenderer renderer = new DefaultTreeCellRenderer();
  Dictionary tipTable;

  public ToolTipTreeCellRenderer (Dictionary tipTable) {
    this.tipTable = tipTable;
  }

  public Component getTreeCellRendererComponent(JTree tree, Object value,
      boolean selected, boolean expanded, boolean leaf, int row,
      boolean hasFocus) {
    renderer.getTreeCellRendererComponent(tree, value, selected, expanded,
      leaf, row, hasFocus);
    if (value != null) {
      Object tipKey;
      if (value instanceof DefaultMutableTreeNode) {
        tipKey = ((DefaultMutableTreeNode)value).getUserObject();
```

```
      } else {
        tipKey = tree.convertValueToText(value, selected, expanded, leaf,
          row, hasFocus);
      }
      renderer.setToolTipText((String)tipTable.get(tipKey));
    }
    return renderer;
  }
}
```

■**Note** The example in Listing 17-6 takes advantage of the JTree method public String convertValueToText(Object value, boolean selected, boolean expanded, boolean leaf, int row boolean hasFocus) to convert the tree node value to a text string. The value parameter is normally a DefaultMutableTreeNode, described later in this chapter. When the value parameter is not a DefaultMutableTreeNode, using convertValueToText() allows the renderer to support other types of tree nodes.

Using the new ToolTipTreeCellRenderer class simply involves creating the Properties list, filling it with tooltip text for the necessary nodes, and then associating the renderer with the tree. Figure 17-11 shows the renderer in action.

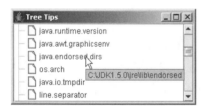

Figure 17-11. *A JTree with tooltips, using the new ToolTipTreeCellRenderer*

The complete sample program used to generate the screen in Figure 17-11 is shown next in Listing 17-7. This tree uses the list of system properties as the tree nodes. The tooltip text is the current setting for the specific property. When using the ToolTipTreeCellRenderer, be sure to register the tree with the ToolTipManager.

Listing 17-7. *Using a Tooltip Cell Renderer*

```java
import javax.swing.*;
import javax.swing.tree.*;
import java.awt.*;
import java.util.*;
```

```
public class TreeTips {
  public static void main(String args[]) {
    Runnable runner = new Runnable() {
      public void run() {
        JFrame frame = new JFrame("Tree Tips");
        frame.setDefaultCloseOperation(JFrame.EXIT_ON_CLOSE);
        Properties props = System.getProperties();
        JTree tree = new JTree(props);
        ToolTipManager.sharedInstance().registerComponent(tree);
        TreeCellRenderer renderer = new ToolTipTreeCellRenderer(props);
        tree.setCellRenderer(renderer);
        JScrollPane scrollPane = new JScrollPane(tree);
        frame.add(scrollPane, BorderLayout.CENTER);
        frame.setSize(300, 150);
        frame.setVisible(true);
      }
    };
    EventQueue.invokeLater(runner);
  }
}
```

Although this example creates a new tree cell renderer, the behavior is only customizing what has already been done for the DefaultTreeCellRenderer. Instead of needing to configure the icons and text yourself, let the default renderer do it for you. Then add the tooltip text.

Editing Tree Nodes

In addition to supporting individualized tree cell renderers, JTree components can be editable, allowing users to change the contents of any node of the tree. By default, trees are read-only. To make a tree editable, just change the editable property setting to return true:

```
aTree.setEditable(true);
```

By default, the editor is a text field. There is also built-in support for picking choices from combo boxes or check boxes. If you prefer, you can create a customized editor for a tree, just as you can create a custom cell renderer.

Note Unfortunately, the built-in check box editor works better within a table than within a tree, where the column label is the name and the value is the cell.

Figure 17-12 shows a tree using the default editor. To enable the editor, select a node, and then double-click it. If the node isn't a leaf node, selecting it will also display or hide the node's children.

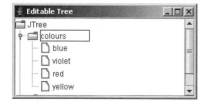

Figure 17-12. *An editable JTree with the default editor*

A series of classes is available to support editing tree nodes. Many are shared with the JTable component because both can support editable cells. The CellEditor interface forms the basis for the TreeCellEditor interface. Any editor implementation for a JTree must implement the TreeCellEditor interface. The DefaultCellEditor (which extends AbstractCellEditor) offers one such editor implementation, and the DefaultTreeCellEditor offers another. Let's now look at these interfaces and classes in more detail.

CellEditor Interface

The CellEditor interface defines the necessary basics for any editor used with a JTree or JTable, as well as for any third-party components that need an editor. Besides defining how to manage a list of CellEditorListener objects, the interface describes how to determine if a particular node or cell is editable and what the new value is after the editor has changed its value.

```
public interface CellEditor {
  // Properties
  public Object getCellEditorValue();
  // Listeners
  public void addCellEditorListener(CellEditorListener l);
  public void removeCellEditorListener(CellEditorListener l);
  // Other methods
  public void cancelCellEditing();
  public boolean isCellEditable(EventObject event);
  public boolean shouldSelectCell(EventObject event);
  public boolean stopCellEditing();
}
```

TreeCellEditor Interface

The TreeCellEditor interface works similarly to the TreeCellRenderer interface. However, the get*XXX*Component() method does not have an argument that tells the editor it has the input focus, because in the case of an editor, it must already have the input focus. Any class implementing the TreeCellEditor interface can serve as an editor for your JTree.

```
public interface TreeCellEditor implements CellEditor {
  public Component getTreeCellEditorComponent(JTree tree, Object value,
    boolean isSelected, boolean expanded, boolean leaf, int row);
}
```

DefaultCellEditor Class

The DefaultCellEditor class serves as an editor for both tree nodes and table cells. The class allows you to easily provide a text editor, combo box editor, or check box editor to modify the contents of a node or cell.

The DefaultTreeCellEditor class, described next, uses this class to provide an editor for a customized text field, maintaining the appropriate node-type icon based on a TreeCellRenderer.

Creating a DefaultCellEditor

When you create a DefaultCellEditor instance, you provide the JTextField, JComboBox, or JCheckBox to use as the editor.

```
public DefaultCellEditor(JTextField editor)
JTextField textField = new JTextField();
TreeCellEditor editor = new DefaultCellEditor(textField);
```

```
public DefaultCellEditor(JComboBox editor)
public static void main (String args[]) {
  JComboBox comboBox = new JComboBox(args);
  TreeCellEditor editor = new DefaultCellEditor(comboBox);
  ...
}
```

```
public DefaultCellEditor(JCheckBox editor)
JCheckBox checkBox = new JCheckBox();
TreeCellEditor editor = new DefaultCellEditor(checkBox);
```

With a JTree, you should use the DefaultTreeCellEditor if you want a JTextField editor. That text field will share the same font and use the appropriate editor border for the tree. When a JCheckBox is used as the editor, the node for the tree should be either a Boolean value or a String that can be converted to a Boolean. (If you are unfamiliar with conversion from String to Boolean, see the Javadoc for the Boolean constructor that accepts a String.)

After creating an editor, you tell the tree to use it with a call similar to tree.setCellEditor(editor). And don't forget to make the tree editable with tree.setEditable(true). For instance, if you wanted an editable combo box as your editor, the following source code would work:

```
JTree tree = new JTree(...);
tree.setEditable(true);
String elements[] = { "Root", "chartreuse", "rugby", "sushi"} ;
JComboBox comboBox = new JComboBox(elements);
comboBox.setEditable(true);
TreeCellEditor editor = new DefaultCellEditor(comboBox);
tree.setCellEditor(editor);
```

This code produces the screen shown in Figure 17-13 when editing the basketball node. Notice that there is no icon to indicate the type of node being edited. This is rectified with the

DefaultTreeCellEditor class. The DefaultCellEditor is primarily for use within a JTable, not a JTree.

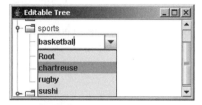

Figure 17-13. *An editable JTree with a JComboBox editor*

■**Caution** When you use a noneditable JComboBox as the cell editor, if the set of choices doesn't include the original node setting, it's impossible to get back to the original setting once the node value changes.

To see how awkward the appearance of a JCheckBox is with the DefaultCellEditor as a TreeCellEditor, take a look at Figure 17-14.

Figure 17-14. *An editable JTree with a JCheckBox editor*

Figure 17-14 uses the following source:

```
Object array[] =
  {Boolean.TRUE, Boolean.FALSE, "Hello"}; // Hello will map to false
JTree tree = new JTree(array);
tree.setEditable(true);
tree.setRootVisible(true);
JCheckBox checkBox = new JCheckBox();
TreeCellEditor editor = new DefaultCellEditor(checkBox);
tree.setCellEditor(editor);
```

■**Note** Use of the JCheckBox with the DefaultCellEditor isn't recommended with a JTree. See the "Creating a Better Check Box Node Editor" section later in this chapter for an implementation that's more appropriate for a tree.

The awkwardness of the JCheckBox editor and custom text field editor within the DefaultTreeCellEditor leaves the JComboBox as the only TreeCellEditor you'll get from DefaultCellEditor. However, you still might want to place the combo box editor within a DefaultTreeCellEditor to display the appropriate type icon next to the node.

DefaultCellEditor Properties

The DefaultCellEditor has only three properties, which are listed in Table 17-4. The editor can be any AWT component, not just a lightweight Swing component. Keep in mind the hazards of mixing heavyweight and lightweight components, if you do choose to use a heavyweight component as the editor. If you want to find out what the current setting is for the editor component, ask for the setting of the cellEditorValue property.

Table 17-4. *DefaultCellEditor Properties*

Property Name	Data Type	Access
cellEditorValue	Object	Read-only
clickCountToStart	int	Read-write
component	Component	Read-only

DefaultTreeCellEditor Class

The DefaultTreeCellEditor class is the TreeCellEditor that is automatically used by a JTree when you make a tree editable but you don't associate an editor with that tree. The DefaultTreeCellEditor combines the icons from a TreeCellRenderer with a TreeCellEditor to return a combined editor.

The default component used as the editor is a JTextField. This text editor is special in that it tries to limit its height to the original cell renderer and prefers the font of the tree so that it won't appear out of place. The editor uses two public inner classes to accomplish this feat: DefaultTreeCellEditor.EditorContainer and DefaultTreeCellEditor.DefaultTextField.

There are two constructors for DefaultTreeCellEditor. Normally, you don't need to call the first constructor because it's automatically created for you by the user interface when it determines that the node is editable. However, it may be necessary if you want to customize the default editor in some manner.

```
public DefaultTreeCellEditor(JTree tree, DefaultTreeCellRenderer renderer)
JTree tree = new JTree(...);
DefaultTreeCellRenderer renderer = (DefaultTreeCellRenderer)tree.getCellRenderer();
TreeCellEditor editor = new DefaultTreeCellEditor(tree, renderer);
```

```
public DefaultTreeCellEditor(JTree tree, DefaultTreeCellRenderer renderer,
  TreeCellEditor editor)
public static void main (String args[]) {
  JTree tree = new JTree(...);
  DefaultTreeCellRenderer renderer =
    (DefaultTreeCellRenderer)tree.getCellRenderer();
```

```
    JComboBox comboBox = new JComboBox(args);
    TreeCellEditor comboEditor = new DefaultCellEditor(comboBox);
    TreeCellEditor editor = new DefaultTreeCellEditor(tree, renderer, comboEditor);
    ...
}
```

Creating a Proper ComboBox Editor for a Tree

As Figure 17-13 showed, using a JComboBox as the TreeCellEditor via a DefaultCellEditor doesn't place the appropriate node-type icon next to the editor. If you want the icons present, you need to combine the DefaultCellEditor with a DefaultTreeCellEditor to get an editor with both an icon and an editor. It's really not as hard as it sounds. It just involves two extra steps: getting the renderer for the tree (from which to get the icons), and then combining the icon with the editor to get a new editor. The following source demonstrates this:

```
JTree tree = new JTree();
tree.setEditable(true);
DefaultTreeCellRenderer renderer = (DefaultTreeCellRenderer)tree.getCellRenderer();
String elements[] = { "Root", "chartreuse", "rugby", "sushi"} ;
JComboBox comboBox = new JComboBox(elements);
comboBox.setEditable(true);
TreeCellEditor comboEditor = new DefaultCellEditor(comboBox);
TreeCellEditor editor = new DefaultTreeCellEditor(tree, renderer, comboEditor);
tree.setCellEditor(editor);
```

The improved output is shown in Figure 17-15.

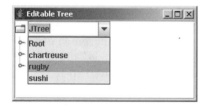

Figure 17-15. *An editable JTree with a JComboBox editor and tree icons*

Creating an Editor Just for Leaf Nodes

In some cases, you will want only the leaf nodes of a tree to be editable. Returning null from the getTreeCellEditorComponent() request effectively makes a node not editable. Unfortunately, this causes a NullPointerException to be thrown by the user interface class.

Instead of returning null, you can override the default behavior of the public boolean isCellEditable(EventObject object) method, which is part of the CellEditor interface. If the original return value is true, you can do an additional check to see if the selected node of the tree is a leaf. Nodes of a tree implement the TreeNode interface (described later in this chapter in the "TreeNode Interface" section). This interface happens to have the method public boolean isLeaf(), which provides the answer you're looking for. The class definition for a leaf node cell editor is shown in Listing 17-8.

Listing 17-8. *Tree Cell Editor for Leaf Nodes*

```
import javax.swing.*;
import javax.swing.tree.*;
import java.awt.*;
import java.util.EventObject;

public class LeafCellEditor extends DefaultTreeCellEditor {

  public LeafCellEditor(JTree tree, DefaultTreeCellRenderer renderer) {
    super(tree, renderer);
  }

  public LeafCellEditor(JTree tree, DefaultTreeCellRenderer renderer,
      TreeCellEditor editor) {
    super(tree, renderer, editor);
  }

  public boolean isCellEditable(EventObject event) {
    // Get initial setting
    boolean returnValue = super.isCellEditable(event);
    // If still possible, check if current tree node is a leaf
    if (returnValue) {
      Object node = tree.getLastSelectedPathComponent();
      if ((node != null) && (node instanceof TreeNode)) {
        TreeNode treeNode = (TreeNode)node;
        returnValue = treeNode.isLeaf();
      }
    }
    return returnValue;
  }
}
```

You use the LeafCellEditor in the same way as a DefaultTreeCellRenderer. It requires a JTree and DefaultTreeCellRenderer for its constructor. In addition, it supports an optional TreeCellEditor. If one isn't provided, a JTextField is used as the editor.

```
JTree tree = new JTree();
tree.setEditable(true);
DefaultTreeCellRenderer renderer = (DefaultTreeCellRenderer)tree.getCellRenderer();
TreeCellEditor editor = new LeafCellEditor(tree, renderer);
tree.setCellEditor(editor);
```

CellEditorListener Interface and ChangeEvent Class

Before exploring the creation of a complete `TreeCellEditor`, take a look at the `CellEditorListener` interface definition. The interface contains two methods that are used with a `CellEditor`.

```
public interface CellEditorListener implements EventListener {
  public void editingCanceled(ChangeEvent changeEvent);
  public void editingStopped(ChangeEvent changeEvent);
}
```

The editor calls the `editingCanceled()` method of the registered listeners to signal that the editing of the node's value has been aborted. The `editingStopped()` method is called to signal the completion of an editing session.

Normally, it's not necessary to create a `CellEditorListener`. However, when creating a `TreeCellEditor` (or any `CellEditor`), it *is* necessary to manage a list of its listeners and notify those listeners when necessary. Thankfully, this is managed for you automatically with the help of the `AbstractCellEditor`.

Creating a Better Check Box Node Editor

Using the `JCheckBox` editor provided by the `DefaultCellEditor` class isn't a good option when working with a `JTree`. Although the editor can be wrapped into a `DefaultTreeCellEditor` to get the appropriate tree icon next to it, you can't display text within the check box (that is, besides true or false). Other text strings can be displayed within the tree, but once a node is edited, the text label for the edited node can only be `true` or `false`.

To have an editable check box with a text label as the tree cell editor, you must create your own. The complete process involves creating three classes—a data model for each node of the tree, a tree cell renderer to render this custom data structure, and the actual editor—plus a test program to connect them all.

■**Note** The renderer and editor created here will support check-box–like data only for editing leaf nodes. If you want to support check boxes for nonleaf nodes, you need to pull out the code that checks for leaf nodes.

Creating the CheckBoxNode Class

The first class to be created is for the data model for each leaf node of the tree. You could use the same data model as the `JCheckBox` class, but that includes extraneous information at each node that you don't need. The only information necessary is the selected state of the node and its text label. With the addition of some setter and getter methods for the state and label, the class is basically defined, as shown in Listing 17-9. The other classes are not quite this easy to formulate.

Listing 17-9. *Custom Node Data for a JTree*

```java
public class CheckBoxNode {
  String text;
  boolean selected;
  public CheckBoxNode(String text, boolean selected) {
    this.text = text;
    this.selected = selected;
  }
  public boolean isSelected() {
    return selected;
  }
  public void setSelected(boolean newValue) {
    selected = newValue;
  }
  public String getText() {
    return text;
  }
  public void setText(String newValue) {
    text = newValue;
  }
  public String toString() {
    return getClass().getName() + "[" + text + "/" + selected + "]";
  }
}
```

Creating the CheckBoxNodeRenderer Class

The renderer will have two parts. For nonleaf nodes, you can use the DefaultTreeCellRenderer because those nodes aren't meant to be CheckBoxNode elements. For the renderer for leaf nodes of type CheckBoxNode, you need to map the data structure into an appropriate renderer. Because these nodes contain a selection state and a text label, the JCheckBox acts as a good renderer for the leaf nodes.

The easier of the two to explain is the nonleaf node renderer. In this example, it simply configures a DefaultTreeCellRenderer as it would normally; nothing special is done.

The renderer for the leaf nodes requires a bit more work. Before even configuring any nodes, you need to make it look like the default renderer. The constructor acquires the necessary fonts and various colors from the look and feel for the renderer, ensuring that the two renderers will appear similar.

The definition for the tree cell renderer, class CheckBoxNodeRenderer, is shown in Listing 17-10.

Listing 17-10. *Custom Node Renderer for a JTree*

```java
import javax.swing.*;
import javax.swing.border.*;
import javax.swing.tree.*;
import java.awt.*;

public class CheckBoxNodeRenderer implements TreeCellRenderer {
  private JCheckBox leafRenderer = new JCheckBox();
  private DefaultTreeCellRenderer nonLeafRenderer = new DefaultTreeCellRenderer();
  Color selectionBorderColor, selectionForeground, selectionBackground,
    textForeground, textBackground;

  protected JCheckBox getLeafRenderer() {
    return leafRenderer;
  }

  public CheckBoxNodeRenderer() {
    Font fontValue;
    fontValue = UIManager.getFont("Tree.font");
    if (fontValue != null) {
      leafRenderer.setFont(fontValue);
    }
    Boolean booleanValue =
      (Boolean)UIManager.get("Tree.drawsFocusBorderAroundIcon");
    leafRenderer.setFocusPainted((booleanValue != null) &&
      (booleanValue.booleanValue()));

    selectionBorderColor = UIManager.getColor("Tree.selectionBorderColor");
    selectionForeground = UIManager.getColor("Tree.selectionForeground");
    selectionBackground = UIManager.getColor("Tree.selectionBackground");
    textForeground = UIManager.getColor("Tree.textForeground");
    textBackground = UIManager.getColor("Tree.textBackground");
  }

  public Component getTreeCellRendererComponent(JTree tree, Object value,
      boolean selected, boolean expanded, boolean leaf, int row, boolean hasFocus) {

    Component returnValue;
    if (leaf) {

      String stringValue = tree.convertValueToText(value, selected, expanded,
        leaf, row, false);
      leafRenderer.setText(stringValue);
      leafRenderer.setSelected(false);

      leafRenderer.setEnabled(tree.isEnabled());
```

```
      if(selected) {
        leafRenderer.setForeground(selectionForeground);
        leafRenderer.setBackground(selectionBackground);
      } else {
        leafRenderer.setForeground(textForeground);
        leafRenderer.setBackground(textBackground);
      }

      if ((value != null) && (value instanceof DefaultMutableTreeNode)) {
        Object userObject = ((DefaultMutableTreeNode)value).getUserObject();
        if (userObject instanceof CheckBoxNode) {
          CheckBoxNode node = (CheckBoxNode)userObject;
          leafRenderer.setText(node.getText());
          leafRenderer.setSelected(node.isSelected());
        }
      }
      returnValue = leafRenderer;
    } else {
      returnValue = nonLeafRenderer.getTreeCellRendererComponent(tree, value,
        selected, expanded, leaf, row, hasFocus);
    }
    return returnValue;
  }
}
```

Note The getLeafRenderer() method is a helper method you'll need in the editor.

Creating the CheckBoxNodeEditor Class

The CheckBoxNodeEditor class is the last part of creating a better check box node editor. It serves as the TreeCellEditor implementation, allowing you to support editing of trees whose leaf node data is of type CheckBoxNode. The TreeCellEditor interface is an extension of the CellEditor implementation, so you must implement the methods of both interfaces. You can't extend DefaultCellEditor or DefaultTreeCellEditor, because they would require you to use the JCheckBox editor implementation they provide, instead of the new one you're creating here. However, you can extend AbstractCellEditor and add the necessary TreeCellEditor interface implementation. An AbstractCellEditor manages the list of CellEditorListener objects for you and has methods to notify the list of listeners upon either stopping or canceling editing.

Because the editor acts as the renderer, you'll need to use the earlier CheckBoxNodeRenderer to get the basic renderer appearance. This will ensure that the editor appears similar to the renderer. Because the renderer for the leaf nodes will be a JCheckBox, this works perfectly well to enable you to change the node state. The editor JCheckBox will be active and changeable, allowing a user to change from a selected state to an unselected state, and vice versa. If instead the editor were the standard DefaultTreeCellRenderer, you would need to manage the creation of selection changes.

Now that the class hierarchy has been set up, the first method to examine is the `public Object getCellEditorValue()` method of `CellEditor`. The purpose of this method is to convert the data as stored within the node editor into the data as stored within the node. The user interface calls this method to get the editor's value after it has determined that the user has successfully changed the data within the editor. In this method, you need to create a new object each time. Otherwise, the same node will be in the tree multiple times, causing all nodes to be equal to the renderer for the last edited node. To convert the editor to the data model, it's necessary to ask the editor what its current label and selected state are, and then create and return a new node.

```
public Object getCellEditorValue() {
  JCheckBox checkbox = renderer.getLeafRenderer();
  CheckBoxNode checkBoxNode =
    new CheckBoxNode(checkbox.getText(), checkbox.isSelected());
  return checkBoxNode;
}
```

■**Note** It's not the job of the editor to directly access the node within the tree to update it. The `getCellEditorValue()` method returns the appropriate node object so that the user interface can notify the tree of any changes.

If you were to implement the `CellEditor` interface yourself, you would also need to manage the list of `CellEditorListener` objects yourself. You would need to manage the list with the `addCellEditorListener()` and `removeCellEditorListener()` methods, and provide methods that notify the list of listeners for each method in the interface. But, because you'll be subclassing `AbstractCellEditor`, it's not necessary to do this yourself. You just need to know that the class provides `fireEditingCanceled()` and `fireEditingStopped()` methods in order to notify the listener list at the appropriate times.

The next `CellEditor` method, `cancelCellEditing()`, is called when a new node of the tree is selected, announcing that the editing process of the prior selection has stopped and any interim update has been aborted. The method is capable of doing anything, such as destroying any necessary interim objects used by the editor. However, what the method should do is call `fireEditingCanceled()`; this ensures that any registered `CellEditorListener` objects are notified of the cancellation. The `AbstractCellEditor` does this for you. Unless you need to do some interim operations, it's not necessary to override this behavior.

The `stopCellEditing()` method of the `CellEditor` interface returns a boolean. This method is called to see if editing of the current node can stop. If any validation needs to be done to determine whether editing can stop, you would check here. For the `CheckBoxNodeEditor` in this example, no validation check is necessary. Therefore, editing can always stop, allowing the method to always return `true`.

You would call the `fireEditingStopped()` method when you want to have the editor stop editing. For instance, if the editor were a text field, pressing Enter within the text field could act as the signal to stop editing. In the case of the `JCheckBox` editor, selection could act as a signal to stop the editor. If `fireEditingStopped()` isn't called, the tree data model isn't updated.

To stop editing after selection of the `JCheckBox`, attach an `ItemListener` to it.

```
ItemListener itemListener = new ItemListener() {
  public void itemStateChanged(ItemEvent itemEvent) {
    if (stopCellEditing()) {
      fireEditingStopped();
    }
  }
};
editor.addItemListener(itemListener);
```

The next method of the CellEditor interface to look at is public boolean
isCellEditable(EventObject event). The method returns a boolean to state whether the node
at the source of the event is editable. To find out if the event happens at a particular node, you
need a reference to the tree where the editor is to be used. You can add this requirement to the
constructor of the editor.

To find out which node is at a specific position during an event, you can ask the tree for the
path of nodes to the event location. The path is returned as a TreePath object, which is examined
again later in this chapter in the "TreePath Class" section. The last component of the tree path
is the specific node where the event happened. It is this node that you must check to determine
if it's editable. If it is editable, the method returns true; if it isn't editable, false is returned. In
the case of the tree to be created here, a node is editable if it's a leaf node and it contains
CheckBoxNode data.

```
JTree tree;

public CheckBoxNodeEditor(JTree tree) {
  this.tree = tree;
}

public boolean isCellEditable(EventObject event) {
  boolean returnValue = false;
  if (event instanceof MouseEvent) {
    MouseEvent mouseEvent = (MouseEvent)event;
    TreePath path = tree.getPathForLocation(mouseEvent.getX(), mouseEvent.getY());
    if (path != null) {
      Object node = path.getLastPathComponent();
      if ((node != null) &&  (node instanceof DefaultMutableTreeNode)) {
        DefaultMutableTreeNode treeNode = (DefaultMutableTreeNode)node;
        Object userObject = treeNode.getUserObject();
        returnValue = ((treeNode.isLeaf()) && (userObject instanceof CheckBoxNode));
      }
    }
  }
  return returnValue;
}
```

The shouldSelectCell() method of the CellEditor interface allows you to decide whether
a node is selectable. For the editor in this example, all editable cells should be selectable. However,

this method allows you to look at a specific node to see if it can be selected. By default, AbstractCellEditor returns true for this method.

The remaining method, getTreeCellEditorComponent(), is from the TreeCellEditor interface. You'll need a reference to a CheckBoxNodeRenderer to get and use that as the editor. There are two minor changes besides just passing through all the arguments. Editors should always be selected and have the input focus. This simply forces two arguments to always be true. When the node is selected, the background is filled in. When focused, a border surrounds the editor when UIManager.get("Tree.drawsFocusBorderAroundIcon") reports true.

```
CheckBoxNodeRenderer renderer = new CheckBoxNodeRenderer();
public Component getTreeCellEditorComponent(JTree tree, Object value,
    boolean selected, boolean expanded, boolean leaf, int row) {

  // Editor always selected / focused
  return renderer.getTreeCellRendererComponent(tree, value, true, expanded, leaf,
    row, true);
}
```

Listing 17-11 shows everything put together, presenting the complete CheckBoxNodeEditor class source.

Listing 17-11. *Custom Node Editor for a JTree*

```
import javax.swing.*;
import javax.swing.event.*;
import javax.swing.tree.*;
import java.awt.*;
import java.awt.event.*;
import java.util.EventObject;

public class CheckBoxNodeEditor extends AbstractCellEditor implements
  TreeCellEditor {

  CheckBoxNodeRenderer renderer = new CheckBoxNodeRenderer();

  ChangeEvent changeEvent = null;

  JTree tree;

  public CheckBoxNodeEditor(JTree tree) {
    this.tree = tree;
  }

  public Object getCellEditorValue() {
    JCheckBox checkbox = renderer.getLeafRenderer();
    CheckBoxNode checkBoxNode =
      new CheckBoxNode(checkbox.getText(), checkbox.isSelected());
    return checkBoxNode;
  }
```

```
public boolean isCellEditable(EventObject event) {
  boolean returnValue = false;
  if (event instanceof MouseEvent) {
    MouseEvent mouseEvent = (MouseEvent)event;
    TreePath path = tree.getPathForLocation(mouseEvent.getX(), mouseEvent.getY());
    if (path != null) {
      Object node = path.getLastPathComponent();
      if ((node != null) &&  (node instanceof DefaultMutableTreeNode)) {
        DefaultMutableTreeNode treeNode = (DefaultMutableTreeNode)node;
        Object userObject = treeNode.getUserObject();
        returnValue = ((treeNode.isLeaf()) &&
          (userObject instanceof CheckBoxNode));
      }
    }
  }
  return returnValue;
}

public Component getTreeCellEditorComponent(JTree tree, Object value,
    boolean selected, boolean expanded, boolean leaf, int row) {

  Component editor = renderer.getTreeCellRendererComponent(tree, value, true,
    expanded, leaf, row, true);

  // Editor always selected / focused
  ItemListener itemListener = new ItemListener() {
    public void itemStateChanged(ItemEvent itemEvent) {
      if (stopCellEditing()) {
        fireEditingStopped();
      }
    }
  };
  if (editor instanceof JCheckBox) {
    ((JCheckBox)editor).addItemListener(itemListener);
  }
  return editor;
}
}
```

Note Notice that there's no direct change of the data in the tree node. It's not the role of the editor to change the node. The editor only gets the new node value, returning it with getCellEditorValue().

Creating the Test Program

The test program in Listing 17-12 consists primarily of creating the CheckBoxNode elements. In addition to creating the tree data, the tree must have the renderer and editor associated with it and be made editable.

Listing 17-12. *Using the Custom Node Editor*

```java
import javax.swing.*;
import javax.swing.tree.*;
import java.awt.*;
import java.util.Vector;

public class CheckBoxNodeTreeSample {
  public static void main(String args[]) {
    Runnable runner = new Runnable() {
      public void run() {
        JFrame frame = new JFrame("CheckBox Tree");
        frame.setDefaultCloseOperation(JFrame.EXIT_ON_CLOSE);

        CheckBoxNode accessibilityOptions[] = {
          new CheckBoxNode("Move system caret with focus/selection changes", false),
          new CheckBoxNode("Always expand alt text for images", true)
        };
        CheckBoxNode browsingOptions[] = {
          new CheckBoxNode("Notify when downloads complete", true),
          new CheckBoxNode("Disable script debugging", true),
          new CheckBoxNode("Use AutoComplete", true),
          new CheckBoxNode("Browse in a new process", false)
        };
        Vector<CheckBoxNode> accessVector =
          new NamedVector<CheckBoxNode>("Accessibility", accessibilityOptions);
        Vector<CheckBoxNode> browseVector =
          new NamedVector<CheckBoxNode>("Browsing", browsingOptions);
        Object rootNodes[] = {accessVector, browseVector};
        Vector<Object> rootVector = new NamedVector<Object>("Root", rootNodes);
        JTree tree = new JTree(rootVector);

        CheckBoxNodeRenderer renderer = new CheckBoxNodeRenderer();
        tree.setCellRenderer(renderer);

        tree.setCellEditor(new CheckBoxNodeEditor(tree));
        tree.setEditable(true);
```

```
        JScrollPane scrollPane = new JScrollPane(tree);
        frame.add(scrollPane, BorderLayout.CENTER);
        frame.setSize(300, 150);
        frame.setVisible(true);
      }
    };
    EventQueue.invokeLater(runner);
  }
}
```

Running the program and selecting a CheckBoxNode will enable the editor. After the editor is enabled, selecting the editor again causes the state of the node within the tree to change. The editor stays enabled until a different tree node is selected. Figure 17-16 shows an example of the editor in use.

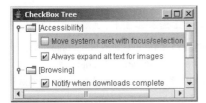

Figure 17-16. *The new CheckBoxNodeEditor in action*

Working with the Nodes of the Tree

When you create a JTree, the type of objects at any spot in the tree can be any Object. There is no requirement that the nodes of the tree implement any interface or subclass any class. Nevertheless, the Swing component libraries provide a pair of interfaces and one class for working with tree nodes. The default data model for the tree, DefaultTreeModel, uses these interfaces and the class. However, the tree data model interface, TreeModel, permits any type of object to be a tree node.

The base interface for nodes is TreeNode, which defines a series of methods describing a read-only, parent-children aggregation relationship. Expanding on TreeNode is the MutableTreeNode interface, which allows you to programmatically connect nodes and store information at each node. The class that implements the two interfaces is the DefaultMutableTreeNode class. Besides implementing the methods of the two interfaces, the class provides a set of methods for traversing the tree and inquiring about the state of various nodes.

Keep in mind that although these node objects are available, much work can be still performed without involving these interfaces and classes, as previously shown in this chapter.

TreeNode Interface

The TreeNode interface describes one possible definition for an individual part of a tree. It's used by one implementation of TreeModel, the DefaultTreeModel class, to store references to the hierarchical data that describes a tree. The interface allows you to find out which node is the parent to the current node, as well as get information about the set of child nodes. When the parent node is null, the node is the root of a tree.

```
public interface TreeNode {
  // Properties
  public boolean getAllowsChildren();
  public int getChildCount();
  public boolean isLeaf();
  public TreeNode getParent();
  // Other methods
  public Enumeration children();
  public TreeNode getChildAt(int childIndex);
  public int getIndex(TreeNode node);
}
```

■**Note** Normally, only nonleaf nodes allow children. However, security restrictions may limit nonleaf nodes from having children, or at least showing them. Imagine a directory tree in which you don't have read access to a particular directory. Although the directory is a nonleaf node, it can't have child nodes because you don't have access to find out what those children are.

MutableTreeNode Interface

Although the TreeNode interface allows you to retrieve information about a hierarchy of tree nodes, it doesn't allow you to create the hierarchy. TreeNode just provides you access to a read-only tree hierarchy. On the other hand, the MutableTreeNode interface allows you to create the hierarchy and store information at a specific node within the tree.

```
public interface MutableTreeNode implements TreeNode {
  // Properties
  public void setParent(MutableTreeNode newParent);
  public void setUserObject(Object object);
  // Other methods
  public void insert(MutableTreeNode child, int index);
  public void remove(MutableTreeNode node);
  public void remove(int index);
  public void removeFromParent();
}
```

When creating the hierarchy of tree nodes, you can either create children nodes and add them to their parent or create parent nodes and add children. To associate a node with a parent node, you set its parent with setParent(). Using insert() allows you to add children to a parent node. The arguments for the insert() method include an index argument. This index represents the position within the set of children to add the child node provided. The index is zero-based, so an index of zero will add the node as the first child of the tree. Adding a node as the last child, instead of the first, requires you to ask the node with getChildCount() how many children it already has and then add 1:

```
mutableTreeNode.insert(childMutableTreeNode, mutableTreeNode.getChildCount()+1);
```

At least for the DefaultMutableTreeNode class described next, setParent() sets a node to be the parent of a child node, even though it doesn't make the child node a child of the parent. In other words, don't call setParent() yourself; call insert(), and it will set the parent accordingly.

■**Caution** The insert() method doesn't allow circular ancestry, where the child node to be added is an ancestor to the parent. If that's attempted, an IllegalArgumentException will be thrown.

DefaultMutableTreeNode Class

The DefaultMutableTreeNode class provides an implementation of the MutableTreeNode interface (which implements the TreeNode interface). When you're creating a tree from a Hashtable, an array, or a Vector constructor, JTree automatically creates the nodes as a set of type DefaultMutableTreeNode. If, on the other hand, you want to create the nodes yourself, you need to create one instance of type DefaultMutableTreeNode for every node in your tree.

Creating a DefaultMutableTreeNode

Three constructors are available for creating instances of DefaultMutableTreeNode:

public DefaultMutableTreeNode()
DefaultMutableTreeNode node = new DefaultMutableTreeNode();

public DefaultMutableTreeNode(Object userObject)
DefaultMutableTreeNode node = new DefaultMutableTreeNode("Node");

public DefaultMutableTreeNode(Object userObject, boolean allowsChildren)
DefaultMutableTreeNode node = new DefaultMutableTreeNode("Node", false);

The information stored at every node is called the *user object*. When not specified by one of the constructors, this user object is null. In addition, you can specify whether a node is allowed to have children.

Building DefaultMutableTreeNode Hierarchies

Building a hierarchy of nodes of type DefaultMutableTreeNode requires creating an instance of type DefaultMutableTreeNode, creating nodes for its children, and then connecting them. Before using DefaultMutableTreeNode directly to create the hierarchy, first let's see how to use the new NamedVector class to create a tree with four nodes: one root and three leaf nodes.

```
Vector vector = new NamedVector("Root", new String[]{ "Mercury", "Venus", "Mars"} );
JTree tree = new JTree(vector);
```

When JTree gets a Vector as its constructor argument, the tree creates a DefaultMutableTreeNode for the root node, and then creates another one for each element in the Vector, making each element node a child of the root node. The data for the root node unfortunately is not the "Root" you specify, but rather root, and isn't shown.

If, instead, you wanted to use DefaultMutableTreeNode to manually create the nodes of a tree, or if you wanted to display the root node, a few more lines would be necessary, as follows:

```
DefaultMutableTreeNode root = new DefaultMutableTreeNode("Root");
DefaultMutableTreeNode mercury = new DefaultMutableTreeNode("Mercury");
root.insert(mercury, 0);
DefaultMutableTreeNode venus = new DefaultMutableTreeNode("Venus");
root.insert(venus, 1);
DefaultMutableTreeNode mars = new DefaultMutableTreeNode("Mars");
root.insert(mars, 2);
JTree tree = new JTree(root);
```

Besides using the insert() method from MutableTreeNode to associate a child with a parent, DefaultMutableTreeNode has an add() method that automatically adds a child node at the end, without providing an index.

```
DefaultMutableTreeNode root = new DefaultMutableTreeNode("Root");
DefaultMutableTreeNode mercury = new DefaultMutableTreeNode("Mercury");
root.add(mercury);
DefaultMutableTreeNode venus = new DefaultMutableTreeNode("Venus");
root.add(venus);
DefaultMutableTreeNode mars = new DefaultMutableTreeNode("Mars");
root.add(mars);
JTree tree = new JTree(root);
```

Both of the previous blocks of source create a tree like the one shown in Figure 17-17.

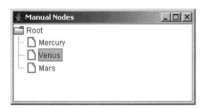

Figure 17-17. *Using DefaultMutableTreeNode*

If you don't need a root node and want the same behavior as if you had used NamedVector at the root of a tree, you could do the following, too:

```
String elements[] = { "Mercury", "Venus", "Mars"} ;
JTree tree = new JTree(elements);
```

DefaultMutableTreeNode Properties

As Table 17-5 shows, there are 22 properties of DefaultMutableTreeNode. Most of the properties are read-only, allowing you to find out information about the tree node's position and relationships. The userObject property contains the data specific to the node that was provided to the DefaultMutableTreeNode when the node was created. The userObjectPath property contains an array of user objects, from the root (at index 0) to the current node (which could be the root).

Table 17-5. *DefaultMutableTreeNode Properties*

Property Name	Data Type	Access
allowsChildren	boolean	Read-write
childCount	int	Read-only
depth	int	Read-only
firstChild	TreeNode	Read-only
firstLeaf	DefaultMutableTreeNode	Read-only
lastChild	TreeNode	Read-only
lastLeaf	DefaultMutableTreeNode	Read-only
leaf	boolean	Read-only
leafCount	int	Read-only
level	int	Read-only
nextLeaf	DefaultMutableTreeNode	Read-only
nextNode	DefaultMutableTreeNode	Read-only
nextSibling	DefaultMutableTreeNode	Read-only
parent	MutableTreeNode	Read-write
path	TreeNode[ ]	Read-only
previousLeaf	DefaultMutableTreeNode	Read-only
previousNode	DefaultMutableTreeNode	Read-only
previousSibling	DefaultMutableTreeNode	Read-only
root	boolean	Read-only
siblingCount	int	Read-only
userObject	Object	Read-write
userObjectPath	Object[ ]	Read-only

Querying Node Relationships

The DefaultMutableTreeNode class provides several ways to determine the relationship between two nodes. In addition, you can check to see if two nodes share a common parent using the following methods:

- isNodeAncestor(TreeNode aNode): Returns true if aNode is the current node or a parent of the current node. This recursively checks getParent() until aNode or null is found.

- isNodeChild(TreeNode aNode): Returns true if the current node is the parent of aNode.

- isNodeDescendant(DefaultMutableTreeNode aNode): Returns true if the current node is aNode or an ancestor of aNode.

- isNodeRelated(DefaultMutableTreeNode aNode): Returns true if both the current node and aNode share the same root (are in the same tree).

- isNodeSibling(TreeNode aNode): Returns true if both nodes share the same parent.

Each method returns a boolean value, indicating whether or not the relationship exists. If two nodes are related, you can ask for the root of the tree to find a shared ancestor. However, this ancestor might not be the closest ancestor within the tree. If a common node exists lower down in the tree, you can use the public TreeNode getSharedAncestor (DefaultMutableTreeNode aNode) method to find this closer ancestor. If none exists because the two nodes aren't in the same tree, null is returned.

■**Note** If a node asks for the shared ancestor of that node and itself, the shared ancestor is the node itself. In other words, a node's closest ancestor to itself is itself.

Traversing Trees

The TreeNode interface and DefaultMutableTreeNode class provide several means of traveling to all the nodes below a specific node. Given a specific TreeNode, you can walk to each descendant node by going through the children() of each node, including the initial node. Given a specific DefaultMutableTreeNode, you can find all the descendants by following both getNextNode() and getPreviousNode() methods until no additional nodes are found. The following code fragment demonstrates the use of the children() method of TreeNode to traverse an entire tree, given a starting node.

```
public void printDescendants(TreeNode root) {
  System.out.println(root);
  Enumeration children = root.children();
  if (children != null) {
    while(children.hasMoreElements()) {
      printDescendants((TreeNode)children.nextElement());
    }
  }
}
```

Although the DefaultMutableTreeNode implementation of TreeNode allows you to traverse a tree via the getNextNode() and getPreviousNode() methods, these methods are extremely inefficient and should be avoided. Instead, use one of the special methods of DefaultMutableTreeNode to produce one Enumeration of all of a node's children. Before looking at the specific methods, review Figure 17-18, which shows a simple tree to traverse.

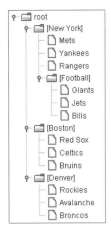

Figure 17-18. *Sample tree for traversal*

Figure 17-18 will help you understand the three special methods of DefaultMutableTreeNode. These methods allow you to traverse a tree in any one of three ways, each public and returning an Enumeration:

- preOrderEnumeration(): Returns an Enumeration of nodes, like the printDescendants() method. The first node in the Enumeration is the node itself. The next node is that node's first child, then it's the first child of that first child, and so on. Once a leaf node with no children is found, the next child of its parent is put in the Enumeration and its children are added to the list accordingly until no nodes are left. Starting at the root for the tree in Figure 17-18, this would result in an Enumeration of nodes in the following order: root, New York, Mets, Yankees, Rangers, Football, Giants, Jets, Bills, Boston, Red Sox, Celtics, Bruins, Denver, Rockies, Avalanche, Broncos.

- depthFirstEnumeration() and postOrderEnumeration(): Return an Enumeration that has practically the opposite behavior of preOrderEnumeration(). Instead of including the current node first and then adding the children, these methods add the children first and then add the current node to the Enumeration. For the tree in Figure 17-18, this results in an Enumeration of nodes in the following order: Mets, Yankees, Rangers, Giants, Jets, Bills, Football, New York, Red Sox, Celtics, Bruins, Boston, Rockies, Avalanche, Broncos, Denver, root.

- breadthFirstEnumeration(): Returns an Enumeration of nodes added by level. For the tree in Figure 17-18, the Enumeration would be in the following order: root, New York, Boston, Denver, Mets, Yankees, Rangers, Football, Red Sox, Celtics, Bruins, Rockies, Avalanche, Broncos, Giants, Jets, Bills.

This leaves but one question: How do you get the starting node? Well, the first node could be selected as the result of a user action, or you can ask a tree's `TreeModel` for its root node. You'll explore `TreeModel` shortly, but the source to get the root node follows. Because `TreeNode` is only one possible type of object that can be stored in a tree, the `getRoot()` method of `TreeModel` returns an `Object`.

```
TreeModel model = tree.getModel();
Object rootObject = model.getRoot();
if ((rootObject != null) && (rootObject instanceof DefaultMutableTreeNode)) {
  DefaultMutableTreeNode root = (DefaultMutableTreeNode)rootObject;

  ...
}
```

■**Note** I can think of only one reason why you would want to create a replacement to the `TreeNode` interface to describe the basic requirements of a node in a `JTree`: if you want to use an `Iterator` from the new Java Collections API, instead of an `Enumeration` to return a list of children, you can create your own replacement to `TreeNode`. This isn't recommended, however.

JTree.DynamicUtilTreeNode Class

The `JTree` class includes an inner class, `JTree.DynamicUtilTreeNode`, which the tree uses to help create the nodes for your trees. The `DynamicUtilTreeNode` is a `DefaultMutableTreeNode` subclass that doesn't create its child nodes until they're needed. The child nodes are needed when you either expand the parent node or try to traverse a tree. Although you normally wouldn't use this class directly, you might find a place for it. To demonstrate, the following example uses a `Hashtable` to create the nodes for a tree. Instead of having an invisible node at the root of the tree (with a `userObject` property setting of root), the root node will have a property of `"Root"`.

```
DefaultMutableTreeNode root = new DefaultMutableTreeNode("Root");
Hashtable hashtable = new Hashtable();
hashtable.put ("One", args);
hashtable.put ("Two", new String[]{"Mercury", "Venus", "Mars"});
Hashtable innerHashtable = new Hashtable();
Properties props = System.getProperties();
innerHashtable.put (props, props);
innerHashtable.put ("Two", new String[]{"Mercury", "Venus", "Mars"});
hashtable.put ("Three", innerHashtable);
JTree.DynamicUtilTreeNode.createChildren(root, hashtable);
JTree tree = new JTree(root);
```

The code just listed creates a tree with the same nodes as shown earlier in the `TreeArraySample` program in Figure 17-2. However, the nodes at the first level of the tree are in a different order. That's because the nodes are in a `Hashtable` in this example, instead of in a `Vector` as in the `TreeArraySample`. The first-level tree elements are added in the order returned by an `Enumeration` of `Hashtable`, instead of being in the order added to the `Vector`, as Figure 17-19 shows.

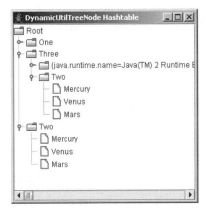

Figure 17-19. *DynamicUtilTreeNode Hashtable tree sample*

TreeModel Interface

The TreeModel interface describes the basic data model structure for a JTree. It describes a parent-child aggregation relationship, which permits any object to be a parent or a child. There is one root to the tree, and all other nodes of the tree are descendants of this node. In addition to returning information about the different nodes, the model requires any implementers to manage a list of TreeModelListener objects so that the listeners can be notified when any nodes in the model have changed. The remaining method, valueForPathChanged(), is meant to provide the means of changing the contents of a node at a particular location.

```
public interface TreeModel {
  // Properties
  public Object getRoot();
  // Listeners
  public void addTreeModelListener(TreeModelListener l);
  public void removeTreeModelListener(TreeModelListener l);
  // Instance methods
  public Object getChild(Object parent, int index);
  public int getChildCount(Object parent);
  public int getIndexOfChild(Object parent, Object child);
  public boolean isLeaf(Object node);
  public void valueForPathChanged(TreePath path, Object newValue);
}
```

DefaultTreeModel Class

The JTree automatically creates a DefaultTreeModel instance to store its data model. The DefaultTreeModel class provides an implementation of the TreeModel interface that uses TreeNode implementations at each node.

In addition to implementing the methods of the TreeModel interface, as well as managing a list of TreeModelListener objects, the DefaultTreeModel class adds several helpful methods:

- `public void insertNodeInto(MutableTreeNode child, MutableParentNode parent, index int)`: Adds the child node to parent's set of children at the child position index (zero-based).

- `public void removeNodeFromParent(MutableTreenode node)`: Causes the node to be removed from tree.

- `public void nodeChanged(TreeNode node)`: Notifies the model that a node has changed.

- `public void nodesChanged(TreeNode node, int childIndices[])`: Notifies the model that the child or children of a node have changed.

- `public void nodeStructureChanged(TreeNode node)`: Notifies the model if the node and children have changed.

- `public void nodesWereInserted(TreeNode node, int childIndices[])`: Notifies the model that nodes were inserted as children of the tree node.

- `public void nodesWereRemoved(TreeNode node, int childIndices[], Object removedChildren[])`: Notifies the model that child nodes were removed from the tree and includes nodes as arguments in the method call.

- `public void reload()` / `public void reload(TreeNode node)`: Notifies the model that there were complex changes made to the nodes and that the model should be reloaded from the root node down or from a specific node down.

The first pair of methods is for directly adding or removing nodes to or from a tree. The remaining methods are for notifying the data model when tree nodes are modified. If you don't insert or remove nodes into or from the model for a displayed tree with one of the first two methods, it's your responsibility to call a method from the second set.

TreeModelListener Interface and TreeModelEvent Class

The `TreeModel` uses a `TreeModelListener` to report any changes to the model. When the `TreeModel` sends a `TreeModelEvent`, any registered listeners are notified. The interface includes notification methods for when nodes are inserted, removed, or changed, as well as one catchall method for when some or all of these operations are done simultaneously.

```
public interface TreeModelListener implements EventListener {
  public void treeNodesChanged(TreeModelEvent treeModelEvent);
  public void treeNodesInserted(TreeModelEvent treeModelEvent);
  public void treeNodesRemoved(TreeModelEvent treeModelEvent);
  public void treeStructureChanged(TreeModelEvent treeModelEvent);
}
```

TreeSelectionModel Interface

In addition to all trees supporting a data model for storing nodes, a renderer for displaying nodes, and an editor for editing them, there is a data model called `TreeSelectionModel` for selective manipulation of tree elements. The `TreeSelectionModel` interface that follows contains methods to describe the selected set of paths to the selected nodes. Each path is stored in a TreePath, which itself contains a path of tree nodes from the root object to a selected node. The TreePath class will be explored shortly.

```
public interface TreeSelectionModel {
  // Constants
  public final static int CONTIGUOUS_TREE_SELECTION;
  public final static int DISCONTIGUOUS_TREE_SELECTION;
  public final static int SINGLE_TREE_SELECTION;
  // Properties
  public TreePath getLeadSelectionPath();
  public int getLeadSelectionRow();
  public int getMaxSelectionRow();
  public int getMinSelectionRow();
  public RowMapper getRowMapper();
  public void setRowMapper(RowMapper newMapper);
  public int getSelectionCount();
  public boolean isSelectionEmpty();
  public int getSelectionMode();
  public void setSelectionMode(int mode);
  public TreePath getSelectionPath();
  public void setSelectionPath(TreePath path);
  public TreePath[] getSelectionPaths();
  public void setSelectionPaths(TreePath paths[]);
  public int[] getSelectionRows();
  // Listeners
  public void addPropertyChangeListener(PropertyChangeListener listener);
  public void removePropertyChangeListener(PropertyChangeListener listener);
  public void addTreeSelectionListener(TreeSelectionListener listener);
  public void removeTreeSelectionListener(TreeSelectionListener listener);
  // Other methods
  public void addSelectionPath(TreePath path);
  public void addSelectionPaths(TreePath paths[]);
  public void clearSelection();
  public boolean isPathSelected(TreePath path);
  public boolean isRowSelected(int row);
  public void removeSelectionPath(TreePath path);
  public void removeSelectionPaths(TreePath paths[]);
  public void resetRowSelection();
}
```

The TreeSelectionModel interface supports three modes of selection, with each mode specified by a class constant: CONTIGUOUS_TREE_SELECTION, DISCONTIGUOUS_TREE_SELECTION, or SINGLE_TREE_SELECTION. When the selection mode is CONTIGUOUS_TREE_SELECTION, only nodes situated next to each other can be selected simultaneously. The DISCONTIGUOUS_TREE_SELECTION mode means that there are no restrictions on simultaneous selection. With the remaining mode, SINGLE_TREE_SELECTION, only one node can be selected at a time. If you don't want anything to be selectable, use a setting of null. This uses the protected JTree.EmptySelectionModel class.

■**Note** The keys used to select multiple nodes are look-and-feel specific. Try using the Ctrl-select or Shift-select keyboard combinations to choose multiple nodes.

Besides changing selection modes, the remaining methods allow you to monitor attributes of the selection path. Sometimes the methods work with row numbers, and other times they work with TreePath objects. The selection model uses a RowMapper to map rows to paths for you. The abstract AbstractLayoutCache class provides a basic implementation of the RowMapper interface that is further specialized by the FixedHeightLayoutCache and VariableHeightLayoutCache classes. You should never need to access or modify the RowMapper or any of its implementations. To map rows to paths (or paths to rows), just ask a JTree.

DefaultTreeSelectionModel Class

The DefaultTreeSelectionModel class provides an implementation of the TreeSelectionModel interface that is initially in DISCONTIGUOUS_TREE_SELECTION mode and that supports all three selection modes. The class introduces some of its own methods for getting listener lists; the other methods are merely implementations of all the TreeSelectionModel interface methods, including methods for accessing the 11 properties listed in Table 17-6. In addition, DefaultTreeSelectionModel overrides the clone() methods of Object to be Cloneable.

Table 17-6. *DefaultTreeSelectionModel Properties*

Property Name	Data Type	Access
leadSelectionPath	TreePath	Read-only
leadSelectionRow	int	Read-only
maxSelectionRow	int	Read-only
minSelectionRow	int	Read-only
rowMapper	RowMapper	Read-write
selectionCount	int	Read-only
selectionEmpty	boolean	Read-only
selectionMode	int	Read-write
selectionPath	TreePath	Read-write
selectionPaths	TreePath[]	Read-write
selectionRows	int[]	Read-only

The primary reason to use the TreeSelectionModel is to change the selection mode of the model. For instance, the following two lines of source code change the model to single-selection mode:

```
TreeSelectionModel selectionModel = tree.getSelectionModel();
selectionModel.setSelectionMode(TreeSelectionModel.SINGLE_TREE_SELECTION);
```

If you're interested in finding out the selected path (or paths), you can ask the JTree directly. You don't need to get the selected path from the model.

TreeSelectionListener Interface and TreeSelectionEvent Class

When the set of selected nodes within a tree changes, a TreeSelectionEvent is generated and any registered TreeSelectionListener objects of the TreeSelectionModel are notified. The TreeSelectionListener can be registered either with the JTree or directly with the TreeSelectionModel. The interface definition follows.

```
public interface TreeSelectionListener implements EventListener {
  public void valueChanged(TreeSelectionEvent treeSelectionEvent);
}
```

TreePath Class

The last major class to examine is TreePath. It has been used in many of the earlier examples in this chapter. It describes a read-only collection of nodes that map a path from the root node to another node, where the root could be the top of a subtree versus the root of the whole tree. Although two constructors exist to create TreePath objects, you'll normally deal with them only as the return value from a method. You can also create a new path by adding an element to an existing TreePath with public TreePath pathByAddingChild(Object child).

A TreePath can be thought of as an Object array, in which the first element of the array is the root of the tree and the last element is called the *last path component*. In between are all the components connecting them. Normally, the elements of the array will be of type TreeNode. However, because TreeModel supports objects of any type, the path property of TreePath is defined to be an array of Object nodes. Table 17-7 lists the four TreePath properties.

Table 17-7. *TreePath Properties*

Property Name	Data Type	Access
lastPathComponent	Object	Read-only
parentPath	TreePath	Read-only
path	Object[ ]	Read-only
pathCount	int	Read-only

To better understand TreePath, let's reuse the tree traversal sample tree from Figure 17-18, shown once more in Figure 17-20.

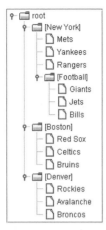

Figure 17-20. *TreePath sample tree*

Using Figure 17-20 to visualize a tree starting from its root, the TreePath for the Jets node would be described by its properties as follows:

- lastPathComponent: A DefaultMutableTreeNode whose user object is Jets.

- parentPath: A TreePath made up of the root, New York, and Football nodes.

- path: An array of DefaultMutableTreeNode nodes whose user objects are root, New York, Football, and Jets.

- pathCount: 4.

That's really all there is to the TreePath class. Just remember that you can't change an existing TreePath—you can only access its elements.

Additional Expansion Events

Two listeners that can be registered with a JTree have yet to be discussed: a TreeExpansionListener and a TreeWillExpandListener.

TreeExpansionListener Interface and TreeExpansionEvent Class

If you're interested in finding out when a tree node has been expanded or collapsed, you can register a TreeExpansionListener with a JTree. Any registered listener will be notified after the expansion or collapse of a parent node.

```
public interface TreeExpansionListener implements EventListener {
  public void treeCollapse(TreeExpansionEvent treeExpansionEvent);
  public void treeExpand(TreeExpansionEvent treeExpansionEvent);
}
```

Each of the methods has a TreeExpansionEvent as its argument. The TreeExpansionEvent class has a single method for getting the path to the expanded or collapsed node: public TreePath getPath().

TreeWillExpandListener Interface and ExpandVetoException Class

The JTree supports the registration of a TreeWillExpandListener, whose definition follows.

```
public interface TreeWillExpandListener implements EventListener {
  public void treeWillCollapse(TreeExpansionEvent treeExpansionEvent)
    throws ExpandVetoException;
  public void treeWillExpand(TreeExpansionEvent treeExpansionEvent)
    throws ExpandVetoException;
}
```

The two method signatures are similar to the TreeExpansionListener, and they can throw an ExpandVetoException. Any registered listener will be notified prior to the expansion or collapse of a parent node. If the listener doesn't want the expansion or collapse to happen, that listener can throw the exception to reject the request, stopping the node from opening or closing.

To demonstrate a TreeWillExpandListener, the following code won't permit either the sports node to be expanded in the default data model or the colors node to be collapsed.

```
TreeWillExpandListener treeWillExpandListener = new TreeWillExpandListener() {
  public void treeWillCollapse(TreeExpansionEvent treeExpansionEvent)
      throws ExpandVetoException {
    TreePath path = treeExpansionEvent.getPath();
    DefaultMutableTreeNode node =
      (DefaultMutableTreeNode)path.getLastPathComponent();
    String data = node.getUserObject().toString();
    if (data.equals("colors")) {
      throw new ExpandVetoException(treeExpansionEvent);
    }
  }
  public void treeWillExpand(TreeExpansionEvent treeExpansionEvent)
      throws ExpandVetoException {
    TreePath path = treeExpansionEvent.getPath();
    DefaultMutableTreeNode node =
      (DefaultMutableTreeNode)path.getLastPathComponent();
    String data = node.getUserObject().toString();
    if (data.equals("sports")) {
      throw new ExpandVetoException(treeExpansionEvent);
    }
  }
};
```

Don't forget to add the listener to a tree with a line of code similar to the following:

```
tree.addTreeWillExpandListener(treeWillExpandListener)
```

Summary

In this chapter, you learned about the many classes related to the use of the JTree component. You looked at tree node rendering with the TreeCellRenderer interface and the DefaultTreeCellRenderer implementation. You delved into tree node editing with the TreeCellEditor interface, and the DefaultCellEditor and DefaultTreeCellEditor implementations.

After reviewing how to display and edit a tree, you dealt with the TreeNode interface, MutableTreeNode interface, and DefaultMutableTreeNode class for manually creating tree objects. You explored the TreeModel interface and DefaultTreeModel implementation for storing the data model of a tree, and the TreeSelectionModel interface and DefaultTreeSelectionModel implementation for storing the selection model for a tree.

In addition, you looked at the many event-related classes for the various tree classes, and the TreePath for describing node connection paths.

In Chapter 18, you'll explore the javax.swing.table package and its many classes that can be used with the JTable component.

CHAPTER 18

Tables

Chapter 17 took an in-depth look at the Swing `JTree` component. In this chapter, you'll explore the many details of the `JTable` component. The component is the standard Swing component for displaying two-dimensional data in the form of a grid.

Introducing Tables

Figure 18-1 shows a simple example of a `JTable`. You'll notice that it includes Japanese fonts. In order to see the Kanji ideographs in this chapter's sample programs, you will need to have the necessary Japanese fonts installed. However, all the examples will work fine without configuring your environment to display Japanese fonts, but instead of seeing the ideographs, you will see characters such as question marks or boxes, depending on your platform.

Note Windows XP Service Pack 2 users will find their systems already have the necessary Japanese fonts for the examples in this chapter. If you don't already have them, one place to get these fonts for Windows systems is `http://ftp.monash.edu.au/pub/nihongo/ie3lpkja.exe`. Solaris users must contact Sun to request the Asian outline fonts for Solaris environments. For more information about configuring fonts in the Java runtime environment, refer to `http://java.sun.com/j2se/1.5.0/docs/guide/intl/fontconfig.html`.

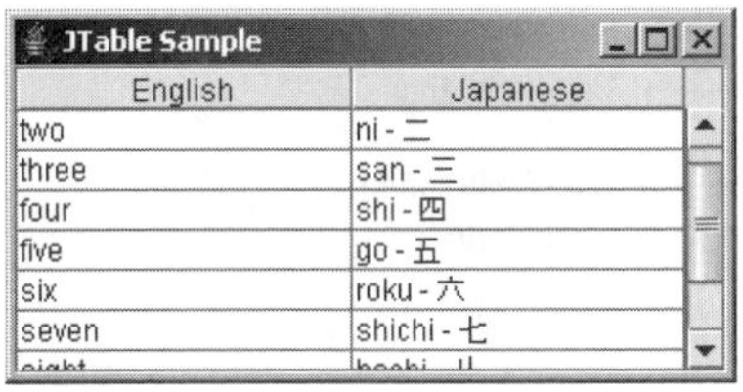

Figure 18-1. *Sample JTable*

Like the `JTree` component, the `JTable` component relies on numerous support classes for its inner workings. For the `JTable`, the support classes are found in the `javax.swing.table` package. The cells within the `JTable` can be selected by row, column, row and column, or individual cell.

It's the responsibility of the current ListSelectionModel settings to control the selection within a table.

The display of the different cells within a table is the responsibility of the TableCellRenderer; the DefaultCellRenderer offers one such implementation of the TableCellRenderer interface in a JLabel subclass.

Managing the data stored in the cells is accomplished through an implementation of the TableModel interface. The AbstractTableModel provides the basics of an implementation of the interface without any data storage. By comparison, the DefaultTableModel encapsulates the TableModel interface and uses a Vector of Vector objects for the data storage. You extend AbstractTableModel if you need a different type of storage than the kind supplied by the DefaultTableModel; for instance, if you already had the data in your own data structure.

The TableColumnModel interface and the DefaultTableColumnModel implementation of the interface manage the table's data as a series of columns. They work together with the TableColumn class to allow for greater flexibility in manipulating individual columns. For example, you can store columns of data in the TableModel in an order that's different from the display order within the JTable. The TableColumnModel manages a second ListSelectionModel to control table column selection.

At the top of every column is a column header. By default, the TableColumn class relies on the JTableHeader class to render a text column header. Nevertheless, you must embed the JTable in a scroll pane to see the default header.

Cells within a JTable can be editable. If a cell is editable, how the editing works depends on the TableCellEditor implementation, such as the DefaultCellEditor implementation, which extends from AbstractCellEditor. In addition, no classes exist to handle individual rows. Rows must be manipulated on a cell-by-cell basis. Behind the scenes, the JTable uses the SizeSequence utility class to deal with variable height rows; you won't need to manipulate it yourself.

There are additional interrelationships among the elements used by the JTable component. These relationships will be explored later in this chapter with each specific interface and class.

To visualize how the JTable elements all fit together, examine Figure 18-2.

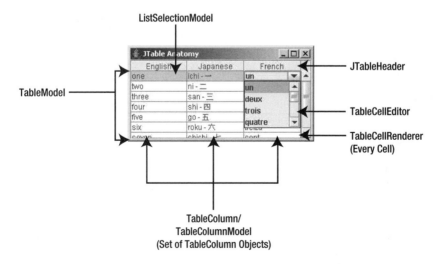

Figure 18-2. *JTable elements*

JTable Class

First, let's look at the JTable class, which gives you a way to display data in tabular form (see Figures 18-1 and 18-2).

Creating a JTable

You have seven different ways to create a JTable. The various constructors allow you to create tables from a number of data sources.

```
public JTable()
JTable table = new JTable();

public JTable(int rows, int columns)
JTable table = new JTable(2, 3);

public JTable(Object rowData[][], Object columnNames[])
Object rowData[][] = { { "Row1-Column1", "Row1-Column2", "Row1-Column3"},
  { "Row2-Column1", "Row2-Column2", "Row2-Column3"} };
Object columnNames[] = { "Column One", "Column Two", "Column Three"};
JTable table = new JTable(rowData, columnNames);

public JTable(Vector rowData, Vector columnNames)
Vector rowOne = new Vector();
rowOne.addElement("Row1-Column1");
rowOne.addElement("Row1-Column2");
rowOne.addElement("Row1-Column3");
Vector rowTwo = new Vector();
rowTwo.addElement("Row2-Column1");
rowTwo.addElement("Row2-Column2");
rowTwo.addElement("Row2-Column3");
Vector rowData = new Vector();
rowData.addElement(rowOne);
rowData.addElement(rowTwo);
Vector columnNames = new Vector();
columnNames.addElement("Column One");
columnNames.addElement("Column Two");
columnNames.addElement("Column Three");
JTable table = new JTable(rowData, columnNames);

public JTable(TableModel model)
TableModel model = new DefaultTableModel(rowData, columnNames);
JTable table = new JTable(model);

public JTable(TableModel model, TableColumnModel columnModel)
// Swaps column order
TableColumnModel columnModel = new DefaultTableColumnModel();
TableColumn firstColumn = new TableColumn(1);
firstColumn.setHeaderValue(headers[1]);
```

```
columnModel.addColumn(firstColumn);
TableColumn secondColumn = new TableColumn(0);
secondColumn.setHeaderValue(headers[0]);
columnModel.addColumn(secondColumn);
JTable table = new JTable(model, columnModel);

public JTable(TableModel model, TableColumnModel columnModel,
  ListSelectionModel selectionModel)
// Set single selection mode
ListSelectionModel selectionModel = new DefaultListSelectionModel();
selectionModel.setSelectionMode(ListSelectionModel.SINGLE_SELECTION);
JTable table = new JTable(model, columnModel, selectionModel);
```

The no-argument constructor creates a table with no rows and no columns. The second constructor takes two integers to create an empty table with a set number of rows and columns.

■**Note** Table cells created from JTable constructors are editable, not read-only. To change their contents in code, just call the public void setValueAt(Object value, int row, int column) method of JTable.

The next two constructors are useful when your tabular data is already in a specially structured form. For instance, if your data is already in the form of an array of arrays or a Vector of Vector objects, you can create a JTable without creating your own TableModel. A two-row-by-three-column table could be created from the array of { { "Row1-Column1", "Row1-Column2", "Row1-Column3"}, { "Row2-Column1", "Row2-Column2", "Row2-Column3"} }, with another array holding the column header names. Similar data structures would be necessary for the vector-based constructor.

The remaining three constructors use JTable-specific data structures. If any one of the three arguments is missing, default settings will be used. For example, if you don't specify a TableColumnModel, the default implementation DefaultTableColumnModel is used and is auto-filled with a display order using the column order of the TableModel. When the selection model is missing, the ListSelectionModel will use multiple-selection mode, which means that noncontiguous rows, but not columns, can be selected.

Scrolling JTable Components

Like other components that may require more space than what is available, the JTable component implements the Scrollable interface and should be placed within a JScrollPane. Scrollbars will appear in a JScrollPane when a JTable is too big for the available screen real estate, and column header names will appear above each column. Figure 18-3 shows how the table in Figure 18-1 would appear if it weren't within a JScrollPane. Notice that neither column headers nor scrollbars appear. This means you can't determine the meaning of the data, nor can you scroll to the undisplayed rows.

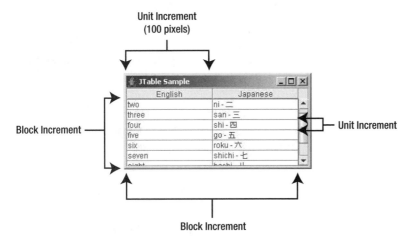

Figure 18-3. *JTable without a JScrollPane*

Therefore, every table you create needs to be placed within a JScrollPane by using code similar to the following:

```
JTable table = new JTable(...);
JScrollPane scrollPane = new JScrollPane(table);
```

Manually Positioning the JTable View

When a JTable within a JScrollPane is added to a window, the table will automatically appear with the table positioned so that the first row and column appear in the upper-left corner. If you ever need to return the position to the origin, you can set the viewport position back to point (0, 0).

```
scrollPane.getViewport().setViewPosition(new Point(0,0));
```

For scrolling purposes, the block increment amount is the visible width and height of the viewport, depending on the direction of the scrollbar. The unit increment is 100 pixels for horizontal scrolling and the height of a single row for vertical scrolling. See Figure 18-4 for a visual representation of these increments.

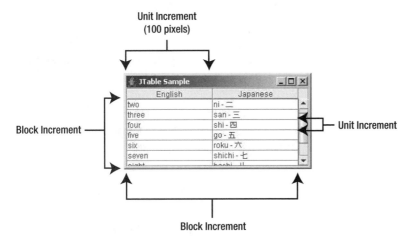

Figure 18-4. *JTable scrolling increments*

Removing Column Headers

As previously stated, placing a JTable within a JScrollPane automatically produces column header labels for the different column names. If you don't want column headers, you can remove them in one of many different ways. Figure 18-5 shows an example of a table without column headers.

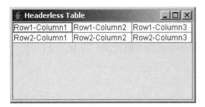

Figure 18-5. *JTable without column headers*

The simplest way to remove the column headers is to provide empty strings as the column header names. With the third JTable constructor in the previous list of seven constructors, this would involve replacing the three column names with "", the empty string.

```
Object rowData[][] = {{"Row1-Column1", "Row1-Column2", "Row1-Column3"},
  {"Row2-Column1", "Row2-Column2", "Row2-Column3"}};
Object columnNames[] = { "", "", ""};
JTable table = new JTable(rowData, columnNames);
JScrollPane scrollPane = new JScrollPane(table);
```

Because this method of removing headers also removes the description of the different columns, you might want to use another way of hiding column headers. The simplest way is to just tell the JTable you don't want table headers:

```
table.setTableHeader(null);
```

You could also remove headers by subclassing JTable and overriding the protected configureEnclosingScrollPane() method, or by telling every TableColumn that its header value is empty. These are more complicated ways of performing the same task.

■**Note** Calling scrollPane.setColumnHeaderView(null) doesn't work to clear out the column headers. Instead, it causes the JScrollPane to use the default column headers.

JTable Properties

As Table 18-1 shows, the JTable has many properties, 40 in all. These 40 are in addition to the many properties inherited from the JComponent, Container, and Component classes.

Table 18-1. *JTable Properties*

Property Name	Data Type	Access
accessibleContext	AccessibleContext	Read-only
autoCreateColumnsFromModel	boolean	Read-write bound
autoResizeMode	int	Read-write bound
cellEditor	TableCellEditor	Read-write bound
cellSelectionEnabled	boolean	Read-write bound
columnCount	int	Read-only
columnModel	TableColumnModel	Read-write bound
columnSelectionAllowed	boolean	Read-write bound
dragEnabled	boolean	Read-write
editing	boolean	Read-only
editingColumn	int	Read-write
editingRow	int	Read-write
editorComponent	Component	Read-only
gridColor	Color	Read-write bound
intercellSpacing	Dimension	Read-write
model	TableModel	Read-write bound
preferredScrollableViewportSize	Dimension	Read-write
rowCount	int	Read-only
rowHeight	int	Read-write bound
rowMargin	int	Read-write bound
rowSelectionAllowed	boolean	Read-write bound
scrollableTracksViewportHeight	boolean	Read-only
scrollableTracksViewportWidth	boolean	Read-only
selectedColumn	int	Read-only
selectedColumnCount	int	Read-only
selectedColumns	int[ ]	Read-only
selectedRow	int	Read-only
selectedRowCount	int	Read-only
selectedRows	int[ ]	Read-only
selectionBackground	Color	Read-write bound
selectionForeground	Color	Read-write bound
selectionMode	int	Write-only

Table 18-1. *JTable Properties (Continued)*

Property Name	Data Type	Access
selectionModel	ListSelectionModel	Read-write bound
showGrid	boolean	Write-only
showHorizontalLines	boolean	Read-write bound
showVerticalLines	boolean	Read-write bound
surrendersFocusOnKeystroke	boolean	Read-write
tableHeader	JTableHeader	Read-write bound
UI	TableUI	Read-write
UIClassID	String	Read-only

Note Row heights are not fixed. You can change the height of an individual row with public void setRowHeight(int row, int rowHeight).

Most of the JTable properties fit into one of three categories: display settings, selection settings, and auto-resizing settings.

Display Settings

The first subset of properties in Table 18-1 allows you to set various display options of the JTable. In addition to the inherited foreground and background properties from Component, you can change the selection foreground (selectionForeground) and background (selectionBackground) colors. You also control which (if any) gridlines appear (showGrid), as well as their color (gridColor). The intercellSpacing property setting deals with the extra space within table cells.

Selection Modes

You can use any one of three different types of selection modes for a JTable. You can select table elements one row at a time, one column at a time, or one cell at a time. These three settings are controlled by the rowSelectionAllowed, columnSelectionAllowed, and cellSelectionEnabled properties. Initially, only the row selection mode is allowed. Because the default ListSelectionModel is in multiselect mode, you can select multiple rows at a time. If you don't like multiselect mode, you can change the selectionMode property of the JTable, causing the selection mode of the rows and columns of the JTable to change accordingly. Cell selection is enabled when both row and column selections are enabled.

If you're interested in whether any of the rows or columns of the JTable are selected, you can inquire with one of the six additional properties of JTable: selectedColumnCount, selectedColumn, selectedColumns, selectedRowCount, selectedRow, and selectedRows.

The ListSelectionModel class provides constants for the different selection modes. The ListSelectionModel interface and DefaultListSelectionModel class were both covered with the JList component information in Chapter 13. They're used to describe the current set of rows and columns within the JTable component. They have three settings:

- MULTIPLE_INTERVAL_SELECTION (the default)

- SINGLE_INTERVAL_SELECTION

- SINGLE_SELECTION

The JTable has independent selection models for both rows and columns. The row selection model is stored with the selectionModel property of the JTable. The column selection model is stored with the TableColumnModel. Setting the selectionMode property of a JTable sets the selection mode for the two independent selection models of the JTable.

Once a selection mode has been set and a user interacts with the component, you can ask the selection model what happened, or, more precisely, what the user has selected. Table 18-2 lists the properties available to facilitate selection with the DefaultListSelectionModel.

Table 18-2. *DefaultListSelectionModel Properties*

Property Name	Data Type	Access
anchorSelectionIndex	int	Read-write
leadAnchorNotificationEnabled	boolean	Read-write
leadSelectionIndex	int	Read-write
listSelectionListeners	ListSelectionListener[ ]	Read-only
maxSelectionIndex	int	Read-only
minSelectionIndex	int	Read-only
selectionEmpty	boolean	Read-only
selectionModel	int	Read-write
valueIsAdjusting	boolean	Read-write

If you're interested in knowing when a selection event happens, register a ListSelectionListener with the ListSelectionModel. The ListSelectionListener was demonstrated in Chapter 13 with the JList component.

Note All table indices are zero-based. So, the first visual column is column 0 internally.

Auto-Resize Modes

The last subset of the JTable properties deals with the column-resize behavior of the JTable. When the JTable is in a column or window that changes sizes, how does it react? Table 18-3 shows the five settings supported by a JTable.

Table 18-3. *Auto-Resize Mode Constants*

Modes	Description
AUTO_RESIZE_ALL_COLUMNS	Adjusts all column widths proportionally.
AUTO_RESIZE_LAST_COLUMN	Adjusts the rightmost column width only to give or take space as required by the column currently being altered. If no space is available within that column, then resizing will work with the previous column until a column with available space to consume is found.
AUTO_RESIZE_NEXT_COLUMN	If you're reducing the width of a neighboring column, the neighboring column will grow to fill the unused space. If you're increasing the width of a column, the neighboring column will shrink.
AUTO_RESIZE_OFF	Turns off the user's ability to resize columns. The columns can still be resized programmatically.
AUTO_RESIZE_SUBSEQUENT_COLUMNS	Adjusts the width by proportionally altering (default) columns displayed to the right of the column being changed.

Listing 18-1 demonstrates what effect each setting has when resizing table columns.

Listing 18-1. *Resizable JTable*

```
import javax.swing.*;
import javax.swing.table.*;
import java.awt.*;
import java.awt.event.*;

public class ResizeTable {
  public static void main(String args[]) {

    final Object rowData[][] = {
      {"1",  "one",   "ichi - \u4E00",  "un",     "I"},
      {"2",  "two",   "ni - \u4E8C",    "deux",   "II"},
      {"3",  "three", "san - \u4E09",   "trois",  "III"},
      {"4",  "four",  "shi - \u56DB",   "quatre", "IV"},
      {"5",  "five",  "go - \u4E94",    "cinq",   "V"},
      {"6",  "six",   "roku - \u516D",  "treiza", "VI"},
      {"7",  "seven", "shichi - \u4E03", "sept",  "VII"},
      {"8",  "eight", "hachi - \u516B", "huit",   "VIII"},
      {"9",  "nine",  "kyu - \u4E5D",   "neur",   "IX"},
      {"10", "ten",   "ju - \u5341",    "dix",    "X"}
    };
```

```
    final String columnNames[] = {"#", "English", "Japanese", "French", "Roman"};

  Runnable runner = new Runnable() {
    public void run() {
      final JTable table = new JTable(rowData, columnNames);
      JScrollPane scrollPane = new JScrollPane(table);

      String modes[] = {"Resize All Columns", "Resize Last Column",
        "Resize Next Column", "Resize Off", "Resize Subsequent Columns"};
      final int modeKey[] = {
        JTable.AUTO_RESIZE_ALL_COLUMNS,
        JTable.AUTO_RESIZE_LAST_COLUMN,
        JTable.AUTO_RESIZE_NEXT_COLUMN,
        JTable.AUTO_RESIZE_OFF,
        JTable.AUTO_RESIZE_SUBSEQUENT_COLUMNS};
      JComboBox resizeModeComboBox = new JComboBox(modes);
      int defaultMode = 4;
      table.setAutoResizeMode(modeKey[defaultMode]);
      resizeModeComboBox.setSelectedIndex(defaultMode);
      ItemListener itemListener = new ItemListener() {
        public void itemStateChanged(ItemEvent e) {
          JComboBox source = (JComboBox)e.getSource();
          int index = source.getSelectedIndex();
          table.setAutoResizeMode(modeKey[index]);
        }
      };
      resizeModeComboBox.addItemListener(itemListener);

      JFrame frame = new JFrame("Resizing Table");
      frame.setDefaultCloseOperation(JFrame.EXIT_ON_CLOSE);

      frame.add(resizeModeComboBox, BorderLayout.NORTH);
      frame.add(scrollPane, BorderLayout.CENTER);

      frame.setSize(300, 150);
      frame.setVisible(true);
    }
  };
  EventQueue.invokeLater(runner);
  }
}
```

Figure 18-6 shows the initial appearance of the program. Change the JComboBox, and you change the column resize behavior.

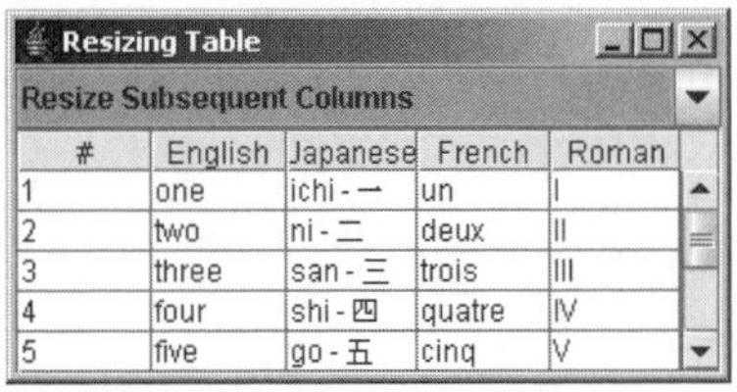

Figure 18-6. *Demonstrating JTable resizing column modes*

Rendering Table Cells

By default, the rendering of table data is done by a JLabel. Whatever value is stored in the table is rendered as a text string. The odd thing is that additional default renderers are installed for classes such as Date and Number subclasses, but they're not enabled. You'll see how to enable these specialized renderers in the "Enabling the Default Table Cell Renderers" section later in this chapter.

Using the TableCellRenderer Interface and DefaultTableCellRenderer Class

The TableCellRenderer interface defines the single method necessary for that class to be a TableCellRenderer.

```
public interface TableCellRenderer {
  public Component getTableCellRendererComponent(JTable table, Object value,
    boolean isSelected, boolean hasFocus, int row, int column);
}
```

By using information given to the getTableCellRendererComponent() method, proper renderer components can be created and sent on their way to display the appropriate content of the JTable. "Proper" means renderers that reflect the table cell state that you've decided to display, such as when you want to display selected cells differently than unselected cells, or how you want the selected cell to appear when it has the input focus.

To see a simple demonstration of this, look at Figure 18-7, which shows a renderer that alternates colors based on which row the renderer is displayed within.

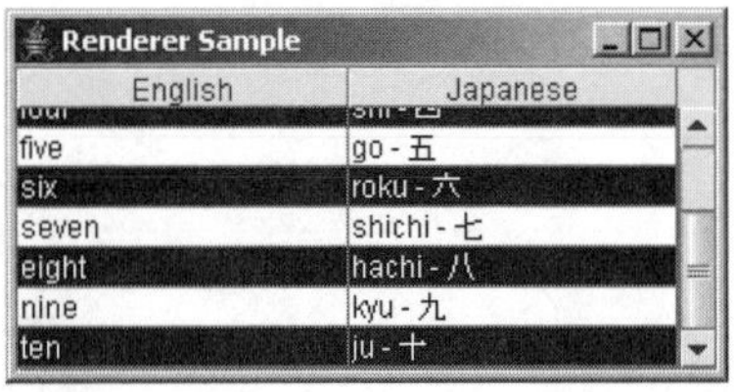

Figure 18-7. *JTable with custom renderer*

The source for the custom renderer used to produce the example in Figure 18-7 is shown in Listing 18-2.

Listing 18-2. *Custom Table Cell Renderer*

```
import java.awt.*;
import javax.swing.*;
import javax.swing.table.*;

public class EvenOddRenderer implements TableCellRenderer {

  public static final DefaultTableCellRenderer DEFAULT_RENDERER =
    new DefaultTableCellRenderer();

  public Component getTableCellRendererComponent(JTable table, Object value,
      boolean isSelected, boolean hasFocus, int row, int column) {
    Component renderer =
      DEFAULT_RENDERER.getTableCellRendererComponent(table, value,
      isSelected, hasFocus, row, column);
    Color foreground, background;
    if (isSelected) {
      foreground = Color.YELLOW;
      background = Color.GREEN;
    } else {
      if (row % 2 == 0) {
        foreground = Color.BLUE;
        background = Color.WHITE;
      } else {
        foreground = Color.WHITE;
        background = Color.BLUE;
      }
    }
    renderer.setForeground(foreground);
    renderer.setBackground(background);
    return renderer;
  }
}
```

Renderers for tables can be installed for individual classes or for specific columns (see the "Enabling the Default Table Cell Renderers" section later in this chapter for details). To install the renderer as the default renderer for the JTable—in other words, for Object.class—use code similar to the following:

```
TableCellRenderer renderer = new EvenOddRenderer();
table.setDefaultRenderer(Object.class, renderer);
```

Once installed, the EvenOddRenderer will be used for any column whose class doesn't have a more specific renderer. It's the responsibility of the public Class getColumnClass() method of TableModel to return the class to be used as the renderer lookup for all the cells in a particular column. The DefaultTableModel returns Object.class for everything; therefore, EvenOddRenderer will be used by all table cells.

■**Note** Keep in mind that one renderer component is used for every cell of every column of a particular class. No individual renderer is created for each cell.

The sample program that used the EvenOddRenderer to generate Figure 18-7 is shown in Listing 18-3.

Listing 18-3. *Using the Custom Table Cell Renderer*

```
import javax.swing.*;
import javax.swing.table.*;
import java.awt.*;

public class RendererSample {

  public static void main(String args[]) {
    final Object rows[][] = {
      {"one",   "ichi - \u4E00"},
      {"two",   "ni - \u4E8C"},
      {"three", "san - \u4E09"},
      {"four",  "shi - \u56DB"},
      {"five",  "go - \u4E94"},
      {"six",   "roku - \u516D"},
      {"seven", "shichi - \u4E03"},
      {"eight", "hachi - \u516B"},
      {"nine",  "kyu - \u4E5D"},
      {"ten",   "ju - \u5341"}
    };
    final Object headers[] = {"English", "Japanese"};
    Runnable runner = new Runnable() {
      public void run() {
        JFrame frame = new JFrame("Renderer Sample");
        frame.setDefaultCloseOperation(JFrame.EXIT_ON_CLOSE);
        JTable table = new JTable(rows, headers);
        TableCellRenderer renderer = new EvenOddRenderer();
        table.setDefaultRenderer(Object.class, renderer);
        JScrollPane scrollPane = new JScrollPane(table);
        frame.add(scrollPane, BorderLayout.CENTER);
        frame.setSize(300, 150);
        frame.setVisible(true);
      }
    };
    EventQueue.invokeLater(runner);
  }
}
```

Using Tooltips

By default, your table cell renderers will display any tooltip text you've configured them to display. Unlike with the JTree component, you don't need to manually register the table with the ToolTipManager. If, however, your table doesn't display tooltip text, the table will respond faster if you unregister the table with the ToolTipManager by using code such as the following:

```
// Explicitly
ToolTipManager.sharedInstance().unregisterComponent(aTable);
// Implicitly
yourTable.setToolTipText(null);
```

Handling JTable Events

There are no JTable events that you can register directly with the JTable. To find out when something happens, you must register with one of the JTable model classes: TableModel, TableColumnModel, or ListSelectionModel.

Customizing a JTable Look and Feel

Each installable Swing look and feel provides a different JTable appearance and set of default UIResource value settings. Figure 18-8 shows the appearance of the JTable component for the preinstalled set of look and feel types: Motif, Windows, and Ocean. In all three cases, the third row is highlighted, where the coloration shows the first column is being edited.

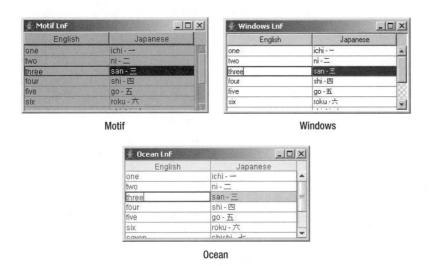

Motif   Windows

Ocean

Figure 18-8. *JTable under different look and feel types*

The available set of UIResource-related properties for a JTable is shown in Table 18-4. The JTable component has 21 different properties.

Table 18-4. *JTable UIResource Elements*

Property String	Object Type
Table.actionMap	ActionMap
Table.ancestorInputMap	InputMap
Table.ancestorInputMap.RightToLeft	InputMap
Table.background	Color
Table.darkShadow	Color
Table.focusCellBackground	Color
Table.focusCellForeground	Color
Table.focusCellHighlightBorder	Border
Table.font	Font
Table.foreground	Color
Table.gridColor	Color
Table.highlight	Color
Table.light	Color
Table.rendererUseTableColors	Boolean
Table.rendererUseUIBorder	Boolean
Table.rowHeight	Integer
Table.scrollPaneBorder	Border
Table.selectionBackground	Color
Table.selectionForeground	Color
Table.shadow	Color
TableUI	String

TableModel Interface

Now that you've looked at the basics of the JTable component, you can learn how it internally manages its data elements. It does this with the help of classes that implement the TableModel interface.

The TableModel interface defines the framework needed by the JTable to acquire column headers and cell values, and modify those cell values when the table is editable. Its definition follows:

```
public interface TableModel {
  // Listeners
  public void addTableModelListener(TableModelListener l);
  public void removeTableModelListener(TableModelListener l);
  // Properties
  public int getColumnCount();
  public int getRowCount();
  // Other methods
  public Class getColumnClass(int columnIndex);
  public String getColumnName(int columnIndex);
  public Object getValueAt(int rowIndex, int columnIndex);
  public boolean isCellEditable(int rowIndex, int columnIndex);
  public void setValueAt(Object vValue, int rowIndex, int columnIndex);
}
```

AbstractTableModel Class

The `AbstractTableModel` class provides the basic implementation of the `TableModel` interface. It manages the `TableModelListener` list and default implementations for several of the `TableModel` methods. When you subclass it, all you need to provide is the actual column and row count, and the specific values (`getValueAt()`) in the table model. Column names default to labels such as *A, B, C, . . ., Z, AA, BB, . . .*, and the data model is read-only unless `isCellEditable()` is overridden.

If you subclass `AbstractTableModel` and make the data model editable, it's your responsibility to call one of the following fire*XXX*() methods of `AbstractTableModel` to ensure that any `TableModelListener` objects are notified when the data model changes:

```
public void fireTableCellUpdated(int row, int column);
public void fireTableChanged(TableModelEvent e);
public void fireTableDataChanged();
public void fireTableRowsDeleted(int firstRow, int lastRow);
public void fireTableRowsInserted(int firstRow, int lastRow);
public void fireTableRowsUpdated(int firstRow, int lastRow);
public void fireTableStructureChanged();
```

When you want to create a `JTable`, it's not uncommon to subclass `AbstractTableModel` in order to reuse an existing data structure. This data structure typically comes as the result of a Java Database Connectivity (JDBC) query, but there's no restriction requiring that to be the case. To demonstrate, the following anonymous class definition shows how you can treat an array as an `AbstractTableModel`:

```
TableModel model = new AbstractTableModel() {
  Object rowData[][] = {
    {"one",   "ichi"},
    {"two",   "ni"},
    {"three", "san"},
    {"four",  "shi"},
    {"five",  "go"},
    {"six",   "roku"},
    {"seven", "shichi"},
```

```
      {"eight", "hachi"},
      {"nine",  "kyu"},
      {"ten",   "ju"}
    };
    Object columnNames[] = {"English", "Japanese"};
    public String getColumnName(int column) {
      return columnNames[column].toString();
    }
    public int getRowCount() {
      return rowData.length;
    }
    public int getColumnCount() {
      return columnNames.length;
    }
    public Object getValueAt(int row, int col) {
      return rowData[row][col];
    }
  };
JTable table = new JTable(model);
JScrollPane scrollPane = new JScrollPane(table);
```

Specifying Fixed JTable Columns

Now that you've seen the basics of how the TableModel and AbstractTableModel describe the data, you can create a JTable with some columns that are fixed columns and some that are not. To create columns that don't scroll, you need to place a second table in the row header view of the JScrollPane. Then when the user scrolls the table vertically, the two tables will remain in sync. The two tables then need to share their ListSelectionModel. That way, when a row in one table is selected, the row in the other table will automatically be selected. Figure 18-9 shows a table with one fixed column and four scrolling columns.

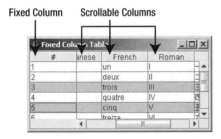

Figure 18-9. *Fixed-column JTable*

The source code used to generate Figure 18-9 is shown in Listing 18-4.

Listing 18-4. *JTable with Fixed Area*

```java
import javax.swing.*;
import javax.swing.table.*;
import java.awt.*;

public class FixedTable {
  public static void main(String args[]) {

    final Object rowData[][] = {
      {"1",  "one",   "ichi",   "un",      "I",    "\u4E00"},
      {"2",  "two",   "ni",     "deux",    "II",   "\u4E8C"},
      {"3",  "three", "san",    "trois",   "III",  "\u4E09"},
      {"4",  "four",  "shi",    "quatre",  "IV",   "\u56DB"},
      {"5",  "five",  "go",     "cinq",    "V",    "\u4E94"},
      {"6",  "six",   "roku",   "treiza",  "VI",   "\u516D"},
      {"7",  "seven", "shichi", "sept",    "VII",  "\u4E03"},
      {"8",  "eight", "hachi",  "huit",    "VIII", "\u516B"},
      {"9",  "nine",  "kyu",    "neur",    "IX",   "\u4E5D"},
      {"10", "ten",   "ju",     "dix",     "X",    "\u5341"}
    };

    final String columnNames[] =
      {"#", "English", "Japanese", "French", "Roman", "Kanji"};

    final TableModel fixedColumnModel = new AbstractTableModel() {
      public int getColumnCount() {
        return 1;
      }
      public String getColumnName(int column) {
        return columnNames[column];
      }
      public int getRowCount() {
        return rowData.length;
      }
      public Object getValueAt(int row, int column) {
        return rowData[row][column];
      }
    };

    final TableModel mainModel = new AbstractTableModel() {
      public int getColumnCount() {
        return columnNames.length-1;
      }
      public String getColumnName(int column) {
        return columnNames[column+1];
      }
    }
```

```
      public int getRowCount() {
        return rowData.length;
      }
      public Object getValueAt(int row, int column) {
        return rowData[row][column+1];
      }
    };

    Runnable runner = new Runnable() {
      public void run() {
        JTable fixedTable = new JTable(fixedColumnModel);
        fixedTable.setAutoResizeMode(JTable.AUTO_RESIZE_OFF);

        JTable mainTable = new JTable(mainModel);
        mainTable.setAutoResizeMode(JTable.AUTO_RESIZE_OFF);

        ListSelectionModel model = fixedTable.getSelectionModel();
        mainTable.setSelectionModel(model);

        JScrollPane scrollPane = new JScrollPane(mainTable);
        Dimension fixedSize = fixedTable.getPreferredSize();
        JViewport viewport = new JViewport();
        viewport.setView(fixedTable);
        viewport.setPreferredSize(fixedSize);
        viewport.setMaximumSize(fixedSize);
        scrollPane.setCorner(JScrollPane.UPPER_LEFT_CORNER,
          fixedTable.getTableHeader());
        scrollPane.setRowHeaderView(viewport);

        JFrame frame = new JFrame("Fixed Column Table");
        frame.setDefaultCloseOperation(JFrame.EXIT_ON_CLOSE);
        frame.add(scrollPane, BorderLayout.CENTER);
        frame.setSize(300, 150);
        frame.setVisible(true);
      }
    };
    EventQueue.invokeLater(runner);
  }
}
```

Enabling the Default Table Cell Renderers

Earlier, I mentioned that the JTable provides default renderers for Date and Number classes. Let's look at the AbstractTableModel class and see how to enable those renderers.

The public Class getColumnClass(int column) method of the TableModel returns the class type for a column in the data model. If the JTable class has a special renderer installed for that particular class, it will use it to display that class. By default, the AbstractTableModel (and DefaultTableModel) implementations of TableModel return Object.class for everything. The AbstractTableModel class doesn't try to be smart about guessing what's in a column. However, if you know that a particular column of the data model will always be numbers, dates, or some other class, you can have the data model return that class type. This allows the JTable to try to be smarter and use a better renderer.

Table 18-5 shows the preinstalled renderers within the JTable. If you have a table full of numbers or just one column of numbers, for example, you can override getColumnClass() to return Number.class for the appropriate columns; your numbers will be right-justified instead of left-justified. With dates, using the default renderer for the Date class produces better-looking, localized output.

Table 18-5. *Default JTable Renderers*

Class	Renderer	Description
Boolean	JCheckBox	Centered
Date	JLabel	Right-aligned; uses DateFormat for output
Double	JLabel	Right-aligned; uses NumberFormat for output
Float	JLabel	Right-aligned; uses NumberFormat for output
Icon	JLabel	Centered
ImageIcon	JLabel	Centered
Number	JLabel	Right-aligned
Object	JLabel	Left-aligned

Figure 18-10 shows how a table might look before and after enabling the renderers.

Before   After

Figure 18-10. *Before and after enabling the renderers.*

You can choose to hard-code the class names for columns or have the getColumnClass() method be generic and just call getClass() on an element in the column. Adding the following code to an AbstractTableModel implementation would allow the JTable to use its default renderers. This implementation assumes that all entries for a particular column are one class type.

```
public Class getColumnClass(int column) {
  return (getValueAt(0, column).getClass());
}
```

DefaultTableModel Class

The DefaultTableModel is a subclass of AbstractTableModel that provides its own Vector data structure for storage. Everything in the data model is stored within vectors internally, even when the data is initially part of an array. In other words, if you already have your data in an adequate data structure, don't use DefaultTableModel. Create an AbstractTableModel that uses the structure, instead of having a DefaultTableModel convert the structure for you.

Creating a DefaultTableModel

There are six constructors for DefaultTableModel:

public DefaultTableModel()
```
TableModel model = new DefaultTableModel()
```

public DefaultTableModel(int rows, int columns)
```
TableModel model = new DefaultTableModel(2, 3)
```

public DefaultTableModel(Object rowData[][], Object columnNames[])
```
Object rowData[][] = {{"Row1-Column1", "Row1-Column2", "Row1-Column3"},
  {"Row2-Column1", "Row2-Column2", "Row2-Column3"}};
Object columnNames[] = {"Column One", "Column Two", "Column Three"};
TableModel model = new DefaultTableModel(rowData, columnNames);
```

public DefaultTableModel(Vector rowData, Vector columnNames)
```
Vector rowOne = new Vector();
rowOne.addElement("Row1-Column1");
rowOne.addElement("Row1-Column2");
rowOne.addElement("Row1-Column3");
Vector rowTwo = new Vector();
rowTwo.addElement("Row2-Column1");
rowTwo.addElement("Row2-Column2");
rowTwo.addElement("Row2-Column3");
Vector rowData = new Vector();
rowData.addElement(rowOne);
rowData.addElement(rowTwo);
Vector columnNames = new Vector();
columnNames.addElement("Column One");
columnNames.addElement("Column Two");
columnNames.addElement("Column Three");
TableModel model = new DefaultTableModel(rowData, columnNames);
```

```
public DefaultTableModel(Object columnNames[], int rows)
TableModel model = new DefaultTableModel(columnNames, 2);
```

```
public DefaultTableModel(Vector columnNames, int rows)
TableModel model = new DefaultTableModel(columnNames, 2);
```

Four of the constructors map directly to JTable constructors, whereas the remaining two allow you to create empty tables from a set of column headers with a fixed number of rows. Once you've created the DefaultTableModel, you pass it along to a JTable constructor to create the actual table, and then place the table in a JScrollPane.

Filling a DefaultTableModel

If you choose to use a DefaultTableModel, you must fill it with data for your JTable to display anything. Along with basic routines to fill the data structure, there are additional methods to remove data or replace the entire contents:
The following methods allow you to add columns:

```
public void addColumn(Object columnName);
public void addColumn(Object columnName, Vector columnData);
public void addColumn(Object columnName, Object columnData[ ]);
```

Use these methods to add rows:

```
public void addRow(Object rowData[ ]);
public void addRow(Vector rowData);
```

These methods insert rows:

```
public void insertRow(int row, Object rowData[ ]);
public void insertRow(int row, Vector rowData);
```

This method removes rows:

```
public void removeRow( int row);
```

And finally, you can replace contents with the following two methods:

```
public void setDataVector(Object newData[ ][ ], Object columnNames[ ]);
public void setDataVector(Vector newData, Vector columnNames);
```

DefaultTableModel Properties

In addition to the rowCount and columnCount properties inherited from AbstractTableModel, DefaultTableModel has two other properties, as shown in Table 18-6. Setting the rowCount property allows you to enlarge or shrink the table size as you please. If you are expanding the model, the additional rows remain empty.

Table 18-6. *DefaultTableModel Properties*

Property Name	Data Type	Access
columnCount	int	Read-only
columnIdentifiers	Vector	Write-only
dataVector	Vector	Read-only
rowCount	int	Read-write

Creating a Sparse Table Model

The default table model implementations are meant for tables that are full of data, not for spreadsheets consisting of mostly empty cells. When the cells in the table are mostly empty, the default data structure for the DefaultTableModel will end up with plenty of wasted space. At the cost of creating a Point for each lookup, you can create a sparse table model that can use a HashMap underneath it. Listing 18-5 demonstrates one such implementation.

Listing 18-5. *Sparsely Populated Table Model*

```
import java.awt.Point;
import java.util.HashMap;
import java.util.Map;
import javax.swing.table.AbstractTableModel;

public class SparseTableModel extends AbstractTableModel {

  static final long serialVersionUID = 57744304026299695111L;

  private Map<Point, Object> lookup;
  private final int rows;
  private final int columns;
  private final String headers[];

  public SparseTableModel(int rows, String columnHeaders[]) {
    if ((rows < 0) || (columnHeaders == null)) {
      throw new IllegalArgumentException("Invalid row count/columnHeaders");
    }
    this.rows = rows;
    this.columns = columnHeaders.length;
    headers = columnHeaders;
    lookup = new HashMap<Point, Object>();
  }
```

```
  public int getColumnCount() {
    return columns;
  }

  public int getRowCount() {
    return rows;
  }

  public String getColumnName(int column) {
    return headers[column];
  }

  public Object getValueAt(int row, int column) {
    return lookup.get(new Point(row, column));
  }

  public void setValueAt(Object value, int row, int column) {
    if ((rows < 0) || (columns < 0)) {
      throw new IllegalArgumentException("Invalid row/column setting");
    }
    if ((row < rows) && (column < columns)) {
      lookup.put(new Point(row, column), value);
    }
  }
}
```

Testing this example involves creating and filling up the model, as follows:

```
String headers[] = { "English", "Japanese"};
TableModel model = new SparseTableModel(10, headers);
JTable table = new JTable(model);
model.setValueAt("one", 0, 0);
model.setValueAt("ten", 9, 0);
model.setValueAt("roku - \ u516D", 5, 1);
model.setValueAt("hachi - \ u516B", 8, 1);
```

Listening to JTable Events with a TableModelListener

If you want to dynamically update your table data, you can work with a TableModelListener to find out when the data changes. The interface consists of one method that tells you when the table data changes.

```
public interface TableModelListener extends EventListener {
  public void tableChanged(TableModelEvent e);
}
```

After the TableModelListener is notified, you can ask the TableModelEvent for the type of event that happened and the range of rows and columns affected. Table 18-7 shows the properties of the TableModelEvent you can inquire about.

Table 18-7. *TableModelEvent Properties*

Property Name	Data Type	Access
column	int	Read-only
firstRow	int	Read-only
lastRow	int	Read-only
type	int	Read-only

The event type can be one of three type constants of TableModelEvent: INSERT, UPDATE, or DELETE.

If the column property setting for the TableModelEvent is ALL_COLUMNS, then all the columns in the data model are affected. If the firstRow property is HEADER_ROW, it means the table header changed.

Sorting JTable Elements

The JTable component doesn't come with built-in support for sorting. Nevertheless, this feature is frequently requested. Sorting doesn't require changing the data model, but it does require changing the view of the data model that the JTable has. This type of change is described by the Decorator pattern, in which you maintain the same API to the data but add sorting capabilities to the view. The participants of the Decorator design pattern are as follows:

- Component: The component defines the service interface that will be decorated.

- ConcreteComponent: The concrete component is the object to be decorated.

- Decorator: The decorator is an abstract wrapper to a concrete component; it maintains the service interface.

- ConcreteDecorator(s) [A, B, C, . . .]: The concrete decorator objects extend the decorator by adding decorating responsibilities while maintaining the same programming interface. They redirect service requests to the concrete component referred to by their abstract superclass.

■**Note** The streams of the java.io package are examples of the Decorator pattern. The various filter streams add capabilities to the basic stream classes and maintain the same API for access.

In the particular case for table sorting, only the Component, ConcreteComponent, and Decorator are required, because there is only one concrete decorator. The Component is the TableModel interface, the ConcreteComponent is the actual model, and the Decorator is the sorted model.

In order to sort, you need to maintain a mapping of the real data to the sorted data. From the user interface, you must allow the user to select a column header label to enable sorting of a particular column.

To use the sorting capabilities, you tell the custom TableSorter class about your data model, decorate it, and create a JTable from your decorated model instead of the original. To enable the sorting by picking column header labels, you need to call the custom install() method of the TableHeaderSorter class shown in the following source code for the TableSorter class:

```
TableSorter sorter = new TableSorter(model);
JTable table = new JTable(sorter);
TableHeaderSorter.install(sorter, table);
```

The main source code for the TableSorter class is shown in Listing 18-6. It extends from the TableMap class, which is shown in Listing 18-7. The TableSorter class is where all the action is. The class does the sorting and notifies others that the data has changed.

Listing 18-6. *Table Column Sorting*

```
import javax.swing.*;
import javax.swing.table.*;
import javax.swing.event.*;
import java.awt.event.*;
import java.util.*;

public class TableSorter extends TableMap implements TableModelListener {
  int indexes[] = new int[0];
  Vector sortingColumns = new Vector();
  boolean ascending = true;

  public TableSorter() {
  }

  public TableSorter(TableModel model) {
    setModel(model);
  }

  public void setModel(TableModel model) {
    super.setModel(model);
    reallocateIndexes();
    sortByColumn(0);
    fireTableDataChanged();
  }

  public int compareRowsByColumn(int row1, int row2, int column) {
    Class type = model.getColumnClass(column);
    TableModel data = model;
```

```
// Check for nulls

Object o1 = data.getValueAt(row1, column);
Object o2 = data.getValueAt(row2, column);

// If both values are null return 0
if (o1 == null && o2 == null) {
  return 0;
} else if (o1 == null) {   // Define null less than everything.
  return -1;
} else if (o2 == null) {
  return 1;
}

if (type.getSuperclass() == Number.class) {
  Number n1 = (Number)data.getValueAt(row1, column);
  double d1 = n1.doubleValue();
  Number n2 = (Number)data.getValueAt(row2, column);
  double d2 = n2.doubleValue();

  if (d1 < d2)
    return -1;
  else if (d1 > d2)
    return 1;
  else
    return 0;
} else if (type == String.class) {
  String s1 = (String)data.getValueAt(row1, column);
  String s2 = (String)data.getValueAt(row2, column);
  int result = s1.compareTo(s2);

  if (result < 0)
    return -1;
  else if (result > 0)
    return 1;
  else
    return 0;
} else if (type == java.util.Date.class) {
  Date d1 = (Date)data.getValueAt(row1, column);
  long n1 = d1.getTime();
  Date d2 = (Date)data.getValueAt(row2, column);
  long n2 = d2.getTime();

  if (n1 < n2)
    return -1;
  else if (n1 > n2)
    return 1;
```

```
      else
        return 0;
  }  else if (type == Boolean.class) {
    Boolean bool1 = (Boolean)data.getValueAt(row1, column);
    boolean b1 = bool1.booleanValue();
    Boolean bool2 = (Boolean)data.getValueAt(row2, column);
    boolean b2 = bool2.booleanValue();

    if (b1 == b2)
      return 0;
    else if (b1) // Define false < true
      return 1;
    else
      return -1;
  }  else {
    Object v1 = data.getValueAt(row1, column);
    String s1 = v1.toString();
    Object v2 = data.getValueAt(row2, column);
    String s2 = v2.toString();
    int result = s1.compareTo(s2);

    if (result < 0)
      return -1;
    else if (result > 0)
      return 1;
    else
      return 0;
  }
}
public int compare(int row1, int row2) {
  for (int level=0, n=sortingColumns.size(); level < n; level++) {
    Integer column = (Integer)sortingColumns.elementAt(level);
    int result = compareRowsByColumn(row1, row2, column.intValue());
    if (result != 0) {
      return (ascending ? result : -result);
    }
  }
  return 0;
}

public void reallocateIndexes() {
  int rowCount = model.getRowCount();
  indexes = new int[rowCount];
  for (int row = 0; row < rowCount; row++) {
    indexes[row] = row;
  }
}
```

```java
  public void tableChanged(TableModelEvent tableModelEvent) {
    super.tableChanged(tableModelEvent);
    reallocateIndexes();
    sortByColumn(0);
    fireTableStructureChanged();
  }

  public void checkModel() {
    if (indexes.length != model.getRowCount()) {
      System.err.println("Sorter not informed of a change in model.");
    }
  }

  public void sort() {
    checkModel();
    shuttlesort((int[])indexes.clone(), indexes, 0, indexes.length);
    fireTableDataChanged();
  }

  public void shuttlesort(int from[], int to[], int low, int high) {
    if (high - low < 2) {
      return;
    }
    int middle = (low + high)/2;
    shuttlesort(to, from, low, middle);
    shuttlesort(to, from, middle, high);

    int p = low;
    int q = middle;

    for (int i = low; i < high; i++) {
      if (q >= high || (p < middle && compare(from[p], from[q]) <= 0)) {
        to[i] = from[p++];
      } else {
        to[i] = from[q++];
      }
    }
  }

  private void swap(int first, int second) {
    int temp          = indexes[first];
    indexes[first]    = indexes[second];
    indexes[second]   = temp;
  }
```

```
  public Object getValueAt(int row, int column) {
    checkModel();
    return model.getValueAt(indexes[row], column);
  }

  public void setValueAt(Object aValue, int row, int column) {
    checkModel();
    model.setValueAt(aValue, indexes[row], column);
  }

  public void sortByColumn(int column) {
    sortByColumn(column, true);
  }

  public void sortByColumn(int column, boolean ascending) {
    this.ascending = ascending;
    sortingColumns.removeAllElements();
    sortingColumns.addElement(new Integer(column));
    sort();
    super.tableChanged(new TableModelEvent(this));
  }
}
```

Note The TableSorter borrows heavily from the TableExample that comes with the JFC/Swing release.

The TableMap class, shown in Listing 18-7, serves as a proxy, passing along all calls to the appropriate TableModel class. It's the superclass of the TableSorter class shown in Listing 18-6.

Listing 18-7. *Table Sorting Support Map*

```
import javax.swing.table.*;
import javax.swing.event.*;

public class TableMap extends AbstractTableModel implements TableModelListener {

  TableModel model;

  public TableModel getModel() {
    return model;
  }
```

```
  public void setModel(TableModel model) {
    if (this.model != null) {
      this.model.removeTableModelListener(this);
    }
    this.model = model;
    if (this.model != null) {
      this.model.addTableModelListener(this);
    }
  }

  public Class getColumnClass(int column) {
    return model.getColumnClass(column);
  }

  public int getColumnCount() {
    return ((model == null) ? 0 : model.getColumnCount());
  }

  public String getColumnName(int column) {
    return model.getColumnName(column);
  }

  public int getRowCount() {
      return ((model == null) ? 0 : model.getRowCount());
  }

  public Object getValueAt(int row, int column) {
    return model.getValueAt(row, column);
  }

  public void setValueAt(Object value, int row, int column) {
    model.setValueAt(value, row, column);
  }

  public boolean isCellEditable(int row, int column) {
    return model.isCellEditable(row, column);
  }

  public void tableChanged(TableModelEvent tableModelEvent) {
    fireTableChanged(tableModelEvent);
  }
}
```

Installation of the sorting routines requires the registration of a MouseListener, as shown in Listing 18-8, so that selection within the table header triggers the sorting process. Regular mouse clicks are ascending sorts; Shift-clicks are descending sorts.

Listing 18-8. *Mouse Listener for Table Sorting*

```java
import javax.swing.*;
import javax.swing.table.*;
import javax.swing.event.*;
import java.awt.event.*;
import java.util.*;

public class TableHeaderSorter extends MouseAdapter {

  private TableSorter sorter;
  private JTable table;

  private TableHeaderSorter() {
  }

  public static void install(TableSorter sorter, JTable table) {
    TableHeaderSorter tableHeaderSorter = new TableHeaderSorter();
    tableHeaderSorter.sorter = sorter;
    tableHeaderSorter.table  = table;
    JTableHeader tableHeader = table.getTableHeader();
    tableHeader.addMouseListener(tableHeaderSorter);
  }

  public void mouseClicked(MouseEvent mouseEvent) {
    TableColumnModel columnModel = table.getColumnModel();
    int viewColumn = columnModel.getColumnIndexAtX(mouseEvent.getX());
    int column = table.convertColumnIndexToModel(viewColumn);
    if (mouseEvent.getClickCount() == 1 && column != -1) {
      System.out.println("Sorting ...");
      int shiftPressed = (mouseEvent.getModifiers() & InputEvent.SHIFT_MASK);
      boolean ascending = (shiftPressed == 0);
      sorter.sortByColumn(column, ascending);
    }
  }
}
```

■**Note** Chapter 19 includes a demonstration using the `TableSorter` to sort a table of system properties.

TableColumnModel Interface

`TableColumnModel` is one of those interfaces that lives in the background and usually doesn't require much attention. It basically manages the set of columns currently being displayed by a `JTable`. Unless triggered to do otherwise, when a `JTable` is created, the component builds a default column model from the data model, specifying that the display column order remains in the data model order.

When the autoCreateColumnsFromModel property of JTable is set (true) prior to setting the data model of the JTable, the TableColumnModel is automatically created. In addition, you can manually tell the JTable to create the default TableColumnModel if the current settings need to be reset. The public void createDefaultColumnsFromModel() method does the creation for you, assigning the new creation to the TableColumnModel of the JTable.

With all that automatically done for you, why do you need to look at the TableColumnModel? Usually, you'll need to work with this interface only when you don't like the defaults or when you want to manually move things around. In addition to maintaining a set of TableColumn objects, the TableColumnModel manages a second ListSelectionModel, which allows users to select columns and rows from the table.

Let's take a look at the interface definition before getting into the default implementation.

```
public interface TableColumnModel {
  // Listeners
  public void addColumnModelListener(TableColumnModelListener l);
  public void removeColumnModelListener(TableColumnModelListener l);
  // Properties
  public int getColumnCount();
  public int getColumnMargin();
  public void setColumnMargin(int newMargin);
  public Enumeration getColumns();
  public boolean getColumnSelectionAllowed();
  public void setColumnSelectionAllowed(boolean flag);
  public int getSelectedColumnCount();
  public int[ ] getSelectedColumns();
  public ListSelectionModel getSelectionModel();
  public void setSelectionModel(ListSelectionModel newModel);
  public int getTotalColumnWidth();
  // Other methods
  public void addColumn(TableColumn aColumn);
  public TableColumn getColumn(int columnIndex);
  public int getColumnIndex(Object columnIdentifier);
  public int getColumnIndexAtX(int xPosition);
  public void moveColumn(int columnIndex, int newIndex);
  public void removeColumn(TableColumn column);
}
```

DefaultTableColumnModel Class

The DefaultTableColumnModel class defines the implementation of the TableColumnModel interface used by the system. It describes the general appearance of the TableColumn objects within the JTable by tracking margins, width, selection, and quantity. Table 18-8 shows the nine properties for accessing the DefaultTableColumnModel settings.

Table 18-8. *DefaultTableColumnModel Properties*

Property Name	Data Type	Access
columnCount	int	Read-only
columnMargin	int	Read-write
columnModelListeners	TableColumnModelListener[ ]	Read-only
columns	Enumeration	Read-only
columnSelectionAllowed	boolean	Read-write
selectedColumnCount	int	Read-only
selectedColumns	int[ ]	Read-only
selectionModel	ListSelectionModel	Read-write
totalColumnWidth	int	Read-only

In addition to the class properties, you can use the following methods to add, remove, and move columns through the TableColumn class, which will be discussed shortly.

```
public void addColumn(TableColumn newColumn);
public void removeColumn(TableColumn oldColumn);
public void moveColumn(int currentIndex, int newIndex);
```

Listening to JTable Events with a TableColumnModelListener

One of the things you might want to do with a TableColumnModel is listen for TableColumnModelEvent objects with a TableColumnModelListener. The listener will be notified of any addition, removal, movement, or selection of columns, or changing of column margins, as shown by the listener interface definition. Note that the different methods don't all receive TableColumnModelEvent objects when the event happens.

```
public interface TableColumnModelListener extends EventListener {
  public void columnAdded(TableColumnModelEvent e);
  public void columnMarginChanged(ChangeEvent e);
  public void columnMoved(TableColumnModelEvent e);
  public void columnRemoved(TableColumnModelEvent e);
  public void columnSelectionChanged(ListSelectionEvent e);
}
```

Because the listener definition identifies the event type, the TableColumnModelEvent definition defines only the range of columns affected by the change, as shown in Table 18-9.

Table 18-9. *TableColumnModelEvent Properties*

Property Name	Data Type	Access
fromIndex	int	Read-only
toIndex	int	Read-only

To see a demonstration of the TableColumnModelListener, you can attach a listener to one of your TableColumnModel objects:

```
TableColumnModel columnModel = table.getColumnModel();
columnModel.addColumnModelListener(...);
```

One such listener is shown in Listing 18-9. It doesn't do much besides print a message. Nevertheless, you can use it to see when different events happen.

Listing 18-9. *Table Column Model Listener*

```
TableColumnModelListener tableColumnModelListener =
    new TableColumnModelListener() {
  public void columnAdded(TableColumnModelEvent e) {
    System.out.println("Added");
  }
  public void columnMarginChanged(ChangeEvent e) {
    System.out.println("Margin");
  }
  public void columnMoved(TableColumnModelEvent e) {
    System.out.println("Moved");
  }
  public void columnRemoved(TableColumnModelEvent e) {
    System.out.println("Removed");
  }
  public void columnSelectionChanged(ListSelectionEvent e) {
    System.out.println("Selected");
  }
};
```

Of course, you do need to create some code to elicit certain events. For instance, margins don't appear out of thin air. But you can add the same column multiple times to add more columns (or remove them). The program shown in Listing 18-10 tests the new TableColumnModelListener.

Listing 18-10. *Playing with Table Columns*

```
import javax.swing.event.*;
import javax.swing.table.*;
import javax.swing.*;
import java.awt.*;

public class ColumnModelSample {
  public static void main(String args[]) {
    final Object rows[][] = {
      {"one",   "ichi - \u4E00"},
      {"two",   "ni - \u4E8C"},
      {"three", "san - \u4E09"},
      {"four",  "shi - \u56DB"},
      {"five",  "go - \u4E94"},
```

```
     {"six",   "roku - \u516D"},
     {"seven", "shichi - \u4E03"},
     {"eight", "hachi - \u516B"},
     {"nine",  "kyu - \u4E5D"},
     {"ten",   "ju - \u5341"}
};
final Object headers[] = {"English", "Japanese"};
Runnable runner = new Runnable() {
  public void run() {
    JFrame frame = new JFrame("Scrollless Table");
    frame.setDefaultCloseOperation(JFrame.EXIT_ON_CLOSE);
    JTable table = new JTable(rows, headers);

    TableColumnModelListener tableColumnModelListener =
        new TableColumnModelListener() {
      public void columnAdded(TableColumnModelEvent e) {
        System.out.println("Added");
      }
      public void columnMarginChanged(ChangeEvent e) {
        System.out.println("Margin");
      }
      public void columnMoved(TableColumnModelEvent e) {
        System.out.println("Moved");
      }
      public void columnRemoved(TableColumnModelEvent e) {
        System.out.println("Removed");
      }
      public void columnSelectionChanged(ListSelectionEvent e) {
        System.out.println("Selection Changed");
      }
    };

    TableColumnModel columnModel = table.getColumnModel();
    columnModel.addColumnModelListener(tableColumnModelListener);

    columnModel.setColumnMargin(12);

    TableColumn column = new TableColumn(1);
    columnModel.addColumn(column);

    JScrollPane pane = new JScrollPane(table);
    frame.add(pane, BorderLayout.CENTER);
    frame.setSize(300, 150);
    frame.setVisible(true);
  }
};
```

```
        EventQueue.invokeLater(runner);
    }
}
```

TableColumn Class

TableColumn is another important class that lives behind the scenes. Swing tables consist of a group of columns, which are made up of cells. Each of those columns is described by a TableColumn instance. Each instance of the TableColumn class stores the appropriate editor, renderer, name, and sizing information. TableColumn objects are then grouped together into a TableColumnModel to make up the current set of columns to be displayed by a JTable. One useful trick to remember is if you don't want a column to be displayed, remove its TableColumn from the TableColumnModel but leave it in the TableModel.

Creating a TableColumn

If you choose to create your TableColumn objects yourself, you can use any one of four constructors. They cascade by adding more constructor arguments.

public TableColumn()
```
TableColumn column = new TableColumn()
```

public TableColumn(int modelIndex)
```
TableColumn column = new TableColumn(2)
```

public TableColumn(int modelIndex, int width)
```
TableColumn column = new TableColumn(2, 25)
```

public TableColumn(int modelIndex, int width, TableCellRenderer
   renderer, TableCellEditor editor)
```
TableColumn column = new TableColumn(2, 25, aRenderer, aEditor)
```

■**Note** All column settings start at zero. Therefore, new TableColumn(2) uses column 3 from the TableModel.

With no arguments, such as in the first constructor in this list, you get an empty column with a default width (75 pixels), a default editor, and a default renderer. The modelIndex argument allows you to specify which column from the TableModel you would like the TableColumn to display within the JTable. You can also specify a width, a renderer, or an editor if you don't like the defaults. If you like one default but not the other, you can also specify null for the renderer or editor.

TableColumn Properties

Table 18-10 lists the 12 properties of the TableColumn. These properties allow you to customize a column beyond the initial set of constructor arguments. Most of the time, everything is configured for you based on the TableModel. However, you can still customize individual columns through the TableColumn class. Yes, all the properties are bound, except for the listener list.

> ■**Note** If an identifier isn't specified, the headerValue setting is used instead.

Table 18-10. *TableColumn Properties*

Property Name	Data Type	Access
cellEditor	TableCellEditor	Read-write bound
cellRenderer	TableCellRenderer	Read-write bound
headerRenderer	TableCellRenderer	Read-write bound
headerValue	Object	Read-write bound
identifier	Object	Read-write bound
maxWidth	int	Read-write bound
minWidth	int	Read-write bound
modelIndex	int	Read-write bound
preferredWidth	int	Read-write bound
propertyChangeListeners	PropertyChangeListener[ ]	Read-only
resizable	boolean	Read-write bound
width	int	Read-write bound

> ■**Caution** If headerRenderer is null, the default header renderer is used by the column:
> TableCellRenderer headerRenderer = table.getTableHeader().getDefaultRenderer();.
> The default is not returned by the getHeaderRenderer() method.

Using Icons in Column Headers

By default, the header renderer for a table displays text or HTML. Although you can get multiple lines of text and images with HTML, there may come a time when you want to display regular Icon objects within a header, as shown in the example in Figure 18-11. To do this, you must change the header's renderer. The header renderer is just another TableCellRenderer.

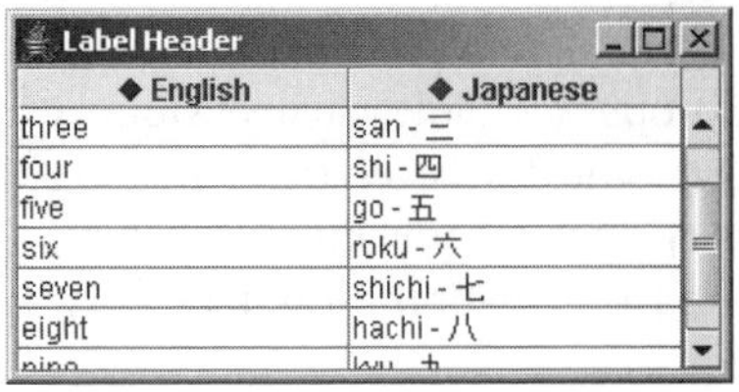

Figure 18-11. *Icons in table headers*

To create a flexible renderer that can display icons, have the renderer treat the value data as a JLabel, instead of using the value to fill the JLabel (or for that, matter any JComponent). Listing 18-11 shows one such renderer, which is used in the program that created Figure 18-11.

Listing 18-11. *Custom Table Cell Renderer for JComponents*

```java
import java.awt.*;
import javax.swing.*;
import javax.swing.table.*;

public class JComponentTableCellRenderer implements TableCellRenderer {
  public Component getTableCellRendererComponent(JTable table, Object value,
      boolean isSelected, boolean hasFocus, int row, int column) {
    return (JComponent)value;
  }
}
```

Figure 18-11 shows how this renderer might appear with the DiamondIcon as the Icon. The source for the sample program is shown in Listing 18-12.

Listing 18-12. *Customizing Column Headers with Icons*

```java
import javax.swing.*;
import javax.swing.border.*;
import javax.swing.table.*;
import java.awt.*;

public class LabelHeaderSample {
  public static void main(String args[]) {
    final Object rows[][] = {
      {"one",   "ichi - \u4E00"},
      {"two",   "ni - \u4E8C"},
      {"three", "san - \u4E09"},
      {"four",  "shi - \u56DB"},
      {"five",  "go - \u4E94"},
      {"six",   "roku - \u516D"},
      {"seven", "shichi - \u4E03"},
      {"eight", "hachi - \u516B"},
      {"nine",  "kyu - \u4E5D"},
```

```
      {"ten",   "ju - \u5341"}
    };
    Runnable runner = new Runnable() {
      public void run() {
        JFrame frame = new JFrame("Label Header");
        frame.setDefaultCloseOperation(JFrame.EXIT_ON_CLOSE);
        String headers[] = {"English", "Japanese"};
        JTable table = new JTable(rows, headers);
        JScrollPane scrollPane = new JScrollPane(table);

        Icon redIcon = new DiamondIcon(Color.RED);
        Icon blueIcon = new DiamondIcon(Color.BLUE);

        Border headerBorder = UIManager.getBorder("TableHeader.cellBorder");

        JLabel blueLabel = new JLabel(headers[0], blueIcon, JLabel.CENTER);
        blueLabel.setBorder(headerBorder);
        JLabel redLabel = new JLabel(headers[1], redIcon, JLabel.CENTER);
        redLabel.setBorder(headerBorder);

        TableCellRenderer renderer = new JComponentTableCellRenderer();

        TableColumnModel columnModel = table.getColumnModel();

        TableColumn column0 = columnModel.getColumn(0);
        TableColumn column1 = columnModel.getColumn(1);

        column0.setHeaderRenderer(renderer);
        column0.setHeaderValue(blueLabel);

        column1.setHeaderRenderer(renderer);
        column1.setHeaderValue(redLabel);

        frame.add(scrollPane, BorderLayout.CENTER);
        frame.setSize(300, 150);
        frame.setVisible(true);
      }
    };
    EventQueue.invokeLater(runner);
  }
}
```

JTableHeader Class

Each JTableHeader instance represents one of a set of headers for all the different columns.
The set of JTableHeader objects is placed within the column header view of the JScrollPane.

You rarely need to work with the JTableHeader directly. Nevertheless, you can configure some characteristics of column headers.

Creating a JTableHeader

The JTableHeader has two constructors. One uses the default TableColumnModel, whereas the other explicitly specifies the model.

```
public JTableHeader()
JComponent headerComponent = new JTableHeader()
```

```
public JTableHeader(TableColumnModel columnModel)
JComponent headerComponent = new JTableHeader(aColumnModel)
```

JTableHeader Properties

As Table 18-11 shows, the JTableHeader has ten different properties. These properties allow you to configure what the user can do with a particular column header or how the column header is shown.

Table 18-11. *JTableHeader Properties*

Property Name	Data Type	Access
accessibleContext	AccessibleContext	Read-only
columnModel	TableColumnModel	Read-write bound
draggedColumn	TableColumn	Read-write
draggedDistance	int	Read-write
reorderingAllowed	boolean	Read-write bound
resizingAllowed	boolean	Read-write bound
resizingColumn	TableColumn	Read-write
table	JTable	Read-write bound
UI	TableHeaderUI	Read-write
UIClassID	String	Read-only

Using Tooltips in Table Headers

By default, if you set tooltip text for the table header, all of the column headers will share the same tooltip text. To specify a tooltip for a given column, you need to create or get the renderer, and then set the tooltip for the renderer. This is true for the individual cells, too. Figure 18-12 shows how the results of this customization would appear.

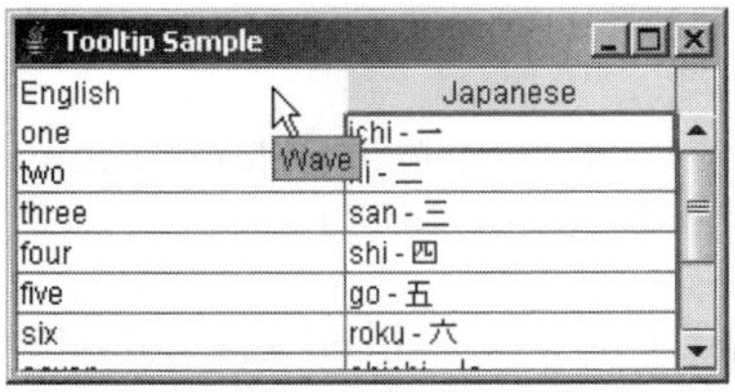

Figure 18-12. *Header tooltips*

The source for the customization in Figure 18-12 is shown in Listing 18-13. Unless you previously set the headers, it's not really necessary to check if the header for a specific column is null first.

Listing 18-13. *Showing Tooltip Text in a Table Header*

```
JLabel headerRenderer = new DefaultTableCellRenderer();
String columnName = table.getModel().getColumnName(0);
headerRenderer.setText(columnName);
headerRenderer.setToolTipText("Wave");
TableColumnModel columnModel = table.getColumnModel();
TableColumn englishColumn = columnModel.getColumn(0);
englishColumn.setHeaderRenderer((TableCellRenderer)headerRenderer);
```

Customizing a JTableHeader Look and Feel

The available set of UIResource-related properties for a JTableHeader is shown in Table 18-12. The five settings control the color, font, and border for the header renderers.

Table 18-12. *JTableHeader UIResource Elements*

Property String	Object Type
TableHeader.background	Color
TableHeader.cellBorder	Border
TableHeader.font	Font
TableHeader.foreground	Color
TableHeaderUI	String

■**Note** For an example of creating column headers spanning multiple columns, see CodeGuru at http://www.codeguru.com/java/Swing.

Editing Table Cells

Editing JTable cells is nearly identical to editing JTree cells. In fact, the default table cell editor, DefaultCellEditor, implements both the TableCellEditor and TreeCellEditor interfaces, allowing you to use the same editor for both tables and trees.

Clicking an editable cell will place the cell in edit mode. (The number of clicks required depends on the type of editor.) The default editor for all cells is a JTextField. Although this works great for many data types, it's not always appropriate for many others. So, you should either not support editing of nontextual information or set up specialized editors for your JTable. With a JTable, you register an editor for a particular class type or column. Then, when the table runs across a cell of the appropriate type, the necessary editor is used.

■**Caution** When no specialized editor is installed, the JTextField is used, even when it's inappropriate for the content.

TableCellEditor Interface and DefaultCellEditor Class

The TableCellEditor interface defines the single method necessary to get an editor cell for a JTable. The argument list for TableCellEditor is identical to the TableCellRenderer, with the exception of the hasFocused argument. Because the cell is being edited, it's already known to have the input focus.

```
public interface TableCellEditor extends CellEditor {
  public Component getTableCellEditorComponent(JTable table, Object value,
    boolean isSelected, int row, int column);
}
```

As described in Chapter 17, the DefaultCellEditor provides an implementation of the interface. It offers a JTextField as one editor, a JCheckBox for another, and a JComboBox for a third.

As Table 18-13 shows, in most cases the default editor is the JTextField. If the cell data can be converted to and from a string, and the class provides a constructor with a String argument, the editor offers the text representation of the data value for the initial editing value. You can then edit the contents.

Table 18-13. *Default JTable Editors*

Class	Editor	Information
Boolean	JCheckBox	Centered
Object	JTextField	Left-aligned

Creating a Simple Cell Editor

As a simple example of changing a non-String cell in a JTable, you can provide a fixed set of color choices to the user. Then when the user picks a color, you have the appropriate Color value to return to the table model. The DefaultCellEditor offers a JComboBox for just this situation. After configuring the ListCellRenderer for the JComboBox to display colors properly, you have a TableCellEditor for picking colors. Figure 18-13 shows how this might appear.

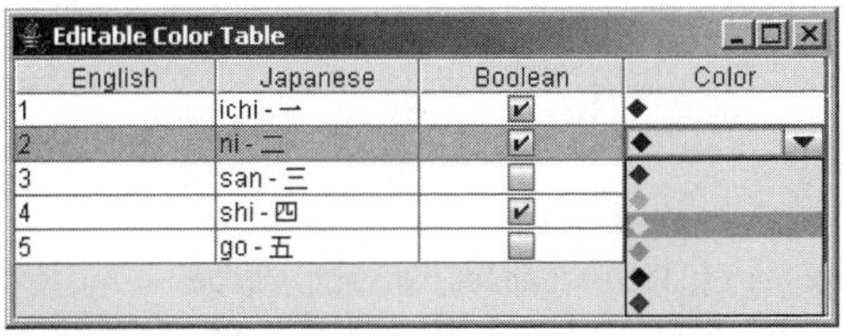

Figure 18-13. *JComboBox color editor*

■**Tip** Any time you can predefine all the choices, you can use the JComboBox as your editor through DefaultCellEditor.

Listing 18-14 shows the class that represents the TableCellRenderer for the Color column of the example shown in Figure 18-13 and the ListCellRenderer for the JComboBox TableCellEditor. Because of the many similarities of the two renderer components, their definitions are combined into one class.

Listing 18-14. *JComboBox As Table Cell Renderer*

```
import java.awt.*;
import javax.swing.*;
import javax.swing.table.*;

public class ComboTableCellRenderer
    implements ListCellRenderer, TableCellRenderer {
  DefaultListCellRenderer listRenderer = new DefaultListCellRenderer();
  DefaultTableCellRenderer tableRenderer = new DefaultTableCellRenderer();

  private void configureRenderer(JLabel renderer, Object value) {
    if ((value != null) && (value instanceof Color)) {
      renderer.setIcon(new DiamondIcon((Color)value));
      renderer.setText("");
    } else {
      renderer.setIcon(null);
      renderer.setText((String)value);
    }
  }
```

```
  public Component getListCellRendererComponent(JList list, Object value,
      int index, boolean isSelected, boolean cellHasFocus) {
    listRenderer =
      (DefaultListCellRenderer)listRenderer.getListCellRendererComponent(
        list, value, index, isSelected, cellHasFocus);
    configureRenderer(listRenderer, value);
    return listRenderer;
  }

  public Component getTableCellRendererComponent(JTable table, Object value,
      boolean isSelected, boolean hasFocus, int row, int column) {
    tableRenderer =
      (DefaultTableCellRenderer)tableRenderer.getTableCellRendererComponent(
        table, value, isSelected, hasFocus, row, column);
    configureRenderer(tableRenderer, value);
    return tableRenderer;
  }
}
```

To demonstrate the use of this new combined renderer and show a simple table cell editor, the program shown in Listing 18-15 creates a data model in which one of the columns is a Color. After installing the renderer twice and setting up the table cell editor, the table can be shown and the Color column can be edited.

Listing 18-15. *Table Cell Editor Sample*

```
import javax.swing.*;
import javax.swing.table.*;
import java.awt.*;

public class EditableColorColumn {

  public static void main(String args[]) {
    Runnable runner = new Runnable() {
      public void run() {
        Color choices[] = {Color.RED, Color.ORANGE, Color.YELLOW,
          Color.GREEN, Color.BLUE, Color.MAGENTA};
        ComboTableCellRenderer renderer = new ComboTableCellRenderer();
        JComboBox comboBox = new JComboBox(choices);
        comboBox.setRenderer(renderer);
        TableCellEditor editor = new DefaultCellEditor(comboBox);

        JFrame frame = new JFrame("Editable Color Table");
        frame.setDefaultCloseOperation(JFrame.EXIT_ON_CLOSE);
        TableModel model = new ColorTableModel();
        JTable table = new JTable(model);
```

```
        TableColumn column = table.getColumnModel().getColumn(3);
        column.setCellRenderer(renderer);
        column.setCellEditor(editor);

        JScrollPane scrollPane = new JScrollPane(table);
        frame.add(scrollPane, BorderLayout.CENTER);
        frame.setSize(400, 150);
        frame.setVisible(true);
      }
    };
    EventQueue.invokeLater(runner);
  }
}
```

Listing 18-16 shows the table model used for this example and the next one.

Listing 18-16. *Table Model*

```
import java.awt.*;
import javax.swing.table.*;

public class ColorTableModel extends AbstractTableModel {

  Object rowData[][] = {
    {"1", "ichi - \u4E00", Boolean.TRUE, Color.RED},
    {"2", "ni - \u4E8C", Boolean.TRUE, Color.BLUE},
    {"3", "san - \u4E09", Boolean.FALSE, Color.GREEN},
    {"4", "shi - \u56DB", Boolean.TRUE, Color.MAGENTA},
    {"5", "go - \u4E94", Boolean.FALSE, Color.PINK},
  };
  String columnNames[] = {"English", "Japanese", "Boolean", "Color"};
  public int getColumnCount() {
    return columnNames.length;
  }
  public String getColumnName(int column) {
    return columnNames[column];
  }
  public int getRowCount() {
    return rowData.length;
  }
  public Object getValueAt(int row, int column) {
    return rowData[row][column];
  }
  public Class getColumnClass(int column) {
    return (getValueAt(0, column).getClass());
  }
```

```
  public void setValueAt(Object value, int row, int column) {
    rowData[row][column]=value;
  }
  public boolean isCellEditable(int row, int column) {
    return (column != 0);
  }
}
```

Creating a Complex Cell Editor

Although the previous example demonstrates how to provide a fixed set of choices to the user in a combo box TableCellEditor, offering the JColorChooser as an option seems to be a better choice (at least, in the case of color selection). When defining your own TableCellEditor, you must implement the single TableCellEditor method to get the appropriate component. You must also implement the seven methods of the CellEditor because they manage and notify a list of CellEditorListener objects, as well as control when a cell is editable. Starting with an AbstractCellEditor subclass makes defining your own TableCellEditor much simpler.

By extending the AbstractCellEditor class, only the getCellEditorValue() method from the CellEditor methods requires customization for the editor. Doing that and providing a JButton that pops up a JColorChooser when clicked provides the entire editor component. Listing 18-17 shows the code for this custom editor.

Listing 18-17. *JColorChooser As Table Cell Editor*

```
import java.awt.*;
import java.awt.event.*;
import javax.swing.*;
import javax.swing.table.*;
public class ColorChooserEditor extends AbstractCellEditor
    implements TableCellEditor {

  private JButton delegate = new JButton();

  Color savedColor;

  public ColorChooserEditor() {
    ActionListener actionListener = new ActionListener() {
      public void actionPerformed (ActionEvent actionEvent) {
        Color color = JColorChooser.showDialog(
          delegate, "Color Chooser", savedColor);
        ColorChooserEditor.this.changeColor(color);
      }
    };
    delegate.addActionListener(actionListener);
  }
```

```
public Object getCellEditorValue() {
  return savedColor;
}

private void changeColor(Color color) {
  if (color != null) {
    savedColor = color;
    delegate.setIcon(new DiamondIcon(color));
  }
}

public Component getTableCellEditorComponent (JTable table, Object value,
    boolean isSelected, int row, int column) {
  changeColor((Color)value);
  return delegate;
}
}
```

Figure 18-14 shows the ColorChooserEditor in action, with the associated table in the background.

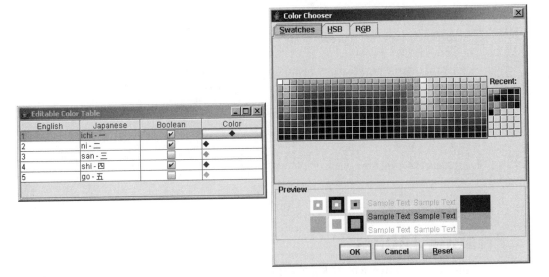

Figure 18-14. *Pop-up color editor*

A sample program using the new ColorChooserEditor is shown in Listing 18-18. The example reuses the earlier ColorTableModel data model shown in Listing 18-16. Setting up the ColorChooserEditor simply involves setting the TableCellEditor for the appropriate column.

Listing 18-18. *Testing Another Custom Table Cell Editor*

```java
import java.awt.*;
import javax.swing.*;
import javax.swing.table.*;

public class ChooserTableSample {

  public static void main(String args[]) {

    Runnable runner = new Runnable() {
      public void run() {
        JFrame frame = new JFrame("Editable Color Table");
        frame.setDefaultCloseOperation(JFrame.EXIT_ON_CLOSE);
        TableModel model = new ColorTableModel();
        JTable table = new JTable(model);

        TableColumn column = table.getColumnModel().getColumn(3);

        ComboTableCellRenderer renderer = new ComboTableCellRenderer();
        column.setCellRenderer(renderer);

        TableCellEditor editor = new ColorChooserEditor();
        column.setCellEditor(editor);

        JScrollPane scrollPane = new JScrollPane(table);
        frame.add(scrollPane, BorderLayout.CENTER);
        frame.setSize(400, 150);
        frame.setVisible(true);
      }
    };
    EventQueue.invokeLater(runner);
  }
}
```

Printing Tables

One of the newer features with JDK 5.0 is also one of the easiest to use: the ability to print tables. Through the simple method of `public boolean print() throws PrinterException` of JTable, you can print a large table across multiple pages on the printer. It will even spread the columns across multiple pages if you don't like the default behavior of fitting the table's entire width on each page.

To demonstrate this behavior, Listing 18-19 takes the basic JTable sample code used to generate Figure 18-1, adds some more rows to the table, and adds a print button.

Listing 18-19. *Printing Tables Sample*

```java
import javax.swing.*;
import java.awt.*;
import java.awt.event.*;
import java.awt.print.*;

public class TablePrint {
  public static void main(String args[]) {
    final Object rows[][] = {
      {"one",   "ichi - \u4E00"},
      {"two",   "ni - \u4E8C"},
      {"three", "san - \u4E09"},
      {"four",  "shi - \u56DB"},
      {"five",  "go - \u4E94"},
      {"six",   "roku - \u516D"},
      {"seven", "shichi - \u4E03"},
      {"eight", "hachi - \u516B"},
      {"nine",  "kyu - \u4E5D"},
      {"ten",   "ju - \u5341"},
... Repeat section at least 10 times ...
      {"one",   "ichi - \u4E00"},
      {"two",   "ni - \u4E8C"},
      {"three", "san - \u4E09"},
      {"four",  "shi - \u56DB"},
      {"five",  "go - \u4E94"},
      {"six",   "roku - \u516D"},
      {"seven", "shichi - \u4E03"},
      {"eight", "hachi - \u516B"},
      {"nine",  "kyu - \u4E5D"},
      {"ten",   "ju - \u5341"},
    };
    final Object headers[] = {"English", "Japanese"};
    Runnable runner = new Runnable() {
      public void run() {
        JFrame frame = new JFrame("Table Printing");
        frame.setDefaultCloseOperation(JFrame.EXIT_ON_CLOSE);
        final JTable table = new JTable(rows, headers);
        JScrollPane scrollPane = new JScrollPane(table);
        frame.add(scrollPane, BorderLayout.CENTER);
        JButton button = new JButton("Print");
        ActionListener printAction = new ActionListener() {
          public void actionPerformed(ActionEvent e) {
```

```
            try {
              table.print();
            } catch (PrinterException pe) {
              System.err.println("Error printing: " + pe.getMessage());
            }
          }
        };
        button.addActionListener(printAction);
        frame.add(button, BorderLayout.SOUTH);
        frame.setSize(300, 150);
        frame.setVisible(true);
      }
    };
    EventQueue.invokeLater(runner);
  }
}
```

After clicking the Print button, the user is prompted with a typical printer selection dialog box, as shown in Figure 18-15.

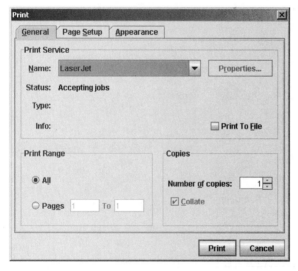

Figure 18-15. *Print dialog box displayed by the printing tables example*

After the user clicks the Print button in the Print dialog box, the printing begins. A dialog window like the one shown in Figure 18-16 appears for each page printed.

Figure 18-16. *Printing progress dialog box displayed by the printing tables example*

Yes, it really is that easy to print a multiple-page table with JDK 5.0. The print() method returns a boolean, so you can discover if the user canceled the operation.

For those looking for more control over the printing operation, there are several other overloaded versions of the print() method of JTable. Like the simple print() method, they all can throw a PrinterException.

One print() version lets you specify the print mode:

```
public boolean print(JTable.PrintMode printMode)
```

The JTable.PrintMode argument is an enumeration of FIT_WIDTH and NORMAL. When not specified with the no-argument version of print(), the default is FIT_WIDTH.

Another version lets you specify a page header or footer:

```
public boolean print(JTable.PrintMode printMode, MessageFormat headerFormat,
  MessageFormat footerFormat)
```

MessageFormat comes from the java.text package. The one argument to the header and footer formatting string is the page number. To display the page number, include {0} in your formatting string where you want the page number to appear. Both will appear centered on the page, with the header in a larger font. To demonstrate, change the print() call in Listing 18-19 to the following (and add an import line):

```
MessageFormat headerFormat = new MessageFormat("Page {0}");
MessageFormat footerFormat = new MessageFormat("- {0} -");
table.print(JTable.PrintMode.FIT_WIDTH, headerFormat, footerFormat);
```

The final print() version is the all inclusive one, allowing you to not show the printer dialog box and configure what the default print request attribute set entails, such as how many copies to print.

```
public boolean print(JTable.PrintMode printMode, MessageFormat headerFormat,
MessageFormat footerFormat, boolean showPrintDialog,
PrintRequestAttributeSet attr, boolean interactive)
```

For those times when you desire no user interaction to print, consider using this last version.

Summary

In this chapter, you explored the inner depths of the JTable component. You looked at customizing the TableModel, TableColumnModel, and ListSelectionModel for the JTable. You delved into both the abstract and concrete implementations of the different table models. In addition, you examined the inner elements of the various table models, such as the TableColumn and JTableHeader classes. You also looked into how to customize the display and editing of the JTable cells by providing a custom TableCellRenderer and TableCellEditor. Finally, you learned about printing tables via the new print() method.

In Chapter 19, you'll explore the drag-and-drop architecture of the JFC/Swing component set.

CHAPTER 19

■ ■ ■

Drag-and-Drop Support

Drag-and-drop support allows a user to highlight something in one program or area of the screen, select it, and relocate it to another program or area of the screen. For example, in Microsoft Word, you can select a paragraph and drag it to a new location.

As Java has evolved, not only has the printing support changed with nearly every release, but so has the drag-and-drop support. The last major change in drag-and-drop support happened with the J2SE 1.4 release. Prior releases had support that was extremely difficult to use, especially to get proper drag-and-drop behavior for complex (nontext) types. The JDK 5.0 version adds some bug fixes and enhancements to drag-and-drop support.

You can implement drag-and-drop within your Java program in three ways:

- For the components that come with built-in support, just enable it by calling their setDragEnabled() method with an argument of true. Those components are JColorChooser, JFileChooser, JList, JTable, JTree, and all the subclasses of JTextComponent, except JPasswordField.

- For components without built-in support, you typically just need to configure the TransferHandler for that component.

- You can also go directly to the classes found in the java.awt.dnd package. Thanks to the built-in support and configurability, this approach is rarely necessary.

Built-in Drag-and-Drop Support

Table 19-1 shows the components that offer built-in support for drag-and-drop. Initially, only dropping is enabled for the components that support it, but after calling setDragEnabled(true) for the component in question, you can enable dragging, too, if it's supported. The drag-and-drop capabilities of the Java platform involve the underlying java.awt.datatransfer package to move data around. Classes in this package allow you to describe the type of data to transfer.

Table 19-1. *Components with Built-in Support for Drag-and-Drop*

Component	Drag	Drop
JColorChooser	X	X
JEditorPane	X	X
JFileChooser	X	
JFormattedTextField	X	X
JList	X	
JPasswordField		X
JTable	X	
JTextArea	X	X
JTextField	X	X
JTextPane	X	X
JTree	X	

■Note For security reasons, you cannot drag text out of a JPasswordField component.

For the JColorChooser component, what you drag is a java.awt.Color object. The other oddball of the bunch is the JFileChooser, where you literally drag a java.io.File object around and drop it into a drop target. If the drop target doesn't support working with File objects, a string representing the path is dropped instead.

As a simple demonstration, Listing 19-1 shows a program with two JColorChooser components on a single screen. The setDragEnabled(true) call is made for both choosers, so you can drag-and-drop colors between the two components with minimal coding effort.

Listing 19-1. *Dragging-and-Dropping Colors Across JColorChooser Components*

```
import javax.swing.*;
import java.awt.*;

public class DoubleColor {
  public static void main(String args[]) {
    Runnable runner = new Runnable() {
      public void run() {
        JFrame frame = new JFrame("Double Color Choosers");
        frame.setDefaultCloseOperation(JFrame.EXIT_ON_CLOSE);

        JColorChooser left = new JColorChooser();
        left.setDragEnabled(true);
        frame.add(left, BorderLayout.WEST);
```

```
        JColorChooser right = new JColorChooser();
        right.setDragEnabled(true);
        frame.add(right, BorderLayout.EAST);

        frame.pack();
        frame.setVisible(true);
      }
    };
    EventQueue.invokeLater(runner);
  }
}
```

Figure 19-1 shows this program in action, after dragging several colors. The drag area is the Preview panel at the bottom. Dropping doesn't adjust the Recent list on the right side of each color chooser, and you can drop across different color chooser panels.

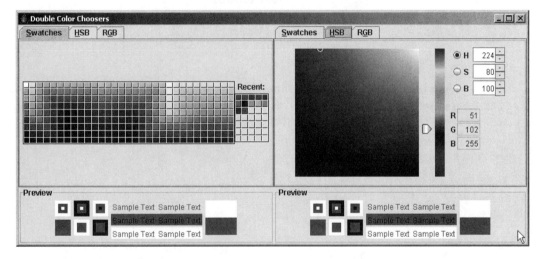

Figure 19-1. *Dueling JColorChoosers*

TransferHandler Class

The magic of drag-and-drop happens because of the java.swing.TransferHandler class, introduced with the J2SE 1.4 release. "What's magical about it?" you might ask. With this class, you can pick which property you would like to be transferable in a drag-and-drop operation.

When you call setDragEnabled(true) to tell a component to support the drag gesture, the component asks the installed TransferHandler what to transfer. If you don't like the default object being transferred, you can call the setTransferHandler() method of the component, passing in an appropriate replacement. You can also call setTransferHandler() when you want to enable drag-and-drop support for a component that doesn't come with support built in.

The TransferHandler class has one public constructor:

```
public TransferHandler(String property)
```

The parameter to the constructor represents the property of the component that you wish to transfer. In other words, you identify the JavaBeans component property as the transferable object for the drag-and-drop operation.

For instance, to transfer the text label of a JLabel, you would do the following:

```
JLabel label = new JLabel("Hello, World");
label.setTransferHandler(new TransferHandler("text"));
```

Since JLabel doesn't have a setDragEnabled() method, you must tell the component what the start of the drag gesture is. Typically, this would be pressing the mouse button, so you would also need to add a MouseListener to the button. When you tell the TransferHandler to exportAsDrag(), that enables the dragging operation for the component.

```
MouseListener listener = new MouseAdapter() {
  public void mousePressed(MouseEvent me) {
    JComponent comp = (JComponent)me.getSource();
    TransferHandler handler = comp.getTransferHandler();
    handler.exportAsDrag(comp, me, TransferHandler.COPY);
  }
};
button.addMouseListener(listener);
```

The default behavior when the drop gesture happens—releasing the mouse in this example—would drop what was registered with the TransferHandler.

Listing 19-2 demonstrates a program that enables drag-and drop for the text in a JLabel.

Listing 19-2. *Dragging Text from a JLabel*

```
import javax.swing.*;
import java.awt.*;
import java.awt.event.*;

public class DragLabel {
  public static void main(String args[]) {
    Runnable runner = new Runnable() {
      public void run() {
        JFrame frame = new JFrame("Drag Label");
        frame.setDefaultCloseOperation(JFrame.EXIT_ON_CLOSE);

        JLabel label = new JLabel("Hello, World");
        label.setTransferHandler(new TransferHandler("foreground"));
        MouseListener listener = new MouseAdapter() {
          public void mousePressed(MouseEvent me) {
            JComponent comp = (JComponent)me.getSource();
            TransferHandler handler = comp.getTransferHandler();
            handler.exportAsDrag(comp, me, TransferHandler.COPY);
          }
        };
```

```
      label.addMouseListener(listener);
      frame.add(label, BorderLayout.SOUTH);

      JTextField text = new JTextField();
      frame.add(text, BorderLayout.NORTH);

      frame.setSize(300, 150);
      frame.setVisible(true);
    }
  };
  EventQueue.invokeLater(runner);
 }
}
```

Figure 19-2 shows this program during the drag operation. Notice how the cursor changes to indicate the operation.

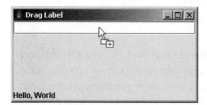

Figure 19-2. *Dragging text from a JLabel to a JTextField*

If instead of dragging the text of the JLabel, you wanted to drag the foreground color, the only change to the program would be to the setTransferHandler() line:

```
label.setTransferHandler(new TransferHandler("foreground"));
```

Then, assuming you had some place to drop the color, as in the program in Listing 19-1, you could drag the foreground color out of the label to the JColorChooser, and then drop the color out of the JColorChooser into the JLabel. Since the TransferHandler is registered for a specific property of the component, there is no explicit code necessary to handle dropping. Instead, the setter method for the property passed into the handler constructor is notified of the change.

Drag-and-Drop Support for Images

If you wish to transfer something other than a simple property, you need to create an implementation of the Transferable interface, found in the java.awt.datatransfer package. Transferable implementations are typically meant for transfers through the clipboard, but by having your implementation be a TransferHandler subclass, you can use it to drag-and-drop the object. The three methods of the Transferable interface are shown here:

```
public interface Transferable{
  public DataFlavor[] getTransferDataFlavors();
  public boolean isDataFlavorSupported(DataFlavor);
  public Object getTransferData(java.awt.datatransfer.DataFlavor)
    throws UnsupportedFlavorException, IOException;
}
```

One common application for this is the ability to transfer images. The exposed property of a JLabel or JButton is a javax.swing.Icon object, not a java.awt.Image object. While you can certainly transfer Icon objects within and across Java programs, a more useful behavior is to transfer Image objects to external entities, like Paint Shop Pro or Photoshop.

To create a transferable image object, the ImageSelection class, you must implement the three Transferable interface methods and override four methods of TransferHandler: getSourceActions(), canImport(), createTransferable(), and importData().

■**Note** The class for transferring strings is called StringSelection.

The getSourceActions() method needs to report which actions you are going to support. By default, this is the TransferHandler.COPY operation when a property is set via the constructor, or TransferHandler.NONE when it is not. Since the ImageSelection class implicitly uses the icon property to get the component's image, just have the method return TransferHandler.COPY:

```
public int getSourceActions(JComponent c) {
  return TransferHandler.COPY;
}
```

There is also a TransferHandler.MOVE operation, but you typically don't want the image to be removed from the label it was copied from.

You pass the canImport() method a component and an array of DataFlavor objects. You need to verify that the component is supported and one of the flavors in the array matches the supported set:

```
private static final DataFlavor flavors[] = {DataFlavor.imageFlavor};
...
public boolean canImport(JComponent comp, DataFlavor flavor[]) {
  if (!(comp instanceof JLabel) && !(comp instanceof AbstractButton)) {
    return false;
  }
  for (int i=0, n=flavor.length; i<n; i++) {
    for (int j=0, m=flavors.length; j<m; j++) {
      if (flavor[i].equals(flavors[j])) {
        return true;
      }
    }
  }
  return false;
}
```

The createTransferable() method returns a reference to the Transferable implementation. When the clipboard paste operation is executed, or the drop gesture is performed while dragging, the Transferable object will be notified to get the object to transfer.

```java
public Transferable createTransferable(JComponent comp) {
  // Clear
  image = null;

  if (comp instanceof JLabel) {
    JLabel label = (JLabel)comp;
    Icon icon = label.getIcon();
    if (icon instanceof ImageIcon) {
      image = ((ImageIcon)icon).getImage();
      return this;
    }
  } else if (comp instanceof AbstractButton) {
    AbstractButton button = (AbstractButton)comp;
    Icon icon = button.getIcon();
    if (icon instanceof ImageIcon) {
      image = ((ImageIcon)icon).getImage();
      return this;
    }
  }
  return null;
}
```

The importData() method is called when data is dropped into the component or pasted from the clipboard. It has two parameters: a JComponent to paste the clipboard data and the clipboard data via a Transferable object. Assuming the method receives a format supported by the Java platform, the component associated with the transfer handler gets a new image to display.

```java
public boolean importData(JComponent comp, Transferable t) {
  if (comp instanceof JLabel) {
    JLabel label = (JLabel)comp;
    if (t.isDataFlavorSupported(flavors[0])) {
      try {
        image = (Image)t.getTransferData(flavors[0]);
        ImageIcon icon = new ImageIcon(image);
        label.setIcon(icon);
        return true;
      } catch (UnsupportedFlavorException ignored) {
      } catch (IOException ignored) {
      }
    }
  } else if (comp instanceof AbstractButton) {
    AbstractButton button = (AbstractButton)comp;
```

```
    if (t.isDataFlavorSupported(flavors[0])) {
      try {
        image = (Image)t.getTransferData(flavors[0]);
        ImageIcon icon = new ImageIcon(image);
        button.setIcon(icon);
        return true;
      } catch (UnsupportedFlavorException ignored) {
      } catch (IOException ignored) {
      }
    }
  }
  return false;
}
```

Putting all this code together with the three methods implemented for the Transferable interface produces Listing 19-3.

Listing 19-3. *Implementing a Draggable Image*

```java
import java.awt.*;
import java.awt.image.*;
import java.awt.datatransfer.*;
import java.io.*;
import javax.swing.*;

public class ImageSelection extends TransferHandler
    implements Transferable {

  private static final DataFlavor flavors[] = {DataFlavor.imageFlavor};

  private Image image;

  public int getSourceActions(JComponent c) {
    return TransferHandler.COPY;
  }

  public boolean canImport(JComponent comp, DataFlavor flavor[]) {
    if (!(comp instanceof JLabel) && !(comp instanceof AbstractButton)) {
      return false;
    }
    for (int i=0, n=flavor.length; i<n; i++) {
      for (int j=0, m=flavors.length; j<m; j++) {
        if (flavor[i].equals(flavors[j])) {
          return true;
        }
      }
    }
```

```
      return false;
    }

    public Transferable createTransferable(JComponent comp) {
      // Clear
      image = null;

      if (comp instanceof JLabel) {
        JLabel label = (JLabel)comp;
        Icon icon = label.getIcon();
        if (icon instanceof ImageIcon) {
          image = ((ImageIcon)icon).getImage();
          return this;
        }
      } else if (comp instanceof AbstractButton) {
        AbstractButton button = (AbstractButton)comp;
        Icon icon = button.getIcon();
        if (icon instanceof ImageIcon) {
          image = ((ImageIcon)icon).getImage();
          return this;
        }
      }
      return null;
    }

    public boolean importData(JComponent comp, Transferable t) {
      if (comp instanceof JLabel) {
        JLabel label = (JLabel)comp;
        if (t.isDataFlavorSupported(flavors[0])) {
          try {
            image = (Image)t.getTransferData(flavors[0]);
            ImageIcon icon = new ImageIcon(image);
            label.setIcon(icon);
            return true;
          } catch (UnsupportedFlavorException ignored) {
          } catch (IOException ignored) {
          }
        }
      } else if (comp instanceof AbstractButton) {
        AbstractButton button = (AbstractButton)comp;
        if (t.isDataFlavorSupported(flavors[0])) {
          try {
            image = (Image)t.getTransferData(flavors[0]);
            ImageIcon icon = new ImageIcon(image);
            button.setIcon(icon);
            return true;
```

```
        } catch (UnsupportedFlavorException ignored) {
        } catch (IOException ignored) {
        }
      }
    }
    return false;
  }

  // Transferable
  public Object getTransferData(DataFlavor flavor) {
    if (isDataFlavorSupported(flavor)) {
      return image;
    }
    return null;
  }

  public DataFlavor[] getTransferDataFlavors() {
    return flavors;
  }

  public boolean isDataFlavorSupported(DataFlavor flavor) {
    return flavors[0].equals(flavor);
  }
}
```

To test this, you need to create a program with a draggable JLabel or AbstractButton subclass. This is basically the same program as shown in Listing 19-2, but with only a JLabel with an associated image located in the center of the screen.

Listing 19-4. *Draggable Image*

```
import javax.swing.*;
import java.awt.*;
import java.awt.event.*;

public class DragImage {
  public static void main(String args[]) {
    Runnable runner = new Runnable() {
      public void run() {
        JFrame frame = new JFrame("Drag Image");
        frame.setDefaultCloseOperation(JFrame.EXIT_ON_CLOSE);
```

```
      Icon icon = new ImageIcon("dog.jpg");
      JLabel label = new JLabel(icon);
      label.setTransferHandler(new ImageSelection());
      MouseListener listener = new MouseAdapter() {
        public void mousePressed(MouseEvent me) {
          JComponent comp = (JComponent)me.getSource();
          TransferHandler handler = comp.getTransferHandler();
          handler.exportAsDrag(comp, me, TransferHandler.COPY);
        }
      };
      label.addMouseListener(listener);
      frame.add(new JScrollPane(label), BorderLayout.CENTER);

      frame.setSize(300, 150);
      frame.setVisible(true);
    }
  };
  EventQueue.invokeLater(runner);
 }
}
```

Figure 19-3 shows the program in action.

Figure 19-3. *Dragging-and-dropping an image*

Summary

Drag-and-drop support in Swing is rich and varied. You get quite a bit of behavior for free for several of the standard components. If you need more, you can dig down a layer at a time until you expose the features you need.

Typically, you don't need to dig all the way into `java.awt.dnd` classes like `DragSourceDragEvent`, `DragSourceDropEvent`, or `DropTargetDragEvent` (to name a few). They are there and doing their work under the covers, but you don't need to worry about them. Instead, drag-and-drop support is typically delegated to the `TransferHandler` associated with a property of the component to drag. Just `setDragEnabled(true)` on that component, and you're ready to go. You can also set up drag-and-drop support for other items, such as images, by creating an implementation of the `Transferable` interface.

In the next chapter, you'll explore Swing's pluggable look and feel architecture. You'll learn how to customize your user interfaces without changing the code for the program.

CHAPTER 20

■■■

The Pluggable Look and Feel Architecture

In Chapter 19, you examined Swing's drag-and-drop support. In this chapter, you will take an in-depth look at the pluggable look and feel (PLAF) architecture that's available when you're working with the Swing component library.

All aspects of the Swing components are Java-based. Therefore, no native source code exists, as there is with the AWT component set. If you don't like the way the components are, you can change them, and you often have many ways to do so.

The abstract LookAndFeel class is the root class for a specific look and feel. Each one of the installable look and feel classes, as they're described by the UIManager.LookAndFeelInfo class, must be a subclass of the LookAndFeel class. The LookAndFeel subclass describes the default appearance of Swing components for that specific look and feel.

The set of currently installed look and feel classes is provided by the UIManager class, which also manages the default display properties of all the components for a specific LookAndFeel. These display properties are managed within a special UIDefaults hash table. The display properties are either tagged with the empty UIResource interface or are UI delegates and therefore a subclass of the ComponentUI class. These properties can be stored as either UIDefaults.LazyValue objects or UIDefaults.ActiveValue objects, depending on their usage.

LookAndFeel Class

Implementations of the abstract LookAndFeel class describe how each of the Swing components will appear and how the user will interact with them. Each component's appearance is controlled by a UI delegate, which serves as both the view and the controller in the MVC architecture. Each of the predefined look and feel classes is contained within its own package, along with its associated UI delegate classes. When configuring the current look and feel, you can use one of the predefined look and feel classes or create your own. When you create your own look and feel, you can build on an existing look and feel, such as the BasicLookAndFeel class and its UI delegates, instead of creating all the UI delegates from scratch. Figure 20-1 shows the class hierarchy of the predefined look and feel classes.

Figure 20-1. *LookAndFeel class hierarchy diagram*

Each of the look and feel classes has six properties, as shown in Table 20-1.

Table 20-1. *LookAndFeel Properties*

Property Name	Data Type	Access
defaults	UIDefaults	Read-only
description	String	Read-only
ID	String	Read-only
name	String	Read-only
nativeLookAndFeel	boolean	Read-only
supportedLookAndFeel	boolean	Read-only

These properties are all read-only and mostly describe the look and feel. The defaults property is slightly different, though. Once you get its UIDefaults value, you can then modify its state directly through its own methods. In addition, the UIDefaults for a LookAndFeel can be directly accessed and modified through the UIManager class.

The nativeLookAndFeel property enables you to determine if a particular look and feel implementation is the native look and feel for the user's operating system. For instance, the WindowsLookAndFeel is native to any system running one of the Microsoft Windows operating systems. The supportedLookAndFeel property tells you if a particular look and feel implementation can be used. With the WindowsLookAndFeel implementation, this particular look and feel class is supported only if the current operating system is Microsoft Windows. Where available, the MacLookAndFeel implementation is supported only on MacOS computers. MotifLookAndFeel and MetalLookAndFeel are native look and feel classes that are not locked to a particular operating system.

Listing the Installed Look and Feel Classes

To discover which look and feel classes are installed in your current environment, ask the UIManager, as shown in Listing 20-1. The UIManager has a UIManager.LookAndFeelInfo[] getInstalledLookAndFeels() method that returns an array of objects providing the textual name (public String getName()) and class name (public String getClassName()) for all the installed look and feel classes.

Listing 20-1. *Listing Looking and Feel Classes*

```
import javax.swing.*;

public class ListPlafs {
  public static void main (String args[]) {
    UIManager.LookAndFeelInfo plaf[] = UIManager.getInstalledLookAndFeels();
    for (int i=0, n=plaf.length; i<n; i++) {
      System.out.println("Name: " + plaf[i].getName());
      System.out.println("  Class name: " + plaf[i].getClassName());
    }
  }
}
```

Running the program might generate the following output. Your current system configuration and/or changes to future versions of the Swing libraries could alter this result somewhat.

```
Name: Metal
  Class name: javax.swing.plaf.metal.MetalLookAndFeel
Name: CDE/Motif
  Class name: com.sun.java.swing.plaf.motif.MotifLookAndFeel
Name: Windows
  Class name: com.sun.java.swing.plaf.windows.WindowsLookAndFeel
```

■Note Ocean is not a look and feel in and of itself. Instead, it is a built-in theme of the Metal look and feel. This theme happens to be the default for Metal.

Changing the Current Look and Feel

Once you know which look and feel classes are available on your system, you can have your programs use any one of them. The UIManager has two overloaded setLookAndFeel() methods for changing the installed look and feel class:

```
public static void setLookAndFeel(LookAndFeel newValue) throws
  UnsupportedLookAndFeelException
```

```
public static void setLookAndFeel(String className) throws
  ClassNotFoundException, InstantiationException, IllegalAccessException,
  UnsupportedLookAndFeelException
```

Although the first version might seem to be the more logical choice, the second one is the more frequently used version. When you ask for the installed look and feel classes with UIManager.getInstalledLookAndFeels(), you get back the class names as strings of the objects, not instances. Because of the exceptions that can occur when changing the look and feel, you need to place the setLookAndFeel() call within a try/catch block. If you're changing the look and feel for an existing window, you need to tell the component to update its appearance with a call to the `public static void updateComponentTreeUI(Component rootComponent)` method of `SwingUtilities`. If the component hasn't been created yet, this isn't necessary.

The following source fragment demonstrates changing a look and feel:

```
try {
  UIManager.setLookAndFeel(finalLafClassName);
  SwingUtilities.updateComponentTreeUI(frame);
} catch (Exception exception) {
  JOptionPane.showMessageDialog (
    frame, "Can't change look and feel",
    "Invalid PLAF", JOptionPane.ERROR_MESSAGE);
}
```

Figure 20-2 illustrates the results of a demonstration program that can change the look and feel at runtime through either a `JComboBox` or `JButton` component. Frequently, you won't want to allow a user to change the look and feel; you may just want to set the look and feel at startup time.

Metal   Motif

Figure 20-2. *Before and after changing the look and feel*

Listing 20-2 shows the complete source of the program shown in Figure 20-2.

Listing 20-2. *Changing the Look and Feel*

```
import java.awt.*;
import java.awt.event.*;
import javax.swing.*;
import javax.swing.plaf.*;

public class ChangeLook {

  public static void main (String args[]) {
    Runnable runner = new Runnable() {
      public void run() {

        final JFrame frame = new JFrame("Change Look");
        frame.setDefaultCloseOperation(JFrame.EXIT_ON_CLOSE);
```

```
ActionListener actionListener = new ActionListener() {
  public void actionPerformed(ActionEvent actionEvent) {
    Object source = actionEvent.getSource();
    String lafClassName = null;
    if (source instanceof JComboBox) {
      JComboBox comboBox = (JComboBox)source;
      lafClassName = (String)comboBox.getSelectedItem();
    } else if (source instanceof JButton) {
      lafClassName = actionEvent.getActionCommand();
    }
    if (lafClassName != null) {
      final String finalLafClassName = lafClassName;
      Runnable runnable = new Runnable() {
        public void run() {
          try {
            UIManager.setLookAndFeel(finalLafClassName);
            SwingUtilities.updateComponentTreeUI(frame);
          } catch (Exception exception) {
            JOptionPane.showMessageDialog (
              frame, "Can't change look and feel",
                "Invalid PLAF", JOptionPane.ERROR_MESSAGE);
          }
        }
      };
      EventQueue.invokeLater(runnable);
    }
  }
};

UIManager.LookAndFeelInfo looks[] =
  UIManager.getInstalledLookAndFeels();

DefaultComboBoxModel model = new DefaultComboBoxModel();
JComboBox comboBox = new JComboBox(model);

JPanel panel = new JPanel();

for (int i=0, n=looks.length; i<n; i++) {
  JButton button = new JButton(looks[i].getName());
  model.addElement(looks[i].getClassName());
  button.setActionCommand(looks[i].getClassName());
  button.addActionListener(actionListener);
  panel.add(button);
}

comboBox.addActionListener(actionListener);
```

```
        frame.add(comboBox, BorderLayout.NORTH);
        frame.add(panel, BorderLayout.SOUTH);
        frame.setSize(350, 150);
        frame.setVisible(true);
      }
    };
    EventQueue.invokeLater(runner);
  }
}
```

■**Note** Notice that the actual look and feel change is made in a call to `EventQueue.invokeLater()`. This is necessary because the handling of the current event must finish before you can change the look and feel, and the change must happen on the event queue.

Besides programmatically changing the current look and feel, you can start up a program from the command line with a new look and feel. Just set the `swing.defaultlaf` system property to the look and feel class name. For instance, the following startup line would start the ChangeLook program, making the Motif look and feel the initial look and feel.

```
java -Dswing.defaultlaf=com.sun.java.swing.plaf.motif.MotifLookAndFeel ChangeLook
```

If you want a different default look and feel every time a program starts up, you can create a file, `swing.properties`, under the Java runtime directory (`jre` by default) with the appropriate setting. The `swing.properties` file needs to be in the `lib` directory of the Java runtime directory (`jre/lib`). For instance, the following line would cause the initial look and feel to be Motif all the time, unless changed programmatically or from the command line.

```
swing.defaultlaf=com.sun.java.swing.plaf.motif.MotifLookAndFeel
```

In addition to the `swing.defaultlaf` setting, the `swing.properties` file supports several other entries, as listed in Table 20-2. Each property allows you to override the default settings for the predefined look and feel setup. The auxiliary and multiplexing look and feel classes support accessibility, among other things. They will be discussed later in this chapter, in the "Using an Auxiliary Look and Feel" section.

Table 20-2. *Swing Properties File Entries*

Property Name	Default Value When Unset
swing.defaultlaf	javax.swing.plaf.metal.MetalLookAndFeel
swing.auxiliarylaf	None
swing.plaf.multiplexinglaf	javax.swing.plaf.multi.MultiLookAndFeel
swing.installedlafs	Metal, Motif, Windows
swing.installedlaf.*.name	N/A
swing.installedlaf.*.class	N/A

■**Tip** The `swing.installedlafs` and `swing.auxiliarylaf` property settings are comma-separated lists of installed look and feel classes.

You may notice that the Synth class shown in the class hierarchy in Figure 20-1 is not listed in the default set of installed look and feel classes. Synth requires a secondary configuration file; it isn't something you can just switch to on the fly without defining the custom appearances. This base look and feel class provides the framework for customization. You'll learn how to use the Synth look and feel in the "SynthLookAndFeel Class" section later in this chapter.

The `WindowsClassicLookAndFeel` is used when the Windows XP style is not appropriate for the user's platform or the `swing.noxp` system property is set.

Customizing the Current Look and Feel

In Chapter 3, you looked at the MVC architecture as well as how the Swing components combine the view and the controller into a UI delegate. Now, you will delve into the UI delegate for the Swing components. Basically, if you don't like how a Swing component looks, you tell the `UIManager` to change it, and then it will never again look the way it did.

UIManager Class

Whenever you need to create a Swing component, the `UIManager` class acts as a proxy to get information about the currently installed look and feel. That way, if you want to install a new look and feel or change an existing one, you don't need to tell the Swing components directly; you just inform the `UIManager`.

Each discussion of components in earlier chapters has been accompanied by a table of all the settings that can be changed through the `UIManager`. In addition, this book's appendix provides an alphabetical listing of all available settings for JDK 5.0. Once you know the property string for the setting you want to change, you call the `public Object UIManager.put(Object key, Object value)` method, which changes the property setting and returns the previous setting (if one existed). For instance, the following line changes the background to red for `JButton` components. After you put a new setting into the `UIManager` class lookup table, any components created in the future will use the new value, `Color.RED`.

```
UIManager.put("Button.background", Color.RED);
```

Once you place new settings into the lookup table for the `UIManager`, the new settings will be used when you create a new Swing component. Old components aren't automatically updated; you must call their `public void updateUI()` method if you want them to be individually updated (or call `updateComponentTreeUI()` to update a whole window of components). If you're creating your own components, or you're just curious about the current setting for one of the different component properties, you can ask the `UIManager` with one of the methods listed in Table 20-3.

Table 20-3. *UIManager UIDefaults Getter Methods*

Method Name	Return Type
getObject(Object key)	Object
getBorder(Object key)	Border
getColor(Object key)	Color
getDimension(Object key)	Dimension
getFont(Object key)	Font
getIcon(Object key)	Icon
getInsets(Object key)	Insets
getInt(Object key)	int
getString(Object key)	String
getUI(JComponent component)	ComponentUI

Each of these methods, except getUI(), has a second version that accepts a Locale argument for localization support.

In addition to the defaults property, which is used when you call the different put() and get() methods, the UIManager has eight class-level properties. These are listed in Table 20-4, which includes two entries for lookAndFeel, with two different setter methods.

Table 20-4. *UIManager Class Properties*

Property Name	Data Type	Access
auxiliaryLookAndFeels	LookAndFeel[ ]	Read-only
crossPlatformLookAndFeelClassName	String	Read-only
defaults	UIDefaults	Read-only
installedLookAndFeels	UIManager.LookAndFeelInfo[ ]	Read-write
lookAndFeel	LookAndFeel	Read-write
lookAndFeel	String	Write-only
lookAndFeelDefaults	UIDefaults	Read-only
propertyChangeListeners	PropertyChangeListener[ ]	Read-only
systemLookAndFeelClassName	String	Read-only

The systemLookAndFeelClassName property allows you to determine what the specific look and feel class name is for the user's operating system. The crossPlatformLookAndFeelClassName property enables you to find out what class name, by default, represents the cross-platform look and feel: javax.swing.plaf.metal.MetalLookAndFeel. Initially, the lookAndFeelDefaults property and the defaults property are equivalent. When you want to make changes to the look and feel, you use the defaults property. That way, the settings for a predefined look and feel don't change.

UIManager.LookAndFeelInfo Class

When you ask the UIManager for the list of installed look and feel classes, you're returned an array of UIManager.LookAndFeelInfo objects. From this array, you can find out the descriptive name of the look and feel (from the name property of the LookAndFeel implementation), as well as the class name for the implementation. As Table 20-5 shows, the two settings are read-only.

Table 20-5. *UIManager.LookAndFeelInfo Properties*

Property Name	Data Type	Access
className	String	Read-only
name	String	Read-only

UIDefaults Class

The LookAndFeel classes and the UIManager use a special UIDefaults hash table to manage the Swing component properties that depend on the look and feel. The special behavior is that whenever a new setting is placed in the hash table with put(), a PropertyChangeEvent is generated and any registered PropertyChangeListener objects are notified. Many of the BasicLookAndFeel classes automatically register the UI delegate to be interested in property change events at the appropriate times.

If you need to change a number of properties at once, you can use the public void putDefaults(Object keyValueList[]) method, which causes only one notification event. With putDefaults(), the key/value entries alternate in a single-dimension array. For instance, to cause buttons to have a default background color of pink and a foreground color of magenta, you would use the following:

```
Object newSettings[] = {"Button.background", Color.PINK,
                        "Button.foreground", Color.MAGENTA};
UIDefaults defaults = UIManager.getDefaults();
defaults.putDefaults(newSettings);
```

Because UIDefaults is a Hashtable subclass, you can discover all the installed settings by using an Enumeration to loop through all the keys or values. To simplify things a little, Listing 20-3 presents a program that lists the properties sorted within a JTable. It reuses several of the table sorting classes from Chapter 18.

■**Note** Feel free to change the UIDefaults property lister program in Listing 20-3 to support modification of property values.

Listing 20-3. *Listing UIDefault Properties*

```java
import javax.swing.*;
import javax.swing.table.*;
import java.awt.*;
import java.awt.event.*;
import java.util.*;

public class ListProperties {
  static class CustomTableModel extends AbstractTableModel {
    Vector<Object> keys = new Vector<Object>();
    Vector<Object> values = new Vector<Object>();
    private static final String columnNames[] = {"Property String", "Value"};

    public int getColumnCount() {
      return columnNames.length;
    }

    public String getColumnName(int column) {
      return columnNames[column];
    }

    public int getRowCount() {
      return keys.size();
    }

    public Object getValueAt(int row, int column) {
      Object returnValue = null;
      if (column == 0) {
        returnValue = keys.elementAt(row);
      } else if (column == 1) {
        returnValue = values.elementAt(row);

      }
      return returnValue;
    }

    public synchronized void uiDefaultsUpdate(UIDefaults defaults) {
      Enumeration newKeys = defaults.keys();
      keys.removeAllElements();
      while (newKeys.hasMoreElements()) {
        keys.addElement(newKeys.nextElement());
      }
```

```java
      Enumeration newValues = defaults.elements();
      values.removeAllElements();
      while (newValues.hasMoreElements()) {
        values.addElement(newValues.nextElement());
      }

      fireTableDataChanged();
    }
  }

  public static void main(String args[]) {
    Runnable runner = new Runnable() {
      public void run() {
        final JFrame frame = new JFrame("List Properties");
        frame.setDefaultCloseOperation(JFrame.EXIT_ON_CLOSE);

        final CustomTableModel model = new CustomTableModel();
        model.uiDefaultsUpdate(UIManager.getDefaults());
        TableSorter sorter = new TableSorter(model);

        JTable table = new JTable(sorter);
        TableHeaderSorter.install(sorter, table);

        table.setAutoResizeMode(JTable.AUTO_RESIZE_ALL_COLUMNS);

        UIManager.LookAndFeelInfo looks[] =
          UIManager.getInstalledLookAndFeels();

        ActionListener actionListener = new ActionListener() {
          public void actionPerformed(ActionEvent actionEvent) {
            final String lafClassName = actionEvent.getActionCommand();
            Runnable runnable = new Runnable() {
              public void run() {
                try {
                  UIManager.setLookAndFeel(lafClassName);
                  SwingUtilities.updateComponentTreeUI(frame);
                  model.uiDefaultsUpdate(UIManager.getDefaults());
                } catch (Exception exception) {
                  JOptionPane.showMessageDialog (
                    frame, "Can't change look and feel",
                    "Invalid PLAF", JOptionPane.ERROR_MESSAGE);
                }
              }
            };
            EventQueue.invokeLater(runnable);
          }
        };
```

```
        JToolBar toolbar = new JToolBar();
        for (int i=0, n=looks.length; i<n; i++) {
          JButton button = new JButton(looks[i].getName());
          button.setActionCommand(looks[i].getClassName());
          button.addActionListener(actionListener);
          toolbar.add(button);
        }

        frame.add(toolbar, BorderLayout.NORTH);
        JScrollPane scrollPane = new JScrollPane(table);
        frame.add(scrollPane, BorderLayout.CENTER);
        frame.setSize(400, 400);
        frame.setVisible(true);
      }
    };
    EventQueue.invokeLater(runner);
  }
}
```

Figure 20-3 shows an example of running the property lister.

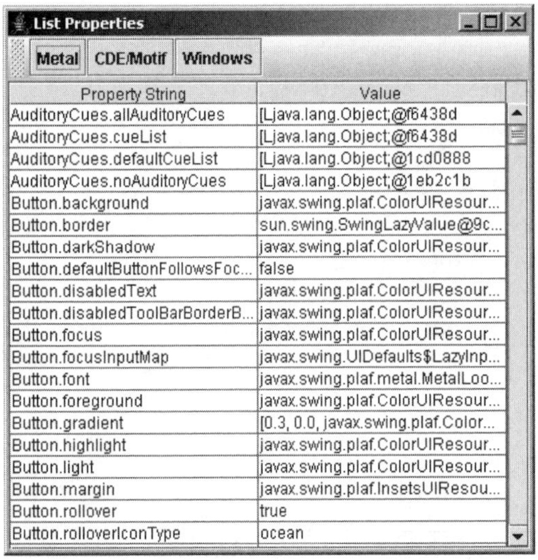

Figure 20-3. *Sample property lister display*

■Tip To reset a property to the default for the currently installed look and feel, set it to `null`. This will cause the component to get the original default from the look and feel.

UIResource Interface

Every UIDefaults setting for the predefined look and feel classes uses a special marker interface, UIResource, that lets the UI delegate determine if a default value has been overridden. If you've changed a specific setting to a new value (for example, the Button.background setting to Color.PINK), then the UIManager won't replace this setting when the installed look and feel changes. This is also true of a call to setBackground(Color.PINK). Only when the value for a specific property implements the UIResource interface will the setting change when the look and feel changes.

The javax.swing.plaf package contains many classes that implement the UIResource interface. For example, the ColorUIResource class treats Color objects as UIResource elements. Table 20-6 lists all of the predefined UIResource components available for customizing the installed look and feel.

Table 20-6. *UIResource Collection*

UIResource Implementation	Wrapped Class/Interface
ActionMapUIResource	ActionMap
BasicBorders.ButtonBorder	Border
BasicBorders.FieldBorder	Border
BasicBorders.MarginBorder	Border
BasicBorders.MenuBarBorder	Border
BasicBorders.RadioButtonBorder	Border
BasicBorders.RolloverButtonBorder	Border
BasicBorders.SplitPaneBorder	Border
BasicBorders.ToggleButtonBorder	Border
BasicComboBoxEditor.UIResource	ComboBoxEditor
BasicComboBoxRenderer.UIResource	ListCellRenderer
BasicTextUI.BasicCaret	Caret
BasicTextUI.BasicHighlighter	Highlighter
BorderUIResource	Border
BorderUIResource.BevelBorderUIResource	Border
BorderUIResource.CompoundBorderUIResource	Border
BorderUIResource.EmptyBorderUIResource	Border
BorderUIResource.EtchedBorderUIResource	Border
BorderUIResource.LineBorderUIResource	Border
BorderUIResource.MatteBorderUIResource	Border
BorderUIResource.TitledBorderUIResource	Border
ColorUIResource	Color

Table 20-6. *UIResource Collection (Continued)*

UIResource Implementation	Wrapped Class/Interface
ComponentInputMapUIResource	InputMap / ComponentInputMap
DefaultListCellRenderer.UIResource	ListCellRenderer
DefaultMenuLayout	LayoutManager / LayoutManager2
DefaultTableCellRenderer.UIResource	TableCellRenderer
DimensionUIResource	Dimension
FontUIResource	Font
IconUIResource	Icon
InputMapUIResource	InputMap
InsetsUIResource	Insets
JScrollPane.ScrollBar	JScrollBar
MetalBorders.ButtonBorder	Border
MetalBorders.Flush3DBorder	Border
MetalBorders.InternalFrameBorder	Border
MetalBorders.MenuBarBorder	Border
MetalBorders.MenuItemBorder	Border
MetalBorders.OptionDialogBorder	Border
MetalBorders.PaletteBorder	Border
MetalBorders.PopupMenuBorder	Border
MetalBorders.RolloverButtonBorder	Border
MetalBorders.ScrollPaneBorder	Border
MetalBorders.TextFieldBorder	Border
MetalBorders.ToggleButtonBorder	Border
MetalBorders.ToolBarBorder	Border
MetalCheckBoxIcon	Icon
MetalComboBoxEditor.UIResource	ComboBoxEditor
MetalIconFactory.PaletteCloseIcon	Icon
ScrollPaneLayout.UIResource	ScrollPaneLayout

The following code demonstrates the use of the ColorUIResource class to set the button background to a value that *will* change when the installed look and feel changes.

```
Color background = new ColorUIResource(Color.PINK);
UIManager.put("Button.background", background);
```

Without the wrapped `ColorUIResource` constructor call, the color would remain pink after a look and feel change.

■**Note** Use of the specific `UIResource` implementation classes tends to be limited to those times when you're creating a custom look and feel or customizing an existing one.

UIDefaults.ActiveValue, UIDefaults.LazyValue, and UIDefaults.ProxyLazyValue Classes

Besides implementing the `UIResource` interface, elements in the `UIDefaults` lookup table can be lazy or active if they implement one of the inner classes of `UIDefaults`: `LazyValue` or `ActiveValue`. For example, since `Color` and `Dimension` objects aren't very resource-intensive, when such an element is placed in the `UIDefaults` table, the `Color` or `Dimension` is created and placed in the table immediately—this is called *active*. On the other hand, in the case of a resource like an `Icon`, and especially an `ImageIcon`, you want to defer creating and loading the icon class file until it's needed—this is called *lazy*. Another example of an element you might want to make lazy is a `ListCellRenderer` that needs a separate renderer for every `JList` component. Because you don't know how many renderers you'll need or which renderer will be installed, you can defer creation to a later time and get a unique version of the current renderer whenever you ask for one.

Take a look at the `public Object makeIcon(Class baseClass, String imageFile)` method of `LookAndFeel`. In order to handle the late loading of icon image files, the `LookAndFeel` class can automatically create a `LazyValue` class for loading an `Icon`. Because the image file won't be loaded until later, you need to provide the icon loader with the location of the icon image file (`baseClass`) and the file name (`imageFile`).

```
Object iconObject = LookAndFeel.makeIcon(this.getClass(), "World.gif");
UIManager.put("Tree.leafIcon", iconObject);
```

Next, look at the `UIDefaults.LazyValue` definition and create a lazy version of the `DiamondIcon`.

```
public interface UIDefaults.LazyValue {
  public Object createValue(UIDefaults table);
}
```

In classes that implement the `LazyValue` interface, their constructors need to save any information that will be passed along to the real constructor through the `createValue()` interface method. To help with creating custom lazy values, the `UIDefaults.ProxyLazyValue` class provides a way of saving this information to pass along. There are four ways to use `ProxyLazyValue` to defer object creation, which each uses reflection to create the actual object, getting the specific how (and what) from the constructor arguments:

- `public UIDefaults.ProxyLazyValue(String className)`: If object creation will use the no-argument constructor, just pass the class name as an argument.

- `public UIDefaults.ProxyLazyValue(String className, String method)`: If object creation will use a factory method that doesn't require arguments, pass the factory method along with the class name.

- public UIDefaults.ProxyLazyValue(String className, Object[] arguments): If object creation will use a constructor that requires some arguments, pass the class name and array of arguments to the ProxyLazyValue constructor.

- public UIDefaults.ProxyLazyValue(String className, String method, Object[] arguments): If object creation will use a factory method that does require arguments, pass the factory method name along with the class name and array of arguments.

For the lazy diamond icon implementation that's about to be created, you'll need to pass state information that consists of the color, selected state, and dimensions.

To test the lazy diamond icon, you can associate an instance of UIDefaults.ProxyLazyValue to the Tree.openIcon setting, as follows:

```
Integer fifteen = new Integer(15);
Object lazyArgs[] = new Object[] { Color.GREEN, Boolean.TRUE, fifteen, fifteen} ;
Object lazyDiamond = new UIDefaults.ProxyLazyValue("DiamondIcon", lazyArgs);
UIManager.put("Tree.openIcon", lazyDiamond);
```

Together with the previous change of the Tree.leafIcon setting to the World.gif icon, and using the default tree data model, the tree would look like Figure 20-4.

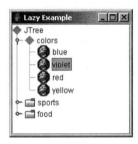

Figure 20-4. *A tree created with lazy values*

Listing 20-4 shows the source code for the example that generated Figure 20-4 by using the two lazy values.

Listing 20-4. *Lazy UIResources*

```
import java.awt.*;
import java.awt.event.*;
import javax.swing.*;
import javax.swing.plaf.*;

public class LazySample {
  public static void main (String args[]) {
    Runnable runner = new Runnable() {
      public void run() {
        JFrame frame = new JFrame("Lazy Example");
        frame.setDefaultCloseOperation(JFrame.EXIT_ON_CLOSE);
```

```
        Object iconObject =
          LookAndFeel.makeIcon(LazySample.class, "World.gif");
        UIManager.put("Tree.leafIcon", iconObject);

        Integer fifteen = new Integer(15);
        Object lazyArgs[] =
          new Object[] {Color.GREEN, Boolean.TRUE, fifteen, fifteen};
        Object lazyDiamond =
          new UIDefaults.ProxyLazyValue("DiamondIcon", lazyArgs);
        UIManager.put("Tree.openIcon", lazyDiamond);

        JTree tree = new JTree();
        JScrollPane scrollPane = new JScrollPane(tree);

        frame.add(scrollPane, BorderLayout.CENTER);
        frame.setSize(200, 200);
        frame.setVisible(true);
      }
    };
    EventQueue.invokeLater(runner);
  }
}
```

Unlike lazy values, active values act like instance-creation factories. Every time they're asked for a value with one of the get() methods of UIManager, a new instance is created and returned. The interface method is the same as that for the UIDefault.LazyValue interface; only the interface name is different.

```
public interface UIDefaults.ActiveValue {
  public Object createValue(UIDefaults table);
}
```

To demonstrate, Listing 20-5 defines a factory that constructs JLabel components. The text of the label will function as a counter to show how many labels have been created. Whenever the createValue() method is called, a new JLabel is created.

Listing 20-5. *Active Label Factory*

```
import javax.swing.*;

public class ActiveLabel implements UIDefaults.ActiveValue {
  private int counter = 0;

  public Object createValue(UIDefaults defaults) {
    JLabel label = new JLabel(""+counter++);
    return label;
  }
}
```

To create the component, you need to install the `ActiveLabel` class with `UIManager.put()`. Once the class is installed, each call to `get()` the key out of the `UIManager` results in a new component being created.

```
UIManager.put(LABEL_FACTORY, new ActiveLabel());
...
JLabel label = (JLabel)UIManager.get(LABEL_FACTORY);
```

Figure 20-5 shows the component in use. Whenever the button is clicked, the `UIManager.get()` method is called, and the component is added to the screen.

Figure 20-5. *Using active values*

Listing 20-6 shows the source for the sample program in Figure 20-5.

Listing 20-6. *Active UIResources*

```java
import java.awt.*;
import java.awt.event.*;
import javax.swing.*;

public class ActiveSample {

  private static final String LABEL_FACTORY = "LabelFactory";

  public static void main (String args[]) {
    Runnable runner = new Runnable() {
      public void run() {
        JFrame frame = new JFrame("Active Example");
        frame.setDefaultCloseOperation(JFrame.EXIT_ON_CLOSE);

        UIManager.put(LABEL_FACTORY, new ActiveLabel());

        final JPanel panel = new JPanel();

        JButton button = new JButton("Get");
```

```
      ActionListener actionListener = new ActionListener() {
        public void actionPerformed(ActionEvent actionEvent) {
          JLabel label = (JLabel)UIManager.get(LABEL_FACTORY);
          panel.add(label);
          panel.revalidate();
        }
      };
      button.addActionListener(actionListener);

      frame.add(panel, BorderLayout.CENTER);
      frame.add(button, BorderLayout.SOUTH);
      frame.setSize(200, 200);
      frame.setVisible(true);
    }
  };
  EventQueue.invokeLater(runner);
  }
}
```

■**Note** There is a special lazy class for creating an `InputMap` lazily: the `UIDefaults.LazyInputMap` class.

Using Client Properties

If changing all the `UIResource` properties known to the `UIManager` still doesn't give you the look and feel you desire, some of the UI delegate classes can provide their own customized capabilities that are hidden from API views. These customized capabilities are provided as client properties and are accessible from two `JComponent` methods: `public final Object getClientProperty(Object key)` and `public final void putClientProperty(Object key, Object value)`. Keep in mind that the key and value here are of type `Object`. While typically the key will be a `String` and the value an object of any type, the key can also be an object of any type.

Client properties tend to be attributes of the component that are specific to the look and feel. Instead of subclassing the look and feel delegate to expose a property through a pair of getter/setter methods, the get/put client property methods provide access to a *private* instance-level lookup table to store a new property setting. In addition, as when making changes to the `UIDefaults`, modifying the client properties of a component notifies any registered property change listeners of the component.

Most of the specific client properties have already been discussed throughout this book with their respective components. Table 20-7 provides a single resource for finding all the configurable client properties. The left column shows the class the property is used in, excluding the package name. The middle column shows the property name, which can include both the raw text string and any class constants that are available. The right column contains the class type to store with the property name. If the class type is a `String`, a list of valid values is provided, if appropriate.

Table 20-7. *Swing's Client Properties*

Class Accessed By	Property Name	Type
AbstractButton	hideActionText	Boolean
AbstractButton	html / BasicHTML.propertyKey	View
BasicButtonListener	initialDefaultButton	JButton
BasicButtonUI	html / BasicHTML.propertyKey	View
BasicComboBoxUI	JComboBox.isTableCellEditor / BasicComboBoxUI.IS_TABLE_CELL_EDITOR	Boolean
BasicEditorPaneUI	JEditorPane.honorDisplayProperties / JEditorPane.HONOR_DISPLAY_PROPERTIES	Boolean
BasicEditorPaneUI	JEditorPane.w3cLengthUnits / JEditorPane.W3C_LENGTH_UNITS	Boolean
BasicHTML	html.base / BasicHTML.documentBaseKey	URL
BasicHTML	html / BasicHTML.propertyKey	View
BasicHTML	html.disable / BasicHTML.htmlDisable	Boolean
BasicLabelUI	html / BasicHTML.propertyKey	View
BasicListUI	List.isFileList	Boolean
BasicMenuItemUI	html / BasicHTML.propertyKey	View
BasicMenuItemUI	maxTextWidth / BasicMenuItemUI.MAX_TEXT_WIDTH	Integer
BasicMenuItemUI	maxAccWidth / BasicMenuItemUI.MAX_ACC_WIDTH	Integer
BasicPopupMenuUI	doNotCancelPopup	Boolean
BasicRadioButtonUI	html / BasicHTML.propertyKey	View
BasicRootPaneUI	temporaryDefaultButton	Object
BasicSliderUI	Slider.paintThumbArrowShape	Boolean
BasicTabbedPaneUI	__index_to_remove__	Integer
BasicTableUI	Table.isFileList	Boolean
BasicTextUI	JPasswordField.cutCopyAllowed	Boolean
BasicToggleButtonUI	html / BasicHTML.propertyKey	View
BasicToolBarUI	JToolBar.focusedCompIndex / BasicToolBarUI.FOCUSED_COMP_INDEX	Integer
BasicToolBarUI	JToolBar.isRollover / BasicToolBarUI.IS_ROLLOVER	Boolean
BasicToolTipUI	html / BasicHTML.propertyKey	View
BluePrintEngine	__arrow_direction__	Integer
DefaultCaret	caretAspectRatio	Number
DefaultCaret	caretWidth	Integer

Table 20-7. *Swing's Client Properties (Continued)*

Class Accessed By	Property Name	Type
DefaultCaret	JPasswordField.cutCopyAllowed	Boolean
DefaultDesktopManager	JDesktopPane.dragMode	String; valid values are null, outline, and faster
FrameView	charset	String
GTKFileChooserUI	GTKFileChooser.showDirectoryIcons	Boolean
GTKFileChooserUI	GTKFileChooser.showFileIcons	Boolean
JInternalFrame	wasIconOnce / DefaultDesktopManager.HAS_BEEN_ICONIFIED_PROPERTY	Boolean
JComponent	nextFocus / JComponent.NEXT_FOCUS	Component
JComponent	InputVerifier / JComponent.INPUT_VERIFIER_KEY	InputVerifier
JComponent	_WhenInFocusedWindow / JComponent.WHEN_IN_FOCUSED_WINDOW_BINDINGS	Hashtable
JComponent	ToolTipText / JComponent.TOOL_TIP_TEXT_KEY	String
JComponent	TransferHandler / JComponent.TRANSFER_HANDLER_KEY	TransferHandler
JComponent	AncestorNotifier / JComponent.ANCESTOR_NOTIFIER_KEY	AncestorNotifier
JComponent	labeledBy / JLabel.LABELED_BY_PROPERTY	JComponent / Accessible
JEditorPane	charset	String
JLabel	html / BasicHTML.propertyKey	View
JLayeredPane	layeredContainerLayer / JLayeredPane.LAYER_PROPERTY	Integer
JPasswordField	JPasswordField.cutCopyAllowed	Boolean
JPopupMenu	JPopupMenu.firePopupMenuCanceled	Boolean
JTable	JTable.autoStartsEdit	Boolean
JTable	terminateEditOnFocusLost	Boolean
JToolBar	JToolBar.isRollover	Boolean
MetalBorders	NoButtonRollover / MetalBorders.NO_BUTTON_ROLLOVER	Boolean
MetalBorders	JInternalFrame.messageType	Integer
MetalFileChooserUI	FileChooser.useShellFolder	Boolean
MetalIconFactory	paintActive	Boolean
MetalInternalFrame➥ TitlePane	JInternalFrame.messageType	Integer

Table 20-7. *Swing's Client Properties (Continued)*

Class Accessed By	Property Name	Type
MetalInternalFrameUI	JInternalFrame.isPalette / MetalInternalFrameUI.IS_PALETTE	Boolean
MetalRadioButtonUI	html / BasicHTML.propertyKey	View
MetalScrollBarUI	JScrollBar.isFreeStanding / MetalScrollBarUI.FREE_STANDING_PROP	Boolean
MetalSliderUI	JSlider.isFilled / MetalSliderUI.SLIDER_FILL	Boolean
MetalTreeUI	JTree.lineStyle / MetalTreeUI.LineStyle	String; valid values are Angled (MetalTreeUI.LEG_LINE_STYLE_STRING), Horizontal (MetalTreeUI.HORIZ_STYLE_STRING), and None (MetalTreeUI.NO_STYLE_STRING)
MotifGraphicsUtils	html / BasicHTML.propertyKey	View
MotifGraphicsUtils	maxAccWidth / MotifGraphicsUtils.MAX_ACC_WIDTH	Integer
PopupFactory	__force_heavy_weight_popup__ / PopupFactory.forceHeavyWeightPopupKey	Boolean
SpringLayout	SpringLayout.class	SpringLayout.Constraints
SwingUtilities	html / BasicHTML.propertyKey	View
SynthEditorPaneUI	JEditorPane.honorDisplayProperties / JEditorPane.HONOR_DISPLAY_PROPERTIES	Boolean
SynthGraphicUtils	html / BasicHTML.propertyKey	View
SynthMenuItemUI	html / BasicHTML.propertyKey	View
SynthToolTipUI	html / BasicHTML.propertyKey	View
WindowsDesktopManager	JInternalFrame.frameType	String; valid values are null and optionDialog
WindowsFileChooserUI	FileChooser.useShellFolder	Boolean
WindowsSliderUI	Slider.paintThumbArrowShape	Boolean
WindowsToolBarUI	XPStyle.subclass	String

■**Note** Many of the properties in Table 20-7 are used internally by the specific component delegate implementations, and you'll never need to use them. Other properties, such as the drag mode for the desktop manager, were interim means to add capabilities while keeping the API unaltered until a new JDK version was released.

To demonstrate the use of client properties, the following two lines change the JToolBar.isRollover attribute of a JToolBar to Boolean.TRUE. Other toolbars might not want this attribute set to Boolean.TRUE and would therefore leave that setting at Boolean.FALSE.

```
JToolBar toolbar = new JToolBar();
toolbar.putClientProperty("JToolBar.isRollover", Boolean.TRUE);
```

Creating a New UI Delegate

Sometimes, modifying a few of the UIResource elements of the Swing component isn't quite enough to get the appearance or behavior you desire. When this is the case, you need to create a new UI delegate for the component. Each Swing component has its own UI delegate for controlling the view and controller aspects of its MVC architecture.

Table 20-8 provides a listing of the Swing components, the abstract class that describes the UI delegate for each component, and the specific implementations for the predefined look and feel classes. For instance, calling the getUIClassID() method of a JToolBar will return the class ID string of "ToolBarUI" for its UI delegate. If you then ask the UIManager for the specific implementation of this UI delegate for the currently installed look and feel with a call to UIManager.get("ToolBarUI"), an implementation of the abstract ToolBarUI class is returned. Therefore, if you want to develop a custom look and feel for the JToolBar component, you must create an implementation of the abstract ToolBarUI class.

Table 20-8. *Swing Component Delegates*

Swing Component	Class ID String	Implementation Class
JButton	ButtonUI	ButtonUI
JCheckBox	CheckBoxUI	ButtonUI
JCheckBoxMenuItem	CheckBoxMenuItemUI	MenuItemUI
JColorChooser	ColorChooserUI	ColorChooserUI
JComboBox	ComboBoxUI	ComboBoxUI
JComponent	n/a	ComponentUI
JDesktopPane	DesktopPaneUI	DesktopPaneUI
JEditorPane	EditorPaneUI	TextUI
JFileChooser	FileChooserUI	FileChooserUI
JFormattedTextField	FormattedTextFieldUI	TextUI
JInternalFrame	InternalFrameUI	InternalFrameUI
JInternalFrame.JDesktopIcon	DesktopIconUI	DesktopIconUI
JLabel	LabelUI	LabelUI
JList	ListUI	ListUI
JMenu	MenuUI	MenuItemUI
JMenuBar	MenuBarUI	MenuBarUI

Table 20-8. *Swing Component Delegates (Continued)*

Swing Component	Class ID String	Implementation Class
JMenuItem	MenuItemUI	MenuItemUI
JOptionPane	OptionPaneUI	OptionPaneUI
JPanel	PanelUI	PanelUI
JPasswordField	PasswordFieldUI	TextUI
JPopupMenu	PopupMenuUI	PopupMenuUI
JPopupMenu.Separator	PopupMenuSeparatorUI	SeparatorUI
JProgressBar	ProgressBarUI	ProgressBarUI
JRadioButton	RadioButtonUI	ButtonUI
JRadioButtonMenuItem	RadioButtonMenuItemUI	MenuItemUI
JRootPane	RootPaneUI	RootPaneUI
JScrollBar	ScrollBarUI	ScrollBarUI
JScrollPane	ScrollPaneUI	ScrollPaneUI
JSeparator	SeparatorUI	SeparatorUI
JSlider	SliderUI	SliderUI
JSpinner	SpinnerUI	SpinnerUI
JSplitPane	SplitPaneUI	SplitPaneUI
JTabbedPane	TabbedPaneUI	TabbedPaneUI
JTable	TableUI	TableUI
JTableHeader	TableHeaderUI	TableHeaderUI
JTextArea	TextAreaUI	TextUI
JTextField	TextFieldUI	TextUI
JTextPane	TextPaneUI	TextUI
JToggleButton	ToggleButtonUI	ButtonUI
JToolBar	ToolBarUI	ToolBarUI
JToolBar.Separator	ToolBarSeparatorUI	SeparatorUI
JToolTip	ToolTipUI	ToolTipUI
JTree	TreeUI	TreeUI
JViewport	ViewportUI	ViewportUI

■Note Classes such as JWindow, JFrame, and JApplet are heavyweight components and therefore lack a UI delegate.

The PopupComboSample example from Chapter 13 demonstrated the creation of a new UI delegate. Listing 20-7 is a slightly changed customized ComboBoxUI piece, where the normal down arrow for showing the drop-down menu is replaced with a right arrow.

Listing 20-7. *Customized ComboBoxUI*

```
import javax.swing.*;
import javax.swing.plaf.*;
import javax.swing.plaf.basic.*;

public class MyComboBoxUI extends BasicComboBoxUI {
  public static ComponentUI createUI(JComponent c) {
    return new MyComboBoxUI();
  }
  protected JButton createArrowButton() {
    JButton button = new BasicArrowButton(BasicArrowButton.EAST);
    return button;
  }
}
```

To use the new UI delegate, you just need to create the class and associate it with the component using the setUI() method.

```
JComboBox comboBox = new JComboBox(labels);
comboBox.setUI((ComboBoxUI)MyComboBoxUI.createUI(comboBox));
```

Changing the PopupComboSample from Chapter 13 (Listing 13-16) to show two combo boxes, with the custom ComboBoxUI on the top and the bottom without, results in the screen shown in Figure 20-6.

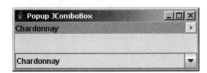

Figure 20-6. *Using the new ComboBoxUI*

Listing 20-8 shows the updated source used to produce Figure 20-6.

Listing 20-8. *Using Customized ComboBoxUI*

```
import java.awt.*;
import javax.swing.*;
import javax.swing.plaf.*;

public class PopupComboSample {
  public static void main(String args[]) {
    Runnable runner = new Runnable() {
      public void run() {
        String labels[] = {"Chardonnay", "Sauvignon", "Riesling", "Cabernet",
          "Zinfandel", "Merlot", "Pinot Noir", "Sauvignon Blanc", "Syrah",
          "Gewürztraminer"};
        JFrame frame = new JFrame("Popup JComboBox");
        frame.setDefaultCloseOperation(JFrame.EXIT_ON_CLOSE);

        JComboBox comboBox = new JComboBox(labels);
        comboBox.setMaximumRowCount(5);
        comboBox.setUI((ComboBoxUI)MyComboBoxUI.createUI(comboBox));
        frame.add(comboBox, BorderLayout.NORTH);

        JComboBox comboBox2 = new JComboBox(labels);
        frame.add(comboBox2, BorderLayout.SOUTH);

        frame.setSize (300, 100);
        frame.setVisible (true);
      }
    };
    EventQueue.invokeLater(runner);
  }
}
```

If you want to use the new UI delegate for all components, you can let the UIManager know about the delegate before creating the components, instead of manually calling setUI() after creating one. In the example in Listing 20-8, you would add the following line:

```
UIManager.put("ComboBoxUI", "MyComboBoxUI")
```

If you did this, both combo boxes would then look the same.

The actual creation of the UI delegate is done somewhat indirectly, as shown by Figure 20-7. A call to the component constructor asks the UIManager for the UI delegate class. The UIManager maintains the list of delegates in its defaults property, a UIDefaults object. When the UIDefaults is queried for the delegate, it goes back to the component to ask which delegate is needed. After it finds the appropriate delegate implementation, the UIDefaults object tells the ComponentUI to create it, resulting in the actual UI delegate class being created. Once the UI delegate is created, it needs to be configured for the state of the specific model.

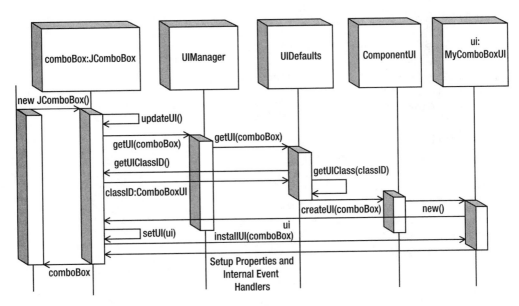

Figure 20-7. *UI delegate creation sequence diagram*

Creating a New Look and Feel

Unless a company wants you to customize everything to provide a unique experience, it typically isn't necessary to create a whole new look and feel from scratch. Usually, developers make minor modifications to an existing look and feel by providing some customized UI delegates. However, if you do want to create a new look and feel class, you just need to create a subclass of the LookAndFeel class. You still must provide the UI delegates, but their classes can now be more hidden from the Swing components, since their usage will not be known directly from the javax.swing component class.

Using the WindowsLookAndFeel on a Non-Windows Machine

To demonstrate the creation of a new look and feel class, let's create a look and feel implementation that cancels out the platform requirement for the Windows UI delegate. By simply overriding the public boolean isSupportedLookAndFeel() method to return true, you effectively remove the platform requirement for the Windows look and feel class.

■**Note** The Java license expressly forbids you from delivering applications that remove the platform requirements for the Windows look and feel class. So, you can work through the example here, as long as you don't deliver it.

The class definition in Listing 20-9 shows how simple the creation of a new look and feel implementation can be.

Listing 20-9. *Custom Look and Feel*

```
import javax.swing.UIDefaults;
import com.sun.java.swing.plaf.windows.WindowsLookAndFeel;
public class MyWindows extends WindowsLookAndFeel {
  public String getID() {
    return "MyWindows";
  }
  public String getName() {
    return "MyWindows Look and Feel";
  }
  public String getDescription() {
    return "The MyWindows Look and Feel";
  }
  public boolean isNativeLookAndFeel() {
    return false;
  }
  public boolean isSupportedLookAndFeel() {
    return true;
  }
}
```

If you use this Swing class on a non-Windows machine, you can get the look and feel to be the Windows look and feel. Just set your look and feel to be MyWindows and make the look and feel class file available. The class file only needs to be available in your CLASSPATH and will be started with the following command line:

```
java -Dswing.defaultlaf=MyWindows ClassFile
```

For the Windows look and feel change to work properly, you need to provide the image files used for the icons of the look and feel from within the icons subdirectory of the MyWindows directory structure. Table 20-9 lists those icons appropriate to the predefined look and feel types. The MyWindows look and feel needs all of the Windows image files.

▪**Note** Although Ocean is a theme of Metal, it does provide its own set of images.

Table 20-9. *Look and Feel Image Files*

File Name	Basic	Metal	Motif	Ocean	Windows
close-pressed.gif				X	
close.gif				X	
collapsed-rtl.gif				X	
collapsed.gif				X	
computer.gif				X	

Table 20-9. *Look and Feel Image Files (Continued)*

File Name	Basic	Metal	Motif	Ocean	Windows
Computer.gif					X
DesktopIcon.gif			X		
DetailsView.gif					X
directory.gif				X	
Directory.gif					X
Error.gif		X	X		X
error.png				X	
expanded.gif				X	
file.gif				X	
File.gif					X
floppy.gif				X	
FloppyDrive.gif					X
hardDrive.gif				X	
HardDrive.gif					X
homeFolder.gif				X	
HomeFolder.gif					X
iconify-pressed.gif				X	
iconify.gif				X	
info.png				X	
Inform.gif		X	X		X
JavaCup16.png	X				
JavaCup32.png					X
ListView.gif					X
maximize-pressed.gif				X	
maximize.gif				X	
menu.gif				X	
minimize-pressed.gif				X	
minimize.gif				X	
newFolder.gif				X	
NewFolder.gif					X
paletteClose-pressed.gif				X	
paletteClose.gif				X	

Table 20-9. *Look and Feel Image Files (Continued)*

File Name	Basic	Metal	Motif	Ocean	Windows
Question.gif		X	X		X
question.png				X	
ScrollDownArrow.gif			X		
ScrollDownArrowActive.gif			X		
ScrollKnobH.gif			X		
ScrollLeftArrow.gif			X		
ScrollLeftArrowActive.gif			X		
ScrollRightArrow.gif			X		
ScrollRightArrowActive.gif			X		
ScrollUpArrow.gif			X		
ScrollUpArrowActive.gif			X		
StandardBackground.gif			X		X
TrayBottom.gif			X		
TrayLeft.gif			X		
TrayRight.gif			X		
TrayTop.gif			X		
TreeClosed.gif			X		X
TreeCollapsed.gif					
TreeLeaf.gif					X
TreeOpen.gif			X		X
upFolder.gif				X	
UpFolder.gif					X
Warn.gif		X	X		X
warning.png				X	

> **■Note** At the very least, images for the JOptionPane message types are needed within every look and feel. Typically, these are named Error.gif, Inform.gif, Question.gif, and Warn.gif, though that isn't an absolute requirement.

If you don't want to sidestep the "native" requirement of the Windows look and feel, you can install individual UI delegates, such as the following, which uses the Windows UI delegate for the JButton component:

```
UIManager.put("ButtonUI","com.sun.java.swing.plaf.windows.WindowsButtonUI");
```

Adding UI Delegates

Creating a new look and feel that has custom UI delegates involves creating a subclass of the LookAndFeel class. More likely, you'll create a subclass of BasicLookAndFeel or another predefined look and feel class, and then provide your custom delegates for some of the components.

If you subclass the BasicLookAndFeel class, it has a protected void initClassDefaults(UIDefaults table) method to be overridden to install your custom UI delegates. Just put the delegates in the UIDefaults table for the look and feel, instead of in your program that wants to use the new delegate.

The extension to the MetalLookAndFeel in Listing 20-10 adds the previously defined MyComboBoxUI delegate (Listing 20-7) as the ComboBoxUI delegate for the look and feel. As you define more customized components, you can add them in a similar way.

Listing 20-10. *MyMetal Look and Feel*

```
import javax.swing.UIDefaults;
import javax.swing.plaf.metal.MetalLookAndFeel;
public class MyMetal extends MetalLookAndFeel {
  public String getID() {
    return "MyMetal";
  }
  public String getName() {
    return "MyMetal Look and Feel";
  }
  public String getDescription() {
    return "The MyMetal Look and Feel";
  }
  public boolean isNativeLookAndFeel() {
    return false;
  }
  public boolean isSupportedLookAndFeel() {
    return true;
  }
  protected void initClassDefaults(UIDefaults table) {
    super.initClassDefaults(table);
        table.put("ComboBoxUI", "MyComboBoxUI");
  }
}
```

Note When creating your own look and feel, be sure to copy or create icons for the `JOptionPane` pop-up windows. Unless you're customizing Ocean, these icons should be named `Error.gif`, `Inform.gif`, `Question.gif`, and `Warn.gif`, and they belong in the `icons` directory under the directory where the look and feel class file exists.

Working with Metal Themes

The Metal look and feel class (`javax.swing.plaf.metal.MetalLookAndFeel`) provides the means to define *themes* to describe the default settings for the colors, fonts, and all the `UIDefaults` managed by the `UIManager`. By allowing users to change themes, they can get preferred coloration or font sizes with minimal work from the developer. By developing corporate themes, you can easily customize an interface without creating new look and feel classes or manually inserting new settings into current `UIDefaults`.

MetalTheme Class

Table 20-10 lists the 49 different properties that are available through the `MetalTheme` class. The various `primary` and `secondary` properties are abstract and must be implemented in a subclass. Of the remaining properties, the six whose names end with `Font`—`controlTextFont`, `menuTextFont`, `subTextFont`, `systemTextFont`, `userTextFont`, and `windowTextFont`—are also abstract and must be implemented by a subclass. The remaining properties, by default, reuse one of the 11 `primary`/`secondary` values (or black and white) for their settings.

Table 20-10. *MetalTheme Properties*

Property Name	Data Type	Access
acceleratorForeground	ColorUIResource	Read-only
acceleratorSelectedForeground	ColorUIResource	Read-only
black	ColorUIResource	Read-only
control	ColorUIResource	Read-only
controlDarkShadow	ColorUIResource	Read-only
controlDisabled	ColorUIResource	Read-only
controlHighlight	ColorUIResource	Read-only
controlInfo	ColorUIResource	Read-only
controlShadow	ColorUIResource	Read-only
controlTextColor	ColorUIResource	Read-only
controlTextFont	FontUIResource	Read-only

Table 20-10. *MetalTheme Properties (Continued)*

Property Name	Data Type	Access
desktopColor	ColorUIResource	Read-only
focusColor	ColorUIResource	Read-only
highlightedTextColor	ColorUIResource	Read-only
inactiveControlTextColor	ColorUIResource	Read-only
inactiveSystemTextColor	ColorUIResource	Read-only
menuBackground	ColorUIResource	Read-only
menuDisabledForeground	ColorUIResource	Read-only
menuForeground	ColorUIResource	Read-only
menuSelectedBackground	ColorUIResource	Read-only
menuSelectedForeground	ColorUIResource	Read-only
menuTextFont	FontUIResource	Read-only
name	String	Read-only
primary1	ColorUIResource	Read-only
primary2	ColorUIResource	Read-only
primary3	ColorUIResource	Read-only
primaryControl	ColorUIResource	Read-only
primaryControlDarkShadow	ColorUIResource	Read-only
primaryControlHighlight	ColorUIResource	Read-only
primaryControlInfo	ColorUIResource	Read-only
primaryControlShadow	ColorUIResource	Read-only
secondary1	ColorUIResource	Read-only
secondary2	ColorUIResource	Read-only
secondary3	ColorUIResource	Read-only
separatorBackground	ColorUIResource	Read-only
separatorForeground	ColorUIResource	Read-only
subTextFont	FontUIResource	Read-only
systemTextColor	ColorUIResource	Read-only
systemTextFont	FontUIResource	Read-only
textHighlightColor	ColorUIResource	Read-only
userTextColor	ColorUIResource	Read-only

Table 20-10. *MetalTheme Properties (Continued)*

Property Name	Data Type	Access
userTextFont	FontUIResource	Read-only
white	ColorUIResource	Read-only
windowBackground	ColorUIResource	Read-only
windowTextFont	FontUIResource	Read-only
windowTitleBackground	ColorUIResource	Read-only
windowTitleForeground	ColorUIResource	Read-only
windowTitleInactiveBackground	ColorUIResource	Read-only
windowTitleInactiveForeground	ColorUIResource	Read-only

DefaultMetalTheme and OceanTheme Classes

Contrary to the class name, the DefaultMetalTheme class is not the default Metal theme; the default is OceanTheme. DefaultMetalTheme calls itself the Steel theme and uses a blue and gray color scheme for the primary and secondary settings, respectively. OceanTheme, named Ocean, uses a light-blue palette with frequent gradient fills for backgrounds.

To use the Steel theme instead of the Ocean theme, you need to set the swing.metalTheme system property to steel, as shown here:

```
java -Dswing.metalTheme=steel ClassName
```

Most people prefer the newer look of Ocean, but Steel is still available for backward-compatibility, as Ocean is new to 5.0.

If you create your own Metal theme, you need to subclass either OceanTheme or DefaultMetalTheme, and then install the custom theme by setting the static currentTheme property of the MetalLookAndFeel class to your theme.

```
MetalTheme myTheme = new MyTheme();
MetalLookAndFeel.setCurrentTheme(myTheme);
```

Whereas most of the customizations of a MetalTheme are related to fonts and colors, the public void addCustomEntriesToTable(UIDefaults table) method allows you to override the default UIDefaults settings for the Metal look and feel. Therefore, not only do themes customize the fonts and colors of the Swing components, but they also can customize any one of the many UIResource-related properties of the Swing components.

The following code demonstrates how to set two of the scrollbar settings for a specific theme. Remember to tag these settings with the UIResource interface when appropriate, and don't forget to initialize the table argument by your superclass implementation (eventually, this would be MetalTheme).

```java
public void addCustomEntriesToTable(UIDefaults table) {
  super.addCustomEntriesToTable(table);

  ColorUIResource thumbColor = new ColorUIResource(Color.MAGENTA);
  table.put("Scrollbar.thumb", thumbColor);
  table.put("ScrollBar.width", new Integer(25));
}
```

The Metalworks system demo provided with the JDK installation (jdk1.5.0\demo\
jfc\Metalworks) comes with examples for customizing themes. One of the themes it defines
reads the theme color settings from a property file. Instead of needing to create a new class file
every time you want to change the theme of your Swing application, you can read it from a file
at runtime.

```
name=Charcoal
primary1=33,66,66
primary2=66,99,99
primary3=99,99,99
secondary1=0,0,0
secondary2=51,51,51
secondary3=102,102,102
black=255,255,255
white=0,0,0
```

Figure 20-8 shows the Charcoal theme just described used within the Metalworks demonstration program. Figure 20-9 shows the Presentation theme it defines.

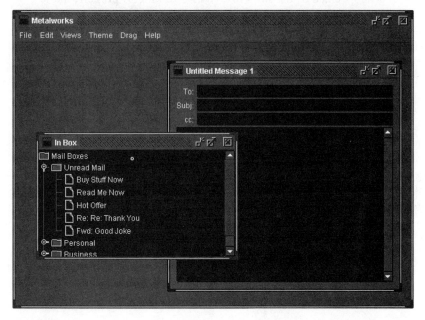

Figure 20-8. *Charcoal theme within the Metalworks demonstration program*

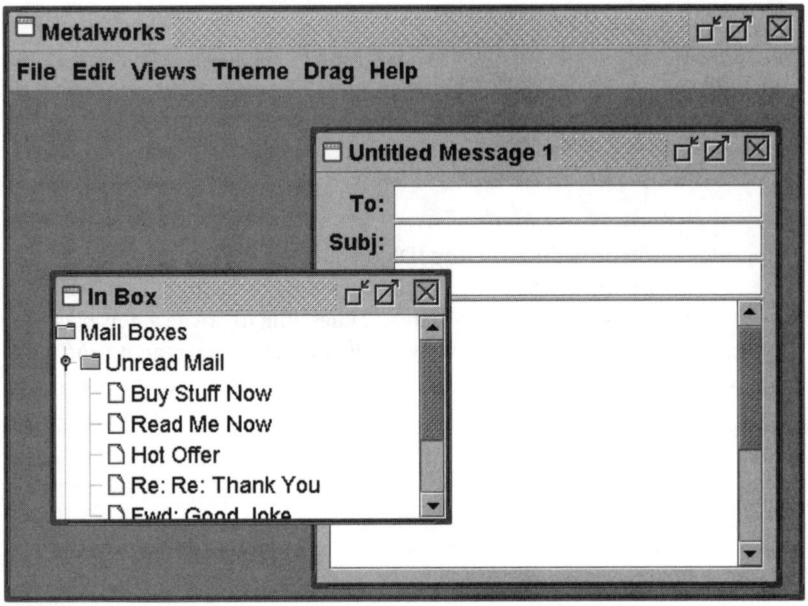

Figure 20-9. *Presentation theme within the Metalworks demonstration program*

Using an Auxiliary Look and Feel

Swing provides for multiple look and feel classes to be active at any one time through the MultiLookAndFeel, or as specified by the swing.plaf.multiplexinglaf property in the swing.properties file. When multiple look and feel classes are installed, only one look and feel will be visual and paint the screen. The remaining versions are called *auxiliary* look and feel classes and tend to be associated with accessibility options, such as for screen readers. Another possible auxiliary look and feel is that of a logger, which records those components that are interacted with in a log file.

Auxiliary look and feel classes are registered with the runtime environment by configuring the swing.auxiliarylaf property within the swing.properties file. If multiple classes are specified, the entries need to be separated by commas. In addition to using the properties file, you can install a look and feel within a program by calling the public static void addAuxiliaryLookAndFeel(LookAndFeel lookAndFeel) method of UIManager. Once installed, the multiplexing look and feel class automatically creates and manages UI delegates for all the installed look and feel classes.

To find out which auxiliary look and feel classes are installed, you can ask the UIManager through its public static LookAndFeel[ ] getAuxiliaryLookAndFeels() method. This returns an array of the actual LookAndFeel objects, unlike the UIManager.LookAndFeelInfo array returned by the getInstalledLookAndFeels() method.

Note Nothing stops multiple look and feel classes from rendering to the screen for the same component. It's the responsibility of the auxiliary look and feel creator to take care not to compete with the primary look and feel when rendering to the screen.

SynthLookAndFeel Class

The Synth look and feel is a full-fledged look and feel, not just a themed extension to Metal, Windows, or Motif. Instead of working with a UIResource table though, the class starts with a blank canvas and gets its entire definition from a single XML file.

Configuring Synth

The configuration of the Synth look and feel might go something like this:

```
SynthLookAndFeel synth = new SynthLookAndFeel();
Class aClass = SynthSample.class;
InputStream is = aClass.getResourceAsStream("config.xml");
synth.load(is, aClass);
UIManager.setLookAndFeel(synth);
```

And what exactly goes into the configuration file, config.xml here? In your configuration file, you specify how you want the specific components used in your program to appear. This is commonly called *skinning your application*, or creating a custom skin. By simply modifying an XML file, the entire appearance of your program changes; no programming is required.

The DTD is available from http://java.sun.com/j2se/1.5.0/docs/api/javax/swing/plaf/synth/doc-files/synth.dtd. The file format is fully described in http://java.sun.com/j2se/1.5.0/docs/api/javax/swing/plaf/synth/doc-files/synthFileFormat.html. The parser does not validate, so until tools are available to help automate the process, you'll need to use care in creating the XML file.

There are many configuration options available with Synth, but the basic XML concept is to define a style and bind it to a component. The <style> tag allows you to customize properties like the font, colors, insets, and background or border image.

To demonstrate, Listing 20-11 defines a custom style named button. Normally, the text will appear in bold 24-point, Monospaced font. When the mouse moves over the associated control, the font changes to a 48-point italic SansSerif font, and the background color changes to blue. When the component is pressed, the font changes again, this time to a 36-point bold-italic Serif font, and the background becomes red. The final part of the configuration file associates the style named button with the JButton control, via the <bind> tag.

Listing 20-11. *Synth Configuration*

```
<synth>
  <style id="button">
    <font name="Monospaced" size="24" style="BOLD"/>
    <state value="MOUSE_OVER">
      <font name="SansSerif" size="48" style="ITALIC"/>
      <opaque value="TRUE"/>
      <color value="BLUE" type="BACKGROUND"/>
    </state>
    <state value="PRESSED">
      <font name="Serif" size="36" style="BOLD AND ITALIC"/>
      <opaque value="TRUE"/>
      <color value="RED" type="BACKGROUND"/>
    </state>
  </style>
  <bind style="button" type="region" key="Button"/>
</synth>
```

Figure 20-10 shows what the component might look like on the screen by itself.

Figure 20-10. *Synth sample button screens*

Listing 20-12 contains the complete sample code used to generate Figure 20-10.

Listing 20-12. *Synth Sample*

```java
import java.awt.*;
import java.io.*;
import java.text.*;
import javax.swing.*;
import javax.swing.plaf.synth.*;

public class SynthSample {
  public static void main(String args[]) {
    Runnable runner = new Runnable() {
      public void run() {
        SynthLookAndFeel synth = new SynthLookAndFeel();
        try {
          Class aClass = SynthSample.class;
          InputStream is = aClass.getResourceAsStream("config.xml");
          if (is == null) {
            System.err.println("Unable to find theme configuration");
            System.exit(-1);
          }
          synth.load(is, aClass);
        } catch (ParseException e) {
          System.err.println("Unable to load theme configuration");
          System.exit(-2);
        }
        try {
          UIManager.setLookAndFeel(synth);
        } catch (javax.swing.UnsupportedLookAndFeelException e) {
          System.err.println("Unable to change look and feel");
          System.exit(-3);
        }
        JFrame frame = new JFrame("Synth Sample");
        frame.setDefaultCloseOperation(JFrame.EXIT_ON_CLOSE);
        JButton button = new JButton("Hello, Synth");
        frame.add(button, BorderLayout.CENTER);
        frame.setSize(300, 200);
        frame.setVisible(true);
      }
    };
    EventQueue.invokeLater(runner);
  }
}
```

Default Synth Properties

The configuration file isn't limited to just styles and bindings. In fact, if you truly do want to set a UIResource property, you still can, but only a limited subset is available. The file located at http://java.sun.com/j2se/1.5.0/docs/api/javax/swing/plaf/synth/doc-files/ componentProperties.html specifies the full set. It is much smaller than the list you'll find in this book's appendix. These settings are configured with either a <property> tag or a <defaultProperty> tag. Defaults end up in the UIDefaults table for the look and feel; properties are just that—settings for the specific control. Tags similar to the following would be placed within a specific <style> tag to be configured:

```
<property key="ScrollPane.viewportBorderInsets" type="insets" value="5 5 5 5"/>
```

or

```
<object class="javax.swing.plaf.ColorUIResource" id="color">
  <int>255</int>
  <int>0</int>
  <int>0</int>
</object>
<defaultsProperty key="Table.focusCellForeground" type="idref" value="color"/>
```

Working with Synth Images

Indirectly, using the SynthPainter class, you can provide images that can be used for borders around components. However, the image must be specially created, as the painter doesn't just draw the image. That one image must be used for components of all sizes, of that type, such as for all text fields. The painter shares the image across different-sized controls by breaking the component into multiple regions. The four corners are always drawn as is. The middle regions are stretched vertically and horizontally.

Figure 20-11 shows a possible border image to use. Notice how there are curves around the corners, but the middle areas don't have curves. The curves stay fixed when the border is stretched.

Figure 20-11. *Text component border*

To use the image in Figure 20-11 within your configuration file, you need to use the <imagePainter> tag and specify an appropriate method attribute. These map directly to the paint*XXX*(SynthContext context, Graphics g, int x, int y, int w, int h, int orientation) methods of the SynthPainter class. Since this image will be used for painting the text field border, the method attribute should be set to textFieldBorder. You also need to specify the path to the image (its file name and path relative to the location specified as the second argument to the SynthLookAndFeel.load() method). Insets and colors are the other items you need to specify. Here's the full style definition for just such a usage.

```
<style id="textfield">
   <opaque value="true"/>
   <state>
      <color value="#C2E2CF" type="BACKGROUND"/>
      <color value="#000000" type="TEXT_FOREGROUND"/>
   </state>
   <imagePainter method="textFieldBorder" path="text.png"
      sourceInsets="3 3 3 3" paintCenter="false"/>
   <insets top="3" left="3" bottom="3" right="3"/>
</style>
<bind style="textfield" type="region" key="TextField"/>
```

Adding a JTextField to the program in Listing 20-12 generates a screen similar to Figure 20-12. When you resize the screen, the text field border grows. Technically speaking, a similar definition would also work for a JTextArea, as there is no height restriction to the image being used here.

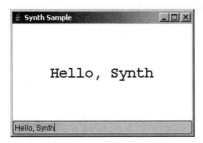

Figure 20-12. *Using the custom text component border*

■**Tip** Much more is in store for the SynthLookAndFeel. In time, expect tools to help with the creation of the XML configuration files. Also expect to be able to purchase libraries that let you just plug in complete look and feel classes created with Synth. Be sure to explore SourceForge for just such a collection.

Summary

In this chapter, you explored the pluggable look and feel architecture of the Swing components. Because all aspects of the Swing components are written in the Java programming language, if you don't like a particular aspect of a component, you can simply change it. And changing it is what this chapter showed you how to do.

First, you learned how to query for the preinstalled LookAndFeel classes and how to change your current look and feel. Next, you learned how to customize the current look and feel by modifying its UIDefaults through the UIManager. You saw how these default settings can implement the UIResource interface so that the settings change when the look and feel class changes. In addition, you saw how these resources can implement the UIDefaults.LazyValue and UIDefaults.ActiveValue interfaces for better use of resources. Moreover, you saw how client properties are hidden from the API view but are available for customizing the look and feel of a component.

To customize the look and feel of various components, you explored creating new UI delegates as well as new look and feel classes, some of which could be nonvisual or auxiliary. You also saw how the Metal look and feel contains a specialized behavior through its use of themes. Lastly, you explored customizing the Synth look and feel.

In Chapter 21, you'll look at the Swing undo framework, which is used for designing undo-able and redoable operations.

■■■

The Undo Framework

In Chapter 20, you discovered how to customize your Swing-based applications by examining the pluggable look and feel architecture support. In this chapter, you'll examine the Undo Framework provided with the JFC as part of the Swing packages.

The Swing packages from Sun include a facility for supporting undo operations within your applications. It allows you to support undoable and redoable operations that change the state of your data. Although the framework is part of the Swing package hierarchy, it's usable within any application, not just component-based applications.

Working with the Undo Framework

Found in the `javax.swing.undo` package, the Undo Framework includes five classes, two interfaces, and two exceptions. To support the Undo Framework, a related interface and event are included in the `javax.swing.event` package. At the root of it all is the `UndoableEdit` interface. The interface forms the basis for encapsulating operations that can be undone or redone using the Command design pattern.

■**Note** Although technically part of the JFC/Project Swing release as an element in the `javax.swing.undo` package, the undo facility actually belongs in the `java.util` package. Unfortunately, when Swing first came out, it needed to be usable within JDK 1.1. Because Swing text packages use this undo facility, that facility needed to be in the Swing package hierarchy. Because Sun couldn't alter the Core API set for JDK 1.1, you'll find the undo support as part of the JFC/Swing packages, and it is therefore usable under the old JDK 1.1, as well as the 1.2 and later platforms, where Swing is standard.

The root implementation class of the undoable command is the `AbstractUndoableEdit` class. Don't let the class name fool you, though—it isn't abstract. The children of the root command are the `CompoundEdit` and `StateEdit` command classes.

The `CompoundEdit` class allows you to combine multiple undoable operations, in which some of the undoable operations could be `StateEdit` objects that store state changes. The Swing text components create `DefaultDocumentEvent` commands when their contents change. The command is a subclass of `CompoundEdit` as well as an inner class of `AbstractDocument`. An additional encapsulated command is the `UndoManager`, which is a subclass of `CompoundEdit`.

The UndoManager manages the edit operations on an editable object by serving as an UndoableEditListener and responding to the creation of each UndoableEditEvent. When an UndoableEdit can't be undone, a CannotUndoException is thrown. In addition, when an UndoableEdit can't be redone, a CannotRedoException is thrown.

If you want to create objects that support undoable and redoable operations, the objects need to implement the StateEditable interface, and they can use the UndoableEditSupport class to help manage the list of UndoableEdit objects.

Before going into the details of the individual pieces of the Undo Framework, let's explore how to use it with the Swing text components. If this is all you want to do, you don't need to understand how the rest works.

Using the Undo Framework with Swing Text Components

The Swing text components already support the necessary undo and redo capabilities. You merely need to manage them with an UndoManager and tell the manager when to undo/redo something.

As an example, consider a program that includes a JTextArea with two toolbar buttons for undoing and redoing a text operation, as shown in Figure 21-1.

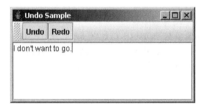

Figure 21-1. *Undo Swing text component usage example*

To enable the JTextArea shown in Figure 21-1 to support undoable operations, you must attach an UndoableEditListener to the Document of the component. Using an UndoManager as the listener is all you need to do. First, you create the manager, and then you attach it.

```
UndoManager manager = new UndoManager();
textArea.getDocument().addUndoableEditListener(manager);
```

Once the manager is attached to the document of the JTextArea, it will monitor all changes to the contents of the text area. Because each of the Swing text components has a Document data model, you can associate an UndoManager with each of these components directly.

After attaching the manager to the text component, you must provide some means to tell the manager to undo/redo an operation. Normally this would be done through a menu selection or a toolbar button selection. In Figure 21-1, this is done with the help of buttons on a JToolBar, with one button for each command. For the Undo button, you want the manager to undo an operation. Therefore, the ActionListener for the button should call the public void undo() method of the UndoManager. The Redo button's ActionListener should call the manager's public void redo() method. The undo() method and redo() method each throws a different exception that must be dealt with.

Because the functionality necessary for the Undo and Redo buttons is the same for all managers, you'll find a helper UndoManagerHelper class included in Listing 21-1 to create Action objects for you. These objects can be used by a JMenuBar, JToolBar, or anything else that can respond with an ActionListener for dealing with the undo and redo operations. You need to ask the helper class for each Action, and then associate that Action with the appropriate component. For instance, the following five lines of source code will take a previously created UndoManager and add the necessary buttons for a JToolBar:

```
JToolBar toolbar = new JToolBar();
JButton undoButton = new JButton(UndoManagerHelper.getUndoAction(manager));
toolbar.add(undoButton);
JButton redoButton = new JButton(UndoManagerHelper.getRedoAction(manager));
toolbar.add(redoButton);
```

Using the undo facility with the Swing text components is that easy. The UndoManagerHelper class definition is shown in Listing 21-1. If you don't like the default button labels (shown in Figure 21-1), additional methods are available that support customization. In addition, if an exception is thrown during the undo/redo operation, a warning message pops up. The warning message and pop-up window title are also customizable.

Listing 21-1. *The UndoManagerHelper Class Definition*

```
import javax.swing.*;
import javax.swing.undo.*;
import java.awt.*;
import java.awt.event.*;

public class UndoManagerHelper {

  public static Action getUndoAction(UndoManager manager, String label) {
    return new UndoAction(manager, label);
  }
  public static Action getUndoAction(UndoManager manager) {
    return new UndoAction(manager,
      (String)UIManager.get("AbstractUndoableEdit.undoText"));
  }
  public static Action getRedoAction(UndoManager manager, String label) {
    return new RedoAction(manager, label);
  }
  public static Action getRedoAction(UndoManager manager) {
    return new RedoAction(manager,
      (String)UIManager.get("AbstractUndoableEdit.redoText"))
  }
```

```java
  private abstract static class UndoRedoAction extends AbstractAction {
    UndoManager undoManager = new UndoManager();
    String errorMessage = "Cannot undo";
    String errorTitle = "Undo Problem";
    protected UndoRedoAction(UndoManager manager, String name) {
      super(name);
      undoManager = manager;
    }
    public void setErrorMessage(String newValue) {
      errorMessage = newValue;
    }
    public void setErrorTitle(String newValue) {
      errorTitle = newValue;
    }
    protected void showMessage(Object source) {
      if (source instanceof Component) {
        JOptionPane.showMessageDialog((Component)source, errorMessage,
          errorTitle, JOptionPane.WARNING_MESSAGE);
      } else {
        System.err.println(errorMessage);
      }
    }
  }

  public static class UndoAction extends UndoRedoAction {
    public UndoAction(UndoManager manager, String name) {
      super(manager, name);
      setErrorMessage("Cannot undo");
      setErrorTitle("Undo Problem");
    }
    public void actionPerformed(ActionEvent actionEvent) {
      try {
        undoManager.undo();
      } catch (CannotUndoException cannotUndoException) {
        showMessage(actionEvent.getSource());
      }
    }
  }

  public static class RedoAction extends UndoRedoAction {
    public RedoAction(UndoManager manager, String name) {
      super(manager, name);
      setErrorMessage("Cannot redo");
      setErrorTitle("Redo Problem");
    }
```

```
    public void actionPerformed(ActionEvent actionEvent) {
      try {
        undoManager.redo();
      } catch (CannotRedoException cannotRedoException) {
        showMessage(actionEvent.getSource());
      }
    }
  }
}
```

> **Note** One thing you can do to improve these helper actions is to have them enabled only when the particular operation is available. The `AbstractUndoableEdit.redoText` and `AbstractUndoableEdit.undoText` usages are listed in Table 21-1.

The rest of the source for the example shown in Figure 21-1 is provided in Listing 21-2. With the help of the new `UndoManagerHelper` class, the most difficult part of using the Undo Framework with the Swing text components has been greatly simplified.

Listing 21-2. *UndoManager Example with Swing Text Components*

```
import javax.swing.*;
import javax.swing.undo.*;
import java.awt.*;

public class UndoSample {
  public static void main(String args[]) {
    Runnable runner = new Runnable() {
      public void run() {
        JFrame frame = new JFrame("Undo Sample");
        frame.setDefaultCloseOperation(JFrame.EXIT_ON_CLOSE);
        JTextArea textArea = new JTextArea();
        JScrollPane scrollPane = new JScrollPane(textArea);

        UndoManager manager = new UndoManager();
        textArea.getDocument().addUndoableEditListener(manager);

        JToolBar toolbar = new JToolBar();
        JButton undoButton =
          new JButton(UndoManagerHelper.getUndoAction(manager));
        toolbar.add(undoButton);
        JButton redoButton =
          new JButton(UndoManagerHelper.getRedoAction(manager));
        toolbar.add(redoButton);
```

```
            frame.add(toolbar, BorderLayout.NORTH);
            frame.add(scrollPane, BorderLayout.CENTER);
            frame.setSize(300, 150);
            frame.setVisible(true);
        }
    };
    EventQueue.invokeLater(runner);
  }
}
```

If you plan to use the Undo Framework only with the Swing text components, you can skip reading the rest of the chapter. On the other hand, if you want to use the framework with other components, or even in a noncomponent setting, you'll want to read the remaining sections, which describe the inner workings of the framework in more detail.

The Command Design Pattern

The undo facility of the `javax.swing.undo` package utilizes the Command design pattern, which has the following participants:

- **Command:** The `UndoableEdit` interface defines the interface for executing the undo/redo operations.

- **Concrete Command:** Instances of the `AbstractUndoableEdit` class, or more specifically its subclasses, implement the necessary Command interface. They bind the commands to the receiver (`Document`) to modify its contents.

- **Client:** In the case of the Swing text components, the `Document` does the creation of the actual `AbstractUndoableEdit` subclass, an `AbstractDocument.DefaultDocumentEvent` by default.

- **Invoker:** The `UndoManager` serves as the Invoker of the `UndoableEdit` command. Normally, someone else tells the Invoker when to do the invoking. However, it's the Invoker who notifies the specific `UndoableEdit` instance when to undo/redo the command.

- **Receiver:** The `Document` is the receiver of the command from the actual `AbstractUndoableEdit` subclass. It knows how to process the request.

If you were using the Undo Framework outside the Swing text components, the Document element would be replaced with a receiver specific to your client application. You would need to create your own UndoableEdit interface implementation to act as the Concrete Command for the pattern. Instead of implementing the interface directly, you merely need to subclass the AbstractUndoableEdit class to encapsulate the specific information about your command.

The design pattern is quite powerful. No matter which command class you're using within the pattern, you can set up capabilities, such as macros for tasks along the lines of automated testing, because the Invoker can sequence the commands at its leisure.

Undo Framework Components

You've seen the Undo Framework in action with the Swing text components and reviewed the Command design pattern. Let's now look at the individual pieces of the framework.

UndoableEdit Interface

The first Undo Framework piece is the UndoableEdit interface, which has the following definition:

```
public interface UndoableEdit {
  // Properties
  public String getPresentationName();
  public String getRedoPresentationName();
  public boolean isSignificant();
  public String getUndoPresentationName();
  // Other Methods
  public boolean addEdit(UndoableEdit anEdit);
  public boolean canRedo();
  public boolean canUndo();
  public void die();
  public void redo() throws CannotRedoException;
  public boolean replaceEdit(UndoableEdit anEdit);
  public void undo() throws CannotUndoException;
}
```

This interface defines the operations that can be done to an object that should support undo and redo capabilities. In addition to describing the supported operations, the interface implicitly defines the three states that an undoable operation can be in, as shown in Figure 21-2.

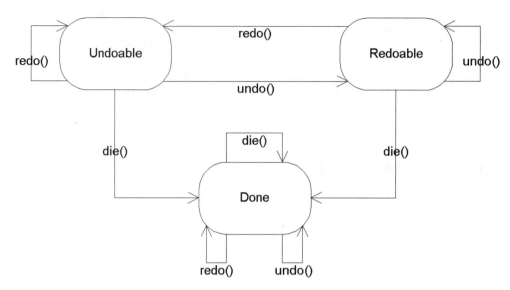

Figure 21-2. *UndoableEdit states*

The flow between states goes as follows:

Undoable state: When an UndoableEdit command is first created, the operation is in the Undoable state. The purpose of the die() method is to release resources for an UndoableEdit before the garbage collector decides to clean things up and to place the command in the Done state. Calling the undo() method either throws a CannotUndoException or causes the command to be undone and the state to change to Redoable. Calling the redo() method either throws a CannotRedoException or causes the command to be done again and the state to stay at Undoable.

Redoable state: When the operation is in the Redoable state, the command has already been undone. Calling the die() method releases any resources and places the command in the Done state. Calling the undo() method either throws a CannotUndoException or causes the command to be undone again and the state to stay at Redoable. Calling the redo() method either throws a CannotRedoException or causes the command to be redone, returning the state to the Undoable state.

Done state: When the operation is in the Done state, calling any of the undo(), redo(), or die() methods leaves the operation in the Done state.

Some state changes aren't commonplace; however, all state changes are supported. The specifics are left to the Command that you're using (as described in the preceding "The Command Design Pattern" section). For instance, Microsoft Word allows you to continuously repeat the last command if the capabilities make sense—such as when formatting a paragraph or just typing a phrase.

AbstractUndoableEdit Class

The AbstractUndoableEdit class provides a default implementation for all the methods of the UndoableEdit interface. Although you might guess from the name that the class is abstract, it isn't. However, developers tend to work with subclasses of the class, not with a direct instance of this class.

By default, AbstractUndoableEdit commands are *significant* (where isSignificant() returns true). What significance you place on the significant property setting depends on your usage of the command. In addition, the class restricts repetition of undoable state changes. Unless overridden by a subclass, exceptions are thrown if you try to redo something in the Undoable state or undo something in the Redoable state. The class doesn't support adding or replacing UndoableEdit operations.

The default presentation names for the undoPresentationName and redoPresentationName properties are Undo and Redo, respectively. These are found by looking up the UIResource-related properties shown in Table 21-1. There is no default for the presentationName property. Subclasses should provide at least a presentation name to provide something more meaningful than the default settings.

Table 21-1. *AbstractUndoableEdit UIResource Elements*

Property String	Object Type
AbstractUndoableEdit.undoText	String
AbstractUndoableEdit.redoText	String

■**Tip** By having the Undo and Redo presentation names as UIResource elements, they can be translated to foreign languages, with their new text available in the same way as other UIResource elements.

CompoundEdit Class

The CompoundEdit class allows you to combine multiple undoable operations into a single operation. For instance, you may want to combine all the keystrokes for typing a whole word into a single CompoundEdit command. This would allow you to continuously redo the typing of a whole word in multiple places. Without combining the separate keystrokes, redoing the last command would redo only the last single keystroke.

The CompoundEdit class uses a read-only inProgress property to report whether the command is still being combined. Initially, the property is true. When in progress, additional commands can be added to the compound command with addEdit(UndoableEdit). To mark the end of a set of commands, you call the end() method. Only after you combine all the commands can they be undone or redone. Figure 21-3 illustrates this.

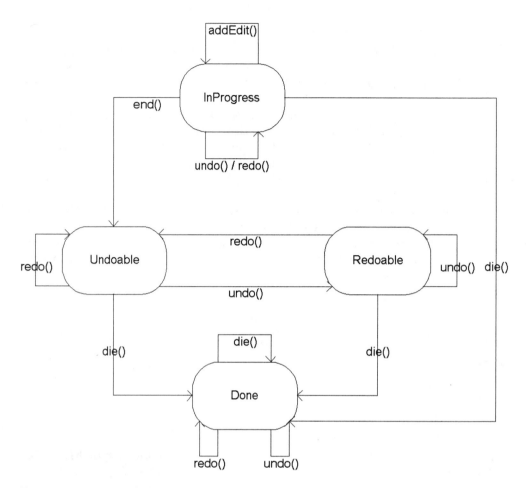

Figure 21-3. *CompoundEdit states*

With a CompoundEdit, if you undo() the edit, all added commands are undone. This is the same with redo(): All commands in the set are redone.

UndoManager Class

The UndoManager class is a specific subclass of CompoundEdit that tracks the history of edit commands, potentially for an entire application. The number of undoable commands the manager can track is defined by a configurable limit property whose initial value is 100.

When isInProgress() reports true for a specific CompoundEdit, the UndoManager acts somewhat like a backward CompoundEdit, in which individual edits can be undone and redone. Once end() has been called, the UndoManager acts like a CompoundEdit, but without the ability to undo or redo individual edit commands. In addition, the UndoManager has one more available state—*Undoable or Redoable*—for when the manager has undone at least one command, can still undo more, but can also redo the undone command(s).

Besides being able to directly add editable operations with addEdit(), the manager also serves as an UndoableEditListener. When the UndoableEditEvent happens, the listener adds the event's UndoableEdit command to the manager with addEdit(). In addition, you can clear the edit queue with public void discardAllEdits(). After the manager receives the end() method, the sequence goes back to looking like Figure 21-3, leaving the bottom three states (Undoable, Redoable, and Done) shown in the chart. The whole sequencing is shown in Figure 21-4.

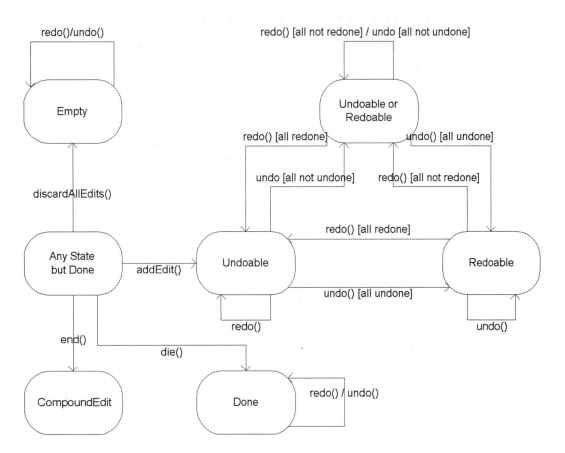

Figure 21-4. *UndoManager states*

Keep in mind that certain undo() and redo() calls can throw exceptions. In addition, when you ask the UndoManager to undo or redo an edit command, the request undoes (or redoes) all commands up to the last significant one.

The transformation of the UndoManager into a CompoundEdit might seem confusing to some users. This transformation allows you to have a secondary UndoManager for certain suboperations that, once completed, become a single CompoundEdit to be passed along to the primary UndoManager.

■**Note** Some developers might find it useful to extend the UndoManager to expose the UndoableEdit list
that it is managing. Then they can display the presentation names of the various edit commands. Fortunately
(or unfortunately), by default, these aren't exposed.

UndoableEditListener Interface and UndoableEditEvent Class

The UndoManager implements the UndoableEditListener interface so that it can be notified
when undoable operations happen. The listener has the following definition:

```
public interface UndoableEditListener extends EventListener {
  public void undoableEditHappened(UndoableEditEvent undoableEditEvent);
}
```

The UndoableEditListener uses an UndoableEditEvent to tell interested objects when a
command that can be undone has happened. The UndoableEditEvent class includes one property,
edit, which returns the UndoableEdit object for the event: public UndoableEdit getEdit().
Of all the classes in the Swing-related packages, only the AbstractDocument class (as defined
in the Document interface) comes with built-in support to add these listeners. When creating
your own classes that support undoable operations, you'll need to maintain your own list of
listeners with the help of the UndoableEditSupport class, described next.

UndoableEditSupport Class

The UndoableEditSupport class is similar to the JavaBeans-related classes of
PropertyChangeSupport and VetoableChangeSupport. All three of these classes manage
a list of a specific type of listener. In the case of the UndoableEditSupport class, that
type of listener is the UndoableEditListener. You add listeners with public void
addUndoableListener(UndoableEditListener) and remove them with public void
removeUndoableListener(UndoableEditListener).
When you want to notify listeners that an UndoableEdit operation has happened, you call
the public void postEdit(UndoableEdit) method, which creates an UndoableEditEvent and
calls the undoableEditHappened() method of each listener.

■**Note** The UndoableEditSupport class also includes support for combining multiple undoable edit
commands into a CompoundEdit with the public void beginUpdate() and public void endUpdate()
methods.

The basic framework for the class usage follows in Listing 21-3. Normally, you tie the undoable event to some other operation. In this example, it's tied to the moment an ActionEvent
happens, and therefore any registered ActionListener objects need to be notified.

Listing 21-3. *Managing UndoableEditListener Objects with UndoableEditSupport*

```java
import javax.swing.undo.*;
import javax.swing.event.*;
import java.awt.event.*;
import java.awt.*;

public class AnUndoableComponent {
  UndoableEditSupport undoableEditSupport = new UndoableEditSupport(this);
  ActionListener actionListenerList = null;

  public void addActionListener(ActionListener actionListener) {
    actionListenerList = AWTEventMulticaster.add(actionListener,
      actionListenerList);
  }

  public void removeActionListener(ActionListener actionListener) {
    actionListenerList = AWTEventMulticaster.remove(actionListener,
      actionListenerList);

  }

  public void addUndoableEditListener(
      UndoableEditListener undoableEditListener) {
    undoableEditSupport.addUndoableEditListener(undoableEditListener);
  }

  public void removeUndoableEditListener(
      UndoableEditListener undoableEditListener) {
    undoableEditSupport.removeUndoableEditListener(undoableEditListener);
  }

  protected void fireActionPerformed(ActionEvent actionEvent) {
    if (actionListenerList != null) {
      actionListenerList.actionPerformed(actionEvent);
    }
    // Need to create your custom type of undoable operation
    undoableEditSupport.postEdit(new AbstractUndoableEdit());
  }
}
```

A Complete Undoable Program Example

Now that you've seen the main classes for the Swing Undo Framework, let's look at a complete example that defines a custom undoable class. The undoable class is a drawing panel in which each mouse click defines a point to be drawn in a polygon. Figure 21-5 shows the drawable panel in action, before and after an undo operation.

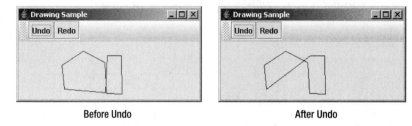

Before Undo　　　　　　　　　　After Undo

Figure 21-5. *The undoable drawing panel at work*

The main program in Listing 21-4 looks practically identical to the earlier example of supporting undo and redo operations in a Swing text component, in Listing 21-2. You simply need to create an UndoManager to manage the undoable operations and associate it to the undoable object. The usage of the Undo Framework works the same here, except that the undoable object is the yet-to-be-created UndoableDrawingPanel class (Listing 21-5).

Listing 21-4. *The UndoDrawing Test Driver*

```
import javax.swing.*;
import javax.swing.undo.*;
import java.awt.*;
public class UndoDrawing {
  public static void main(String args[]) {
    Runnable runner = new Runnable() {
      public void run() {
        JFrame frame = new JFrame("Drawing Sample");
        frame.setDefaultCloseOperation(JFrame.EXIT_ON_CLOSE);

        UndoableDrawingPanel drawingPanel = new UndoableDrawingPanel();

        UndoManager manager = new UndoManager();
        drawingPanel.addUndoableEditListener(manager);

        JToolBar toolbar = new JToolBar();
        JButton undoButton =
          new JButton(UndoManagerHelper.getUndoAction(manager));
        toolbar.add(undoButton);
        JButton redoButton =
          new JButton(UndoManagerHelper.getRedoAction(manager));
        toolbar.add(redoButton);
```

```
            frame.add(toolbar, BorderLayout.NORTH);
            frame.add(drawingPanel, BorderLayout.CENTER);
            frame.setSize(300, 150);
            frame.setVisible(true);
        }
    };
    EventQueue.invokeLater(runner);
  }
}
```

The `UndoableDrawingPanel` class is a component that draws a polygon within itself based on a set of points within the polygon. New points are added to the polygon whenever the mouse is released. If you don't want the component to support undoable operations, you don't need to do anything beyond collecting points for the drawing panel.

For the panel to support undoable operations, it must do two things:

- It must maintain a list of `UndoableEditListener` objects. This can be easily done with the help of the `UndoableEditSupport` class, as shown earlier in Listing 21-3.

- The second task involves creating an `UndoableEdit` object, prior to any state changes, and posting it to the registered listeners. Because the state of the drawing panel is the polygon, this property must be exposed in the drawing class.

Listing 21-5 shows the definition for the `UndoableDrawingPanel` class. Nothing in the class is particularly complicated. The important thing to remember when defining an undoable class is that the undoable event must be created *before* the state of the component changes. (The implementation class of the `UndoableEdit` interface, `UndoableDrawEdit`, is shown later, in Listing 21-6.)

Listing 21-5. *The UndoableDrawingPanel Main Component*

```
import javax.swing.*;
import javax.swing.event.*;
import javax.swing.undo.*;
import java.awt.*;
import java.awt.event.*;

public class UndoableDrawingPanel extends JPanel {
  UndoableEditSupport undoableEditSupport = new UndoableEditSupport(this);
  Polygon polygon = new Polygon();
```

```
  public UndoableDrawingPanel() {
    MouseListener mouseListener = new MouseAdapter() {
      public void mouseReleased(MouseEvent mouseEvent) {
        undoableEditSupport.postEdit(
          new UndoableDrawEdit(UndoableDrawingPanel.this));
        polygon.addPoint(mouseEvent.getX(), mouseEvent.getY());
        repaint();
      }
    };
    addMouseListener(mouseListener);
  }

  public void addUndoableEditListener(
      UndoableEditListener undoableEditListener) {
    undoableEditSupport.addUndoableEditListener(undoableEditListener);
  }

  public void removeUndoableEditListener(
      UndoableEditListener undoableEditListener) {
    undoableEditSupport.removeUndoableEditListener(undoableEditListener);
  }

  public void setPolygon(Polygon newValue) {
    polygon = newValue;
    repaint();
  }

  public Polygon getPolygon() {
    Polygon returnValue;
    if (polygon.npoints == 0) {
      returnValue = new Polygon();
    } else {
      returnValue = new Polygon(
        polygon.xpoints, polygon.ypoints, polygon.npoints);
    }
    return returnValue;
  }

  protected void paintComponent(Graphics g) {
    super.paintComponent(g);
    g.drawPolygon(polygon);
  }
}
```

When defining the custom implementation of the UndoableEdit interface, you can choose to implement the complete interface, or you can subclass the AbstractUndoableEdit class and override any appropriate methods. More typically, you'll just subclass AbstractUndoableEdit.

The minimum methods to override are undo() and redo(), although you'll probably also choose to override getPresentationName() to give a better name to the undoable operation.

Because the Command design pattern has the Concrete Command (that is, the UndoableEdit implementation) invoke the operation, the constructor must save any information necessary to make the operation undoable. In the case of the drawing panel, you need to save a reference to the panel and its current polygon. Then when the operation is asked to undo itself, the original polygon can be restored. To support redoing the undo operation, the undo() method must also save the new polygon; otherwise, the redo() operation wouldn't know how to change things back. It may sound like quite a bit of work, but it really isn't. The complete class definition for the UndoableEdit implementation follows in Listing 21-6.

Listing 21-6. *The UndoableDrawEdit Undoable Command*

```java
import javax.swing.undo.*;
import java.awt.*;

public class UndoableDrawEdit extends AbstractUndoableEdit {
  UndoableDrawingPanel panel;
  Polygon polygon, savedPolygon;

  public UndoableDrawEdit(UndoableDrawingPanel panel) {
    this.panel = panel;
    polygon = panel.getPolygon();
  }

  public String getPresentationName() {
    return "Polygon of size " + polygon.npoints;
  }

  public void redo() throws CannotRedoException {
    super.redo();
    if (savedPolygon == null) {
      // Should never get here, as super() doesn't permit redoing
      throw new CannotRedoException();
    } else {
      panel.setPolygon(savedPolygon);
      savedPolygon = null;
    }
  }

  public void undo() throws CannotUndoException {
    super.undo();
    savedPolygon = panel.getPolygon();
    panel.setPolygon(polygon);
  }
}
```

And that's it! The last two classes make the UndoDrawing example class (Listing 21-4) work. When creating your own undoable classes, you will need to subclass a nonundoable class and then add the necessary support to make it undoable. In addition, you will need to define an UndoableEdit implementation to support your specific class.

Using an Outside Object to Manage Undo States

In the previous example, it was the responsibility of your custom UndoableEdit implementation to maintain the before-and-after state of the undoable object. The Swing Undo Framework also supports the ability of an object outside the undoable edit implementation to manage the state. When using an outside object for state management, it isn't necessary to implement the UndoableEdit interface yourself. Instead, you can use the StateEdit class as the UndoableEdit implementation. The StateEdit class then relies on a class to implement the StateEditable interface to manage the before-and-after storage of the state of an undoable object (within a Hashtable).

StateEditable Interface

The StateEditable interface consists of two methods and a meaningless string constant.

```
public interface StateEditable {
  public final static String RCSID;
  public void restoreState(Hashtable state);
  public void storeState(Hashtable state);
}
```

An object that supports the undoing of its operations stores its state with the storeState(➥ Hashtable) method. This is all the information about the state of the object that can change. Then restoring the state of the object is done in the restoreState(Hashtable) method.

To demonstrate, let's see how to rewrite the UndoableDrawingPanel example. Using this interface with the updated, undoable drawing panel involves implementing the interface, and storing and getting the polygon shown earlier in Figure 21-5. That's because the polygon is the only state information we care about undoing. The source code is shown in Listing 21-7.

Listing 21-7. *The StateEditable Implementation of the Updated Component*

```
public class UndoableDrawingPanel2 extends JPanel implements StateEditable {

  private static String POLYGON_KEY = "Polygon";
  public void storeState(Hashtable state) {
    state.put(POLYGON_KEY, getPolygon());
  }
```

```
  public void restoreState(Hashtable state) {
    Polygon polygon = (Polygon)state.get(POLYGON_KEY);
    if (polygon != null) {
      setPolygon(polygon);
    }
  }
}
```

The Hashtable that the restoreState() method returns contains only key/value pairs that changed. It's possible that the get() method of the Hashtable returns null for something that you explicitly put() in the hash table. Therefore, as shown in Listing 21-7, you're required to add an if-null check after getting any state information from the hash table.

StateEdit Class

After you've implemented the StateEditable interface, you can use the StateEdit class as the UndoableEdit implementation. Where the previous UndoableDrawingPanel example created a custom UndoableDrawEdit, the new class creates a StateEdit instance.

The StateEdit constructor accepts a StateEditable object that you're going to change and an optional presentation name. After creating the StateEdit object, modify the StateEditable object and then tell the StateEdit to end() the modifications to the StateEditable object. When the StateEdit object is told that the modifications have ended, it compares the before-and-after states of the state editable object and removes any key/value pairs that didn't change from the hash table. You can then post the UndoableEdit to the list of UndoableEditListener objects through the list maintained by the UndoableEditSupport class.

```
StateEdit stateEdit = new StateEdit(UndoableDrawingPanel2.this);
// Change state of UndoableDrawingPanel2
polygon.addPoint(mouseEvent.getX(), mouseEvent.getY());
// Done changing state
stateEdit.end();
undoableEditSupport.postEdit(stateEdit);
```

After the edit is posted, the UndoManager manages the StateEdit instance of UndoableEdit, just like any other undoable edit object. The UndoManager can then request the StateEdit object to tell its StateEditable object to restore its previous state. This holds for any other UndoableEdit object. Therefore, no other source code needs to change.

A Complete StateEditable/StateEdit Example

The reworking of the UndoableDrawingPanel example is presented in Listing 21-8, with the differences from Listing 21-5 shown in boldface. This version uses the StateEditable/StateEdit combination just described. The earlier test program is included as the main() method to keep the complete example together. With the exception of the class name change for the drawing panel, the test program didn't change and will still result in what you see in Figure 21-5, assuming the same set of points in the polygon.

Listing 21-8. *The Updated UndoableDrawingPanel2 Main Component*

```java
import javax.swing.*;
import javax.swing.event.*;
import javax.swing.undo.*;
import java.awt.*;
import java.awt.event.*;
import java.util.Hashtable;

public class UndoableDrawingPanel2 extends JPanel implements StateEditable {
  private static String POLYGON_KEY = "Polygon";
  UndoableEditSupport undoableEditSupport = new UndoableEditSupport(this);
  Polygon polygon = new Polygon();

  public UndoableDrawingPanel2() {
    MouseListener mouseListener = new MouseAdapter() {
      public void mouseReleased(MouseEvent mouseEvent) {
        StateEdit stateEdit = new StateEdit(UndoableDrawingPanel2.this);
        polygon.addPoint(mouseEvent.getX(), mouseEvent.getY());
        stateEdit.end();
        undoableEditSupport.postEdit(stateEdit);
        repaint();
      }
    };
    addMouseListener(mouseListener);
  }
  public void addUndoableEditListener(
      UndoableEditListener undoableEditListener) {
    undoableEditSupport.addUndoableEditListener(undoableEditListener);
  }

  public void removeUndoableEditListener(
      UndoableEditListener undoableEditListener) {
    undoableEditSupport.removeUndoableEditListener(undoableEditListener);
  }

  public void storeState(Hashtable state) {
    state.put(POLYGON_KEY, getPolygon());
  }

  public void restoreState(Hashtable state) {
    Polygon polygon = (Polygon)state.get(POLYGON_KEY);
    if (polygon != null) {
      setPolygon(polygon);
    }
  }
```

```java
public void setPolygon(Polygon newValue) {
  polygon = newValue;
  repaint();
}

public Polygon getPolygon() {
  Polygon returnValue;
  if (polygon.npoints == 0) {
    returnValue = new Polygon();
  } else {
    returnValue = new Polygon(
      polygon.xpoints, polygon.ypoints, polygon.npoints);
  }
  return returnValue;
}

protected void paintComponent(Graphics g) {
  super.paintComponent(g);
  g.drawPolygon(polygon);
}

public static void main(String args[]) {
  Runnable runner = new Runnable() {
    public void run() {
      JFrame frame = new JFrame("Drawing Sample2");
      frame.setDefaultCloseOperation(JFrame.EXIT_ON_CLOSE);
      UndoableDrawingPanel2 drawingPanel = new UndoableDrawingPanel2();

      UndoManager manager = new UndoManager();
      drawingPanel.addUndoableEditListener(manager);

      JToolBar toolbar = new JToolBar();
      JButton undoButton =
        new JButton(UndoManagerHelper.getUndoAction(manager));
      toolbar.add(undoButton);
      JButton redoButton =
        new JButton(UndoManagerHelper.getRedoAction(manager));
      toolbar.add(redoButton);

      frame.add(toolbar, BorderLayout.NORTH);
      frame.add(drawingPanel, BorderLayout.CENTER);
      frame.setSize(300, 150);
      frame.setVisible(true);
    }
  };
```

```
      EventQueue.invokeLater(runner);
    }
}
```

Summary

This chapter took both a short look and a long look at the Undo Framework found in the javax.swing.undo package with support from javax.swing.event. You saw how the framework support arrives already built in to the Swing text components. In addition, you learned how to build support into your own classes. With the interfaces and classes found in the Undo Framework, you can make any editable object support both undo and redo capabilities.

The next chapter introduces the accessibility support for the Swing component set. There, you'll learn about the support for using assistive technologies with the components and working with audio cues.

CHAPTER 22

■ ■ ■

Accessibility

A standard part of the Swing framework is support for assistive technologies. These technologies allow your Swing-based programs to be accessible to those with physical challenges. Some users need screen readers, audio cues, or just an input mode that doesn't require the mouse. Mouse-less input is typically through the keyboard, but it also could be through specialized input devices, such as those that are voice-activated.

Users don't need to be physically challenged to take advantage of options you, as the developer, can use to make your programs more accessible. For example, you might add tooltip text, which users can see by resting their mouse over the component. Limited-vision users taking advantage of accessibility devices could rely on that text to describe the component with a screen reader. Other options include keyboard accelerators and menu mnemonics, which allow users to navigate around the screen and activate actions with minimal hand movement.

This chapter offers some suggestions to help you create programs that follow federal guidelines in the United States, known as Section 508 Accessibility Requirements. For details on these requirements, refer to *Accessibility for Everybody: Understanding the Section 508 Accessibility Requirements*, by John Paul Mueller (Apress, 2003; ISBN 1-59059-086-4). Sun also offers a resource at `http://www.sun.com/access/background/laws.html`, which includes references to international resources, as well as those in the United States. And, of course, there is the JFC Assistive Technologies home page, at `http://java.sun.com/products/jfc/accessibility/`.

Accessibility Classes

The `javax.accessibility` package is both the most and least used package. Provided you configure your Swing components properly, everything happens behind the scenes. When a user taking advantage of an accessibility device runs the program, the Java Accessibility API steps in and provides the necessary information to the device. For instance, when creating an `ImageIcon`, there are two sets of constructors: those without a `description` argument and those with a `description` argument.

```
// Without description argument
public ImageIcon()
public ImageIcon(Image image)
public ImageIcon(String filename)
public ImageIcon(URL location)
public ImageIcon(byte imageData[])
```

```
// With description argument

public ImageIcon(Image image, String description)
public ImageIcon(String filename, String description)
public ImageIcon(URL location, String description)
public ImageIcon(byte imageData[], String description)
```

By creating an ImageIcon with a description, your program automatically becomes more accessible. In addition to creating the icon with a description argument to the constructor, you can also assign the text later by calling the setDescription() method.

One important interface, Accessible, and an abstract class, AccessibleContext, provide the core framework for the Java Accessibility API.

Accessible Interface

For a Swing component to work within the accessibility framework, it must implement the Accessible interface.

```
public interface Accessible {
  // Property
  public AccessibleContext getAccessibleContext();
}
```

As the interface definition shows, there is only one method, which gets the current AccessibleContext instance for the implementing class. All the standard AWT and Swing components implement the interface. Several internal aspects of components, like the system menu bar on the title pane of the JInternalFrame, also implement the Accessible interface.

AccessibleContext Class

While the Accessible interface is all that a component must implement, the work is actually done in the AccessibleContext instance that it returns. The returned context is practically another component. It maps the accessible properties to the properties of the component. For example, with the JLabel component, when you get its AccessibleContext, you are getting the concrete subclass known as AccessibleJLabel. This subclass maps JLabel properties, such as the accessibleName property to the text property. As shown in Table 22-1, the abstract class itself is larger than the interface.

Table 22-1. *AccessibleContext Properties*

Property Name	Data Type	Access
accessibleAction	AccessibleAction	Read-only
accessibleChildrenCount	int	Read-only
accessibleComponent	AccessibleComponent	Read-only
accessibleDescription	String	Read-write bound
accessibleEditableText	AccessibleEditableText	Read-only

Table 22-1. *AccessibleContext Properties (Continued)*

Property Name	Data Type	Access
accessibleIcon	AccessibleIcon	Read-only
accessibleIndexInParent	int	Read-only
accessibleName	String	Read-write bound
accessibleParent	Accessible	Read-write
accessibleRelationSet	AccessibleRelationSet	Read-only
accessibleRole	AccessibleRole	Read-only
accessibleSelection	AccessibleSelection	Read-only
accessibleStateSet	AccessibleStateSet	Read-only
accessibleTable	AccessibleTable	Read-only
accessibleText	AccessibleText	Read-only
accessibleValue	AccessibleValue	Read-only
locale	Locale	Read-only

As Table 22-1 shows, there are several other classes found in the `javax.accessibility` package. However, typically, you don't need to worry about them, provided that you create your components and screens to be accessible.

Creating Accessible Components

This section presents some hints to help you create applications that will be accessible when used with assistive technologies. This is not meant to be an exhaustive list, but it does provide an overview of some helpful techniques.

- As a first task, try to use your program without a mouse. Do your menus support accelerators and mnemonics? Do your buttons have mnemonics associated with them? Do your text fields have labels associated with them via the `setLabelFor()` method, and does each label have a mnemonic?

- Make sure your components have a short string associated with them. If a component, such as an image-only button, doesn't have a string, call the `setAccessibleName()` method of the `AccessibleContext`. Remember to localize this name if your program is targeting an internationalized audience.

- Work with tooltip text wherever possible. If it is not appropriate to have tooltip text with a component, be sure to call `setAccessibleDescription()`.

- Are your custom components accessible? If you've subclassed `JComponent`, that class doesn't implement the `Accessible` interface. But, if you've subclassed `JPanel`, it does. However, even though `JPanel` implements the interface, your component might not be providing the necessary accessibility information. Consider having your custom `AccessibleContext` extend `JComponent.AccessibleJComponent` when appropriate.

- Components that are inside containers that aren't accessible are themselves not accessible. Be sure to use JPanel as your container, rather than the AWT Container class, to ensure your screens are accessible.

■**Note** To see how well you've done creating accessible programs, you can try using the Java Accessibility Utilities, available from the JFC Assistive Technologies home page at http://java.sun.com/products/ jfc/accessibility/. These downloadable utilities are designed to let you see exposed accessibility properties in different forms. However, I personally couldn't get them to work. The jaccess.jar and jaccess-examples.jar files needed weren't available, nor were the imported classes for the code that was provided.

Working with the Java Access Bridge

If you happen to be working on a Microsoft Windows platform, you can try out the Java Access Bridge, available from http://java.sun.com/products/accessbridge/. This utility is easy to use.

■**Caution** To get the Java Access Bridge, do not follow the link from the main Accessibility page. The link available there in early 2005 pointed to the 1.0.4 beta version of the product. You should download at least version 1.2, available directly from http://java.sun.com/products/accessbridge/.

After downloading accessbridge-1_2.zip, unpack it and run the Install program, found in the installer subdirectory. After the program checks Java virtual machines (JVMs) for compatibility, it prompts you to select in which of the compatible JVMs you want the bridge installed. As Figure 22-1 shows, if you happen to have a few JVMs on your system, this may be in several places. Just pick the ones you are most likely to use. The program might also prompt you to remove some of the older versions on your machine. The directories that begin with c:\program files\java are the different versions of Java Plug-in for the browser.

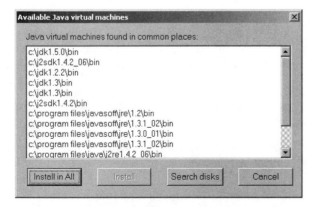

Figure 22-1. *Installing the Java Access Bridge*

After clicking the Install (or Install in All) button, you'll see a success window, as shown in Figure 22-2 (assuming everything succeeded). Installation is quick.

Figure 22-2. *Java Access Bridge successfully installed*

Once you've installed the bridge, you can run programs like Java Monkey and Java Ferret (yes, those are their real names). Once running, these programs attach themselves to any Java programs that run through the same JVM. For instance, you can try running the tooltip sample program presented in Chapter 4 with Java Monkey, repeated here in Listing 22-1.

Listing 22-1. *Tooltip Sample*

```java
import javax.swing.*;
import java.awt.*;

public class TooltipSample {

  public static void main(String args[]) {
    Runnable runner = new Runnable() {
      public void run() {
        JFrame frame = new JFrame("Tooltip Sample");
        frame.setDefaultCloseOperation(JFrame.EXIT_ON_CLOSE);

        JPanel panel = new JPanel();
        panel.setToolTipText("<HtMl>Tooltip<br>Message");
        frame.add(panel, BorderLayout.CENTER);

        JButton button = new JButton("Hello, World") {
          public JToolTip createToolTip() {
            JToolTip tip = super.createToolTip();
            tip.setBackground(Color.YELLOW);
            tip.setForeground(Color.RED);
            return tip;
          }
          public boolean contains(int x, int y) {
            if (x < 100) {
              setToolTipText("Got Green Eggs?");
            } else {
              setToolTipText("Got Ham?");
            }
```

```
                return super.contains(x, y);
              }
            };
            button.setToolTipText("Hello, World");
            frame.add(button, BorderLayout.NORTH);

            frame.setSize(300, 150);
            frame.setVisible(true);
          }
        };
        EventQueue.invokeLater(runner);
    }
}
```

You'll see the screen shown in Figure 22-3. If you don't immediately see the component tree, select the Refresh Tree option under the File menu in the Java Monkey window.

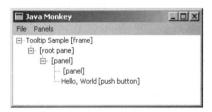

Figure 22-3. *Main Java Monkey screen*

Select the Accessibility API Panel option under the Panels menu to see the information available through the AccessibleContext, such as the name, description, and role. Figure 22-4 shows an example. Be sure to scroll down to see all the available information.

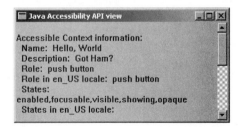

Figure 22-4. *Secondary Java Monkey screen*

The other program that comes with the Java Access Bridge is Java Ferret. This is more of a tracking program, where you can enable the tracking of different events, such as mouse, focus, and menu selection. If you've enabled mouse tracking, you'll see the program updated. Figure 22-5 shows an example of the Java Ferret information displayed when you move the mouse over the JButton in the sample tooltip program (Listing 22-1).

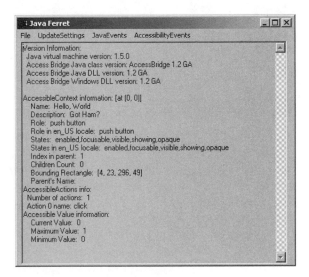

Figure 22-5. *Java Ferret interface*

■**Note** Does anyone else find it ironic that the Java Monkey and Java Ferret programs are not themselves very accessible? Where are the mnemonics and menu accelerators?

Summary

This chapter explored how the Swing APIs help make your programs more accessible, both for the normal user and the physically challenged. By following the suggestions in this chapter, your programs should be well on their way to meeting federal and international guidelines. With the help of the Java Monkey and Ferret programs, you can discover if sufficient attributes are exposed to users needing the accessibility features.

And this wraps up your tour of Swing. Be sure to visit The Swing Connection maintained by Sun at http://www.theswingconnection.com/ to follow the latest happenings.

UI Manager Properties

Throughout this book are tables that list the property names and data types for all the UIResource elements of specific Swing components. Although these tables show all the information about a specific component, it is handy to have the information about property names for all of the components in one place.

With that in mind, this appendix provides a complete, alphabetical list of properties used by the predefined look and feel classes—Motif, Metal/Ocean, Windows, GTK, and Synth— provided with the Swing release for the Java 2 Platform Standard Edition, version 5.0 (J2SE 5.0). The table indicates with an *X* which of the five look and feel classes uses a particular property. For properties defined within the base Basic look and feel, these are assumed to be used by all the look and feel types, since all of the system-defined look and feel classes extend from BasicLookAndFeel. It is possible that a subclass masks the use of a property defined for the Basic look and feel, and in fact doesn't physically use one flagged as such in the table. Also, since the GTK look and feel is a subclass of Synth, a similar situation arises with GTK, too.

To change the default setting for any of these properties, you need to notify the UIManager by storing a new setting in the lookup table of the UIManager. For instance, to change the default text for the Yes button in a JOptionPane, you need to replace the OptionPane.yesButtonText property with the new setting (*Si*, in this example):

```
UIManager.put("OptionPane.yesButtonText", "Si");
```

Then any component created after the setting change will get the new value: Si. If you want a displayed component to get the new setting, you must call its updateUI() method after changing the setting.

When you change the current look and feel, any custom settings you install may be lost. If the class of the property value setting implements the UIResource interface (an empty marker interface such as Serializable), the setting will be replaced by the default setting of the look and feel. For example, the following setting would be saved when the look and feel changes:

```
UIManager.put("OptionPane.background", Color.RED);
```

Conversely, the following setting would not be saved when the look and feel changes:

```
UIManager.put("OptionPane.background", new ColorUIResource(Color.RED));
```

If the property value setting does not implement the UIResource interface, the property setting is retained when the look and feel changes.

> **Note** The specific set of available properties changes with each JFC/Project Swing release. The listing here reflects the current settings for J2SE 5.0. Some properties did not exist in earlier versions, and others may get replaced in later versions. The changes tend to be minor, but they do exist.

UIResource Elements for the Predefined Look and Feel Classes

Property String	Object Type	CDE/Motif	Metal	Windows	GTK	Synth
AbstractButton.clickText	String	X	X	X	X	X
AbstractDocument.additionText	String	X	X	X	X	X
AbstractDocument.deletionText	String	X	X	X	X	X
AbstractDocument.redoText	String	X	X	X	X	X
AbstractDocument.styleChangeText	String	X	X	X	X	X
AbstractDocument.undoText	String	X	X	X	X	X
AbstractUndoableEdit.redoText	String	X	X	X	X	X
AbstractUndoableEdit.undoText	String	X	X	X	X	X
activeCaption	Color	X	X	X	X	X
activeCaptionBorder	Color	X	X	X	X	X
activeCaptionText	Color	X	X	X	X	X
Application.useSystemFontSettings	Boolean		X	X		
ArrowButton.size	Integer				X	X
ArrowButtonUI	String				X	X
AuditoryCues.allAuditoryCues	String[ ]	X	X	X	X	X
AuditoryCues.cueList	String[ ]	X	X	X	X	X
AuditoryCues.defaultCueList	String[ ]		X			
AuditoryCues.noAuditoryCues	String[ ]	X	X	X	X	X
AuditoryCues.playList	String[ ]	X	X	X	X	X
black	Color				X	
Button.actionMap	ActionMap	X	X	X	X	X
Button.background	Color	X	X	X	X	X
Button.border	Border	X	X	X	X	X
Button.contentAreaFilled	Boolean				X	X
Button.darkShadow	Color	X	X	X	X	X
Button.dashedRectGapHeight	Integer			X		
Button.dashedRectGapWidth	Integer			X		

UIResource Elements for the Predefined Look and Feel Classes (Continued)

Property String	Object Type	CDE/Motif	Metal	Windows	GTK	Synth
Button.dashedRectGapX	Integer			X		
Button.dashedRectGapY	Integer			X		
Button.defaultButtonFollowsFocus	Boolean	X	X	X	X	X
Button.disabledForeground	Color			X		
Button.disabledGrayRange	Integer[ ]		X			
Button.disabledShadow	Color			X		
Button.disabledText	Color		X			
Button.disabledToolBarBorder➡ Background	Color		X			
Button.focus	Color		X	X		
Button.focusInputMap	InputMap	X	X	X	X	X
Button.font	Font	X	X	X	X	X
Button.foreground	Color	X	X	X	X	X
Button.gradient	List		X			
Button.highlight	Color	X	X	X	X	X
Button.icon	Icon				X	X
Button.iconTextGap	Integer				X	X
Button.light	Color	X	X	X	X	X
Button.margin	Insets	X	X	X	X	X
Button.rollover	Boolean	X	X	X	X	X
Button.rolloverIconType	String		X			
Button.select	Color	X	X			
Button.shadow	Color	X	X	X	X	X
Button.showMnemonics	Boolean			X		
Button.textIconGap	Integer	X	X	X	X	X
Button.textShiftOffset	Integer	X	X	X	X	X
Button.toolBarBorderBackground	Color		X			
ButtonUI	String	X	X	X	X	X
caretColor	Color				X	
CheckBox.background	Color	X	X	X	X	X
CheckBox.border	Border	X	X	X	X	X
CheckBox.darkShadow	Color			X		

UIResource Elements for the Predefined Look and Feel Classes (Continued)

Property String	Object Type	CDE/Motif	Metal	Windows	GTK	Synth
CheckBox.disabledText	Color		X			
CheckBox.focus	Color	X	X	X		
CheckBox.focusInputMap	InputMap	X	X	X	X	X
CheckBox.font	Font	X	X	X	X	X
CheckBox.foreground	Color	X	X	X	X	X
CheckBox.gradient	List		X			
CheckBox.highlight	Color			X		
CheckBox.icon	Icon	X	X	X	X	X
CheckBox.interiorBackground	Color			X		
CheckBox.light	Color			X		
CheckBox.margin	Insets	X	X	X	X	X
CheckBox.rollover	Boolean		X			
Checkbox.select[a]	Color		X			
CheckBox.shadow	Color			X		
CheckBox.textIconGap	Integer	X	X	X	X	X
CheckBox.textShiftOffset	Integer	X	X	X	X	X
CheckBoxMenuItem.acceleratorFont	Font	X	X	X	X	X
CheckBoxMenuItem.accelerator➡Foreground	Color	X	X	X	X	X
CheckBoxMenuItem.accelerator➡SelectionForeground	Color	X	X	X	X	X
CheckBoxMenuItem.actionMap	ActionMap	X	X	X	X	X
CheckBoxMenuItem.arrowIcon	Icon	X	X	X	X	X
CheckBoxMenuItem.background	Color	X	X	X	X	X
CheckBoxMenuItem.border	Border	X	X	X	X	X
CheckBoxMenuItem.borderPainted	Boolean	X	X	X	X	X
CheckBoxMenuItem.checkIcon	Icon	X	X	X	X	X
CheckBoxMenuItem.commandSound	String	X	X	X	X	X
CheckBoxMenuItem.disabled➡Foreground	Color	X	X	X	X	X
CheckBoxMenuItem.font	Font	X	X	X	X	X
CheckBoxMenuItem.foreground	Color	X	X	X	X	X
CheckBoxMenuItem.gradient	List		X			

UIResource Elements for the Predefined Look and Feel Classes (Continued)

Property String	Object Type	CDE/Motif	Metal	Windows	GTK	Synth
CheckBoxMenuItem.margin	Insets	X	X	X	X	X
CheckBoxMenuItem.opaque	Boolean	X	X	X	X	X
CheckBoxMenuItem.selection➦Background	Color	X	X	X	X	X
CheckBoxMenuItem.selection➦Foreground	Color	X	X	X	X	X
CheckBoxMenuItemUI	String	X	X	X	X	X
CheckBoxUI	String	X	X	X	X	X
ColorChooser.background	Color	X	X	X	X	X
ColorChooser.cancelText	String	X	X	X	X	X
ColorChooser.font	Font	X	X	X	X	X
ColorChooser.foreground	Color	X	X	X	X	X
ColorChooser.hsbBlueText	String	X	X	X	X	X
ColorChooser.hsbBrightnessText	String	X	X	X	X	X
ColorChooser.hsbDisplayed➦MnemonicIndex	Integer	X	X	X	X	X
ColorChooser.hsbGreenText	String	X	X	X	X	X
ColorChooser.hsbHueText	String	X	X	X	X	X
ColorChooser.hsbMnemonic	Integer	X	X	X	X	X
ColorChooser.hsbNameText	String	X	X	X	X	X
ColorChooser.hsbRedText	String	X	X	X	X	X
ColorChooser.hsbSaturationText	String	X	X	X	X	X
ColorChooser.okText	String	X	X	X	X	X
ColorChooser.panels	AbstractColor➦ChooserPanel[ ]				X	X
ColorChooser.previewText	String	X	X	X	X	X
ColorChooser.resetMnemonic	Integer	X	X	X	X	X
ColorChooser.resetText	String	X	X	X	X	X
ColorChooser.rgbBlueDisplayed➦MnemonicIndex	Integer	X	X	X	X	X
ColorChooser.rgbBlueMnemonic	Integer	X	X	X	X	X
ColorChooser.rgbBlueText	String	X	X	X	X	X
ColorChooser.rgbDisplayed➦MnemonicIndex	Integer	X	X	X	X	X

UIResource Elements for the Predefined Look and Feel Classes (Continued)

Property String	Object Type	CDE/Motif	Metal	Windows	GTK	Synth
ColorChooser.rgbGreenDisplayed➡ MnemonicIndex	Integer	X	X	X	X	X
ColorChooser.rgbGreenMnemonic	Integer	X	X	X	X	X
ColorChooser.rgbGreenText	String	X	X	X	X	X
ColorChooser.rgbMnemonic	Integer	X	X	X	X	X
ColorChooser.rgbNameText	String	X	X	X	X	X
ColorChooser.rgbRedDisplayed➡ MnemonicIndex	Integer	X	X	X	X	X
ColorChooser.rgbRedMnemonic	Integer	X	X	X	X	X
ColorChooser.rgbRedText	String	X	X	X	X	X
ColorChooser.sampleText	String	X	X	X	X	X
ColorChooser.showPreviewPanelText	Boolean	X	X	X	X	X
ColorChooser.swatchesDefault➡ RecentColor	Color	X	X	X	X	X
ColorChooser.swatchesDisplayed➡ MnemonicIndex	Integer	X	X	X	X	X
ColorChooser.swatchesMnemonic	Integer	X	X	X	X	X
ColorChooser.swatchesNameText	String	X	X	X	X	X
ColorChooser.swatchesRecent➡ SwatchSize	Dimension	X	X	X	X	X
ColorChooser.swatchesRecentText	String	X	X	X	X	X
ColorChooser.swatchesSwatchSize	Dimension	X	X	X	X	X
ColorChooserUI	String	X	X	X	X	X
ComboBox.actionMap	ActionMap	X	X	X	X	X
ComboBox.ancestorInputMap	InputMap	X	X	X	X	X
ComboBox.background	Color	X	X	X	X	X
ComboBox.border	Border	X	X	X	X	X
ComboBox.buttonBackground	Color	X	X	X	X	X
ComboBox.buttonDarkShadow	Color	X	X	X	X	X
ComboBox.buttonHighlight	Color	X	X	X	X	X
ComboBox.buttonShadow	Color	X	X	X	X	X
ComboBox.control	Color	X				
ComboBox.controlForeground	Color	X				
ComboBox.disabledBackground	Color	X	X	X	X	X

UIResource Elements for the Predefined Look and Feel Classes (Continued)

Property String	Object Type	CDE/Motif	Metal	Windows	GTK	Synth
ComboBox.disabledForeground	Color	X	X	X	X	X
ComboBox.font	Font	X	X	X	X	X
ComboBox.foreground	Color	X	X	X	X	X
ComboBox.rendererUseListColors	Boolean				X	X
ComboBox.selectionBackground	Color	X	X	X	X	X
ComboBox.selectionForeground	Color	X	X	X	X	X
ComboBox.showPopupOnNavigation	Boolean	X	X	X	X	X
ComboBox.timeFactor	Long	X	X	X	X	X
ComboBox.togglePopupText	String	X	X	X	X	X
ComboBoxUI	String	X	X	X	X	X
ComponentUI	String	X	X	X	X	X
control	Color	X	X	X	X	X
controlDkShadow	Color	X	X	X	X	X
controlHighlight	Color	X	X	X	X	X
controlLightShadow	Color	X				
controlLtHighlight	Color	X	X	X	X	X
controlShadow	Color	X	X	X	X	X
controlText	Color	X	X	X	X	X
dark	Color				X	
desktop	Color	X	X	X	X	X
Desktop.ancestorInputMap	InputMap	X	X	X	X	X
Desktop.background	Color	X	X	X	X	X
Desktop.windowBindings	Object[ ] [b]	X	X	X	X	X
DesktopIcon.background	Color		X			
DesktopIcon.border	Border	X	X	X	X	X
DesktopIcon.font	Font		X			
DesktopIcon.foreground	Color		X			
DesktopIcon.icon	Icon	X				
DesktopIcon.width	Integer		X	X		
DesktopIcon.windowBindings	Object[ ] [c]	X				
DesktopIconUI	String	X	X	X	X	X
DesktopPane.actionMap	ActionMap	X	X	X	X	X

UIResource Elements for the Predefined Look and Feel Classes (Continued)

Property String	Object Type	CDE/Motif	Metal	Windows	GTK	Synth
DesktopPaneUI	String	X	X	X	X	X
DirectoryPaneUI	String	X	X	X	X	X
EditorPane.actionMap	ActionMap	X	X	X	X	X
EditorPane.background	Color	X	X	X	X	X
EditorPane.border	Border	X	X	X	X	X
EditorPane.caretAspectRatio	Number				X	
EditorPane.caretBlinkRate	Integer	X	X	X	X	X
EditorPane.caretForeground	Color	X	X	X	X	X
EditorPane.focusInputMap	InputMap	X	X	X	X	X
EditorPane.font	Font	X	X	X	X	X
EditorPane.foreground	Color	X	X	X	X	X
EditorPane.inactiveForeground	Color	X	X	X	X	X
EditorPane.keyBindings	KeyBinding[ ]	X	X	X	X	X
EditorPane.margin	Insets	X	X	X	X	X
EditorPane.selectionBackground	Color	X	X	X	X	X
EditorPane.selectionForeground	Color	X	X	X	X	X
EditorPaneUI	String	X	X	X	X	X
FileChooser.acceptAllFile➡FilterText	String	X	X	X	X	X
FileChooser.ancestorInputMap	InputMap	X	X	X	X	X
FileChooser.cancelButtonMnemonic	Integer	X	X	X	X	X
FileChooser.cancelButtonText	String	X	X	X	X	X
FileChooser.cancelButton➡ToolTipText	String	X	X	X	X	X
FileChooser.deleteFileButton➡Mnemonic	Integer				X	
FileChooser.deleteFileButtonText	String				X	
FileChooser.deleteFileButton➡ToolTipText	String				X	
FileChooser.detailsViewButton➡AccessibleName	String		X	X		
FileChooser.detailsViewButton➡ToolTipText	String		X	X		
FileChooser.detailsViewIcon	Icon	X	X	X	X	X

UIResource Elements for the Predefined Look and Feel Classes (Continued)

Property String	Object Type	CDE/Motif	Metal	Windows	GTK	Synth
FileChooser.directoryDescription➡Text	String	X	X	X	X	X
FileChooser.directoryOpenButton➡Mnemonic	Integer	X	X	X	X	X
FileChooser.directoryOpenButton➡Text	String	X	X	X	X	X
FileChooser.directoryOpenButton➡ToolTipText	String	X	X	X	X	X
FileChooser.enterFileNameLabel➡Mnemonic	Integer	X				
FileChooser.enterFileNameLabel➡Text	String	X				
FileChooser.fileDescriptionText	String	X	X	X	X	X
FileChooser.fileNameLabelMnemonic	Integer		X	X		
FileChooser.fileNameLabelText	String		X	X		
FileChooser.filesLabelMnemonic	Integer	X				
FileChooser.filesLabelText	String	X			X	
FileChooser.filesOfTypeLabel➡Mnemonic	Integer		X	X		
FileChooser.filesOfTypeLabelText	String		X	X		
FileChooser.filterLabelMnemonic	Integer	X			X	
FileChooser.filterLabelText	String	X			X	
FileChooser.foldersLabelMnemonic	String	X				
FileChooser.foldersLabelText	String	X			X	
FileChooser.helpButtonMnemonic	Integer	X	X	X	X	X
FileChooser.helpButtonText	String	X	X	X	X	X
FileChooser.helpButtonToolTipText	String	X	X	X	X	X
FileChooser.homeFolder➡AccessibleName	String		X	X		
FileChooser.homeFolderIcon	Icon	X	X	X	X	X
FileChooser.homeFolderToolTipText	String		X	X		
FileChooser.listFont	Font		X			
FileChooser.listViewBackground	Color		X			
FileChooser.listViewBorder	Border		X			
FileChooser.listViewButton➡AccessibleName	String		X	X		

UIResource Elements for the Predefined Look and Feel Classes (Continued)

Property String	Object Type	CDE/Motif	Metal	Windows	GTK	Synth
FileChooser.listViewButton➡ ToolTipText	String		X	X		
FileChooser.listViewIcon	Icon	X	X	X	X	X
FileChooser.listViewWindowsStyle	Boolean			X		
FileChooser.lookInLabelMnemonic	Integer		X	X		
FileChooser.lookInLabelText	String		X	X		
FileChooser.newFolderAccessible➡ Name	String		X	X		
FileChooser.newFolderButton➡ Mnemonic	Integer				X	
FileChooser.newFolderButtonText	String				X	
FileChooser.newFolderButtonTool➡ TipText				X		
FileChooser.newFolderDialogText	String				X	
FileChooser.newFolderError➡ Separator	String	X	X	X	X	X
FileChooser.newFolderErrorText	String	X	X	X	X	X
FileChooser.newFolderIcon	Icon	X	X	X	X	X
FileChooser.newFolderToolTipText	String		X	X		
FileChooser.openButtonMnemonic	Integer	X	X	X	X	X
FileChooser.openButtonText	String	X	X	X	X	X
FileChooser.openButtonToolTipText	String	X	X	X	X	X
FileChooser.openDialogTitleText	String	X	X	X	X	X
FileChooser.other.newFolder	String	X	X	X	X	X
FileChooser.other.newFolder. subsequent	String	X	X	X	X	X
FileChooser.pathLabelMnemonic	Integer	X			X	
FileChooser.pathLabelText	String	X			X	
FileChooser.readOnly	Boolean	X	X	X	X	X
FileChooser.renameFileButton➡ Mnemonic	Integer				X	
FileChooser.renameFileButtonText	String				X	
FileChooser.renameFileButton➡ ToolTipText	String				X	
FileChooser.renameFileDialogText	String				X	

UIResource Elements for the Predefined Look and Feel Classes (Continued)

Property String	Object Type	CDE/Motif	Metal	Windows	GTK	Synth
FileChooser.renameFileErrorText	String				X	
FileChooser.renameFileErrorTitle	String				X	
FileChooser.saveButtonMnemonic	Integer	X	X	X	X	X
FileChooser.saveButtonText	String	X	X	X	X	X
FileChooser.saveButtonToolTipText	String	X	X	X	X	X
FileChooser.saveDialogTitleText	String	X	X	X	X	X
FileChooser.saveInLabelText	String		X	X		
FileChooser.updateButtonMnemonic	Integer	X	X	X	X	X
FileChooser.updateButtonText	String	X	X	X	X	X
FileChooser.updateButtonToolTip➡Text	String	X	X	X	X	X
FileChooser.upFolderAccessible➡Name	String		X	X		
FileChooser.upFolderIcon	Icon	X	X	X	X	X
FileChooser.upFolderToolTipText	String		X	X		
FileChooser.usesSingleFilePane	Boolean	X	X	X	X	X
FileChooser.useSystemExtension➡Hiding	Boolean	X	X	X	X	X
FileChooser.win32.newFolder	String	X	X	X	X	X
FileChooser.win32.newFolder.subsequent	String	X	X	X	X	X
FileChooserUI	String	X	X	X	X	X
FileView.computerIcon	Icon	X	X	X	X	X
FileView.directoryIcon	Icon	X	X	X	X	X
FileView.fileIcon	Icon	X	X	X	X	X
FileView.floppyDriveIcon	Icon	X	X	X	X	X
FileView.hardDriveIcon	Icon	X	X	X	X	X
FormattedTextField.actionMap	ActionMap	X	X	X	X	X
FormattedTextField.background	Color	X	X	X	X	X
FormattedTextField.border	Border	X	X	X	X	X
FormattedTextField.caret➡AspectRatio	Number				X	
FormattedTextField.caretBlinkRate	Integer	X	X	X	X	X
FormattedTextField.caret➡Foreground	Color	X	X	X	X	X

UIResource Elements for the Predefined Look and Feel Classes (Continued)

Property String	Object Type	CDE/Motif	Metal	Windows	GTK	Synth
FormattedTextField.focusInputMap	InputMap	X	X	X	X	X
FormattedTextField.font	Font	X	X	X	X	X
FormattedTextField.foreground	Color	X	X	X	X	X
FormattedTextField.inactive➡Background	Color	X	X	X	X	X
FormattedTextField.inactive➡Foreground	Color	X	X	X	X	X
FormattedTextField.keyBindings	KeyBinding[ ]	X	X	X	X	X
FormattedTextField.margin	Insets	X	X	X	X	X
FormattedTextField.selection➡Background	Color	X	X	X	X	X
FormattedTextField.selection➡Foreground	Color	X	X	X	X	X
FormattedTextFieldUI	String	X	X	X	X	X
FormView.browseFileButtonText	String	X	X	X	X	X
FormView.resetButtonText	String	X	X	X	X	X
FormView.submitButtonText	String	X	X	X	X	X
GTKColorChooserPanel.displayed➡MnemonicIndex	Integer				X	
GTKColorChooserPanel.mnemonic	Integer				X	
GTKColorChooserPanel.nameText	String				X	
inactiveCaption	Color	X	X	X	X	X
inactiveCaptionBorder	Color	X	X	X	X	X
inactiveCaptionText	Color	X	X	X	X	X
info	Color	X	X	X	X	X
infoText	Color	X	X	X	X	X
InternalFrame.actionMap	ActionMap	X	X	X	X	X
InternalFrame.activeBorderColor	Color			X		
InternalFrame.activeTitle➡Background	Color	X	X	X	X	X
InternalFrame.activeTitle➡Foreground	Color	X	X	X	X	X
InternalFrame.activeTitleGradient	List		X	X		
InternalFrame.border	Border	X	X	X	X	X
InternalFrame.borderColor	Color	X	X	X	X	X

UIResource Elements for the Predefined Look and Feel Classes (Continued)

Property String	Object Type	CDE/Motif	Metal	Windows	GTK	Synth
InternalFrame.borderDarkShadow	Color	X	X	X	X	X
InternalFrame.borderHighlight	Color	X	X	X	X	X
InternalFrame.borderLight	Color	X	X	X	X	X
InternalFrame.borderShadow	Color	X	X	X	X	X
InternalFrame.borderWidth	Integer			X		
InternalFrame.closeButtonToolTip	String	X	X	X	X	X
InternalFrame.closeIcon	Icon	X	X	X	X	X
InternalFrame.closeSound	String	X	X	X	X	X
InternalFrame.icon	Icon	X	X	X	X	X
InternalFrame.iconButtonToolTip	String	X	X	X	X	X
InternalFrame.iconifyIcon	Icon	X	X	X	X	X
InternalFrame.inactiveBorderColor	Color			X		
InternalFrame.inactiveTitle➡ Background	Color	X	X	X	X	X
InternalFrame.inactiveTitle➡ Foreground	Color	X	X	X	X	X
InternalFrame.inactiveTitle➡ Gradient	List		X	X		
InternalFrame.layoutTitlePane➡ AtOrigin	Boolean	X	X	X	X	X
InternalFrame.maxButtonToolTip	String	X	X	X	X	X
InternalFrame.maximizeIcon	Icon	X	X	X	X	X
InternalFrame.maximizeSound	String	X	X	X	X	X
InternalFrame.menuIcon	Icon		X			
InternalFrame.minimizeIcon	Icon	X	X	X	X	X
InternalFrame.minimizeIcon➡ Background	Color			X		
InternalFrame.minimizeSound	String	X	X	X	X	X
InternalFrame.optionDialogBorder	Border		X			
InternalFrame.paletteBorder	Border		X			
InternalFrame.paletteCloseIcon	Icon		X			
InternalFrame.paletteTitleHeight	Integer		X			
InternalFrame.resizeIconHighlight	Color			X		
InternalFrame.resizeIconShadow	Color			X		

UIResource Elements for the Predefined Look and Feel Classes (Continued)

Property String	Object Type	CDE/Motif	Metal	Windows	GTK	Synth
InternalFrame.restoreButton➥ ToolTip	String	X	X	X	X	X
InternalFrame.restoreDownSound	String	X	X	X	X	X
InternalFrame.restoreUpSound	String	X	X	X	X	X
InternalFrame.titleButtonHeight	Integer			X		
InternalFrame.titleButtonWidth	Integer			X		
InternalFrame.titleFont	Font	X	X	X	X	X
InternalFrame.titlePaneHeight	Integer			X		
InternalFrame.useTaskBar	Boolean				X	X
InternalFrame.windowBindings	Object[ ] [d]	X	X	X	X	X
InternalFrameTitlePane.close➥ ButtonAccessibleName	String	X	X	X	X	X
InternalFrameTitlePane.close➥ ButtonText	String	X	X	X	X	X
InternalFrameTitlePane.closeIcon	Icon				X	X
InternalFrameTitlePane. iconifyButtonAccessibleName	String	X	X	X	X	X
InternalFrameTitlePane. iconifyIcon	Icon				X	X
InternalFrameTitlePane. maximizeButtonAccessibleName	String	X	X	X	X	X
InternalFrameTitlePane. maximizeButtonText	String	X	X	X	X	X
InternalFrameTitlePane. maximizeIcon	Icon				X	X
InternalFrameTitlePane. minimizeButtonText	String	X	X	X	X	X
InternalFrameTitlePane. minimizeIcon	Icon				X	X
InternalFrameTitlePane. moveButtonText	String	X	X	X	X	X
InternalFrameTitlePane. restoreButtonText	String	X	X	X	X	X
InternalFrameTitlePane. sizeButtonText	String	X	X	X	X	X
InternalFrameTitlePane. titlePaneLayout	LayoutManager				X	X
InternalFrameTitlePaneUI	String			X	X	

UIResource Elements for the Predefined Look and Feel Classes (Continued)

Property String	Object Type	CDE/Motif	Metal	Windows	GTK	Synth
InternalFrameUI	String	X	X	X	X	X
IsindexView.prompt	String	X	X	X	X	X
Label.actionMap	ActionMap	X	X	X	X	X
Label.background	Color	X	X	X	X	X
Label.border	Border	X	X	X	X	X
Label.disabledForeground	Color	X	X	X	X	X
Label.disabledShadow	Color	X	X	X	X	X
Label.font	Font	X	X	X	X	X
Label.foreground	Color	X	X	X	X	X
LabelUI	String	X	X	X	X	X
light	Color				X	
List.actionMap	ActionMap	X	X	X	X	X
List.background	Color	X	X	X	X	X
List.border	Border	X	X	X	X	X
List.cellHeight	Integer				X	X
List.cellRenderer	ListCell➡Renderer	X	X	X	X	X
List.focusCellHighlightBorder	Border	X	X	X	X	X
List.focusInputMap	InputMap	X	X	X	X	X
List.focusInputMap.RightToLeft	InputMap	X	X	X	X	X
List.font	Font	X	X	X	X	X
List.foreground	Color	X	X	X	X	X
List.lockToPositionOnScroll	Boolean	X	X	X	X	X
List.rendererUseListColors	Boolean				X	X
List.rendererUseUIBorder	Boolean				X	X
List.selectionBackground	Color	X	X	X	X	X
List.selectionForeground	Color	X	X	X	X	X
List.timeFactor	Long	X	X	X	X	X
ListUI	String	X	X	X	X	X
menu	Color	X	X	X	X	X
Menu.acceleratorDelimiter	String				X	X
Menu.acceleratorFont	Font	X	X	X	X	X

UIResource Elements for the Predefined Look and Feel Classes (Continued)

Property String	Object Type	CDE/Motif	Metal	Windows	GTK	Synth
Menu.acceleratorForeground	Color	X	X	X	X	X
Menu.acceleratorSelection➡Foreground	Color	X	X	X	X	X
Menu.actionMap	ActionMap	X	X	X	X	X
Menu.arrowIcon	Icon	X	X	X	X	X
Menu.background	Color	X	X	X	X	X
Menu.border	Border	X	X	X	X	X
Menu.borderPainted	Boolean	X	X	X	X	X
Menu.checkIcon	Icon	X	X	X	X	X
Menu.crossMenuMnemonic	Boolean	X	X	X	X	X
Menu.delay	Integer				X	X
Menu.disabledForeground	Color	X	X	X	X	X
Menu.font	Font	X	X	X	X	X
Menu.foreground	Color	X	X	X	X	X
Menu.margin	Insets	X	X	X	X	X
Menu.menuPopupOffsetX	Integer	X	X	X	X	X
Menu.menuPopupOffsetY	Integer	X	X	X	X	X
Menu.opaque	Boolean	X	X	X	X	X
Menu.selectionBackground	Color	X	X	X	X	X
Menu.selectionForeground	Color	X	X	X	X	X
Menu.shortcutKeys	int[ ]	X	X	X	X	X
Menu.submenuPopupOffsetX	Integer	X	X	X	X	X
Menu.submenuPopupOffsetY	Integer	X	X	X	X	X
Menu.textIconGap	Integer				X	X
Menu.useMenuBarBackground➡ForTopLevel	Boolean	X	X	X	X	X
MenuBar.actionMap	ActionMap	X	X	X	X	X
MenuBar.background	Color	X	X	X	X	X
MenuBar.border	Border	X	X	X	X	X
MenuBar.borderColor	Color		X			
MenuBar.darkShadow	Color	X				
MenuBar.font	Font	X	X	X	X	X
MenuBar.foreground	Color	X	X	X	X	X

UIResource Elements for the Predefined Look and Feel Classes (Continued)

Property String	Object Type	CDE/Motif	Metal	Windows	GTK	Synth
MenuBar.gradient	List		X			
MenuBar.highlight	Color	X	X	X	X	X
MenuBar.shadow	Color	X	X	X	X	X
MenuBar.windowBindings	Object[ ] [e]	X	X	X	X	X
MenuBarUI	String	X	X	X	X	X
MenuItem.acceleratorDelimiter	String	X	X	X	X	X
MenuItem.acceleratorFont	Font	X	X	X	X	X
MenuItem.acceleratorForeground	Color	X	X	X	X	X
MenuItem.acceleratorSelection➥ Foreground	Color	X	X	X	X	X
MenuItem.actionMap	ActionMap	X	X	X	X	X
MenuItem.arrowIcon	Icon	X	X	X	X	X
MenuItem.background	Color	X	X	X	X	X
MenuItem.border	Border	X	X	X	X	X
MenuItem.borderPainted	Boolean	X	X	X	X	X
MenuItem.checkIcon	Icon	X	X	X	X	X
MenuItem.commandSound	String	X	X	X	X	X
MenuItem.disabledForeground	Color	X	X	X	X	X
MenuItem.font	Font	X	X	X	X	X
MenuItem.foreground	Color	X	X	X	X	X
MenuItem.margin	Insets	X	X	X	X	X
MenuItem.opaque	Boolean	X	X	X	X	X
MenuItem.selectionBackground	Color	X	X	X	X	X
MenuItem.selectionForeground	Color	X	X	X	X	X
MenuItem.textIconGap	Integer				X	X
MenuItemUI	String	X		X	X	X	X
menuPressedItemB	Color			X		
menuPressedItemF	Color			X		
menuText	Color	X	X	X	X	X
MenuUI	String	X	X	X	X	X
MetalTitlePane.closeMnemonic	Integer		X			
MetalTitlePane.closeTitle	String		X			

UIResource Elements for the Predefined Look and Feel Classes (Continued)

Property String	Object Type	CDE/Motif	Metal	Windows	GTK	Synth
MetalTitlePane.iconifyMnemonic	Integer		X			
MetalTitlePane.iconifyTitle	String		X			
MetalTitlePane.maximizeMnemonic	Integer		X			
MetalTitlePane.maximizeTitle	String		X			
MetalTitlePane.restoreMnemonic	Integer		X			
MetalTitlePane.restoreTitle	String		X			
mid	Color				X	
OptionPane.actionMap	ActionMap	X	X	X	X	X
OptionPane.background	Color	X	X	X	X	X
OptionPane.border	Border	X	X	X	X	X
OptionPane.buttonAreaBorder	Border	X	X	X	X	X
OptionPane.buttonClickThreshhold	Integer	X	X	X	X	X
OptionPane.buttonFont	Font	X	X	X	X	X
OptionPane.buttonOrientation	Integer	X	X	X	X	X
OptionPane.buttonPadding	Integer	X	X	X	X	X
OptionPane.cancelButtonMnemonic	String	X	X	X	X	X
OptionPane.cancelButtonText	String	X	X	X	X	X
OptionPane.cancelIcon	Icon	X	X	X	X	X
OptionPane.error➡ Dialog.border.background	Color		X			
OptionPane.error➡ Dialog.titlePane.background	Color		X			
OptionPane.error➡ Dialog.titlePane.foreground	Color		X			
OptionPane.error➡ Dialog.titlePane.shadow	Color		X			
OptionPane.errorIcon	Icon	X	X	X	X	X
OptionPane.errorSound	String	X	X	X	X	X
OptionPane.font	Font	X	X	X	X	X
OptionPane.foreground	Color	X	X	X	X	X
OptionPane.informationIcon	Icon	X	X	X	X	X
OptionPane.informationSound	String	X	X	X	X	X
OptionPane.inputDialogTitle	String	X	X	X	X	X
OptionPane.isYesLast	Boolean	X	X	X	X	X

UIResource Elements for the Predefined Look and Feel Classes (Continued)

Property String	Object Type	CDE/Motif	Metal	Windows	GTK	Synth
OptionPane.messageAnchor	Integer	X	X	X	X	X
OptionPane.messageAreaBorder	Border	X	X	X	X	X
OptionPane.messageDialogTitle	String	X	X	X	X	X
OptionPane.messageFont	Font	X	X	X	X	X
OptionPane.messageForeground	Color	X	X	X	X	X
OptionPane.minimumSize	Dimension	X	X	X	X	X
OptionPane.noButtonMnemonic	String	X	X	X	X	X
OptionPane.noButtonText	String	X	X	X	X	X
OptionPane.noIcon	Icon	X	X	X	X	X
OptionPane.okButtonMnemonic	String	X	X	X	X	X
OptionPane.okButtonText	String	X	X	X	X	X
OptionPane.okIcon	Icon	X	X	X	X	X
OptionPane.questionDialog. border.background	Color		X			
OptionPane.questionDialog. titlePane.background	Color		X			
OptionPane.questionDialog. titlePane.foreground	Color		X			
OptionPane.questionDialog. titlePane.shadow	Color		X			
OptionPane.questionIcon	Icon	X	X	X	X	X
OptionPane.questionSound	String	X	X	X	X	X
OptionPane.sameSizeButtons	Boolean	X	X	X	X	X
OptionPane.separatorPadding	Integer				X	X
OptionPane.setButtonMargin	Boolean	X	X	X	X	X
OptionPane.titleText	String	X	X	X	X	X
OptionPane.warningDialog. border.background	Color		X			
OptionPane.warningDialog. titlePane.background	Color		X			
OptionPane.warningDialog. titlePane.foreground	Color		X			
OptionPane.warningDialog. titlePane.shadow	Color		X			
OptionPane.warningIcon	Icon	X	X	X	X	X

UIResource Elements for the Predefined Look and Feel Classes (Continued)

Property String	Object Type	CDE/Motif	Metal	Windows	GTK	Synth
OptionPane.warningSound	String	X	X	X	X	X
OptionPane.windowBindings	Object[ ] f	X	X	X	X	X
OptionPane.yesButtonMnemonic	String	X	X	X	X	X
OptionPane.yesButtonText	String	X	X	X	X	X
OptionPane.yesIcon	Icon	X	X	X	X	X
OptionPaneUI	String	X	X	X	X	X
Panel.background	Color	X	X	X	X	X
Panel.border	Border	X	X	X	X	X
Panel.font	Font	X	X	X	X	X
Panel.foreground	Color	X	X	X	X	X
PanelUI	String	X	X	X	X	X
PasswordField.actionMap	ActionMap	X	X	X	X	X
PasswordField.background	Color	X	X	X	X	X
PasswordField.border	Border	X	X	X	X	X
PasswordField.caretAspectRatio	Number				X	
PasswordField.caretBlinkRate	Integer	X	X	X	X	X
PasswordField.caretForeground	Color	X	X	X	X	X
PasswordField.disabledBackground	Color			X		
PasswordField.focusInputMap	InputMap	X	X	X	X	X
PasswordField.font	Font	X	X	X	X	X
PasswordField.foreground	Color	X	X	X	X	X
PasswordField.inactiveBackground	Color	X	X	X	X	X
PasswordField.inactiveForeground	Color	X	X	X	X	X
PasswordField.keyBindings	KeyBinding[ ]	X	X	X	X	X
PasswordField.margin	Insets	X	X	X	X	X
PasswordField.selectionBackground	Color	X	X	X	X	X
PasswordField.selectionForeground	Color	X	X	X	X	X
PasswordFieldUI	String	X	X	X	X	X
PopupMenu.actionMap	ActionMap	X	X	X	X	X
PopupMenu.background	Color	X	X	X	X	X
PopupMenu.border	Border	X	X	X	X	X
PopupMenu.consumeEventOnClose	Boolean	X	X	X	X	X

UIResource Elements for the Predefined Look and Feel Classes (Continued)

Property String	Object Type	CDE/Motif	Metal	Windows	GTK	Synth
PopupMenu.font	Font	X	X	X	X	X
PopupMenu.foreground	Color	X	X	X	X	X
PopupMenu.popupSound	String	X	X	X	X	X
PopupMenu.selectedWindow➡InputMapBindings	Object[ ] [g]	X	X	X	X	X
PopupMenu.selectedWindow➡InputMapBindings.RightToLeft	Object[ ] [h]	X	X	X	X	X
PopupMenuSeparatorUI	String	X	X	X	X	X
PopupMenuUI	String	X	X	X	X	X
ProgressBar.background	Color	X	X	X	X	X
ProgressBar.border	Border	X	X	X	X	X
ProgressBar.cellLength	Integer	X	X	X	X	X
ProgressBar.cellSpacing	Integer	X	X	X	X	X
ProgressBar.cycleTime	Integer	X	X	X	X	X
ProgressBar.font	Font	X	X	X	X	X
ProgressBar.foreground	Color	X	X	X	X	X
ProgressBar.highlight	Color			X		
ProgressBar.horizontalSize	Dimension	X	X	X	X	X
ProgressBar.repaintInterval	Integer	X	X	X	X	X
ProgressBar.selectionBackground	Color	X	X	X	X	X
ProgressBar.selectionForeground	Color	X	X	X	X	X
ProgressBar.shadow	Color			X		
ProgressBar.verticalSize	Dimension	X	X	X	X	X
ProgressBarUI	String	X	X	X	X	X
ProgressMonitor.progressText	String	X	X	X	X	X
RadioButton.background	Color	X	X	X	X	X
RadioButton.border	Border	X	X	X	X	X
RadioButton.darkShadow	Color	X	X	X	X	X
RadioButton.disabledText	Color		X			
RadioButton.focus	Color	X	X	X		
RadioButton.focusInputMap	InputMap	X	X	X	X	X
RadioButton.font	Font	X	X	X	X	X
RadioButton.foreground	Color	X	X	X	X	X

UIResource Elements for the Predefined Look and Feel Classes (Continued)

Property String	Object Type	CDE/Motif	Metal	Windows	GTK	Synth
RadioButton.gradient	List		X			
RadioButton.highlight	Color	X	X	X	X	X
RadioButton.icon	Icon	X	X	X	X	X
RadioButton.interiorBackground	Color			X		
RadioButton.light	Color	X	X	X	X	X
RadioButton.margin	Insets	X	X	X	X	X
RadioButton.rollover	Boolean		X			
RadioButton.select	Color		X			
RadioButton.shadow	Color	X	X	X	X	X
RadioButton.textIconGap	Integer	X	X	X	X	X
RadioButton.textShiftOffset	Integer	X	X	X	X	X
RadioButtonMenuItem.acceleratorFont	Font	X	X	X	X	X
RadioButtonMenuItem.accelerator Foreground	Color	X	X	X	X	X
RadioButtonMenuItem.accelerator SelectionForeground	Color	X	X	X	X	X
RadioButtonMenuItem.actionMap	ActionMap	X	X	X	X	X
RadioButtonMenuItem.arrowIcon	Icon	X	X	X	X	X
RadioButtonMenuItem.background	Color	X	X	X	X	X
RadioButtonMenuItem.border	Border	X	X	X	X	X
RadioButtonMenuItem.borderPainted	Boolean	X	X	X	X	X
RadioButtonMenuItem.checkIcon	Icon	X	X	X	X	X
RadioButtonMenuItem.commandSound	String	X	X	X	X	X
RadioButtonMenuItem.disabledForeground	Color	X	X	X	X	X
RadioButtonMenuItem.font	Font	X	X	X	X	X
RadioButtonMenuItem.foreground	Color	X	X	X	X	X
RadioButtonMenuItem.gradient	List		X			
RadioButtonMenuItem.margin	Insets	X	X	X	X	X
RadioButtonMenuItem.opaque	Boolean	X	X	X	X	X
RadioButtonMenuItem.selectionBackground	Color	X	X	X	X	X
RadioButtonMenuItem.selectionForeground	Color	X	X	X	X	X

UIResource Elements for the Predefined Look and Feel Classes (Continued)

Property String	Object Type	CDE/Motif	Metal	Windows	GTK	Synth
RadioButtonMenuItemUI	String	X	X	X	X	X
RadioButtonUI	String	X	X	X	X	X
RootPane.actionMap	ActionMap	X	X	X	X	X
RootPane.ancestorInputMap	InputMap	X	X	X	X	X
RootPane.colorChooserDialogBorder	Border		X			
RootPane.defaultButton➥WindowKeyBindings	Object[ ] [i]	X	X	X	X	X
RootPane.errorDialogBorder	Border		X			
RootPane.fileChooserDialogBorder	Border		X			
RootPane.frameBorder	Border		X			
RootPane.informationDialogBorder	Border		X			
RootPane.plainDialogBorder	Border		X			
RootPane.questionDialogBorder	Border		X			
RootPane.warningDialogBorder	Border		X			
RootPaneUI	String	X	X	X	X	X
scrollbar	Color	X	X	X	X	X
ScrollBar.actionMap	ActionMap	X	X	X	X	X
ScrollBar.allowsAbsolute➥Positioning	Boolean	X	X	X	X	X
ScrollBar.ancestorInputMap	InputMap	X	X	X	X	X
ScrollBar.ancestorInputMap.RightToLeft	InputMap	X	X	X	X	X
ScrollBar.background	Color	X	X	X	X	X
ScrollBar.border	Color	X	X	X	X	X
ScrollBar.darkShadow	Color		X			
ScrollBar.focusInputMap	InputMap	X	X	X	X	X
ScrollBar.focusInputMap.RightToLeft	InputMap	X	X	X	X	X
ScrollBar.foreground	Color	X	X	X	X	X
ScrollBar.gradient	List		X			
ScrollBar.highlight	Color		X			

UIResource Elements for the Predefined Look and Feel Classes (Continued)

Property String	Object Type	CDE/Motif	Metal	Windows	GTK	Synth
ScrollBar.maximumThumbSize	Dimension	X	X	X	X	X
ScrollBar.minimumThumbSize	Dimension	X	X	X	X	X
ScrollBar.shadow	Color		X			
ScrollBar.squareButtons	Boolean	X	X	X	X	X
ScrollBar.thumb	Color	X	X	X	X	X
ScrollBar.thumbDarkShadow	Color	X	X	X	X	X
ScrollBar.thumbHeight	Integer				X	X
ScrollBar.thumbHighlight	Color	X	X	X	X	X
ScrollBar.thumbShadow	Color	X	X	X	X	X
ScrollBar.track	Color	X	X	X	X	X
ScrollBar.trackForeground	Color			X		
ScrollBar.trackHighlight	Color	X	X	X	X	X
ScrollBar.trackHighlight➥Foreground	Color			X		
ScrollBar.width	Integer	X	X	X	X	X
ScrollBarUI	String	X	X	X	X	X
ScrollPane.actionMap	ActionMap	X	X	X	X	X
ScrollPane.ancestorInputMap	InputMap	X	X	X	X	X
ScrollPane.ancestorInputMap.RightToLeft	InputMap	X	X	X	X	X
ScrollPane.background	Color	X	X	X	X	X
ScrollPane.border	Border	X	X	X	X	X
ScrollPane.font	Font	X	X	X	X	X
ScrollPane.foreground	Color	X	X	X	X	X
ScrollPane.viewportBorder	Border	X	X	X	X	X
ScrollPane.viewportBorderInsets	Insets				X	X
ScrollPaneUI	String	X	X	X	X	X
Separator.background	Color	X	X	X	X	X
Separator.foreground	Color	X	X	X	X	X
Separator.highlight[j]	Color	X	X	X	X	X
Separator.insets	Insets				X	
Separator.shadow[k]	Color	X	X	X	X	X
Separator.thickness	Integer				X	X

UIResource Elements for the Predefined Look and Feel Classes (Continued)

Property String	Object Type	CDE/Motif	Metal	Windows	GTK	Synth
SeparatorUI	String	X	X	X	X	X
Slider.actionMap	ActionMap	X	X	X	X	X
Slider.altTrackColor	Color		X			
Slider.background	Color	X	X	X	X	X
Slider.border	Border	X	X	X	X	X
Slider.darkShadow	Color		X			
Slider.focus	Color	X	X	X	X	X
Slider.focusGradient	List		X			
Slider.focusInputMap	InputMap	X	X	X	X	X
Slider.focusInputMap.RightToLeft	InputMap	X	X	X	X	X
Slider.focusInsets	Insets	X	X	X	X	X
Slider.foreground	Color	X	X	X	X	X
Slider.gradient	List		X			
Slider.highlight	Color	X	X	X	X	X
Slider.horizontalSize	Dimension	X	X	X	X	X
Slider.horizontalThumbIcon	Icon		X			
Slider.majorTickLength	Integer		X			
Slider.minimumHorizontalSize	Dimension	X	X	X	X	X
Slider.minimumVerticalSize	Dimension	X	X	X	X	X
Slider.paintThumbArrowShape	Boolean	X	X	X	X	X
Slider.paintValue	Boolean				X	X
Slider.shadow	Color	X	X	X	X	X
Slider.thumb	Color		X			
Slider.thumbHeight	Integer				X	X
Slider.thumbWidth	Integer				X	X
Slider.tickColor	Color	X	X	X	X	X
Slider.trackBorder	Border				X	X
Slider.trackWidth	Integer		X			
Slider.verticalSize	Dimension	X	X	X	X	X
Slider.verticalThumbIcon	Icon		X			
SliderUI	String	X	X	X	X	X
Spinner.actionMap	ActionMap	X	X	X	X	X

UIResource Elements for the Predefined Look and Feel Classes (Continued)

Property String	Object Type	CDE/Motif	Metal	Windows	GTK	Synth
Spinner.ancestorInputMap	InputMap	X	X	X	X	X
Spinner.arrowButtonBorder	Border	X	X	X	X	X
Spinner.arrowButtonInsets	Insets	X	X	X	X	X
Spinner.arrowButtonSize	Dimension	X	X	X	X	X
Spinner.background	Color	X	X	X	X	X
Spinner.border	Border	X	X	X	X	X
Spinner.editorBorderPainted	Boolean	X	X	X	X	X
Spinner.font	Font	X	X	X	X	X
Spinner.foreground	Color	X	X	X	X	X
SpinnerUI	String	X	X	X	X	X
SplitPane.actionMap	ActionMap	X	X	X	X	X
SplitPane.activeThumb	Color	X				
SplitPane.ancestorInputMap	InputMap	X	X	X	X	X
SplitPane.background	Color	X	X	X	X	X
SplitPane.border	Border	X	X	X	X	X
SplitPane.centerOneTouchButtons	Boolean	X	X	X	X	X
SplitPane.darkShadow	Color	X	X	X	X	X
SplitPane.dividerFocusColor	Color		X			
SplitPane.dividerSize	Integer	X	X	X	X	X
SplitPane.highlight	Color	X	X	X	X	X
SplitPane.leftButtonText	String	X	X	X	X	X
SplitPane.oneTouchButtonOffset	Integer	X	X	X	X	X
SplitPane.oneTouchButtonSize	Integer	X	X	X	X	X
SplitPane.oneTouchButtonsOpaque	Boolean		X			
SplitPane.oneTouchExpandable	Boolean				X	X
SplitPane.oneTouchOffset	Integer				X	
SplitPane.rightButtonText	String	X	X	X	X	X
SplitPane.shadow	Color	X	X	X	X	X
SplitPane.size	Integer				X	X
SplitPane.supportsOneTouchButtons	Boolean	X	X	X	X	X
SplitPaneDivider.border	Border	X	X	X	X	X
SplitPaneDivider.draggingColor	Color	X	X	X	X	X

UIResource Elements for the Predefined Look and Feel Classes (Continued)

Property String	Object Type	CDE/Motif	Metal	Windows	GTK	Synth
SplitPaneDivider.oneTouchButton➡Size	Integer				X	X
SplitPaneUI	String	X	X	X	X	X
StandardDialogUI	String	X	X	X	X	X
swing.boldMetal	Boolean		X			
swing.plaf.metal.controlFont	Font		X			
swing.plaf.metal.smallFont	Font		X			
swing.plaf.metal.systemFont	Font		X			
swing.plaf.metal.userFont	Font		X			
TabbedPane.actionMap	ActionMap	X	X	X	X	X
TabbedPane.ancestorInputMap	InputMap	X	X	X	X	X
TabbedPane.background	Color	X	X	X	X	X
TabbedPane.borderHightlightColor	Color		X			
TabbedPane.contentAreaColor	Color	X	X	X	X	X
TabbedPane.contentBorderInsets	Insets	X	X	X	X	X
TabbedPane.contentOpaque	Boolean	X	X	X	X	X
TabbedPane.darkShadow	Color	X	X	X	X	X
TabbedPane.focus	Color	X	X	X	X	X
TabbedPane.focusInputMap	InputMap	X	X	X	X	X
TabbedPane.font	Font	X	X	X	X	X
TabbedPane.foreground	Color	X	X	X	X	X
TabbedPane.highlight	Color	X	X	X	X	X
TabbedPane.light	Color	X	X	X	X	X
TabbedPane.opaque	Boolean	X	X	X	X	X
TabbedPane.selected	Color	X	X	X	X	X
TabbedPane.selectedForeground	Color	X	X	X	X	X
TabbedPane.selectedTabPadInsets	Insets	X	X	X	X	X
TabbedPane.selectHighlight	Color		X			
TabbedPane.selectionFollowsFocus	Boolean	X	X	X	X	X
TabbedPane.shadow	Color	X	X	X	X	X
TabbedPane.tabAreaBackground	Color	X	X	X	X	X
TabbedPane.tabAreaInsets	Insets	X	X	X	X	X

UIResource Elements for the Predefined Look and Feel Classes (Continued)

Property String	Object Type	CDE/Motif	Metal	Windows	GTK	Synth
TabbedPane.tabInsets	Insets	X	X	X	X	X
TabbedPane.tabRunOverlay	Integer	X	X	X	X	X
TabbedPane.tabsOpaque	Boolean	X	X	X	X	X
TabbedPane.tabsOverlapBorder	Boolean	X	X	X	X	X
TabbedPane.textIconGap	Integer	X	X	X	X	X
TabbedPane.unselectedBackground	Color		X			
TabbedPane.unselectedTab➡Background	Color	X				
TabbedPane.unselectedTab➡Foreground	Color	X				
TabbedPane.unselectedTabHighlight	Color	X				
TabbedPane.unselectedTabShadow	Color	X				
TabbedPaneUI	String	X	X	X	X	X
Table.actionMap	ActionMap	X	X	X	X	X
Table.ancestorInputMap	InputMap	X	X	X	X	X
Table.ancestorInputMap.RightToLeft	InputMap	X	X	X	X	X
Table.background	Color	X	X	X	X	X
Table.darkShadow	Color			X		
Table.focusCellBackground	Color	X	X	X	X	X
Table.focusCellForeground	Color	X	X	X	X	X
Table.focusCellHighlightBorder	Border	X	X	X	X	X
Table.font	Font	X	X	X	X	X
Table.foreground	Color	X	X	X	X	X
Table.gridColor	Color	X	X	X	X	X
Table.highlight	Color			X		
Table.light	Color			X		
Table.rendererUseTableColors	Boolean				X	X
Table.rendererUseUIBorder	Boolean				X	X
Table.rowHeight	Integer				X	X
Table.scrollPaneBorder	Border	X	X	X	X	X
Table.selectionBackground	Color	X	X	X	X	X
Table.selectionForeground	Color	X	X	X	X	X

UIResource Elements for the Predefined Look and Feel Classes (Continued)

Property String	Object Type	CDE/Motif	Metal	Windows	GTK	Synth
Table.shadow	Color			X		
TableHeader.background	Color	X	X	X	X	X
TableHeader.cellBorder	Border	X	X	X	X	X
TableHeader.font	Font	X	X	X	X	X
TableHeader.foreground	Color	X	X	X	X	X
TableHeaderUI	String	X	X	X	X	X
TableUI	String	X	X	X	X	X
text	Color	X	X	X	X	X
TextArea.actionMap	ActionMap	X	X	X	X	X
TextArea.background	Color	X	X	X	X	X
TextArea.border	Border	X	X	X	X	X
TextArea.caretAspectRatio	Number				X	
TextArea.caretBlinkRate	Integer	X	X	X	X	X
TextArea.caretForeground	Color	X	X	X	X	X
TextArea.focusInputMap	InputMap	X	X	X	X	X
TextArea.font	Font	X	X	X	X	X
TextArea.foreground	Color	X	X	X	X	X
TextArea.inactiveForeground	Color	X	X	X	X	X
TextArea.keyBindings	KeyBinding[ ]	X	X	X	X	X
TextArea.margin	Insets	X	X	X	X	X
TextArea.selectionBackground	Color	X	X	X	X	X
TextArea.selectionForeground	Color	X	X	X	X	X
TextAreaUI	String	X	X	X	X	X
TextField.actionMap	ActionMap	X	X	X	X	X
TextField.background	Color	X	X	X	X	X
TextField.border	Border	X	X	X	X	Synth
TextField.caretAspectRatio	Number				X	X
TextField.caretBlinkRate	Integer	X	X	X	X	X
TextField.caretForeground	Color	X	X	X	X	X
TextField.darkShadow	Color	X	X	X	X	X
TextField.disabledBackground	Color	X	X	X	X	X
TextField.focusInputMap	InputMap	X	X	X	X	X

UIResource Elements for the Predefined Look and Feel Classes (Continued)

Property String	Object Type	CDE/Motif	Metal	Windows	GTK	Synth
TextField.font	Font	X	X	X	X	X
TextField.foreground	Color	X	X	X	X	X
TextField.highlight	Color	X	X	X	X	X
TextField.inactiveBackground	Color	X	X	X	X	X
TextField.inactiveForeground	Color	X	X	X	X	X
TextField.keyBindings	KeyBinding[ ]	X	X	X	X	X
TextField.light	Color	X	X	X	X	X
TextField.margin	Insets	X	X	X	X	X
TextField.selectionBackground	Color	X	X	X	X	X
TextField.selectionForeground	Color	X	X	X	X	X
TextField.shadow	Color	X	X	X	X	X
TextFieldUI	String	X	X	X	X	X
textHighlight	Color	X	X	X	X	X
textHighlightText	Color	X	X	X	X	X
textInactiveText	Color	X	X	X	X	X
TextPane.actionMap	ActionMap	X	X	X	X	X
TextPane.background	Color	X	X	X	X	X
TextPane.border	Border	X	X	X	X	X
TextPane.caretAspectRatio	Number				X	
TextPane.caretBlinkRate	Integer	X	X	X	X	X
TextPane.caretForeground	Color	X	X	X	X	X
TextPane.focusInputMap	InputMap	X	X	X	X	X
TextPane.font	Font	X	X	X	X	X
TextPane.foreground	Color	X	X	X	X	X
TextPane.inactiveForeground	Color	X	X	X	X	X
TextPane.keyBindings	KeyBinding[ ]	X	X	X	X	X
TextPane.margin	Insets	X	X	X	X	X
TextPane.selectionBackground	Color	X	X	X	X	X
TextPane.selectionForeground	Color	X	X	X	X	X
TextPaneUI	String	X	X	X	X	X
textText	Color	X	X	X	X	X
TitledBorder.border	Border	X	X	X	X	X

UIResource Elements for the Predefined Look and Feel Classes (Continued)

Property String	Object Type	CDE/Motif	Metal	Windows	GTK	Synth
TitledBorder.font	Font	X	X	X	X	X
TitledBorder.titleColor	Color	X	X	X	X	X
ToggleButton.background	Color	X	X	X	X	X
ToggleButton.border	Border	X	X	X	X	X
ToggleButton.darkShadow	Color	X	X	X	X	X
ToggleButton.disabledText	Color		X			
ToggleButton.focus	Color		X	X		
ToggleButton.focusInputMap	InputMap	X	X	X	X	X
ToggleButton.font	Font	X	X	X	X	X
ToggleButton.foreground	Color	X	X	X	X	X
ToggleButton.gradient	List		X			
ToggleButton.highlight	Color	X	X	X	X	X
ToggleButton.light	Color	X	X	X	X	X
ToggleButton.margin	Insets	X	X	X	X	
ToggleButton.select	Color	X	X			
ToggleButton.shadow	Color	X	X	X	X	X
ToggleButton.textIconGap	Integer	X	X	X	X	X
ToggleButton.textShiftOffset	Integer	X	X	X	X	X
ToggleButtonUI	String	X	X	X	X	X
ToolBar.actionMap	ActionMap	X	X	X	X	X
ToolBar.ancestorInputMap	InputMap	X	X	X	X	X
ToolBar.background	Color	X	X	X	X	X
ToolBar.border	Border	X	X	X	X	X
ToolBar.borderColor	Color		X			
ToolBar.darkShadow	Color	X	X	X	X	X
ToolBar.dockingBackground	Color	X	X	X	X	X
ToolBar.dockingForeground	Color	X	X	X	X	X
ToolBar.floatingBackground	Color	X	X	X	X	X
ToolBar.floatingForeground	Color	X	X	X	X	X
ToolBar.font	Font	X	X	X	X	X
ToolBar.foreground	Color	X	X	X	X	X
ToolBar.handleIcon	Icon				X	X

UIResource Elements for the Predefined Look and Feel Classes (Continued)

Property String	Object Type	CDE/Motif	Metal	Windows	GTK	Synth
ToolBar.highlight	Color	X	X	X	X	X
ToolBar.isRollover	Boolean	X	X	X	X	X
ToolBar.light	Color	X	X	X	X	X
ToolBar.nonrolloverBorder	Border	X	X	X	X	X
ToolBar.rolloverBorder	Border	X	X	X	X	X
ToolBar.separatorSize	Dimension	X	X	X	X	X
ToolBar.shadow	Color	X	X	X	X	X
ToolBarSeparatorUI	String	X	X	X	X	X
ToolBarUI	String	X	X	X	X	X
ToolTip.background	Color	X	X	X	X	X
ToolTip.backgroundInactive	Color	X	X	X	X	X
ToolTip.border	Border	X	X	X	X	X
ToolTip.borderInactive	Color	X	X	X	X	X
ToolTip.font	Font	X	X	X	X	X
ToolTip.foreground	Color	X	X	X	X	X
ToolTip.foregroundInactive	Color	X	X	X	X	X
ToolTip.hideAccelerator	Boolean		X			
ToolTipUI	String	X	X	X	X	X
Tree.actionMap	ActionMap	X	X	X	X	X
Tree.ancestorInputMap	InputMap	X	X	X	X	X
Tree.background	Color	X	X	X	X	X
Tree.changeSelectionWithFocus	Boolean	X	X	X	X	X
Tree.closedIcon	Icon	X	X	X	X	X
Tree.collapsedIcon	Icon	X	X	X	X	X
Tree.drawDashedFocusIndicator	Boolean			X		
Tree.drawHorizontalLines	Boolean				X	X
Tree.drawsFocusBorderAroundIcon	Boolean	X	X	X	X	X
Tree.drawVerticalLines	Boolean				X	X
Tree.editorBorder	Border	X	X	X	X	X
Tree.editorBorderSelectionColor	Color	X				
Tree.expandedIcon	Icon	X	X	X	X	X
Tree.expanderSize	Integer				X	

UIResource Elements for the Predefined Look and Feel Classes (Continued)

Property String	Object Type	CDE/Motif	Metal	Windows	GTK	Synth
Tree.focusInputMap	InputMap	X	X	X	X	X
Tree.focusInputMap.RightToLeft	InputMap	X	X	X	X	X
Tree.font	Font	X	X	X	X	X
Tree.foreground	Color	X	X	X	X	X
Tree.hash	Color	X	X	X	X	X
Tree.iconBackground	Color	X				
Tree.iconForeground	Color	X				
Tree.iconHighlight	Color	X				
Tree.iconShadow	Color	X				
Tree.leafIcon	Icon	X	X	X	X	X
Tree.leftChildIndent	Integer	X	X	X	X	X
Tree.line	Color		X			
Tree.lineTypeDashed	Boolean	X	X	X	X	X
Tree.openIcon	Icon	X	X	X	X	X
Tree.padding	Integer				X	X
Tree.paintLines	Boolean	X	X	X		
Tree.rendererUseTreeColors	Boolean				X	X
Tree.rightChildIndent	Integer	X	X	X	X	X
Tree.rowHeight	Integer	X	X	X	X	X
Tree.scrollsHorizontally➡AndVertically	Boolean	X	X	X	X	X
Tree.scrollsOnExpand	Boolean	X	X	X	X	X
Tree.selectionBackground	Color	X	X	X	X	X
Tree.selectionBorderColor	Color	X	X	X	X	X
Tree.selectionForeground	Color	X	X	X	X	X
Tree.showsRootHandles	Boolean	X	X	X	X	X
Tree.textBackground	Color	X	X	X	X	X
Tree.textForeground	Color	X	X	X	X	X
Tree.timeFactor	Integer	X	X	X	X	X
TreeUI	String	X	X	X	X	X
Viewport.background	Color	X	X	X	X	X
Viewport.font	Font	X	X	X	X	X

UIResource Elements for the Predefined Look and Feel Classes (Continued)

Property String	Object Type	CDE/Motif	Metal	Windows	GTK	Synth
Viewport.foreground	Color	X	X	X	X	X
ViewportUI	String	X	X	X	X	X
white	Color				X	
win.ansiVar.font.height	Integer		X	X		
win.frame.captionFont.height	Integer		X	X		
win.menu.font.height	Integer		X	X		
win.tooltip.font.height	Integer		X	X		
window	Color	X	X	X	X	X
windowBorder	Color	X	X	X	X	X
windowText	Color	X	X	X	X	X

a. Lowercase "b" is correct.
b. Flattened ComponentInputMap pieces. Describes the InputMap, with every even number item being a String giving the KeyStroke as specified in KeyStroke.getKeyStroke(String) (or a KeyStroke), and every odd number item the Object used to determine the associated Action in an ActionMap.
c. Flattened ComponentInputMap pieces. Describes the InputMap, with every even number item being a String giving the KeyStroke as specified in KeyStroke.getKeyStroke(String) (or a KeyStroke), and every odd number item the Object used to determine the associated Action in an ActionMap.
d. Flattened ComponentInputMap pieces. Describes the InputMap, with every even number item being a String giving the KeyStroke as specified in KeyStroke.getKeyStroke(String) (or a KeyStroke), and every odd number item the Object used to determine the associated Action in an ActionMap.
e. Flattened ComponentInputMap pieces. Describes the InputMap, with every even number item being a String giving the KeyStroke as specified in KeyStroke.getKeyStroke(String) (or a KeyStroke), and every odd number item the Object used to determine the associated Action in an ActionMap.
f. Flattened ComponentInputMap pieces. Describes the InputMap, with every even number item being a String giving the KeyStroke as specified in KeyStroke.getKeyStroke(String) (or a KeyStroke), and every odd number item the Object used to determine the associated Action in an ActionMap.
g. Flattened ComponentInputMap pieces. Describes the InputMap, with every even number item being a String giving the KeyStroke as specified in KeyStroke.getKeyStroke(String) (or a KeyStroke), and every odd number item the Object used to determine the associated Action in an ActionMap.
h. Flattened ComponentInputMap pieces. Describes the InputMap, with every even number item being a String giving the KeyStroke as specified in KeyStroke.getKeyStroke(String) (or a KeyStroke), and every odd number item the Object used to determine the associated Action in an ActionMap.
i. Flattened ComponentInputMap pieces. Describes the InputMap, with every even number item being a String giving the KeyStroke as specified in KeyStroke.getKeyStroke(String) (or a KeyStroke), and every odd number item the Object used to determine the associated Action in an ActionMap.
j. Deprecated, do not use. Property still set and available though.
k. Deprecated, do not use. Property still set and available though.

INDEX

■A

AbstractAction class, 170
  default implementation of Action
    interface, 38
  lookup property keys, 41
  properties, 41
  Swing-specific event handling, 37
  TextAction class as extension of, 535
  using actions, 38–41
AbstractBorder class
  creating, 216
  extending to create borders, 232
  implements Border interface, 212
  javax.swing.border package, 216
  methods, 217
AbstractButton class
  as parent class, 64
  ButtonModel interface, 99
  components grouped into ButtonGroup
    class, 115
  DefaultButtonModel interface, 99
  handling events, 102
  icons, 102
  internal positioning, 102
  mnemonics, 101
  parent class to JButton class, 67
  properties, 98
AbstractCellEditor class, 623, 676
  creating CheckBoxNodeEditor class
    653–658
  managing CellEditorListener objects, 653
AbstractColorChooserPanel class, 301
  getDefaultChooserPanels() method, 320
  implementing methods, 313
  installChooserPanel() method, 312
  represented by tabs in upper part of
    JColorChooser, 310
  subclassing, 311
AbstractDocument class, 521
  attaching DocumentFilter to, 538
  introduction, 540

PlainDocument class as specific
    implementation of, 541
  properties, 540
  setDocumentFilter() method, 542
AbstractDocument.Content class
  implementations, 596
AbstractFormatter class
  as mask for formatted text, 566
AbstractFormatterFactory class, 566
  as mask for formatted text, 566
AbstractLayoutCache class
  implements RowMapper interface, 670
AbstractListModel class, 451
  extended by DefaultComboBoxModel
    class, 460
  introduction, 452
  subclassing, 462
AbstractSpinnerModel class
  AbstractSpinnerModel class
    implements, 514
  introduction, 513
  SpinnerListModel class implements, 513
  SpinnerNumberModel class
    implements, 513
AbstractTableModel class
  data storage, 676
  enabling default table cell renderers,
    694–695
  introduction, 691, 692
  specifying fixed JTable columns, 692–694
AbstractUndoableEdit class, 783, 788
  subclassing, 798
  UIResource Elements, 791
Abstract Window Toolkit (AWT), 1
accelerator property
  JMenu class, 171
  JMenuItem class, 164
acceleratorForeground property
  MetalLookAndFeel class, 772
accelerators, 46

acceleratorSelectedForeground property
    MetalLookAndFeel class, 772
accept() method
    filechooser class, 331
acceptAllFileFilter property
    JFileChooser class, 327
acceptAllFileFilterUsed property
    JFileChooser class, 327
accessibility, 805
    classes, 805, 806
        Accessible interface, 806
        AccessibleContext class, 806
    creating accessible components, 807
    Java Access Bridge, 808–810
accessibility classes
    javax.accessibility package, 805
Accessible interface, 806
    implementation of, 807
accessibleAction property
    AccessibleContext class, 806
accessibleChildrenCount property
    AccessibleContext class, 806
accessibleComponent property
    AccessibleContext class, 806
AccessibleContext class
    extending JComponent.
        AccessibleJComponent, 807
    introduction, 806
    setAccessibleDescription() method, 807
accessibleContext property
    Box class, 379
    JButton class, 105
    JCheckBox class, 127
    JCheckBoxMenuItem component, 185
    JColorChooser class, 307
    JComboBox class, 492
    JComponent class, 79
    JDesktopPane component, 263
    JDialog class, 250
    JEditorPane class, 575
    JFileChooser class, 327
    JFrame class, 243
    JInternalFrame class, 254
    JLabel class, 89
    JLayeredPane class, 242
    JList class, 464
    JMenu class, 171
    JMenuBar class, 159
    JMenuItem class, 164

JOptionPane class, 281
JPasswordField class, 564
JPopupMenu class, 179
JProgressBar component, 440
JRadioButton class, 136
JRadioButtonMenuItem component, 191
JRootPane class, 237
JScrollBar component, 426
JScrollPane class, 407
JSeparator class, 175
JSlider component, 431
JSpinner class, 510
JSplitPane class, 385
JTabbedPane class, 399
JTable class, 681
JTableHeader class, 716
JTextArea class, 571
JTextComponent class, 523
JTextField class, 529
JToggleButton class, 120
JToolBar class, 203
JToolTip class, 85
JTree class, 628
JViewport class, 412
JWindow class, 248
ProgressMonitor class, 296
accessibleDescription property
    AccessibleContext class, 806
accessibleEditableText property
    AccessibleContext class, 806
accessibleIcon property
    AccessibleContext class, 807
accessibleIndexInParent property
    AccessibleContext class, 807
AccessibleJLabel class
    JLabel class, 806
accessibleName property
    AccessibleContext class, 807
    AccessibleJLabel class, 806
accessibleParent property
    AccessibleContext class, 807
accessibleRelationSet property
    AccessibleContext class, 807
accessibleRole property
    AccessibleContext class, 807
accessibleSelection property
    AccessibleContext class, 807
accessibleStateSet property
    AccessibleContext class, 807

accessibleTable property
    AccessibleContext class, 807
accessibleText property
    AccessibleContext class, 807
accessibleValue property
    AccessibleContext class, 807
accessory property
    JFileChooser class, 327
Action interface
    as extension of the ActionListener
        interface, 37, 170
    definition, 37
    Swing-specific event handling, 37
Action objects
    adding to JMenuBar class, 589
    Swing text components come with, 585
action property
    AbstractButton class, 98
    JComboBox class, 492
    JTextField class, 529
actionCommand property
    AbstractButton class, 98
    DefaultButtonModel interface, 100
    JButton class, 107
    JComboBox class, 492
    JTextField class, 529, 557
ActionEvent event
    JButton class, 107
ActionFocusMover class
    programmatically moving focus, 49
ActionListener interface
    AbstractButton class, 102
    Action interface is extension of, 37, 170
    adding to JFileChooser class, 324, 325
    creating, 19
    creating to handle input focus, 48
    customizing for JColorChooser class,
        305–307
    focusNextComponent() method, 48
    handling JCheckBox selection events, 130
    handling JCheckBoxMenuItem selection
        events with ItemListener, 186
    handling JRadioButton selection events,
        139, 140
    handling JRadioButtonMenuItem
        selection events, 190, 192
    handling JToggleButton selection
        events, 121
    listening to JComboBox events, 493–496

listening to JMenuItem events, 166
    listening to JTextField events, 556
actionListeners property
    AbstractButton class, 98
    JComboBox class, 492
    JTextField class, 529
    Timer class, 36
ActionMap class
    InputMap class, 37
    Keymap interface, 554
    sharing instances to share actions, 44
actionMap property
    JComponent class, 41, 79
actionPerformed() method, 21
actions property
    JFormattedTextField class, 567
    JTextComponent class, 523, 535
    JTextField class, 529
ActiveValue class, 755
    constructing JLabel components, 757
activeWindow property
    KeyboardFocusManager class, 55
add() method
    ButtonGroup class, 117
    Container class, 157, 381, 397
    DefaultListModel class, 453
    DefaultMutableTreeNode interface, 662
    JMenu class, 169
    JMenuBar class, 158
    JPopupMenu class, 177
    JToolBar class, 203
addActionForKeyStroke() method
    Keymap interface, 45
addActionListener() method
    JButton class, 20
addAuxiliaryLookAndFeel() method
    UIManager class, 776
addCellEditorListener() method
    CellEditor interface, 654
addChoosableFileFilter() method
    JFileChooser class, 330
addChooserPanel() method
    JColorChooser class, 314
addComponent() method
    Seven-Button GridBagLayout example, 352
addCustomEntriesToTable() method
    MetalLookAndFeel class, 774
addEdit() method
    CompoundEdit class, 791
    UndoManager class, 792

addElement() method
DefaultListModel class, 453
addLayoutComponent() method
LayoutManager interface, 345
LayoutManager2 interface, 345
addListSelectionListener() method
JList class, 476
addSelectedInterval() method
JList class, 479
addSeparator() method
JMenu class, 169, 175
JPopupMenu class, 177, 178, 182
JToolBar class, 208
addTab() method
JTabbedPane class, 398
addUndoableListener() method
UndoableEditSupport class, 794
AdjustmentListener interface
handling JScrollBar events, 423
adjustmentListeners property
JScrollBar component, 426
alignment property
TabStop class, 604
alignmentX property
JComponent class, 78
alignmentY property
JComponent class, 78
allFrames property
JDesktopPane component, 263
allowsChildren property
DefaultMutableTreeNode interface, 663
AncestorListener event handler
JComponent class, 81
anchorSelectionIndex property
DefaultListSelectionModel class, 475, 683
JList class, 464
anchorSelectionPath property
JTree class, 628, 630
approveButtonMnemonic property
JFileChooser class, 327
approveButtonText property
JFileChooser class, 327
approveButtonToolTipText property
JFileChooser class, 327
armed property
DefaultButtonModel interface, 100
JMenuItem class, 164
ArrayList class
converting data structure to ListModel, 453

asynchronousLoadPriority property
AbstractDocument class, 540
AttributeContext interface, 595
attributeCount property
SimpleAttributeSet class, 598
attributeNames property
SimpleAttributeSet class, 598
attributes property
HTMLDocument.Iterator class, 609
AttributeSet interface, 585
changing and checking status with
StyleConstants class, 603
constants, 598, 599
introduction, 597
setting JTextPane text attributes, 580
SimpleAttributeSet class
implementation, 597
specifying with Style interface, 606
styles, 595
autoCreateColumnsFromModel property
JTable class, 681, 708
autoResizeMode property
JTable class, 681
autoscrolls property
JComponent class, 79
auxiliaryLookAndFeels property
UIManager class, 748
AWT (Abstract Window Toolkit), 1
AWT 1.1 event model
handling JScrollBar events, 423
AWT components
AWT containers compared to Swing
containers, 235
distinction between equivalent Swing
components, 3
layout managers, 343
mapping to Swing components, 3
replacements, 3
resizing, 388
Swing menu components, 156
to Swing Window mapping, 4
AWTEvent class
getID() method, 257
AWTEventMulticaster class
managing listener lists, 29, 31, 32
AWTKeyStroke class
KeyStroke class as subclass of, 42

B

background property
  Component class, 682
  DefaultTreeCellRenderer class, 635
  JComponent class, 78
backgroundNonSelectionColor property
  DefaultTreeCellRenderer class, 635
backgroundSelectionColor property
  DefaultTreeCellRenderer class, 635
backgroundSet property
  JComponent class, 78
BadLocationException class, 599
BasicColorChooserUI class, 309
BasicComboBoxEditor class
  javax.swing.plaf.basic package, 499
BasicDirectoryModel class
  ListModel implementation, 452
BasicLookAndFeel class, 741
  initClassDefaults() method, 771
  look and feel classes extend from, 813
BasicMenuUI class, 199
BasicSplitPaneDivider subclass, 389
BasicSplitPaneUI subclass
  createDefaultDivider() method, 389
BasicTextAreaUI interface, 60
beginUpdate() method
  UndoableEditSupport class, 794
BevelBorder class, 220
  methods, 221
bidiRootElement property
  AbstractDocument class, 540
black property
  MetalLookAndFeel class, 772
blinkRate property
  Caret interface, 548
blockIncrement property
  JScrollBar component, 421, 426
Border interface
  javax.swing.border package, 212
  methods, 212
border property
  JComponent class, 78, 441
  JViewport class, 412
  TitledBorder class, 229
BorderFactory class
  javax.swing package, 215
BorderLayout class
  introduction, 347, 348, 349
  using LayoutManager2 interface, 345

BorderLayout manager, 204
  default layout manager for JApplet
    class, 252
borderOpaque property
  CompoundBorder class, 227
  LineBorder class, 220
  TitledBorder class, 229
borderPainted property
  AbstractButton class, 98
  JMenuBar class, 159
  JPopupMenu class, 179
  JProgressBar component, 440, 441
  JToolBar class, 203
borderPaintedFlat property
  JCheckBox class, 127, 128
borders, 211
  basics, 211
    AbstractBorder class, 216
    Border interface, 212
    BorderFactory class, 215
  creating, 232, 234
  predefined borders, 218
    BevelBorder class, 220
    CompoundBorder class, 226
    EmptyBorder class, 218
    EtchedBorder class, 223
    LineBorder class, 219
    MatteBorder class, 224
    SoftBevelBorder class, 222
    TitledBorder class, 227
borderSelectionColor property
  DefaultTreeCellRenderer class, 635
bottomComponent property
  JSplitPane class, 385, 386
bounded range components
  available components, 419
  BoundedRangeModel interface, 419
  DefaultBoundedRangeModel class, 420
  JProgressBar class, 439–447
  JScrollBar class, 421–428
  JSlider class, 428–438
BoundedRangeModel interface
  definition, 420
  getModel() method, 426
  JTextField class, 447, 449
  properties, 419
bounds property
  JComponent class, 77

Box class
  BoxLayout class as default layout manager
      of container, 357
  creating, 378
  creating areas that grow, 380–381
  creating rigid areas, 382–383
  introduction, 377
  properties, 379
Box.Filler class. *See* Filler class
BoxLayout class
  as default layout manager of Box class, 377
  creating, 358
  filling box with JLabel, JTextField, and
      JButton, 378
  growing components, 380
  introduction, 357, 358
  laying out components, 359
    with different alignments, 362
    with same alignments, 359–361
  laying out larger components, 363, 364
  layout manager for JMenuBar class, 381
breadthFirstEnumeration() method
  DefaultMutableTreeNode class, 665
ButtonGroup class
  grouping JRadioButton components in,
      136–139
  grouping objects into, 98
  introduction, 116–118
  logical grouping of AbstractButton
      components, 115
  placing JCheckBoxMenuItem component
      in, 184
  placing JRadioButtonMenuItem
      components within, 189
ButtonModel interface, 98
  AbstractButton class, 99
  DefaultButtonModel class implements, 115

■C

Calendar class
  constants, 514
calendarField property
  SpinnerDateModel class, 515
cancelCellEditing() method
  CellEditor interface, 654
canceled property
  ProgressMonitor class, 296
canImport() method
  TransferHandler class, 734
CannotRedoException class, 784, 790

CannotUndoException class, 784, 790
CardLayout class
  compared to JTabbedPane class, 394
  introduction, 357
  using LayoutManager2 interface, 345
caret category of properties
  JTextComponent class, 524
Caret interface, 522
  introduction, 547–550
  properties, 548
caret property
  JTextComponent class, 523
caretColor property
  JTextComponent class, 523
CaretEvent class
  introduction, 550–552
CaretListener interface
  associating with JTextComponent, 550
  introduction, 550–552
caretListeners property
  JTextComponent class, 523
caretPosition property
  JTextComponent class, 523
caretUpdate() method
  CaretListener interface, 551
cell editor, 718
  creating complex version, 722–724
  creating simple version, 718–722
CellEditor interface, 644
  and CellEditorListener interface
      methods, 650
  creating the CheckBoxNodeEditor class, 653
  editing tree nodes, 644
  methods, 654–655
    getCellEditorValue() method, 654
    isCellEditable() method, 648
cellEditor property
  JTable class, 681
  JTree class, 628
  TableColumn class, 713
CellEditorListener interface
  definition, 650
  list of objects managed by
      AbstractCellEditor class, 653
cellEditorValue property
  DefaultCellEditor class, 647
cellRenderer property
  JList class, 464, 469
  JTree class, 628
  TableColumn class, 713

cellSelectionEnabled property
JTable class, 681, 682
changedUpdate() method
DocumentListener interface, 558
ChangeListener, 420
AbstractButton class, 102
adding to JSlider component, 284
attaching to Style interface, 606
handling JCheckBox selection events
131, 133
handling JProgressBar events, 445, 446
handling JRadioButton selection events,
142, 145
handling JScrollBar events, 424, 425
handling JSlider events, 430
handling JToggleButton selection
events, 121
listening to JMenu events, 173
listening to JMenuItem events, 165
ChangeListener interface
listening for JSpinner class events,
511–512
changeListener property
JSpinner class, 510
changeListeners property
AbstractButton class, 98
JProgressBar component, 440
JSlider component, 431
JTabbedPane class, 399
JViewport class, 412
changeUpdate() method
DocumentListener interface, 546
characterAttributes property
JTextPane class, 580
CharacterConstants class
keys for attributes, 598
check box node editor
creating CheckBoxNode class, 650–651
creating CheckBoxNodeEditor class,
653–658
creating CheckBoxNodeRenderer class,
651–653
creating test program, 658–659
introduction, 650
CheckBoxUI class
user interface delegate, 126
checkIcon property
JCheckBoxMenuItem component, 188

childCount property
DefaultMutableTreeNode interface, 663
children() method
TreeNode class, 664
choosableFileFilters property
JFileChooser class, 327
chooserPanels property
JColorChooser class, 307, 320
choosers
JColorChooser class
creating, 301
customizing look and feel, 320–322
introduction, 300–301
properties, 307–320
using, 302–307
JFileChooser class
creating, 323
customizing look and feel, 336–341
introduction, 322
properties, 326–327
using, 323–326
working with file filters, 328–336
className property
UIManager.LookAndFeelInfo class, 749
clearSelection() method
JList class, 479
clickCountToStart property
DefaultCellEditor class, 647
clipboard access operations
JTextComponent class, 526
operations with JTextField class,
534–537
closable property
JInternalFrame class, 254
closed property
JInternalFrame class, 254, 255
closedIcon property
DefaultTreeCellRenderer class, 635
coalesce property
Timer class, 36
color category of properties
JTextComponent class, 524
Color class
decode() method, 499
displaying list of colors from, 311
dragging-and-dropping, 730
color property
JColorChooser class, 307, 308

ColorChooserComponentFactory class 301, 308
  getPreviewPanel() method, 320
  panels provided to JColorChooser class, 310
  using, 320
ColorChooserUI class, 320
  bug in implementation class, 309
ColorConstants class
  keys for attributes, 598
colorModel property
  JComponent class, 78
ColorSelectionModel interface
  changing color chooser, 313
  color changes, 313
  data model for JColorChooser, 303
  DefaultColorSelectionModel class implements, 301
column property
  TableModelEvent class, 700
columnCount property
  DefaultTableColumnModel class, 709
  DefaultTableModel class, 697
  JTable class, 681
columnHeader property
  JScrollPane class, 407
columnHeaderView property
  JScrollPane class, 407, 409
columnIdentifiers property
  DefaultTableModel class, 698
columnMargin property
  DefaultTableColumnModel class, 709
columnModel property
  JTable class, 681
  JTableHeader class, 716
columnModelListeners property
  DefaultTableColumnModel class, 709
columns property
  DefaultTableColumnModel class, 709
  JTextArea class, 571
  JTextField class, 529
columnSelectionAllowed property
  DefaultTableColumnModel class, 709
  JTable class, 681, 682
ComboBoxEditor interface
  editing JComboBox class elements, 499
  entering choices for JComboBox class, 491
ComboBoxModel interface, 64, 451
  extended by MutableComboBoxModel interface, 460

introduction, 460
  storing labels and colors arrays, 314
ComboBoxUI example, 765–766
Command design pattern
  Concrete Command, 799
  participants, 788
commitEdit() method
  JFormattedTextField component, 612
component anchoring
  GridBagConstraints class, 354
Component class
  background property, 682
  compared to JComponent class, 67
  foreground property, 682
  methods
    getComponentOrientation() method, 345
    getListeners() method, 29
    getName() method, 397
    setFocusable() method, 49
    setFocusTraversalKeys() method, 55
  shortcut API methods, 55
component property
  DefaultCellEditor class, 647
  JMenu class, 171
  JMenuBar class, 159
  JMenuItem class, 164
  JPopupMenu class, 179
  JToolTip class, 85
component resizing
  GridBagConstraints class, 354
componentCount property
  JComponent class, 78
ComponentListener interface
  supported by JFrame class, 245
componentOrientation property
  JComponent class, 78
  JScrollPane class, 407
  JTextComponent class, 523
componentPopupMenu property
  JComponent class, 79
components property
  JComponent class, 78
ComponentUI class
  UI delegates a subclass of, 741
CompoundBorder class, 226
  configuring properties, 227
  creating, 226

CompoundEdit class, 783
    inProgress property, 791
    methods, 791
Concrete Command
    Command design pattern, 799
configureEnclosingScrollPane() method
    JTable class, 680
Constraints class, 371
Container class
    add() method, 157, 381, 397
    compared to JComponent class, 67
    setLayout() method, 344
    transferFocusDownCycle() method, 55
ContainerListener interface
    supported by JFrame class, 245
ContainerOrderFocusTraversalPolicy
            class, 53
contains() method
    DefaultListModel class, 460
    JToolTip class, 85
contentAreaFilled property
    AbstractButton class, 98
contentPane property
    JDialog class, 250
    JFrame class, 243
    JInternalFrame class, 254
    JRootPane class, 237
    JWindow class, 248
CONTENTS_CHANGED type constant
    ListDataEvent class, 455
contentType property
    JEditorPane class, 575
CONTIGUOUS_TREE_SELECTION mode
    TreeSelectionModel interface, 669
continuousLayout property
    JSplitPane class, 384, 385, 391
control property
    MetalLookAndFeel class, 772
controlButtonsAreShown property
    JFileChooser class, 327
controlDarkShadow property
    MetalLookAndFeel class, 772
controlDisabled property
    MetalLookAndFeel class, 772
controlHighlight property
    MetalLookAndFeel class, 772
controlInfo property
    MetalLookAndFeel class, 772

controlShadow property
    MetalLookAndFeel class, 772
controlTextColor property
    MetalLookAndFeel class, 772
controlTextFont property
    MetalLookAndFeel class, 772
conversion operations
    JTextComponent class, 526
convertValueToText() method
    JTree class, 642
copy() method
    JTextComponent class, 534
copyAction class constant
    DefaultEditorKit class, 592
copyInto() method
    DefaultListModel class, 460
createBevelBorder() method
    BevelBorder class, 221
createBlackLineBorder() method
    LineBorder class, 219
CreateColorSamplePopup program
    modified version, 318–320
createCompoundBorder() method
    CompoundBorder class, 226
createDefaultColumnsFromModel() method
    JTable class, 708
createDefaultDivider() method
    BasicSplitPaneUI subclass, 389
createDialog() method
    JColorChooser class, 305
    JOptionPane class, 272, 276, 292
createDisabledImage() method
    GrayFilter class, 97
createEtchedBorder() method
    EtchedBorder class, 224
createGlue() method
    Box class, 380, 382
createGrayLineBorder() method
    LineBorder class, 220
createHorizontalBox() method
    Box class, 378
createInternalFrame() method
    JOptionPane class, 272, 276
createLineBorder() method
    LineBorder class, 220
createLoweredBevelBorder() method
    BevelBorder class, 221
createMatteBorder() method
    MatteBorder class, 226

createRadioButtonGrouping() method
  JRadioButton class, 139
  RadioButtonUtils class, 137, 140, 141
createRaisedBevelBorder() method
  BevelBorder class, 222
createRigidArea() method
  Box class, 382
createRootPane() method
  JApplet class, 252
  JDialog class, 250, 252
  JFrame class, 246
  JWindow class, 248
createStandardLabels() method
  Hashtable class, 435
createTitledBorder() method
  TitledBorder class, 229
createToolTip() method
  JToolTip class, 84
createTransferable() method
  TransferHandler class, 734, 735
createValue() method
  LazyValue interface, 755
createVerticalBox() method
  Box class, 378
crossPlatformLookAndFeelClassName
    property
  UIManager class, 748
current() method
  ElementIterator class, 611
currentDirectory property
  JFileChooser class, 327
currentManager() method
  JComponent class, 70
currentTheme property
  MetalLookAndFeel class, 774
cursor property
  JComponent class, 79
cursorSet property
  JComponent class, 79
cut() method
  JTextComponent class, 534
cutAction class constant
  DefaultEditorKit class, 592
cutAction() method
  DefaultEditorKit class, 535

■D
data model category of properties
  JTextComponent class, 524

data model modification methods
  DefaultComboBoxModel class, 461
dataVector property
  DefaultTableModel class, 698
Date object
  providing to JFormattedTextField
    constructor, 612
date property
  SpinnerDateModel class, 515
DateEditor class
  introduction, 519
  properties, 519
DateFormat class, 612
DateFormatter class, 566
debugGraphicsOption property
  JComponent class, 78
DecimalFormat class
  associated with NumberEditor class, 520
decode() method
  Color class, 499
Decorator pattern
  sorting JTable elements, 700
DefaultBoundedRangeModel class
  getListeners() method, 421
  implementing BoundedRangeModel
    interface, 420
defaultButton property
  JButton class, 105
  JRootPane class, 237
DefaultButtonModel class, 98
  AbstractButton class, 99
  properties, 100
  ToggleButtonModel class customizes
    behavior of, 115
defaultCapable property
  JButton class, 105
DefaultCaret class, 547
DefaultCellEditor class, 644, 676, 719
  as cell editor with JTable, 624
  combining with DefaultTreeCellEditor
    class, 648
  creating, 645, 646
  editing table cells, 718
  editing tree nodes, 645
  implementation of TreeCellEditor
    class, 623
  properties, 647
DefaultCellRenderer class, 676

defaultClosedIcon property
DefaultTreeCellRenderer class, 635
defaultCloseOperation property
JDialog class, 250
JFrame class, 243, 246
JInternalFrame class, 254, 255
DefaultColorSelectionModel class
javax.swing.colorchooser package, 301
DefaultComboBoxModel class
implements ComboBoxModel
interface, 451
introduction, 460–463
DefaultDesktopManager class, 252
implementation of DesktopManager
interface, 266
DefaultEditor class
properties, 518
DefaultEditorKit class
class constants, 591
copyAction class constant, 592
cutAction class constant, 592
cutAction() method, 535
pasteAction class constant, 592
readOnlyAction class constant, 592
writableAction class constant, 592
DefaultFocusManager class, 47
DefaultFocusTraversalPolicy
FocusTraversalPolicy class, 53
DefaultFormatterFactory class
javax.swing.text package, 620, 621
DefaultHighlighter class, 547
DefaultHighlighter.HighlightPainter class, 547
DefaultKeyboardFocusManager class, 37, 55
defaultLeafIcon property
DefaultTreeCellRenderer class, 635
DefaultListCellRenderer class, 468
and ListCellRenderer interface, 468, 470
DefaultListModel class
data model implementation of JList, 451
introduction, 453
methods, 459
DefaultListSelectionModel class
properties, 475, 683
defaultLookAndFeelDecorated property
JDialog class, 250
JFrame class, 244
DefaultMenuLayout class
javax.swing.plaf.basic package, 381

DefaultMetalTheme class
introduction, 774
DefaultMutableTreeNode class, 624
building hierarchies, 661, 662
creating, 661
DynamicUtilTreeNode as subclass of, 666
properties, 663
traversing trees, 664
userObject property, 640, 666
working with tree nodes, 661–664
DefaultMutableTreeNode interface
querying node relationships, 664
defaultOpenIcon property
DefaultTreeCellRenderer class, 635
defaultRootElement property
AbstractDocument class, 540
DefaultStyledDocument class, 596
defaults property
LookAndFeel class, 742
UIManager class, 748
DefaultSingleSelectionModel class, 395
default implementation of
SingleSelectionModel interface, 162
DefaultStyledDocument class, 521, 574, 595
creating, 596
implementation of StyledDocument
interface, 596
properties, 596
DefaultTableCellRenderer class, 686, 687
DefaultTableColumnModel class
implementation of TableColumnModel
interface, 676
properties, 708
used when TableColumnModel interface
is not specified, 678
DefaultTableModel class
creating, 696, 697
creating sparse table model, 698, 699
encapsulates TableModel interface, 676
filling, 697
introduction, 696
listening to JTable events with
TableModelListener, 699
properties, 697
DefaultTreeCellEditor class, 644
combining with DefaultCellEditor class, 648
implementation of TreeCellEditor class, 623
introduction, 647
using for a JTextField editor with JTree, 645

DefaultTreeCellRenderer class
    configuring, 651
    creating custom renderer, 637–641
    implementation of TreeCellRenderer
        interface, 623
    introduction, 635
    properties, 635, 636
DefaultTreeModel class
    introduction, 667, 668
    storing TreeModel for JTree, 624
    working with tree nodes, 659
DefaultTreeSelectionModel class
    implementation of TreeSelectionModel, 624
    introduction, 670
delay property
    JMenu class, 171
    Timer class, 36
delegation-based event handling, 17
    event delegation model, 17, 18
    event listeners as observers, 19
        creating listener instance, 20
        defining the listener, 19
        registering listener with component, 20
    sequence diagram, 18
depth property
    DefaultMutableTreeNode interface, 663
depthFirstEnumeration() method
    DefaultMutableTreeNode class, 665
description property
    ImageIcon class, 96
    LookAndFeel class, 742
desktopColor property
    MetalLookAndFeel class, 773
desktopIcon property
    JInternalFrame class, 254
DesktopManager interface, 262, 265
    management of frames within desktop, 252
desktopManager property
    JDesktopPane component, 263
desktopPane property
    JInternalFrame class, 254
dialogInit() method
    JDialog class, 252
dialogTitle property
    JFileChooser class, 327
dialogType property
    JFileChooser class, 327
DiamondAbstractButtonStateIcon icon
    using with component that is not
        AbstractButton type, 189

Dictionary class, 435
    java.util package, 641
die() method
    UndoableEdit interface, 790
directorySelectionEnabled property
    JFileChooser class, 327, 331
disabledIcon property
    AbstractButton class, 98, 102
    JLabel class, 89
disabledSelectedIcon property
    AbstractButton class, 98, 102
disabledTextColor property
    JTextComponent class, 523
discardAllEdits() method
    UndoManager class, 793
DISCONTIGUOUS_TREE_SELECTION mode
    TreeSelectionModel interface, 669
dismissDelay property
    ToolTipManager class, 87
displayable property
    JComponent class, 79
displayedMnemonic property
    JLabel class, 89, 91
displayedMnemonicIndex property
    AbstractButton class, 98, 101
    JLabel class, 89, 91
dividerLocation property
    JSplitPane class, 385, 387, 388
dividerSize property
    JSplitPane class, 385
Document interface, 788
    AbstractDocument class provides basic
        implementation, 540
    binding commands to, 788
    displaying contents with EditorKit class, 607
    extended by StyledDocument interface, 595
    filtering document models, 542–546
    implementations, 521
        AbstractDocument class, 60
    insertString() method, 583
    introduction, 537–540
    PlainDocument implementation, 526, 570
    specifying Document data model for
        JPasswordField class, 564
document property
    JFormattedTextField class, 567
    JTextComponent class, 523
    JTextField class, 529, 530
    JTextPane class, 580

DocumentEvent interface
   introduction, 546
DocumentEvent.ElementChange class, 547
DocumentEvent.EventType class
   constants, 546
DocumentFilter class
   attaching to AbstractDocument, 538
   customizing, 542–545
   filtering document models, 542
   methods, 542
documentFilter property
   AbstractDocument class, 540
DocumentListener interface
   attaching to data model, 538
   introduction, 546
   listening to JTextField events, 558, 559
documentListeners property
   AbstractDocument class, 540
documentProperties property
   AbstractDocument class, 540
dot property
   Caret interface, 548
doubleBuffered property
   JComponent class, 70, 78
doubleBufferingEnabled property
   RepaintManager class, 71
doubleBufferMaximumSize property
   RepaintManager class, 71
downFocusCycle() method
   KeyboardFocusManager class, 55
drag-and-drop support, 729
   built-in drag-and-drop support, 729–731
   support for images, 733
   TransferHandler class, 731–733
dragEnabled property
   JColorChooser class, 307
   JFileChooser class, 327
   JList class, 464
   JTable class, 681
   JTextComponent class, 523
   JTree class, 628
draggable image
   implementing, 736–740
draggedColumn property
   JTableHeader class, 716
draggedDistance property
   JTableHeader class, 716
dragMode property
   JDesktopPane component, 263

dropTarget property
   JComponent class, 79
dump-model action, 591
DynamicUtilTreeNode class
   inner class of JTree, 624, 666

■E

echoChar property
   JPasswordField class, 564
echoCharIsSet() method
   JPasswordField class, 564
edit property
   UndoableEditEvent class, 794
editable property
   JComboBox class, 492
   JTextComponent class, 523
   JTree class, 628, 643
editing property
   JTable class, 681
   JTree class, 628
editingCanceled() method
   CellEditorListener interface, 650
editingColumn property
   JTable class, 681
editingPath property
   JTree class, 628
editingRow property
   JTable class, 681
editingStopped() method
   CellEditorListener interface, 650
editor property
   JComboBox class, 492
   JSpinner class, 510
editorComponent property
   JTable class, 681
EditorContainer class
   placing custom editors within, 623
EditorKit class
   capabilities of TextAction objects, 607
editorKit property
   JEditorPane class, 575
   JTextPane class, 580
editValid property
   JFormattedTextField class, 567
Element interface
   and Document interface, 538
elementAt() method
   DefaultListModel class, 459
ElementChange class, 547

ElementIterator class
  introduction, 611
elements() method
  DefaultListModel class, 460
empty property
  DefaultListModel class, 453
  SimpleAttributeSet class, 598
EmptyBorder class
  methods, 218
EmptySelectionModel class, 669
  inner class of JTree, 624
enabled property
  AbstractAction class, 41
  AbstractButton class, 98
  DefaultButtonModel interface, 100
  JComboBox class, 492
  JComponent class, 79
  JMenuItem class, 164
  JScrollBar component, 426
  ToolTipManager class, 87
end property
  SpinnerDateModel class, 515
end() method
  CompoundEdit class, 791
  StateEdit class, 801
  UndoManager class, 793
endOffset property
  HTMLDocument.Iterator class, 609
endPosition property
  AbstractDocument class, 540
endUpdate() method
  UndoableEditSupport class, 794
ensureCapacity() method
  DefaultListModel class, 460
ensureIndexIsVisible() method
  JList class, 468
Enumeration class
  using instead of Iterator class, 666
equals() methods
  problems with DefaultComboBoxModel
    class, 462
EtchedBorder class, 223
  constructors and methods, 223
event delegation model, 17, 18
event handling, 17
  delegation-based event handling, 17
    event delegation model, 17, 18
  Swing components, 10, 11

EventListenerList class, 29
  managing listener lists, 32, 33, 34
EventQueue class
  invokeAndWait() method, 21, 34
  invokeLater() method, 21, 22, 34, 746
  isDispatchThread() method, 21
events category of properties
  JTextComponent class, 524
EventType class, 576
  constants, 546
expandsSelectedPath property
  JTree class, 628, 630
ExpandVetoException class, 673
exportAsDrag() method
  TransferHandler class, 732
extent property
  BoundedRangeModel interface, 419
  JSlider component, 431
extentSize property
  JViewport class, 412

■F

File class
  dragging-and-dropping, 730
  java.io package, 333
filechooser class
  accept() method, 331
FileFilter class
  compared to java.io.FileFilter interface, 323
  creating subclasses, 331
  javax.swing.filechooser package, 322
  working with JFileChooser class, 328–330
FileFilter interface
  java.io package, 331
fileFilter property
  JFileChooser class, 327
fileHidingEnabled property
  JFileChooser class, 327
FilenameFilter class
  compared to FileFilter class, 328
fileSelectionEnabled property
  JFileChooser class, 327, 331
fileSelectionMode property
  JFileChooser class, 327, 331
FileSystemView class, 323
  custom views as subclasses, 333
  javax.swing.filechooser package, 322
  selectable buttons, 324
  using with JFileChooser class, 333, 334

fileSystemView property
    JFileChooser class, 327
FileView class
    using with JFileChooser class, 334–336
fileView property
    JFileChooser class, 327, 334
Filler class
    inner class of Box class, 377
    working with, 380
final keyword, 23
findColorLabel() method
    SystemColorChooserPanel class, 314
findColorPosition() method
    SystemColorChooserPanel class, 313
fireContentsChanged() method
    AbstractListModel class, 452
fireEditingStopped() method
    AbstractCellEditor class, 654
fireIntervalAdded() method
    AbstractListModel class, 452
fireIntervalRemoved() method
    AbstractListModel class, 452
first() method
    ElementIterator class, 611
firstChild property
    DefaultMutableTreeNode interface, 663
firstIndex property
    ListSelectionEvent class, 476
firstLeaf property
    DefaultMutableTreeNode interface, 663
firstRow property
    TableModelEvent class, 700
firstVisibleIndex property
    JList class, 464, 468
fixedCellHeight property
    JList class, 464, 466
fixedCellWidth property
    JList class, 464, 466
fixedRowHeight property
    JTree class, 628, 629
floatable property
    JToolBar class, 203
FlowLayout class
    compared to BoxLayout class, 357
    introduction, 345, 346, 347
focus cycle, 50
    restricting focus cycle example, 51, 52
focusable property
    JComponent class, 78

focusAccelerator property
    JTextComponent class, 523
focusColor property
    MetalLookAndFeel class, 773
focusCycleRoot property, 50
    JComponent class, 78
    JInternalFrame class, 254
focusCycleRootAncester property
    JInternalFrame class, 254
focusCycleRootAncestor property
    JComponent class, 78
focusedWindow property
    KeyboardFocusManager class, 55
FocusListener
    supported by JFrame class, 245
FocusListener interface
    focus management, 47
focusLostBehavior property
    JFormattedTextField class, 567
    JFormattedTextField component, 612
FocusManager class, 47
focusNextComponent() method
    ActionListener interface, 48
    KeyboardFocusManager class, 55
focusOwner property
    JComponent class, 78
    JInternalFrame class, 254
    KeyboardFocusManager class, 55
focusPainted property
    AbstractButton class, 98
focusPreviousComponent() method
    KeyboardFocusManager class, 55
focusTraversablePolicySet property
    JComponent class, 78
focusTraversalKeysEnabled property
    JComponent class, 78
FocusTraversalPolicy class, 37
    focus management, 47
    methods for controlling traversal order, 52
    predefined traversal policies, 53
    reversing focus traversal, 53, 55
focusTraversalPolicy property
    JComponent class, 78
focusTraversalPolicyProvider property
    JComponent class, 50, 78
font property
    DefaultTreeCellRenderer class, 635
    JComponent class, 78
    JTextArea class, 571
    JTextField class, 529

FontConstants class
  keys for attributes, 598
fontSet property
  JComponent class, 78
foreground property
  Component class, 682
  JComponent class, 78
foregroundSet property
  JComponent class, 78
Format class
  java.text package, 566
format property
  DateEditor class, 519
  NumberEditor class, 520
formatter property
  JFormattedTextField class, 567
formatterFactory property
  JFormattedTextField class, 567
frameIcon property
  JInternalFrame class, 254
frameInit() method
  JFrame class, 246, 247
French version
  JOptionPane class, 290
fromIndex property
  TableColumnModelEvent class, 709

■G
GapContent class
  AbstractDocument.Content
    implementation, 596
get() method
  DefaultListModel class, 459
  UIManager class, 758, 763
getAcceptAllFileFilter() method
  JFileChooser class, 330
getActionListeners() method
  JButton class, 29
getActionMap() method
  JComponent class, 593
getActions() method
  JTextComponent class, 586
getBorder() method
  UIManager class, 747
getBorderInsets() method
  AbstractBorder class, 217
  Border interface, 214
  MotifButtonUI class, 217
getCellEditorValue() method
  CellEditor interface, 654

getChange() method
  DocumentEvent interface, 547
getChildCount() method
  MutableTreeNode interface, 660
getClientProperty() method
  JComponent class, 759
getColor() method
  UIManager class, 747
getColumnClass() method
  TableModel interface, 687, 695
getComponent() method
  MenuElement interface, 195
getComponentAfter() method
  FocusTraversalPolicy class, 52
getComponentBefore() method
  FocusTraversalPolicy class, 52
getComponentOrientation() method
  Component class, 345
getComponentPopupMenu() method
  JComponent class, 178
getConstraint() method
  SpringLayout class, 372
getContentType() method
  predefined editor kits, 576
getDefaultChooserPanels() method
  AbstractColorChooserPanel class, 320
getDefaultComponent() method
  FocusTraversalPolicy class, 52
getDimension() method
  UIManager class, 747
getEditorComponent() method
  ComboBoxEditor class, 499
getElementAt() method
  DefaultListModel class, 459
getElements() method
  ButtonGroup class, 118
getFileSystemView() method
  FileSystemView class, 333
getFirstComponent() method
  FocusTraversalPolicy class, 52
getFont() method
  UIManager class, 747
getHeaderRenderer() method
  TableColumn class, 713
getIcon() method
  UIManager class, 747
getID() method
  AWTEvent class, 257

getIheritsPopupMenu() method
    JComponent class, 178
getInitialComponent() method
    FocusTraversalPolicy class, 52
getInputMap() method
    JComponent class, 43
getInputValue() method
    JOptionPane class, 272
getInsets() method
    UIManager class, 747
getInstalledLookAndFeels() method
    UIManager class, 743, 776
    UIManager.LookAndFeelInfo class, 742
getInt() method
    UIManager class, 747
getInteriorRectangle() method
    AbstractBorder class, 217
getInternalFrame() method
    InternalFrameEvent class, 257
getItem() method
    ComboBoxEditor class, 499
getKeymap() method
    JTextComponent class, 586
getKeyStroke() method
    KeyStroke class, 43
getKeyStrokeForEvent() method
    KeyStroke class, 43
getKeyText() method
    KeyEvent class, 29
getLastComponent() method
    FocusTraversalPolicy class, 52
getListCellRendererComponent() method
    ListCellRenderer interface, 469
getListDataListeners() method
    AbstractListModel class, 452
getListeners() method
    Component class, 29
    DefaultBoundedRangeModel class, 421
getMaxCharactersPerLineCount() method
    JOptionPane class, 281
getModel() method
    BoundedRangeModel interface, 426, 431
getName() method
    Component class, 397
getNextMatch() method
    JList class, 481
getNextNode() method
    DefaultMutableTreeNode class, 664

getNextVisualPositionFrom() method
    NavigationFilter class, 552
getObject() method
    UIManager class, 747
getPaintTicks() method
    JSlider component, 435
getPath() method
    TreePath class, 673
getPopupLocation() method
    JComponent class, 178
getPreviewPanel() method
    ColorChooserComponentFactory class, 320
getPreviousNode() method
    DefaultMutableTreeNode class, 664
getProgress() method
    ProgressMonitor class, 293
getProperty() method
    AbstractDocument class, 540
getPropertyName() method
    JInternalFrame class, 255
getRoot() method
    TreeModel class, 666
getSelectedElements() method
    JRadioButton class, 141
getSelectedIndex() method
    JComboBox class, 495, 497
getSelectedItem() method
    JComboBox class, 495
getSelection() method
    OptionPaneUtils class, 273, 274
getSharedOwnerFrame() method
    SwingUtilities class, 277
getSourceActions() method
    TransferHandler class, 734
getString() method
    UIManager class, 747
getSubElements() method
    MenuElement interface, 195
getSupportsWindowDecorations() method
    JRootPane class, 238
getTableCellRendererComponent() method
    TableCellRenderer interface, 686, 687
getTreeCellEditorComponent() method
    TreeCellEditor interface, 648, 656
getUI() method
    UIManager class, 747
getUIClassID() method
    JToolBar class, 763

getValue() method
    JOptionPane class, 272
    SpinnerDateModel class, 515
glassPane property
    JDialog class, 250
    JFrame class, 243
    JInternalFrame class, 254
    JRootPane class, 237
    JWindow class, 248
glue, creating, 380–381
Graphics class
    translate() method, 214
graphics property
    JComponent class, 78
graphicsConfiguration property
    JComponent class, 78
GrayFilter class, 97
    createDisabledImage() method, 97
grid positioning
    GridBagConstraints class, 355, 356
GridBagConstraints class
    and GridBagLayout class, 351
    component anchoring, 354
    component resizing, 354
    grid positioning, 355–356
    introduction, 353
    padding, 356
    weight, 357
GridBagLayout class
    associating GridBagConstraints object to
        component, 345
    compared to BoxLayout class, 357
    components should have
        GridBagConstraints associated, 353
    introduction, 350–352
    rows and columns, 353
    using LayoutManager2 interface, 345
gridColor property
    JTable class, 681–682
GridLayout class
    compared to BoxLayout class, 357
    compared to GridBagLayout class, 350
    introduction, 349–350
group property
    DefaultButtonModel interface, 100
growing components, creating, 380–381

■H

Hashtable class, 41
    createStandardLabels() method, 435
    creating JTree from, 625
    UIDefaults class as subclass, 749
headerRenderer property
    TableColumn class, 713
headerValue property
    TableColumn class, 713
height property
    JComponent class, 77
helpMenu property
    JMenuBar class, 159
hide() method
    Popup class, 200
HierarchyBoundsListener
    supported by JFrame class, 246
HierarchyListener
    supported by JFrame class, 246
highestLayer() method
    JLayeredPane class, 240
Highlight class, 547
highlightedTextColor property
    MetalLookAndFeel class, 773
highlighter category of properties
    JTextComponent class, 524
Highlighter interface, 522
    introduction, 547–550
highlighter property
    JTextComponent class, 523
Highlighter.Highlight class, 547
HighlightPainter class, 547
horizontalAlignment property
    AbstractButton class, 98, 102
    JLabel class, 89
    JTextField class, 529, 530
horizontalScrollBar property
    JScrollPane class, 407
horizontalScrollBarPolicy property
    JScrollPane class, 407
horizontalTextPosition property
    AbstractButton class, 98, 102
    JLabel class, 89
horizontalVisibility property
    JTextField class, 529, 530
HTML documents
    iterating through, 608–612
    loading as StyledDocument into
        JEditorPane, 607

HTML.Tag class
    constants, 608, 609
    searching for tag types in document, 611
HTMLDocument interface, 522
HTMLDocument.Iterator class
    next() method, 609
    properties, 609
    using, 608, 610, 611
HTMLEditorKit class, 585
HTMLEditorKit.Parser class
    javax.swing.text.html package, 607
HTMLEditorKit.ParserCallback class, 607
HTMLEditorKit.ParserDelegator class, 607
HyperlinkEvent class, 574
HyperlinkEvent.EventType class, 576
HyperlinkListener interface, 574
    handling JEditorPane events example,
        577–578
    hyperlinkUpdate() method, 576
hyperlinkListeners property
    JEditorPane class, 575
hyperlinkUpdate() method
    HyperlinkListener interface, 576

■I
I/O operations
    JTextComponent class, 526
icon argument
    JOptionPane class, 270
Icon interface, 92
    creating, 93, 94
    displaying images within components, 67
    javax.swing package, 734
    paintIcon() method, 93
    using, 94
icon property
    AbstractButton class, 98
    ImageSelection class, 734
    JInternalFrame class, 254, 255
    JLabel class, 89
    JOptionPane class, 281
iconHeight property
    ImageIcon class, 96
iconifiable property
    JInternalFrame class, 254
iconImage property
    JFrame class, 243
icons
    JMenuItem and subclasses inherit
        support, 156

iconTextGap property
    JLabel class, 89
iconWidth property
    ImageIcon class, 96
ID property
    LookAndFeel class, 742
identifier property
    TableColumn class, 713
ignoreRepaint property
    JComponent class, 78
IllegalArgumentException class
    and GridLayout class, 350
    can be caused by
        MutableTreeNode.insert(), 661
    changing border of JViewport class, 412
    creating JProgressBar components, 440
    creating JScrollbar components, 423
    creating JSlider components, 429
    creating JTabbedPane class, 396
    moving JSplitPane divider, 387
    setting delay property of JMenu class, 172
    setting orientation of JSplitPane class, 386
    setting policies for JScrollPane class, 405
image property
    ImageIcon class, 96
ImageIcon class, 94
    creating, 95, 805–806
    predefined images, 67
    properties, 96
    using, 95
imageLoadStatus property
    ImageIcon class, 96
imageObserver property
    ImageIcon class, 96
images, drag-and-drop support, 733
ImageSelection class
    creating, 734
    icon property, 734
importData() method
    TransferHandler class, 734–735
inactiveControlTextColor property
    MetalLookAndFeel class, 773
inactiveSystemTextColor property
    MetalLookAndFeel class, 773
indeterminate property
    JProgressBar component, 440
index0 property
    ListDataEvent class, 454

index1 property
    ListDataEvent class, 454
indexOf() method
    DefaultListModel class, 460
INFORMATION_MESSAGE pop-up
    JOptionPane class, 277
inheritsPopupMenu property
    JComponent class, 79
initClassDefaults() method
    BasicLookAndFeel class, 771
initialDelay property
    Timer class, 36
    ToolTipManager class, 87
initialSelectionValue property
    JOptionPane class, 281
initialValue argument
    JOptionPane class, 271
initialValue property
    JOptionPane class, 281
inProgress property
    CompoundEdit class, 791
inputAttributes property
    JTextPane class, 581
inputContext property
    JComponent class, 79
InputEvent class, 23
InputMap class
    ActionMap class, 37
    getting for component based on focus
        activation condition, 43
    Keymap interface, 544
inputMap property
    JComponent class, 41, 79
InputMethodListener
    supported by JFrame class, 246
inputMethodRequests property
    JComponent class, 79
    JTextComponent class, 523
inputValue property
    JOptionPane class, 281, 284
InputVerifier interface, 37
    component-level verification during focus
        traversal, 56
    listening to JTextField events, 558
    setVerifyInputWhenFocusTarget()
        method, 57
inputVerifier property
    JComponent class, 78

insert() method
    MutableTreeNode interface, 660, 662
insertElementAt() method
    DefaultListModel class, 453
insertNodeInto() method
    DefaultTreeModel class, 668
insertSeparator() method
    JMenu class, 175
insertString() method
    Document interface, 583
    DocumentFilter class, 542
insertUpdate() method
    DocumentListener interface, 546
insets property
    JComponent class, 78
    JViewport class, 412
insideBorder property
    CompoundBorder class, 227
installChooserPanel() method
    AbstractColorChooserPanel class, 312, 313
installedLookAndFeels property
    UIManager class, 748
intercellSpacing property
    JTable class, 681, 682
InternalFrameAdapter class, 253
    InternalFrameListener methods, 256
InternalFrameEvent class, 253
    constants for event subtypes, 257
InternalFrameFocusTraversalPolicy
    FocusTraversalPolicy class, 53
InternalFrameIconifyListener class, 264
InternalFrameListener interface, 253
    definition, 256
    methods, 256
internalFrameListeners property
    JInternalFrame class, 254
InternationalFormatter class
    java.swing.text package, 612
INTERVAL_ADDED type constant
    ListDataEvent class, 455
INTERVAL_REMOVED type constant
    ListDataEvent class, 455
inverted property
    JSlider component, 431
invokeAndWait() method
    EventQueue class, 21, 34
    SwingUtilities class, 23

invokeLater() method
    EventQueue class, 21, 22, 34, 746
    SwingUtilities class, 23
invoker property
    JPopupMenu class, 179
invokesStopCellEditing property
    JTree class, 628
IOException class
    thrown by read/write methods of
        JTextComponent class, 530
isBorderOpaque() method
    AbstractBorder class, 217
    Border interface, 214
isCellEditable() method
    CellEditor interface, 648, 655
isDispatchThread() method
    EventQueue class, 21
isEventDispatchThread() method
    SwingUtilities class, 21
isFilled property
    JSlider component, 438
isInProgress() method
    UndoManager class, 792
isLeftMouseButton() method
    SwingUtilities class, 24
isMiddleMouseButton() method
    SwingUtilities class, 24
isNodeAncestor() method
    DefaultMutableTreeNode interface, 664
isNodeChild() method
    DefaultMutableTreeNode interface, 664
isNodeDescendant() method
    DefaultMutableTreeNode interface, 664
isNodeRelated() method
    DefaultMutableTreeNode interface, 664
isNodeSibling() method
    DefaultMutableTreeNode interface, 664
isRightMouseButton() method
    SwingUtilities class, 24
isSelectedIndex() method
    DefaultListSelectionModel class, 475
isTraversable() method
    FileSystemView class, 334
itemCount property
    JComboBox class, 492
    JMenu class, 171
ItemListener interface
    handling JCheckBox selection events, 130
    handling JCheckBoxMenuItem selection
        events, 187

handling JRadioButton selection
    events, 142
handling JRadioButtonMenuItem
    selection events, 192
handling JToggleButton selection events,
    121–124
listening to JComboBox events, 493–496
itemListeners property
    AbstractButton class, 98
    JComboBox class, 492
Iterator class
    using instead of Enumeration class, 666

■J

Japanese-language buttons
    JOptionPane class, 291
JApplet class
    BorderLayout class as default layout
        manager for, 347
    extending, 252
    introduction, 252
JAR files, 1
Java Access Bridge
    working with, 808–810
Java archive, 1
Java Ferret, introduction, 810
java.awt package
    Color class, 730
    FocusTraversalPolicy class, 47
    KeyboardFocusManager, 47
java.awt.datatransfer package
    drag-and-drop capabilities, 729
    Transferable interface, 733
java.awt.event package
    KeyEvent class, 163
java.beans package
    PropertyChangeListener, 420
java.io package
    File class, 333, 730
    FileFilter interface, 331
java.swing package
    TransferHandler class, 731
java.swing.text package
    InternationalFormatter class, 612
java.text package
    DecimalFormat class, 520
    Format class, 566
    MessageFormat class, 727
    NumberFormat class, 615

java.util package
    Dictionary class, 641
    Hashtable class, 41
    Map interface, 41
    Timer class, 36
    Undo Framework, 783
javax.accessibility package
    accessibility classes, 805
javax.swing package, 2
    BorderFactory class, 215
    DefaultFocusManager class, 47
    filechooser class, 331
    FocusManager class, 47
    Icon class, 734
javax.swing.border package
    AbstractBorder class, 216
    Border interface, 212
javax.swing.colorchooser package
    support classes for JColorChooser
        class, 301
javax.swing.event package, 32
    EventListenerList class, 29, 33
    event-related classes, 624
    support for Undo Framework, 783
javax.swing.filechooser package
    support classes for JFileChooser, 322
javax.swing.plaf package, 2
    classes that implement UIResource
        interface, 753–754
javax.swing.plaf.basic package
    BasicComboBoxEditor class, 499
    DefaultMenuLayout class, 381
javax.swing.plaf.metal package
    MetalLookAndFeel class, 748, 772
javax.swing.table package
    support classes for JTable class, 675
javax.swing.text package
    DefaultFormatterFactory class, 620, 621
javax.swing.text.html package
    HTMLEditorKit.Parser class, 607
javax.swing.tree package
    tree specific classes, 624
javax.swing.undo package, 11
    Undo Framework, 783
JButton class, 67, 104, 722
    ActionEvent event, 107
    addActionListener() method, 20
    changing look and feel at runtime
        through, 744–746

configuring a default button, 105
creating, 104
customizing look and feel, 108
    UIResource-related properties, 109
generating ActionEvent objects, 19
getActionListeners() method, 29
handling events, 106, 107
placing icon onto, 271
properties, 105
using on JOptionPane, 285
JCheckBox class
    appearance with DefaultCellEditor as
        TreeCellEditor, 646
    compared to JCheckBoxMenuItem
        component, 185
    creating, 126–127
    creating CheckBoxNodeEditor class,
        653–658
    customizing look and feel, 133
        UIResource-related properties, 134
    editing table cells, 718
    handling selection events, 130–133
    introduction, 125
    properties, 127–130
JCheckBoxMenuItem component, 8
    compared to JRadioButtonMenuItem
        component, 190
    creating, 184
    customizing look and feel, 187
        UIResource-related properties, 187, 189
    handling selection events, 186
        with ActionListener, 186
        with ItemListener, 187
    introduction, 184
    properties, 185
JColorChooser class, 9, 722
    built-in drag-and-drop support, 730
    changing color chooser panels, 310–320
    changing preview panel, 308–309
    creating, 301
    creating and showing in pop-up window,
        303–307
    dragging-and-dropping colors across, 730
    introduction, 300–301
    listening for color selection changes, 303
    properties, 307
    providing OK/cancel event listeners, 305
    using, 302

JComboBox class, 64, 314, 719
   changing look and feel at runtime
      through, 744–746
   creating components, 491
   customizing look and feel, 503–506
   data model provided by
      DefaultComboBoxModel class, 460
   demonstrating use of, 462–463
   editing elements, 497–503
   editing table cells, 718
   introduction, 490, 491
   properties, 491, 492
   rendering elements, 493
   selecting elements, 493–497
   sharing data model with JList, 506, 508
   uses implementation of ComboBoxModel
      interface, 460
   using with DefaultCellEditor as
      TreeCellEditor, 647
JComboBoxMenuItem class
   using with MenuElement interface, 195
JComponent class
   adding to JColorChooser, 308
   compared to AWT Component and
      Container classes, 67
   customizing display characteristics tooltip
      objects, 84
   descendent classes, 67
   handling events, 80
      listening to inherited events, 82, 84
      with AncestorListener, 81
      with PropertyChangeListener, 80
      with VetoableChangeListener, 81
   implements Accessible interface, 807
   introduction, 67
   methods
      currentManager() method, 70
      getActionMap() method, 593
      getClientProperty() method, 759
      getInputMap() method, 43
      putClientProperty() method, 759
      setComponentPopupMenu()
        method, 178
      setMinimumSize() method, 388
      setToolTipText() method, 84, 87
   painting JComponent objects, 69
   properties, 41, 74–77
      border property, 441
      client properties, 73

      component-set-oriented properties, 78
      event support properties, 79
      focus-oriented properties, 78
      focusTraversalPolicyProvider
        property, 50
      internationalization support
        properties, 79
      layout-oriented properties, 78
      opaque property, 525
      other properties, 79
      painting properties, 70, 78
      painting support properties, 78
      position-oriented properties, 77
      state support properties, 79
   Swing menu elements are subclasses
      of, 156
   UIResource properties, 72
JDesktopIcon class
   changing, 261
   inner class of JInternalFrame, 252
JDesktopPane component, 8
   adding internal frames to, 262
   and JInternalFrame class, 253
   as a specialized JLayeredPane, 252
   complete desktop example, 263–265
   creating, 262
   customizing look and feel, 263
   introduction, 262
   properties, 262
JDialog class
   BorderLayout class as default layout
      manager for, 347
   creating, 248–249
   extending, 252
   handling events, 250–252
   introduction, 248
   placing JOptionPane class within, 271–272
   properties, 250
   setUndecorated() method, 237
JEditorPane class, 5
   as subclass of JTextComponent class, 521
   built-in drag-and-drop support, 730
   creating, 575
   customizing look and feel, 579
      UIResource-related properties, 579
   handling events, 576–579
   HTMLDocument interface, 522
   JTextPane as subclass of, 521
   introduction, 574

loading HTML documents as
    StyledDocument, 607
properties, 575–576
JFileChooser class, 452
  adding ActionListener, 324–325
  creating, 323
  customizing look and feel, 336
  dragging-and-dropping File object, 730
  introduction, 322
  properties, 326
  showing in pop-up window, 326
  using, 323–324
  working with file filters, 328
    adding accessory panels, 331
    choosing directories instead of files, 331
    using FileSystemView class, 333
    using FileView class, 334–336
JFormattedTextField class, 7
  and DefaultFormatterFactory class, 621
  and JSpinner class, 509
  built-in drag-and-drop support, 730
  creating, 566–567
  customizing look and feel, 569
    UIResource-related properties, 569–570
  date and time formats, 612–614
  example, 567–569
  finding actions, 591
  formats, 612
  input masks, 618–620
  introduction, 566
  properties, 567
  notify-field-accept action, 587
  number formats, 615–617
  setMask() method, 618
  setText() method, 615
  setValue() method, 615
  using formatted input options and
    validation available, 585
  working with editors based on, 518
JFormattedTextField.
    AbstractFormatterFactory class
  manages use of formatter objects, 617
JFrame class
  adding components, 245
  BorderLayout class as default layout
    manager for, 347
  close operation constants, 244
  compared to JInternalFrame class, 253

creating, 243
defaultLookAndFeelDecorated
    property, 244
extending, 246
handling events, 245
introduction, 242
properties, 243
setting window decoration style, 244
setUndecorated() method, 237
JInternalFrame class, 8
  and JDesktopPane, 266
  BorderLayout class as default layout
    manager for, 347
  changing JDesktopIcon, 261
  creating, 253
  customizing look and feel, 257
    UIResource-related properties, 259–261
  handling events, 256–257
  introduction, 253
  palette with other frames, 261
  placing JOptionPane class within, 271
  properties, 254–255
  property constants, 255–256
  without AWT counterpart, 235
JIT compilers, 1
JLabel class, 67
  AccessibleJLabel class, 806
  creating, 89
  customizing look and feel, 92
    UIResource value settings, 92
  DefaultListCellRenderer class as subclass
    of, 468
  dragging text from, 732
  event handling, 91
  implementation of within
    TableCellRenderer interface, 676
  introduction, 88
  properties, 89
  setDisplayedMnemonic() method, 527
  setLabelFor() method, 528
JLayeredPane class
  adding components in layers, 240–241
  as component of JRootPane class, 235
  component layers and positions, 241
  creating, 240
  introduction, 239–240
  properties, 242

JList class
    adding element level tooltips, 488–490
    creating components, 463–464
    creating dual list box, 481–488
    customizing look and feel, 480
        UIResource-related properties, 480–481
    data model implementation, 451
    displaying multiple columns, 479–480
    introduction, 463
    properties, 464–465
    rendering elements, 468–470
        creating complex ListCellRenderer,
            471–473
    scrolling components, 466–468
    scrolling support, 406
    selecting elements, 473–479
    sharing data model with JComboBox
        506, 508
JMenu class
    adding menu items to, 169
    addSeparator() method, 175
    creating, 168–169
    customizing look and feel, 173
        UIResource-related properties, 173–175
    insertSeparator() method, 175
    introduction, 168
    listening to events
        with ChangeListener, 173
        with MenuListener, 173
    properties, 171
    setting menu components, 172
    using Action objects, 170, 171
JMenuBar class
    adding Action objects, 589
    adding glue component to, 381
    adding to or removing menus from menu
        bars, 157–158
    and JApplet class, 252
    changing layout manager, 161
    contained in JLayeredPane class, 236
    creating, 157
    customizing look and feel, 159
        UIResource-related properties, 160
    introduction, 157
    properties, 158–159
    setHelpMenu() method, 381
jMenuBar property
    JDialog class, 250
    JFrame class, 243

JInternalFrame class, 254
JRootPane class, 237
JMenuItem class
    creating, 162–163
    customizing look and feel, 167
        UIResource-related properties, 167–168
    handling events, 164–167
    introduction, 162
    properties, 163
    setText() method, 589
JOptionPane class, 9
    adding components to button area, 285
    adding components to message area, 284
    automatically creating in pop-up window,
        274–275
    arguments for factory methods, 276
    confirm pop-ups, 278
    input pop-ups, 278–279
    message pop-ups, 277
    option pop-ups, 280
    createDialog() method, 292
    creating, 268–269
    creating JDialog class, 249
    creating pop-up dialogs hosted by
        JInternalFrame class, 254
    customizing look and feel, 287–291
    displaying, 271–274
    displaying multiline messages, 281–282
    initialValue argument, 271
    introduction, 267–268
    listening for property changes, 286
    message argument, 269–270
    message property, 283
    messageType argument, 270
    options argument, 271
    optionType argument, 270
    properties, 280–281
    showInternalMessageDialog()
        method, 277
    showMessageDialog() method, 277
JPanel class, 67
    AbstractColorChooserPanel as JPanel
        subclass, 312
    creating, 110
    customizing look and feel, 112
        UIResource-related properties, 112
    FlowLayout class as default layout
        manager for, 345
    implementing Accessible interface, 807

mixing lightweight and heavyweight
    components, 179
placing JRadioButton objects within, 227
setting previewPanel property to empty
    JPanel, 308
using, 110–112
JPasswordField class, 5
    built-in drag-and-drop support, 730
    creating, 563–564
    customizing look and feel, 565
        UIResource-related properties, 565
    finding actions, 591
    introduction, 563
    notify-field-accept action, 587
    properties, 564
    subclass of JTextField class, 521
JPopupMenu class
    adding menu item to JMenu, 170
    adding menu items to, 177
    creating, 176
    customizing look and feel, 180
        UIResource-related properties, 181
    displaying, 178
    example, 182–184
    introduction, 176
    JMenu contained within, 168
    properties, 179
    Separator class, 182
    watching for pop-up menu visibility, 180
JProgressBar component, 6
    creating, 439–440
    customizing look and feel, 446
        UIResource-related properties, 446
    handling events, 445–446
    introduction, 439
    labeling, 441
    painting borders, 441
    process of step through, 442–445
    properties, 440
    using an indeterminate progress bar, 442
JRadioButton class
    compared to JRadioButtonMenuItem
        component, 189
    creating, 135–136
    customizing look and feel, 147
        UIResource-related properties, 148
    grouping in a ButtonGroup, 136–139
    handling selection events, 139–145
    introduction, 134

listing text actions, 586
placing within JPanel, 227
properties, 136
JRadioButtonMenuItem component, 8
    configuring properties, 191
    creating, 190
    customizing look and feel, 191
        UIResource-related properties, 191–192
    example, 192–194
    handling selection events, 190
    introduction, 184, 189
JRootPane class
    and JDialog class, 248
    creating, 236
    creating JLayeredPane class, 240
    customizing look and feel, 238–239
    introduction, 235
    layering effect, 180
    properties, 236–238
    RootLayout inner class, 343
    windowDecorationStyle property, 244
JScrollBar component
    BoundedRangeModel interface
        properties, 419
    compared to JSlider component, 6
    creating, 422
    customizing look and feel, 427
        UIResource-related properties, 427–428
    handling scrolling events, 423
    introduction, 421
    listening to scrolling events
        with AdjustmentListener, 423
        with ChangeListener, 424–425
    methods, 426
    properties, 14, 426
JScrollPane class
    creating, 404–405
    creating columns that don't scroll, 692
    creating viewport view, 406
    customizing look and feel, 410
        UIResource-related properties, 410
    introduction, 403
    JScrollBar component used within, 421
    JTextComponent text components can be
        placed within, 523
    JViewport class used with, 371
    manually positioning JTable view, 679
    placing JList component within, 466
    placing JTableHeader objects within, 715

placing JTextArea within, 570
placing JTree within, 627
placing tree within, 623
policies, 405
properties, 407
resetting viewport position, 410
Scrollable interface, 406
use of ScrollPaneLayout class, 370
using with JTable class, 678
working with headers and corners, 409
working with ScrollPaneLayout
    manager, 408
JScrollPane.ScrollBar. *See* Scrollable
    interface
JSeparator class, 8
    creating, 175
    customizing look and feel, 176
        UIResource-related properties, 176
    does not implement MenuElement
        interface, 195
    introduction, 175
    properties, 175
    setOrientation() method, 182, 208
JSlider class, 6
    adding to JOptionPane, 284
    client properties, 438
    creating, 428–429
    customizing look and feel, 435–438
    displaying tick marks within, 432
    handling events, 430
    introduction, 428
    labeling positions, 434
    methods, 431
    properties, 431
    snapping thumb into position, 434
    UIResource-related properties, 437
JSpinner class, 6
    creating, 510
    custom models, 517
    customizing look and feel, 512
        UIResource properties, 512–513
    editors, 518
        DateEditor class, 519
        DefaultEditor class, 518
        ListEditor class, 519
        NumberEditor class, 520
    introduction, 509
    listening for events with ChangeListener
        interface, 511–512

properties, 510–511
    SpinnerModel interface as data model, 513
JSplitPane class, 10
    changing components, 386
    creating, 384
    customizing look and feel, 393
        UIResource-related properties, 393
    introduction, 383
    listening for property changes, 390–392
    moving divider, 387
    one-touch expandable divider, 388
    properties, 385
    resizing, 389
    resizing components, 388
    setting orientation, 386
JTabbedPane class, 10
    adding and removing tabs, 397–398
    addTab() method, 398
    creating, 395–396
    customizing look and feel, 401
        UIResource-related properties, 402–403
    displaying multiple chooser panels in
        JColorChooser, 301
    introduction, 394
    listening for changing tab selection,
        399–401
    properties, 398–399
    used instead of CardLayout class, 357
JTable class, 7, 677
    autoCreateColumnsFromModel
        property, 708
    auto-resize modes, 683–685
    createDefaultColumnsFromModel()
        method, 708
    creating, 677–678
    customizing look and feel, 689
        UIResource-related properties, 689–690
    display settings, 682
    editing table cells, 718
    example, 675
    handling events, 689
    listening to events with
        TableColumnModelListener, 709–712
    listing properties within with UIDefaults
        class, 749
    manually positioning view, 679
    preinstalled renderers, 695
    print() method, 724, 727
    properties, 680, 682

removing column headers, 680
rendering table cells, 686–689
scrolling components, 678–679
scrolling support, 406
selection modes, 682, 683
sorting elements, 700–707
support classes, 675
JTableHeader class, 676
  creating, 716
  customizing look and feel, 717
  introduction, 715
  properties, 716
  using tooltips in headers, 716, 717
JTextArea class
  adding to window, 476
  as subclass of JTextComponent class, 521
  as view part of MVC, 59
  built-in drag-and-drop support, 730
  creating, 570
  customizing look and feel, 572
    UIResource-related properties, 573–574
  handling events, 572
  introduction, 570
  model and UI delegate, 60
  properties, 571, 572
  supporting undoable operations, 784
JTextComponent class
  associating CaretListener interface
      with, 550
  associating NavigationFilter class with, 552
  drawing in the background of component,
      525–526
  getActions() method, 586
  getKeymap() method, 586
  introduction, 523
  modelToView() method, 549
  operations, 526
  operations with JTextField class, 530–537
  properties, 523
  read() method, 607
  registerKeyboardAction() method, 554
  scrolling support, 406
  setKeymap() method, 586
  subclasses, 521
  write() method, 607
JTextComponent.KeyBinding class, 556

JTextField class, 499
  as editor for JTree, 645
  as subclass of JTextComponent class, 521
  BoundedRangeModel interface, 447, 449
  built-in drag-and-drop support, 730
  creating, 527
  customizing look and feel, 562–563
  dragging text from JLabel class to
      JTextField class, 733
  editing JComboBox class elements, 498
  editing table cells, 718
  handling events, 556–562
  introduction, 526
  JPasswordField as subclass of, 521, 565
  JTextComponent operations, 530
    accessing the clipboard, 534–537
    loading and saving content, 530–534
  notify-field-accept action, 587
  properties, 529
  using JLabel mnemonics, 527–529
JTextPane class, 5
  as subclass of JEditorPane component, 521
  built-in drag-and-drop support, 730
  creating, 580
  creating stylized text for display, 585
  customizing look and feel, 581
  DefaultStyledDocument class as data
      model, 596
  Hello, Java example, 600–601
      introduction, 580
  loading with content, 582–583
  populating StyledDocument for, 599
  properties, 580–581
JToggleButton class, 6
  creating, 119–120
  customizing look and feel, 124
    UIResource elements, 125
  handling selection events, 121–124
  introduction, 119
  properties, 120
  ToggleButtonModel class as inner class
      of, 115
JToggleButtonMenuItem example, 195–199
JToolBar class, 8, 784
  adding components to, 202
  creating, 202
  customizing look and feel, 205
  getUIClassID() method, 763

handling events, 205
introduction, 202
properties, 203
Separator class, 208
usage example, 206–208
JToolTip class, 7
creating, 84
creating customized objects, 84
customizing look and feel, 86
displaying positional tooltip text, 85
properties, 85
JTree class, 7
convertValueToText() method, 642
creating a proper ComboBox editor for, 648
creating, 624–627
creating custom renderer, 637–641
customizing look and feel, 630–634
DefaultTreeCellEditor class, 647
DefaultTreeModel class, 667
DynamicUtilTreeNode inner class, 624, 666
editable property, 643
EmptySelectionModel inner class, 624, 669
introducing trees, 623–624
properties, 628–630
scrolling support, 406
scrolling trees, 627–628
should use DefaultTreeCellEditor for JTextField editor, 645
working with tree tooltips, 641–643
JViewport class
contained within JScrollPane, 403
creating, 412
customizing look and feel, 417
introduction, 412
keyboard movement control, 414–417
properties, 412
scroll modes, 414
use of ViewportLayout class, 371
usually used with JScrollPane class, 371
JWindow class
BorderLayout class as default layout manager for, 347
creating, 247
extending, 248
fitting JPopupMenu menu items, 179
handling events, 248
introduction, 247
properties, 248

K

KeyBinding class, 556
KeyboardFocusManager class, 37, 48
activeWindow property, 55
focus management, 47
focusedWindow property, 55
focusOwner property, 55
input focus behavior of Swing components, 55
methods, 55
KeyEvent class
getKeyText() method, 29
java.awt.event package, 163
KeyListener class
listening to JTextField events, 557
sending keystrokes to ActionListener, 30
supported by JFrame class, 246
using, 586
Keymap interface, 37
addActionForKeyStroke() method, 45
implementation as a wrapper to InputMap/ActionMap combination, 586
introduction, 554–556
maps KeyStroke to TextAction, 586
keymap property
JTextComponent class, 523, 554
keys property
AbstractAction class, 41
KeySelectionManager interface, 195, 493
keystroke manager for JComboBox class, 491
listening to JComboBox keyboard events, 494
keySelectionManager property
JComboBox class, 492, 494
KeyStroke class
creating, 42
getKeyStroke() method, 43
getKeyStrokeForEvent() method, 43
keystroke registration conditions, 42
registering, 43, 44, 45
registering to JTextComponent class, 554
Swing-specific event handling, 37
using, 586
KeyTextComponent class
registering ActionListener, 31

L

label property
  AbstractButton class, 99
  JPopupMenu class, 179
labelFor property
  JLabel class, 90, 91
labelTable property
  JSlider component, 431
largeModel property
  JTree class, 628, 630
lastChild property
  DefaultMutableTreeNode interface, 663
lastDividerLocation property
  JSplitPane class, 385, 389, 390, 392
lastIndex property
  ListSelectionEvent class, 476
lastIndexOf() method
  DefaultListModel class, 460
lastLeaf property
  DefaultMutableTreeNode interface, 663
lastPathComponent property
  TreePath class, 671
lastRow property
  TableModelEvent class, 700
lastSelectedPathComponent property
  JTree class, 628, 630
lastVisibleIndex property
  JList class, 465, 468
layer property
  JInternalFrame class, 254
LayeredHighlighter class, 547
LayeredHighlighter.LayerPainter class, 547
layeredPane property
  JDialog class, 250
  JFrame class, 243
  JInternalFrame class, 254
  JRootPane class, 237
  JWindow class, 248
LayerPainter class, 547
layout management
  changing manager for JMenuBar class, 161
  changing manager for JTabbedPane
    class, 399
  Swing components, 10, 11
layout managers
  See also AWT layout managers and Swing
    layout managers
  BorderLayout class, 347–349
  BoxLayout class, 357–364

CardLayout class, 357
FlowLayout class, 345–347
GridBagConstraints class, 353–357
GridBagLayout class, 350–353
GridLayout class, 349–350
introduction, 343
LayoutManager interface, 344–345
OverlayLayout class, 365–370
responsibilities, 343–344
ScrollPaneLayout class, 370
SizeRequirements class, 370
SpringLayout class, 371–375
ViewportLayout class, 371
layout property
  AbstractButton class, 98
  Box class, 379
  JComponent class, 78
  JDialog class, 250
  JFrame class, 243
  JInternalFrame class, 255
  JLayeredPane class, 240
  JScrollPane class, 407
  JToolBar class, 203
  JWindow class, 248
LayoutFocusTraversalPolicy class
  focus management, 47
  FocusTraversalPolicy class, 53
LayoutManager interface
  introduction, 344
  methods, 344
LayoutManager2 interface
  methods, 345
layoutOrientation property
  JList class, 465
lazy, definition, 755
LazyValue interface, 755
  creating, 755
  createValue() method, 755
leadAnchorNotificationEnabled property
  DefaultListSelectionModel class, 475, 683
leader property
  TabStop class, 604
leadSelectionIndex property
  DefaultListSelectionModel class, 475, 683
  JList class, 465
leadSelectionPath property
  DefaultTreeSelectionModel class, 670
  JTree class, 628, 630

leadSelectionRow property
  DefaultTreeSelectionModel class, 670
  JTree class, 629–630
leaf nodes
  creating editor for, 648–649
leaf property
  DefaultMutableTreeNode interface, 663
leafCount property
  DefaultMutableTreeNode interface, 663
leafIcon property
  DefaultTreeCellRenderer class, 635
leftComponent property
  JSplitPane class, 385–386
length property
  AbstractDocument class, 540
level property
  DefaultMutableTreeNode interface, 663
lightweight property
  JComponent class, 79
lightWeightPopupEnabled property
  JComboBox class, 492
  JPopupMenu class, 179
  ToolTipManager class, 87
LineBorder class
  configuring properties, 220
  creating, 219
lineColor property
  LineBorder class, 220
lineCount property
  JTextArea class, 571
lineWrap property
  JTextArea class, 571
list model controls, 451
  See also individual controls
list property
  SpinnerListModel class, 516
ListCellRenderer interface, 719
  and DefaultListCellRenderer class, 468, 470
  cell renderer for JComboBox class, 491
  creating complex version, 471–473
  drawing elements of JList class, 463
  getListCellRendererComponent()
    method, 469
  making lazy, 755
listData property
  JList class, 465
ListDataEvent class
  properties, 454

ListDataListener class, 451
  list managed by DefaultListModel class, 453
  list management provided by
    AbstractListModel, 452
  listening for ListModel events, 454–460
  listening to JComboBox events, 497
  managed by ListModel interface, 452
  using, 455
ListEditor class
  introduction, 519
ListModel interface
  converting ArrayList data structure, 453
  data model for JList class, 463
  defines data model for JComboBox
    class, 491
  extended by
    ComboBoxModel interface, 460
  introduction, 451
  management of ListDataListener, 452
  partially implemented by
    AbstractListModel, 452
ListSelectionEvent class
  properties, 476
ListSelectionListener interface
  listening to JList events, 476–478
  registering with ListSelectionModel
    class, 683
listSelectionListeners property
  DefaultListSelectionModel class, 475, 683
  JList class, 465
ListSelectionModel interface, 676
  allowing users to select columns and rows
    from table, 708
  attaching ListSelectionListener, 476
  constants for different selection
    modes, 683
  controls selection process for JList, 473
  creating columns that do not scroll, 692
  default implementation is
    DefaultListSelectionModel class, 475
  handling JTable events, 689
  model for selecting elements of JList
    class, 463
  modes, 474
  multiple-selection mode, 678
  registering ListSelectionListener, 683
  settings control selection within table, 676
load() method
  SynthLookAndFeel class, 780

locale property
 AccessibleContext class, 807
 JComponent class, 79
localization
 NumberFormat class, 615
locationOnScreen property
 JComponent class, 77
locationToIndex() method
 JList class, 478
logicalStyle property
 JTextPane class, 581
look and feel architecture, 741
 creating new look and feel, 767–772
 LookAndFeel class, 741–766
 metal themes, 772
 SynthLookAndFeel class, 777–781
 using auxiliary look and feel, 776
look and feel image files, 768–770
LookAndFeel class
 as root class for specific look and feel, 741
 changing current look and feel, 743–747
 customizing current look and feel, 747
  creating new UI delegate, 763–766
  UIDefaults class, 749–752
  UIDefaults.ActiveValue,
   UIDefaults.LazyValue, and
   UIDefaults.ProxyLazyValue classes,
   755–759
  UIManager class, 747–749
  UIManager.LookAndFeelInfo class, 749
  UIResource interface, 753–755
  using client properties, 759–763
 introduction, 741–742
 listing installed classes, 742
 makeIcon() method, 755
lookAndFeel property
 UIManager class, 748
lookAndFeelDefaults property
 UIManager class, 748
lowestLayer() method
 JLayeredPane class, 240

■M

MacLookAndFeel implementation
 LookAndFeel.supportedLookAndFeel, 742
magicCaretPosition property
 Caret interface, 548
majorTickSpacing property
 JSlider component, 431

makeIcon() method
 LookAndFeel class, 755
Map interface, 41
margin property
 AbstractButton class, 98
 JMenuBar class, 159
 JPopupMenu class, 179
 JTextComponent class, 523, 524
 JToolBar class, 203
mark property
 Caret interface, 548
MaskFormatter class, 566
 overwriteMode property, 620
 placeholderCharacter property, 620
 validCharacters property, 620
MatteBorder class, 224
 color implementation, 225
 constructors and methods, 225
 Icon implementation, 225
maxCharactersPerLineCount property
 JOptionPane class, 281, 282, 292
maximizable property
 JInternalFrame class, 255
maximum property
 BoundedRangeModel interface, 419
 JInternalFrame class, 255
 JProgressBar component, 440
 JScrollBar component, 426
 JSlider component, 431
 ProgressMonitor class, 296
 SpinnerNumberModel class, 517
maximumDividerLocation property
 JSplitPane class, 385
maximumRowCount property
 JComboBox class, 492
maximumSize property
 JComponent class, 78
 JScrollBar component, 426
maximumSizeSet property
 JComponent class, 78
maxSelectionIndex property
 DefaultListSelectionModel class, 475, 683
maxSelectionRow property
 DefaultTreeSelectionModel class, 670
 JTree class, 629, 630
maxWidth property
 TableColumn class, 713
menu components
 example, 152
 hierarchy, 156

menuBackground property
    MetalLookAndFeel class, 773
menuComponentCount property
    JMenu class, 171
menuComponents property
    JMenu class, 171
menuCount property
    JMenuBar class, 159
menuDisabledForeground property
    MetalLookAndFeel class, 773
MenuDragMouseEvent class
    definition, 167
MenuDragMouseListener interface
    listening to JMenuItem events, 167
menuDragMouseListeners property
    JMenuItem class, 164
MenuElement interface, 157
    creating custom components, 195
menuForeground property
    MetalLookAndFeel class, 773
MenuKeyListener interface
    listening to JMenuItem events, 166
menuKeyListeners property
    JMenuItem class, 164
    JPopupMenu class, 179
MenuListener interface
    listening to JMenu events, 173
menuListeners property
    JMenu class, 172
menus, adding to or removing from menu
        bars, 157, 158
menuSelectedBackground property
    MetalLookAndFeel class, 773
menuSelectedForeground property
    MetalLookAndFeel class, 773
menuSelectionChanged() method
    MenuElement interface, 195
MenuSelectionManager class, 167, 195
menuTextFont property
    MetalLookAndFeel class, 773
message property
    JOptionPane class, 269, 270, 281, 283
MessageFormat class
    java.text package, 727
messageType property
    JOptionPane class, 270, 281
Metal themes, creating, 774

MetalLookAndFeel class
    addCustomEntriesToTable() method, 774
    currentTheme property, 774
    javax.swing.plaf.metal package, 748, 772
    properties, 772
MetalLookAndFeel implementation
    LookAndFeel.supportedLookAndFeel, 742
Metalworks system demo
    examples for customizing themes, 775
millisToDecideToPopup property
    ProgressMonitor class, 292, 296
millisToPopup property
    ProgressMonitor class, 292, 296
minimum property
    BoundedRangeModel interface, 419
    JProgressBar component, 440
    JScrollBar component, 426
    JSlider component, 431
    ProgressMonitor class, 296
    SpinnerNumberModel class, 517
minimumDividerLocation property
    JSplitPane class, 385
minimumSize property
    JComponent class, 78
    JScrollBar component, 426
minimumSizeSet property
    JComponent class, 78
minorTickSpacing property
    JSlider component, 431
minSelectionIndex property
    DefaultListSelectionModel class, 475, 683
    JList class, 465
minSelectionRow property
    DefaultTreeSelectionModel class, 670
    JTree class, 629, 630
minWidth property
    TableColumn class, 713
mnemonic property
    AbstractButton class, 98
    DefaultButtonModel interface, 100
mnemonics, 46
model property
    AbstractButton class, 99
    DateEditor class, 519
    JComboBox class, 492
    JList class, 465
    JMenu class, 172

JProgressBar component, 440
JScrollBar component, 426
JSlider component, 431
JSpinner class, 510
JTabbedPane class, 399
JTable class, 681
JTree class, 629
ListEditor class, 520
NumberEditor class, 520
modelIndex property
  TableColumn class, 713
modelToView() method
  JTextComponent class, 549
ModifyModelSample program
  using DefaultListModel class modifying
      methods, 455–459
mostRecentFocusOwner property
  JInternalFrame class, 255
MotifButtonUI class
  getBorderInsets() method, 217
MotifLookAndFeel implementation
  LookAndFeel.supportedLookAndFeel, 742
mouseClicked() method
  MouseInputListener interface, 23
mouseDragged() method
  MouseMotionListener interface, 23
mouseEntered() method
  MouseInputListener interface, 23
MouseEnterFocusMover class
  programmatically moving focus, 49
mouseExited() method
  MouseInputListener interface, 23
MouseInputListener interface
  methods, 23
MouseListener interface
  creating to handle input focus, 48
  requestFocusInWindow() method, 48
  supported by JFrame class, 246
MouseMotionListener interface
  methods, 23
  supported by JFrame class, 246
mouseMoved() method
  MouseMotionListener interface, 23
mousePosition property
  JComponent class, 79
mousePressed() method
  MouseInputListener interface, 23
mouseReleased() method
  MouseInputListener interface, 23

moveDot() method
  Caret interface, 549
  NavigationFilter class, 552
moveToBack() method
  JLayeredPane class, 241
moveToFront() method
  JLayeredPane class, 241
multiClickThreshhold property
  AbstractButton class, 99
multiline messages
  displaying in JOptionPane, 281, 282
MULTIPLE_INTERVAL_SELECTION mode
  ListSelectionModel interface, 474
multiSelectionEnabled property
  JFileChooser class, 327
multithreaded Swing event handling, 21, 23
  managing listener lists, 29
    AWTEventMulticaster class, 29–32
    EventListenerList, 32–34
  selectable button example, 22
  Timer class, 34–36
  using PropertyChangeListeners as
      Observers, 26–28
  using SwingUtilities class for mouse
      button identification, 23–26
MutableAttributeSet interface, 585, 595
  adding name to with Style interface, 606
  introduction, 597
  modifying with StyleConstants class,
      602–603
  setting JTextPane text attributes, 580
MutableComboBoxModel interface, 64, 451
  implementing DefaultComboBoxModel
      class, 461
  introduction, 460
MutableTreeNode interface, 659
  insert() method, 662
  nodes of JTree are implementations of, 624
  working with tree nodes, 660
MVC architecture, 11, 59
  BoundedRangeModel interface, 419
  flow described
    communication, 59
    UI delegates for Swing components, 60
  handling JScrollBar events, 423
  predefined data models, 63–64
  sharing data models, 61–63

■N

name property
  JComponent class, 79
  LookAndFeel class, 742
  MetalLookAndFeel class, 773
  UIManager.LookAndFeelInfo class, 749
NamedStyle class, 595, 606
nativeLookAndFeel property
  LookAndFeel class, 742
NavigationFilter class, 522
  introduction, 552
  restricting caret movement example
    552, 554
navigationFilter property
  JTextComponent class, 523
next() method
  ElementIterator class, 611
  HTMLDocument.Iterator class, 609
nextLeaf property
  DefaultMutableTreeNode interface, 663
nextNode property
  DefaultMutableTreeNode interface, 663
nextSibling property
  DefaultMutableTreeNode interface, 663
nextValue property
  JSpinner class, 510
  SpinnerDateModel class, 515
  SpinnerListModel class, 516
  SpinnerNumberModel class, 517
nodeChanged() method
  DefaultTreeModel class, 668
nodesChanged() method
  DefaultTreeModel class, 668
nodeStructureChanged() method
  DefaultTreeModel class, 668
nodesWereInserted() method
  DefaultTreeModel class, 668
nodesWereRemoved() method
  DefaultTreeModel class, 668
non-AWT upgraded components, 5
normalBounds property
  JInternalFrame class, 255
note property
  ProgressMonitor class, 296
notify-field-accept action
  extra action for JTextField,
    JFormattedTextField, and
    JPasswordField, 587

Number object
  providing to JFormattedTextField
    constructor, 612
number property
  SpinnerNumberModel class, 517
NumberEditor class
  introduction, 520
  properties, 520
NumberFormat class, 612
  java.text package, 615
NumberFormatter class, 566

■O

Observer design pattern
  delegation-based event handling, 17, 18
  event listeners as observers, 19
OceanTheme class
  introduction, 774
oneTouchExpandable property
  JSplitPane class, 386, 388
opaque property
  JComponent class, 70, 78
  JDesktopPane component, 263
  JTextComponent class, 525
openIcon property
  DefaultTreeCellRenderer class, 635
optimizedDrawingEnabled property
  JComponent class, 70, 78
  JLayeredPane class, 242
  JRootPane class, 237
  JViewport class, 412
OptionPaneUtils class
  creating narrow JOptionPane, 281, 282
  getSelection() method, 273, 274
options property
  JOptionPane class, 271, 281
optionType property
  JOptionPane class, 270, 281
orientation property
  JProgressBar component, 440
  JScrollBar component, 426
  JSeparator class, 175
  JSlider component, 431
  JSplitPane class, 386
  JToolBar class, 203
outsideBorder property
  CompoundBorder class, 227
OvalPanel class, 391

OverlayLayout class
    introduction, 365–370
overwriteMode property
    MaskFormatter class, 620

■P
padding
    GridBagConstraints class, 356
page property
    JEditorPane class, 575
paint() method
    JComponent class, 69
paintBorder() method
    AbstractBorder class, 217, 232
    Border interface, 212
    JComponent class, 69, 70
paintChildren() method
    JComponent class, 69, 70
paintComponent() method
    JComponent class, 69, 70
    JPanel class, 111
paintIcon() method
    Icon interface, 93
paintImmediately() method
    JComponent class, 70, 78
paintingTile property
    JComponent class, 78
paintLabels property
    JSlider component, 431
paintTicks property
    JSlider component, 431
paintTrack property
    JSlider component, 431
Panel class
    displaying the menu choices, 179
paragraphAttributes property
    JTextPane class, 581
ParagraphConstants class
    keys for attributes, 598
    TabSet attribute, 603
parent property
    DefaultMutableTreeNode interface, 663
    JComponent class, 77
parentPath property
    TreePath class, 671
password property
    JPasswordField class, 564
paste() method
    JTextComponent class, 534

pasteAction class constant
    DefaultEditorKit class, 592
path property
    DefaultMutableTreeNode interface, 663
    TreePath class, 671
pathByAddingChild() method
    TreePath class, 671
pathCount property
    TreePath class, 671
percentComplete property
    JProgressBar component, 441
placeholderCharacter property
    MaskFormatter class, 620
plaf, 2
PlainDocument class, 60, 521
    implementation of Document
        interface, 526
        as data model for JTextArea, 570
    introduction, 541, 542
PlainView view
    BasicTextAreaUI interface, 60
Popup class
    creating, 200
pop-up menu usage example, 182–184
pop-up usage example, 200–202
pop-up window
    showing JFileChooser in, 326
PopupFactory class
    creating Popup objects, 200
popupMenu property
    JMenu class, 172
PopupMenuEvent event
    PopupMenuListener class, 180
PopupMenuListener class
    watching for pop-up menu visibility, 180
popupMenuListeners property
    JComboBox class, 492
    JPopupMenu class, 179
popupMenuVisible property
    JMenu class, 172
pop-ups, 267
    JOptionPane class
        automatically creating in pop-up
            window, 274–280
        creating, 268–271
        customizing look and feel, 287–291
        displaying, 271–274
        introduction, 267–268
        properties, 280–287

ProgressMonitor class
  creating, 292
  customizing look and feel, 297
  introduction, 291–292
  properties, 296–297
  using, 293–296
ProgressMonitorInputStream class
  creating, 297
  introduction, 297
  properties, 299
  using, 298–299
popupSize property
  JPopupMenu class, 179
popupVisible property
  JComboBox class, 492
position constants
  JOptionPane class, 274
position property
  TabStop class, 604
positioning operations
  JTextComponent class, 526
postEdit() method
  UndoableEditSupport class, 794
preferredScrollableViewportSize property
  JList class, 465, 466
  JTable class, 681
  JTextArea class, 571
  JTextComponent class, 523
  JTree class, 629
preferredSize property
  DefaultTreeCellRenderer class, 635
  JComponent class, 78
  JEditorPane class, 575
  JTextArea class, 571
  JTextField class, 529
preferredSizeSet property
  JComponent class, 78
preferredWidth property
  TableColumn class, 713
preOrderEnumeration() method
  DefaultMutableTreeNode class, 665
pressed property
  DefaultButtonModel interface, 100
pressedIcon property
  AbstractButton class, 99
previewPanel property
  JColorChooser class, 307, 308
previous() method
  ElementIterator class, 611

previousLeaf property
  DefaultMutableTreeNode interface, 663
previousNode property
  DefaultMutableTreeNode interface, 663
previousSibling property
  DefaultMutableTreeNode interface, 663
previousValue property
  JSpinner class, 510
  SpinnerDateModel class, 515
  SpinnerListModel class, 516
  SpinnerNumberModel class, 517
primary1 property
  MetalLookAndFeel class, 773
primary2 property
  MetalLookAndFeel class, 773
primary3 property
  MetalLookAndFeel class, 773
primaryControl property
  MetalLookAndFeel class, 773
primaryControlDarkShadow property
  MetalLookAndFeel class, 773
primaryControlHighlight property
  MetalLookAndFeel class, 773
primaryControlInfo property
  MetalLookAndFeel class, 773
primaryControlShadow property
  MetalLookAndFeel class, 773
print() method
  JTable class, 724, 727
PrinterException class, 727
printing tables, 724
processKeyEvent() method
  MenuElement interface, 195
processMouseEvent() method
  MenuElement interface, 195
progress property
  ProgressMonitor class, 296
ProgressMonitor class
  creating, 292
  introduction, 291–292
  properties, 296–297
  using, 293–296
progressMonitor property
  ProgressMonitorInputStream class, 300
ProgressMonitorHandler inner class, 294
ProgressMonitorInputStream class
  creating, 297
  introduction, 297
  properties, 299
  using, 298–299

PropertiesList example
demonstrating tooltips, 488, 490
PropertyChangeListener, 420
AbstractButton class, 102
as accessory component for JFileChooser
class, 331, 333
JOptionPane, 287
listening for JSplitPane property
changes, 390
supported by JFrame class, 246
PropertyChangeListener interface
event handler for JComponent class, 80
using as Observers, 26, 27, 28
propertyChangeListeners property
AbstractAction class, 41
TableColumn class, 713
UIManager class, 748
PropertyChangeSupport class, 26
prototypeCellValue property
JList class, 465, 466
prototypeDisplayValue property
JComboBox class, 492
ProxyLazyValue class, 755
associating with Tree.openIcon setting,
756, 757
deferring object creation, 755, 756
put() method
UIManager class, 747, 758
putClientProperty() method
JComponent class, 759
putConstraint() method
SpringLayout class, 372, 373
putDefaults() method
UIDefaults class, 749
putProperty() method
AbstractDocument class, 540

■Q
QUESTION_MESSAGE pop-up
JOptionPane class, 278

■R
RadioButtonUtils class
complete definition, 145
createRadioButtonGrouping() method,
137, 140
listing text actions, 587
read() method
JTextComponent class, 530

readOnlyAction class constant
DefaultEditorKit class, 592
redo() method
CompoundEdit class, 792
UndoableEdit interface, 790
UndoManager class, 784
registeredKeyStrokes property
JComponent class, 79
registerKeyboardAction() method
JTextComponent class, 554
reload() method
DefaultTreeModel class, 668
remove() method
DocumentFilter class, 542
JMenuBar class, 158
JPopupMenu class, 178
removeCellEditorListener() method
CellEditor interface, 654
removeChooserPanel() method
JColorChooser class, 320
removeElement() method
DefaultListModel class, 454
removeListenerListener() method
JList class, 476
removeNodeFromParent() method
DefaultTreeModel class, 668
removeSelectedInterval() method
JList class, 479
removeUpdate() method
DocumentListener interface, 546
renderer property
JComboBox class, 492
renderers, preinstalled
JTable class, 695
reorderingAllowed property
JTableHeader class, 716
repaint() method
JComponent class, 69
RepaintManager class
customizing painting behavior, 69
introduction, 70, 71
properties, 71
repeats property
Timer class, 36
replace() method
DocumentFilter class, 542
requestFocusEnabled property
JComponent class, 78

requestFocusInWindow() method
    MouseListener interface, 48
resetToPreferredSizes() method
    JSplitPane class, 387
reshowDelay property
    ToolTipManager class, 87
resizable property
    JInternalFrame class, 255
    TableColumn class, 713
resizeWeight property
    JSplitPane class, 386, 389
resizingAllowed property
    JTableHeader class, 716
resizingColumn property
    JTableHeader class, 716
resolveParent property
    SimpleAttributeSet class, 598
restart() method
    Timer class, 35
restoreState method
    StateEditable interface, 800
restoreState() method
    StateEditable interface, 801
restricting focus cycle example, 51
revalidate() method
    JComponent class, 70, 79
reversing focus traversal, 53–55
rightComponent property
    JSplitPane class, 386
rigid component, creating, 382, 383
rollover property
    DefaultButtonModel interface, 100
    JToolBar class, 203, 205
rolloverEnabled property
    AbstractButton class, 99, 102
rolloverIcon property
    AbstractButton class, 99, 102
rolloverSelectedIcon property
    AbstractButton class, 99, 102
root pane containers
    introduction, 235
    JApplet class, 252
    JDialog class, 248–252
    JFrame class, 242–247
    JLayeredPane class, 239–242
    JRootPane class, 235–239
    JWindow class, 247–248
    RootPaneContainer interface, 239
    working with a desktop, 252

JDesktopPane class, 262–266
    JInternalFrame class, 253–262
root property
    DefaultMutableTreeNode interface, 663
rootElements property
    AbstractDocument class, 540
RootLayout class
    layout manager for JRootPane class,
        235–236
RootLayout inner class, 343
rootPane property
    JComponent class, 78
    JDialog class, 250
    JFrame class, 243
    JInternalFrame class, 255
    JWindow class, 248
RootPaneContainer interface
    adding components to JFrame class, 245
    getting root pane, 236
    implemented by JApplet class, 252
    implemented by JDialog class, 248
    implemented by JInternalFrame class, 253
    introduction, 239
rootVisible property
    JTree class, 629, 630
roundedCorners property
    LineBorder class, 220
rowCount property
    DefaultTableModel class, 697
    JTable class, 681
    JTree class, 629
rowHeader property
    JScrollPane class, 407
rowHeaderView property
    JScrollPane class, 407, 409
rowHeight property
    JTable class, 681
    JTree class, 629
RowMapper class
    implementation of TreePath class, 624
RowMapper interface
    AbstractLayoutCache class
        implements, 670
rowMapper property
    DefaultTreeSelectionModel class, 670
rowMargin property
    JTable class, 681
rows property
    JTextArea class, 571

rowSelectionAllowed property
    JTable class, 681, 682
Runnable objects
    creating with EventQueue class, 21
running property
    Timer class, 36

■S

Scrollable interface, 404, 466
    definition, 406
    implemented by JTable class, 678
    implemented by JTextComponent
        class, 523
        implementation properties, 524
    implemented by JTree, 623, 627
scrollableTracksViewportHeight property
    JEditorPane class, 575
    JList class, 465
    JTable class, 681
    JTextComponent class, 523
    JTree class, 629
scrollableTracksViewportWidth property
    JEditorPane class, 575
    JList class, 465
    JTable class, 681
    JTextArea class, 571
    JTextComponent class, 523
    JTree class, 629
Scrollbar component
    compared to JScrollBar and JSlider
        components, 6
scrolling support
    Swing components, 406
scrollMode property
    JViewport class, 412, 414
scrollOffset property
    JTextField class, 529, 530
ScrollPaneLayout class
    introduction, 370
ScrollPaneLayout manager class
    locations, 408
scrollPathToVisible() method
    JTree class, 627
scrollRowToVisible() method
    JTree class, 627
scrollsOnExpand property
    JTree class, 629, 630
secondary1 property
    MetalLookAndFeel class, 773

secondary2 property
    MetalLookAndFeel class, 773
secondary3 property
    MetalLookAndFeel class, 773
selectAll() method
    ComboBoxEditor class, 499
selected property
    AbstractButton class, 99
    DefaultButtonModel interface, 100
    JInternalFrame class, 255
    JMenu class, 172
    JMenuBar class, 159
    JPopupMenu class, 179
selectedColor property
    ColorSelectionModel interface, 303
selectedColumn property
    JTable class, 681–682
selectedColumnCount property
    DefaultTableColumnModel class, 709
    JTable class, 681–682
selectedColumns property
    DefaultTableColumnModel class, 709
    JTable class, 681–682
selectedComponent property
    JTabbedPane class, 399
selectedFile property
    JFileChooser class, 327
selectedFiles property
    JFileChooser class, 327
selectedFrame property
    JDesktopPane component, 263
selectedIcon property
    AbstractButton class, 99
selectedIndex property
    JComboBox class, 492
    JList class, 465
    JTabbedPane class, 399
selectedIndices property
    JList class, 465
selectedItem property
    DefaultComboBoxModel class, 461
    extended by ComboBoxModel
        interface, 460
    JComboBox class, 492
selectedObjects property
    AbstractButton class, 99
    DefaultButtonModel interface, 100
    JCheckBoxMenuItem component, 185
    JComboBox class, 492

selectedRow property
    JTable class, 681–682
selectedRowCount property
    JTable class, 681–682
selectedRows property
    JTable class, 681–682
selectedText property
    JTextComponent class, 524
selectedTextColor property
    JTextComponent class, 524
selectedValue property
    JList class, 465
selectedValues property
    JList class, 465
selection operations
    JTextComponent class, 526
selectionBackground property
    JList class, 465
    JTable class, 681, 682
    TextField class, 547
selectionColor property
    JTextComponent class, 524
selectionCount property
    DefaultTreeSelectionModel class, 670
    JTree class, 629
selectionEmpty property
    DefaultListSelectionModel class, 475, 683
    DefaultTreeSelectionModel class, 670
    JList class, 465
    JTree class, 629
selectionEnd property
    JTextComponent class, 524
selectionForeground property
    JList class, 465
    JTable class, 681, 682
selectionForKey() method
    KeySelectionManager interface, 494
selectionMode property
    DefaultListSelectionModel class, 475
    DefaultTreeSelectionModel class, 670
    JList class, 465, 475
    JTable class, 681–682
selectionModel property
    DefaultListSelectionModel class, 683
    DefaultTableColumnModel class, 709
    JColorChooser class, 307
    JList class, 465
    JMenuBar class, 159
    JPopupMenu class, 179

    JTable class, 682, 683
    JTree class, 629
selectionPath property
    DefaultTreeSelectionModel class, 670
    JTree class, 629
selectionPaths property
    DefaultTreeSelectionModel class, 670
    JTree class, 629, 630
selectionRow property
    JTree class, 629
selectionRows property
    DefaultTreeSelectionModel class, 670
    JTree class, 629, 630
selectionStart property
    JTextComponent class, 524
selectionValues property
    JOptionPane class, 281
selectionVisible property
    Caret interface, 548
Separator class, 182
    JToolBar class, 208
separatorBackground property
    MetalLookAndFeel class, 773
separatorForeground property
    MetalLookAndFeel class, 773
set() method
    DefaultListModel class, 453
setAcceptAllFileFilterUsed() method
    JFileChooser class, 331
setAccessibleDescription() method
    AccessibleContext class, 807
setAccessibleName() method
    AccessibleContext class, 807
setAction() method
    JComboBox class, 494
    JPopupMenu class, 177
setAlignment() method
    StyleConstants class, 602
setBackgroundAt() method
    JTabbedPane class, 398
setBorder() method
    JViewport class, 412
setBorderPainted method
    hiding border, 219
setBorderPainted() method
    JProgressBar component, 441
setBottomComponent() method
    JSplitPane class, 386

setColor() method
    JColorChooser class, 313
setComponentAt() method
    JTabbedPane class, 398
setComponentPopupMenu() method
    JComponent class, 178
setContraints() method
    SpringLayout.Constraints class, 371
setCorner() method
    JScrollPane class, 409
setCurrentManager() method
    RepaintManager class, 70
setDefaultCloseOperation() method
    JFrame class, 246
setDescription() method
    ImageIcon class, 806
setDisabledIconAt() method
    JTabbedPane class, 398
setDisplayedMnemonic() method
    JLabel class, 527
setDisplayedMnemonicIndexAt() method
    JTabbedPane class, 398
setDividerLocation() method
    JSplitPane class, 387
setDocumentFilter() method
    AbstractDocument class, 542
setDot() method
    NavigationFilter class, 552
setDragEnabled() method
    components with built-in drag-and-drop
        support, 729
setEditor() method
    JSpinner class, 518
setElementAt() method
    DefaultListModel class, 453
setEnabled property
    AbstractButton class, 102
setEnabled() method
    disables selection of component, 232
setEnabledAt() method
    JTabbedPane class, 398
setExtent method
    JScrollBar component, 426
    JSlider component, 431
setFileFilter() method
    JFileChooser class, 330
setFocusable() method
    Component class, 49

setFocusTraversalKeys() method
    Component class, 55
setForegroundAt() method
    JTabbedPane class, 398
setHelpMenu() method
    JMenuBar class, 381
setIconAt() method
    JTabbedPane class, 398
setIheritsPopupMenu() method
    JComponent class, 178
setIndeterminate() method
    JProgressBar component, 442
setInverted() method
    JSlider component, 436
setItem() method
    ComboBoxEditor class, 499
setJMenuBar() method
    adding JMenuBar to a window, 157
setKeymap() method
    JTextComponent class, 586
setLabelFor() method
    JLabel class, 528, 807
setLabelTable() method
    JSlider component, 435
setLayer() method
    JLayeredPane class, 240
setLayout() method
    Container class, 344
    JToolBar class, 204
setLayoutOrientation() method
    JList class, 479
setLookAndFeel() method
    UIManager class, 743
setMajorTickSpacing() method
    JSlider component, 432
setMask() method
    JFormattedTextField component, 618
setMaximum method
    JScrollBar component, 426
    JSlider component, 431
setMinimum method
    JScrollBar component, 426
    JSlider component, 431
setMinimumSize() method
    JComponent class, 388
setMinorTickSpacing() method
    JSlider component, 432
setMnemonic() method
    AbstractButton class, 101

setMnemonicAt() method
  JTabbedPane class, 398
setModel() method
  JTree class, 625
setOrientation() method
  JSeparator class, 182, 208
setPaintLabels() method
  JSlider component, 435
setPaintTicks() method
  JSlider component, 432
setPaintTrack() method
  JSlider component, 436
setParent() method
  MutableTreeNode interface, 660
setPopupLocation() method
  JComponent class, 178
setPosition() method
  JLayeredPane class, 241
setPreviewPanel() method
  JColorChooser class, 309, 320
setProgress() method
  ProgressMonitor class, 293
setRowHeight() method
  JTable class, 682
setSelected() method
  ButtonGroup class, 118
setSelectedIcon() method
  JCheckBox class, 127, 128
  JRadioButton class, 136
setSelectedIndex() method
  JComboBox class, 493
setSelectedInterval() method
  JList class, 479
setSelectedItem() method
  JComboBox class, 493
setSelectedValue() method
  JList class, 479
setSnapToTicks() method
  JSlider component, 434
setStringPainted() method
  JProgressBar component, 441
setText() method
  JFormattedTextField component, 615
  JMenuItem class, 589
setTitleAt() method
  JTabbedPane class, 398
setToolTipText() method
  JComponent class, 84, 87
setToolTipTextAt() method
  JTabbedPane class, 398

setTopComponent() method
  JSplitPane class, 386
setTransferHandler() method
  passing in replacement object to be
    transferred, 731
setUndecorated() method
  JDialog class, 237
  JFrame class, 237
setValue() method
  JFormattedTextField component, 615
  JOptionPane, 286
  JScrollBar component, 426
  JSlider component, 431
setValueAt() method
  JTable class, 678
setVerifyInputWhenFocusTarget() method
  InputVerifier interface, 57
setView() method
  JViewport class, 412
setVisibleRowCount() method
  JList class, 467
sharedInstance() method
  ToolTipManager class, 86
shouldSelectCell() method
  CellEditor interface, 655
show() method
  Popup class, 200
showDialog() method
  JColorChooser class, 304, 305, 314
  JFileChooser class, 327
showGrid property
  JTable class, 682
showHorizontalLines property
  JTable class, 682
showing property
  JComponent class, 79
showInputDialog() method
  JOptionPane class, 276, 278
showInternalInputDialog() method
  JOptionPane class, 278
showInternalMessageDialog() method
  JOptionPane class, 277
showInternalOptionDialog() method
  JOptionPane class, 280
showInternalXXXDialog() methods
  JOptionPane class, 274
showMessageDialog() method
  JOptionPane class, 277
showOptionDialog() method
  JOptionPane class, 280

showsRootHandles property
    JTree class, 629, 630
showVerticalLines property
    JTable class, 682
showXXXDialog() methods
    JOptionPane class, 274, 275
siblingCount property
    DefaultMutableTreeNode interface, 663
simple numeric text field verification
        example, 56–57
SimpleAttributeSet class, 585
    creating, 598
    implementation of MutableAttributeSet
        interface, 595
    introduction, 597
    properties, 598
    using, 598–601
SINGLE_INTERVAL_SELECTION mode
    ListSelectionModel interface, 474
SINGLE_SELECTION mode
    ListSelectionModel interface, 474
SINGLE_TREE_SELECTION mode
    TreeSelectionModel interface, 669
SingleSelectionModel interface
    introduction, 161
size property
    DefaultComboBoxModel class, 461
    DefaultListModel class, 453
    JComponent class, 77
SizeRequirements class, 370
SmallAttributeSet class, 595
snapToTicks property
    JSlider component, 431, 434
SoftBevelBorder class, 222
    constructors, 223
SortingFocusTraversalPolicy
    FocusTraversalPolicy class, 53
spinner property
    DefaultEditor class, 518
SpinnerDateModel class
    getValue() method, 515
    introduction, 514–515
    properties, 515
SpinnerListModel class
    introduction, 515–516
    properties, 516
    subclassing, 517–518
    working with ListEditor class, 519

SpinnerModel interface
    data model for JSpinner, 513
    properties, 515
SpinnerNumberModel class
    introduction, 516–517
    properties, 517
SpringLayout class
    Constraints inner class, 371
    introduction, 371–375
SpringLayout.Constraints class, 371
    setContraints() method, 371
StackOverflowError, 214
start property
    SpinnerDateModel class, 515
start() method
    Timer class, 35
startOffset property
    HTMLDocument.Iterator class, 609
startPosition property
    AbstractDocument class, 540
state of text properties
    JTextComponent class implementation
        properties, 525
state property
    JCheckBoxMenuItem component, 185
StateEdit class, 783
    as UndoableEdit implementation, 800–801
    end() method, 801
    example with StateEditable, 801–804
StateEditable interface
    example with StateEdit class, 801–804
    implementation of updated document, 800
    methods, 800
    restoreState() method, 801
stepSize property
    SpinnerNumberModel class, 517
stop() method
    Timer class, 35
stopCellEditing() method
    CellEditor interface, 654
storeState method
    StateEditable interface, 800
StreamDescriptionProperty constant
    Document interface, 531
string property
    JProgressBar component, 441
StringContent class
    AbstractDocument.Content
        implementation, 596

stringPainted property
    JProgressBar component, 441
strut, creating, 382–383
Style interface, 595
    introduction, 606
    setting JTextPane text attributes, 580
StyleConstants class, 595
    constants, 601–602
    introduction, 601
    methods, 602–603
    sharing between multiple documents, 596
StyleContext class
    introduction, 606
StyleContext.NamedStyle class, 606
StyleContext.SmallAttributeSet class, 595
StyledDocument interface, 521
    Document interface extension of, 595
    extending Document interface, 595
    implemented by DefaultStyledDocument
        class, 596
    loading JTextPane class with content,
        582–583
    manages Style objects, 595
    using with JTextField class, 530
styledDocument property
    JTextPane class, 581
StyledDocument.NamedStyle class, 595
StyledEditorKit class
    finding actions, 591
styleNames property
    DefaultStyledDocument class, 596
subElements property
    JMenu class, 172
    JMenuBar class, 159
    JMenuItem class, 164
    JPopupMenu class, 179
subTextFont property
    MetalLookAndFeel class, 773
supportedLookAndFeel property
    LookAndFeel class, 742
surrendersFocusOnKeystroke property
    JTable class, 682
Swing
    advanced containers, 377
        Box class, 377–383
        JScrollPane class, 403–412
        JSplitPane class, 383–394
        JTabbedPane class, 394–403
        JViewport class, 412–417

client properties, 759–763
introduction, 1
layout management, 10, 11
menus, 151
    JCheckBoxMenuItem class, 184–189
    JMenu class, 168–175
    JMenuBar class, 157–161
    JMenuItem class, 162–168
    JPopupMenu class, 176–184
    JRadioButtonMenuItem class, 189–195
    JSeparator class, 175–176
    menu class hierarchy, 156
    MenuElement interface, 195–199
    SingleSelectionModel interface, 161–162
    working with, 152–156
pop-ups, 200–202
toolbars, 151
    JToolBar class, 202–208
Swing components, 2
    See also text components
    AbstractButton class, 98–103
    AWT component replacements, 3
    chapter mapping, 12
    containers compared to AWT
        containers, 235
    delegates, 763–765
    distinction between equivalent AWT
        components, 3
    event handling, 10–11
    GrayFilter class, 97
    Icon interface, 92–94
    ImageIcon class, 94–97
    JButton class, 104–110
    JComponent class, 67
        component pieces, 69–73
        events, 80–84
        properties, 74–79
    JLabel class, 88–92
    JPanel class, 110–112
    JToolTip class, 84–88
    layout managers, 343
    non-AWT upgraded components, 5
    predefined models, 64
    resizing, 388
    scrolling support, 406
    SwingSet demonstration, 11
    undo framework, 11

Swing focus management, 46, 47
  examining focus cycles, 50–52
  FocusTraversalPolicy class, 52, 53, 55
  KeyboardFocusManager class, 55
  moving the focus, 48–50
  verifying input during focus traversal, 56–57
swing.auxiliarylaf property
  registering auxiliary look and feel classes, 776
swing.properties file, 746
SwingPropertyChangeSupport class, 29
SwingSet demonstration, 11
Swing-specific event handling, 37
  AbstractAction class, 38–41
  Action interface, 37–38
  KeyStroke class41–45
    mnemonics and accelerators, 46
SwingUtilities class
  getSharedOwnerFrame() method, 277
  isEventDispatchThread() method, 21
  mouse button identification, 23, 24, 26
  updateComponentTreeUI() method, 743
  wrapper methods, 23
synchronous painting
  JComponent class, 70
SynthLookAndFeel class, 777
  configuring, 777, 779
  default properties, 780
  working with Synth images, 780–781
SystemColor class
  displaying list of colors from, 311
SystemColorChooserPanel class, 312, 313
  changing color chooser, 313
  complete source, 314–318
systemLookAndFeelClassName property
  UIManager class, 748
systemTextFont property
  MetalLookAndFeel class, 773

■T

tabCount property
  JTabbedPane class, 399
tabLayoutPolicy property
  JTabbedPane class, 399
table property
  JTableHeader class, 716

TableCellEditor class, 676, 719, 723
  defining, 722
  editing table cells, 718
TableCellRenderer interface, 676
  display of cells within table, 676
  getTableCellRendererComponent() method, 686, 687
TableColumn class, 676
  creating, 712
  introduction, 712
  properties, 713
  removing column headers, 680
  using icons in column headers, 713–715
TableColumnModel interface, 676
  definition, 708
  handling JTable events, 689
  introduction, 708
  listening for TableColumnModelEvent objects, 709
  removing TableColumn, 712
  specifying when creating JTable class, 678
  storing column selection model, 683
TableColumnModelEvent class
  properties, 709
TableColumnModelListener
  attaching to TableColumnModel object, 710
  listening to JTable events, 709–712
tableHeader property
  JTable class, 682
TableModel interface, 676
  AbstractTableModel class, 691–696
    default implementation, 695
  DefaultTableModel class, 696–700
  getColumnClass() method, 687, 695
  handling JTable events, 689
  implemented by AbstractTableModel class, 691
  introduction, 690
  leaving TableColumn in, 712
  ordering stored columns of data, 676
  sorting JTable elements, 700–707
  using column order of, 678
TableModelEvent class
  properties, 699
TableModelListener interface
  list managed by AbstractTableModel class, 691
  listening to JTable events, 699

tables, 675
    editing table cells
        creating complex cell editor, 722–724
        creating simple cell editor, 718–722
    editing table cells, 718–724
    introducing, 675–676
    JTable class, 677–690
    JTableHeader class, 715–718
    printing tables, 724–727
    TableColumnModel interface
        DefaultTableColumnModel class,
            708–709
        listening to JTable events with
            TableColumnModelListener,
            709–712
        TableColumn class, 712–715
    TableColumnModel interface, 707–708, 712
    TableModel interface, 690
        AbstractTableModel class, 691–696
        DefaultTableModel class, 696–700
        sorting JTable elements, 700–707
tabPlacement property
    JTabbedPane class, 399
tabRunCount property
    JTabbedPane class, 399
TabSet attribute
    ParagraphConstants class, 603
TabSet class
    introduction, 603
tabSize property
    JTextArea class, 571
TabStop class
    alignment settings, 604
    creating, 603
    introduction, 603
    properties, 604
    using, 605–606
tag property
    HTMLDocument.Iterator class, 609
tearOff property
    JMenu class, 172
text capabilities, 585
    creating styled text, 595–607
    editor kits, 607–612
    JFormattedTextField component, 612–621
    using actions, 585–594
text components
    finding actions, 591–594
    JFormattedTextField class, 566–570

JPasswordField class, 563–566
JTextArea class, 570–580
JTextComponent class, 523–526
JTextField class, 526–563
JTextPane class, 580–583
listing actions, 586–589
overview, 521–522
using actions, 585–586, 589–591
text justification
    TitledBorder class, 230
text property
    AbstractButton class, 99
    JEditorPane class, 575
    JLabel class, 89
    JTextComponent class, 524
TextAction class, 522, 585
    as extension of AbstractAction class, 535
    listing text actions, 587
    provides concrete Action
        implementations, 585
    Swing-specific event handling, 37
    using, 586
TextField class
    selectionBackground property, 547
textField property
    DefaultEditor class, 518
textHighlightColor property
    MetalLookAndFeel class, 773
textNonSelectionColor property
    DefaultTreeCellRenderer class, 635
textSelectionColor property
    DefaultTreeCellRenderer class, 635
TextUI interface, 60
TextUtilities class, 537
thickness property
    LineBorder class, 220
Timer class
    creating objects, 34
    notifying an ActionListener after a
        predefined number of milliseconds,
        34, 35
    properties, 35–36
    using objects, 35
tipText property
    JToolTip class, 85
title justification
    TitledBorder class, 230
title positioning
    TitledBorder class, 231

title property
    JInternalFrame class, 255
    TitledBorder class, 229
titleColor property
    TitledBorder class, 229
TitledBorder class, 227
    configuring properties, 229
    creating, 228
    customizing look and feel, 232
titleFont property
    TitledBorder class, 229
titleJustification property
    TitledBorder class, 229
titlePosition property
    TitledBorder class, 229
toArray() method
    DefaultListModel class, 460
toggle buttons, 115
    ButtonGroup class, 116–118
    JCheckBox class, 125–134
    JRadioButton class, 134–149
    JToggleButton class, 119–125
    ToggleButtonModel class, 115–116
ToggleButtonModel class
    button model for JRadioButtonMenuItem
        components, 189
    data model for JCheckBoxMenuItem
        class, 184
    defining JToggleButton structure, 119
    introduction, 115–116
ToggleButtonUI class
    defining JToggleButton structure, 119
toggleClickCount property
    JTree class, 629, 630
toIndex property
    TableColumnModelEvent class, 709
toolkit property
    JComponent class, 79
ToolTipManager class
    adding element level tooltips, 488
    disabling, 87
    properties, 87
    registering component with, 641
    sharedInstance() method, 86
    unregistering table, 689
tooltips
    PropertiesList example, 488, 490
toolTipText property
    JComponent class, 79

ToolTipTreeCellRenderer class, 642
topComponent property
    JSplitPane class, 386
topLevelAncestor property
    JComponent class, 78
topLevelMenu property
    JMenu class, 172
totalColumnWidth property
    DefaultTableColumnModel class, 709
Transferable interface
    creating transferable image object, 734
    java.awt.datatransfer package, 733
    methods, 733
transferFocus() method
    Component class, 55
transferFocusBackward() method
    Component class, 55
transferFocusDownCycle() method
    Container class, 55
transferFocusUpCycle() method
    Component class, 55
TransferHandler class
    canImport() method, 734
    createTransferable() method, 735
    creating a transferable image object, 734
    importData() method, 735
    introduction, 731
transferHandler property
    JComponent class, 79
translate() method
    Graphics class, 214
tree nodes
    creating proper ComboBox editor for a
        tree, 648
    DefaultMutableTreeNode class, 661–664
    editing, 643
        with CellEditor interface, 644
        with DefaultCellEditor class, 645
        with DefaultTreeCellEditor class, 647
        with TreeCellEditor interface, 644
    MutableTreeNode interface, 660
    traversing trees, 664
    TreeNode interface, 659
tree tooltips
    working with, 641–643
TreeCellEditor interface, 644
    creating CheckBoxNodeEditor class,
        653–658
    editing table cells, 718

editing tree nodes, 623, 644
getTreeCellEditorComponent() method, 648, 656
TreeCellRenderer interface
  creating custom renderer, 637–641
  DefaultTreeCellRenderer class, 635
  implementations, 623
  introduction, 634
TreeExpansionEvent class, 672
  TreePath getPath() method, 673
TreeExpansionListener interface, 672
treeExpansionListeners property
  JTree class, 629
treelock property
  JComponent class, 79
TreeModel interface
  DefaultTreeModel class implements, 667
  introduction, 667
  getRoot() method, 666
  storing within DefaultTreeModel class, 624
  working with tree nodes, 659
TreeModelEvent class
  notifying registered listeners, 668
TreeModelListener interface
  DefaultTreeModel class manages, 667
  reporting changes to model, 668
TreeNode interface
  nodes of JTree are implementations of, 624
  traversing trees, 664
  working with tree nodes, 659
TreePath class, 624
  introduction, 671–672
trees
  additional expansion events, 672–673
  editing tree nodes, 643–659
  introduction, 623–624
  JTree class, 624–634
  TreeCellRenderer interface, 634–643
  TreeModel interface, 667
  TreeSelectionModel interface, 668–672
  working with tree nodes, 659–667
TreeSelectionEvent class, 671
TreeSelectionListener interface, 671
treeSelectionListeners property
  JTree class, 629
TreeSelectionModel interface
  DefaultTreeSelectionModel class, 670
  introduction, 668–670
  tree selection management, 624

TreeWillExpandListener interface, 673
treeWillExpandListeners property
  JTree class, 629
trimToSize() method
  DefaultListModel class, 460
type property
  ListDataEvent class, 454
  TableModelEvent class, 700

■U
UI delegates
  adding, 771–772
  creating, 763–766
UI property
  AbstractButton class, 99
  JColorChooser class, 307
  JComboBox class, 492
  JDesktopPane component, 263
  JFileChooser class, 327
  JInternalFrame class, 255
  JLabel class, 90
  JList class, 465
  JMenuBar class, 159
  JMenuItem class, 164
  JOptionPane class, 281
  JPopupMenu class, 179
  JProgressBar component, 441
  JRootPane class, 237
  JScrollBar component, 426
  JScrollPane class, 407
  JSeparator class, 175
  JSlider component, 431
  JSpinner class, 510
  JSplitPane class, 386
  JTabbedPane class, 399
  JTable class, 682
  JTableHeader class, 716
  JTextComponent class, 524
  JToolBar class, 203
  JToolTip class, 85
  JTree class, 629
  JViewport class, 412
UIClassID property
  JButton class, 105
  JCheckBox class, 127
  JCheckBoxMenuItem component, 185
  JColorChooser class, 307
  JComboBox class, 492
  JDesktopPane component, 263

JEditorPane class, 575
JFileChooser class, 327
JFormattedTextField class, 567
JInternalFrame class, 255
JLabel class, 90
JList class, 465
JMenu class, 172
JMenuBar class, 159
JMenuItem class, 164
JOptionPane class, 281
JPasswordField class, 564
JPopupMenu class, 179
JProgressBar component, 441
JRadioButton class, 136
JRadioButtonMenuItem component, 191
JRootPane class, 237
JScrollBar component, 426
JScrollPane class, 407
JSeparator class, 175
JSlider component, 431
JSpinner class, 510
JSplitPane class, 386
JTabbedPane class, 399
JTable class, 682
JTableHeader class, 716
JTextArea class, 571
JTextField class, 529
JTextPane class, 581
JToggleButton class, 120
JToolBar class, 203
JToolTip class, 85
JTree class, 629
JViewport class, 412
uiClassID property
    JComponent class, 79
UIDefaults class
    inner classes, 755
    introduction, 71, 749
    listing properties within JTable, 749–752
UIDefaults.ActiveValue class, 755
    look and feel properties stored as, 741
UIDefaults.LazyValue class, 755
    look and feel properties stored as, 741
UIDefaults.ProxyLazyValue class, 755
UIManager class
    addAuxiliaryLookAndFeel() method, 776
    checking component settings in
        UIDefaults lookup table, 72
    currently installed look and feel classes
        provided by, 741

get() method, 758, 763
getInstalledLookAndFeels() method
    743, 776
getter methods, 747
introduction, 747
properties, 748, 813–846
put() method, 758
setLookAndFeel() method, 743
UIManager.LookAndFeelInfo class, 741
    getInstalledLookAndFeels() method, 742
    introduction, 749
UIResource interface, 741
    classes that implement, 753–754
    introduction, 753
UIResource properties, fetching, 72
Undo Framework, 783
    Command design pattern, 788, 789
    components, 789
        AbstractUndoableEdit class, 791
        CompoundEdit class, 791
        defining custom undoable class, 795–800
        UndoableEdit interface, 789–790
        UndoableEditEvent class, 794
        UndoableEditListener interface, 794
        UndoableEditSupport class, 794
        UndoManager class, 792, 793
    using an outside object to manage Undo
        states, 800
        example, 801–804
        StateEdit class, 801
        StateEditable interface, 800
    using with Swing text components, 784–788
    working with, 783, 784
undo() method
    CompoundEdit class, 792
    UndoableEdit interface, 790
    UndoManager class, 784
undoable program example, 795–800
UndoableDrawingPanel class, 797
UndoableEdit command
    posting to UndoableEditListener
        objects, 801
    UndoManager class, 788, 799
UndoableEdit interface, 788
    creating, 797
    definition, 789
    flow between states, 790
    StateEdit class implementation, 800
UndoableEditEvent class
    edit property, 794

UndoableEditEvent event
    UndoableEditListener interface, 794
    UndoableEditSupport class, 794
    UndoManager class, 793
undoableEditHappened() method
    listener objects, 794
UndoableEditListener interface, 794
    attaching to document of component, 784
    managing objects with
        UndoableEditSupport class, 794
    UndoableEditEvent event, 794
    UndoableEditSupport class, 794
    UndoManager class, 784
undoableEditListeners property
    AbstractDocument class, 540
UndoableEditSupport class, 801
    addUndoableListener() method, 794
    beginUpdate() method, 794
    endUpdate() method, 794
    managing UndoableEditListener
        objects, 794
    postEdit() method, 794
    UndoableEditListener listener, 794
UndoManager class, 783
    extending to expose UndoableEdit list, 794
    managing undo and redo capabilities for
        Swing text components, 784
    methods, 792
    UndoableEdit command, 788
UndoManagerHelper class, 785
    definition, 785, 787
    using the Undo Framework with the Swing
        text components, 787
uninstallChooserPanel() method
    AbstractColorChooserPanel class, 313
unitIncrement property
    JScrollBar component, 422, 426
updateChooser() method
    AbstractColorChooserPanel class, 313
updateComponentTreeUI() method
    SwingUtilities class, 743
updateUI() method
    changing look and feel setting of
        component, 813
upFocusCycle() method
    KeyboardFocusManager class, 55

userObject property
    DefaultMutableTreeNode class, 640, 666
    DefaultMutableTreeNode interface, 663
userObjectPath property
    DefaultMutableTreeNode interface, 663
userTextColor property
    MetalLookAndFeel class, 773
userTextFont property
    MetalLookAndFeel class, 774

■V

validateRoot property
    JTextField class, 529
valid property
    HTMLDocument.Iterator class, 609
    JComponent class, 79
validateRoot property
    JComponent class, 79
    JRootPane class, 237
    JScrollPane class, 407
    JSplitPane class, 386
validCharacters property
    MaskFormatter class, 620
value property
    BoundedRangeModel interface, 419
    JFormattedTextField class, 567
    JOptionPane class, 281, 285
    JProgressBar component, 441
    JScrollBar component, 426
    JSlider component, 431
    JSpinner class, 510
    SpinnerDateModel class, 515
    SpinnerListModel class, 516
    SpinnerNumberModel class, 517
valueForPathChanged() method
    TreeModel interface, 667
valueIsAdjusting property
    BoundedRangeModel interface, 420, 424
    DefaultListSelectionModel class, 475, 683
    JList class, 465
    JScrollBar component, 426
    JSlider component, 431
    ListSelectionEvent class, 476
Vector class
    creating JTree from, 625–627

verifyInputWhenFocusTarget property
   JComponent class, 78
verticalAlignment property
   AbstractButton class, 99, 102
   JLabel class, 90
verticalScrollBar property
   JScrollPane class, 407
verticalScrollBarPolicy property
   JScrollPane class, 407
verticalTextPosition property
   AbstractButton class, 99, 102
   JLabel class, 90
VetoableChangeListener event handler
   JComponent class, 81
View class
   displaying Document contents with
      EditorKit class, 607
view property
   JViewport class, 412
ViewFactory class
   displaying Document contents with
      EditorKit class, 607
viewport property
   JScrollPane class, 407
viewportBorder property
   JScrollPane class, 407
viewportBorderBounds property
   JScrollPane class, 407
ViewportLayout class, 371, 412
viewportView property
   JScrollPane class, 406, 407
viewPosition property
   JViewport class, 412, 414
viewRect property
   JViewport class, 412, 413
viewSize property
   JViewport class, 412, 413
visible property
   Caret interface, 548
   JComponent class, 79
   JPopupMenu class, 179
visibleAmount property
   JScrollBar component, 426
visibleRect property
   JComponent class, 77
visibleRowCount property
   JList class, 465
   JTree class, 629, 630

W
wantsInput property
   JOptionPane class, 281, 285
warningString property
   JInternalFrame class, 255
weight
   GridBagConstraints class, 357
wheelScrollingEnabled property
   JScrollPane class, 407
white property
   MetalLookAndFeel class, 774
width property
   JComponent class, 77
   TableColumn class, 713
WindowAdapter class
   WindowListener methods, 256
windowBackground property
   MetalLookAndFeel class, 774
WindowConstants interface
   close operation constants, 244
   implemented by JDialog class, 248
   working with JFrame class to manage
      closing operations, 242
windowDecorationStyle property
   JRootPane class, 237, 244
      class constants, 237
windowInit() method
   JWindow class, 248
WindowListener interface
   supported by JFrame class, 246
   WindowAdapter class, 256
WindowsClassicLookAndFeel
      implementation
   LookAndFeel.supportedLookAndFeel, 747
WindowsLookAndFeel implementation
   LookAndFeel.supportedLookAndFeel, 742
   using on non-Windows machine, 767–768
windowTextFont property
   MetalLookAndFeel class, 774
windowTitleBackground property
   MetalLookAndFeel class, 774
windowTitleForeground property
   MetalLookAndFeel class, 774
windowTitleInactiveBackground property
   MetalLookAndFeel class, 774
windowTitleInactiveForeground property
   MetalLookAndFeel class, 774
WORA (write-once, run anywhere), 1

WrappedPlainView view
    BasicTextAreaUI interface, 60
wrapStyleWord property
    JTextArea class, 571
writableAction class constant
    DefaultEditorKit class, 592
write() method
    JTextComponent class, 531

■**X**
x property
    JComponent class, 77

■**Y**
y property
    JComponent class, 77